ANTIQUES&
COLLECTIBLES

2012 PRICE GUIDE • 28th Edition

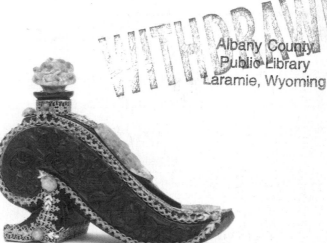

Pub

Krause Publications, a division of F+W Media, Inc.
700 East State Street • Iola, WI 54990-0001
715-445-2214 • 888-457-2873
www.krausebooks.com

To order books or other products call toll-free 1-800-258-0929
or visit us online at www.krausebooks.com or www.Shop.Collect.com

ISSN: 1536-2884

ISBN-13: 978-1-4402-1695-4
ISBN-10: 1-4402-1695-9

Cover Design by Heidi Zastrow
Designed by Marilyn McGrane
Edited by Eric Bradley

Printed in the United States of America

More Great Books in the Antique Trader Series

Antique Trader Book Collector's Price Guide

Antique Trader Bottles Identification & Price Guide

Antique Trader Collectible Cookbooks Price Guide

Antique Trader Collectible Paperback Price Guide

Antique Trader Furniture Price Guide

Antique Trader Indian Arrowheads Price Guide

Antique Trader Jewelry Price Guide

Antique Trader Kitchen Collectibles Price Guide

Antique Trader Perfume Bottles Price Guide

Antique Trader Pottery & Porcelain Ceramics Price Guide

Antique Trader Salt and Pepper Shaker Price Guide

Antique Trader Tools Price Guide

Table of Contents

Listings

Introduction

By Eric Bradley

Eric Bradley

It's a confusing time in the antiques market. After emerging from the recessions of 2000-2001 and 2007-2010, buyers and sellers find themselves on an alien landscape.

Longtime antiques shows have vanished; the size of such events now favoring quality rather than quantity. Auctions dominate the sales landscape. "Antiques Roadshow" now has competition, and the audience for programs about antiques and collectibles rival those of late night talk shows. The average age of collectibles sellers on trendy vintage websites is 34, folks who are noticeably absent from shows and traditional auctions.

This is definitely not your father's hobby anymore.

The 28th edition of the *Antique Trader Antiques & Collectibles Price Guide* represents a new approach to our hobby and the market. Not only will you find thousands of entries across a field of areas, you'll also find enhanced identification methods and tips on how you can excel at both buying and selling no matter your budget or passion.

In this edition, we've introduced new collecting areas as well as reliable favorites. Although dollar values continue to rise for the best of the market, the volume of items moving on the lower end is attracting new collectors every day. This demand for items and information is creating new businesses. Here are a few observations on today's market and what you can expect for 2012:

BUYING TRENDS

The highflying Asian art and antiques "bubble" isn't a bubble at all. It is the new norm. As Asian countries rise to "catch up" with our standard of living, their disposable income will be more assertively directed at collecting cultural art and antiques. Americans and Europeans have enjoyed the escalation of wealth during the last 300 years, and now it's Asians who are consuming a larger segment of the market. Sure, prices may fluctuate (perhaps even decline in stressed periods), but auction houses and dealers are right to bank on a long term, sustainable trend of an increase of demand in Asian art and antiques.

Vintage technology is gearing up for the long haul. Once relegated to a small segment of the collecting public, vintage technology is hot, and young people are getting interested in old typewriters, electric fans, microscopes, and oddities. The hobby supports several collectors' websites, a new book, and an international auction house. The appetite comes from affluent, accomplished tech industry workers as well as nostalgia buffs reminded of a simpler, less-connected way of life. The fondness Baby Boomers shared for their first bicycle is akin to the fondness those ages 35 and younger share for their first computer.

A NEW AUDIENCE

By the end of 2011, more than 16 new television shows involving the antiques and collectibles trade were in production or in early planning stages. Production crews are eager to satisfy this so far unexplored (or unexploited) segment of the reality television genre and you can expect more to come. In mid-2011, Leslie and Leigh Keno announced the formation of their own television show – the first post-"Antiques Roadshow" members to strike out on their own television endeavor. Dealers and auction houses yearned for this phenomenon as early as 2006 as a way to spark demand among younger buyers. Now's the time to capitalize on the publicity and enjoy the new faces flooding into shops, shows, yard sales, and storage locker auctions.

THINK OUTSIDE THE BOX

What we share at *Antique Trader* are universal lessons to improve the hobby of antiques no matter what region you live in or what method you use to buy and sell. They all boil down to one truism – the time for change is now. In order to take advantage of greater trends happening in our hobby, buyers and sellers must change how they meet. Take a look at some of the case examples:

- A San Francisco dealer of trains and vintage American toys is using interesting and innovative displays at a major airport to promote his business and his inventory.
- Dealers are moving away from the bureaucracy and fees of online auction sites by launching their own "digital storefronts" on their own websites. Breakthroughs from major Internet search engines are making it easier for a dealer's well-written inventory descriptions to be found.
- It's time to free up capital currently held up in merchandise that's not selling. Successful dealers make friends with their local estate auction house (or set up at well-trafficked shows) to sell their "mistakes." Now is a good time to admit that some purchases need to be sold at cost to free up cash for items in better condition, which may be undervalued.
- Nothing replaces knowledge. Collectors must pursue up-to-the-minute pricing. Websites sites such as LiveAuctioneers, Artfact, and Worthpoint.com all offer pricing results from auctions every day. In most cases the resources are free or at a nominal cost. Such as you cultivated a comprehensive reference library before the digital age, so should you bookmark and subscribe to reliable reference information on the market.

This is an exciting, vibrant time in our hobby. Whether your passion is Old Master paintings or yard sale treasures, opportunity abounds around every corner. Now is the time to open your mind and eyes and find the things you didn't know you wanted.

ABOUT ANTIQUETRADER.COM

We think you'll be impressed with the new layout, sections and information in this year's annual. Because the antiques world (like everything else) is constantly changing, I invite you to visit AntiqueTrader.com and make it your main portal into the world of antiques.

Like our magazine, AntiqueTrader.com's team of collectors, dealers and bloggers share information daily on events, auctions, new discoveries and tips on how to buy more for less. Here's what's offered everyday on AntiqueTrader.com.

- **Free eNewsletters:** Get a recap of the world of antiques sent to your inbox every week.
- **Free Classified Ads:** Inventory (great and small) from around the world offered for buy, sell or trade.
- **Exclusive video featuring stars from all the shows you love:** "Antiques Roadshow," "American Pickers," "Pawn Stars," "Cash & Cari," "Storage Wars" and more!
- **Experts' Q&A** on how to value and sell your collections online at the best prices.
- **The Internet's largest free antiques library:** More than 10,000 articles of research, show reports, auction results and more.
- **Blogs** on where to sell online, how to buy more for less, restoration, fakes and reproductions, displaying your collections and how to find hidden gems in your town!
- **The largest online events calendar** in the world of antiques with links to more than 1,000 shows worldwide.

ERIC BRADLEY is the editor of *Antique Trader* magazine, AntiqueTrader.com and the Antique Trader Blog. In addition to writing hundreds of articles on antiques, collecting and the trade, he has been a producer of the Atlantique City Antiques Show and a lifelong student of antiques. Bradley is often spotted haunting country auctions and outdoor shows to feed his collection of American art pottery, World War II homefront collectibles and Midwest folk art.

The Art of Evaluating Collectible Art

By Mary Manion

Mary Manion

It was a snowy New Year's Eve day, and the appraisers were making a house call. The client was a woman with a family heirloom, a piece of cut and painted paper silhouette art from a genre known by its German name, scherenschnitte. Her story ran like this: Her mother brought the paper art to the United States from Austria in the 1950s and had the piece appraised many years ago by a Boston dealer, at a value of $16,000.

She fervently believed her story but, alas, the family lore was obviously wrong. The piece, while nice work, had been framed in the 1960s before archival materials were available. The scherenschnitte had been glued down to a matt board, and acid from the board migrated over the decades onto the artwork. The paper was pocked by breaks and foxing. Moreover, it was impossible to find auction records higher than $2,000 for a comparable scherenschnitte in good condition. The client was indignant when the appraisers determined its value was only $400.

Witness the growing problem in the art market of customer over-expectation, a trend fanned by the popularity of "Antiques Roadshow," aided by ill-informed amateur websites and often abetted by family legends that just seem to sound better with each passing generation.

In the current economic climate, people are re-evaluating their finances, taking inventory of their personal property, and in some cases, downsizing the manor. The demand for appraisals has multiplied exponentially and, like a kind of "cross your fingers" lottery logic, people hope it's the winning ticket to prosperity.

The problem is that unlike investing in gold, the value of art can be illusory. Also, the authenticity of gold can easily be established. With art, what looks like the real thing can, upon evaluation, turn into mere fool's gold. And the appraiser is also faced with a disadvantage not endured by dealers in gold. The value of precious metal is measured by the ounce and determined by the world market. The value of artwork will always be more subjective.

Portrait of Rev. Gryllis of Helston Cornwall.
Copake Auction, 266 Route 7A, Copake, NY 12516

"Antiques Roadshow," the ever-popular appraisal program on PBS, has become the bellwether for appraisal events that have sprung up across the country in recent years. Patterned after "Antiques Roadshow's" presentation, appraisal affairs feature qualified appraisers from numerous disciplines who are brought together for a day to assess and provide a quick verbal value to whatever antique is put in front of them. My experience as a fine art appraiser at these events indicates all that glitters is not gold.

At a recent appraisal fair more than 1,800 advance ticket sales were offered and sold out weeks before the date. I was among a team of 38 appraisers who volunteered their knowledge and time for a 10-hour event. In my line, the majority of ticket holders had researched their artwork beforehand on the Internet and told me what they believed to be the value of their work as I was examining

"La Famile" 1976, by Orville Bulman.
Concept Art Gallery, 1031 South Braddock Avenue, Pittsburgh, PA 15218

their piece. Often, what they thought they had was not quite what they actually had. The most popular misconception is the difference between original works of art and their deceptive imitators: a reproduction, a copy or a "pretender" — a paper print on canvas, which can look like a painting to the amateur but holds little value to its original counterpart.

Picasso reproductions are the frequent item of disappointment brought in by people who gather their information randomly from the Internet. Two Picasso-hopefuls were brought to my table: one a faded reproduction from the '70s, and the other a rather cheap-looking image of a rooster that had been transferred onto a plastic plaque with a wall hook attached on the back. I had a bit of a struggle trying to set the record straight about its value. The client insisted that someone at a museum had told him it was valuable. Maintaining levity at such moments is a vital part of the assignment.

Another common misunderstanding comes in determining value with an artwork that has prospective worth. An oil painting, for example, may be less desirable if it is in poor condition, has a questionable provenance or aesthetically is not good quality work, or the market for that artist might be low. People seldom realize the parameters involved in the evaluation process.

A watercolor I encountered recently comes to mind as an example of a listed artist with a strong sale history ($20,000 to $50,000 at Sotheby's and Christie's, among other houses) but currently is generating no interest in consignment at auction houses. The local collector acquired the well-rendered, mixed-media floral several years ago.

He researched the French artist, Andre Dunoyer de Segonzac (1884-1974), and eventually had it authenticated by a specialist who determined the watercolor was in excellent condition, well executed and consistent with other works by the same artist that sold around $50,000 at auction. Several years had passed, and the client decided to place it at auction.

Contacting the appropriate specialist at several auction houses within a six-week period culminated in the finding that currently, the artist's work is of "little interest" in the market. As these inquiries were being made, Christie's, one of the houses contacted for the consignment, had several De Segonzac watercolors up for auction. A New York sale brought in $4,200 (hammer) for a watercolor landscape; a week later in Paris, Christie's sale of a floral watercolor sold for $3,780 (hammer).

In November 2009, a De Segonzac watercolor similar in composition and size as our client's, sold at Christie's (New York) for $41,500 (hammer). Within the following year, auction records indicate 43 watercolors by De Segonzac appeared at auction. The 21 lots that sold ranged in price from $257 to $14,141 (hammer). Nineteen lots did not sell, and two sales were not communicated.

Because the art market fluctuates, determining value involves a skillful process that includes ongoing research and a good eye on market sales. If Christie's takes a pass, keep it in your portfolio. The market may possibly change.

Paris street scene signed M. Passoni.
King Galleries, 854 Atlanta St., Roswell, GA 30075

MARY MANION is the associate director of Landmarks Gallery and Restoration Studio in Milwaukee. A columnist for *Antique Trader* since 2006, Manion is a member of the New England Appraisers Association. She regularly writes about the market's most popular and active artists and themes. A library of her work can be found at AntiqueTrader.com.

Furniture Styles and Designs

The antique furniture market continues to reward the finest examples, celebrity designers, and impeccable provenance. Despite changing tastes and decorating style, quality and craftsmanship help good furniture sell.

Especially desirable are pristine examples from the American Arts & Crafts period, monumental pieces such as bookcases or breakfronts, and pieces made by R.J. Horner, John Henry Belter, or the talented craftsmen in 18th century New England. Danish modern furniture continues to hold its value as new buyers appreciate the craftsmanship as well as the minimalist design. Expect to see utilitarian pieces such as occasional tables, bookcases, country kitchen canning cupboards, and nightstands rise in value as they are adapted into the modern home's demand that a single piece of furniture serve double duty.

In this primer, antique furniture expert Fred Taylor shares his list of the most commonly traded styles and design elements pursued by 21st century collectors and decorators. Furniture can be determined by careful study and remembering what design elements each one embraces. To help understand what defines each period, here are some of the major design elements for each period.

George III mahogany secretary bookcase.
Photo courtesy Bonhams & Butterfields

William and Mary, 1690-1730: The style is named for the English King William of Orange and his consort, Mary. New colonists in America brought their English furniture traditions with them and tried to translate these styles using native woods. Their furniture was practical and sturdy. Lines of this furniture style tend to be crisp, while facades might be decorated with bold grains of walnut or maple veneers, framed by inlaid bands. Moldings and turnings are exaggerated in size. Turnings are baluster-shaped, and the use of C-scrolls is quite common. Feet found in this period generally are round or oval. One exception to this is known as the Spanish foot, which flares to a scroll. Woods tend to be maple, walnut, white pine, or southern yellow pine. One type of decoration that begins in the William and Mary period and extends through to Queen Anne and Chippendale styles is known as "japanning," referring to a lacquering process that combines ashes and varnish.

Queen Anne, 1720-1760: Evolution of this design style is from Queen Anne's court, 1702 to 1714, and lasted until the Revolution. This style of furniture is much more delicate than its predecessor. It was one way for the young Colonists to show their own unique style, with each regional area initiating special design elements. Forms tend to be attenuated in New England. Chair rails were more often mortised through the back legs when made in Philadelphia. New England furniture makers preferred pad feet, while the makers in Philadelphia used triffid feet. Makers in Connecticut and New York often preferred slipper and claw and ball feet. The most popular woods were walnut, poplar, cherry, and maple. Japanned decoration tends to be in red, green, and gilt, often on a blue-green field. A new furniture form of this period was the tilting tea table.

Chippendale, 1755-1790: This period is named for the famous English cabinetmaker, Thomas Chippendale, who wrote a book of furniture designs, *Gentlemen and Cabinet-Maker's Directory*, published in 1754, 1755, and 1762. This book gave cabinetmakers real direction, and they soon eagerly copied the styles presented. Chippendale was influenced by ancient cultures, such as the Romans, and Gothic influences. Look for Gothic arches,

Chinese fretwork, columns, capitals, C-scrolls, S-scrolls, ribbons, flowers, leaves, scallop shells, gadrooning, and acanthus leaves. The most popular wood used in this period was mahogany, with walnut, maple, and cherry also present. Legs become straight and regional differences still existed in design elements, such as feet. Claw and ball feet become even larger and more decorative. Pennsylvania cabinetmakers used Marlborough feet, while other regions favored ogee bracket feet. One of the most popular forms of this period was a card table that sported five legs instead of the four of Queen Anne designs.

Federal (Hepplewhite), 1790-1815: This period reflects the growing patriotism felt in the young American states. Their desire to develop their own distinctive furniture style was apparent. Stylistically it also reflects the architectural style known as Federal, where balance and symmetry were extremely important. Woods used during this period were mahogany and mahogany veneer, but other native woods, such as maple, birch, or satinwood, were used. Reflecting the architectural ornamentation of the period, inlays were popular, as was carving and even painted highlights. The motifs used for inlay included bellflowers, urns, festoons, acanthus leaves, and pilasters, to name but a few. Inlaid bands and lines were also popular and often used in combination with other inlay. Legs of this period tend to be straight or tapered to the foot. The foot might be a simple extension of the leg, or bulbous or spade shaped. Two new furniture forms were created in this period. They are the sideboard and the worktable. Expect to find a little more comfort in chairs and sofas, but not very thick cushions or seats.

When a piece of furniture is made in England, or styled after an English example, it may be known as Hepplewhite. The time frame is the same. Robert Adam is credited with creating the style known as Hepplewhite during the 1760s and leading the form. Another English book heavily influenced the designers of the day. This one was by Alice Hepplewhite, and titled *The Cabinet Maker and Upholsterer's Guide*, published in 1788, 1789, and 1794.

Sheraton, 1790-1810: The style known as Sheraton closely resembles Federal. The lines are somewhat straighter and the designs plainer than Federal. Sheraton pieces are more closely associated with rural cabinetmakers. Woods include mahogany, mahogany veneer, maple, and pine, as well as other native woods. This period was heavily influenced by the work of Thomas Sheraton and his series of books, *The Cabinet Maker and Upholsterer's Drawing Book*, from 1791-1794, *The Cabinet Directory*, 1803, and *The Cabinet-Maker, Upholsterer, and General Artist's Encyclopedia* of 1804.

Empire (Classical), 1805-1830: By the beginning of the 19th century, a new design style was emerging. Known as Empire, it had an emphasis on the classical world of Greece, Egypt, and other ancient European influences. The American craftsmen began to incorporate more flowing patriotic motifs, such as eagles with spread wings. The basic wood used in the Empire period was mahogany. However, during this period, dark woods were so favored that often mahogany was painted black. Inlays were popular when made of ebony or maple veneer. The dark woods offset gilt highlights, as were the brass ormolu mountings often found in this period. The legs of this period are substantial and more flowing than those found in the Federal or Sheraton periods. Feet can be highly ornamental, as when they are carved to look like lion's paws, or plain when they extend to the floor with a swept leg. Regional differences in this style are very apparent, with New York City being the center of the design style, as it was also the center of fashion at the time.

New furniture forms of this period include the sleigh bed, with the headboard and footboard forming a graceful arch. Several new forms of tables also came into being, especially the sofa table. Because the architectural style of the Empire period used big, open rooms, the sofa was now allowed to be in the center of the room, with a table behind it. Former architectural periods found most furniture placed against the outside perimeter of the walls and brought forward to be used.

Victorian, 1830-1890: The Victorian period as it relates to furniture styles can be divided into several distinct styles. However, not every piece of furniture can be dated or definitely identified, so the generic term "Victorian" will apply to those pieces. Queen Victoria's reign affected the design styles of furniture, clothing, and all sorts of items used in daily living. Her love of ornate styles is well known. When thinking of the general term, think of a cluttered environment, full of heavy furniture, and surrounded by plants, heavy fabrics, and lots of china and glassware.

French Restoration, 1830-1850: This is the first sub-category of the Victoria era. This style is best simplified as the plainest of the Victorian styles. Lines tend to be sweeping, undulating curves. It is named for the style that was popular in France as the Bourbons tried to restore their claim to the French throne, from 1814 to 1848. The Empire (Classical) period influence is felt, but French Restoration lacks some of the ornamentation and fussiness of that period. Design motifs continue to reflect an interest

Walnut parlor table with pierced barley twist column on four scroll carved feet.
California Auctioneers, 8597 Ventura Ave., Ventura, CA 93001

in the classics of Greece and Egypt. Chair backs are styled with curved and concave crest rails, making them a little more comfortable than earlier straight-back chairs. The use of bolster pillows and more upholstery is starting to emerge. The style was only popular in clusters, but did entice makers from larger metropolitan areas, such as Boston and New Orleans, to embrace the style.

The Gothic Revival, 1840-1860: This is relatively easy to identify for collectors. It is one of the few styles that celebrates elements found in the corresponding architectural themes: turrets, pointed arches, and quatrefoils—designs found in 12th through 16th centuries that were adapted to this mid-century furniture style. The furniture shelving form known as an étagère was born in this period, allowing Victorians to have more room to display their treasured collections. Furniture that had mechanical parts was also embraced by the Victorians of this era. The woods preferred by makers of this period were walnut and oak, with some use of mahogany and rosewood. The scale used ranged from large and grand to small and petite. Carved details gave dimension and interest.

Rococo Revival, 1845-1870: This design style features the use of scrolls, either in a "C" shape or the more fluid "S" shape. Carved decoration in the form of scallop shells, leaves and flowers, particularly roses, and acanthus further add to the ornamentation of this style of furniture. Legs and feet of this form are cabriole or scrolling. Other than what might be needed structurally, it is often difficult to find a straight element in Rococo Revival furniture. The use of marble for tabletops was quite popular, but expect to find the corners shaped to conform to the overall scrolling form. To accomplish all this carving, walnut, rosewood, and mahogany were common choices. When lesser woods were used, they were often painted to reflect these more expensive woods. Some cast-iron elements can be found on furniture from this period, especially if it was cast as scrolls. The style began in France and England, but eventually migrated to America where it evolved into two other furniture styles, Naturalistic and Renaissance Revival.

Elizabethan, 1850-1915: This sub-category of the Victorian era is probably the most feminine-influenced style. It also makes use of the new machine-turned spools and spiral profiles that were fast becoming popular with furniture makers. New technology advancements allowed more machined parts to be generated. By adding flowers, either carved or painted, the furniture pieces of this era had a softness to them. Chair backs tend to be high and narrow, having a slight back tilt. Legs vary from straight to baluster-turned forms to spindle turned. This period of furniture design saw more usage of needlework upholstery and decoratively painted surfaces.

Louis XVI, 1850-1914: One period of the Victorian era that flies away with straight lines is Louis XVI. However, this furniture style is not austere; it is adorned with ovals, arches, applied medallions, wreaths, garlands, urns, and other Victorian flourishes. As the period aged, more ornamentation became present on the finished furniture styles. Furniture of this time was made from more expensive woods, such as ebony or rosewood. Walnut was popular

INTRODUCTION

Dresser, oak, three drawers, first quarter 20th century.

Montrose Auction Inc., 1702 Second St., Montrose, GA 31065

around the 1890s. Other dark woods were featured, often to contrast the lighter ornaments. Expect to find straight legs or fluted and slightly tapered legs.

Naturalistic, 1850-1914: This furniture period takes the scrolling effects of the Rococo Revival designs and adds more flowers and fruits to the styles. More detail is spent on the leaves—so much that one can tell if they are to represent grape, rose, or oak leaves. Technology advances enhanced this design style, as manufacturers developed a way of laminating woods together. This layered effect was achieved by gluing thin layers together, with the grains running at right angles on each new layer. The thick panels created were then steamed in molds to create the illusion of carving. The woods used as a basis for the heavy ornamentation were mahogany, walnut and some rosewood. Upholstery of this period is often tufted, eliminating any large flat surface. The name of John Henry Belter is often connected with this period, for it was when he did some of his best design work. John and Joseph W. Meeks also enjoyed success with laminated furniture. Original labels bearing these names are sometimes found on furniture pieces from this period, giving further provenance.

Renaissance Revival, 1850-1880: Furniture made in this style period reflects how cabinetmakers interpreted 16th- and 17th-century designs. Their motifs range from curvilinear and florid early in the period to angular and almost severe by the end of the period. Dark woods, such as mahogany and walnut, were primary with some use of rosewood and ebony. Walnut veneer panels were a real favorite in the 1870s designs. Upholstery, usually of a more generous nature, was also often incorporated into this design style. Ornamentation and high relief carving included flowers, fruits, game, classical busts, acanthus scrolls, strapwork, tassels, and masks. Architectural motifs, such as pilasters, columns, pediments, balusters, and brackets are another prominent design feature. Legs are usually cabriole or have substantial turned profiles.

Néo-Greek, 1855-1885: This design style easily merges with both the Louis XVI and Renaissance Revival. It is characterized by elements reminiscent of Greek architecture, such as pilasters, flutes, columns, acanthus, foliate scrolls, Greek key motifs, and anthemion high-relief carving. This style originated with the French, but was embraced by American furniture manufacturers. Woods are dark and often ebonized. Ornamentation may be gilded or bronzed. Legs tend to be curved to scrolled or cloven hoof feet.

Eastlake, 1870-1890: This design style is named for Charles Locke Eastlake, who wrote a popular book in 1872 called *Hints on Household Taste*. It was originally published in London. One of his principles was the relationship between function, form, and craftsmanship. Shapes of furniture from this style tend to be more rectangular. Ornamentation was created through the use of brackets, grooves, chamfers, and geometric designs. American furniture manufacturers were enthusiastic about this style, since it was so easy to adapt for mass production. Woods used were again dark, but more native woods, such as oak, maple, and pine were incorporated. Legs and chair backs are straighter, often with incised decoration.

Art Furniture, 1880-1914: This period represents furniture designs gone mad, almost an "anything goes" school of thought. The style embraces both straight and angular with some pieces that are much more fluid, reflecting several earlier design periods. This era saw the wide usage of turned moldings and dark woods, but this time stained to imitate ebony and lacquer. The growing Oriental influence is seen in furniture from this period, including the use of bamboo, which was imported and included in the designs. Legs tend to be straight; feet tend to be small.

Arts & Crafts, 1895-1915: The Arts & Crafts period of furniture represents one of the strongest trends for current collectors. Quality period Arts & Crafts furniture is available through most of the major auction houses. And, for those desiring the look, good quality modern furniture is also made in this style. The Arts & Crafts period furniture is generally rectilinear and a definite correlation is seen between form and function. The primary influences of this period were the Stickley brothers (especially Gustav, Leopold, and John George), Elbert Hubbard, Frank Lloyd Wright, and Harvey Ellis. Their furniture designs often overlapped into architectural and interior design, including rugs, textiles, and other accessories. Wood used for Arts & Crafts furniture is primarily oak. Finishes were natural, fumed, or painted. Hardware was often made in copper. Legs are straight and feet are small, if present at all, as they were often a simple extension of the leg. Some inlay of natural materials was used, such as silver, copper, and abalone shells.

Art Nouveau, 1896-1914: Just as the Art Nouveau period is known for women with long hair, flowers, and curves, so is Art Nouveau furniture. The Paris Exposition of 1900 introduced furniture styles reflecting what was happening in the rest of the design world, such as jewelry and silver. This style of furniture was not warmly embraced, as the sweeping lines were not very conducive to mass production. The few manufacturers that did interpret it for their factories found interest to be slight in America. The French held it in higher esteem. Legs tend to be sweeping or cabriole. Upholstery becomes slimmer.

Walnut hall tree, style of Henry II, with beveled mirror.
Morton Kuehnert Auctioneers & Appraisers, 4901 Richmond Ave., Houston, TX 77027

Art Deco, 1920-1945: The Paris "L'Exposition International des Arts Décorative et Industriels Modernes" became the mantra for designs of everything in this period. Lines are crisp, with some use of controlled curves. The Chrysler Building in New York City remains among the finest example of Art Deco architecture and those same straight lines and gentle curves are found in furniture. Makers used expensive materials, such as veneers, lacquered woods, glass, and steel. The cocktail table first enters the furniture scene during this period. Upholstery can be vinyl or smooth fabrics. Legs are straight or slightly tapered; chair backs tend to be either low or extremely high.

Modernism, 1940-present: Furniture designed and produced during this period is distinctive, as it represents the usage of some new materials, like plastic, aluminum, and molded laminates. The Bauhaus and also the Museum of Modern Art heavily influenced some designers. In 1940, the museum organized competitions for domestic furnishings. Designers Eero Saarien and Charles Eames won first prize for their designs. A new chair design combined the back, seat, and arms together as one unit. Tables were designed that incorporated the top, pedestal, and base as one. Shelf units were also designed in this manner.

Louis XVI style gilt bronze mounted mahogany suite of bedroom furniture, late 19th century.

All That Glitters is Great Jewelry

By Kathy Flood

Kathy Flood

Recently I purchased an enameled base-metal pin clip for $15 and sold it for $1,500. If that doesn't get your juices flowing for costume jewelry, I don't know what will. Why, you could even pay for a week of your ungrateful child's college tuition with such a sale. This just in: Another pin from the same company sold even more recently for $2,500. (It wasn't mine.)

You probably want to know what these profitable pins are. I only hesitate to say because, if you're new to the jewelry world, you shouldn't immediately run out to buy every Trifari piece you spot. Old Trifari figurals can be uncannily lucrative. Keep an eye out for them. Chances are, though, before you hit a jackpot, you'll first accumulate at least seven dozen pieces of Trifari you won't be able to unload — ever. It's part of the learning process.

Jewelry collectors can be a tough crowd. The costume-jewelry category, specifically, still has much more glory than gory, but it's not the '80s anymore, when American and international buyers from all over the world threw gobs of mad money at it. And that was pre-Internet. Now, with everyone spoiled and choosy, delicious gems even by names long considered sexy, from Eisenberg Original to Schiaparelli, may languish in well-trafficked shops.

The first time I came face to face with the steely resistance of jewelry collectors was when I set up at my first show. I had great jewelry to sell and modestly estimated I'd do about $1,000 in business that day. Instead, the take was $350. The show manager noticed I looked, let's say, glum while packing up and said to me, "You'll have to show up three to six times before your sales are good. Jewelry collectors don't like new dealers." I thought it was the most ridiculous thing I'd ever heard; how long a seller was around never mattered to me as a collector, but then, "Dancing With the Stars" and "The Office" make my skin crawl, so what do I know?

The other thing you might find if you decide to dip your toe in the sparkling waters of jewelry is that one seller's goldmine is another seller's coal mine. For example, vintage silver jewelry is highly coveted when it's well-designed and well-crafted. After all, we're talking precious metal and sometimes exceptional aesthetics. Last year, I decided to target sterling as an area to invest in for resale. Huge mistake for me. I just can't sell it. Others can.

Vintage Bakelite is another slightly cold category in my case, and it's such a dreamy medium, it's hard to resist. But I strictly limit myself to purchases of only the rarest Bakelite pieces. Even then, sales take a while. Maybe collectors eventually will come banging loudly at the door again for these nicest of niches. All it takes is Mila Kunis or Natalie Portman being photographed in some great Bakelite to change things around in a huge way, similar to what Sarah Jessica Parker and Angelina Jolie helped do for pearls. (See Warman's Jewelry, 4th edition.) Patience is an underrated virtue. Initially you'll be as petulant as a two-year-old. A mellower attitude comes with time.

The flip side for me, to mention just three stars in my

Kenneth J. Lane pink bead bracelet with enameled sea creature clasp.
Wickliff & Associates Auctioneers, 12232 Hancock St., Carmel, IN 46032

own sales constellation, includes Kenneth J. Lane, Trifari and many figural categories, especially fur-clip pins. People like them — a lot. Within these groups, though, are some hard-core cold spots, which is where you'll make your mistakes, cut your teeth, and get a great education.

But this primer is meant to help you avoid as many faux pas as possible. First, all you have to do is look around at results from live auctions to see that fine jadeite, large-diamond, and fancy-color diamond jewelry are off the charts in hammer prices at auction houses. That's one venue. When I spoke with some successful jewelry dealers in the course of business recently, I asked what's simmery vs. shivery for them as well, since what's hot or not can vary depending on vehicle, venue, and exactly who the veteran is. Here's what four active jewelry dealers had to

Fourteen karat gold and enamel jaguar clip/brooch designed by Kenneth J. Lane.
Skinner, Massachusetts

say. Pay special attention not just to what's hot, but what's icy, too, because that's where steals are sleeping. Meaning: you buy them now, tuck them away and pull them out another day — when everyone wants them once again.

P.S. The $1,500 piece was the Art Deco Trifari bartender. The $2,500 price was a Trifari figural from designer Alfred Philippe's Ming series.

At one shop, The More the Merrier, proprietor Merry Shugart didn't equivocate in either category, dreamy or unsteamy. Her list of the hot-hot:

- Victorian sterling hinged bracelets. "I can't get enough of them!"
- Juliana (DeLizza & Elster) necklaces and bracelets (pins, less so).
- Victorian overall, but mourning jewelry not so much.
- Better Haskell. "I especially sell a lot to collectors in Japan."
- Saphirets (old and new)
- Native American silver
- "In fine jewelry, Deco diamond rings are selling like hotcakes."
- Italian silver. "Peruzzi and Parenti, especially; Cini less so."
- Enamel lockets = hottish
- Big, glitzy bracelets
- Hobe — the drippier the better

Her list of the fairly frigid:

Gem-set gold fur-clip, 18 karat yellow gold diamond accented feathers, ruby and sapphire cabochons and leaf-shaped diamond triplet clusters, circa 1955.
Rago Arts and Auction Center, 333 North Main St., Lambertville, NJ 08530

- Weiss thermoset clamper bracelets. " ...Super hot three years ago, pretty dead now."
- Matisse enamels. "Not commanding the high prices they were."
- Mexican silver. "I have gorgeous pieces that are languishing."
- Mourning jewelry
- Lockets in general ... "although I still buy good ones when possible."
- "Puffy hearts have really slowed down."

Meanwhile, at Linda Lombardo's shop, Worn to Perfection, she says, "What seems to have cooled are the fabulous Edwardian and Transitional Deco filigree pieces: usually rhodium plated, delicate, with colored glass. These happen to be among my favorites, and I absolutely believe they will make a comeback." (Look at a few and you'll see how fickle jewelry tastes can be. How can any pieces this pretty ever cool?)

Higher temps at Worn to Perfection can be found in these popular categories, according to Lombardo (in no particular order): Victorian lockets and Victorian in general; bolder brass or gold-toned pieces with attitude ... ("I recently had four sets of Haskell, simple sets and the Maria Teresa or Teresia coin necklace. They flew out of my shop. The only one remaining is a white set, which may require some warmer weather to inspire someone.") "Pearls are also stronger sellers right now, both real or faux. Multi-strand pearl bracelets with rhinestone clasps are very 'Mad Men' — and hot."

OK, I admit it was a relief to have Claudia Roach, owner of The Pink Lady, commiserate with me over Bakelite. "I cannot give Bakelite away," Claudia actually exclaimed. "This has been going on for a while. It may have something to do with geography?" (Claudia's in California; I'm in the Midwest, so, maybe not. But can there be any doubt Bakelite will live to rise again to its former glory? It'll be back with a vengeance eventually. So for now, keep an eye out for any great Bake sale.)

"What's hot for me at The Pink Lady are reasonably priced $50 to $80 sparkly pins and bracelets. I also sell a ton of earrings, but I don't see any pattern to it — just earrings purchased to go with outfits. With young people, costume rings are really hot, one for every finger, $25 tops each."

At Sandi DiDio's shop, Zi-Glitterati, she explained, "I had a vintage shop for 10 years, but recently moved my inventory to an antiques mall. When I opened my shop 10 years ago, everyone went crazy over vintage jewelry in general, especially rhinestone brooches. It didn't matter if they were designer signed, big and sparkly or small and dainty. Antique jewelry didn't sell nearly as fast as the '50s-'60s pieces. But brooch sales have slowed down for me, and antique jewelry sells far better now: Victorian, Edwardian, Art Deco, Art Nouveau ... all are really hot! So is enamel jewelry — very hot. Anything unusual sells, of course, so I love figural brooches and clips. Rings have always sold well for me. Cold for me has always been something I really love: porcelain jewelry. It just doesn't sell. I also love old plastics — Bakelite, celluloid, Lucite — but they haven't been selling at all. I love dress and fur clips but can't get customers to buy them, and you can do so much with a dress clip, even clip over a chain as a necklace. I do believe they will become a hot item in the next few years."

It makes sense. Especially if we can get Blake Lively to wear some on "Gossip Girl."

European 18k gold, amethyst, rose diamond and purple enamel necklace, circa 1890s.
Steve Fishbach Collection; photo by Linda Lombardo

Cushion-cut fancy natural yellow diamond ring in platinum, rose gold and 18k yellow gold, accented by fancy yellow diamonds, fancy pink diamonds and colorless diamonds.
Maidi Corp courtesy of Natural Color Diamond Association

KATHY FLOOD is a journalist, author of three Warman's jewelry books, and the proprietor of several jewelry businesses including Fabulous Figurals on Ruby Lane and ChristmasTreePins.com. A library of her books is available for sale on Shop.Collect.com.

Advertising Items

Thousands of advertising items made in various materials, some intended as gifts with purchases, others used for display or given away for publicity, are actively collected.

Before the days of mass media, advertisers relied on colorful product labels and advertising giveaways to promote their products. Containers were made to appeal to the buyer through the use of stylish lithographs and bright colors. Many of the illustrations used the product in the advertisement so that even an illiterate buyer could identify a product.

Advertisements were put on almost every household object imaginable and became constant reminders to use the product or visit a certain establishment.

Advertisement, 'Auto-Lite Spark Plugs,' promotion tied in to Rita Hayworth movie 'You'll Never Got Rich,' color photo of Hayworth in grass skirt, a spark plug in the foreground, stylized illustration of Art Deco style movie theater in background w/marquee showing name of movie, a row of movie goers at bottom, text reads 'Theatres! Look at this sensational Auto-Lite Tip-up - featuring Rita Hayworth - It's Free - It's Colorful - It's Box Office - It's One of Many Valuable Auto-Lite Tie-ins' & 'Auto-Lite Dealers Offer You 100% Cooperation!' at bottom, 1941....**$100**

Calendar, 1903, 'Bemis Bros. Bag Co.,' rectangular, lithographed cloth, red w/white & yellow lettering, center w/white circle depicting head of a buffalo in black & white & surrounded by a circle of white dots, flanked by torches above bags & marked above 'Animals that Are Hunted,' Bemis Bros. Bag Co., St. Louis, Missouri, each page features different animal & colors, ca. 1903, 11 x 16" **$450-650**

Calendar, 1909, 'Osborne Harvesting Machines,' full color illustration of cowboy on galloping horse aiming rifle at antelope in distance, 'Osborne - Harvesting Machines - and - Farm Implements' in upper right, w/full calendar pad for 1909 & band at top, 13 1/2 x 20".....................**$935**

Calendar, 1920, 'Winchester,' long rectangular print w/a large color image of a duck hunter carrying his game & stepping out of a small boat where his son sits, water in the background, full pad at the bottom, 19 3/4 x 38 1/2"......**$805**

Clock, 'Milkmaid Milk,' Baird-style wall-mounted round embossed metal frame in brown w/raised white wording 'Milkmaid Milk - Now's The Time to Buy It,' stained paper dial w/Roman numerals, hinged glass dial cover w/brass trim, includes the pendulum, 17 1/2" d......................**$460**

Calendar, 1907, 'Metropolitan Life Insurance Co.,' long narrow rolldown paper-style, four round color reserves showing the stages in a woman's life, flowers & small calendar blocks joining the images, excellent condition, 12 x 33".....................**$345**

Counter display/container, 'Planters Peanuts,' papier-maché two-piece peanut, embossed w/ 'Planters' in script, the end coming off for filling w/one pound of peanuts, 5 x 6", 12" l. **$44**

Counter display case, 'J. & P. Coats Boilfast Thread,' low rectangular wood-grained metal three-drawer case, black printing on top & front of top drawer, early 20th c., 17 x 19", 6 1/2" h. **$288**

Counter display, 'Winchester Firearms,' cardboard cutout gun rack, colorful dual rack for .22 rifles or shotguns, top shows two men holding guns on either side of circular advertising area that can display one of three rounded attachments, one a Christmas wreath w/'Give a 22' inside, one w/image of a crow in the center w/'Get him with a new Winchester 22' around rim & across bottom, & one w/image of gopher in center w/'Get him with a new Winchester 22' around rim & across bottom, red & white striped gun rack w/gold oval panels reading 'Winchester' in red, 1950s, 12 x 18", 20" h. **$633**

Counter display box, 'Briggs Bros. & Co. Seeds,' wooden w/applied paper labels, a long low rectangular box w/a string-hinged flat lid, the interior w/a large color-printed label showing various vegetables, front of box w/long advertising label centered by a small spread-winged eagle, contains about 190 original full seed packets, late 19th - early 20th c., 10 1/4 x 24", 5 1/4" h. **$1,380**

Counter display jar, 'Curtiss Chicos Spanish Peanuts 5¢,' upright squared clear glass w/rounded corners, colorful fitted metal id & embossed yellow band base w/advertising & dispensing flap, early 20th c., 8" w., 11" h. **$403**

Counter display cabinet, 'Humphreys' Veterinary Specifics,' walnut, front-opening, w/heavily embossed composition panel w/a profile of a horse, scarce version reading 'Humphreys' Veterinary Homeopathic Specifics,' dated 12/14/87, 10 x 21", 34" h. **$5,500-7,000**

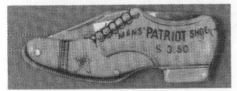

Penknife, 'Men's Patriot Shoes - $3.50 - Star Brand Shoes Are Better,' yellow celluloid case shaped like a man's shoe, one-blade, early 20th c., 2 3/4" l.... **$587**

Display card, 'Wheatlet,' cardboard easel-back display w/full-color illustration of Uncle Sam standing on globe of world, holding hat in one hand & gesturing toward box of Wheatlet & bowl of cereal sitting atop it, bowing to crowd of men looking up at him, 'Eaten and Enjoyed by all Nations' in red below figure, 'Made only by - The Franklin Mills Co. - Lockport, N.Y. U.S.A.' at bottom of display, 1899, 3 1/2 x 6 1/4" **$121**

Pin, 'Selby,' celluloid over tin, round, 'SELBY' in center, 'B.B.' curved above & 'Split Shot' curved below, litho by American Artworks, 1 1/2" d. **$66**

Pinback button, 'Sportsman's League,' celluloid, round, gold-colored edge reading 'Sportsman's League' in black, the center w/ illustration of fishing lure in orange & grey & reading 'Bradshaw's Fancy - Wet Fly for Trout,' 1 1/4" d. **$77**

Pocket mirror, 'Ohio Blue Tip Matches,' round, celluloid, dark blue border w/white letters reading 'Ohio Blue Tip Matches - The Ohio Match Co.' & 'J.C. Orrick & Son Co. - Cumberland, MD. Distributors' above scene of factory w/white & blue product package below, Ohio Match Company, Wadsworth, Ohio, ca. 1900, 3 1/2" d........**$175-225**

Asian (Chinese – Art & Antiques)

Art and antiques from China, Japan, Korea, the Pacific Rim, and Southeast Asia have fascinated collectors for centuries because they are linked with the rich culture and fascinating history of the Far East. Their beauty, artistry and fine craftsmanship have lured collectors through the ages.

The category is vast and includes objects ranging from jade carvings to cloisonné to porcelain, the best-known of these being porcelain.

Large quantities of porcelain have been made in China for export to America from the 1780s. A major source of this porcelain was Ching-te-Chen in the Kiangsi province, but the wares were also made elsewhere. The largest quantities were blue and white.

Nippon is the term used to describe a wide range of porcelain wares produced in Japan from the late 19th century until about 1921. Many Japanese factories produced Nippon porcelain, much of it hand-painted with ornate floral or landscape decoration.

Prices for Asian antiques and art fluctuate considerably depending on age, condition, decoration, etc.

Bronze Censer, foliate designs and double handles, seal to base, 3-1/2" h. **$57**

Blue and White Porcelain Fish Bowl, Chinese, unidentified maker, late 16th c., late Ming Dynasty, Wanli period (1573-1619), porcelain, unmarked, base has old professional repair to crack along the luting line, firing flaws characteristic of porcelain from this period, 21-1/2" h. x 24-3/4" w...**$10,755**

◄Carved Carnelian Tripod Koro, Chinese, reticulated cover, double loose ring handles and loose ring handles to finial, with wood stand, 8-1/4" h. **$179**
►Carved Hardstone of Standing Buddah, Chinese, holding an orb and staff with a bag tied to the end and thrown over his shoulder, 3-1/2" h. **$39**

Carved Ivory Floral Planter, with wood base, Chinese, 20th c., relief-carved ivory, some shrinkage cracks, 11" h. x 15-1/2" w. not including base......... **$2,629**

Carved Ivory Chess Set, Chinese, c.1900, winged dogs of Foo pawns, elephant rooks, winged horse knights, turtle bishops, Phoenix queen, dragon king, hand carved, with fitted wooden box, tallest piece 6" h. **$1,551**

Carved Jade Horses, Chinese, 20th c., a carved jade group of six horses in full stride atop rockery, wood stand, small chips to mane, 11-3/4" h. x 13-1/2" w. x 2-3/4" d..**$896**

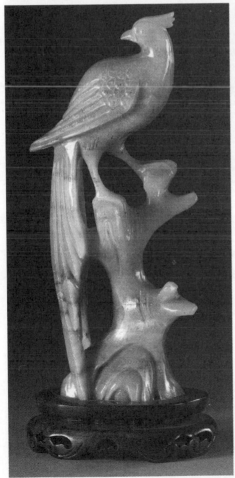

Carved Jade/Hardstone Figure, Chinese, carved jade/hardstone figure of a phoenix, perched on tree branches on a wood stand, 8-1/2" h. **$102**

▶Carved Snuff Bottle, Chinese carved snuff bottle, probably bone, with stopper carved in the form of a chilong, 4" h. x 2-3/4" w................................. **$72**

ASIAN

TOP! LOT!

Chinese gilt bronze figure of Vajrasattva, with an incised six-character Xuande mark................ **$1,530,000**

Chinese gold and silver inlaid bronze animal-form censer from the 17th/18th century. **$81,000**

Embroidered blue silk dragon robe having nine five-claw dragons with couched gold-wrapped threads leaping amidst clouds, bats and other auspicious emblems, all above a hem of crusting waves with other auspicious objects and the lishui stripe. **$10,925**

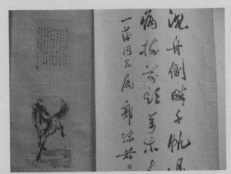

Two Oriental scrolls, one featuring characters and the other with two panels of a galloping horse and characters.................................**$6,325**

Chinese carved jade mortar, spinach-colored jade, motif features scrolling dragons, clouds, waves, 10-1/4" tall, late 19th/early 20th century. **$14,760**

Southeast Asian Gilt-Bronze Covered Bowl on Stand with Seated Figure of Buddha, shaped in the form of a lotus, the bowl topped by a seated Buddha figure whose hand touches the earth – a gesture meant to represent a renunciation of worldly desires. **$22,000**

◄Chinese translucent white jade carving of two crickets atop a cabbage, late-19th-century (Qing/early Republic) 6-1/2" long, 3.25 pounds...**$1,800**

Chinese brass mounted Jichimu long table (Huazbo). **$41,125**

ASIAN

Woodblock in colors by Hasui Kawase (Jap., 1883-1957), titled Zojoji Temple. **$5,500**

Ovoid form Chinese vase with puce ground and turquoise, 19th century, 6-3/8". **$11,500**

Chinese Ming Dynasty landscape painting on silk, dated 1535, 66" long by 16-3/4" wide, formerly the property of the Honolulu Academy of Arts. **$14,760**

Left: Chinese blue and white Imari figure of a seated Buddha, signed. $1,100

Right: Asian blue and white floral vase, 12". $3,080

▲Late Ming dynasty Jing du Jiang blue and white bowl, 16" in diameter. . **$4,760**

◄Rare intact set of 10 Canton porcelain nesting bowls with figural scenes on each... **$5,060**

Chinese silver export tray, Wang Hing & Co., pierce carved dragon design, 145.87 ozt. $17,360

White jade vase with cover, ovoid with lion-form finial, 10" tall. $22,320

Chinese yellow jade rhyton, relief carved with spiraling design, 10" tall...........$17,360.

ASIAN

◄Carved Wood Figure, Chinese, unidentified maker, c.1900, portraying the dual nature of Li Tie Gwai, one of the eight Immortals, the carved face with inset green glass eyes near the bottom of the carving depicts Li's non-corporal traveling spirit, the standing figure with inset amber glass eyes depicts the elderly crippled beggar's body that Tie Gwai Li stole when his own body was misplaced, unsigned, 20-1/2" h.........**$191**

▲Celadon Ginger Jar, Chinese, unidentified maker, 20th c., smooth slightly domed wooden lid, signed underside in Chinese characters, lid shows signs of previous repair, two pieces reconstructed, insert has been non-professionally restored, 6" h..............**$54**

►Cloisonne Vase, Chinese, unidentified maker, late Qing Dynasty, unsigned 11-3/4" h. ..**$448**

▼Cloisonne Oil Lamp, Chinese, unidentified maker, c.1920, gilt metal spine ridge, elbows, feet, and tail, and brass tubular connector of head with impressed with number 40, unmarked, 12" l. x 8.25" h...**$335**

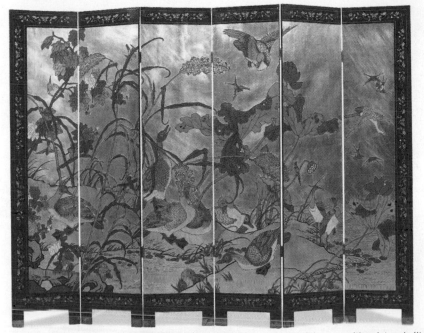

Coromandel Screen, Asian, unidentified maker, c.1820, six panel, black lacquer with paint and gilt, unmarked, some restoration to corners and minor chips, 72" h. x 96" w. **$3,585**

Hardwood Plant Stand, Chinese, late 19th-early 20th c., marble inset top, 18-5/8 x 13-1/2 x 13-1/2" **$131**

Coromandel-Style Cabinet on Giltwood Stand, Chinese cabinet with English stand, late 19th c. lacquer, brass, giltwood, unmarked, 54 x 32 x 18" **$11,950**

Silver Bowl, Chinese export, unidentified maker, Canton, China, c.1825-1875, marks: KC, (shop mark), 6-1/4 x 12" d., minor surface scratching and denting **$4,929**

Lacquered Tea Caddy, Chinese export, late 18th-early 19th c., 8-5/8 x 13-3/4 x 11" closed..........**$717**

Porcelain Vases, Chinese export, c.1840, unmarked, 10" h., small chip under rim, pair............**$717**

Porcelain Storage Jar with Lid, Chinese, unidentified maker, c.1750, porcelain with polychrome enamel and gilt decoration, domed lid with foo dog knop, unmarked, 16" h.................**$657**

Rose Medallion Porcelain Vase, Chinese export, c.1890, unmarked, 15 x 11" d. **$508**

▲Taoist Shrine, Chinese, unidentified maker, c.1900, unmarked, flat top with age cracks, old repair, and loss of detachable pediment, loss of carved 'rail' element between front columns, alterations to door, loss of original back, new mirrored glass and wooden back added, 36-1/2" h.
....**$263**

◄Ivory Figure of Guanyin, Chinese, Qing Dynasty, 1644-1911, 1-7/8" h.
....**$239**

Banks - Mechanical

Original early mechanical and cast-iron still banks are in great demand with collectors. Their scarcity has caused numerous reproductions of both types, and the novice collector is urged to exercise caution.

Numbers after the bank name refer to those in John Meyer's *Handbook of Old Mechanical Banks*. However, *Penny Lane—A History of Antique Mechanical Toy Banks* by Al Davidson, provides updated information, and the number from this volume is indicated at the end of each listing. A well illustrated book, *The Penny Lane Bank Book—Collecting Still Banks* by Andy and Susan Moore, pictures and describes numerous additional banks, and the Moore numbers appear after the name of each listing. Other books on still banks include *Iron Safe Banks* by Bob and Shirley Peirce (SBCCA publication), *The Bank Book* by Bill Norman (N), *Coin Banks by Banthrico* by James Redwine (R), and *Monumental Miniatures* by Madua & Weingarten (MM). We indicate the Whiting or other book reference number, with the abbreviation noted above, at the end of the listing.

Bull Dog Bank - 63 -, seated, coin on nose, brown & red, rare white variant known, J. & E. Stevens, 1880, old paint restoration, PL 64 .... **$1,668**

Bad Accident - 9 -, man riding in cart pulled by donkey w/boy hiding behind cat-tail plant, J. & E. Stevens, multicolored, fair paint, old repair to top of card, trap missing, PL 20 .... **$834**

Goat, Frog & Old Man (Initiating 2nd Degree) - 114 -, bearded old man on goat facing frog, similar action to Initiating, 1st Degree bank, black, yellow & green paint, Mechanical Novelty Works, 1880s, large areas of overpaint, PL 220 .... **$805**

Hall's Excelsior - 118 -, cast iron & wood, considered the first cast-iron mechanical bank, string-pull mechanism, building w/pop-up monkey in roof, paper 'Cashier' label, multicolored, J. & E. Stevens, ca. 1869, PL 228 ...... **$316**

Home Bank (No Dormer Windows) - 124 -, door w/ three-paneled windows on each side & three steps, seated man in doorway, no Dormer windows, small chip on corner of roof, PL 243 .... **$690**

Mama Katzenjammer - 140 -, Mama Katzenjammer wearing rose-colored dress & holding kids at her side, one dressed in blue, one in tan, when coin is dropped in bank, Mama rolls her eyes, rare, older repaint, 3 1/2", PL 317 ....**$780**

Paddy & His Pig - 185 -, Irish figure holding pig in his lap, multicolored, J. & E. Stevens, ca. 1885, PL 376 ...... **$1,323**

Tammany Bank (Little Fat Man) - 224 -, seated figure representing William 'Boss' Tweed, moving head & arm, various color variations, J. & E. Stevens, pat. Dec. 23, 1873, repaint to face, erratic nodding action, PL 455 .... **$200-400**

Mule Entering Barn - 169 -, multicolored, J. & E. Stevens, marked 'Pat'd. Aug. 30, 1880,' paint faded, PL 342...........................**$460**

Tank & Cannon, Starkie's, Burnley, Lancaster, England, ca. 1919, repair to base, PL 456 ....**$575**

William Tell - 237 -, figure firing rifle at boy w/apple on head, into the tower & strikes the bell, multicolored, J. & E. Stevens, ca. 1896, PL 565 ....**$1,093**

Uncle Remus - 230 -, cast iron, figure holding chicken in doorway of chicken coop w/policeman holding stick outside, Kyser & Rex Co. or Mechanical Novelty Works, if in near mint condition, PL 492 ....**$3,500-4,500**

Trick Pony - 196 -, pony lowers head to deposit the coin in the trough trap door which opens & closes to receive the coin , red, brown, black & yellow paint, Shepard Hardware, coin trap missing, PL 484 ....**$805**

(The) Robot (Aluminum), figure of black-painted mail carrier robot standing in front of red-painted building reading 'The Robot' above door, when coin is placed in right hand of robot & mechanism is activated, the hand comes forward & deposits the coin in slot on door, rare, Starkie's, England, early 20th c., PL 416 ....**$4,600**

Barbie

At the time of her introduction in 1959, no one could have guessed that this statuesque doll would become a national phenomenon and eventually the most famous girl's plaything ever produced.

Over the years, Barbie and her growing range of family and friends have evolved with the times, serving as an excellent mirror of the fashion and social changes taking place in American society. Today, after more than 50 years of continuous production, Barbie's popularity remains unabated among both young girls and older collectors. Early and rare Barbies can sell for remarkable prices, and it is every Barbie collector's hope to find a mint condition #1 Barbie.

▶Bubblecut Barbie, introduced 1961, rounded hairstyle, blonde, brunette, or titian (red) hair, red jersey one-piece swimsuit, matching red open toe heels and a gold wrist tag, mint in box... **$1,400**

Ponytail #1 Barbie, introduced 1959, unique feature is drilled holes in feet lined with copper tubing to allow it to rest on stand, stand included with box, produced with both blond and brunette hair, brunette variation more valuable because of rarity, mint in box with stand................................**$9,000**

Ponytail #2 Barbie, no holes in feet, produced in blond and brunette hair, mint in box..... **$7,000**

Fashion Queen Barbie, introduced 1963, original packaging included three wigs, mint in box........ **$500**

Miss Barbie, introduced 1964, with "sleep eyes" that open and close, mint in box..........**$1,200**

Swirl Ponytail Barbie, introduced 1964, wide variation of hair and lip color, mint in box . **$1,200**

American Girl Barbie, introduced 1965, bendable leg, first issued in 1965, mint in box **$1,900**

Color Magic Barbie, introduced 1966, includes Color Magic liquid changer A and B, sponge applicator with pink handle, and instruction booklet allowing hair, swimsuit, and headband colors to change back and forth between two alternatives; when swabbed with color changing solution, Golden Blonde hair changed to Scarlet Flame, and Midnight changed to Ruby Red. The yellow and green swimsuit changed to red and burgundy, as did Barbie doll's matching headband, mint in box.............. **$3,500**

Twist 'n Turn Barbie (also known as TNT), introduced 1967, with bendable waist, mint in box......... **$500**

Talking Barbie, introduced 1968, with Twist 'n Turn body and pull-string talking feature, mint in box............. **$425**

Talking Busy Barbie, introduced 1972, with gripping hands and twist 'n' turn waist, mint in box........... **$300**

Walk Lively Barbie, introduced 1971, packaged with special stand that allowed her to walk and swing her arms, mint in box **$225**

Malibu Barbie (also known as The Sun Set) introduced 1971, mint in box **$60**

Growin' Pretty Hair Barbie, introduced 1971, with retractable ponytail, included came with hairpieces and accessories, mint in box **$300**

BARBIE

Free Moving Barbie, introduced 1974, with lever on back to swing arms and upper torso, mint in box........... **$100**

▲Montgomery Ward 100th Anniversary "Original Barbie" reissue, released in 1972 to commemorate Montgomery Wards' 100 years in business, with reproduction Barbie dressed in black-and-white swimsuit of an early Ponytail, sold in a sparsely illustrated pink box under the name "The Original Barbie;" dolls ordered through the store's catalog were shipped in plain boxes, mint in box **$800**

Sweet 16 Barbie, introduced 1974, accessories include scented sticker barrettes, mint in box **$125**

Miss America Barbie, introduced 1974, mint in box **$75**

Supersize Barbie, introduced 1977, 18" alternative to the standard 11-1/2" size, mint in box.........**$200**

Baseball Memorabilia

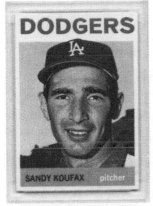

Baseball card, Sandy Koufax, Topps, 1964, graded NM-MT 8, cased **$237**

Baseball was reputedly invented by Abner Doubleday as he laid out a diamond-shaped field with four bases at Cooperstown, New York. A popular game from its inception, by 1869 it was able to support its first all-professional team, the Cincinnati Red Stockings. The National League was organized in 1876, and though the American League was first formed in 1900, it was not officially recognized until 1903. Today, the "national pastime" has millions of fans, and collecting baseball memorabilia has become a major hobby with enthusiastic collectors seeking out items associated with players such as Babe Ruth, Lou Gehrig, and others who became legends in their own lifetimes. Although baseball cards, issued as advertising premiums for bubble gum and other products, seem to dominate the field, there are numerous other items available.

Baseball, 1937 St. Louis Cardinals team-signed ball, twenty-five team members including Mize, Frisch, Martin, Durocher, Dean & Don Padgett, unofficial model, signed in blue fountain pen, well-toned **$658**

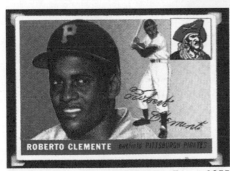

Baseball card, Roberto Clemente, Topps 1955 'rookie' card, graded EX-NM +6.5, cased **$981**

Baseball card set, 1951 Topps 'Red Back' set, includes Kiner, Feller, Snider, Berra, Wynn, Hodges & more, grades EX/MT to VG, complete set of 52 . **$754**

BASEBALL

Book, 'Smitty at the Ball Game,' based on the 1920s comic strip, the storyline featuring Smitty & Babe Ruth, copyright 1929, 86 pp., original dust jacket in color, overall excellent condition, 7 x 8 3/4"...**$185**

Cigar box, 'Base Ball Cigar,' printed labels on a wooden box, inside top label showing the ring logo w/crossed bats, tax stamps dating to 1883, very light traces of ink damage, overall excellent condition, 5 x 8", closed 4" h. **$414**

First Day postal cover, envelope postmarked Milwaukee, October 10, 1957, left half of front printed in red, white & blue w/Milwaukee Braves logo & promotion of their World Champion status, signed on the right front by Spahn, Mathews, Schoendienst & Burdette, excellent condition **$144**

Game, 'Baseball and Checkers - Two Game Combination,' board-type, two-sided folding board w/baseball diamond on one side & checkerboard on other, Milton Bradley, early 20th c., only one baseball token missing, overall excellent condition, colorfully printed box top, box 8 1/2 x 18" **$225**

Game, 'Batter Rou Baseball Game,' board-type, endorsed by Dizzy Dean, made by Memphis Plastic Enterprises, 1955, complete & near mint, box 9 x 19" **$160**

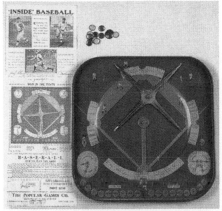

Game, 'Inside' Baseball,' board-type, square board w/ rounded corners in lithographed tin showing a baseball diamond in green w/yellow & orange details, large metal spinner, w/all 20 of its player disks, featuring a 1913 World Series game between the Athletics & the Giants, w/original instructions, produced by Popular Games Co., overall excellent condition, board 17 1/2" sq. **$506**

Gloves, souvenir-type, heavy white cloth w/thin black stripes, printed 'Go Go - Sox,' probably made for fans of the Chicago White Sox to wear during cold weather at games, handwritten illegible date on the wrist '1959,' palms mildly soiled, pr. **$244**

Lapel pin, oval celluloid center w/a photograph & name of Johnny Evers, ornate stamped scrolling brass frame, ca. 1915, minor damage but overall very good condition **$332**

Mug, stoneware, commemorative-type, yellow exterior printed in dark blue 'Globe Base Ball Association - Warwick Club - Sept. 15, 1907,' central caricature figure of the league-sponsoring Globe newspaper, excellent condition, 4 3/8" h. **$562**

Pinback button, souvenir-type, celluloid printed in red & white to resemble a baseball w/crossed bats in the lower section, red & white wording reads 'Booster - Federals - 1914,' from the short-lived Federal League, near mint condition, 7/8" d..**$185**

Pinback button, souvenir-type, large celluloid w/black & white half-length photo of Babe Ruth at bat, sold by vendors at Yankee Stadium, ca. 1920s-30s, excellent condition, 1 3/4" d. **$591**

Pinback button, souvenir-type, oval celluloid w/black & white composite photo of the 1929 National League Champion Chicago Cubs, reads 'Champions - 1929 - Cubs Team,' overall excellent condition, 2 3/4" l.. **$511**

Pinback button, souvenir-type, white printed in dark blue w/ crossed flags & wording 'World Series - New York Yankees - Brooklyn Dodgers - Ebbets Field - 1955,' minor paint restoration at rim, 2 1/4" d. **$301**

The Magnificent Yankee: Mickey Mantle

During his 18-year Major League career, Mickey Mantle led the New York Yankees to seven World Series titles while being named American League MVP three times. In 1956 Mantle won the Triple Crown, by leading the league in home runs, runs batted in, and batting average. In 1961 he and Yankee teammate Roger Maris produced one of the most memorable home run races in the history of baseball. Maris hit 61 homers that year, breaking Babe Ruth's home run record set in 1927. Mantle hit 54 home runs in an injury-shortened season.

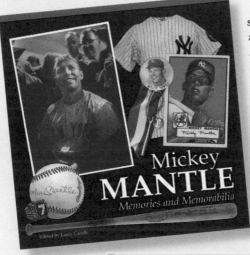

By the time he retired after the 1968 season, Mantle had hit 536 home runs and was selected to the American League All-Star team 16 times. Inducted into the Baseball Hall of Fame in 1974, Mantle died in 1995. But he remains one of the most popular baseball players of all time. His baseball cards, associated memorabilia, and signed items are highly collectible.

For more information on Mickey Mantle, see *Mickey Mantle: Memories and Memorabilia* by Larry Canale.

Photograph, 1949 Independence (Kansas) Yankees, signed, Mickey Mantle (first row, far right), 8" x 10", black and white............**$4,182**

1948 Mickey Mantle High School Junior Yearbook, Bengal Tales, leather bound, 8.5" x 11". $823

Advertising counter display for Haggar Slacks, features Mickey Mantle, cardboard, 14" x 18.75". **$3,819**

Above left: Mickey Mantle signed photograph, 18" x 10". $448

Above right: Mickey Mantle signed high school basketball photograph....................$537

Left: Photograph, New York Yankees 1984 Old Timer's Day, signed by Joe Dimaggio, Mickey Mantle, and Roger Maris.........................$1,880

▶Mickey Mantle artwork, artist Willard Mullin original pen-and-ink on coquille board, early 1950s, 14.5" x 19.75", signed by artist. **$3,525**

▼1952 Topps Mickey Mantle card. **$250,000**

Ron Lewis print featuring 11 members of the 500 Home Run Club, signed by (from left) Ted Williams, Frank Robinson, Harmon Killebrew, Reggie Jackson, Mickey Mantle, Willie Mays, Hank Aaron, Mike Schmidt, Ernie Banks, Eddie Mathews, and Willie McCovey. **$1,400**

Mickey Mantle original painting, 1962, signed by artist LeRoy Neiman, framed, 42" x 42". **$119,500**

Mickey Mantle World Series Display, 40" x 52.5", framed, features 16 World Series ticket stubs from games in which Mantle hit a record 18 home runs. Also features cut signatures of the 15 pitchers who gave up the home runs to Mantle.................................... **$6,463**

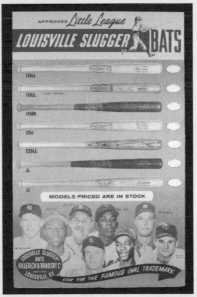

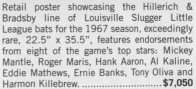

Retail poster showcasing the Hillerich & Bradsby line of Louisville Slugger Little League bats for the 1967 season, exceedingly rare, 22.5" x 35.5", features endorsements from eight of the game's top stars: Mickey Mantle, Roger Maris, Hank Aaron, Al Kaline, Eddie Mathews, Ernie Banks, Tony Oliva and Harmon Killebrew. **$7,050**

Print, advertising-type, black & white photo of Mickey Mantle & Roger Maris posed holding a bat, advertising the Holiday Inn in Joplin, Missouri, where Mantle had been a member of their Minor League team, 1960s, two minor creases, excellent condition, 8 x 10"............**$346**

Program, 'Chicago National League Ball Club - Wrigley Field - World's Series - 1929 - Chicago Cubs vs Philadelphia Athletics,' the cover printed in a bold Art Deco design in black, orange, yellow & white, black & white photos of Connie Mack & Joe McCarthy on the lower front, some penciled scoring, very good to excellent condition **$369**

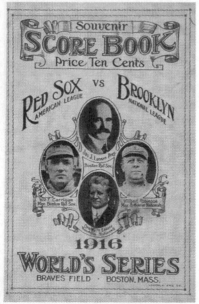

Program - score book, 'Souvenir Score Book - Price Ten Cents - Red Sox - American League vs Brooklyn - National League - 1916 - World's Series - Braves Field - Boston, Mass.,' the cover printed in red & dark blue & including photos of league & team officials, important because Babe Ruth was still a member of the Boston team & his photo is shown on the back cover, mild vertical crease, moderate cover stain, overall very good condition **$1,180**

Schedule, '1915 Schedule - Joe Tinker's Whales - Federal League,' printed in red, white & blue w/ comic figures of Uncle Sam & a Whales ballplayer, overall excellent, 36 pp., 2 1/4 x 4 1/2"......**$974**

Sign, reproduction of the classic 'Ted's Creamy Root Beer' sign printed in yellow, black, white, blue & red, actually autographed by Ted Williams in black Sharpie beside his image, 10 x 15" **$304**

Sign, 'Yoo-hoo Frozen Energy Bar,' long rectangular shape w/a bright green background printed in dark blue, red & white, features a baseball & a photo of Yogi Berra holding one of the ice cream bars, reads 'take it from Hall of Famer...Yogi Berra - Go Big League - Yoo-hoo Frozen Energy Bar,' ca. 1950s, near mint, 7 1/2 x 15" **$301**

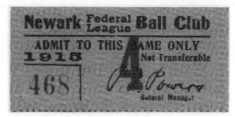

Ticket, full ticket for a 1915 game of the Newark, New Jersey, Federal League ball club, last year of the league, excellent condition, 1 x 2" **$449**

Stock certificate, 'The Federal Baseball Club of Baltimore,' issued to Douglas H. Gordon on March 19, 1914, cost $2,500, deep red border design, logo of the Federal League at the top center, issued for the Baltimore Terrapins team, minor holes, overall excellent condition, 8 1/4 x 11 1/2" **$1,787**

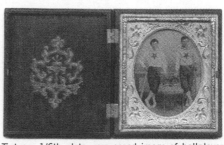

Tintype, 1/6th plate, rare cased image of ballplayer Candy Cummings, inventor of the curveball, posed on the left w/an unknown player, one of only four known images of Cummings, mid-19th c., closed 3 1/4 x 3 3/4" **$407**

Baskets

The American Indians were the first basket weavers on this continent and, of necessity, the early Colonial settlers and their descendants pursued this artistic handicraft to provide essential containers for berries, eggs and endless other items to be carried or stored. Rye straw, split willow and reeds are but a few of the wide variety of materials used. Nantucket baskets, plainly and sturdily constructed, along with those made by specialized groups, would seem to draw the greatest attention to this area of collecting.

'Buttocks' basket, forty-nine rib, wide wrapped oval rim, central arched bentwood handle, 13 x 16 1/2", overall 12" h. **$316**

Market basket, woven splint w/round wrapped rim, bentwood swing handle, dark red paint, 11 1/2" d., 7 1/2" h. **$575**

Market basket, woven splint, round w/wrapped rim & swing bentwood splint handle, green paint, few breaks to top wrap, 12" d., 8" h. **$518**

◀'Buttocks' basket, woven splint, 24-rib construction, bentwood handle, original blue paint, 12 1/2" l., 6 1/2" h. **$460**

▶'Melon' basket, woven splint, 34-rib construction, oblong w/bentwood handle, tightly woven w/good patina, minor splint break on bottom, America, 19th c., 18" l., 16" h. **$201**

Laundry basket, wide woven splint, rectangular w/two end rim handles, decorated w/ red & blue stripes w/vertical stamped blue decoration, 10 1/2 x 14 3/4", 6" h. **$230**

Nantucket basket, finely woven splint, deep round sides w/wrapped rim & carved swing handle, turned wooden base w/two incised lines, America, late 19th - early 20th c., 5 3/8" d., overall 7" h. **$3,819**

Utility basket, woven splint, rectangular w/deep sides, wrapped rim & bentwood handle, old blue paint, America, 19th c., a few splint breaks, 8 x 16 1/2", 14 3/4" h. **$407**

Utility basket, woven splint, Shaker-type, round push-up bottom & deep rounded sides w/a thick wrapped bentwood rim & fixed bentwood handle, 13 1/2" d., overall 13" h. **$120**

Utility basket, woven splint, a flat square bottom w/ deep sides, a bentwood gallery rim & central bentwood fixed handle, found in Connecticut, minor damage, 13" sq., 7 1/2" h. **$144**

Utility basket, finely woven wicker, Shaker-type, flat rounded push-up bottom w/deep swelled sides & a wrapped bentwood rim, high bentwood swing handle, 12" d., 7" h.. **$345**

Wall basket, woven splint, the high stepped back topped by a hanging loop above the tightly woven back, a front loop-woven arched band above the rectangular basket, old dark green paint, possibly Passamaquoddy, late 19th - early 20th c., 10" w., back overall 9 1/2" h.. **$431**

Wall basket, woven splint, the tall peaked solid-weave back w/curls down the side, deep basket w/a rectangular bottom & rounded sides w/a half-round bentwood wrapped rim, old salmon red paint, possibly Passamaquoddy, late 19th - early 20th c., 12" w., 19" h. **$920**

Bells

Bells—one of the oldest forms of art—hearken back centuries to ancient civilizations long gone. They are steeped in mystery, surrounded by legends of special powers ranging from thwarting demons to invoking curses and lifting spells.

In general, bells were most often used as a signal, marking significant points of ritual, calling to worship, tolling the hours, announcing events, and helping communities to rejoice, mourn, or send warning. Their power was at one time extremely significant to many religions. Bells have also been treasured as patriotic symbols and war trophies.

Most cultures today have turned these utilitarian objects into works of art with respect to shape, materials, and ornamentation. Created of porcelain, wood, metal, china, crystal, and other materials, the melodious chimers are a double joy for collectors because they are both lovely to hear and to look at.

American Peach Blow Glass Bell, maker unknown, circa 1900, unsigned, 7" h., no clapper **$335**

American Bronze Liberty Bell Replica, unknown maker, 20th c., cast bronze, fixed to wooden pedestal, 40-1/2" h. x 34-3/4" w. including pedestal **$478**

American Iron Bell, O.S. Bell Co., Hillsboro, Ohio, 19th c., cast iron, yoke marked 'No. 2 Yoke', 24" h. x 20" w. **$359**

American Bronze Ship's Bell with Wooden Stand, unknown maker, 19th c., cast bronze, hallmark on top of bell, 31-1/2" h. x 14" w. x 17" d. including frame **$1,434**

American Silver Dinner Bell, Towle Silversmiths, Newburyport, Massachusetts, 20th c., marks: (lion on T), STERLING 7405, B 4-1/2 x 2-3/8", fine surface scratches **$287**

American Silver Plate Dinner Bell, Gorham Manufacturing Company, Providence, Rhode Island, circa 1900, marks: G.MFG (anchor), 046, 5 x 2-1/2" d. **$359**

American Silver Repousse Bell, Mark of Mauser, New York, circa 1900, body entirely repousse, handle plain tear drop shape, 4" h. **$168**

Danish Silver Dinner Bell, Georg Jensen Silversmithy, Copenhagen, Denmark, circa 1930, Marks: GEORG JENSEN (within beaded oval), STERLING, DENMARK, DESSIN (intertwined GA), 148, 3-1/4" h., minor surface scratches **$263**

American Silver Dinner Bell, Tiffany & Co., New York, New York, circa 1888, marks: TIFFANY & CO., 9993 M 7353, STERLING-SILVER, 5" h. x 4-3/4" inches w., scratches to bottom **$5,975**

▶Chinese Bronze Bell, unknown maker, 19th c., bronze, unmarked, 37" h. **$5,975**

Mexican Silver Dinner Bell, William Spratling, Taxco, Mexico, circa 1940, marks: SPRAT-LING MADE IN MEXICO (circling) WS, SPRAT-LING SILVER, 3-3/8 x 1-3/4 x 1-5/8", fine surface scratches **$717**

Mexican Silver Dinner Bell, William Spratling, Taxco, Mexico, circa 1960, marks: WILLIAM SPRATLING, TAXCO MEXICO, script WS 925, 4-1/2" h. x 3-1/8" w. **$2,390**

Bookends

Once a staple in many homes, bookends serve both functional and decorative purposes. They not only keep a person's books in order, they look good while they're doing it.

Bookends are commonly made of a variety of metals (bronze, brass, pewter, silver plate) as well as organic materials (marble, wood). The art they feature represents many subjects, with wildlife, domesticated animals and pets, sports figures or items, nautical themes, and fantasy themes as favorites.

The value of an antique bookend is determined by its age, the material it is made from, what it represents, the company that created it, and how scarce it is.

Abraham Lincoln: Bradley and Hubbard, brass shell back / base with bronze-finished bust of Lincoln on plinth, both are marked on back w/letters "B&H" w/ printer's flowers above and below, 4-1/2" w. x 6-1/2" h., light finish loss to the busts, pair................**$310**

Lalique Birds, 20th c., landing birds, both frosted and clear, signature to the underside, Lalique France, 6-1/8" h., pair... **$598**

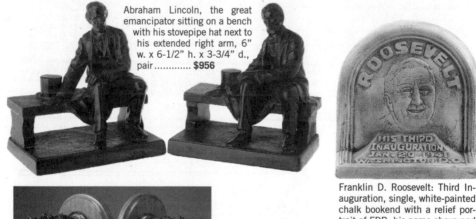

Abraham Lincoln, the great emancipator sitting on a bench with his stovepipe hat next to his extended right arm, 6" w. x 6-1/2" h. x 3-3/4" d., pair **$956**

Franklin D. Roosevelt: Third Inauguration, single, white-painted chalk bookend with a relief portrait of FDR, his name above and "His Third Inauguration / Jan. 20. 1941 / Washington, D.C." below, bottom bears a label that reads "Made and Sold / by/ Harry Grimm / 107 - 14th Street / Wheeling. W. Va.", 6-1/2" x 6-1/4", slight finish loss and minor chipping.......................**$37**

George B. Marks (American, 1923-1983), Horse Head Bookends, 1979, bronze, 9 x 5 x 6", Ed. 29/40 and 30/40, signed on base: GB Marks, inscribed on base: A&S U.S.A., pair **$598**

Louis C. Tiffany Furnaces Inc., gilt bronze "Landscape" circa 1900, marks: stamped FAVRILE LOUIS C. TIFFANY FURNACES INC. 605 with circular trademark, 4-1/2" h., pair...................................... **$837**

Mahonri Mackintosh Young (American, 1877-1957), Elephant, bronze, each signed on the base: Young, stamped verso: Cast by Griffoul Newark, N.J., 5-1/2 x 7-1/8 x 2-3/4", pair..................................... **$5,676**

Rookwood, circa 1928, Dutch man and woman face each other behind a brown brick wall with mauve colored tulips, stamped with insignia and date XXVIII, 6-1/2" h., nick on girl's nose, pair.................. **$215**

Roseville, c.1931, open books and pinecones, raised signature Roseville/U.S.A., 4-3/4" h., pair **$215**

Running Terriers, Edith Barretto Stevens Parsons, American (1878-1956), bronze with brown patina, the first, signed E. B. Parsons with copyright symbol, stamped Gorham Co. Founders OFCO. The second, signed E. B. Parsons with copyright symbol, stamped with foundry mark for Kunst Foundry, N.Y., bases 7-3/4" l., pair.. **$1,195**

Theodore Roosevelt , circa early 1900s, bronze, each signed, "Paul Herzel" (American, 1876-1950), probably individual pieces from two separate sets of book ends united later, patinas are slightly different, and one has Roosevelt's name across the front of the base, while the other has it across the back, 6" h. x 4-3/8" w. x 2" d., pair **$403**

Theodore Roosevelt, cast iron w/ bronze finish, 6-1/4" h., surface wear, pair........................... **$253**

Bottles

Interest in bottle collecting is strong and continues to gain popularity, with new bottle clubs forming throughout the United States and Europe.

More collectors are spending their free time digging through old dumps, foraging through ghost towns, digging out old outhouses, exploring abandoned mine shafts, and searching out their favorite bottle at antiques shows, swap meets, flea markets, and garage sales. In addition, the Internet offers collectors opportunities and resources without ever leaving the house.

Most collectors still look beyond the type and value of a bottle to its origin and history. Researching the history of bottles can be as interesting as finding the bottle itself.

Michael Polak, bottle expert

◄Carter's - Liver Bitters - C.M. Co. New York, oval, rounded shoulder, smooth base, tooled mouth, ca. 1890-1900, amber, 8 1/4" h. (front & back) **$448**

Bitters

(Numbers with some listings below refer to those used in Carlyn Ring's *For Bitters Only*.)

Brown's Celebrated Indian Herb Bitters - Patented Feb. 11, 1868, figural Indian queen, inward rolled mouth, smooth base, unusual coloring w/arms & upper body in yellow w/a hint of green, headdress & lower portion in yellowish amber, highlighted by old red & yellow paint, 12 1/8" h. **$1,792**

Dingen's - Napoleon Cocktail Bitters - Dingen Brothers - Buffalo N.Y., banjo shape on pedestal, w/lady's leg neck, iron pontil, applied sloping collar mouth, smoky clear, ca. 1865-75, 10 1/8" h. **$6,160**

Fish (The) Bitters - W.H. Ware, Patented 1866, figural fish, 'W.H. Ware Patent 1866' on bottom, applied small round collared mouth, smooth base, ca. 1866-1875, yellow w/faint amber & olive tones, 11 5/8" h. **$1,456**

German - Hop - Bitters - 1880 - Dr C. D. Warner's - Reading, Mich, square semi-cabin, smooth base, applied sloping double collar mouth, 97% paper label on front & 70% label on rear, ca. 1880-85, amber, 9 3/4" h. (two views) **$672**

Greeley's Bourbon Bitters, barrel-shaped, ten rings above & below center band, applied mouth, smooth base, ca. 1860-75, smoky copper topaz, 9 1/4" h. **$476**

Hertrichs Bitter, Einziger Fabrikant, Hans Hertrich Hof Gesetzlich Geschutzt, footed ball-shaped w/tall ringed neck, applied double collar mouth, smooth base, Germany, ca. 1880-1900, yellowish olive green, 9 1/4" h. **$336**

Holtzermann's Patent Stomach Bitters (on roof), cabin-shaped, two-roof, smooth logs, applied sloping collar mouth, smooth base, ca. 1865-75, amber, smoothed out chip on one log, tiny faint iridescent bruise on one roof, 9 3/8" h. **$784**

National Bitters, figural ear of corn, 'Patent 1867' on base, applied sloping collared mouth w/ring, smooth base, medium golden yellowish amber, ca. 1867-75, 12 1/2" h. **$840**

Nibol Kidney and Liver Bitters - The Best Tonic Laxative & Blood Purifier, square, smooth base, tooled lip, w/98 percent original front & back labels & contents, medium amber, 9 1/2" h. **$728**

Old Sachem Bitters and Wigwam Tonic, barrel-shaped, ten-rib, pontil scarred base, applied mouth, deep bluish aqua w/patch of olive in area of embossing, ca. 1855-70, 10 1/4" h. **$5,040**

Pineapple figural, embossed diamond-shaped panel, applied top, smooth base, ca. 1865-75, medium amber, 9" h.............................. **$308**

Prickly Ash Bitters, square, smooth base, ABM lip, w/99 percent original label on three sides & contents, made by Meyer Brothers Drug. Co., St. Louis, Missouri, medium amber, ca. 1910-15, 9 1/4" h. (two sides)............ **$258**

Thads. Waterman - Warsaw - Stomach Bitters, octagonal, smooth base, applied sloping double collar mouth, many seed bubbles, medium golden amber, ca. 1865-75, 10 1/2" h. **$3,920**

Suffolk Bitters - Philbrook & Tucker Boston, figural pig, smooth base, applied double collar mouth, medium amber shading to more yellow in feet, ca. 1865-75, 10 1/8" l. **$1,064**

Travellers Bitters, rectangular w/rounded side panels, cabin-like shoulder, front panel embossed w/a figure of a man walking w/a cane (Robert E. Lee), applied sloping collared mouth, smooth base, golden amber, 1860-80, small flat chip on base, pinpoint bruise to right of figure, minor exterior wear & scratches, rare, 10 1/2" h. **$5,320**

Tippecanoe (birch bark & canoe design), H.H. Warner & Co., cylindrical, 'Patent Nov. 20. 83 - Rochester - N.Y.' on smooth base, applied disc mouth, ca. 1880-95, yellowish amber, 9" h. **$168**

Figurals

Clam, ground lip, smooth base, threaded neck for metal cap, ca. 1885-95, cobalt blue, no metal cap, 5" h. **$1,064**

Alligator, seated upright animal on a round base, a tall cylindrical neck issuing from the mouth, pontil scar on base, sheared & tooled mouth, milk glass, chip off tail filled in w/white plaster-of-Paris, probably French, ca. 1880-1910, 10" h. **$168**

Shoe, lace-up shoe w/toe protruding from hole in front, ground lip w/original screw-on cap at ankle, 'PAT. APL. 00' on smooth base, black amethyst w/original flesh-color paint on toe, ca. 1890-1910, 3 3/4" h. **$258**

Oyster, closed shell, aqua w/99 percent original grey brown paint, smooth base, ground lip, original metal screw-on cap, ca. 1890-1910, 6" h. **$179**

Bust of George Washington, raised on a socle base marked 'Washington - Patd April 11, 1876,' rough sheared & base base missing the closure, clear, probably a giveaway at the 1876 Centennial Exposition, 4 1/4" h. **$336**

Bear, sitting up w/collar suspending a shield-shaped medallion on its chest, medallion lettered 'BABOAB - WPPMTEPA,' a cylindrical neck w/bulbed base at the top, on a molded rectangular base, dense yellow olive, probably Russia, 1860-70, some separation of glass near left foot & base, chip & bruise w/line below right foot, early Kummel bear, 10 1/4" h. **$308**

Birdcage, a wide disk foot supporting a barrel-shaped birdcage w/ pagoda-shaped lid, smooth base marked 'Pat. Apl'd For,' light teal blue w/original gold paint trim, probably American, ca. 1920-34, 4 3/4" h. **$56**

▪ Flasks

GI-54 -, Washington bust without queue - Taylor bust in uniform, open pontil, applied sloping double collar mouth, medium to deep emerald green, qt. **$952**

GII-106 -, American eagle facing left above oval panel obverse & reverse, w/'Pittsburgh PA' in oval on obverse, narrow vertical rib on edges, smooth base, applied mouth, emerald green, pt. ... **$672**

GIV-43 -, Seeing Eye over 'A.D.' - Star & arm w/'G.R.J.A.,' open pontil, sheared & tooled lip, yellow amber, pt. **$448**

GIX-45 -, Scroll, corset-waist style, elaborate scroll decoration forming acanthus leaves w/four-petal flower at top & diamond at center obverse & reverse, vertical medial ribs, pontil scarred base, sheared & tooled lip, deep aqua, pt..**$840**

GVIII-14a -, Sunburst centered by ring w/a dot in middle, horizontal corrugated edges, pontil scarred base, sheared & tooled lip, extremely rare color, emerald green, 1/2 pt.............................**$4,760**

GX-18 -, Spring Tree (leaves & buds) - Summer Tree, smooth edges, applied sloping double collar mouth, light bluish green, pontil scar w/in-the-making small chip, qt. **$616**

GXII-37 -, Clasped hands above oval all inside shield w/'Union' above shield, reverse similar, smooth base, applied ringed mouth, light cobalt blue, only two known examples known in this color, qt. **$2,352**

GXIII-4 -, Hunter facing left wearing flat-top stovepipe hat, short coat & full trousers, game bag hanging at left side, firing gun at two birds flying upward at left, large puff of smoke from muzzle, two dogs running to left toward section of rail fence - Fisherman standing on shore near large rock, wearing round-top stovepipe hat, V-neck jacket, full trousers, fishing rod held in left hand w/end resting on ground, right hand holding large fish, creel below left arm, mill w/bushes & tree in left background, calabash, edges w/wide flutes, iron pontil, applied mouth, orange amber, 9 1/4" h. **$420**

GXIII-49 -, Anchor w/fork-ended pennants inscribed 'Baltimore' & 'Glassworks' - Sheaf of grain w/ rake & pitchfork crossed behind sheaf, smooth edges, smooth base, applied mouth, yellow olive, 1/2 pt. **$3,080**

GXIII-59 -, Anchor w/fork-ended pennants inscribed 'Spring Garden' & 'Glass Works' - Cabin w/ pebbly ground, smooth base, open pontil, applied double collar, yellow olive, pt. **$5,600**

GXIII-8 -, Sailor dancing a hornpipe on an eight-board hatch cover, above a long rectangular bar - Banjo player sitting on a long bench, smooth edges, smooth base, applied double collar mouth, brilliant light to medium olive yellow, 1/2 pt. **$1,456**

Nailsea, teardrop shape, cranberry red glass w/overall white & pink loop pattern, pontil scarred base, tooled mouth w/original threaded neck collar & fancy screw-on lid, England or America, ca. 1860-80, 7 1/8" h. **$336**

BOTTLES

■ Inks

Beehive teakettle-type fountain inkwell w/neck extending up at angle from base, sapphire blue, octagonal domed & banded form w/ground lip & smooth base, ca. 1875-85, cluster of unmelted sand w/small stress crack, 2 3/8" h.. **$784**

Cone-shaped, medium emerald green, inward rolled rim, open pontil, ca. 1840-60, 2 1/2" h. **$728**

Cylindrical, blown-three-mold, medium sapphire blue, Mt. Vernon Glassworks, geometric design, open pontil, ca. 1815-35, 1 3/4" h., GII-15 .... **$13,440**

Cylindrical, medium bluish green, master-size, applied sloping double collar mouth w/hand-tooled pour spout, open pontil, the side embossed 'Hover - Phila.,' crude whittled glass, ca. 1840-60, 9 3/8" h. **$960**

Cylindrical w/thick shoulder & base ring, medium cobalt blue, short center neck w/tooled lip, smooth base, embossed around sides 'Lyons Ink,' ca. 1880-95, 2 7/8" h. **$235**

Drape pattern cone shape, medium sapphire blue, applied mouth, open pontil, rare color, ca. 1840-60, 2 1/4" h. **$2,690**

Igloo-form w/side neck, bright yellow w/olive tone, tooled mouth, smooth base, molded around the paneled sides 'J. - & - I. - E. - M.,' ca. 1875-90, 1 3/4" h........ **$960**

◆ A pontil is a circular scar left on the bottom center of a handblown bottle. After the glassblower blows a bottle with a blowpipe, he attaches a pontil rod to the bottom of the bottle with a small blob of molten glass. Then he breaks the blowpipe from the neck and forms the lip of the bottle. Once the lip is finished, he snaps the pontil rod off the base of the bottle, leaving the pontil.

◆ While bubbles in glass add interesting visual effects and evidence that a bottle has been hand blown, they do not of themselves raise the value of a bottle. In fact, they are considered flaws and can lower the value of bottles.

Medicines _____

Brinckerhoffs (C.) - Health Restorative - New York - Price One Dollar, rectangular w/beveled corners, applied sloping collared mouth, sticky ball type pontil, olive w/some yellow, 7" h. **$1,540**

Judson's Cherry & Lungwort Extract, rectangular w/arched panels, tall neck w/applied sloping mouth, open pontil scar, ca. 1840-60, bluish aqua, 8 3/8" h. **$840**

Peuser & Kadish Druggists Chicago, cylindrical w/sloping shoulder, smooth base, tooled lip, rare in size & form, medium teal blue, ca. 1875-1890, 7 1/2" h. **$504**

Swaim's Panacea Philada, cylindrical w/ rounded shoulder & paneled sides, pontil scarred base, applied mouth, deep olive green in base shading to lighter color in shoulder area, ca. 1840-60, 7 5/8" h.**$672**

Rushton & Aspinwall New-York - Compound Chlorine Tooth Wash, rectangular w/beveled corners, wide flattened flared lip, tubular pontil, yellowish amber w/ faint olive tone, ca. 1840-60, some faint exterior haze, 5 7/8" h. **$15,680**

U.S.A. Hosp. Dept., cylindrical w/rounded shoulder, smooth base, applied mouth, blown in four-piece mold, emerald green, ca. 1860-75, shallow chip off side of lip, 6" h. **$560**

Warner's Safe Diabetes Cure Rochester, N.Y., smooth base, applied mouth, embossed image of safe, amber, ca. 1880-95, 9 1/2" h. **$213**

Wishart's (L.Q.C.) - Pine Tree Tar Cordial, Phila. - Patent (design of pine tree) 1859, square w/ beveled corners, applied sloping collar mouth, smooth base, emerald green, 9 1/2" h. ... **$224**

Mineral Waters, Sodas & Sarsaparillas

Brown (J.T.) Chemist - Boston - Double Soda Water, ten-pin shape w/ rough textured smooth rounded base, applied mouth, deep bluish green, light interior stain, ca. 1855-75, 8 1/8" h. **$532**

Caladonia Spring - Wheelock VT, cylindrical w/applied sloping collared mouth w/ring, smooth base, possibly Stoddard, New Hampshire, yellowish amber, strong embossing, qt. **$728**

Carpenter - & Cobb - Knickerbocker - Soda - Water - Saratoga - Springs, ten-sided cylindrical form tapering to an applied blob mouth, iron pontil, ca. 1840-60, medium bluish green, very thin small open bubble on one edge, 7 5/8" h. **$960**

Coldbrook Medicinal - Spring Water, cylindrical w/tall tapering neck & applied sloping collared mouth w/ring, smooth base, ca. 1860-80, yellow amber w/olive tone, dug example, two cracks in neck, some staining, very rare bottle, qt.**$560**

Coles (J. & W.) - Superior Soda & Mineral Water - Staten Island, cylindrical tapering to a tall neck w/applied blob mouth, iron pontil, ca. 1840-60, medium cobalt blue, cleaned, 7 3/8" h. **$420**

Congress Water (on shoulder), cylindrical w/ applied sloping double collar mouth w/ring, smooth base, ca. 1850-60, deep yellowish olive, qt..........................**$448**

Dowdall (J.) [in slug plate] - Union Glass Works Phila. - Superior - Mineral Water, cylindrical shape w/panels at base, deep cobalt blue, iron pontil, applied blob mouth, rare, ca. 1840-60, 7 3/8" h. **$2,128**

Highrock Congress Spring (design of a rock), C. & W. Saratoga N.Y., cylindrical w/applied sloping double collared mouth w/ring, smooth base, ca. 1865-75, teal blue, strong embossing, pt.....................**$1,064**

Pickle Bottles & Jars

Aqua, barrel shape, six-rib, half-gallon size, iron pontil, rolled lip, ca. 1855-65, 10 5/8" h..... **$532**

Deep bluish aqua, four-sided cathedral-type w/Gothic windows w/a trefoil at the top, rolled lip, smooth base, deep bluish aqua, heavily whittled, ca. 1860-70, 13 1/8" h **$190**

Medium bluish green, four-sided cathedral-type w/Gothic windows, rolled lip, smooth base, ca. 1860-70, medium bluish green, 11" h. **$728**

Aqua, six-sided cathedral-type w/fancy Gothic windows, one panel embossed 'Yarnall Bros.,' applied collared mouth, smooth base, ca. 1860-80, 13 1/4" h. **$364**

Emerald green, six-sided Cathedral-type, applied mouth, smooth base, ca. 1855, two tiny chips on lip, 12 5/8" h....... **$728**

Honey amber, six-sided cathedral-type w/simple Gothic windows, cylindrical ringed neck w/outward rolled mouth, smooth base, ca. 1860-80, rare color, 13 1/8" h **$960**

Light bluish green, cylindrical w/seven large rounded vertical panels up the body & sixteen flutes on the shoulder, ringed neck w/outward rolled mouth, iron pontil, embossed mark 'Wm. Underwood - & Co. - Boston,' ca. 1845-60, 11 1/2" h. **$1,456**

BOTTLES

■ Poisons

Amber, coffin-shaped, embossed 'Poison - F.A. Thompson & Co. Detroit - Poison,' tooled mouth, smooth base, faint small cooling crack in wording & pinhead flakes on edge of lip & shoulder, ca. 1890-1910, 3 1/8" h. **$392**

Amber, cylindrical w/ tooled lip & smooth base, embossed 'Poison (star) - (skull & crossbones) - (star) Poison' against a fine diamond quilted ground, pinhead flake on edge of lip, ca. 1890-1915, 4 5/8" h. **$532**

Amber, eight-sided w/ tooled mouth & smooth base, sides embossed '[skull & crossbones] - Poison - Jacobs - Bichloride - Tablets - [skull & crossbones] - Poison,' professionally cleaned, ca.1900, 2 1/4" h. **$420**

Cobalt blue, model of a skull w/a cylindrical neck at the top, cross bone base marked 'Poison,' back of neck marked 'Pat. Appl'd For,' lip w/several small & one large chip, 4 1/4" h. **$776**

◆ Be aware of what's in the bottles you are buying and selling, as some bottles may contain their original contents of liquor, cocaine, opium, or poison. All can be dangerous and/or illegal to sell.

◆ A freeblown bottle is one in which the glassblower has used only a blowpipe and has molded the final shape by hand, rather than blowing the blob of glass into a mold.

Cobalt blue, cylindrical w/overall embossed diamond lattice design, tooled lip, smooth base marked 'H.B. Co.,' ca. 1890-1910, 7" h. **$112**

Yellowish amber, cylindrical w/ tooled mouth, overall latticework design w/a central panel w/'Poison' running vertically on each side of a skull & crossbones, a five-point star above & below the skull, tooled lip, smooth base marked 'S&D - 231,' ca. 1890-1910, 4 3/4" h. **$840**

Target Balls

Target ball, Agnew & Brown. circa 1870s. **$29,120**

Target ball with stars (or crosses), three-piece mold, 2.2 ounces, warm amber coloration. **$2,464**

Target ball, from Capt. A.H. Bogardus of Chicago, 2.6-oz., in mint condition............................ **$4,704**

Target ball, E.E. Sage & Co. of Chicago, 2.1-ounce target ball, light to medium amber, near mint condition. **$4,928**

Target ball, E. Barton & Sons (U.K.), sand ball **$1,232**

BOTTLES

Target ball, Jas. Brown & Son of Pittsburgh, three-piece mold, 2.4-ounce. **$10,080**

Target ball, J.H. Johnston of Pittsburgh, extremely rare purple coloration. **$14,560**

Target Balls

◆ Target balls had a brief but colorful life, bursting on the scene around 1876 before fading out altogether by 1895. During that small window of time, glass balls—similar in size and shape to glass Christmas tree ornaments—were stuffed with feathers and sawdust and catapulted from spring-loaded traps to be hit by shooters. They'd explode in the air in a feathery, dusty cloud, as a bird would. In fact, target balls were introduced because the bird population was declining.

During their heyday, target balls were produced by the millions, and not just here in the United States. Manufacturers sprang up in England, France, Germany and Australia, too. These glass orbs sold for a penny apiece back then, but today a rare example like the Agnew & Brown ball can command a hefty price tag. But it's entirely possible to buy a nice ball for around $200.

All photos are courtesy American Bottle Auctions

Whiskey & Other Spirits

Beer, 'Grace Bros. Brewing Co Santa Rosa Cal' embossed around monogram, cylindrical, w/ original stopper, amber **$55**

Beer, 'Raspiller Brewing Co West Berkeley,' cylindrical, tooled top w/ embossed bird, amber **$55**

Spirits, chestnut flask-type, flattened rounded form w/applied mouth & neck handle, pontil, yellowish olive green, ca. 1865-75, 8 1/2" h. **$448**

Spirits, free-blown onion-form w/short neck & applied string lip, pontilled base w/high kick-up, yellowish green, Germany, ca. 1720-1750, 5 5/8" d., 5 3/4" h. **$308**

Spirits, mold-blown, globular, twenty-four ribs swirled to the right, tall neck w/outward rolled lip, pontil scar, Zanesville, Ohio, ca. 1825-35, medium amber, shallow surface bottle, 7 1/2" h. **$616**

Spirits, mold-blown seal-type w/cylindrical body & tall tapering neck w/applied string lip, pontil scar, dark olive amber, seal molded 'HHC,' England, ca. 1790-1810, 10 3/4" h. **$420**

Whiskey, 'Bininger (A.M.) & Co. No. 375 Broadway N.Y.,' square w/beveled corners, applied sloping collar mouth, smooth base, moss green, ca. 1865-75, 9 5/8" h. **$1,456**

Whiskey, 'Booz's (E.G.) Old Cabin Whiskey - 120 Walnut St. Philadelphia' (on roof), '1840 - E.G. Booz's Old Cabin Whiskey' (on sides), cabin-shaped, applied sloping collar mouth, smooth base, medium amber, ca. 1860-65, 7 5/8" h. **$7,840**

Ceramics

Belleek

The name Belleek refers to an industrious village in County Fermanagh, Northern Ireland, on the banks of the River Erne, and to the lustrous porcelain wares produced there.

In 1849, John Caldwell Bloomfield inherited a large estate near Belleek. Interested in ceramics, and having discovered rich deposits of feldspar and kaolin (china clay) on his lands, he soon envisioned a pottery that would make use of these materials, local craftspeople and water power of the River Erne. He was also anxious to enhance Ireland's prestige with superior porcelain products.

Bloomfield had a chance meeting with Robert Williams Armstrong who had established a substantial architectural business building potteries. Keenly interested in the manufacturing process, he agreed to design, build, and manage the new factory for Bloomfield. The factory was to be located on Rose Isle on a bend in the River Erne.

Bloomfield and Armstrong then approached David McBirney, a highly successful merchant and director of railway companies, and enticed him to provide financing. Impressed by the plans, he agreed to raise funds for the enterprise. As agreed, the factory was named McBirney and Armstrong, then later D. McBirney and Company.

Although 1857 is given as the founding date of the pottery, it is recorded that the pottery's foundation stone was laid by Mrs. J.C. Bloomfield on Nov. 18, 1858. Although not completed until 1860, the pottery was producing earthenware from its inception.

With the arrival of ceramic experts from the (William Henry) Goss Pottery in England, principally William Bromley, Sr. and William Wood Gallimore, Parian ware was perfected and, by 1863, the wares we associate with Belleek today were in production.

With Belleek Pottery workers and others emigrating to the United States in the late 1800s and early 1900s, Belleek-style china manufacture, known as American Belleek, commenced at several American firms, including Ceramic Art Company, Colombian Art Pottery, Lenox Inc., Ott & Brewer, and Willets Manufacturing Co.

Throughout its Parian production, Belleek Pottery marked its items with an Irish harp and wolfhound and the Devenish Tower. The 1st Period mark of 1863 through 1890 is shown below. Its 2nd Period began with the advent of the McKinley Tariff Act of 1891 and the (revised) British Merchandise Act as Belleek added the ribbon "Co. FERMANAGH IRELAND" beneath its mark in 1891. Both the 1st and 2nd period marks were black, although they occasionally appeared in burnt orange, green, blue or brown, especially on earthenware items. Its 3rd Period begin in 1926, when it added a Celtic emblem under the 2nd Period mark as well as the government trademark "Reg No 0857," which was granted in 1884. The Celtic emblem was registered by the Irish Industrial Development Association in 1906 and reads "Deanta in Eirinn," and means "Made in Ireland." The pottery is now utilizing its 13th mark, following a succession of three black marks, three green marks, a gold mark, two blue marks and three green. The final green mark was used only a single year, in 2007, to commemorate its 150th anniversary. In 2008, Belleek changed its mark to brown. Early earthenware was often marked in the same color as the majority of its surface decoration. Early basketware has Parian strips applied to its base with the impressed verbiage "BELLEEK" and later on, additionally "Co FERMANAGH" with or without "IRELAND." Current basketware carries the same mark as its Parian counterpart.

The item identification scheme is that followed within the works by Richard K. Degenhardt: *Belleek The Complete Collector's Guide and Illustrated Reference* (both first and second edition). Additional information, as well as a thorough discussion of the early marks, is located in these works as well as on the Internet at Del E. Domke's Web site: http://home.comcast.net/~belleek_website.

The prices given are for items in excellent condition, i.e., no chips, cracks, crazing or repairs. On flowered items, however, minimal chips to the flowering are acceptable, to the extent of the purchaser's tolerance. Earthenware items often exhibit varying degrees of crazing due to the primitive bottle kilns originally utilized at the pottery.

All Irish Belleek photographs used with permission, Rod Kearns, photographer, rkearns bak.rr.com.

CERAMICS

AMERICAN BELLEEK

Marks:

American Art China Works - R&E, 1891-95
AAC (superimposed), 1891-95
American Belleek Company - Company name, banner & globe
Ceramic Art Company - CAC palette, 1889-1906
Colombian Art Pottery - CAP, 1893-1902
Cook Pottery - Three feathers w/"CHC," 1894-1904
Coxon Belleek Pottery - "Coxon Belleek" in a shield, 1926-1930
Gordon Belleek - "Gordon Belleek," 1920-28
Knowles, Taylor & Knowles - "Lotusware" in a circle w/a crown, 1891-96
Lenox China - Palette mark, 1906-1924
Ott & Brewer - crown & shield, 1883-1893
Perlee - "P" in a wreath, 1925-1930
Willets Manufacturing Company - Serpent mark, 1880-1909
Cook Pottery - Three feathers w/"CHC"

Plates and Platters————————————————————

Ceramic Art Company, plate, 10 1/2" d., finely h.p. in the center w/a bust portrait of a young maiden holding a closed book & a stylus, wearing a white wrap on her head, a white gown & red shawl, wide claret border band decorated w/an ornate gilt swag band w/foliate scrolls & flower garlands, gilt rim band, artist-signed, ca. 1905.............................. **$2,880**

◆ The Ceramic Art Company was founded by Walter Scott Lenox in Trenton, New Jersey, in 1889. The firm began as a studio rather than a factory, producing high-end, handpainted wares. Its works were of such high quality that within ten years The Smithsonian was displaying examples of its products. In 1906, the company's name was changed to Lenox. Lenox porcelain was chosen for use at the White House by five U.S. presidents: Wilson, Truman, Reagan, Clinton and George W. Bush. It has also been used in more than 300 U.S. embassies and more than half of the governor's mansions and remains one of the oldest and most respected potteries in the world.

CERAMICS

IRISH BELLEEK

Comports & Centerpieces

Comport, Trihorse Comport, impressed "Belleek Co. Fermanagh," D37-I **$3,400**

Figurines

Boy and Shell, 9" h., D9-II **$3,000**

Tea Ware - Museum Display Patterns (Artichoke, Chinese, Finner, Five O'Clock, Lace, Ring Handle Ivory, Set #36 & Victoria)

Muffin dish, cov., Artichoke Tea Ware, gilt trim, D720-I **$2,000**

▲Plate, Ring Handle Ivory Ware plate, h.p. Irish scene, unsigned but from the School of Eugene Sheerin, 7 1/2" d., D823-II **$1,800**

◄Tray, Lace Tea Ware, gilt decoration, designed as a wall hanging w/pierced hanging holes at the top, 13" d., D803-IV **$4,800**

CERAMICS

Tea Ware - Rare Patterns
(Aberdeen, Blarney, Celtic [low & tall], Cone, Erne, Fan, Institute, Ivy, Lily [high & low], Scroll, Sydney, Thistle & Thorn)

Celtic Candlestick, Low, painted & gilt, 4 3/4" h., D1511-VI **$340**

Celtic Design creamer, Celtic Design tea ware, tall shape, multi-colored, ('mystery' mark, 1st Period over Celtic Scroll, probably a transition from 1st to 2nd period), 4 1/2" h., D1442-II **$400**

Celtic Design bread plate, Celtic Design tea ware, multicolored & gilt, D1425-III **$600**

◆ Replacement value and actual cash value are not the same. Replacement value is the cost required to purchase a comparable item at retail value. Actual cash value is replacement value minus depreciation. Depreciation is a loss in value due to wear and tear. Depreciation is typically calculated by using a depreciation schedule, which mathematically calculates the loss in value according to the number of years the item has been in existence.

CERAMICS

Tea Wares - Miscellaneous

Celtic bowl of roses, h.p. colors of dark pink, yellow & green, D1510-VII **$2,600**

Plate, scenic center of Irish peasant homes w/ornate gilt scroll border, h.p. by former pottery manager Cyril Arnold, artist-signed & w/what appears to be "15 PA" following the signature, 8 1/2" d., D1527-IV . **$1,200**

Plate, pottery, Scenic Celtic Commemorative Plate, painted & gilded, D1553-V........................... **$800**

Wedding cup, three-handled, Shamrock patt., h.p. trim, D2105-II **$640**

◆ Collectors are conscious of the idea of antiques as investments, but it should never be the driving force. The greatest benefit of collecting should be enjoyment, from the thrill of the hunt to learning more about their history. Acquire the highest quality pieces you can afford, learn as much as you can, stay focused, and someday your diligence may be rewarded.

CERAMICS

◼ Bennington

Bennington wares, which ranged from stoneware to parian and porcelain, were made in Bennington, Vermont, primarily in two potteries, one in which Captain John Norton and his descendants were principals, and the other in which Christopher Webber Fenton (also once associated with the Nortons) was a principal. Various marks are found on the wares made in the two major potteries, including J. & E. Norton, E. & L. P. Norton, L. Norton & Co., Norton & Fenton, Edward Norton, Lyman Fenton & Co., Fenton's Works, United States Pottery Co., U.S.P. and others.

The popular pottery with the mottled brown on yellowware glaze was also produced in Bennington, but such wares should be referred to as "Rockingham" or "Bennington-type" unless they can be specifically attributed to a Bennington, Vermont factory.

 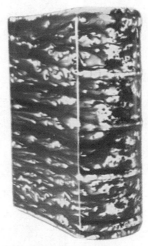 

Book flask, binding marked "Departed Spirits G," Flint Enamel glaze, 5 1/2" h. **$532**

Book flask, noting lettering on binding, mottled brown & cream Rockingham glaze, 5 3/4" h. **$392**

Toby pitcher, figural seated Mr. Toby, dark brown mottled Rockingham glaze, unmarked, 6" h. **$259**

Cuspidor, short round waisted shape w/side hole, Flint Enamel glaze, Type A impress mark on base, mid-19th c., 8" d., 3 3/4" h. **$144**

Picture frame, oval w/wide ringed rounded sides, overall mottled Rockingham glaze, few underside flakes, mid-19th c., 8 3/4 x 9 3/4"... **$489**

Delft

In the early 17th century, Italian potters settled in Holland and began producing tin-glazed earthenwares, often decorated with pseudo-Oriental designs based on Chinese porcelain wares. The city of Delft became the center of this pottery production and several firms produced the wares throughout the 17th and early 18th century. A majority of the pieces featured blue on white designs, but polychrome wares were also made. The Dutch Delftwares were also shipped to England, where eventually the English copied them at potteries in such cities as Bristol, Lambeth and Liverpool. Although still produced today, Delft peaked in popularity by the mid-18th century.

Bowl, 8 5/8" d., 2" h., scalloped rim on low lobed body, h.p. w/blue stylized flowers on a powder blue ground, England, mid-18th c., minor rim chips & glaze wear.. **$470**

Charger, round shallow dished form w/a narrow flanged rim, the center w/a large rounded panel-sided reserve h.p. w/leafy scrolls around a round center w/a stylized leafy blossom, the border band decorated w/ small oval reserves decorated w/scrolls & squiggles, a blue initial or X under the bottom, various glaze & rim chips, Holland, 18th c., 13 3/4" d. **$460**

Plate, 8 3/4" d., shallow dished form w/a wide flanged rim, the center h.p. in dark blue w/a large urn filled w/fruit & fanned & feathery leaves & flowers, the border h.p. in dark blue w/wide half-leaves alternating w/ squiggle bands, Holland, 18th c., tight hairline from rim nearly to center, small rim chip **$230**

Tile, rectangular, decorated in blue & white w/a seaside scene w/women standing on the shore & sailing ships heading out to sea, after a painting by Hendrik Willem Mesdag, marked w/Delft & other painted & impressed marks, late 19th - early 20th c., 7 7/8 x 10" **$500**

CERAMICS

Doulton & Royal Doulton

Doulton & Company, Ltd., was founded in Lambeth, London, in about 1858. It operated there until 1956 and often incorporated the words "Doulton" and "Lambeth" in its marks. Pinder, Bourne & Company Burslem was purchased by the Doultons in 1878 and in 1882 became Doulton & Company Ltd. It added porcelain to its earthenware production in 1884. The "Royal Doulton" mark has been used since 1902 by this factory, which is still in operation. Character jugs and figurines are commanding great attention from collectors at the present time.

John Doulton, the founder, was born in 1793. He became an apprentice at the age of 12 to a potter in south London. Five years later he was employed in another small pottery near Lambeth. His two sons, John and Henry, subsequently joined their father in 1830 in a partnership he had formed with the name of Doulton & Watts. Watts retired in 1864 and the partnership was dissolved. Henry formed a new company that traded as Doulton & Company.

In the early 1870s the proprietor of the Pinder Bourne Company, located in Burslem, Staffordshire, offered Henry a partnership. The Pinder Bourne Company was purchased by Henry in 1878 and became part of Doulton & Company in 1882.

With the passage of time, the demand for the Lambeth industrial and decorative stoneware declined whereas demand for the Burslem manufactured and decorated bone china wares increased.

Doulton & Company was incorporated as a limited liability company in 1899. In 1901 the company was allowed to use the word "Royal" on its trademarks by Royal Charter. The well known "lion on crown" logo came into use in 1902. In 2000 the logo was changed on the company's advertising literature to one showing a more stylized lion's head in profile.

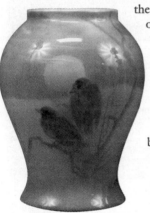

Today Royal Doulton is one of the world's leading manufacturers and distributors of premium grade ceramic tabletop wares and collectibles. The Doulton Group comprises Minton, Royal Albert, Caithness Glass, Holland Studio Craft and Royal Doulton. Royal Crown Derby was part of the group from 1971 until 2000 when it became an independent company. These companies market collectibles using their own brand names.

◀Vase, 7" h., Titanian Ware, bulbous ovoid body w/flared foot & wide flat mouth, h.p. scene of two large perched birds, designed by Edward Raby, ca. 1920.. **$1,000**

MARKS:

CERAMICS

ANIMALS & BIRDS

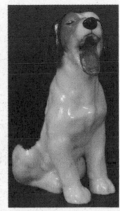

Cat, Siamese, seated, glossy cream & black, DA 129, 4" h **$30**

Dog, Alsatian, "Benign of Picardy," dark brown, HN 1117, 1937-68, 4 1/2"...... **$250**

Dog, character dog yawning, white w/brown patches over ears & eyes, black patches on back, HN 1099, 1934-85, 4" h. **$75**

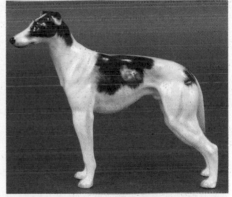

Dog, Bulldog, HN 1074, standing, white & brown, 1932- 85, 3 1/4".. **$195**

Dog, Greyhound, white w/dark brown patches, HN 1077, 1932-55, 4 1/2"................................ **$575**

Dog, Pekinese, Ch. "Biddee of Ifield," golden w/black highlights, HN 1012, 1931-85, 3"   **$95**

Dog, Scottish Terrier, Ch. "Albourne Arthur," black, HN 1015, 1931-60, 5"................................ **$315**

CERAMICS

Dogs, Terrier Puppies in a Basket, three white puppies w/light & dark brown markings, brown basket, HN 2588, 1941-85, 3" h. **$105**

Elephant, trunk in salute, grey w/black, HN 2644, 1952- 85, 4 1/4" **$175**

Tiger on a Rock, brown, grey rock, HN 2639, 1952-92, 10 1/4 x 12"... **$1,150**

Bird, Bullfinch, blue & pale blue feathers, red breast, HN 2551, 1941-46, 5 1/2" h...................... **$80**

Dog, Airedale Terrier, K 5, 1931-55, 1 1/4 x 2 1/4" **$275**

Dog, Bulldog, HN 1044, brown & white, 1931-68, 3 1/4" h. **$250**

Dog, Bulldog Puppy, K 2, seated, tan w/brown patches, 1931-77, 2"..................................... **$85**

Dog, Irish Setter, Ch. "Pat O'Moy," reddish brown, HN 1054, 1931-60, 7 1/2" h. **$725**

Dog, Labrador, standing, black, DA 145, 1990-present, 5" h... **$55**

Dog, Springer Spaniel, "Dry Toast," white coat w/ brown markings, HN 2517, 1938-55, 3 3/4" **$175**

Dogs, Cocker Spaniels sleeping, white dog w/brown markings & golden brown dog, HN 2590, 1941-69, 1 3/4" h. **$105**

Duck, Drake, standing, green, 2 1/2" **$50**

Duck, Drake, standing, white, HN 806, 1923-68, 2 1/2" h. **$105**

Horses, Chestnut Mare and Foal, chestnut mare w/ white stockings, fawn-colored foal w/white stockings, HN 2522, 1938-60, 6 1/2" h. **$695**

Kitten, on hind legs, light brown & black on white, HN 2582, 1941-85, 2 3/4" **$75**

Monkey, Langur Monkey, long-haired brown & white coat, HN 2657, 1960-69, 4 1/2" h. **$255**

Penguin, grey, white & black, green patches under eyes, K 23, 1940-68, 1 1/2" h. **$170**

Tiger, crouching, brown w/dark brown stripes, HN 225, 1920-36, 2 x 9 1/2".......................... **$575**

Kitten, licking hind paw, brown & white, HN 2580, 2 1/4" **$75**

Pony, Shetland Pony (woolly Shetland mare), glossy brown, DA 47, 1989 to present, 5 3/4"............ **$45**

BUNNYKINS FIGURINES

Airman, DB 199, limited edition of 5000, 1999 **$75**

Astro, Music Box, DB 35, white, red, blue, 1984-89 .... **$300**

Aussie Surfer, DB 133, gold & green outfit, white & blue base, 1994 .... **$115**

Banjo Player, DB 182, white & red striped blazer, black trousers, yellow straw hat, 1999, limited edition of 2,500 .... **$150**

Be Prepared, DB 56, dark green & grey, 1987-96 .... **$60**

Bedtime, DB 63, second variation, red & white striped pajamas, 1987, limited edition **$425**

Bogey, DB 32, green, brown & yellow, 1984-92 .... **$150**

Boy Skater, DB 152, blue coat, brown pants, yellow hat, green boots & black skates, 1995-98 ...... **$45**

Busy Needles, DB 10, white, green & maroon, 1973-88 .... **$75**

Carol Singer, DB 104, dark green, red, yellow & white, 1991, UK backstamp, limited edition of 700 **$250**

Cavalier, DB 179, red tunic, white collar, black trousers & hat, yellow cape, light brown boots, 1998, limited edition of 2,500 .... **$265**

Choir Singer, DB 223, white cassock, red robe, 2001, RDICC exclusive **$45**

Cinderella, DB 231, pink & yellow, RDICC exclusive, 2001 .... **$70**

Clown, DB 129, white costume w/red stars & black pompons, black ruff around neck, 1992, limited edition of 250 .... **$1,500**

Cowboy, DB 201, 1999, limited edition of 2,500 .... **$125**

Cymbals, DB 25, red, blue & yellow, from the Oompah Band series, 1984-90 .... **$115**

Day Trip, DB 260, two Bunnykins in green sports car, 2002, limited edition of 1,500 .... **$175**

Dodgem Car Bunnykins, DB 249, red car, 2001, limited edition of 2,500 .... **$175**

Dollie Bunnykins Playtime, DB 80, white & yellow, 1988, by Holmes, limited edition of 250 ..... **$225**

Double Bass Player, DB 185, green & yellow striped jacket, green trousers, yellow straw hat, 1999, limited edition of 2,500 .... **$150**

Drum-Major, DB 109, dark green, red & yellow, Oompah Band series, 1991, limited edition of 200 .... **$525**

Drummer, DB 89, blue trousers & sleeves, yellow vest, cream & red drum, Royal Doulton Collectors Band series, 1990, limited edition of 250.... **$525**

Drummer, DB 108, dark green & red, white drum, Oompah Band series, 1991, limited edition of 200 **$525**

Eskimo, DB 275, yellow coat & boots, orange trim, Figure of the Year, 2003............................... **$65**

Federation, DB 224, blue, Australian flag, limited edition of 2,500 .... **$165**

Fisherman, DB 170, blue hat & trousers, light yellow sweater, black wellingtons, 1997-2000 .... **$45**

Fortune Teller, DB 218, red, black & yellow, white ball, 2000.. **$65**

Gardener, DB 156, brown jacket, white shirt, grey trousers, light green wheelbarrow, 1996-98.... **$50**

Goalkeeper, DB 120, yellow & black, 1991, limited edition of 250 .... **$650**

Grandpa's Story, DB 14, burgundy, grey, yellow, blue & green, 1975-83..................................... **$350**

Bath Night, DB 141, tableau RDICC exclusive, limited edition of 5,000, 2001 .... **$160**

Halloween, DB 132, orange & yellow pumpkin, 1993-97.. **$80**

Harry the Herald, DB 115, yellow & dark green, 1991, Royal Family series, limited edition of 300 .... **$1,000**

Hornpiper, DB 261, brown, 2003 Special Event **$43**

Jack & Jill, DB 222, tableau, brown pants, yellow & white dress, 2000..................................... **$125**

Jogging, Music Box, DB 37, yellow & blue, 1987-89 .... **$275**

Judy, DB 235, blue & yellow, 2001, limited edition of 2,500... **$180**

King John, DB 91, purple, yellow & white, Royal Family series, 1990, limited edition of 250........ **$550**

Liberty Bell, DB 257, green & black, 2001, limited edition of 2,001 .... **$125**

Little John, DB 243, brown cloak, 2001 .... **$60**

Master Potter, DB 131, blue, white, green & brown, 1992-93, RDICC Special............................ **$250**

Minstrel, DB 211, 1999, limited edition of 2,500 .... **$105**

Mountie, DB 135, red jacket, dark blue trousers, brown hat, 1993, limited edition of 750 ...... **$800**

Mr. Bunnykins at the Easter Parade, DB 18, red, yellow & brown, 1982-93 .... **$85**

Mrs. Bunnykins at the Easter Parade, DB 19, pale blue & maroon, 1982-96............................. **$75**

Old Balloon Seller, DB 217, multicolored, 1999, limited edition of 2,000................................. **$195**

Oompah Band, DB 105, 106, 107, 108, 109, green, 1991, limited edition of 250, the set **$2,750**

Out for a Duck, DB 160, white, beige & green, 1995, limited edition of 1,250 .... **$315**

Piper, DB 191, green, brown & black, 1999, limited edition of 3,000 .... **$150**

Prince Frederick, DB 48, green, white & red, Royal Family series, 1986-90 .... **$125**

Princess Beatrice, DB 93, yellow & gold, Royal Family series, 1990, limited edition of 250............ **$465**

Ringmaster, DB 165, black hat & trousers, red jacket, white waistcoat & shirt, black bow tie, 1996, limited edition of 1,500................................. **$500**

Rock and Roll, DB 124, white, blue & red, 1991, limited edition of 1,000 .... **$395**

CERAMICS

Bride, DB 101, cream dress, grey, blue & white train, 1991 to 2001 .... **$45**

Collector, DB 54, brown, blue & grey, 1987, RDICC **$550**

Footballer, DB 119, red, 1991, limited edition of 250 .... **$650**

Magician, DB 159, black suit, yellow shirt, yellow table cloth w/red border, 1998, limited edition of 1,000 .... **$695**

Mystic, DB 197, green, yellow & mauve, 1999 .... **$55**

Sweetheart, DB 174, white & blue, pink heart, 1997, limited edition of 2,500 .... **$205**

Sands of Time, DB 229, yellow, 2000, limited order period of three months **$60**

Saxophone Player, DB 186, navy & white striped shirt, blue vest, black trousers, 1999, limited edition of 2,500 .... **$180**

Scotsman (The), DB 180, dark blue jacket & hat, red & yellow kilt, white shirt, sporran & socks, black shoes, 1998, limited edition of 2,500 .... **$185**

Sousaphone, DB 86, blue uniform & yellow sousaphone, Oompha Band series, 1990, limited edition of 250 .... **$500**

Susan, DB 70, white, blue & yellow, 1988-93. **$125**

Tally Ho!, DB 12, burgundy, yellow, blue, white & green, 1973-88... **$105**

Touchdown, DB 29B (Boston College), maroon & gold, 1985, limited edition of 50 .... **$2,000**

Touchdown, DB 99 (Notre Dame), green & yellow, 1990, limited edition of 200 .... **$625**

Tyrolean Dancer, DB 246, black & white, 2001 . **$60**

Will Scarlet, DB 264, green & orange, 2002 ..... **$60**

Wizard, DB 168, brown rabbit, purple robes & hat, 1997, limited edition of 2,000 .... **$400**

BURSLEM WARES

Ashtray, earthenware, advertising-type, low squared white shape w/rounded corners w/notches for cigarettes, the rounded sides printed w/advertising for De Reszke Cigarettes, Burslem, ca. 1925, 5 1/2" w. **$250**

Centerpiece, Vellum Ware, low oblong floral-decorated dish w/crimped & ruffled sides curving up at one end to form a high curved handle molded w/a figural gold dragon, designed by Charles Noke, ca. 1895. **$2,000**

Bowl, 16" d., 9" h., a wide round pedestal base in brown & green supporting a wide, deep curved bowl decorated w/a continuous band of large bright yellow tulips on dark green leaves & stems, ca. 1910 . **$3,600**

Bowl, 5 1/4" d., Titanian Ware, shallow rounded shape h.p. on the interior w/flowers, designed by Percy Curnock, ca. 1920............................... **$750**

▲Dessert plate, bone china, rounded w/low ruffled rim, h.p. scene of a polar bear by a river, ca. 1890 .... **$300**

◀Cracker jar, cov., Bewick Birds Series, barrel-shaped w/a low molded rim & inset cover, the sides decorated w/ a design of Bewick birds perched in a leafy branch, done in the print & tint technique in shades of brown, blue, yellow, rose red, green & pale blue, Burslem, ca. 1905 .... **$500**

Bowl, 8 7/8" d., 3 3/4" h., wide shallow rounded form, interior w/transfer-printed polychrome fox hunt scenes, green vintage border w/gilt trim, early 20th c. **$125**

Cabinet plates, 10 1/4" d., each w/a different English garden view within a narrow acid-etched gilt border, transfer-printed & painted by J. Price, ca. 1928, artist- signed, green printed lion, crown & circle mark, impressed year letters, painted pattern numbers "H3587," set of 12 .... **$2,750**

Chocolate set: 8" h. cov. chocolate pot, 6 1/2" h. cov. water pot, creamer, sugar bowl & eight cups & saucers; bone china, each enamel decorated w/relief-molded fox in various poses, crop-form handles, 20th c., England, the set **$650**

Pitcher, 11" h., Poplars at Sunset patt. **$175**

Plate, 9 1/8" d., Peony patt., dark blue floral center w/ rectangular panels around the border, trimmed w/reddish rust & beige, ca. 1900 .... **$65**

Plates, 9" d., slightly dished w/scalloped rim, gilt-trimmed rim w/polychrome leafy vines bordering brown enameled Shakespearean sites, retailed by Theodore B. Starr, New York City, Doulton, Burslem, late 19th c., set of 12 .... **$450**

Match holder, bone china, figural, an upright oblong shape molded on one side w/the smiling face of Mephistopheles & on the other side w/his frowning face, the sides in blue inscribed w/a motto, designed by Charles Noke, Burslem, ca. 1900 .... **$1,000**

Figure group, earthenware, limited edition tribute to George Tinworth, the oval brown base inscribed "The Tug of War," a green grassy mound w/three dark blue frogs pulling against three brown mice, Model No. LW2, one of 150, designed by Martyn Alcock, Burslem, 2005, 5 1/2" l. **$600**

Napkin rings, each decorated w/applied hand-made colorful flowers, ca. 1935, a boxed set of 4 ..... **$400**

Ginger jar, cov., bulbous nearly spherical body w/a domed cover, bright yellow ground painted in colorful enamels w/a long-tailed bird-of-paradise flying among stylized pendent flowers & fruiting branches, Model No. 1256C, date code for December 1925, 10 3/4" h. **$1,315**

Pitcher, Ruby Lustre, wide bulbous body tapering to a short cylindrical wide neck w/spout, simple loop handle, h.p. design of stylized dragons in the style of William de Morgan, ca. 1890 .... **$1,500**

Salt dip, small gilded ball feet supporting the squatty bulbous dish decorated w/flowers on a pale blue ground, gilt rim band, w/a salt spoon, ca. 1900 .... **$400**

Teapot, cov., figural Old Salt model, the body in the image of a sailor mending a net, a mermaid forming the handle, designed by William K. Harper, introduced in 1989 .... **$300**

Teapot, cov., figural Pirate and Captain model, designed by Anthony Cartlidge, limited edition of 1,500, introduced in 2003 .... **$300**

Teapot, cov., Polar Bear Series, footed very wide squatty low body tapering to a flat rim & conical cover w/disk finial, short angled spout & loop handle, overall crackled background w/a center band of walking polar bears, ca. 1920s **$90**

Teapot, cov., bone china, hand-painted w/images of exotic birds & heavy gilt scroll trim, painted by Joseph Birbeck, ca. 1910 .... **$2,000**

Teapot, cov., footed wide squatty bulbous body w/a wide flat neck & inset cover w/button finial, serpentine spout & C-form handle, decorated w/floral clusters, England, early 20th c. **$90**

Teapot, cov., figural Norman and Saxon model, designed by Anthony Cartlidge, limited edition of 1,500, introduced in 2003 .... **$300**

Tray, earthenware, rectangular w/rounded corners & tab end handles, a tan border & scattered pink & yellow floral clusters around the interior, ca. 1895, 17" l. **$400**

Tyg (three-handled mug), Vellum Ware, ornately scroll-molded cylindrical body decorated w/a large panel of Spanish Ware floral decoration, three figural cherub handles, ca. 1895 .... **$800**

Vase, bone china, tall pedestal foot supporting the slightly tapering cylindrical body w/a flared & ruffled rim, gold loop handles at the lower body, h.p. white reserve w/a colorful floral bouquet within a raised gilt border, the cobalt blue background further trimmed w/ornate gold, ca. 1910 .... **$600**

Vase, 5 7/8" h., Natural Foliage Ware, tapering gourd- form body, decorated w/scattered brown leaves on a mottled green & yellow ground, impressed mark, Shape No. 7669 .... **$173**

Vase, 6" h., bone china, footed ovoid body w/a short trumpet neck, dark yellow ground h.p. w/a large bird perched on a blossoming branch, designed by Arthur Eaton, ca. 1920 .... **$400**

Vases, Vellum Ware, buff-colored, a scalloped foot below the wide bell-shaped body molded w/a decoration of a frog & a mouse, a slender ringed neck w/cupped rim, small loop shoulder handles, pr. **$1,000**

Vases, 8" h., earthenware, cylindrical foot supporting the swelled cylindrical body w/a wide flat mouth, printed w/colorful stylized Art Deco florals hanging from the rim, ca. 1935, pr. **$400**

Vase, 18 1/2" h., bulbous tulip-shaped body on a fluted pedestal base, the sides of the body finely h.p. w/a continuous pastoral & wooded landscape, high flaring & fluted mouth w/a ruffled rim matches the base & molded to resemble folds of cloth w/gilt trimmed dark green panels alternating w/gilt-trimmed pale green panels, attributed to Arthur Eaton, ca. 1880.................. **$4,560**

Vase, cov., Vellum exhibition type, round foot & ringed pedestal in gold supporting the wide bulbous body w/a small cylindrical gold neck w/flaring rim & a low domed cover w/knob finial, decorated in the Spanish style w/colorful florals, ca. 1895 .... **$1,000**

Vase, 7" h., bone china, footed bulbous ovoid body tapering to a flaring trumpet form neck flanked by gold loop handles, h.p. in shades of blue w/the scene of a large bear standing beside a rocky shoreline, ca. 1910 .... **$1,200**

Vase, bone china, footed tapering ovoid body w/a small trumpet-form neck, dark blue ground h.p. w/ white swans & trimmed w/raised paste gold, designed by Fred Hodkinson, ca. 1910 .... **$1,000**

Vase, bone china, footed gently flaring cylindrical body w/a flat rim, h.p. scene of a man & his dog in an autumnal landscape, designed by Harry Allen, ca. 1910 .... **$800**

Whiskey decanter w/stopper, figural bell, shaded dark to light brown, advertising Bells Whisky (sic), 1955, 10 1/2" h. **$150**

CERAMICS

CHARACTER JUGS

Apothecary, small, D 6574, 4" h...................... $65

Aramis, small, D 6454, 3 1/2" h. $48

'Arriet, miniature, D 6250, 2 1/4" h................ $65

Cap'n Cuttle "A", small, D 5842, 4" h. $95

Dick Turpin, horse handle, small, D 6535, 3 3/4" h. $60

Don Quixote, miniature, D 6511, 2 1/2" h........ $55

Falstaff, small, D 6385, 3 1/2" h..................... $45

Fortune Teller (The), miniature, D 6523, 2 1/2" h. $375

Gondolier, small, D 6592, 4" h. $395

Henry VIII, small, D 6647, 3 3/4" h. $65

Jarge, small, D 6295, 3 1/2" h....................... $135

Jockey, second version, small, D 6877, 4" h..... $55

John Peel, small, D 5731, 3 1/2" h.................. $60

Lobster Man, small, D 6620, 3 3/4" h.............. $50

Long John Silver, large, D 6335, 7" h. $90

Lumberjack, small, D 6613, 3 1/2" h............... $55

Merlin, miniature, D 6543, 2 3/4" h. $50

Mine Host, large, D 6468, 7" h. $105

Mr. Micawber, miniature, D 6138, 2 1/4" h. $60

Mr. Pickwick, miniature, D 6254, 2 1/4" h. $55

Mr. Quaker, large, D 6738, 7 1/2" h............... $650

North American Indian, small, D 6614, 4 1/4" h. $45

Old Charley, tiny, D 6144, 1 1/4" h.................. $75

Old Salt, miniature, D 6557, 2 1/2" h.............. $50

Parson Brown "A", small, D 5529, 3 1/4" h. ... $63

Pearly Queen, small, D 6843, 3 1/2" h. $60

Pied Piper, large, D 6403, 7" h. $75

Poacher (The), small, D 6464, 4" h. $45

Porthos, large, D 440, 7 1/4" h. $90

Red Queen (The), large, D 6777, 7 1/4" h...... $125

Robin Hood, 1st version, miniature, D 6252, 1/4" h. $50

Robin Hood, large, D 6205, 6 1/4" h. $125

Robinson Crusoe, small, D 6539, 4" h. $60

Sairey Gamp, miniature, D 6045, 2 1/8" h. $40

Sancho Panza, large, D 6456, 6 1/2" h............ $85

Sancho Panza, small, D 6461, 3 1/4" h. $60

Santa Claus, reindeer handle, large, D 6675, 1/4" h. $265

Scaramouche, small, D 6561, 3 1/4" h. $525

Sir Francis Drake, large, D 6805, 7" h. $105

Sleuth (The), miniature, D 6639, 2 3/4" h........ $65

Snooker Player (The), small, D 6879, 4" h....... $55

Tam O'Shanter, small, D 6636, 3 1/4" h. $70

Toby Philpots, small, D 5737, 3 1/4" h. $60

Trapper (The), large, D 6609, 7 1/4" h........... $125

Ugly Duchess, small, D 6603, 3 1/2" h. $395

Veteran Motorist, miniature, D 6641, 2 1/2" h. $135

Viking, small, D 6502, 4" h. $150

Walrus & Carpenter (The), miniature, D 6608, 2 1/2" h. $175

Winston Churchill pitcher, large, D 6907, 7" h. $135

Witch (The), large, D 6893, 7" h. $290

Night Watchman, large, D 6569, 7" h. $130

Rip Van Winkle, large, D 6438, 6 1/2" h. $115

Sam Weller, large, D 6064, 6 1/2" h................ $80

CERAMICS

FLAMBÉ GLAZES

Animals & Birds

Cat, reclining curled up w/head slightly raised to the side, Rouge Flambé glaze, Model 70, ca. 1920, 3 1/2" h. **$1,600**

Elephant, Shanxi, w/howdah on back, Rouge Flambé glaze, Model BA 42, designed by Alan Maslankowski, limited edition of 250, 2004, 11 1/2" l. **$1,700**

Water buffalo, standing on an oblong base, Rouge Flambé, Model BA 59, limited edition of 150, designed by Martyn Alcock, 2005, 7" h. **$1,500**

MISCELLANEOUS PIECES

Bowl, Rouge Flambé, round shallow shape w/inner bands of stylized flowers in black on a red ground, black border band, ca. 1930 .... **$3,000**

Bowl, 9" d., Sung Ware glaze, black ground w/a red border band decorated w/rabbits & meandering berry vines, ca. 1930 ..... **$3,000**

Charger, Sung Ware glaze, deep round center w/a wide flat flanged rim, the center decorated w/a large stylized stag & vines, the rim inscribed in black "Many a Race Is Lost Ere Ever a Step is Taken," ca. 1925 .... **$6,000**

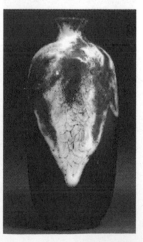

◄Vases, 11" h., Sung Ware glaze, tall gently swelled cylindrical body w/a low flared mouth, decorated w/colorful flying peacock against a swirled red, black & yellow ground, ca. 1985, pr. **$4,000**

►Vase, Chang Ware glaze, swelled cylindrical body tapering to a rounded shoulder & tiny trumpet neck, boldly contrasting colors, ca. 1955.. **$3,000**

CERAMICS

KINGSWARE

This line of earthenware featured a very dark brown background often molded with scenes or figures trimmed in color and covered with a glossy glaze. All pieces in this line were designed by the leading Royal Doulton designer, Charles Noke.

Shaving mug, ovoid body w/a flared rim & projecting brush spout, molded Friar portrait **$1,500**

Flask, figural, man wearing a top hat seated astride a large barrel, known as the Bacchus model, 8 1/2" h. **$3,000**

LAMBETH ART WARES

Candlesticks, stoneware, funnel-shaped base tapering w/a flaring drip pan centered by a tall cylindrical shaft w/ looped base handles, decorated w/incised designs trimmed in blue & brown, ca. 1872, 11" h., pr. **$2,000**

Clock, stoneware, spherical case enclosing a round dial w/Arabic numerals, ca. 1900 .... **$1,200**

Jardiniere, stoneware, squatty bulbous shape w/a wide, low cylindrical neck, molded in high-relief w/stylized long fish in green & brown swimming through large scrolling brown, grey & tan waves, designed by Mark Marshall, ca. 1900, 9" h. .. **$2,000**

Isobath, stoneware, a round domed foot supporting a wide cylindrical cup-shaped body w/a side cup spout & a conical cover w/knob finial, brown w/blue band rim, the body & cover decorated w/ornate large cream-colored floral & scrolling leaf panels, made for Thos. de la Rue, ca. 1893, 6" h. **$500**

Potpourri jar, cov., stoneware, a bulbous ovoid body tapering to a wide cylindrical neck, the mottled bluish black ground applied around the shoulder w/pierced blue flower blossoms below an upper band of pierced trefoils, the domed cover w/a knob finial pieced w/small holes separated w/a thin molded scroll band, ca. 1900 .... **$1,500**

▲Pitcher, stoneware, tankard-style, flared base ring below the tall cylindrical body w/a neck ring & short neck w/ rim spout, C-form handle, the main body applied & incised w/a stylized scrolling blue & green foliate design, designed by George Tinworth, ca. 1880. .... **$1,500**

▶Teapot, cov., Marqueterie Ware, spherical body w/ribs around the lower half, short angled spout, squared handle, small domed cover, Doulton & Rix patent, ca. 1890. .... **$2,000**

CERAMICS

Teapot, cov., stoneware, molded swimming fish decoration around the body, Doulton-Lambeth, ca. 1895 .... **$2,000**

Tyg, stoneware, cylindrical body w/a tan ground & tan brown-lined handles & brown rim, the sides incised & painted w/large pale blue & brown daisy-like flowers & cobalt blue leaves flanked by brown bands, made for the Royal Canoe Club, 1895, 6" h. **$1,200**

Vase, faience, footed ovoid body tapering to a short trumpet neck, the tan foot below the dark cobalt blue body decorated w/large yellow irises & long green leaves, the neck decorated w/brick red blossoms on a tan ground, ca. 1880 .... **$1,200**

Vase, 7 1/2" h., stoneware, footed ovoid urn-form w/flaring neck & squared shoulder handles, a base band w/ incised blue pointed leaves, the neck decorated w/a band of stylized blue blossoms, the body decorated w/a repeating design of large incised dark blue crosses enclosing large dark blue diamonds centered by a molded florette, tan ground, designed by Rosina Harris, ca. 1885... **$1,000**

◄Vase, 14" h., faience, moon flask-shaped, the flattened round sides in shaded dark green h.p. w/a large cluster of white wild roses w/greenish yellow leaves all issuing from a small brick red circle, raised on pointed flaring brick red feet, ca. 1880 .... **$1,500**

BLUE CHILDREN - BABES IN WOOD SERIES

Plaque, oval, scene of a girl & boy peeping into a tree hole, ca. 1900 .... **$1,500**

Dish, low-sided oblong diamond-shape w/a patterned border band, the center w/a scene of a woman w/a child holding her cloak, ca. 1900 .... **$1,500**

Plaque, oval, scene of a little girl carrying a basket, ca. 1900 .... **$1,500**

Plaque, oval, scene of two girls sheltering under an umbrella, ca. 1900 .... **$1,500**

CERAMICS

DICKENS WARE SERIES

Bowl, Lennox shape, round foot below the wide cylindrical body w/a molded rim band, color scene of the Artful Dodger, Charles Noke, 1912 .... **$1,000**

Pitcher, jug-type, cylindrical body w/rim spout & brown angled handle w/White Hart sign, relief-molded w/a scene of Poor Jo & Fat Boy, No. D5864, Charles Noke, 1937 .... **$600**

Dish on pedestal foot, shallow squared shape, color scene of Alfred Jingle, Charles Noke, 1912..... **$500**

Teapot, cov., Joan shape, color scene of Tony Weller, Charles Noke, 1912....................................... **$500**

BARLOW FAMILY DOULTON WARES

Jug, stoneware, footed ovoid body tapering to a cylindrical slightly flaring neck w/ pinched rim spout, strap handle, in-cised w/a large scene of a hunts-man, his horse & a fox, decorated by Hannah Barlow, ca. 1880 .... **$2,000**

Cache pot, stoneware, bulbous ovoid form w/a wide, short cylindrical neck, the sides incised w/panels of horses framed by bold cobalt blue scrolling legs, tan neck, decorated by Hannah Barlow & Eliza Sim-mance, ca. 1885... **$2,000**

TINWORTH DOULTON PIECES

Menu holder, stoneware, figural, two white mouse musicians on a brown & blue molded round base, titled "Harp and Concertina," ca. 1884, 4" h. $3,000

Ewer, stoneware, footed tall ovoid body w/a tall gently flaring neck w/rim spout & large C-form handle, the base band incised w/ vertical pale blue lappets alternating w/ beaded bands on a dark blue ground below a white beaded band, the wide brown central band incised w/a continuous scrolling band of pale green leaves & applied blue florettes, an upper thin white beaded band below the round shoulder incised w/alternating dark green spearpoints & pale blue petals, the brown neck applied w/blue florettes, ca. 1880 .... **$3,000**

Vase, stoneware, large ovoid body w/a wide short cylindrical neck, applied & incised overall w/ornate scrolling & leaf designs in dark blue, brick red, brown & blue, ca. 1880 .... **$3,500**

◆ Hannah Barlow was one of nine children born to Iram and Hannah Barlow in Hertfordshire, England, in the mid-1800s. Hannah and the two siblings, Florence and Albert, gained recognition as superb Doulton studio artists.

◆ Repairing valuable ceramics should be left to professionals who can do the job expertly and minimize loss of value to the piece. Of course, the cost of the repair should be weighed against the value of the piece. But keep in mind that poorly done, do-it-yourself repairs can generally not be undone and will permanently lower a piece's value.

CERAMICS

Fiesta

The Homer Laughlin China Company originated with a two-kiln pottery on the banks of the Ohio River in East Liverpool, Ohio. Built in 1873-'74 by Homer Laughlin and his brother, Shakespeare, the firm was first known as the Ohio Valley Pottery, and later Laughlin Bros. Pottery. It was one of the first white-ware plants in the country.

After a tentative beginning, the company was awarded a prize for having the best white-ware at the 1876 Centennial Exposition in Philadelphia.

Three years later, Shakespeare sold his interest in the business to Homer, who continued on until 1897. At that time, Homer Laughlin sold his interest in the newly incorporated firm to a group of investors, including Charles, Louis, and Marcus Aaron and the company bookkeeper, William E. Wells.

Under new ownership in 1907, the headquarters and a new 30-kiln plant were built across the Ohio River in Newell, West Virginia, the present manufacturing and headquarters location.

In the 1920s, two additions to the Homer Laughlin staff set the stage for the company's greatest success: the Fiesta line.

Dr. Albert V. Bleininger was hired in 1920. A scientist, author, and educator, he oversaw the conversion from bottle kilns to the more efficient tunnel kilns.

In 1927, the company hired designer Frederick Hurten Rhead, a member of a distinguished family of English ceramists. Having previously worked at Weller Pottery and Roseville Pottery, Rhead began to develop the artistic quality of the company's wares, and to experiment with shapes and glazes. In 1935, this work culminated in his designs for the Fiesta line.

For more information on Fiesta, see *Warman's Fiesta Identification and Price Guide* by Glen Victorey.

FIESTA COLORS

From 1936 to 1972, Fiesta was produced in 14 colors (other than special promotions). These colors are usually divided into the "original colors" of cobalt blue, light green, ivory, red, turquoise, and yellow (cobalt blue, light green, red, and yellow only on the Kitchen Kraft line, introduced in 1939); the "1950s colors" of chartreuse, forest green, gray, and rose (introduced in 1951); medium green (introduced in 1959); plus the later additions of Casuals, Amberstone, Fiesta Ironstone, and Casualstone ("Coventry") in antique gold, mango red, and turf green; and the striped, decal, and Lustre pieces. No Fiesta was produced from 1973 to 1985. The colors that make up the "original" and "1950s" groups are sometimes referred to as "the standard 11."

In many pieces, medium green is the hardest to find and the most expensive Fiesta color.

FIESTA COLORS AND YEARS OF PRODUCTION TO 1972

Antique Gold—Dark Butterscotch	(1969-1972)	Ivory—Creamy, Slightly Yellowed	(1936-1951)
Chartreuse—Yellowish Green	(1951-1959)	Mango Red—Same As Original Red	(1970-1972)
Cobalt Blue—Dark Or "Royal" Blue	(1936-1951)	Medium Green—Bright Rich Green	(1959-1969)
Forest Green—Dark "Hunter" Green	(1951-1959)	Red—Reddish Orange (1936-1944 and 1959-1972)
Gray—Light Or Ash Gray	(1951-1959)	Rose—Dusty, Dark Rose	(1951-1959)
Green—Often Called Light Green When Comparing		Turf Green—Olive	(1969-1972)
It To Other Green Glazes, Also Called "Original"		Turquoise—Sky Blue, like the stone	(1937-1969)
Green	(1936-1951)	Yellow—Golden Yellow	(1936-1969)

Ashtray in red.. **$65-$72**

Ashtray in light green................................ **$42-$48**

Covered onion soup bowl in cobalt blue. ..**$680-$739**

Cream soup cup in gray.............................. **$61-$72**

Dessert bowl in rose................................... **$45-$55**

Dessert bowl in chartreuse......................... **$46-$51**

Footed salad bowl in yellow....................**$375-$395**

4-3/4" fruit bowl in red.............................. **$31-$33**

11-3/4" fruit bowl in yellow. ....**$280-$315**

5-1/2" fruit bowl in chartreuse.................... **$32-$39**

#1 mixing bowl in red, $249-$295, with an ivory lid
.... **$875-$1,000**

Individual salad bowl in turquoise. .... **$89-$95**

#3 mixing bowl, $138-$165, and lid in cobalt blue
.... **$900-$1,100**

#2 mixing bowl in yellow. ....**$115-$140**

#4 mixing bowl in turquoise. ....**$130-$157**   #5 mixing bowl in ivory. ....**$225-$265**

#6 mixing bowl in red. ....**$282-$327**

#7 mixing bowl in light green.................**$449-/$589**

Very rare bowl lids in red
....................**$900-$1,100**
light green ....**$800-$900**
and yellow....... **$800-$900**

8-1/2" nappy in rose.................................**$59-$62**

9-1/2" nappy in ivory. ....**$69-$71**

CERAMICS

Bulb candleholder in cobalt blue ....$115-$125/pair

Tripod candleholders in cobalt blue ....$575-$630/pair
and red...$635-$699/pair

Carafes in red..$295-$335
and ivory...$310-$320

Carafe in light green. ....$275-$295

Coffeepot in cobalt blue. ....$238-$270

Demitasse coffeepot in light green...........$475-$525

Comport in ivory. ....$170-$190

Comport in red. ....$190-$200

Demitasse coffeepot in yellow. ....$450-$500

Sweets comport in cobalt blue. .... $85-$95

Covered sugar in turquoise........................ $49-$58

Ring-handle creamer and covered sugar bowl in medium green
Creamer ....$120-$135
Sugar bowl..$195-$215

Demitasse cup and saucer in yellow.
....$60-$79/set

CERAMICS

Eggcup in turquoise. ...... **$56-$65**

Eggcup in ivory. .... **$66-$72**

Tom & Jerry mug in medium green. ....**$125-$140**

Teacup and saucer in gray. .... **$36-$43/set**

Teacup and saucer in forest green. .... **$44-$49/set**

Teacup and saucer in rose .... **$42-$51/set**

Marmalade jar in ivory. **$350-$370**

Three mustards in yellow ....**$270-$295**
light green ....**$260-$280**
turquoise ....**$295-$320**

Disk water pitcher in rose. ....**$245-$285**

Disk water pitcher in medium green. . **$1,500-$1,600**

Ice pitcher in yellow. ....$135-$145

Two-pint jug in chartreuse. ....$130-$140

DripCut syrup pitcher in cobalt blue with a blue top, marked Fiesta. ....$420-$440

6" plate in gray. .... $10-$11

9" plate in turquoise...... $13-$17

9" plate in red............... $18-$20

10" plate in medium green......................$140-$165

10" plate in ivory... $40-$46

CERAMICS

Top and side views of a cake plate in yellow.
....**$1,200-$1,300**

Unopened original box of Fiesta containing two salad plates in yellow. Boxes can double or triple the overall value of the pieces they contain.

7" plates (top to bottom): yellow, **$9-$10**, turquoise, **$9-$10**, red, **$12-$15**, forest green, **$15-$17**, light green, **$10-$11**, chartreuse, **$14-$16**, cobalt blue, **$10-$12**, rose, **$15-$17**, and ivory, **$10-$12**.

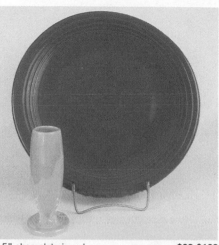

13" chop plate in rose. .... **$85-$90**

15" chop plate in red.............................**$90-$100**
Yellow bud vase...**$85-$92**

10-1/2" compartment plate in red..**$65-$75**
12" compartment plate in light green ....**$58-$65**

12" compartment plate in cobalt blue. .... **$72-$80**

Deep plate in medium green....................**$135-$150**

CERAMICS

Oval platter in chartreuse. .... **$50-$60**

Oval platter in turquoise. .... **$40-$48**

Shakers in gray. .... **$48-$52/pair**

Sauceboat in forest green. .... **$72-$84**

Sauceboat in ivory. .... **$70-$79**

Medium teapot in rose. .... **$275-$295**

Medium teapot in medium green. .... **$1,475-$1,595**

Large teapot in yellow. .... **$290-$300**

Relish tray and inserts in light green, as it would have come from the factory. .... **$295-$310/set**

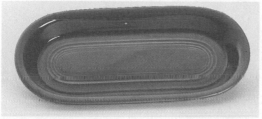

Utility tray in red. .... **$50-$55**

Tidbit tray in ivory, light green, and cobalt blue. .... **$100-$200**

Water tumbler in yellow. .... **$67-$70**

Bud vase in cobalt blue. ....**$100-$130**

8" vase in ivory...**$740-$780**

10" vase in light green. ....**$900-$975**

12" vase in light green............**$1,100-$1,200**

Bottom Marks

Bottom of 6" bread plate in turquoise, showing "Genuine Fiesta" stamp.

An ink stamp on the bottom of a piece of Fiesta.

Examples of impressed Fiesta bottom marks.

Two different impressed marks on the bottoms of relish tray inserts.

Notice the different bottoms of two ashtrays. The left one has a set of rings with no room for a logo. The right ashtray has rings along the outer edge, opposite of the ring pattern on the ashtray above. The red example is an older example. The yellow ashtray with the logo can be dated to a time period after 1940.

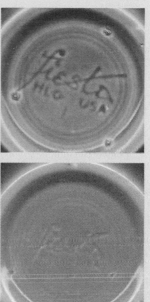

Bottom of a teacup saucer in turquoise, showing sagger pin marks and the "Genuine Fiesta" stamp.

Bottom of No. 1 mixing bowl in green, showing sagger pin marks, the "Fiesta/HLCo. USA" impressed mark, and the faint "1" size indicator. The impressed size mark on the bottom of the No. 2 mixing bowl in yellow is too faint to be seen in this image.

Fiesta pieces were glazed on the underside, so before being fired, each piece was placed on a stilt to keep it off the floor of the kiln. The stilt was made up of three sagger pins positioned an equal distance from each other to form three points of a triangle. If you inspect the underside of any piece of Fiesta, which has a completely glazed bottom, you will notice three small blemishes in a triangular pattern. Later in Fiesta's production run, the undersides of pieces were glazed and then wiped, creating a dry foot, before going into the kiln to be fired.

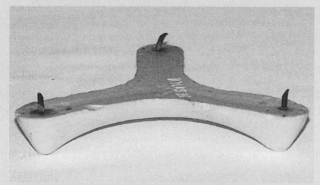

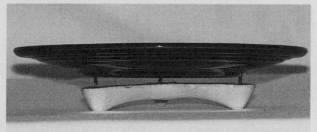

A 9" cobalt blue plate rests on a stilt with sagger pins to show the basic idea of how it worked. Please note that this stilt is not the exact one that would have been used by Homer Laughlin China Company, but rather an updated style in use today by many ceramic studios.

CERAMICS

Frankoma

John Frank started his pottery company in 1933 in Norman, Oklahoma. However, when he moved the business to Sapulpa, Oklahoma, in 1938, he felt he was home. Still, Mr. Frank could not know the horrendous storms and trials that would follow him. Just after his move, on November 11, 1938, a fire destroyed the entire operation, which included the pot and leopard mark he had created in 1935. Then, in 1942, the war effort needed men and materials so Frankoma could not survive. In 1943, John and Grace Lee Frank bought the plant as junk salvage and began again.

The time in Norman had produced some of the finest art ware that John would ever create and most of the items were marked either "Frank Potteries," "Frank Pottery," or to a lesser degree, the "pot and leopard" mark. Today these marks are avidly and enthusiastically sought by collectors. Another elusive mark wanted by collectors shows "Firsts Kiln Sapulpa 6-7-38." The mark was used for one day only and denotes the first firing in Sapulpa. It has been estimated that perhaps 50 to 75 pieces were fired on that day.

The clay Frankoma used is helpful to collectors in determining when an items was made. Creamy beige clay know as "Ada" clay was in use until 1953. Then a red brick shale was found in Sapulpa and used until about 1985 when, by the addition of an additive, the clay became a reddish pink.

Rutile glazes were used early in Frankoma's history. Glazes with rutile have caused more confusion among collectors than any other glazes. For example, a Prairie Green piece shows a lot of green and it also has some brown. The same is true for the Desert Gold glaze; the piece shows a sandy-beige glaze with some amount of brown. Generally speaking, Prairie Green, Desert Gold, White Sand, and Woodland Moss are the most puzzling to collectors.

In 1970 the government closed the rutile mines in America and Frankoma had to buy it from Australia. It was not the same so the results were different. Values are higher for the glazes with rutile. Also, the pre-Australian Woodland Moss glaze is more desirable than that created after 1970.

After John Frank died in 1973, his daughter Joniece Frank, a ceramic designer at the pottery, became president of the company. In 1983 another fire destroyed everything Frankoma had worked so hard to create. They rebuilt but in 1990, after the IRS shut the doors for nonpayment, Joniece, true to the Frank legacy, filed for Chapter 11 (instead of bankruptcy) so she could reopen and continue the work she loved. In 1991 Richard Bernstein purchased the pottery and the name was changed to Frankoma Industries.

The company was sold again in 2006. The new buyers are concentrating mostly on dinnerware, none of which is like the old Frankoma. They have a "Collectors Series," "Souvenir & State Items," and "Heartwarming Trivets." None of these is anything like what Frankoma originally created. The company is doing some Frankoma miniatures such as a dolphin on a wave, a fish, a wolf, a bear, etc. These, too, do not resemble Frankoma miniatures, and all their glazes are new.

Book ends, Walking Ocelot on a two-tiered oblong base, black high glaze, Model No. 424, signed on reverse of tiered base "Taylor" denoting designer Joseph Taylor, pot & leopard mark on bottom, 7" l., 3" h., pr. **$1,900**

Book ends, model of leopard, Pompeian Bronze glaze, Model No. 431, 9" l., 5 1/2" h., pr. **$1,800**

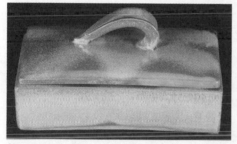

Cigarette box, cov., rectangular, cover w/single raised & hard-to-find curved leaf handle, Bronze Green glaze, Ada clay, marked "Frankoma," 4 x 6 3/4", 3 1/2" h. **$175**

Ornament, "The ABCs of life," gift w/purchase from Tulsa shopping mall, 1987, white background w/ sketch of three children, 3 1/2" d...................... **$69**

Bowl, 5 3/4" d., shallow form, advertising "Oklahoma Gas Company - Golden Anniversary," 1956, Desert Gold, marked "Frankoma" **$186**

Mortar & pestle, advertising "Schreibers Drug Store," White Sand, marked "Frankoma," 3 1/4" **$145**

▲Sign, dealer teepee, Prairie Green, 1940s, marked "Frankoma," 6 1/2" h. **$725**

◄Teapot, cov., Wagon Wheel patt., Desert Gold glaze, Sapulpa, Oklahoma, ca. 1942 .... **$25**

CERAMICS

Fulper Pottery

The Fulper Pottery was founded in Flemington, New Jersey, in 1805 and operated until 1935, although operations were curtailed in 1929 when its main plant was destroyed by fire. The name was changed in 1929 to Stangl Pottery, which continued in operation until July of 1978, when Pfaltzgraff, a division of Susquehanna Broadcasting Company of York, Pennsylvania, purchased the assets of the Stangl Pottery, including the name.

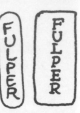

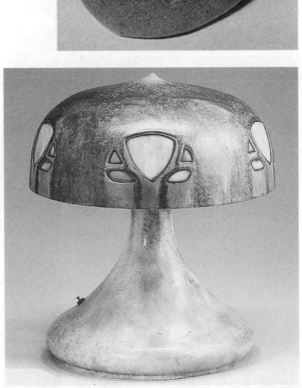

Flower frog, figural, model of a large oval scarab beetle, nice matte green glaze, unmarked, 3 1/4" l., 1 1/2" h.......................................$150

Vase, 10 1/2" h., 4 1/2" d., simple tall baluster-form body, Ivory Flambé glaze dripping over a mustard yellow matte ground, ink racetrack mark $805

Lamp, table model, a wide pottery mushroom-shaped shade w/a fine Leopard Skin Crystalline glaze, the border pierced w/clusters of small openings centered by a large triangular opening, all inset w/leaded slag glass pieces, on a widely flaring matching pottery pedestal base, original sockets & switch, hairline in a ceramic bridge between the two pieces of slag glass, rectangular ink mark on both pieces, shade 15 1/4" d., overall 18 1/2" h..$10,925

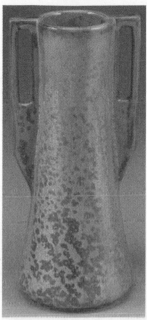

Vase, 11" h., 4 3/4" d., tall gently tapering cylindrical body w/a flat mouth flanked by long squared buttressed handles, fine Leopard Skin Crystalline glaze, rectangular ink mark. **$1,093**

Vase, 12 3/4" h., 4 3/4" d., "Cattail" patt., tall cylindrical form molded overall w/cattails, Leopard Skin crystalline glaze, minor burst bubble at rim, rectangular ink mark. **$4,025**

Vase, 13" h., 4 3/4" d., tall slightly tapering cylindrical body molded in relief overall in cattails, glossy bluish grey & Moss Flambé glaze, rectangular ink mark. **$4,313**

Jug, bulbous ovoid body w/a wide shoulder centered by a short cylindrical neck, a high arched handle from base of neck to edge of shoulder, Copper Dust Crystalline glaze, small in-the-making grinding chip on base, incised racetrack mark, 7 3/4" d., overall 11 1/2" h..**$2,760**

Vase, 11 1/2" h., 9" d., footed baluster-form body w/ flaring rim, molded w/vertical low ribs forming panels up the sides, fine mirrored Cat's-eye Flambé glaze, raised racetrack mark.....................................**$4,025**

CERAMICS

Vase, 7 1/2" h., 6" d., bulbous ovoid gourd-form body w/a slightly tapering cylindrical neck flanked by curved handles to the shoulder, blue & amber Crystalline glaze, incised racetrack mark........... **$546**

Vase, 5 1/2" h., 5" d., bulbous ovoid body tapering to a low wide molded mouth, Copper Dust Crystalline glaze, raised racetrack mark.............**$1,035**

Vase, 7 1/2" h., 4" d., corseted cylindrical body, dripping frothy ivory, blue & mahogany Flambé glaze, rectangular ink mark **$1,035**

Vase, 4 3/4" h., 5 3/4" d., wide low squatty lower body w/a wide tapering shoulder to the wide flat mouth flanked by squared scroll handles, Copper Dust Crystalline glaze, incised racetrack mark........... **$575**

Vase, 7" h., 9 1/2" d., wide squatty bulbous tapering form w/a flat closed rim flanked by square buttressed handles, cafe-au-lait glaze, rectangular ink mark **$748**

Right: Vase, 6" h., 8 1/2" d., footed wide squatty bulbous body w/a short wide cylindrical neck surrounded by three short loop handles, Cucumber Crystalline glaze, raised racetrack mark **$1,150**

Far right: Wall pocket, triple, a central tapering cone w/a high upturned back rim flanked down the sides w/ smaller entwined open-topped cones, matte blue glaze, remnant of rectangular ink mark, 11 1/2" h. **$374**

Grueby

Some fine art pottery was produced by the Grueby Faience and Tile Company, established in Boston in 1891. Choice pieces were created with molded designs on a semi-porcelain body. The ware is marked and often bears the initials of the decorators. The pottery closed in 1907.

GRUEBY

Bowl, 5 3/8" d., 1 7/8" h., wide low rounded sides & a wide flat molded rim, overall medium-dark blue matte glaze, impressed mark **$345**

Bowl, 3" d., 4 1/4" h., a small footring supporting the deep vertical & slightly uneven sides, wide flat rim, dappled green matte glaze, impressed mark, two pinhead-sized glaze pops............................... **$805**

Paperweight, model of a scarab beetle, oval, matte blue glaze, impressed circular mark, some small glaze chips at base, 3 7/8" l.................................... **$196**

Candlestick, a wide flat dished base w/low vertical sides, centered by a tapering ringed shaft w/an ovoid socket w/a flattened flared rim, mottled yellow & brown matte glaze, circular tulip-style insignia, No. 227, glazed-over chip at top rim, 5 3/8" h. **$460**

Paperweight, model of a scarab beetle, oval, matte oatmeal glaze, impressed circular mark, glaze peppering, 3 7/8" l... **$345**

CERAMICS

Plaque, rectangular, architectural-type, carved & modeled w/a family of elephants in black against a bluish grey ground, mounted in a black box frame, two firing lines in body, restoration to one, small chip to one corner, stamped mark, 14 x 23"...**$9,775**

Tile, square, a large white rabbit crouched behind a small stylized leafy shrub in white, both outlined in dark blue against a pale blue ground, impressed tulip-style mark, burst glaze bubbles, some small edge nicks, 3 7/8" w. **$690**

▲Vase, 12 1/2" h., 8 1/4" d., rare large form w/bulbous body centered by a flaring cylindrical neck, tooled & applied w/large wide pointed overlapping leaves, fine organic matte green glaze, couple of very minor edge nicks, by Marie Seaman, stamped round mark **$11,500**

◄Vase, 6 1/4" h., squatty bulbous form w/a wide flat mouth, molded around the shoulder w/seven flower buds alternating w/seven wide leaves down the sides, mottled matte yellow glaze, unmarked, restoration to center of base, ca. 1908...**$5,288**

Vase, 6 3/4" h., footed simple ovoid body tapering to a flat mouth, textured matte blue glaze, impressed Grueby mark **$690**

Vase, 9 1/2" h., footed squatty bulbous lower body tapering to a wide cylindrical neck w/a molded rim, dark green matte glaze **$1,265**

Vase, 7 3/4" h., squatty bulbous base w/an angled shoulder to the tall gently flaring neck, tooled floral designs, dark matte green glaze, impressed tulip mark **$1,610**

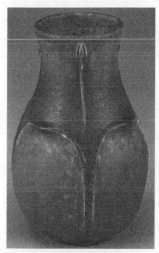

Above: Vase, 5 1/2" h., 4 1/2" d., bulbous ovoid body w/a wide rolled rim, crisply tooled w/broad leaves up the sides, covered in a leathery dark green glaze, some highpoint nicks, circular mark **$2,875**

Above left: Vase, 7 1/2" h., 4 1/2" d., ovoid body tapering to a wide gently flaring neck, tooled & applied w/rounded leaves around the lower half w/ four buds up the sides, medium matte green glaze, small nick to one leaf edge, mark obscured by glaze **$2,875**

Left: Vase, 12 1/2" h., swelled cylindrical body tapering to a short flared neck, matte green glaze w/a number of pinhead burst bubbles, area of thin glaze on side **$1,265**

Hall China

Founded in 1903 in East Liverpool, Ohio, this still-operating company at first produced mostly utilitarian wares. It was in 1911 that Robert T. Hall, son of the company founder, developed a special single-fire, lead-free glaze that proved to be strong, hard and nonporous. In the 1920s the firm became well known for its extensive line of teapots (still a major product), and in 1932 it introduced kitchenwares, followed by dinnerwares in 1936 and refrigerator wares in 1938.

HALL CHINA (HALL)
MADE IN U.S.A.

The imaginative designs and wide range of glaze colors and decal decorations have led to the growing appeal of Hall wares with collectors, especially people who like Art Deco and Art Moderne design. One of the firm's most famous patterns was the "Autumn Leaf" line, produced as premiums for the Jewel Tea Company. For listings of this ware see "Jewel Tea Autumn Leaf."

Helpful books on Hall include *The Collector's Guide to Hall China* by Margaret & Kenn Whitmyer, and *Superior Quality Hall China - A Guide for Collectors* by Harvey Duke (An ELO Book, 1977).

Batter bowl, Five Band shape, Chinese Red........**$95**

Casserole, cov., Art Deco w/chrome reticulated handled base...**$55**

Casserole w/inverted pie dish lid, Radiance shape, No. 488, 6 1/2" d., 4" h....................................**$60**

Coffeepot, cov., Terrace shape, Crocus patt. **$80**

CERAMICS

Bean pot, cov., Sani-Grid (Pert) shape, Chinese Red **$100**

Cookie jar, cov., Flareware **$65**

Cookie jar, cov., Five Band shape, Meadow Flower patt. **$325**

Creamer, Radiance shape, Autumn Leaf patt. **$45**

Humidor, cov., Indian Decal, walnut lid **$55**

Leftover, cov., Zephyr shape, Chinese Red **$110**

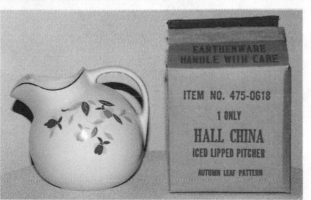

Pitcher, ball shape, Autumn Leaf patt., 1978, w/box...................... **$65**

Mug, Irish coffee, footed, commemorative, "Hall China Convention 2000" **$40**

Pitchers, Sani-Grid (Pert) shape, Chinese Red, three sizes (ILLUS. of three) **$35-55**

Salt & pepper shakers, Sani-Grid (Pert) shape, Chinese Red, pr... **$35**

CERAMICS

Teapot, cov., Adele shape, Art Deco style, Olive Green **$200**

Teapot, cov., Aladdin shape, round opening for cover & insert, Gold Swag decoration **$70-75**

Teapot, cov., Aladdin shape, round opening w/insert, Marine Blue **$65-75**

Teapot, cov., Aladdin shape, round opening w/insert, Maroon **$65-75**

Teapot, cov., Aladdin shape, w/infuser, Serenade patt. **$350**

Teapot, cov., Aladdin shape, Wildfire patt., w/oval infuser, 1950s **$75**

▲Teapot, cov., Automobile shape, Autumn Leaf patt., reissue for China Specialties w/commemorative stamp on the bottom, 1993 .... **$175**

▶Teapot, cov., Birdcage shape, Canary Yellow w/ "Gold Special" decoration **$450**

Teapot, cov., Donut shape, Orange Poppy patt... **$450**

Teapot, cov., Football shape, commemorative, "Hall 2000 Haul, East Liverpool, Ohio" Ivory............ **$125**

Teapot, cov., Hook Cover shape, Cameo Rose patt., part of a limited edition produced exclusively for China Specialties, Strongsville, Ohio, fewer than 500 made.. **$95**

Teapot, cov., Hook Cover shape, Chinese Red ... **$250**

Teapot, cov., Illinois shape, Maroon w/gold decoration **$225**

Teapot, cov., Philadelphia shape, Chinese Red. **$250**

Teapot, cov., Morning Set shape, Blue Garden patt. **$350**

Teapot, cov., Lipton Tea shape, Mustard Yellow... **$40**

CERAMICS

Teapot, cov., Radiance shape, Acacia patt........ **$225**

Teapot, cov., Rutherford shape, ribbed, Chinese Red
.... **$300**

▲Teapot, cov., Star shape, Turquoise w/
gold decoration.......................**$100-125**

Teapot, cov., Streamline shape, Fantasy patt. **$400**

Teapot, cov., Sundial shape, Blue Blossom patt.
.... **$300**

Teapot, cov., Tea-for-Two shape, Pink w/gold deco-
ration **$150**

Haviland

Haviland porcelain was originated by Americans in Limoges, France, shortly before the mid-19th century and continues in production. Some Haviland was made by Theodore Haviland in the United States during the last World War. Numerous other factories also made china in Limoges.

Chocolate set: tall tapering pot & six tall cups & saucers; Albany patt., white w/narrow floral rim bands & gold trim, late 19th - early 20th c., the set **$450-650**

Cups & saucers, Papillon butterfly handles w/Meadow Visitors decoration, six sets (ILLUS. of one set) **$900**

Dinner service: twelve 8-piece place settings w/additional open & cov. vegetable dishes & oval platter; Albany patt., white w/narrow floral rim bands & gold trim, late 19th - early 20th c., the set...................**$2,700**

Comport, pedestal on three feet w/ornate gold shell design, top w/reticulated edge, peach & gold design around base & top, 9" d. **$595**

Dinner service: service for eight w/five-piece place settings & additional bowls, pitcher, gravy boat & other pieces; mostly Blank No. 5 w/delicate pink floral decoration, late 19th - early 20th c., 54 pcs. (ILLUS. of part) **$2,500**

Fish set: 22" l. oval platter & twelve 8 1/2" d. plates; each piece w/a different fish in the center, the border in two shades of green design w/gold trim, h.p. scenes by L. Martin, mark of Theodore Haviland, 13 pcs. (ILLUS. of plate) **$2,750**

CERAMICS

Hair receiver, cov., squatty round body on three gold feet, h.p. overall w/small flowers in blues & greens w/ gold trim, mark of Charles Field Haviland......... **$225**

Pitcher, 9" h., lemonade-type, Schleiger 1026B variation, Blank 117, decorated w/lavender flowers & brushed gold trim, Theodore Haviland.......... **$250**

Plate, bread & butter, 6 1/2" d., Paisley patt., smooth blanks w/gold edge, brownish red ground w/flowers in yellow, bright blue, green & white border design w/ yellow flowers & bright blue leaves, turquoise scroll trim, Haviland & Co. mark **$28**

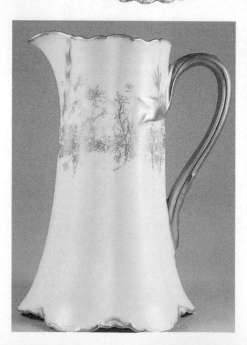

▲Pitcher, 7" h., milk-type, tankard style w/tapering cylindrical white body w/a large relief-molded anchor under the heavy rope-twist loop handle, bright gold trim, old Haviland & Co. mark **$175**

◄Pitcher, 9" h., tankard-shaped lemonade-type, Ranson blank, delicate floral band around the upper body trimmed in gold, gold handle & trim bands, factory-decorated, Haviland & Co. mark **$250**

Hull Pottery

The A.E. Hull Pottery Company grew from the clay soil of Perry County, Ohio, in 1905. By the 1930s, its unpretentious line of ware could be found in shops and, more importantly, homes from coast to coast, making it one of the nation's largest potteries. Leveled by flood and ensuing fire in 1950, like a phoenix, Hull rose from the ashes and reestablished its position in the marketplace. Less than four decades later, however, the firm succumbed after eight bitter strikes by workers, leaving behind empty buildings, memories and the pottery shown in this volume.

Addis Emmet Hull founded A.E. Hull Pottery in July 1905. By the time the company was formed, the Crooksville/Roseville/Zanesville area was already well established as a pottery center. Hull constructed an all-new pottery, featuring six kilns, four of them large natural gas-fired beehive kilns.

The early years were good to Hull. In fact, after only two years of operation, Hull augmented the new plant by taking over the former facilities of the Acme pottery. By 1910, Hull was claiming to be the largest manufacturer of blue-banded kitchenware in the United States. By 1925 production reached three million pieces annually.

This early ware included spice and cereal jars and salt boxes. Some of these items were lavishly decorated with decals, high-gloss glazes or bands. This evolved into some early art ware pieces including vases and flowerpots. However, Hull could not keep up with the demand, especially the growing demand for artwares, which could be sold in five and dime stores. Hence, Addis Hull visited Europe and made arrangements to import decorative items from Czechoslovakia, England, France, Germany and Italy. To accommodate the influx of these items, Hull opened a facility in Jersey City, N.J. This arrangement continued until 1929, when import operations were discontinued.

In 1926 Plant 1 was converted to manufacture decorative floor and wall tiles, which were popular at the time. But by the time of Addis Hull's death in 1930, the company bearing his name was exiting the tile business. Plant 1, Hull's original, which had been converted to the now-discontinued line of tile production as well as being elderly, was closed in 1933.

When Addis Hull Sr. died in 1930, management of the works was passed to his son, Addis Hull Jr., who was involved in the formation of the Shawnee Pottery Company. By the late 1930s, Addis Junior left the family business and assumed the presidency of Shawnee.

World War II affected the entire nation, and Hull was no exception. This time period saw the production of some of Hull's most famous lines, including Orchid, Iris, Tulip and Poppy. Their airbrushed matte hues of pink, blue, green and yellow became synonymous with the Hull name. Sales of such wares through chain and dime stores soared.

The close of the decade saw the emergence of high-gloss glazed art pottery as the growing trend in decorative ceramics. Hull responded initially by merely changing the glaze applied to some of its earlier lines. Another significant development of the time was the growing influence of designer Louise Bauer on Hull's lines. First and most notable was her 1943 Red Riding Hood design, but also significant were her Bow-Knot and Woodland lines.

While the late 1940s and early 1950s saw the demise of long-time rivals Weller and Roseville, business at Hull flourished. This is particularly surprising given that on June 16, 1950, the pottery was completely destroyed by a flood, which in turn caused the kiln to explode, and the ensuing fire finished off the venerable plant.

B-17 Bow-Knot candleholders, 4"... **$150-$175 each**

A new plant officially opened on Jan. 1, 1952. With the new plant came a new company name – Hull Pottery Company.

Hull entered into dinnerware manufacture in the early 1960s at the behest of one of its largest customers, the J.C. Penney Company. Penney, whose offers to purchase Pfaltzgraff dinnerware were declined by the manufacturer, turned to Hull to create a competitive line. Hull's response to this was the new House 'n Garden line, which would remain in production until 1967 and would grow to 100 items.

During the 1970s and 1980s, the pottery was closed by no fewer than eight strikes, one of which lasted for seven weeks. The eighth and final strike by workers sounded the death knell for the pottery. In 1986, the Hull Pottery Company ceased business operations. For more information on Hull pottery, see *Warman's Hull Pottery Identification and Price Guide* by David Doyle.

T-2 Blossom Flite basket, 6"........**$75-$100**

T14 Blossom Flite teapot, 8"............................**$125-$175**

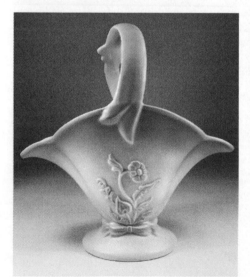

B-12 Bow-Knot basket, 10-1/2". ....**$750-$1,000**

B-24 Bow-Knot cup and saucer wall pocket, 6"
....**$250-$300**

B-11 Butterfly ewer, 13 1/2". ....**$100-$150**

B-19 Butterfly creamer, 5". ....**$50-$75**

Like its smaller cousins, the Calla Lily 9" No. 530/33 vase appeared in various color schemes. ..**$350-$450**

No. 506/10 Calla Lily ewer, 10" .... **$350-$450**

No. 107 6" Camellia basket. ....**$325-$375**

No. 136 Camellia 6-1/4" vase. ....**$125-$150**

CERAMICS

C525 Capri 6-1/4" pitcher vase. ....$75-$125

C53 Continental vase, 8-1/2". ....$20-$40

C87 Capri 12" ewer. ...$100-$150

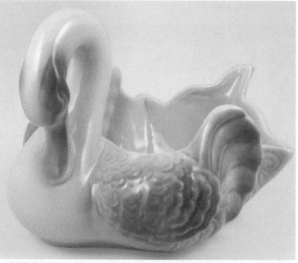

C55 Continental basket, 12-3/4" ....$125-$200

No. 213 Coronet swan. ....$20-$40

No. 201 Coronet flowerpot, 5" x 3-1/2" or 5-1/2" x 4" .... $5-$10

B-8 Crescent cookie jar, 9-1/2"............... $50-$75

CERAMICS

This Crestone pitcher, mold number 349, is finished in a non-standard glaze. Experimental pieces such as this are highly sought after by collectors............. **$40-$50**

Shown here are examples of Debonair partitioned Dutch oven and individual casserole dishes, both with covers. They are marked "Oven Proof Hull USA 0-7 and 0-17," and 6-1/4" and 10" wide respectively.
0-7 .... **$10-20**
0-17 ....**$20-$30**

No. 502 Dogwood vase, 6-1/2"...............**$225-$275**

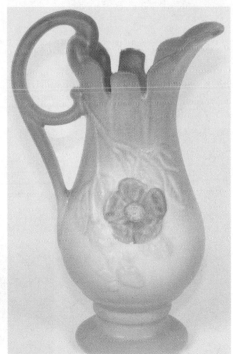

No. 505 Dogwood ewer, 6-1/2"...............**$225-$275**

Among Hull's Early Art stoneware offerings was this hanging basket in green, blue and red high glaze. The unmarked basket measures 7-1/2" wide by 4-3/4" tall. ....**$75-$125**

A Hull early stoneware utility bowl............. **$20-$30**

Ebb Tide, like most of Hull's art pottery lines, came in multiple color schemes. E-10 ewer, 14".. **$200-$250**

E-13 Ebb Tide candleholder, 2-3/4". ...**$15-$25 each**

This is a No. 45 Fiesta strawberry vase with gold trim, 8-1/2" x 4-1/2", marked Hull USA 45........ **$20-$40**

No. 71 Fantasy vase, 9".......**$10-$20**

No. 46 Floral pitcher, one quart. .... **$40-$50**

No. 215 Granada vase, 9".
.... **$50-$75**

No. 216 Granada vase, 9"
.... **$50-$75**

F482 Imperial fish gurgling ewer,
11"............................**$75-$100**

A-18 Heritageware cookie jar.
.... **$25-$35**

No. 592 House 'n Garden oval hen
on nest. .... **$50-$65**

Typical of Hull's production, the
front and rear faces of this 10"
No. 403 vase are not decorated
alike..........................**$325-$375**

No. 198 House 'n Garden gingerbread man server, 10"............**$50-$60**

F72 Imperial flower dish, 11-3/4" x 5" x 3"............................**$10-$20**

No. 414 Iris vase, 10-1/2".
..................................**$250-$325**

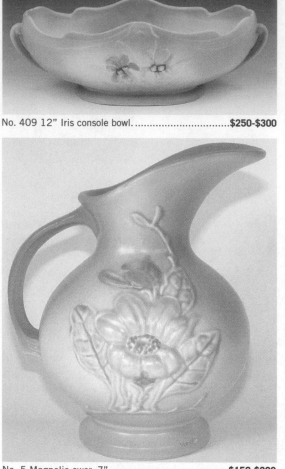

No. 409 12" Iris console bowl. ....**$250-$300**

No. 5 Magnolia ewer, 7". ....$150-$200

No. 411 "Dutchess" Jubilee planter, 12-1/2". ....**$30-$50**

No. 47 9" Mardi Gras vase. ....$75-$100

This unmarked Lusterware bottleneck vase in golden yellow is 13-1/2" tall by 6-1/2" wide. .... **$50-$75**

No. 17 Magnolia vase, 12-1/4"
......................................**$300-$350**

No. 18 Magnolia ewer, 13-1/2"
......................................**$350-$425**

No. 84 7-1/4" Mayfair planter or wall pocket .... **$25-$40**

No. 809 11" Medley cat vase.
......................................**$50-$75**

These 8" Mirror Black candy dishes were originally part of the Fantasy line. `...**$30-$50 each**

H-16 12-1/2" New Magnolia vase. ....**$200-$250**

New Magnolia teapot, creamer and sugar bowl.
No. H-20 teapot ....**$150-$200**
No. H-21 creamer and H-22 sugar bowl......................**$40-$60 each**

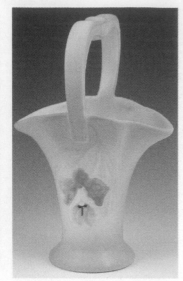

No. 305 7" Orchid basket. **$500-$600**

The pair of 4" No. 315 Orchid candleholders provide a nice accent for the 13" console bowl. ....**$500-$700**

S-5 11" Parchment and Pine window box. ....**$80-$120**

S-9 16" Parchment and Pine console bowl. ....**$75-$125**

No. 306 6-3/4" Orchid bud vase .... **$150-$200**

Pink 6-1/2" Pine Cone vase. ....**$150-$200**

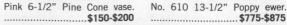

No. 610 13-1/2" Poppy ewer. ....**$775-$875**

No. 612 6-1/2" Poppy vase.
...................................**$75-$100**

No. 540 Rainbow leaf serve-all. ....**$35-$45**

No. 914 Tangerine two-quart ice jug............ **$25-$30**

R-12 7" Rosella basket. ....**$225-$275**

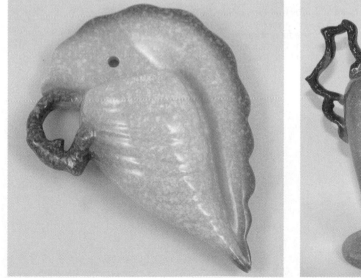

W13 Royal wall pocket, 7-1/2". .... **$75-$125**

W24 Royal pitcher vase, 13-1/2". **$50-$75**

CERAMICS

S4 Serenade puritan vase, 5-1/4". .... **$50-$75**

S21 Serenade pitcher, 10-1/2"............... **$200-$250**

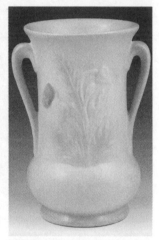

S3 Serenade candy dish, 8-1/4".
.................................**$125-$175**

Although the entire Thistle line was made up of only four molds, one form of variety was the result of using different patterns on the front and rear of the vases. This is the No. 51 6-1/2" vase. **$75-$100**

Variety also came in the form of varying the coloration of the pieces. This is the Thistle No. 53 6-1/2" vase................**$100-$125**

No. 6 Supreme candy box, 6-1/4" x 7". .... **No established value.**

No. 7 Tokay fruit bowl, 9-1/2". .... **$150-$200**

No. 6 Tokay basket, 8"..**$60-$100**

No. T53 Tropicana vase, 8-1/2".. **$325-$425**

No. 102 Tulip basket, 6". .... **$125-$150**

No. 109 Tulip ewer, 8"...**$225-$275**

Like most of Hull's decorative pottery, the Tulip pattern was produced in more than one color combination. No. 115 7" jardinière.. **$275-$325**

No. 28 Vegetable cookie jar. .... **$60-$80**

CERAMICS

L-A Water Lily vase, 8-1/2".....................**$200-$225**

L-14 Water Lily basket, 10-1/2".............**$300-$375**

L-25 Water Lily flowerpot, 5-1/4"............**$150-$175**

No. 54 Wildflower vases, 6-1/4"...... **$150-$175 each**

W-2 Wildflower ewer, 5-1/2". ....**$100-$125**

This pink and blue Wildflower basket is one of the more sought after by "W" series item is this 10-1/2" basket. It is marked "Hull Art USA W-16-10 1/2"."
....**$250-$350**

One of the most desirable of the later "W-series" Hull Wildflower items is this 15-1/2" tall floor vase. Marked "Hull Art USA W-20-15 1/2"," the example shown here is finished in a dusty rose shade........ **$450-$550**

W7 Woodland Hi-Gloss jardinière, 5-1/2". **$150-$200**

W7 Woodland jardinière, 5-1/2"............**$150-$200**

W11 Woodland flowerpot, 5-3/4". ....**$150-$200**

W26 Woodland Hi-Gloss teapot, 6-1/2". ...**$400-$500**

W12 Woodland hanging basket, 7-1/2"....**$400-$500**

W23 Woodland double cornucopia, 14"...**$500-$600**

Ironstone

The first successful ironstone was patented in 1813 by C.J. Mason in England. The body contains iron slag incorporated with the clay. Other potters imitated Mason's ware, and today much hard, thick ware is lumped under the term ironstone. Earlier it was called by various names, including graniteware. Both plain white and decorated wares were made throughout the 19th century. Tea Leaf Lustre ironstone was made by several firms.

GENERAL

Chamber pot, cov., Atlantic shape, all-white, T. & R. Boote $125-150

Sugar bowl, cov., Four Square Wheat shape, all-white, unmarked $80

▶Soup tureen, cover & undertray, Gothic Octagon shape, all-white, Wedgwood & Co., 3 pcs. $900

Compote, open, oval, President shape, all-white, John Edwards..$350-400

Soap slab, rectangular w/molded scroll edges, all-white, marked "ELO" [East Liverpool, Ohio] $20-30

Syllabub cup, Hyacinth shape, all-white, Wedgwood & Co., ca. 1865 .... **$45**

Teapot, cov., all-white, Plain Seashore shape, molded dolphin on handle & finial, by W. & E. Corn, ca. 1885..**$125-150**

Teapot, cov., Full Paneled Gothic shape, all-white, John Alcock, ca. 1850 ....**$275-300**

Vegetable tureen, cov., Sydenham shape, all-white, T. & R. Boote, 1853 ....**$190-240**

TEA LEAF IRONSTONE

Butter dish, cover & insert, Chelsea patt., Alfred Meakin, the set (minor flaws)....................................**$60**

Butter dish, cover & insert. Brocade patt., Alfred Meakin, flanks inside base, chip on insert..............**$110**

Chamber pot, cov., Cable shape, Anthony Shaw **$175**

Compote, open, square w/rounded corners, pedestal base, H. Burgess... **$185**

Creamer & cov. sugar bowl, child's, slant-sided shape, Mellor Taylor, pr. **$100**

Creamer, Chinese shape, Anthony Shaw........... **$410**

Mustache cup & saucer, Edge Malkin, professional rim repair... **$500**

Pitcher, 8" h., Blanket Stitch shape, Alcock..... **$140**

Pitcher, 8" h., Square Ridged shape, Wedgwood **$50**

Pitcher, water, Cable shape, Anthony Shaw, rare **$1,200**

Punch bowl, Cable shape, Anthony Shaw **$400**

Teapot, cov., Scroll shape, Alfred Meakin **$160**

Toothbrush vase, cylindrical w/molded handles near pedestal base, drain holes, no underplate, possibly by Shaw... **$850**

Wash bowl & pitcher set, Cable shape, Anthony Shaw, the set... **$225**

Chamber pot, open, King Charles patt., Mayer.. **$100**

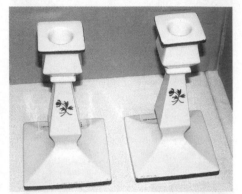

Candlesticks, square, Red Cliff, ca. 1970, pr. .. **$360**

Cake plate, Empress patt., Micratex by Adams, ca. 1960s **$160**

Coffeepot, cov., Woodland patt., W. & E. Corn, minor flaws **$60**

Creamer, Maidenhair Fern patt., T. Wilkinson.... **$150**

Gravy boat with attached undertray, Empress patt., Micratex by Adams, ca. 1960 .... **$80**

Ladle, sauce tureen-size, some crazing. **$200**

Platter, oval, Fleur-de-Lis Chain patt., Wodgwood & Co., large **$50**

Salt & pepper shakers, Empress patt., Micratex by Adams, ca. 1960s, pr. **$130**

Teapot, cov., Ginger Jar patt., unmarked, repair to spout. **$60**

Vegetable dish, cov., Bullet patt., A. Shaw, minor flaws **$65**

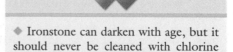

◆ Ironstone can darken with age, but it should never be cleaned with chlorine bleach, as it will destroy the glaze.

◆ The tea leaf decoration probably orginated from a superstition that finding a complete open tea leaf at the bottom of a tea cup would bring good luck.

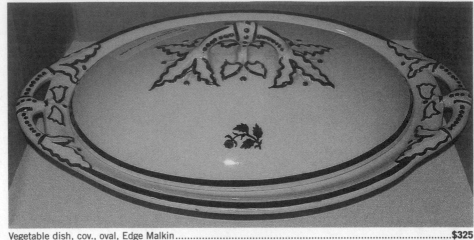

Vegetable dish, cov., oval, Edge Malkin...**$325**

Wash bowl & pitcher set, Chrysanthemum patt., H. Burgess, the set **$575**

TEA LEAF VARIANTS

Chamber pot, cov., Pre-Tea Leaf patt., Niagara shape, E. Walley.................................... **$1,050**

Coffeepot, cov., Wheat in Meadow shape, lustre band trim, Powell & Bishop.................................. **$325**

Creamer, Wrapped Sydenham shape, lustre bands & pinstripes, Edward Walley **$260**

Cup & saucer, handleless, Pre-Tea Leaf patt., Niagara shape, E. Walley **$90**

Gravy boat, Scallops patt., Sydenham shape, E. Walley **$250**

Mug, Gothic shape, paneled sides, lustre band, Livesley & Powell **$100**

Posset cup, Tobacco Leaf patt., Tulip shape, Elsmore & Forster.. **$325**

Sauce tureen, cov., Gothic Cameo shape, lustre band trim, Edward Walley **$250**

Sauce tureen, cover, undertray & ladle, Moss Rose patt., H. Burgess, the set............................ **$375**

Chamber pot, cov., Grape Octagon shape, lustre band trim, E. Walley, minor flaws **$150**

Coffeepot, cov., Pinwheel patt., Grape Octagon shape, E. Walley, slight crazing on cover.................... $200

Pitcher, 7 3/4" h., Laurel Wreath patt., lustre trim, Elsmore & Forster, minor flaws...................... $325

Vegetable dish, cov., Reverse Teaberry patt., Portland shape, Elsmore & Forster.. $380

Toothbrush vase, Teaberry patt., Heavy Square shape, Clementson Bros., slight flaws ... $1,350

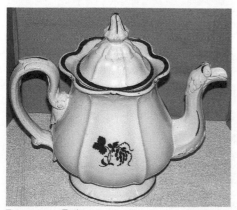

Teapot, cov., Teaberry patt., Ring O' Hearts shape, J. Furnival $650

Soap dish, cover & insert, Lily of the Valley shape, lustre band trim, chip inside lip, Anthony Shaw, the set......... $205

Sugar bowl, cov., Quartered Rose shape, copper lustre bands & cobalt blue plumes, minor flaws, J. Furnival $180

Syrup pitcher w/hinged metal lid, Moss Rose patt., George Scott.............. $325

Teapot, cov., Moss Rose patt.......................... $100

Teapot, cov., Quartered Rose shape, copper lustre bands & cobalt blue plumes, possibly J. Furnival $225

Vegetable dish, cov., Quartered Rose shape, copper lustre bands & trim & cobalt blue plumes, slight flaws......... $250

Waste bowl, Gothic shape, Chelsea Grape patt., minor flaws......... $35

Limoges

Limoges is a magical word for those who love beautiful French porcelain. The word is synonymous with fine porcelain, but the name belongs to a special city in central France. Here, in the 18th and 19th centuries, a number of porcelain factories were established because deposits of the special clays required to produce true hard paste porcelain were located nearby.

The best known of these Limoges factories was founded by the Haviland family; however, there were many other firms that produced wares just as fine. All Limoges-made porcelain is high quality and worthy of collector interest.

Fish set: 11 x 24" oval fish tray, twelve matching 9 1/2" d. plates & a 7 1/4" l. sauceboat & underplate; each piece w/a gently scalloped rim & paneled sides & each h.p. w/a different game fish, a lake landscape & a flower, bases marked "B.B. H. Limoges, France," the set............**$1,668**

Charger, large rounded shape w/ an ornate scroll-molded gold border, h.p. w/a scene of two battling brown stags against a shaded ground w/leaves in shades of yellow, green & lavender, 13" d.. **$201**

Punch set: punch bowl, base & ten champagne-style stems; the footed bowl w/deep rounded & flaring sides h.p. around the sides w/large gold leafy grapevines on stems against a pale blue shaded to white ground, on a matching base w/large gold paw feet, the saucer-shaped matching stems w/a wide shallow round bowl on a simple stem, mark of Tressemann & Vogt, Limoges, late 19th - early 20th c., bowl 16" d., 7" h., base 3 1/2" h., stems each 3 1/2" h., some rubbing to gold, the set....**$1,035**

Pitcher, 14 1/2" h., tankard-type, a gold & brown ringed base below the slightly tapering cylindrical body w/a reddish brown D-form handle, h.p. w/a friar seated at a tavern table, artist-signed **$518**

Tea set: one-cup cov. teapot, open sugar, creamer & oblong tray; each piece painted w/colorful roses, a gold wave scroll band around the teapot & creamer neck, gold loop handles & teapot finial, marks of Gèrard, Dufraisseix & Abbot, Limoges, France, ca. 1900-41, the set............. **$900**

CERAMICS

Majolica

In 1851, an English potter was hoping that his new interpretation of a centuries-old style of ceramics would be well received at the "Great Exhibition of the Industries of All Nations" set to open May 1 in London's Hyde Park.

Potter Herbert Minton had high hopes for his display. His father, Thomas Minton, founded a pottery works in the mid-1790s in Stoke-on-Trent, Staffordshire. Herbert Minton had designed a "new" line of pottery, and his chemist, Leon Arnoux, had developed a process that resulted in vibrant, colorful glazes that came to be called "majolica."

Trained as an engineer, Arnoux also studied the making of encaustic tiles, and had been appointed art director at Minton's works in 1848. His job was to introduce and promote new products. Victorian fascination with the natural world prompted Arnoux to reintroduce the work of Bernard Palissy, whose naturalistic, bright-colored "maiolica" wares had been created in the 16th century. But Arnoux used a thicker body to make pieces sturdier. This body was given a coating of opaque white glaze, which provided a surface for decoration.

Pieces were modeled in high relief, featuring butterflies and other insects, flowers and leaves, fruit, shells, animals and fish. Queen Victoria's endorsement of the new pottery prompted its acceptance by the general public.

When Minton introduced his wares at Philadelphia's 1876 Centennial Exhibition, American potters also began to produce majolica.

For more information on majolica, see *Warman's Majolica Identification and Price Guide* by Mark F. Moran.

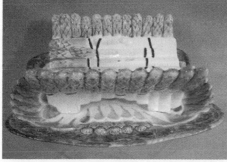

Longchamp French asparagus tray and cradle, good color, 13-1/2" long. .... **$250+**

Etruscan cobalt daisy comport (compote), 8-1/2" diameter. .... **$250+**

Etruscan oak leaf oval bowl with pink center, strong color, 12-1/2" wide. (Collector tip: Made by Griffen, Smith and Hill of Phoenixville, Pa., 1879 to about 1890.) .... **$500+**

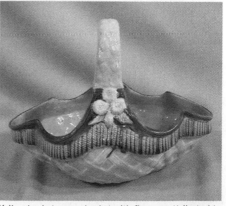

Yellow basket weave basket with flowers, attributed to Holdcroft, 10" long.. **$300+**

CERAMICS

Minton putti shell carriers on cobalt rimmed base, strong color and detail, 11" wide, 11" tall. ...**$3,000+**

Four begonia leaf on basket butter pats. ....**$275+ all**

Pond lily and stork tall cake stand, good detail, 9-1/2" tall, 10-1/2" diameter. ....**$400+**

Holdcroft pond lily foot cachepot strong color and detail, 7" diameter, 5-3/4" tall. (Collector tip: Joseph Holdcroft majolica ware was produced at Daisy Bank in Longton, Staffordshire, England, from 1870 to 1885. Items can be found marked with "JHOLD-CROFT," but many items can only be attributed by the patterns and colors that are documented to have come from the Holdcroft potteries.)...............**$700+**

▲Minton rabbits under cabbage table centerpiece, shape no. 1451, date code for 1873, strong color and detail, 9-1/2" long, 4-1/2" tall. ....**$7,500-$10,000**

◄Minton dolphin candlestick professional repair to top, 8-1/4" tall. (Thomas Minton founded his factory in the mid-1790s in Stoke-on-Trent, Staffordshire, England. His son, Herbert Minton, introduced majolica pottery—with glazes created by Léon Arnoux—at England's Great Exhibition of 1851.) ....**$450+**

George Jones cobalt picket fence and daisy full-size cheese keeper, outstanding color, minor professional rim repair to under plate, 12" diameter, 12" tall. .... **$10,000+**

George Jones rustic floral creamer, Bacall Collection, 3" tall. (Collector tip: The company started operations in the early 1860s as George Jones in Stoke, Staffordshire, England, and in 1873 became George Jones & Sons Ltd.) .... **$350+**

Holdcroft mottled shell comport (or compote) with shells and seaweed on base, good detail, 9-1/2" diameter, 7" tall. .... **$325+**

Wardle floral and leaf covered sugar, 5" tall.... **$130+**

Victoria Pottery Co. (VPC) basket weave game dish with mallard ducks on bed of ferns on cover, good color, with insert, professional repair to duck's wing, 12" wide. (Collector tip: Victoria Pottery Co., Hanley, Staffordshire, England, 1895 to 1927.)......... **$600+**

Fielding bird and fan turquoise cup and saucer. (Collector tip: Railway Pottery, established by S. Fielding & Co., Stoke, Stoke-on-Trent, Staffordshire, England, 1879.) .... **$125+ pair**

Turquoise and pink basket weave egg holder basket, 7-1/4" diameter... **$170+**

▲Large French birds on branch, blackberry, floral and leaves oval jardinière, good detail, 15" wide, 8" tall. .... **$500+**

◄Copeland ewer with angel faces and birds in high relief, band of ivy and berries on cobalt ground, good color, professional spout and handle repair, 10-1/2" tall. (Collector tip: William T. Copeland & Sons pottery of Stoke-on-Trent, England, began producing porcelain and earthenware in 1847.)..................... **$1,200**

Bird and fan turquoise humidor, 5-1/2" tall.... **$150+**

French figural horse inkwell, very unusual, ears professionally restored, 10-1/2" wide................ **$400+**

Thomas Sergent Palissy shells, fern and leaf jardinière, great detail, 7-1/2" tall, 10" diameter. (Collector tip: Thomas-Victor Sergent was one of the School of Paris ceramists of the late 19th century who was influenced by the works of Bernard Palissy, c. 1510-1590, the great French Renaissance potter.)... **$800+**

Minton tower jug with jester finial on hinged pewter lid, shape no. 1231, 13" tall........................ **$850+**

"BB" figural match striker with mouse, melon, flowers and leaves, minor rim repair, 8" wide. .... **$550+**

George Jones apple blossom and basket weave mug, good color and detail, 5-1/2" tall. (Collector tip: The company started operations in the early 1860s as George Jones in Stoke, Staffordshire, England, and in 1873 became George Jones & Sons Ltd.)..... **$2,000+**

CERAMICS

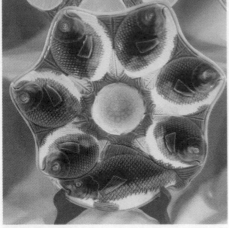

Fish oyster plate with large fish cracker well, 10"
wide. .... **$800+**

Samuel Lear sunflower oyster plate with lavender rim,
minor rim glaze wear, 9-3/4" diameter. (Collector tip:
Samuel Lear, Hanley, Staffordshire, England, 1877 to
1886.) ....**$1,300+**

Wedgwood St. Louis pattern oyster plate with cobalt
and turquoise wells, strong color and detail, 9" diameter. (Collector tip: Founded by Josiah Wedgwood in
1759 at Burslem, Staffordshire, England.)...**$1,300+**

▲Etruscan bamboo syrup pitcher, Bacall Collection.
(Collector tip: Made by Griffen, Smith and Hill of
Phoenixville, Pa., 1879 to about 1890.)........ **$525+**

◄Cobalt wild rose pitcher with butterfly spout, good
color, 9-1/2" tall.. **$300+**

Wild rose on mottled ground pitcher, 8" tall... **$180+**

George Jones turquoise apple blossom and basket pitcher, strong color and detail, Bacall Collection, 8" tall. ....**$1,600+**

Turquoise tree bark and blackberry pitcher, 4-1/2" tall. .... **$175+**

▲Holdcroft cobalt pond lily ice-lip pitcher, great color, 9-1/2" tall. (Collector tip: Joseph Holdcroft majolica ware was produced at Daisy Bank in Longton, Staffordshire, England, from 1870 to 1885. Items can be found marked with "JHOLDCROFT," but many items can only be attributed by the patterns and colors that are documented to have come from the Holdcroft potteries.)................................... **$800-$1,200**

◄Hugo Lonitz small dolphin footed planter with mythological faces on ends, cobalt accents, 6" wide, 5" tall. (Collector tip: Hugo Lonitz operated in Haldensleben, Germany, from 1868-1886, and later Hugo Lonitz & Co., 1886-1904, producing household and decorative porcelain and earthenware, and metal wares. Look for a mark of two entwined fish.) . **$170+**

CERAMICS

Sarreguemines pair of cobalt mythological-head hanging planters with leaves and foliage in high relief, great color, shape no. 557, 11" diameter, 6" tall. (Collector tip: Named for the city in the Alsace-Lorraine region of northeastern France.)... **$850+ pair**

Brownfield strawberry and leaf plate, 8-3/4" diameter. (Collector tip: W. Brownfield & Son, Burslem and Cobridge, Staffordshire, England, 1850 to 1891.)
.... **$275+**

Holdcroft cobalt leaf plate strong color, 8-1/4" diameter. (Collector tip: Joseph Holdcroft majolica ware was produced at Daisy Bank in Longton, Staffordshire, England, from 1870 to 1885. Items can be found marked with "JHOLDCROFT," but many items can only be attributed by the patterns and colors that are documented to have come from the Holdcroft potteries.).. **$385+**

Begonia on basket plate with cobalt rope edge, good color, 8" diameter... **$250+**

Fielding bird and fan cobalt plate, strong color, 7-1/2" diameter. (Collector tip: Railway Pottery, established by S. Fielding & Co., Stoke, Stoke-on-Trent, Staffordshire, England, 1879.) .... **$150+**

Geranium and floral plate with lavender flowers, strong color, 9-1/4" diameter. .... **$300+**

George Jones pineapple plate good color, rim chip to back, 9" diameter.. **$375+**

Samuel Lear floral and fan plate 8" diameter. (Collector tip: Samuel Lear, Hanley, Staffordshire, England, 1877 to 1886.).. **$140+**

Wedgwood yellow grape and leaf plate, strong color, 9" diameter.. **$350+**

Geranium platter with lavender flowers, outstanding color and detail, 12" wide. .... **$550+**

George Jones overlapping ferns and leaves platter with twig handles, strong color and detail, 14" wide. (Collector tip: The company started operations in the early 1860s as George Jones in Stoke, Staffordshire, England, and in 1873 became George Jones & Sons Ltd.)..**$2,300+**

Two-compartment lemon figural salt, attributed to Massier, 4" tall.. **$125+**

CERAMICS

Wedgwood yellow salmon platter, extremely rare in this color, outstanding color, detail and condition, 25" long, 12-3/4" wide. (Collector tip: Founded by Josiah Wedgwood in 1759 at Burslem, Staffordshire, England.) **$12,500+**

Wedgwood grape and vine punch set with large punch bowl, 10-1/2" diameter, 6-1/2" tall, and eight matching cups, strong color and detail to entire set, rare to find a complete set. (Collector tip: Founded by Josiah Wedgwood in 1759 at Burslem, Staffordshire, England.)........................ **$1,500**

George Jones strawberry server with cream and sugar, strong color and detail, 14-1/2" long. .... **$1,500-$2,000**

▲Yellow sardine box with attached under plate.**$200+**

◄Etruscan cobalt sunflower sauce dish, strong color, 5" diameter. (Collector tip: Made by Griffen, Smith and Hill of Phoenixville, Pa., 1879 to about 1890.)
.... **$250+**

Samuel Lear water lily spooner, 5-1/4" tall. (Collector tip: Samuel Lear, Hanley, Staffordshire, England, 1877 to 1886.) .... **$115+**

Fielding ribbon bow, daisy and wheat teapot, great detail, 6" tall. **$350+**

Minton "Spikey" fish figural teapot, extremely rare, professional repair to spout, base rim and rim of lid, outstanding color and detail, 9-1/2" long, 7" tall. .... **$26,000+**

Moth and butterfly toothpick holder, good color, 1-3/4" tall. .... **$190+**

Cobalt fish and seaweed tray, strong color and detail, 13-1/2" wide. .... **$450+**

Fan-shaped dragonfly tray with cobalt ribbon handle, 10" long. .... **$225+**

CERAMICS

Wedgwood turquoise basket weave grape tray with twig handles, 9-1/2" diameter. (Collector tip: Founded by Josiah Wedgwood in 1759 at Burslem, Staffordshire, England.).. **$400+**

George Jones turquoise butterfly, wheat and bamboo two-handled tray, outstanding color and detail, Bacall Collection, 13" wide. ....**$4,000+**

Lavender covered game tureen with liner, good color, professional rim repair to base and rim of lid, 9" wide. .... **$750+**

Pair of Copeland cobalt mantle vases with floral and leaf motif, strong color and detail, each 11-1/2" tall. (Collector tip: William T. Copeland & Sons pottery of Stoke-on-Trent, England, began producing porcelain and earthenware in 1847.) .... **$2,750+ pair**

Above left: Holdcroft cobalt water lily and bamboo umbrella stand, strong color, 23" tall. (Collector tip: Joseph Holdcroft majolica ware was produced at Daisy Bank in Longton, Staffordshire, England, from 1870 to 1885. Items can be found marked with "JHOLDCROFT" but many items can only be attributed by the patterns and colors that are documented to have come from the Holdcroft potteries.) ....**$3,250+**

Delphin Massier figural stork vase, good detail, 8-1/2" tall. (Collector tip: The Massier family began producing ceramics in Vallauris, France, in the mid-18th century.)..................**$350+**

Above right: W.S. & S. vase with mask feet and handles, 12-1/2", (Collector tip: Wilhelm Schiller and Sons, Bodenbach, Bohemia, established 1885.) ....**$500+**

CERAMICS

McCoy Pottery

The first McCoy with clay under his fingernails was W. Nelson McCoy. With his uncle, W.F. McCoy, he founded a pottery works in Putnam, Ohio, in 1848, making stoneware crocks and jugs.

That same year, W. Nelson's son, James W., was born in Zanesville, Ohio. James established the J.W. McCoy Pottery Co. in Roseville, Ohio, in the fall of 1899. The J.W. McCoy plant was destroyed by fire in 1903 and was rebuilt two years later.

It was at this time that the first examples of Loy-Nel-Art wares were produced. The line's distinctive title came from the names of James McCoy's three sons, Lloyd, Nelson, and Arthur. Like other "standard" glazed pieces produced at this time by several Ohio potteries, Loy-Nel-Art has a glossy finish on a dark brown-black body, but Loy-Nel-Art featured a splash of green color on the front and a burnt-orange splash on the back.

George Brush became general manager of J.W. McCoy Pottery Co. in 1909. The company became Brush-McCoy Pottery Co. in 1911, and in 1925 the name was shortened to Brush Pottery Co. This firm remained in business until 1982.

Separately, in 1910, Nelson McCoy Sr. founded the Nelson McCoy Sanitary and Stoneware Co., also in Roseville. By the early 1930s, production had shifted from utilitarian wares to art pottery, and the company name was changed to Nelson McCoy Pottery.

Designer Sydney Cope was hired in 1934, and was joined by his son, Leslie, in 1936. The Copes' influence on McCoy wares continued until Sydney's death in 1966. That same year, Leslie opened a gallery devoted to his family's design heritage and featuring his own original art.

Nelson McCoy Sr. died in 1945, and was succeeded as company president by his nephew, Nelson McCoy Melick.

A fire destroyed the plant in 1950, but company officials—including Nelson McCoy Jr., then 29—decided to rebuild, and the new Nelson McCoy Pottery Co. was up and running in just six months.

Nelson Melick died in 1954. Nelson Jr. became company president, and oversaw the company's continued growth. In 1967, the operation was sold to entrepreneur David Chase. At this time, the words "Mt. Clemens Pottery" were added to the company marks. In 1974, Chase sold the company to Lancaster Colony Corp., and the company marks included a stylized "LCC" logo. Nelson Jr. and his wife, Billie, who had served as a products supervisor, left the company in 1981.

In 1985, the company was sold again, this time to Designer Accents. The McCoy pottery factory closed in 1990.

For more information on McCoy pottery, see *Warman's McCoy Pottery*, 2nd edition, by Mark F. Moran.

CERAMICS

CROCKS AND JUGS

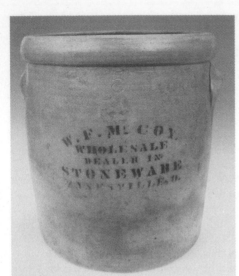

W.F. McCoy 1-1/2-gallon crock, salt glaze with stenciled ink lettering: "W.F. McCoy Wholesale Dealer in Stoneware–Zanesville, O.," late 1800s, 9-1/4" h. .... **$1,000-$1,200**

▲W.F. McCoy 5-gallon crock, salt glaze with stenciled ink lettering: "W.F. McCoy Wholesale Dealer in Stoneware–Zanesville, O.," with impressed "5," late 1800s, 13" h...........**$1,200-$1,400 in mint condition**

▶Three brown-top miniatures: plain crock, pickling crock, and jug, range from 3" to 3-3/4" h. .... **$175-$225 each**

Nelson McCoy Sanitary Stoneware jugs, 1910-20s, shield with M mark, 2- to 6-gallon sizes. Depending on size ....**$75-$125**

DINNERWARE

Basket weave tankard and mugs in green glaze, 1920s stoneware, unmarked.
Tankard, 9" h ....$100-$125
Mugs, 5" h ....$40-$50 each

Cherries and Leaves serving bowl, two individual salad bowls, and two
cups, all in glossy aqua, mid-1930s, unmarked, all very rare.
Serving bowl, 9" diameter ....$450-$550
Salad bowls, 5" diameter ....$225-$275 each
Cups, 2-7/8" h ....$90-$110 each

Three Cherries and Leaves teapots in glossy burgundy, yellow, and aqua,
mid-1930s, unmarked. ....$90-$110 each

Buttermilk pitcher in glossy yellow, late 1920s, unmarked or with shield, usually found in green, sometimes in caramel-tan, 5-1/2" h.................................... **$60-$70**

Covered casserole, 1940s, McCoy USA, 6-1/2" diameter. ... **$55-$65**

Covered butter dish in glossy green, 1960s, McCoy USA mark.
.... **$30-$40**

Bunnies baby set (cup not shown), late 1970s, McCoy LCC mark with serial numbers 1221 and 1222, plate 6" diameter. As shown
.... **$35-$40**

◄Two Parading Ducks pitchers in glossy brown and burgundy, holds 4 pints, late 1930s, stoneware, unmarked, found in a variety of colors. .... **$125-$150 each**

Daisy teapot with sugar and creamer, 1940s, McCoy mark. ....**$150-$175 set**

Biscuit or grease jar in glossy burgundy, 1950s, unmarked. ....**$90-$110**

Two Donkey pitchers (also called pitcher vases) in glossy blue and white, 1940s, NM USA mark, rare in any color. .... **$300-$350 each**

Suburbia creamer in glossy green, 1960s, McCoy USA mark, 5-1/2" h ....**$45-$55**

From left: Cabbage salt and pepper shakers with cork stoppers, 1950s, McCoy USA mark, 4-1/2" h. ....**$75-$85/pair**
Cabbage grease jar, 1950s, McCoy USA, 9" h. .... **$125-$150**

Soup and sandwich luncheon set in yellow, 1960s, McCoy mark, plate 8-1/2" x 11". .... **$35-$45 set**

Three Hobnail ice jugs, in yellow, coral, and blue, early 1940s, unmarked. ....**$150-$175 each**

FLOWERPOTS

Flowerpot in a skyscraper design, with detached saucer, 1930s-40s, found in other colors, unmarked, 9" h, 10-1/2" diameter. ...... **$75+**

Three Lotus Leaf pots and saucers (sometimes saucer is detached) in glossy tan and green, matte brown and green, and glossy green, 1930s, unmarked
6" h ....$75-$85
4" h ....$50-$60

Two Dragonfly pots and saucers in matte coral and yellow, 1940s, unmarked, 3-1/2" diameter. .... **$60-$70 each**

McCoy flowerpot, ribbed with rose design, stoneware, 1920s, unmarked, 4" h, 5-1/2" diameter.................... **$30+**

Two sizes of the "Viney" pots, one with saucer, in matte white, 1930s, unmarked, 9" h, $125-$150; 5" h. **$70-$80**

▲Lotus Leaf pot and saucer (detached) in brown and green, 1930s, unmarked, 10" h.**$350-$450**

◀Two Hobnail pots and saucers with stylized Greek key bands in glossy pink and yellow, 1940s, McCoy mark, 5" and 4" h.**$30-$40 each**

CERAMICS

Butterfly Line pot and saucer in matte aqua, 1940s, NM USA mark, 6-1/2" diameter. .. **$75-$85**

Leaves and Berries flowerpot in matte brown and green, 5-1/2" diameter. .... **$60-$70**

Garden Club pot and saucer in glossy yellow, late 1950s, McCoy USA mark, 8" h............. **$80-$90**

Two Basket-weave with Rings pots and saucers in glossy burgundy and green, 1950s, unmarked.
6" h............................**$75-$85**
4" h............................**$50-$60**

Three sizes of Lily Bud pots and saucers in matte blue, rose, and yellow, 1940s, NM USA mark.
6" h..............................**$65-$75**
5" h..............................**$50-$60**
3-1/2" h. ....**$40-$50**

Two Fish-scale pots and saucers in glossy blue and yellow, 1940s, NM USA mark
7" h...**$55-$65**
4" h...**$40-$45**

Two Speckled pots and saucers in glossy turquoise and pink, 1950s, McCoy USA mark, 6" and 4" h.
....**$25-$35 each**

JARDINIERES AND PEDESTALS

Jardinière in a majolica glaze, stoneware, early 1920s, 9-1/2" h, 10-3/4" diameter.............. **$150+**

Oak Leaves and Acorns jardinière in matte green, late 1920s, unmarked, 6-3/4" h........... **$70-$80**

Jardinière and pedestal in glossy turquoise and cobalt blue drip glaze, circa 1910, 41" h overall, unmarked. .... **$1,500-$2,000**

Basket-Weave jardinière in matte brown and blue, 1930s, unmarked, 9" h...................... **$150**

Holly jardinière in matte white, 1930s, unmarked, 9" h. ....**$175-$225**

Leaves and Berries jardinière in non-production pink and green glaze combination, 1930s, stoneware, unmarked, 4" h. In these colors ....**$75-$100**

Ivy jardinière in brown and green, early 1950s, unmarked, also found in a brighter glossy tan and green with matching pedestal, 8" h...............................**$350-$450**

Fish in Net jardinière in rare gray-green, late 1950s, McCoy mark, also found in brown, 7-1/2" h. ....**$250-$300**

Two jardinières with applied leaves and berries, late 1940s, McCoy USA mark, 7-1/2" h. **$200-$250 each**

Swallows jardinière in brown and green, stoneware, late 1930s, 7" h, 7-1/2" diameter. .... **$75+**

CERAMICS

KITCHENWARE

Two sizes of the batter bowl with spoon rest in glossy green, late 1920s, shield mark #3, diameters without spouts and handles.
7-1/2" ....**$175-$225**
9-1/2" ....**$275-$325**

Ring ware hanging salt box and covered jar (cheese or butter), both in glossy green, 1920s, shield mark "M." Saltbox.
6" h ....**$250-$300**
covered jar, 5" h ....**$175-$200**

Two Islander Line reamers in yellow and white, early 1980s. ....**$50-$60 each**

Ring ware covered butter or cheese crock, 1920s, shield mark "M."
....**$90-$110**

Raspberries and Leaves mixing bowl in glossy white, 1930s, unmarked, 9" diameter. ....**$200-$225**

Complete set of pink and blue banded nesting mixing bowls, 1930s, old mark, 4-1/2"-11-1/2" diameter, smallest bowls are hardest to find and most expensive. ....**$400-$500 set**

Five sizes of Stone Craft mixing bowls (called pink and blue) ranging in diameter from 7" to 14" (also a 5" size), mid-1970s, McCoy LCC mark. Complete set ....**$225-$250**

Mixing bowl in the Wave or Sunrise pattern, size No. 7, from a set of six ranging in size from 5" to 11" diameter, 1920s, square bottom, also found in yellow and burgundy; and three 5" mixing bowls in green, yellow, and burgundy. Complete set ....**about $1,200**
Individual sizes range from ....**$175-$250 each**

PLANTERS

Cope monkey planter, cold-paint details, 1930s, 5" h. .... **$75+**

Singing Bird planter in matte white, 1940s, USA mark, found in other colors, 4-1/2" h .... **$30-$40** (Also found in 6-3/4" size.)

Butterfly hanging basket planter in non-production dark green glaze, early 1940s, NM mark; as shown .... **$500-$600** In pastel colors .... **$225-$250**

Stretch Dog planter (also called "angry dog"), in matte aqua, 1930s, 7-1/2" l, 5-3/4" h. **$125+**

Small Stretch Lion in rare cobalt blue, 1940s, unmarked, 4" h. .... **$250-$300**

Cat with Bow planter with cold paint decoration, 1950s, McCoy USA mark on back, 7" l. **$40-$50**

Antelope planter, 1950s, unmarked, 12" l. ... **400-$450**

Butterfly Line window box in matte aqua, 1940s, unmarked, hard to find this size, 9-1/4" l, ... **$150-$175** If marked **$250**

Lily Bud divided planting dish in matte aqua, 1940s, NM USA mark, 11-1/2" l. .... **$85-$95**

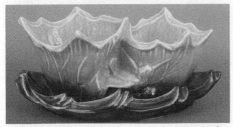

▲Humming Bird planter in blue, late 1940s, McCoy USA mark, 10-1/2" w. .... **$125-$150**

▶Fancy Lily Bud planting dish, late 1940s or early 1950s, hand-painted under glaze, 11" l. .... **$85-$95**

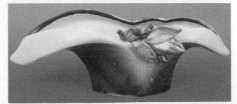

CERAMICS

Pine Cone planter, mid-1940s, McCoy USA mark, 8" wide, rare..............................**$500-$600** (A slightly larger planter in rust glaze **$1,800-$2,000**)

Hunting dog planter in hard-to-find chartreuse glaze with black dog, 1954 McCoy mark, 12" w, 8-1/2" h. ....**$350-$450**

Large Fish planter in pink, green and white, 1950s, McCoy USA mark, 12" l. ....**$1,200+**

Swan planting dish in chartreuse and black, 1950s, McCoy USA mark, 8-1/2" h. ....**$700-$800**

Flying ducks planter in raspberry and chartreuse, 1950s, McCoy USA mark, 10" w. ......**$175-$225**

Large Turtle planter in dark green and pink, 1950s, McCoy USA mark, 12-1/2" l. ....**$175-$225**

Carriage with Umbrella planter in traditional colors, cold paint in excellent condition, mid-1950s, McCoy USA mark, 9" h.......... **$200+**

Cactus flower planter, three pieces, 1950s, marked 677 USA, 7" w..**$50+**

Jewel Line planter with applied butterflies, 1950s, 4-1/4" h, McCoy USA mark. .... **$100+**

From left: Mammy on Scoop planter (also found with yellow scoop), cold-paint decoration, 1950s, McCoy mark, 7-1/2" l. .... **$175-$200**
Boy on Rolling Pin planter (also found with yellow pin), cold-paint decoration, 1950s, McCoy mark, 7-1/2" l. .... **$125-$150**

Sport Fishing planter with cold-paint decoration on brown bisque-style finish, from the 1956 line of sports planters, which also included a golf and bowling planter, USA mark, 6-1/4" l. .... **$125-$150**

Two Crestwood pieces, from left: Pedestal planter, 12" h; Boat planter, 13" long, mid-1960s, McCoy USA with original labels. .... **$60-$70 each**

Petal basket planter, 1950s, McCoy USA mark, 8-3/4" h. .... **$150-$175**

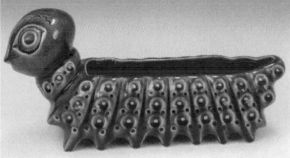

Caterpillar planter, 1960s, Floraline mark, 13-1/2" long, also found in brown, white, and yellow. .... **$40-$50**

Cowboy boots planter (this form also used for lamp base), 1960s, McCoy USA mark, 7" h. .... **$75-$85**

Three-sided ivy planter, 1950s, McCoy USA mark, hard to find, 6" h. .... **$400-$500**

VASES AND FLOWER HOLDERS

J.W. McCoy Olympia vase, with rare cream-drip glaze overflow, early 1900s, marked 28, 5-1/4" h.....................**$195-$225**

From left: "V" vase in glossy green glaze, mid-1920s, V2 mark, this style also found without handles, 9" h..**$90-$110**
"Number 50" vase in glossy burgundy, 1930s, unmarked, 9" h ....**$100-$125**

Blossomtime handled vase with cobalt flowers (rare), 1940s, raised McCoy mark, 6-1/2" h. .... **$125+**

Two Hourglass vases in matte yellow and pink, 1930s, unmarked, 8" h. .... **$90-$110 each**

Ring ware vase, 1920s, unmarked, 9-1/4" h........**$100-$125**

Lizard vase, stoneware, 1930s, unmarked, 9" h. ....**$350-$450**

Leaves and Berries urn-form vase in matte white with small handles and unusual interior ring pattern, hard to find form, stoneware, 1930s, 8" h...............**$300-$350**

Two Disc vases in glossy cobalt blue and burgundy, 1940s, also found in yellow and white, USA mark, 6-3/4" h. ....**$100-$125 each**

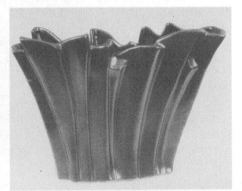

Pine Cone vase, not a production piece, mid-1940s, McCoy USA mark, 9-1/2" h. ....**$800-$1,000**

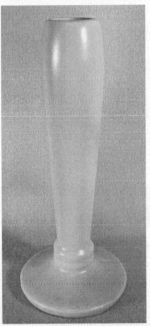

Vesta line vase, 1962, McCoy mark, 8-1/2" h. .... **$25-$35**

Bud vase in matte yellow glaze, 1960s, McCoy mark, 8" h. **$35-$45**

Antique Curio Line gladiolus vase in traditional colors, style #1607, late 1950s, McCoy USA mark, 14-1/4" h. ....**$85+**

Arcature vase in atypical dark lavender glaze (usually green and yellow), early 1950s, McCoy USA mark, 6-3/4" h; in normal colors, $50-$60. ......**$150-$200**

Large Fan vase, also called "Blades of Grass," glossy black, late 1950s, McCoy USA mark, 10" h. ....**$175-$225**

WALL POCKETS

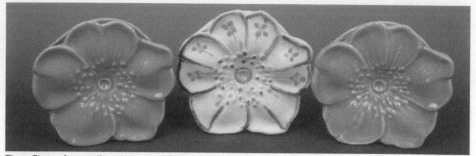

Three Flower form wall pockets, late 1940s, unmarked, 6" h; the blue and coral are common colors.. **$40-$50**
The center pocket, with under-glaze decoration .... **$175-$225**

Butterfly wall pocket with crisp mold, 1940s, NM mark, 6" high."
....**$175-$225**

Cuckoo Clock wall pocket in gold trim (comes with both Roman and Arabic numerals, and in a range of colors), 1950s, McCoy mark, 8" h without weights. ....**$200-$225**

Fan wall pocket with crisp mold and unusual multicolor glaze, 1950s, McCoy USA mark, also signed by Nelson McCoy, 8-1/2" w; two hanging holes and no brace; no other example with these variations is known.
....**$5,000+**

Tongue wall pocket from the Floral Country line, 1970s, with decal decoration, 9-1/4" h. ....**$35+**

MISCELLANEOUS

Lily bookends, 1940s, Mc-Coy Made in USA mark, 6" h. ....**$125-$150/pair**

Flower form bookends/planters, 1950s, McCoy USA mark, also found in green and yellow, cream and green; 6" h. ....**$150-$175/pair**

Rearing-horse bookends, with gold trim, 1970s, USA mark, 8" h. ...... **$125+ with gold trim**

CERAMICS

Meissen

The secret of true hard paste porcelain, known long before to the Chinese, was "discovered" accidentally in Meissen, Germany by J.F. Bottger, an alchemist working with E.W. Tschirnhausen. The first European true porcelain was made in the Meissen Porcelain Works, organized about 1709. Meissen marks have been widely copied by other factories.

Centerpiece, allegorical, the flaring reticulated oblong top base w/open end handles decorated overall w/ encrusted colorful flowers & green leaves among gilt-trimmed scrolls, raised on an ornate flower-encrusted pedestal w/a flower-painted scrolled cartouche above a group of children representing the Four Seasons around the scrolled base, blue crossed-swords mark, modeled by Leuteritz, ca. 1880, overall 17 3/8" h. **$7,768**

Figure group, a young mother in 18th c. costume seated holding her bare-bottomed toddler across her lap w/a switch to spank it in her other hand, her young daughter pulling at her arm to dissuade her, on a round molded & gilt-trimmed base, blue crossed-swords mark, late 19th c., 10 1/4" h. **$3,585**

Dinner service: ten 10" d. dinner plates, nine cups & saucers, eight cream soup bowls & eight underplates; Blue Onion patt., all marked w/the blue crossed swords, 19th c., the set (ILLUS. of part) **$1,725**

Urn, a flaring gadrooned foot joined by a white-beaded disk to the large ovoid urn-form body w/ gold gadrooning around the lower portion below the wide white central band h.p. w/a large bouquet of colorful flowers, the tapering neck in deep pink below the heavy gold rolled & gadrooned rim, white & gold entwined serpent handles at each side, blue crossed-swords mark, late 19th c., 11" h. **$518**

Vase, 6 5/8" h., footed bottle-form body tapering to a ringed neck w/a widely flaring rim, cobalt blue ground enameled in white in the Limoges style w/a pair of amorous putti sitting on a leafy branch, one extending a floral wreath to a third in flight releasing a dove, gold banding at the foot, neck ring & rim, blue crossed-swords mark, probably designed by E.A. Leuteritz, ca. 1880 .... **$2,868**

Vase, 15 1/2" h., classic baluster form, a fluted flaring base & pedestal w/rings supporting the ovoid body w/a band of flutes below the wide cobalt blue body band decorated w/large gilt & silver florals, ringed shoulder & short flaring neck w/incurved molded rim flanked by long looped snake handles from rim to shoulder, gilt trim on base & body & new gilt trim on handles, late 19th c. **$2,300**

Vases, 19" h., baluster form w/entwined snake handles, cobalt blue ground, the mouth, collar & foot molded & trimmed w/gilt, late 19th - early 20th c., blue crossed swords marks & incised & impressed numbers, mounted as lamps, pr. **$2,990**

Teapot, cov., nearly spherical slightly tapering body decorated w/a robin's-egg blue ground, the flat cover w/a gold knob finial, short curved shoulder spout & pointed arch handle, each side centered by a h.p. color scene of merchants haggling at quayside within a gold border, the cover w/two smaller views, "Indianische Blumen" design under spout & on handle, blue crossed-swords mark, 1735-40, overall 4 1/4" l., 4 1/4" h. **$4,780**

CERAMICS

Nippon

"Nippon" is a term used to describe a wide range of porcelain wares produced in Japan from the late 19th century until about 1921. It was in 1891 that the United States implemented the McKinley Tariff Act, which required that all wares exported to the United States carry a marking indicating their country of origin. The Japanese chose to use "Nippon," their name for Japan. In 1921 the import laws were revised and the words "Made in" had to be added to the markings. Japan was also required to replace the "Nippon" with the English name "Japan" on all wares sent to the United States.

Many Japanese factories produced Nippon porcelain, much of it hand-painted with ornate floral or landscape decoration and heavy gold decoration, applied beading and slip-trailed designs referred to as "moriage." We indicate the specific marking used on a piece, when known, at the end of each listing. Be aware that a number of Nippon markings have been reproduced and used on new porcelain wares.

Important reference books on Nippon include: *The Collector's Encyclopedia of Nippon Porcelain, Series One through Three*, by Joan F. Van Patten (Collector Books, Paducah, Kentucky) and *The Wonderful World of Nippon Porcelain, 1891-1921* by Kathy Wojciechowski (Schiffer Publishing, Ltd., Atglen, Pennsylvania).

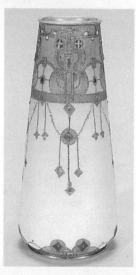

Above left: Humidor, cov., three square block feet supporting the wide slightly tapering cylindrical body w/a slightly tapering cover w/large mushroom finial, the body decorated w/a landscape of a man in a canoe w/a stag in green bushes on the shore, dark yellow to pale cream ground, the feet & top rim decorated w/geometric decorative bands w/stylized symbols, matching band around the cover, 7" h. **$575**

Above center: Vase, 7 1/8" h., "sharkskin" technique, slender slightly tapering cylindrical body w/a narrow shoulder centered by a short neck w/widely flaring mouth, arched & pierced-loop gold shoulder handles, the sides h.p. w/a stylized landscape w/tall trees in the foreground & small houses & a lake in the distance, done in pastel shades of blue, yellow, green, lavender & orange, purple Cherry Blossom mark, tiny glaze nick in the base **$230**

Above right: Vase, 5 3/4" h., bulbous ovoid body tapering to a short flaring neck trimmed in gold & flanked by arched gold shoulder handles, the body centered by a large gold oval reserve painted w/a full-length portrait of an exotic young woman standing in front of a peacock, surrounded by an overall gold lattice & pink rose decoration on the white ground, green Maple Leaf mark, minor gold wear..**$432**

◄Vase, 9 1/2" h., tapestry-type, tall gently tapering cylindrical body w/a flat rim, the upper body decorated w/a wide band of stylized geometric designs in shades of green, blue, rose red & gold & faux jewels, delicate gold beaded swags suspended down the sides, blue Maple Leaf mark **$1,150**

▪ Noritake

Noritake china, still in production in Japan, has been exported in large quantities to this country since early in the last century. Although the Noritake Company first registered in 1904, it did not use "Noritake" as part of its backstamp until 1918. Interest in Noritake has escalated as collectors now seek out pieces made between the "Nippon" era and World War II (1921-41). The Azalea pattern is also popular with collectors.

CERAMICS

◆ Repairing valuable ceramics should be left to professionals who can do the job expertly and minimize loss of value to the piece. Of course, the cost of the repair should be weighed against the value of the piece. But keep in mind that poorly done, do-it-yourself repairs can generally not be undone and will permanently lower a piece's value

▲Basket, short form w/extremely flaring sides, decorated inside & out in/floral motif in peach, pearl grey & black, silvered rim & center handle, 4 1/2" d., 6 1/2" h. . **$188**

◄Calendar holder, narrow rectangular base w/an upright oblong holder at one end & a flattened figural rabbit at the other end, iridized orange & green w/stylized purple & blue blossoms, 5 1/4" l., 2" h................................... **$720**

Breakfast set: cov. teapot, teacup, sugar, creamer, tray; tray w/ruffled sides & four depressions to hold teapot, cup & creamer, all w/yellow C-form handles & decorated w/pastoral scene of woman in ruffled yellow dress & wide brimmed yellow bonnet standing under tree & holding flowers, the cylindrical sugar w/scene of tree & flowers, all w/gilt line trim at rims, tray 8 1/2 x 10 1/2", the set... **$293**

CERAMICS

Chip & dip, cov., round, the attached plate & dip container & lid decorated w/blue ribbons around their rims, the plate & lid w/ red, orange, pink, lavender & yellow flowers, the lid's handle in the form of a seated/kneeling black-haired woman in blue, overall 4 1/2" h., plate 9 1/2" d..**$945**

Chocolate pot, cov., decorated w/figure of black-haired girl in purple knee-length dress w/wide skirt, the hem decorated w/ red flowers, a matching sash flowing out at each side, yellow-trimmed white petti- coats showing where dress appears to be billowing in breeze, the waist decorated w/ yellow & red flowers, a large green floppy- brimmed hat w/floral trim obscuring one eye, one hand reaching up toward hang- ing flowers in yellow, red & caramel w/ green leaves, a purple bird flying by, all on caramel ground, the lid w/handle in the form of a perched bird in red, blue, brown, green & yellow, C-scroll side han- dle, 9" h. **$650**

◀Cigarette holder, footed, figural swan, orange lustre w/black neck & head, black outlining on wing feathers & tail, 3" w., 4 1/2" h..**$310**

Creamer & sugar, the sugar container a round shal- low form w/gilt scroll side handles, slight depression in center to hold creamer, the creamer a cylindrical form w/angled gilt trimmed handle & slightly arched spout, both pieces decorated in alternating black & white panels, the black w/white & gilt oval designs, the white w/stylized floral designs in deep red/orange, black & white, both pieces w/gilt trim, 5 1/2" d., the set **$153**

Dish, cov., caramel colored bowl & lid, the lid w/ embossed daisy-like flowers, the handle in the form of a seated black-haired masked Pierrot-type figure dressed in pearl-grey, black & white w/caramel ruff, holding one leg up to chest, 7" h., 7 1/8" d.....**$2,890**

Jam server, cov., three-legged round container on disk base, the lid w/opening just big enough for handle of serving spoon, in pink, deep orange & black w/green leaf decorations, orange knob handle on lid, white spoon, 4 1/4" w., 5 1/4" h., the set **$203**

Pin tray, round, mauve tray decorated w/applied image of seated dog in caramel & black, 2" h., 2 3/5" d. **$65**

Jug, slender ovoid form w/cut-out handle at top & short cylindrical spout set in body at an angle, the top a deep cyan w/black line trim, the rest of the body a deep red ground decorated w/scene of an 18th-c. woman w/powdered hair & wearing a blue off- the-shoulder top & full white skirt holding a songbird on one out-stretched finger, the birdcage open in front of her, all against a background of shade trees & arbor vitae, the foreground w/yellow roses, 3 1/2 x 4 1/4", 7 1/2" h. **$325**

Plate, 6 1/4" d., caramel ground w/figure of woman wearing elaborate powdered coiffure or wig bedecked w/yellow, deep pink, mauve & apricot flowers w/green leaves & black ribbons, dressed in blue sleeveless gown w/full skirt trimmed in yellow, one hand fingering green bead necklace, the other holding a black mask **$740**

Potpourri pot, cov., ovoid form, the flat lid white w/ black line trim & black & white knob handle, the body decorated w/figure of Oriental woman in deep red ki-mono holding green flower-decorated fan in one hand, a sprig of cherry blossoms in the other, standing beneath branches of cherry trees in bloom, all against a caramel ground, 4" d., 5" h. **$395**

Powder puff box, cov., round, the lid decorated w/ figure of woman sitting w/back to viewer, wearing dark green & cream-colored dress w/full skirt, dark green bodice, festooned w/lavender ribbons at waist & shoulders & pink & yellow flowers decorating skirt, two dark curls escaping from back of the yellow & green flower-bedecked bonnet that hides her face, all on caramel ground, 1 3/4" h., 4 1/4" d. **$420**

Powder box, cov., round, in the form of a woman in full-skirted off-the-shoulder dress in coral-pink decorated w/light pink roses & green leaves, the bottom of the skirt making up the powder container, the top of the skirt the lid, the handle formed by the figure of a fan-holding woman w/powdered hair & a beauty mark, 3 1/2" d., 6 1/4" h. **$875**

Powder puff box, cov., squat circular shape, pale mauve w/black line trim, the cover w/caramel top upon which perches a blue, red, yellow & black bird,1" h., 4" d. **$434**

Sandwich serving plate, round, w/gilt angular handle in middle, the plate decorated w/scene of pink-clad figures on rolling green ground gathering red fruit from large tree, a line of shrubs in the background, all against a pink & green ground, 9 1/2" d. **$385**

Tea set: cov. teapot, creamer, cov. sugar, tray; the teapot, creamer & sugar w/ gold angled loop handles, the 6 x 11" tray w/tab side handles, all in vivid deep orange w/gold & black trim, decorated w/ desert scene of robed, turbaned figure against backdrop of palm trees & a tower, the set........ **$395**

Vase, 6 7/8" h., U-form double vase, the two receptacles joined by double bars, the top one serving as roost for tropical bird in vivid orange, dark blue, green, yellow & pink, the double vases in pale mauve decorated w/deep orange & yellow/gold flowers & green leaves, the scalloped rims w/gilt trim, flared base **$261**

Vase, 6" h., trumpet form w/wavy black-trimmed rim & flared base, the ringed body decorated w/green & white checked sash & rose-like flowers in shades of pink & yellow, all on a caramel ground **$171**

Vase, 8 1/4" h., ovoid shape tapering out to scalloped rim, C-scroll handles, the bottoms of which are applied to the top of vase, w/the tops of the handles unconnected to vase, pale mauve disk base, the body decorated w/ ornate flower in deep red, grape, yellow, pink & blue/grey colors & black dots, green leaves, against caramel ground w/pale mauve & brown trim **$156**

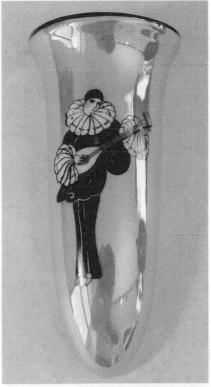

Vase, 8" h., squatty form w/tapering shoulder & high pointed arch handle at top, caramel ground w/black trim on handle & short pink neck, the body decorated w/figure of young woman in powdered hair adorned w/a single red rose, wearing black full-skirted gown trimmed w/red roses, one hand holding a decorative fan **$615**

Wall pocket, trumpet form in caramel w/black rim, decorated w/figure of lute-playing musician dress in black w/extravagant white & red ruff & cuffs, 2 7/8" w. x 6" h. **$505**

CERAMICS

■ Paul Revere Pottery

This pottery was established in Boston, Massachusetts, in 1906, by a group of philanthropists seeking to establish better conditions for underprivileged young girls of the area. Edith Brown served as supervisor of the small "Saturday Evening Girls Club" pottery operation, which was moved, in 1912, to a house close to the Old North Church where Paul Revere's signal lanterns had been placed. The wares were mostly hand decorated in mineral colors, and both sgraffito and molded decorations were employed. Although it became popular, it was never a profitable operation and always depended on financial contributions to operate. After the death of Edith Brown in 1932, the pottery foundered and finally closed in 1942.

S.E.G.

Bowl, 6" d., 3" h., deep rounded sides w/a wide flat rim, brown semi-matte ground decorated around the rim w/a cuerda seca band of Greek key in taupe & ivory on white, signed "SEG - 10.12 - FL" **$1,116**

Bowl, 4 1/4" d., bulbous ovoid body w/a wide flat mouth, decorated around the top w/a yellow band accented by flying scarabs in light green, streaky pale blue glaze, marked "S.E.G. - 05-1-14," crazing, 1914.. **$1,093**

Breakfast set: child's, 7 1/2" d. plate & 3 5/8" h. mug; each h.p. w/a circle enclosing a picture of a white rabbit lying on a green grassy mound, white & blue outer bands, initialed by the artist, early 20th c., the set... **$1,116**

Jardiniere, wide bulbous squatty body w/a closed rim, yellow ground w/a wide rim band in cuerda seca w/ black-outlined white lotus blossoms trimmed w/yellow, stamped mark, firing lines around rim & base, two restored rim chips, 9" d., 7" h. **$1,495**

Plate, dinner, 10" d., dark greyish blue ground decorated around the rim in cuerda seca w/a band of stylized white lotus blossoms, signed "SEG - AM - 11-14," rim bruise, small chips to footring..**$646**

▶Vase, 6 1/4" h., 3 3/4" d., simple ovoid body w/a wide flat rim, dark bluish grey lower body, a wide shoulder band in cuerda seca decorated w/a band of stylized oak leaves & acorns in green, brown & pale blue, inkstamped "SEG - AM - 12-17," 1917 ....**$4,025**

Plates, 8 1/2" d., luncheon, creamy white w/a dark blue border band decorated w/stylized white lotus blossoms, Saturday Evening Girls mark & dated 1910, set of 12............**$2,645**

Tea set: cov. bulbous 4 3/4" h. teapot, 4 1/4" h. cylindrical creamer, 4" h. cylindrical cov. sugar bowl & 5 1/4" w. square tea tile; each decorated w/a dark blue glaze w/a border band of stylized white lotus blossoms, all marked w/the Saturday Evening Girls mark & dated 1910, teapot cover cracked, glued chip on inner rim of teapot, the set **$1,955**

CERAMICS

Red Wing Pottery

Various potteries operated in Red Wing, Minnesota, from 1868, the most successful being the Red Wing Stoneware Co., organized in 1877. Merged with other local potteries through the years, it became known as Red Wing Union Stoneware Co. in 1906 and was one of the largest producers of utilitarian stoneware items in the United States. After a decline in the popularity of stoneware products, an art pottery line was introduced to compensate for the loss. This was reflected in a new name for the company, Red Wing Potteries, Inc., in 1936. Stoneware production ceased entirely in 1947, but vases, planters, cookie jars, and dinnerware of art pottery quality continued in production until 1967, when the pottery ceased operation altogether.

For more information on Red Wing pottery, see *Warman's Red Wing Pottery Identification and Price Guide* by Mark F. Moran.

CHURNS

One-of-a-kind "lunch hour" churn about 1-1/2 gallon, with a row of birch leaves stamped all around the base, 11" tall without lid, made in about 1890-1910. (Collector Tip: Lid is a new salt-glaze style reproduction, 6" diameter.) .... **No established value**

Two-gallon salt-glaze churn with cobalt decoration of "target," circa 1890, 12-1/2" tall, unmarked, and cover in Albany slip. ....**$1,000-$1,200**

Two-gallon white stoneware churn with birch leaves, and cover, 12-1/2" tall without cover.**$500-$700**

Two-gallon churn with Utah advertising, 12-5/8" tall, otherwise unmarked. **$4,000**

Five-gallon white stoneware "ball lock" jar, 18-1/2" tall with locking device, but not handle, found in several sizes. .... **$250+**

Transitional three-gallon churn with long-stem leaf, in a zinc glaze, 14-3/4" tall with original cover. .... **$4,000-$5,000**

Three-gallon churn-form store advertisement with "elephant ears," with original churn cover, 14-3/8" tall including lid. .... **$7,500+**

Three-gallon salt-glaze churn with cobalt decoration of "target," circa 1890, 13-3/4" tall, with recessed Albany slip cover, unmarked. ....**$700-$800**

Three-gallon white stoneware churn with cover, with wing and oval placement reversed, 14-1/4" tall with cover.................... **$400+**

Four-gallon salt-glaze churn with cobalt decoration of "lazy 8" and "tornado," circa 1890, and cover in Albany slip glaze, 16" tall, unmarked. ....**$800-$900**

Five-gallon white stoneware churn with birch leaves, and cover, 16-3/4" tall without cover.**$400-$600**

CERAMICS

Five-gallon salt-glaze churn with cobalt leaf, circa 1890, 16-1/2" tall, with cover in Albany slip glaze, unmarked. .... **$2,000-$2,400**

Five-gallon churn-form store advertisement with "elephant ears," with lid adapted from a churn cover with button handle, 16-3/4" tall. ....**$10,000+**

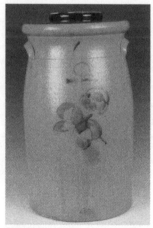

Six-gallon salt-glaze churn with cobalt butterfly and flower, circa 1890, 17-3/4" tall, with cover in Albany slip glaze, unmarked. .... **$2,000+**

Six-gallon white stoneware churn with birch leaves called "elephant ears," 17-1/2" tall... **$800-$1,000**

Ten-gallon salt-glaze churn with "lazy eight," and a target with a tail. .... **$4,000-$5,000**

Cover for five-gallon churn-form store advertisement, 8-1/2" diameter. .... **$250+**

COLLECTOR TIPS

◆ Any marked or stamped salt-glaze pieces are usually almost double the price of an unmarked example.

◆ Of all sizes of Red Wing stoneware, the two-gallon churns and water coolers are the most highly prized, and are among the highest in price.

CROCKS

Transitional crocks with hand-lettered gallon markings, two with stamped "elephant ear" leaves.................................**$300-$1,000 each**

Close-up of the hand-decorated butterfly and flower on a 20-gallon salt-glaze crock. Signed .**$2,000-$2,500**

One-of-a-kind 20-gallon stoneware crock/cooler with cover, jar form, but with bunghole, circa 1908............ **No established value**

White stoneware advertising crocks 5" and 3-3/4" tall, unmarked. ....**$900-$1,200 each**

Two-gallon white stoneware crock with tilted birch leaves, 10" tall, impressed mark, "Minnesota Stoneware Co. Red Wing, Minn." .... **$70-$90**

Blue and white covered butter crock in a daisy pattern, left, 4-1/2" tall with lid, 5-1/2" diameter. .... **$400+**
Right, blue and white bail-handle covered butter crock with advertising, 5-1/2" tall without handle. .... **$500+**

Two-gallon crock with tilted birch leaves and oval stamp with "Minnesota Stoneware Company" (spelled out, commonly found as "Co."), 12" tall with lid, otherwise unmarked. **$1,500+**

White stoneware bail-handle butter crock with advertising (cover missing), left, 7-1/4" tall without handle, unmarked. .... **$400+**
Right, sponge-decorated butter crock with lid, 7" tall, unmarked. .... **$300+**

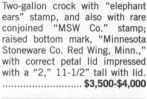

Two-gallon crock with "elephant ears" stamp, and also with rare conjoined "MSW Co." stamp; raised bottom mark, "Minnesota Stoneware Co. Red Wing, Minn.," with correct petal lid impressed with a "2," 11-1/2" tall with lid. .... **$3,500-$4,000**

One-gallon salt-glaze crock circa 1890, 8" tall, marked on bottom, "Minnesota Stoneware Co. Red Wing, Minn." Second photo shows rare one-gallon "petal" cover with Albany slip, 8" diameter.
Crock.. **$70+**
Lid **$400**

Two-gallon crock with "elephant ears" stamp and rare single-line "Minn. Stoneware Co." mark; raised bottom mark, "Minnesota Stoneware Co. Red Wing, Minn.," with correct petal lid impressed with a "2," 11-1/2" tall with lid. .... **$3,000-$3,500**

Two-gallon salt-glaze crock with strong cobalt decoration of "target with tail," circa 1890, marked on bottom, "Minnesota Stoneware Co. Red Wing, Minn." Second photo shows "petal" lid with glaze drippings known as "turkey droppings."
Crock.. **$175+**
Lid **$300**

Two-gallon crock with atypical department stores advertising from Hooper, Neb., 9-3/4" tall, otherwise unmarked. .... **$4,500+**

Two-gallon crock with Utah advertising, with what collectors call the "ski oval," named for the mark between Red Wing and Union Stoneware, 10-1/8" tall. .... **$2,500+ if perfect**

Two-gallon crock with Washington advertising and original lid, 12" tall with lid. **$2,500**

Two-gallon crock with double "elephant ears" stamp, 9-3/4" tall. .... **$1,500+**

Two-gallon crock with double markings, 10" tall. **$2,200**

Three-gallon white stoneware crock with tilted birch leaves and original lid, and rarely seen "Minnesota Stoneware Company" oval mark, 10-3/4" tall without lid; lid, 11" diameter.................... **$900+**

Three-gallon salt-glaze crock with cobalt decoration referred to as "double P ribcage" and "target," circa 1890, 10-1/4" tall, with impressed back stamp, "Minnesota Stoneware Co., Red Wing." Second photo shows "petal" lid with Albany slip glaze, 10-1/4" diameter
Crock... **$500+**
Lid **$300**

Three-pound butter crock with Hormel advertising, 4-3/8" tall, soft impressed mark, "Red Wing Stoneware Co.".............. **$2,500+**

CERAMICS

Three-pound butter crock with Owatonna, Minn., advertising, with button lid, 4-1/4" tall without lid, otherwise unmarked. **$2,500+**

Four-gallon salt-glaze crock with strong cobalt decoration of "target with tail," circa 1890, 12" tall. Second photo shows "petal" lid with glaze drippings known as "turkey droppings," 11" diameter.
Crock.. **$200+**
Lid **$300**

Four-gallon white stoneware crock with birch leaves called "elephant ears," and original lid, 11-1/2" tall without lid.................. **$150+**

Five-gallon white stoneware crock with oval and large wing, the most commonly found size for crocks and jugs. .... **$70+**

Transitional five-gallon crock with hand-decorated blue-black number and "bowtie," circa 1900, the glaze on this crock is between white and tan, 13-1/4" tall, unmarked. .... **$300+**

Five-gallon crock with 6" wing, no oval, also with double trim line and a stamped "5" on base; base also shows a firing ring from the smaller crock it sat on in the kiln, 13" tall. .... **$250+**

Eight-gallon transitional zinc-glaze crock with stamped Minnesota oval and hand-decorated birch leaf. .... **$3,500+**

Detail of a 10-gallon "double el-ephant ear" crock. **$3,000**

Detail of a 10-gallon crock with birch leaves and Nebraska adver-tising............................ **$2,800+**

Detail of transitional 10-gallon zinc-glaze crock with hand-deco-rated leaf and "Union" oval.**$1,000**

10-pound butter crock with Osage, Iowa, advertising, 6-3/4" tall, otherwise unmarked. . **$1,500**

Ten-gallon crock with Washington advertising that includes the word crockery. .... **$1,500+ if perfect**

12-gallon salt-glaze crock with large hand-decorated birch leaf pointing up. **$2,500**

Fifteen-gallon salt-glaze crock with cobalt decoration of "bowtie" and double leaves, circa 1890, 18 1/2" tall, unmarked. (Collector Tip: The leaves seen here are precursors to the stenciled or stamped birch-leaf decoration used on white hand-thrown stoneware made just a few years later.) .... **$800-$1,000**

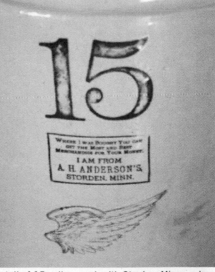

Detail of 15-gallon crock with Storden, Minn., adver-tising and large wing..................................**$3,500+**

CERAMICS

White stoneware 20-pound butter crock with hand-decorated numbers, a transitional mark before stamping was regularly used, circa 1900, 8" tall, 11-1/2" diameter, raised mark on bottom, "Minnesota Stoneware Red Wing, Minn." .... **$800-$1,000**

White stoneware 20-pound butter crock with 4" wing, 7-1/2" tall, 11-1/2" diameter. .... **$1,000+**

Twenty-gallon crock detail with double-stamped wing (red over blue), with original lid.... **$600+**

Detail of a 25-gallon crock double-stamped. **$2,000**

Detail of a 20-gallon crock with North Dakota advertising. . **$3,000**

Stoneware bread crock in glossy green glaze, also found with matte Brushed Ware surface, and in tan; lid missing, 11" tall, 14" diameter, rare. .... **$2,800+ (as is)**
With lid .... **$4,000+**

COLLECTOR TIPS

◆ With double-stamped stoneware pieces, the proximity of the stamps to each other also determines value. The closer together the stamps, the higher the value.

JUGS

Eight souvenir mini jugs commemorating outings, sports rivalries, businesses and communities, each 2-1/2" to 3" tall. .... **$250+ each**

Eighth-pint fancy jug with rare blue sponge decoration, 2-3/4" tall. ....**$1,800+**

Eight souvenir mini jugs commemorating outings, sports rivalries, businesses and communities, and one marked "Mercury," each 2-1/2" to 3" tall. ....**$250+ each** (with a high range of $800 depending on markings)

Two brown-top stoneware jugs with small red wings; left, half gallon, 9" tall; right, one gallon, wide mouth, 10-1/2" tall. .... **$150-$225 each**

Three brown-top mini jugs two with advertising and one a souvenir, each 4-1/4" tall, found unmarked and with raised "R.W.S.W. Co." ....**$250+ each** (with a high range of $800 depending on markings)

Three small domed brown-top jugs, one with advertising; from left, 4-1/2", 6-1/4" and 5-1/2" tall.
Plain ....**$50-$75 each**
Advertising..**$200+**

CERAMICS

Courtesy Red Wing Collectors Society

Jug, four-gallon Red Wing, "Griesel Bros., Winona, Minn." advertising............................**$450**

Five-gallon transitional Ice Water cooler, front-stamped "Red Wing Stoneware Company," mint condition. **$1,250**

Two-gallon ice water cooler with Elephant Ear decoration, Red Wing Potteries, hairline in the back.............................**$2,100**

Jugs, "Jos. Bernard Wines & Brandies, Chicago, Ill." advertising, Red Wing, from left to right ....**$110, $225, $150, and $90**

Red Wing stoneware Mason jars, complete set, graduated. **$900**

Garden ware urn, 23-1/2-inch, bottom-signed "Red Wing Art Pottery", bronze tan color..............**$900**

Bean pot, Red Wing, "Goodyear Tires" advertising and "Brookings, S. Dak." **$280**

Cow and calf figure, Red Wing, maker unknown. **$2,300**

Salt glaze "lunch hour" cat figure, Red Wing, 5-1/2" long. **$850**

Ten-gallon Red Wing double-handled threshing jug with birch leaves..**$7,100**

Water cooler, five-gallon, straight-sided salt glazing, front-stamped "Red Wing Stoneware Company," hairline crack. **$2,300**

Art pottery, Red Wing Gray Engobe line, example at left..**$110**
Example at right...**$550**

Art pottery vase, Red Wing.........................**$1,500**
Mason jar, quart-sized....................................**$90**

CERAMICS

White stoneware bail-handle jugs in three sizes with advertising; from left, 6", 10" and 7-1/2" tall. ....**$300-$400 each**

Half-gallon shoulder jug with Cannon Falls, Minn., advertising, 8-1/2" tall, impressed bottom mark, "Minnesota Stoneware Co. Red Wing, Minn." ....**$500+**

Two white stoneware shoulder jugs one with elaborate advertising for a Chicago liquor store; left, 7-1/2" tall, with rare mark, "Minn. S. Co. Red Wing, Minn." .... **$70+**
Right, 8-3/4" tall, unmarked. ....**$300-$500**

Two white stoneware shoulder jugs with advertising; left, 10-1/2" tall; right, 8-1/2" tall.. **$275-$350 each**

Two half-gallon shoulder jugs, one with a white top and one brown, late 19th and early 20th century, with advertising for the same liquor store in Lead, S.D., but identifying different owners, each 8-3/4" tall.
White ....**$500-$600**
Brown...**$600-$800**

1915 Potters Excursion shoulder jug one gallon, 11" tall. ....**$7,000+**

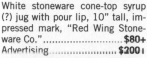

White stoneware cone-top syrup (?) jug with pour lip, 10" tall, impressed mark, "Red Wing Stoneware Co."............................ **$80+**
Advertising **$200**

Brown-top stoneware field jug or "monkey jug" with bail handle and advertising, about 1-1/2 gallons, 9-1/2" tall.......... **$500-$700**

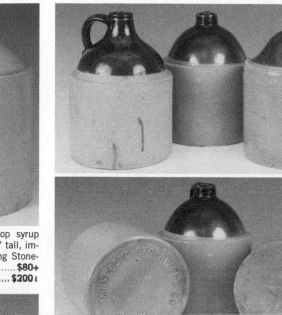

Red Wing-produced one-gallon jugs three styles, from left: funnel, dome and pear; each 10" tall. Second photo shows bottom marks of Minnesota Stoneware and North Star potteries. .... **$80-$110 each**

Two white stoneware half-gallon jugs with advertising, each about 7-1/2" tall, found in scores of advertising variations. ....**$500-$700 each**

Wide-mouth, brown-top one-gallon jug left, with raised star on bottom, 10" tall. .... **$75+**
Right, dome-top one-gallon jug with unglazed top, with raised letters, "Wm. R. Adams Microbe Killer," 10-1/2" tall, unmarked. .... **$325+**

Two one gallon white stoneware shoulder jugs with cobalt trim, with narrow and wide mouths, 11" and 10-1/4" tall, both marked on bottom, "Minnesota Stoneware Co. Red Wing, Minn.".....**$375-$450 each**

CERAMICS

One-gallon brown-top stoneware jug with rare original paper label, 11" tall. ....**$300+**

Rare "dome top" jug also called the "bird jug," about 1-1/2 gallons, in Albany slip glaze, circa 1895, 9-1/4" tall. Second photo shows impressed mark, "Red Wing Stoneware Co." and two marks resembling flying birds. ....**$150+**

Two brown-top stoneware shoulder jugs with advertising, one-gallon and half-gallon sizes, 11-1/4" and 9-1/2" tall. .... **$500-$700 each**

Two-gallon stoneware "fancy jug" with 4" wing, 11-1/2" tall. **$400+**

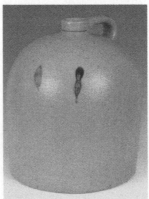

Two-gallon salt-glaze "beehive" jug circa 1890, with glaze drippings known as "turkey droppings," 11" tall, unmarked................**$60-$80**

Three-gallon "beehive" jug in Albany slip glaze, 13-1/2" tall, unmarked. ....**$80+**

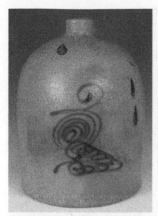

Three-gallon salt-glaze "beehive" jug with elaborate "3" and stylized leaf, circa 1890, with glaze drippings known as "turkey droppings," 14" tall, unmarked...........**$2,000+**

White stoneware jug three Imperial gallons (Canada), with oval and large wing, 16" tall......**$125-$160**

Four-gallon salt-glaze "beehive" jug with cobalt decoration referred to as "ribcage" and "target," circa 1890, 15" tall, unmarked. .... **$2,500+**

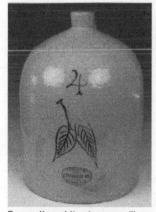

Four-gallon white stoneware "beehive" jug with birch leaves, 15-1/2" tall. ....**$800+**

White stoneware "beehive" jug four Imperial gallons (Canada), with advertising, rare this form, 17" tall. .... **$2,000+**

Five-gallon stoneware "beehive" jug Albany slip glaze, with sgraffito number, 17" tall, with rare handle stamp, "RWS Co."..**$1,100-$1,500**

Five-gallon white stoneware "threshing jug" beehive form with reinforced bunghole, 16-1/2" tall ....**$1,800-$2,300**

Five-gallon white stoneware "beehive" jug, 17" tall.............**$400+**

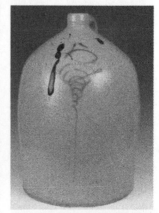

Five-gallon salt-glaze "beehive" jug with cobalt "tornado" decoration, circa 1890, with glaze drippings called "turkey droppings," 17" tall, unmarked. ......**$2,750-$3,000**

CERAMICS

Left: Five-gallon white stoneware "beehive" two-handle jug with advertising, 17" tall, rare. (Note glaze variation between this jug and the next.).......**$4,000+**

Right: Five-gallon white stoneware "beehive" two-handle jug with advertising, 17" tall, rare. .... **$4,000+**

Five-gallon salt-glaze "beehive" jug with stylized leaf, circa 1890, with pocked surface typical of many pieces made at this time, 17" tall, unmarked. **$3,000**

Five-gallon white stoneware jug made for Waconda Water, with oval and large wing, 17-1/2" tall, rare. .... **$900-$1,100**

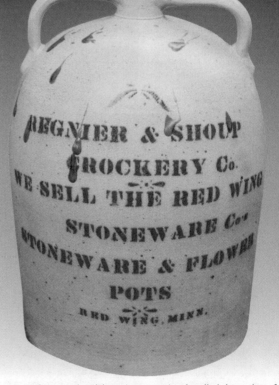

Large and rare advertising stoneware two-handled jug, circa 1890, 15-gallon salt-glazed, promoting "Regnier & Shoup Crockery Co. — 'We sell the Red Wing Stoneware Co.'s Stoneware and Flower Pots' — Red Wing, Minn.," with glaze drips on body (Collector's Tip: These globs of glaze are called "turkey droppings."), cracks around mouth, overall excellent condition. .... **No established value**

Rockingham Wares

The Marquis of Rockingham first established an earthenware pottery in the Yorkshire district of England around 1745, and it was occupied afterwards by various potters. The well-known mottled brown Rockingham glaze was introduced about 1788 by the Brameld Brothers and became immediately popular. It was during the 1820s that the production of true porcelain began at the factory, and it continued to be made until the firm closed in 1842. Since that time the so-called Rockingham glaze has been used by various potters in England and the United States, including some famous wares produced in Bennington, Vermont. Very similar glazes were also used by potteries in other areas of the United States including Ohio and Indiana, but only wares specifically attributed to Bennington should use that name. The following listings will include mainly wares featuring the dark brown mottled glaze produced at various sites here and abroad.

Foot warmer, wide flattened half-round form w/two molded indentations on the top for feet, a small spout at the top end, overall mottled brown glaze, American-made, ca. 1860, underside crazing, small flakes in the glaze, 7" w., 10" h. **$230**

Creamer, tapering ovoid body w/ an undulating rim & wide arched spout, C-scroll handle, yellow-ware w/overall mottled dark brown Rockingham glaze, 19th c., 5 1/2" h. **$44**

Flask, figural Mermaid design, dark brown glaze, ca. 1860, 8" h. **$187**

Right: Flask, flattened ovoid body w/small neck, yellowware molded in relief w/an oval reserve enclosing a half-length portrait of a man snorting snuff on each side, overall dark mottled brown Rockingham glaze, possibly Bennington, Vermont, or East Liverpool, Ohio, excellent condition, first half 19th c., 7 1/2" h. **$248**

Far right: Flask, flattened ovoid shape tapering to a fluted neck & ringed mouth, molded on one side w/the American Eagle & on the other w/a morning glory vine, dark brown Rockingham glaze, No. G11-19, several old glaze chips, ca. 1840-60, pt. **$308**

Inkwell, figural, modeled as a woman reclining asleep on an oblong rockwork base, yellowware w/overall mottled dark brown Rockingham glaze, several old edge chips, reportedly made by the Larkin Bros. Company, Newell, West Virginia, ca. 1850-80, 3 7/8" h. **$101**

Model of a lion, recumbent animal raised on a deep rectangular base, mottled dark brown glaze, restoration to minor surface roughness along base, ca. 1860, 6 3/4 x 9" **$303**

Pitcher, 9 1/2" h., yellowware w/overall mottled dark brown glaze, molded hound handle, wide baluster form shape molded in relief w/eight panels of hanging game & fowl, a molded eagle under the wide spout, minor hairline in bottom, minor glaze wear, ca. 1850 .... **$121**

Jug, advertising-type, figural, model of a walking pig, impressed on the rear "Bieler's Ronny Club," yellowware w/a mottled brown Rockingham glaze, original white porcelain stopper marked "Brookfield Rye Bieler," reportedly from Cincinnati, Ohio, ca. 1880-1900, 9 1/2" l., 5 1/4" h. **$1,232**

Pitcher, 6 1/2" h., hound-handled, wide bulbous body w/a flattened shoulder to the wide flared neck & wide arched spout, relief- molded w/stag hunting scene, overall very dark brown glaze, possibly Bennington, Vermont, ca. 1850... **$144**

Pitcher, 6 1/2" h., hound-handled, flat-bottomed swelled cylindrical body w/a flattened shoulder to the neck w/a wide arched spout, the body molded in relief w/a continuous hound & deer hunting scene, molded vine band around the neck, yellowware w/overall dark brown Rockingham glaze, possibly West Troy Factory, Troy, New York, ca. 1860, excellent condition **$275**

Teapot, cov., footed ovoid body w/swan's-neck spout & C-form handle, domed cover w/bud-form finial, mottled brown glaze w/relief-molded scene of Rebecca at the well, early 20th c., Ohio, 8 1/2" h. **$200**

Rookwood Pottery

Maria Longworth Nichols founded Rookwood Pottery in 1880. The name, she later reported, paid homage to the many crows (rooks) on her father's estate and was also designed to remind customers of Wedgwood. Production began on Thanksgiving Day 1880 when the first kiln was drawn.

Rookwood's earliest productions demonstrated a continued reliance on European precedents and the Japanese aesthetic. Although the firm offered a variety of wares (Dull Glaze, Cameo, and Limoges for example), it lacked a clearly defined artistic identity. With the introduction of what became known as its "standard glaze" in 1884, Rookwood inaugurated a period in which the company won consistent recognition for its artistic merit and technical innovation.

Rookwood's first decade ended on a high note when the company was awarded two gold medals: one at the Exhibition of American Art Industry in Philadelphia and another later in the year at the Exposition Universelle in Paris. Significant, too, was Maria Longworth Nichols' decision to transfer her interest in the company to William W. Taylor, who had been the firm's manager since 1883. In May 1890, the board of a newly reorganized Rookwood Pottery Company purchased "the real estate, personal property, goodwill, patents, trademarks... now the sole property of William W. Taylor" for $40,000.

Under Taylor's leadership, Rookwood was transformed from a fledgling startup to successful business that expanded throughout the following decades to meet rising demand.

Throughout the 1890s, Rookwood continued to attract critical notice as it kept the tradition of innovation alive. Taylor rolled out three new glaze lines—Iris, Sea Green and Aerial Blue—from late 1894 into early 1895.

At the Paris Exposition in 1900, Rookwood cemented its reputation by winning the Grand Prix, a feat largely due to the favorable reception of the new Iris glaze and its variants.

Over the next several years, Rookwood's record of achievement at domestic and international exhibitions remained unmatched.

Throughout the 1910s, Rookwood continued in a similar vein and began to more thoroughly embrace the simplified aesthetic promoted by many Arts and Crafts figures. Production of the Iris line, which had been instrumental in the firm's success at the Paris Exposition in 1900, ceased around 1912. Not only did the company abandon its older, fussier underglaze wares, but the newer lines the pottery introduced also trended toward simplicity.

Unfortunately, the collapse of the stock market in October 1929 and ensuing economic depression dealt Rookwood a blow from which it did not recover. The Great Depression took a toll on the company and eventually led to bankruptcy in April 1941.

Rookwood's history might have ended there were it not for the purchase of the firm by a group of investors led by automobile dealer Walter E. Schott and his wife, Margaret. Production started once again. In the years that followed, Rookwood changed hands a number of times before being moved to Starkville, Mississippi, in 1960. It finally closed its doors there in 1967.

CERAMICS

ROOKWOOD MARKS

Rookwood employed a number of marks on the bottom of its vessels that denoted everything from the shape number, to the size, date, and color of the body, to the type of glaze to be used.

Company Marks:

1880-1882

In this early period, a number of marks were used to identify the wares.

1. "ROOKWOOD" followed by the initials of the decorator, painted in gold. This is likely the earliest mark, and though the wares are not dated, it seems to have been discontinued by 1881-1882.

2. "ROOKWOOD / POTTERY. / [DATE] CIN. O." In *Marks of American Potters* (1904), Edwin AtLee Barber states, "The most common marks prior to 1882 were the name of the pottery and the date of manufacture, which were painted or incised on the base of each piece by the decorator."

3. "R. P. C. O. M. L. N." These initials stand for "Rookwood Pottery, Cincinnati, Ohio, Maria Longworth Nichols," and were either painted or incised on the base.

4. Kiln and crows stamp. Barber notes that in 1881 and 1882, the trademark designed by the artist Henry Farny was printed beneath the glaze.

5. Anchor stamp: Barber notes that this mark is "one of the rarest."

6. Oval stamp.

7. Ribbon or banner stamp: According to Barber, "In 1882 a special mark was used on a trade piece... the letters were impressed in a raised ribbon.

8. Ribbon or banner stamp II: A simpler variation of the above stamp, recorded by Herbert Peck.

1883-1886

1. Stamped name and date.
2. Impressed kiln: Appears only in 1883.

1886-1960

Virtually all of the pieces feature the conjoined RP monogram. Pieces fired in the anniversary kilns carry a special kiln-shaped mark with the number of the anniversary inside of it.

1955

A diamond-shaped mark that reads: "ROOKWOOD / 75th / ANNIVERSARY / POTTERY" was printed on wares.

1960-1967

Occasionally pieces are marked "ROOKWOOD POTTERY / STARKVILLE MISS"; from 1962 to 1967 a small "®" occasionally follows the monogram.

Date Marks

Unlike many of their contemporaries, Rookwood seems very early on to have adopted a method of marking its pottery that was accurate and easy to understand.

From 1882-1885, the company impressed the date, often with the company name, in block letters (see 1883-86, No. 1).

Although the date traditionally given for the conjoined RP mark is June 23, 1886, this marks the official introduction of the monogram rather than the first use.

Stanley Burt, in his record of the Rookwood at the Cincinnati Museum noted two pieces from 1883 (Nos. 2 and 3) that used the monogram. The monogram was likely designed by Alfred Brennan, since it first appears on his work.

From 1886 on, the date of the object was coded in the conjoined "RP" monogram.

1886: conjoined "RP" no additional flame marks.

1887-1900: conjoined "RP" with a flame added for each subsequent year. Thus, a monogram with seven flames would represent 1893.

1900-1967: conjoined "RP" with fourteen flames and a Roman numeral below the mark to indicate the year after 1900. Thus, a monogram with fourteen flames and the letters "XXXVI" below it signifies 1936.

Clay-Type Marks

From 1880 until around 1895, Rookwood used a number of different colored bodies for production and marked each color with a letter code. These letters were impressed and usually found grouped together with the shape number, sometimes following it, but more often below it.

The letter "S" is a particularly vexing designation since the same initial was used for two other unrelated designations. As a result, it is particularly important to take into account the relative position of the impressed letter.

R = Red
Y = Yellow
S – Sage
G = Ginger
W = White
O = Olive
P = From 1915 on Rookwood used an impressed "P" (often found perpendicular to the orientation of the other marks) to denote the soft porcelain body.

Size and Shape Marks

Almost all Rookwood pieces have a shape code consisting of three or four numbers, followed by a size letter. "A" denotes the largest available size, "F" is the smallest. According to Herbert Peck, initial designs were given a "C" or "D" designation so that variations could be made. Not every shape model, however, features a variation in every size.

Glaze Marks

In addition to marking the size, shape and year of the piece, Rookwood's decorators also used a number of letters to designate the type of glaze to be used upon a piece. Generally speaking, these marks are either incised or impressed.

"S" = Standard Glaze to be used. (Incised.)

"L" = Decorators would often incise an "L" near their monogram to indicate that the light variation of the Standard Glaze was to be used. (Incised.)

"SG" = Sea Green Glaze to be used.

"Z" = from 1900-1904 designated any piece with a mat glaze. (Impressed.)

"W" = Iris Glaze to be used.

"V" = Vellum Glaze to be used; variations include "GV" for Green Vellum and "YV" for Yellow Vellum.

Other Marks

"S" = If found away from the shape number, this generally indicates a piece that was specially thrown at the pottery in the presence of visitors. (Impressed.)

"S" = If this precedes the shape number than it denotes a piece that was specifically thrown and decorated from a sketch with a corresponding number. Because of the size and quality of pieces this letter has been found on, this probably signifies a piece made specifically for an important exhibition.

"X" = Rookwood used a wheel ground "x" to indicate items that were not of first quality. There has been some suggestion that decorators and salespersons might have conspired to "x" certain pieces that they liked, since this designation would reduce the price. Since there are a number of items that appear to have been marked for no apparent reason, there may be some truth to this idea. Unfortunately, as this idea has gained credence, many pieces with obvious flaws have been listed as "marked x for no apparent reason," and collectors should be cautious.

Generally, the mark reduces the value and appeal of the piece. Peck describes a variation of the "x" that resembles an asterisk as indicating a piece that could be given away to employees.

"T" = An impressed T that precedes a shape number indicates a trial piece.

➤ ⑤

▲ = These shapes (crescents, diamonds, and triangles) are used to indicate a glaze trial.

◆

"K1" and "K3" = c. 1922, used for matching teacups and saucers

"SC" = Cream and Sugar sets, c. 1946-50

"2800" = Impressed on ship pattern tableware

For more information on Rookwood, see *Warman's Rookwood Pottery Identification and Price Guide* by Denise Rago and Jonathan Clancy.

SOME LINES OF NOTE

Aerial Blue: Commercially, this line was among the least successful. As a result, there are a limited number of pieces, and this scarcity has increased their values relative to other wares.

Black Iris: This line is among the most sought after by collectors, commanding significantly more than examples of similar size and design in virtually any other glaze. In fact, the current auction record for Rookwood—over $350,000—was set in 2004 for a Black Iris vase decorated by Kitaro Shirayamadani in 1900.

Iris: Uncrazed examples are exceptionally rare, with large pieces featuring conventional designs commanding the highest prices. Smaller, naturalistically painted examples, though still desirable, are gradually becoming more affordable for the less advanced collector.

Production Ware: This commercial and mass-produced artware is significantly less expensive than pieces in most other lines.

Standard Glaze: These wares peaked in the 1970s-1980s, and the market has remained thin in recent years, but regardless of the state of the market, examples of superlative quality, including those with silver overlay, have found their places in the finest of collections.

Wax Mat: This is among the most affordable of the hand-decorated lines.

Black Iris Glaze tankard, painted and carved by Kitaro Shirayamadani.

EARLY WARES

Large Limoges-style basket on lion's head feet, painted by A.R. Valentien with butterflies, 1882, stamped ROOKWOOD 1882 45 A.R.V., 9-3/4" x 20". .... **$800-$1,200**

Limoges-style humidor with double-lid by Maria Longworth Nichols, 1882, painted with spiders and bats on a mottled ground, stamped ROOKWOOD/1882/MLN, 6" x 6" **$2,000-$3,000**

Rare pitcher decorated by Laura Fry with incised fronds covered in indigo and dark green glaze, 1882, stamped ROOKWOOD 1882, incised Cincinnati Pottery Club, LAF, 7" x 5" .... **$1,500-$2,500.**
Laura Fry was a member of the Women's Pottery Club of Cincinnati, a china-painting group, along with Clara Chipman Newton and Mary Louise McLaughlin, before joining the first generation of decorators at Rookwood. During her 10-year stay at the pottery, she developed and patented the atomizer for glazing purposes. From Rookwood, she moved on to the Lonhuda Pottery in Steubenville, Ohio.

Rare and important red clay "Indian" portrait charger by H.F. Farny, 1881, with a Native American chief in headdress painted in black surrounded by geometric and abstract designs, 11" d.......... **$12,500-$17,500.**
Henry Francois Farny (1847-1916), a well-known Cincinnati artist, designed the first trademark for Rookwood and was the first to suggest "Indian designs" for its pottery. The charger is recorded in the Shape Record Book as: "189. Red clay plaque. Pressed. Decorated by H. Farny. Could not be fired hard enough to set the colors in manner desired by artist without destroying effect," (*The Book of Rookwood Pottery* by Herbert Peck, 1968, p. 15).

◄Cincinnati Art Club/E. G. Winslow bulbous vase with applied blue and red morning glories on barbotine-painted ground, on Rookwood blank, 1882, stamped ROOKWOOD 1882, incised E.G. Winslow, 1882, 11-1/2" x 7-1/2". .... **$700-$1,000**

CERAMICS

Carved Iris Glaze vase decorated by Matthew A. Daly, 1901, with indigo hyacinths and tall green leaves in high relief against an indigo and violet ground, 8" x 5-1/2". .... **$4,000-$6,000**

Rare Aerial Blue baluster vase painted by artist CW with a classical maiden as fertility goddess in front of a full moon on a blue ground, 1894, flame mark/E/538/273/CW/crescents, 7-1/2" x 3-1/2".... **$2,500-$3,500**

Exceptional and rare tall Cameo cylindrical vase painted by A.R. Valentien with a wisteria branch in white pate-sur-pate on a dead matte indigo ground, 1893, flame mark/C/644/A.R.V./W., 14-1/2" x 4".....................**$10,000-$15,000**

Standard Glaze Light large urn finely painted by Matt Daly with branches of yellow dogwood, a gently tooled underglaze design encircling the collar, 1888, flame mark/MAD/L/425/W, 13" x 10-1/2". .... **$3,000-$5,000**

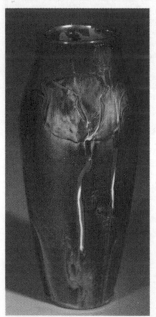

Tiger Eye vase, probably by Kitaro Shirayamadani, carved with full-length russet poppies on a silky brown, green and gold ground, mark obscured by glaze, 9-1/4" x 3-3/4". .... **$4,500-$6,500**

Sea Green pillow vase with crescent rim, decorated by Edward Diers, 1899, with tall stems and leaves in green against a blue and celadon ground, wrapped in a bronze overlay of iris blossoms, 4-1/2" x 4". ....**$17,500-$25,000**

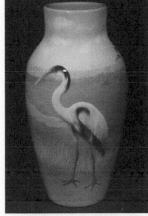

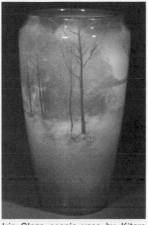

Iris Glaze vase painted by Carl Schmidt, 1902, with a blue and white water bird standing in tall grasses near a stream in tones of lavender, brown and green, 11" x 5-1/4"............. **$8,000-$12,000**

Iris Glaze scenic vase by Kitaro Shirayamadani, 1907, painted with a panoramic scene of tall trees and distant mountains around a lake in celadon, gray and pink, 9-1/4" x 5"........**$18,000-$24,000**

Iris Glaze landscape vase painted by Kitaro Shirayamadani, 1911, with a panoramic view of birches at dusk showing tall white trees through green foliage against a blue-to-yellow and pink sky, 16-1/4" x 7".....**$30,000-$40,000**

Silver-overlaid Standard Glaze two-handled vase by Kitaro Shirayamadani, 1898, painted with orange and golden yellow chrysanthemums and green leaves, and covered in Gorham silver with whiplash strands, 12" x 6-1/2". ....**$10,000-$15,000**

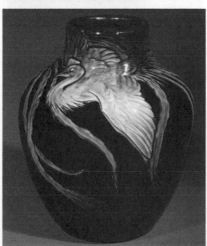

Silver-overlaid Standard Glaze cylindrical vase, "Edelweiss," painted by Bruce Horsfall with a golden-haired maiden dropping blossoms, 1893, half the vase covered in GORHAM floral silver overlay, flame mark/B-/Edelweiss/589C W, 12-3/4" x 3-3/4".............**$17,500-$25,000**

Black Carved Iris Glaze bulbous vase by Matthew A. Daly, 1899, its rim encircled by blue birds-of-paradise in relief against a black ground, 8-3/4" x 7". .... **$35,000-$55,000**

CERAMICS

MAT GLAZE

Z-Line mug with wave pattern under a matt green glaze, 1902, marked, 5". ....**$600-$800**

Incised Mat corn jug by Kitaro Shirayamadani in matte greens and browns, 1904, flame mark/ IV/765BZ/X/artist cipher, 9" x 5-1/2". .... **$5,000-$6,000**

Fine Incised Mat ovoid vase by Elizabeth Lincoln, 1918, beautifully-decorated with bright red fruit and green and purple leaves on a purple and umber butterfat ground, flame mark/XVIII/943C/LNL, 10-1/2" x 5-1/2". .... **$2,000-$3,000**

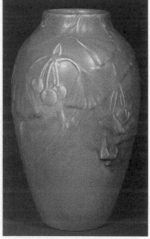

Modeled Mat ovoid vase by Kitaro Shirayamadani, 1905, with modeled branches of ginkgo leaves and berries in relief under a green and yellow mat glaze, 10-1/2" x 6-1/2". .... **$9,500-$12,500**

Fine Incised Mat vase by unidentified artist MF, with stylized purple flowers on whiplash green stems on a green ground, 1909, flame mark/MF, 10"....... **$1,500-$2,500**

Z-Line squat vessel by A. M. Valentien with reclining nude under a cherry red matte glaze, 1901, flame mark/?51Z/A.M.V., 3-1/2" x 4-1/2"................. **$2,000-$3,000**

Incised Mat spherical vase decorated by Sallie Coyne with trillium in green on a matte red ground, 1905, flame mark/V/911E/artist's cipher, 4-1/4" x 5".. **$800-$1,200**

Painted Mat vase by O.G. Reed with pink roses and yellow centers on an indigo-to-rose ground, 1906, flame mark/VI/907DD/O.G.R., 9-1/2" x 3-3/4"....**$9,000-$13,000**

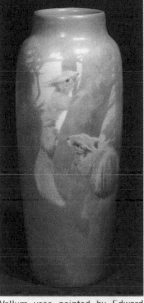

Fine banded Vellum cylindrical vase by Kitaro Shirayamadani, 1911, elegantly painted with flying Canadian geese and bamboo on a shaded blue, pink and green ground, elegantly painted, almost no crazing, flame mark/XI/952E/V/artist's cipher, 7-1/2" x 3-1/2" .... **$8,000-$10,000**

Vellum vase painted by Ed Diers with a fall landscape, 1916, flame mark/XVI/904D/V/ED., 8-3/4" x 3-3/4"................ **$4,000-$6,000**

Vellum vase painted by Edward Diers, 1901, with squirrels amidst branches in a panoramic forest scene in tones of brown, sky blue and green, 11-1/2" x 4-1/2". .... **$8,000-$12,000**

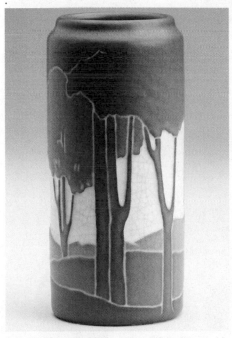

Carved Vellum cylindrical vase beautifully decorated in the Arts & Crafts style by Sara Sax with an abstracted landscape of silhouetted trees and mountains in blue-grays and ivory, 1908, purchased from the famous 1942 B. Altman's sale, flame mark/VIII/952E/artist cipher/V, 7-1/2" x 3-1/2". .... **$15,000-$25,000**

Vellum ovoid vase by Carl Schmidt, 1916, painted with ships at sea against a distant city skyline under gray clouds, in tones of cream, blue, green, brown and pink, 12-3/4" x 7-1/2". ....**$8,500-$12,500**

Incised Mat squat vessel by William Hentschell with stylized peacock feathers, 1912, flame mark/XII/494BWEH, 4-1/2" x 7-3/4" ....$1,500-$2,000

Vellum bulbous vase by Kitaro Shirayamadani, 1907, decorated with dragonflies on tall grasses in gray and white on a shaded yellow and blue-green ground, flame mark/VII/1097C/V/artist's cipher/X, 9-1/4" x 5-1/2"......$3,000-$4,000

Green Vellum ovoid vase by Sara Sax, 1908, incised with a band of stylized peacock feathers in matte teal glaze on a medium green ground, flame mark VIII/951D/V/ artist's cipher, 9" x 3-3/4" ....$2,750-$3,500

Vellum vase painted by Fred Rothenbusch with trees by a lake, against a pink and blue sky, 1924, flame mark/XXIV/926B/FR, 11" x 6"........................$6,000-$8,000

Ombroso vase by Elizabeth Barrett with large blue fruit and green leaves on a butterfat mustard ground, 1915, flame mark/XV/1917/artist's cipher, 6" x 6-1/4"....................$900-$1,400

Yellow Vellum baluster vase painted by Lenore Asbury with red berries and green leaves on an amber ground, 1924, flame mark/XXIV/546C/L.A./Y.V, 9-1/2" x 5". ....$3,000-$4,000

Vellum vase painted by Carl Schmidt with irises on shaded pink and blue ground, 1926, flame mark/XXVI/2544/V/artist cipher, 8-1/4" x 4".. $7,000-$9,000

Ombroso bulbous vase by William Hentschel with spade-shaped leaves in green on a flambe brown ground, 1911, flame mark, WEH, 7-1/2".................$2,000-$3,000

NEW PORCELAIN BODY

Fine Yellow Tinted vase by Sara Sax, 1923, with flaring rim decorated with honeysuckle blossoms and leaves on a yellow ground, uncrazed, flame mark/XXIII/2545C/ artist's cipher, 10" x 3-1/4". .... **$2,500-$3,500**

Large Turquoise Blue bulbous vase painted by Sara Sax with birds and magnolia on a rich blue and black ground, 1917, flame mark/ XVII/2272/P/artist's cipher, 12-1/4" x 7-1/2"....... **$4,000-$6,000**

Tiger Eye ovoid vase, beautifully painted by Harriet Wilcox with stylized green poppies, 1929, flame mark/XXIX/2544/H.E.W., 8" x 3-3/4". .... **$3,000-$4,000**

French Red tall baluster vase enamel-decorated by Sara Sax with flowers on a gunmetal ground, 1921, flame mark/XXI/2551/artist's cipher, 14" x 6"...... **$1,500-$2,000**

Butterfat tall bottle-shaped vase painted by Lorinda Epply with blue and green blossoms under thick ivory curdled glaze, 1928, flame mark/XXVIII/2983/LE, 15-1/2" x 8". .... **$3,000-$4,000**

Decorated Mat bottle-shaped vase painted by C.S. Todd with abstract red flowers and yellow band against a blue-green ground, 1921, flame mark/XXI/497/CST, 7-3/4" x 5-1/4".... **$1,500-$2,000**

Decorated Mat two-handled center bowl painted by Elizabeth Lincoln with red chrysanthemums and pink flowers on a yellow butterfat ground, 1929, flame mark/XXXIV/2951/LNL, 5" x 10"......... **$950-$1,250**

CERAMICS

Fine and large Decorated Mat baluster vase incised and painted by Louise Abel with fleshy vermillion magnolias on a rich gold and orange butterfat ground, 1926, flame mark/XXVI/424B/artist cipher, 14-1/4" x 7". **$2,750-$3,750**

Decorated Mat vase painted by Sallie Coyne with abstract flowers in jewel tones on a vermillion ground, 1927, flame mark/XXVII/2785/artist's cipher, 13-1/4" x 5-1/2". .... **$1,500-$2,500**

Decorated Mat vase beautifully painted by Kitaro Shirayamadani with purple and ivory hollyhocks, 1939, flame mark/XXXIX, 10" x 5-1/2". .... **$3,500-$4,500**

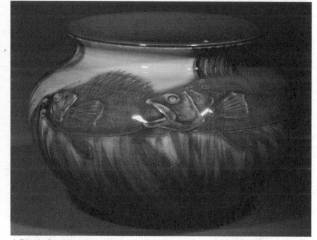

Large Decorated Mat vase by Jens Jensen with plums on a peach ground, 1930, flame mark/XXX/264OC/artist's cipher, 13-3/4" x 9-1/2".. **$1,500-$2,000**

▲Black Opal vase by Kitaro Shirayamadani, 1925, its exterior painted and modeled with gray-green fish swimming through brown and red seaweed under a dripping cobalt glaze, and its interior in a deep mauve glaze, 5" x 7"..**$8,500-$12,500**

◄Decorated Mat bulbous vase painted by unidentified artist with red hollyhocks in relief on a red and green ground, 1928, flame mark, 6-3/4". ....**$1,000-$2,000**

◆ To celebrate its 35th anniversary in 1915, Rookwood introduced an entirely new "soft porcelain" body and developed a number of new glazes to promote this new body. The company also continued its longevity by responding to changing tastes and embracing a more Art Deco/Moderne sensibility.

Wax Mat bulbous vase painted by E.T. Hurley with orange roses and green foliage on ivory ground, 1933, uncrazed, flame mark/ XXXIII/S/E.T.H. 6-1/4" x 4". .... **$1,000-$1,500**

Tall Later Mat/Mat Moderne vase by Elizabeth Barrett with sprigs of leaves, 1927, flame mark/XXVII/2368/EB, 17" x 7". .... **$1,500-$2,250**

Later Mat/Mat Moderne vase by William Hentschel with white leaves on turquoise ground, 1929, flame mark/XXIX/927D/WEH, 9-1/4" x 7".......... **$1,400-$1,900**

Wax Mat flaring vase by Elizabeth Barrett with a geometric butterfat decoration in gray, black, and brown, 1943, flame mark/ XLIII/2193/artist's cipher, 5" x 5-1/2".................... **$900-$1,400**

Coromandel bulbous vase embossed with stylized decoration under a rich, metallic gold and deep brown glaze, 1937, Rookwood/2857, 4" X 6". ...**$600-$900**

Jewel Porcelain squat potpourri jar painted by Arthur Conant with rabbits in a Persian floral pattern, 1919, complete with two lids, flame mark/XIX/2337/C, 4-3/4" x 5"....................... **$3,000-$5,000**

Later Mat/Mat Moderne urn decorated by Wilhelmine Rehm with stylized foliage in brown on a verdigris ground, 1930, flame mark/XXX/6010E/WR, 8" x 7". ....**$700-$1,000**

Later Mat/Mat Moderne vase by Wilhelmine Rehm, 1934, with rose matte antelope in relief on a mottled blue matte ground, flame mark/XXXIV/S/WR, 6" x 3-1/2". .... **$1,000-$1,500**

Jewel Porcelain ovoid vase decorated in a Persian floral pattern by Arthur Conant, 1921, flame mark/ XXI/551/artist cipher, 6-1/2" x 3"....................... **$1,250-$1,750**

CERAMICS

Jewel Porcelain plate painted by William Hentschel in blue and white Chinoiserie, 1924 (exhibited in "After the China Taste: China's Influence in America, 1730-1930," catalog #53, p. 69), flame mark/XXIV/K2A/artist's cipher, 10-1/4" d. **$1,250-$1,750**

Jewel Porcelain baluster vase painted and incised by Jens Jensen with green and blue birds, fish and oversized leaves on a white and amber ground under a crackled overglaze, 1944, flame mark XLIV/614B/artist's cipher, 15-1/2" x 7-1/2".. **$3,000-$4,000**

Jewel Porcelain barrel-shaped vase painted by Lorinda Epply with amber fish on a butter yellow ground, 1930, flame mark/XXX/6203C/LE, 8" x 6-1/4". .... **$3,500-$4,500**

Jewel Porcelain large, classically-shaped vase painted by Arthur Conant with peacocks perched on blooming apple branches and over paperwhites, in jewel tones on a gray ground, 1919, flame mark/XIX/2273/artist's cipher, 17-1/4" x 7-3/4". ....**$10,000-$15,000**

Jewel Porcelain vase painted by E. Timothy Hurley, 1924, with peacocks in brilliant polychrome resting on branches of flowers against a bright emerald green and black ground, 13" x 7".**$8,000-$11,000**

Jewel Porcelain squat vase by Sara Sax, 1922, its exterior painted with abstract circular designs in mauve, violet and gold, and its interior in bright green glaze, 6" x 7-1/4". .... **$4,500-$6,500**

Jewel Porcelain vase painted by Carl Schmidt, 1925, with full-height lavender and white irises and green leaves against a light blue and white ground, 11-3/4" x 4-1/2". .... **$15,000-$20,000**

Jewel Porcelain hemispherical vessel painted by E.T. Hurley with large birds and blooming branches, 1929, flame mark/XXIX/2254D/E.T.H., 5-1/4" x 6-1/4". .... **$1,250-$1,750**

PRODUCTION WARES

Production Z-line cabinet vase, c. 1900, incised with key motif at rim and covered in a mottled mauve matte glaze, flame mark, 3-1/2" x 2-3/4"..........**$300-$400**

Production pitcher embossed with triangles under a good frothy mint green glaze, 1907, flame mark, 4-1/2"......................**$300-$400**

Incised Mat ovoid vase by Cecil Duell, 1908, its rim carved with a band of free-form shapes, covered in a matte green glaze, flame mark/artist's cipher, 6-1/4" x 4-3/4"......................**$550-$750**

Early Production chamberstick in the form of a poppy in mustard and brown, 1903, flame mark, 8-1/4". ....**$550-$750**

Rare Production rook inkwell covered in dark teal glaze, 1908, missing lid, flame mark, 7-1/2" x 12". ....**$700-$900**

Large Production vase embossed with swirling blossoms under cobalt glaze, 1914, flame mark/XIV/516, 11" x 12"..................**$1,750-$2,250**

CERAMICS

Rare and early Production squat bowl embossed with gingko leaves and fruit under purple and green matte glaze, 1913, flame mark/XIII/1680, 2-1/4" x 6-1/2" .... **$1,000-$1,500**

Production porcelain creamer and sugar bowl covered in glossy blue glaze, 1916, marked, 4" .... **$75-$125 each**

Production bookends with goddesses under matte indigo glaze, 1918, marked, 8". .... **$450-$650**

Pair of Bassett hound bookends designed by Louise Abel covered in tobacco brown matte glaze, 1930, flame marks, 4-3/4" x 6-1/2". .... **$500-$700**

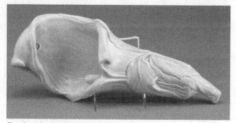

Production calla lily wall pocket covered in matte yellow glaze, 1922, flame mark, 15-1/2"..... **$750-$950**

Pair of Production double penguin bookends in metallic gray and beige, 1924, flame marks, 5-1/2". .... **$1,500-$2,000**

Production tall candlesticks, 1922, embossed with tulips and covered in a dark pink matte glaze, flame mark, 10-1/2".. **$400-$600**

Production ginger jar designed by Arthur Conant with a double lid and embossed rabbits in a Persian floral motif, and covered in raspberry semi-matte glaze, 1926, marked, 15" x 8". **$1,000-$1,500**

Tall Production vase designed by Louise Abel, 1922, embossed with a classical Greek scene of maidens and a flute player under a matte green glaze, flame mark, 11". ....**$500-$700**

Production bulbous vase, 1925, embossed with a broad band of flowers and leaves, covered in a brownish-green matte glaze, flame mark, 9-1/4"..............**$500-$700**

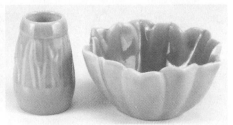

Two Production porcelain pieces: faceted covered nut jar with peanut finial, 1949, and four-sided vase with daisies, 1951, both covered in glossy green glaze, 5-1/2" and 5-1/4"......... **$150-$250 and $100-$200**

Production pieces from 1928: a pair of faceted bud vases and a swirled low bowl, all covered in blue butterfat matte glaze, flame marks, 6-3/4" h and 4-1/2" d.. **$100-$150 each**

Pair of Production oak tree bookends designed by William P. McDonald, 1928, flame mark/XXVIII/6023/WMcD, 5-1/2" x 5-1/2". .... **$1,000-$1,500**

Two Production porcelain pieces covered in celadon glaze, an ovoid vase with cattails and a lotus bowl, 1953-4, flame marks, 5" and 7-1/4" d. .... **$100-$200 each**

CERAMICS

Production ovoid vase, 1916, embossed with panels of berries and leaves on a shaded green and umber matte ground, flame mark, 7-1/2" x 3"................**$600-$900**

Five Production vessels in glossy glazes: bulbous vase with water lilies in mauve, vase molded with Southwestern scene in ivory, two cream pitchers in yellow and blue, and ribbed covered dish in celadon, all marked, tallest: 6-1/4"; pitchers..**$50-$100 each**
Vases...**$100-$250 each**

Massive Production urn embossed with Classical scene in indigo matte glaze, 1929, flame mark, 13" x 9"............. **$1,000-$1,400**

Production porcelain bud vase embossed with blue flowers on a brown ground, 1946, marked, 5" x 2-3/4". ....**$250-$350**

Porcelain classically-shaped vase by R. E. Menzel, 1957, covered in a feathered blue-green glossy glaze, flame mark LVII/S/REM, 7-3/4" x 3-3/4"..........**$350-$500**

Production porcelain vase with flat shoulder, 1932, covered in a turquoise crystalline and lavender flambe glaze, flame mark/ XXXII/6310, 5" x 5". ..**$250-$350**

Production eagle paperweight designed by Louise Abel and covered in gunmetal brown glaze, 1934, flame mark, 5-1/2" x 8". ....**$900-$1,400**

Large Production figure of a rook designed by William MacDonald, 1944, in apple green high glaze, flame mark, 10" x 9"..**$500-$700**

Roseville Pottery

Roseville is one of the most widely recognizable of potteries across the United States. Having been sold in flower shops and drug stores around the country, its art and production wares became a staple in American homes through the time Roseville closed in the 1950s.

The Roseville Pottery Company, located in Roseville, Ohio, was incorporated on Jan. 4, 1892, with George F. Young as general manager. The company had been producing stoneware since 1890, when it purchased the J. B. Owens Pottery, also of Roseville.

The popularity of Roseville Pottery's original lines of stoneware continued to grow. The company acquired new plants in 1892 and 1898, and production started to shift to Zanesville, just a few miles away. By about 1910, all of the work was centered in Zanesville, but the company name was unchanged.

Young hired Ross C. Purdy as artistic designer in 1900, and Purdy created Rozane—a contraction of the words "Roseville" and "Zanesville." The first Roseville artwork pieces were marked either Rozane or RPCO, both impressed or ink-stamped on the bottom.

In 1902, a line was developed called Azurean. Some pieces were marked Azurean, but often RPCO. In 1904 at the St. Louis Exposition, Roseville's Rozane Mongol, a high-gloss oxblood red line, captured first prize, gaining recognition for the firm and its creator, John Herold.

Many Roseville lines were a response to the innovations of Weller Pottery, and in 1904 Frederick Rhead was hired away from Weller as artistic director. He created the Olympic and Della Robbia lines for Roseville. His brother Harry took over as artistic director in 1908, and in 1915 he introduced the popular Donatello line.

By 1908, all handcrafting ended except for Rozane Royal. Roseville was the first pottery in Ohio to install a tunnel kiln, which increased its production capacity.

Frank Ferrell, who was a top decorator at the Weller Pottery by 1904, was Roseville's artistic director from 1917 until 1954. This Zanesville native created many of the most popular lines, including Pine Cone, which had scores of individual pieces.

Many collectors believe Roseville's circa 1925 glazes were the best of any Zanesville pottery. George Krause, who had become Roseville's technical supervisor, responsible for glaze, in 1915, remained with Roseville until the 1950s.

Company sales declined after World War II, especially in the early 1950s when cheap Japanese imports began to replace American wares, and a simpler, more modern style made many of Roseville's elaborate floral designs seem old-fashioned.

In the late 1940s, Roseville began to issue lines with glossy glazes. Roseville tried to offset its flagging artware sales by launching a dinnerware line—Raymor—in 1953. The line was a commercial failure.

Roseville issued its last new designs in 1953. On Nov. 29, 1954, the facilities of Roseville were sold to the Mosaic Tile Company. For more information on Roseville, see *Warman's Roseville Pottery*, 2nd edition, by Denise Rago.

CERAMICS

Bottom Marks

There is no consistency to Roseville bottom marks. Even within a single popular pattern like Pine Cone, the marks vary.

Several shape numbering systems were implemented during the company's almost 70-year history, with some denoting a vessel style and some applied to separate lines. Though many pieces are unmarked, from 1900 until the late teens or early 1920s, Roseville used a variety of marks including "RPCo," "Roseville Pottery Company," and the word "Rozane," the last often with a line name, i.e., "Egypto."

The underglaze ink script "Rv" mark was used on lines introduced from the mid-to-late teens through the mid-1920s. Around 1926 or 1927, Roseville began to use a small, triangular black paper label on lines such as Futura and Imperial II. Silver or gold foil labels began to appear around 1930, continuing for several years on lines such as Blackberry and Tourmaline, and on some early Pine Cone.

From 1932 to 1937, an impressed script mark was added to the molds used on new lines, and around 1937 the raised script mark was added to the molds of new lines. The relief mark includes "U.S.A."

All of the following bottom mark images appear courtesy of Adamstown Antique Gallery, Adamstown, Pennsylvania.

Impressed mark on Azurean vase, 8" h.

Raised mark on a Bushberry vase.

Ink stamp on a Cherry Blossom pink vase, 10" h.

Wafer mark on a Della Robbia vase, 10-1/2" h.

Gold foil label and grease pencil marks on an Imperial II vase, 10" h.

Impressed mark on an Iris vase.

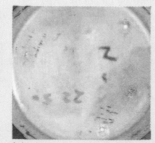

Ink stamps on a Wisteria bowl, 5" h.

Impressed mark on a Rozane portrait vase, 13" h.

Blue Apple Blossom tall vase, 393-18", raised mark. **$400-$600**

Artcraft jardinière in brown and green glaze, unmarked, 6" x 8". ....**$300-$500**

Artwood Ikebana vase with thistle, 1059-10", covered in a glossy green and brown glaze, raised mark. ....**$400-$450**

Two early Landscape pitchers, unmarked, 7-1/2"..........**$150-$250 each**

Autumn jardinière, unmarked, 8-1/2" x 11-1/2"........**$600-$900**

Aztec bulbous vase, decorated in squeezebag with a band of spade-shaped flowers in brown and white against a blue ground, unmarked, 6-1/2" x 4-1/2"..........**$500-$700**

Exceptional Azurean vase finely painted by W. Myers with a wooded trail, impressed mark/artist's signature, 15" x 4-1/4"..**$4,000-$6,000**

CERAMICS

Pink Baneda urn, 589-6", un-marked, 6-1/2" x 4". ...**$350-$550**

Green Bittersweet bowl, 829-12", raised mark. ....**$100-$150**

Blended Iris jardinière, unmarked, 11" x 12". ....**$300-$500**

Blue Bushberry sand jar, 778-14", raised mark. ....**$700-$900**

Blackberry wall pocket, 1267-8", unmarked, 8-1/4". ....**$650-$950**

Two Burmese green sconces, 80-B, raised marks, 8" h.**$100-$200 each**

Two Capri shell-shaped dishes, one ivory and one brown, marked, 1-1/2" x 6-1/2" and 1-1/2" x 5-1/2". ....**$25-$45 each**

Cameo jardinière and pedestal set in matte green with medallions in ivory and brown, unmarked, 33-3/4" overall. .... **$2,500-$3,500**

Pink Bleeding Heart jardinière and pedestal set, 651-8", both marked. ....**$750-$1,000**

◄Carnelian II ribbed bowl cov-ered in a fine deep red, green, and ochre dripping glaze, Rv ink mark, 4" x 10"...................**$350-$450**

CERAMICS

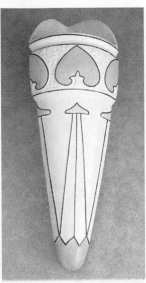

Carnelian I tall ewer in gray and beige, 1315-15", Rv ink mark, 15-1/4"......................**$250-$400**

Fine Ceramic Design Persian-type corner wall pocket, #336, decorated with geometric and leaf designs in green and yellow, unmarked, 17". .... **$1,350-$1,850**

Chloron pitcher with a swirled design and ring handle, 20-7", unmarked, 7-1/2" x 4-1/2". .... **$350-$500**

Above left: Pink Cherry Blossom bulbous vase, 619-5", unmarked, 5-1/4" x 5".....................**$350-$550**

Above: Blue Clematis cookie jar, 3-8", raised mark. ....**$150-$250**

◄Two Corinthian bulbous vases, 5-3/4" and 8-1/2", unmarked. ....**$50-$100 and $75-$125**

CERAMICS

Green Clemana vase, 753-8", impressed mark..............**$250-$350**

Brown Columbine bulbous vase, 23-10", raised mark. ..**$200-$350**

Tall blue Cosmos ewer, 957-15", unmarked. ....**$300-$400**

►Creamware smoking set painted with a Native American and geometric designs in red and green, unmarked, 7-1/4" x 9-1/2" ....**$600-$800**

▼Cremo rare corseted vase decorated with squeezebag floral design on a shaded red, yellow, blue, and green ground, unmarked, 9-3/4" x 3"........... **$6,500-$8,500**

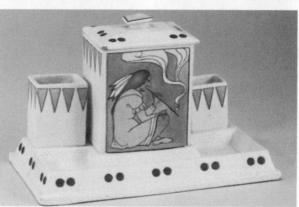

Pink Cremona flaring vase with two buttressed handles, 362-12" unmarked, 12" x 6"....**$300-$400**

Crystalis ring-handle vase in an Egypto shape (E 58) with a mottled salmon and gold glaze, with "Rozane Ware/Egypto" wafer, 14-7/8" h. ....**$1,500-$1,800**

Pair of Dahlrose candlesticks, soft mold, 1069-3". ....$200-$300/pair

Pair of Dawn pink bookends, impressed mark, 5-1/4" x 4-1/4" x 4-1/2". ....$450-$550/pair

▲ Decorated Matt jardinière, in gray-blue with geometric design along rim in cream, yellow, and brown, unmarked, 6-1/4" h. .... $1,500-$1,800
▶ Donatello bulbous vase with two long, angular handles, a rare Donatello form, unmarked, 10-1/4". ....$250-$400

Della Robbia teapot excised with stylized tulips and hearts in a two-tone green glaze, incised E Dutrow/medallion mark, 4-1/2" x 9". **$2,000-$3,000**

Egypto Aladdin lamp, Rozane seal, 4-1/2". .... **$450-$650**

Dogwood I tall vase on squat base, unmarked, 15-3/4" x 6-1/2". ....$350-$500

CERAMICS

Fine and large Earlam two-handled vase, unmarked, 15-1/2" x 9-1/4"............................. **$1,750-$2,500**

Borden Milk Company three-piece child's breakfast set commemorating Elsie the Cow and Beauregard the Bull, consisting of a plate (7-1/2" d), bowl (5-1/2" d) and mug (2-1/2" d), all covered in a glossy pumpkin glaze, raised marks................... **$750-$850**

Blue Falline vase with ribbed base and tapered neck, 652-9", unmarked............................ **$1,750-$2,250**

Red Ferella flaring two-handled vase, 501-6", unmarked, 6-1/4" x 4-1/2". ....**$600-$900**

Brown Florentine jardinière, unmarked, 9" x 12". ....**$100-$200**

Green Freesia bookends, #15, both marked, 5" each. ....**$125-$225**

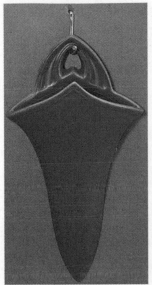

Florane I brown wall pocket, Rv ink stamp, in a style also found in Rosecraft-Color, 9-1/2". $90-$110

Green Foxglove jardinière and pedestal set, 659-8", raised mark. .... **$750-$1,250**

Blue Fuchsia floor vase, 905-18", impressed mark....... **$750-$1,000**

Futura hanging basket, 344-6", with leaves in polychrome on an orange ground, unmarked, 6-1/4" x 9-1/2". .... **$400-$600**

Brown Hexagon vase, Rv ink mark, 4-1/2" x 6-1/2"..........**$250-$400**

Pair of brown Gardenia bookends, #659, both marked.....**$150-$250**

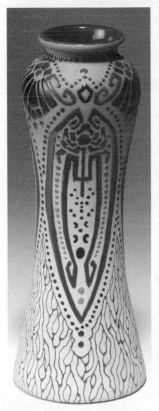

Fudji corseted vase decorated in squeezebag with stylized crab-like design, Rozane seal, 10-3/4". .... **$1,500-$2,500**

Fudjiyama gourd-shaped vase decorated with brown blossoms and green leaves, ink mark, 11-1/2"............... **$1,500-$2,000**

CERAMICS

Home Art three-footed jardinière painted with tulips on a teal and ivory ground, unmarked, rare, 10" x 12". ....**$325-$375**

Imperial I basket, unmarked, 10-1/4" x 6"..............**$150-$250**

Fine Imperial II flaring vase covered in a curdled green over orange glaze, 476-8", unmarked..**$3,000-$4,000**

▲Old Ivory jardinière with leafy and floral motif, 503, impressed mark, 7-3/4" h. ....**$350-$450**

◄Blue Iris jardinière and pedestal set, 647-8", impressed mark. ....**$650-$950**

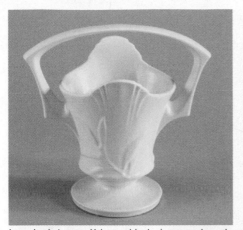

Ivory basket on a Velmoss blank, impressed mark, 9"..**$75-$150**

Two Ivory Tint wall pockets, one with floral designs, the other with medallions and scrolled designs, unmarked, 14-1/4" each..... **$150-$250 and $200-$300**

Ixia green vase, 064-12", some peppering to body, impressed mark and remnant of foil label to body. ....**$110-$140**

Jonquil large bulbous vase, this example has a very crisp mold, unmarked, 12-1/4". ....**$600-$900**

La Rose wall pocket, 1233-7", Rv ink stamp. ....**$400-$450**

Landscape teapot, creamer, and sugar set with transfer seascapes in blue. ....**$300-$350**

▶Green Laurel flaring vase, unmarked, 8" x 7". ....**$350-$500**

Lombardy wall pocket covered in a blue-gray glossy glaze, unmarked, 9" h. ....**$250-$300**

Lotus tapering vase, L3-10", covered in a glossy sky blue and beige trial glaze, raised mark and glaze codes to bottom..........**$800-$900**

Orange Lustre vase, foil label, 16"...........................**$350-$550**

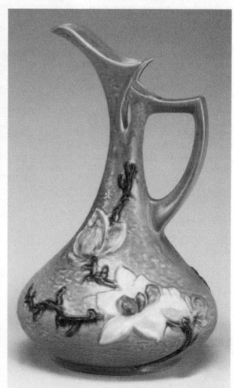

Blue Magnolia ewer, 15-15", raised mark....**$150-$250**

◄ Green Luffa 10" jardinière and pedestal set, unmarked. .... **$1,000-$1,500**

Matt Color jardinière covered in an unusual cobalt glaze, unmarked, 9".......**$350-$500**

Mara vase, K-22, with contrasting scroll design on a glossy raspberry glaze, faint impressed mark, 8-1/2" h. ....**$500-$600**

Mayfair basket in glossy brown with tan interior, 1012-10", raised mark, 8-1/2" x 10" ....**$150-$175**

Matt Green footed jardinière with spade-shaped buttresses and checkerboard pattern, unmarked, 10-1/4" x 12-1/2"......**$600-$800**

Ming Tree blue vase, 510-14", raised mark...............**$150-$200**

Pink Mock Orange flaring vase, 985-12", raised mark. ....**$200-$300**

CERAMICS

Blue Moderne triple candlestick, #1112, impressed mark, 6".
......................................**$100-$200**

Mongol vase in a Mara shape, K-22, Rozane Ware wafer, 8" h.
......................................**$550-$650**

Brown Montacello flaring vase covered in an exceptional mottled glaze, 565-10", unmarked.
...............................**$950-$1,350**

Green Morning Glory bowl, unmarked, 5" x 11-1/2".
....**$350-$450**

Mostique large planter, unmarked, 10"....**$200-$300**

Pink Moss vase, 784-10", impressed mark..**$300-$400**

Normandy umbrella stand, blue ink stamp, 20" x 10"...**$375-$425**

Olympic pitcher, "Ulysses at the Table of Circe," signed and titled, 7" x 8-1/2"............ **$2,000-$3,000**

Red Orian footed bowl, unmarked, 5" x 13". ....**$150-$250**

Green Panel ovoid vase, Rv ink mark, 10-1/2". ....**$750-$1,250**

Fine and large Pauleo vase covered in a mottled olive, red, and ochre, and brown glaze, unmarked, 24" x 13-1/2".. **$6,000-$8,000**

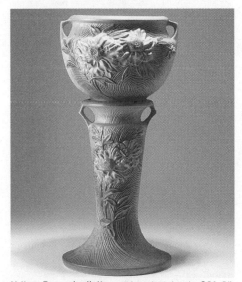

Yellow Peony jardinière and pedestal set, 661-8", raised mark...**$450-$650**

Persian jardinière decorated with orange berries and green leaves, unmarked, 5" x 6-1/2".......**$350-$500**

Large and rare brown Pine Cone urn, 912-15", impressed mark.................................... **$1,500-$2,500**

Green Pine Cone pitcher, 415-9", raised mark.
....**$300-$400**

A pair of Poppy vases, 868-7", one pink and one green, both marked........................ **$125-$200 each**

Blue Pine Cone ewer, 851-15", impressed mark.
....**$750-$1,250**

▶Pink Primrose sand jar, 772, impressed mark, 14" x 10". ....**$450-$650**

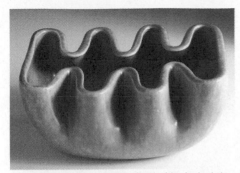

Rare Raymor Modern Artware bowl with pinched rim, covered in ochre glaze, 29-11", marked. .**$650-$950**

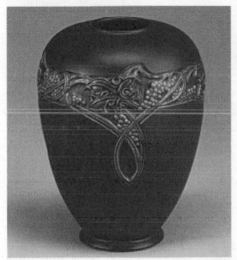

Three Rosecraft Color wall pockets in purple, green, and blue, unmarked, 9-3/4". .... **$150-$300 each**

Rosecraft Vintage bulbous vase, a very nice example of this form, Rv ink mark, 10-1/2" x 7". ...**$450-$650**

Royal Capri scalloped bowl, 526-7", raised mark. ....**$175-$200**

Two Rozane 1917 pieces: green jardinière and ivory vase, Rozane stamp mark to one; jardinière: 9" h..**$150-$200/pair**

Brown Rozane Pattern flower frog, #44, in a glossy glaze, marked, 7-1/2"......................**$100-$200**

CERAMICS

Tall Rozane ewer painted by Adams with ears of corn, Rozane seal, 15-1/2" x 7". .....**$400-$600**

Fine Rozane Royal Light bulbous bud vase painted by W. M. with pink and lavender pansies, unmarked, 4-3/4" x 3-3/4". ....**$600-$800**

Silhouette red vase decorated with a nude in the forest, 787-10", raised mark. ....**$400-$600**

Russco spherical vase with a fine dark green to yellow crystalline glaze, unmarked, 6-1/2" x 7-1/2". ....**$300-$400**

Savona yellow covered vessel, black paper label, 4" x 8". ....**$750-$950**

Blue Snowberry floor vase, IV-18", raised mark. ....**$300-$500**

Sunflower umbrella stand, crisply decorated, strong color, unmarked, 20-1/4" x 11-1/2". .... **$3,000-$5,000**

Teasel sea foam bulbous vase, 889-15", impressed mark. ....**$500-$600**

Blue Thorn Apple vase, 324-16", Impressed mark.........**$450-$650**

Sylvan jardinière decorated with hunting dogs, with olive-green glossy glazed interior, unmarked, 10" x 12-1/2"... **$1,500-$1,600**

Blue Topeo vase with flaring rim, unmarked, 10-1/2" x 6". ....**$550-$750**

Tourist wall pocket, unmarked........**$15,000-$20,000**

CERAMICS

Tourmaline ribbed flaring vase, unmarked, 10"..........**$300-$500**

Pink Tuscany four-sided vase, unmarked, 7-1/4" x 3-1/2"..................................**$100-$200**

Early Velmoss vase embossed with leaves under a green-brown glaze, unmarked, 7-3/4".......**$450-$650**

Rare blue Velmoss II flaring vase with twisted leaves forming two handles, 119-10", unmarked, 10-1/2" x 6-1/4".. **$850-$1,150**

Velmoss Scroll jardinière, unmarked, 9" x 10-1/2".
....**$200-$300**

Venetian ovenware bowl in blue glaze, came with wire handle and wooden grip, impressed mark "Venetian Fireproof," 10-3/4" x 5-1/8". ....**$200-$250**

Victorian Art Pottery blue bulbous vase, unmarked, 6-1/2" x 6-1/2" ....$300-$500

Rare Vista basket, unmarked, 10-1/2".....$600-$800

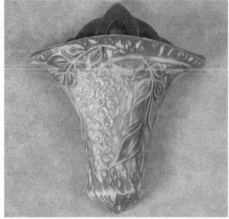

Brown Wisteria wall pocket, unmarked, 8-1/4". ....$700-$1,000

▶Rare blue Windsor basket with curved handle, paper label, 5" x 6-1/2". ....$1,250-$1,750

Brown Water Lily ewer, 12-15", raised mark...............$300-$400

Pink White Rose floor vase, 994-18", raised mark. ....$300-$400

Tall blue Wincraft vase, 2V-15", raised mark................$250-$350

R.S. Prussia

Bob Welter has collected R.S. Prussia for 12 years, but his admiration for the porcelain china made by the Schlegelmilch family before 1917 dates back to his formative years, when he dished potato salad from a beautifully decorated bowl given to his grandparents as a wedding present in 1907.

In 2010, he discovered he had purchased a rare R.S. Prussia picture frame at a Woody Auction in August 2009. Welter said he bought the unmarked 8-inch by 10-inch frame thinking it was French, probably Limoges, even though Woody had listed it in his catalog as possibly being R.S. Prussia.

A photo of the frame in the auction catalog had Bob Welter thinking it was Limoges, but a hands-on inspection confirmed it was R.S. Prussia. **$225**

"I just thought it was so pretty that it would be something my wife would enjoy," said Welter, who asked auctioneer Jason Woody to hold it until they met up at the national convention in July.

"As soon as I saw it I said, 'Ooh!' and ran to our author in residence, Lee Marple, and said, 'Is it possible?' He looked at it and said, 'Oh, yes. That's R.S. Prussia.' I thought, 'A home run!'" said Welter.

Auctioneer Woody said he thought the unmarked frame was R.S. Prussia right from the start.

"R.S. Prussia collectors can tell by the style, the mold shape, the colors and decoration. Persons familiar with R.S. Prussia can identify it," said Woody.

Welter said that he thought Marple recognized the transfer decoration on the frame. Welter also suggested the frame was left unmarked because it was intended for the German market.

"Everybody knew who they were; they didn't need to mark it," said Welter.

Making the buy all the sweeter, the final auction price ended at only $225.

"I always ask the auctioneers what they think something will go for in their market. Woody said he thought it would go for $400 to $600. I bid (absentee) $750 and got it for $225," said Welter, adding, "It all depends on who's there and what they think."

Tom Hoepf

R.S. Prussia & Related Marks

A selection of various R.S. Prussia marks.

Icicle mold chocolate pot with six matching cups and saucers, all decorated in a swan scene.......... **$3,750**

This pink and white rose decorated urn with gold trim and opal jewels **$500**

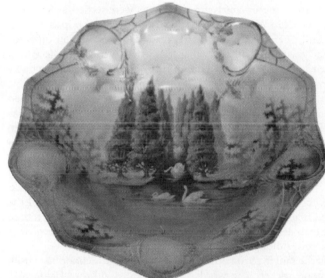

R.S. Prussia embossed bowl with swan and landscape design, 10-3/4 inches in diameter. .. **$300**

Group of four porcelain serving pieces, including an R.S. Prussia hand-painted, two-handled pastry tray in "Poppies" decor, 1904-1908; a smaller R.S. Prussia fruit bowl, also in "Poppies" decor; a German polychromed and parcel-gilt porcelain berry bowl in the R.S. Prussia style; and an Altrohlau richly decorated porcelain berry bowl in "Peonies" decor, 1884-1909; the R. S. Prussia and Altrohlau examples all signed; the largest diameter is 11-3/8 inches. **$70**

CERAMICS

Schoop (Hedi) Art Creations —————————

By far one of the most talented artists working in California in the 1940s and 1950s was Hedi Schoop. She designed and modeled almost every piece in her line. She began her business in 1940 in Hollywood, California. Barker Brothers department store in Los

Hedi Schoop
HOLLYWOOD CAL.

Angeles discovered Schoop's work which encouraged her to open the small Hollywood studio. Shortly after a move to larger quarters, financed by her mother, Hedi began calling her business Hedi Schoop Art Creations. It would remain under that name throughout Schoop's career which was ended when a fire destroyed the operation in 1958. At that time, Hedi decided to free-lance for other companies (see: Cleminson Clay). Probably one of the most imitated artists of the time, other people began businesses using Schoop's designs and techniques. Hedi Schoop decided to sue in court and the results were settled in Schoop's favor. Among those imitators were Kim Ward, and Ynez and Yona. Hedi Schoop saw forms differently than other artists and, therefore, was able to create with ease and in different media. While Hedi made shapely women with skirts that flared out to create bowls as well as women with arms over their heads holding planters, she also produced charming bulky looking women with thick arms and legs. When TV lamps became popular, Hedi was able to easily add her talents to creating those designs with roosters, tragedy and comedy joined together in an Art Deco fashion, and elegant women in various poses. A variety of marks were used by Schoop including her signature (incised or stamped) which also, on occasion, shows "Hollywood, Cal." or "California," and there was also a sticker used but such pieces are hard to find.

Hedi Schoop left Germany in 1930, then immigrated to Hollywood, California, in 1933. She began producing ceramics of her own designs in 1940. Schoop turned out as many as 30,000 pieces per year once her production was running smoothly. A fire destroyed the pottery in 1958, and Hedi did freelance work for several California companies. She retired from working full-time in the early 1960s, but her talents would not let her quit completely. She died in 1996 and had painted, although sparingly, until then.

There were a variety of marks ranging from the stamped or incised Schoop signature to the hard-to-find Hedi Schoop sticker. The words "Hollywood, Cal." or "California" can also be found in conjunction with the Hedi Schoop name. You can find items with a production number, artists' names or initials.

Schoop was imitated by many artists, especially some decorators who opened businesses of their own after working with Schoop. Mac and Yona Lippen owned Yona Ceramics, and Katherine Schueftan owned Kim Ward Studio. They used many of Schoop's designs and today have their own following among collectors. There were others, but Schueftan lost a lawsuit Hedi had brought against her in 1942 for design infringements. It is important to buy pieces marked "Hedi Schoop" or buy from a reputable dealer if you want to be sure you have the real thing.

Considering the number of products created, it would be easy to assume that Schoop pieces are plentiful. This would be an erroneous assumption. Collectors will indeed be fortunate to find any Schoop figurines for less than $100, and to amass many of her products takes dedication and determination.

Ashtray, in the shape of a butterfly w/spread wings, yellow w/ gold trim & "eyes" on wings, inkstamp overglaze, 5 1/2" w.
.... **$66**

Console set: "Young China Musicians," Chinese boy & Chinese girl w/rectangular planter; planter 11" l., girl 10 1/4" h., boy 10 3/4" h., the set **$300-350**

Figures, "Lantern Girls," squatting Chinese girls each holding a stick suspending a lantern, accompanying figures for the "Young China Musicians" console set, in red, 8 1/2" h., each............................. **$100-125**

Figural group, cowboy & woman dancing, bisque faces & hands, cowboy wears hat & kerchief, woman wears black top & ruffled yellow full-length skirt, cowboy has one hand around woman's waist, woman holds skirt out w/one hand, incised unglazed mark "Hedi Schoop, California," 11" h. **$400**

Figure of Chinese woman, standing on a round black base, white floor-length skirt, black, white & green blouse w/long sleeves flaring at wrists, a white flower in black hair above each ear, right fingers bent to hold a pot w/black cloth handle & in same colors as blouse, right leg bent at knee, woman 9" h., pot 2 1/2" h., 2 pcs................................**$215**

▲Figure of woman, in 19th-c. mint-green off-the-shoulder dress decorated w/h.p. pink flowers on bodice & skirt, light hair w/gold hair bow & curls cascading down one side, holds parasol in one hand, other hand holds skirt, ink-stamp underglaze "Hedi Schoop, Hollywood, Cal.," 13" h.......**$258**

▶Figure of woman, standing on one foot & holding large basket above her head w/both hands, dressed in yellow top & full yellow skirt w/blue & green stripes, on yellow oval base, incised overglaze "Hedi Schoop Design, California U.S.A.," 14" h.......**$395**

Figures, Oriental couple each holding a basket, black & gold shirts & white pants, woman 11 1/2" h., man 12 1/2" h., pr. **$275-300**

CERAMICS

Figure of girl, standing on cobalt blue-glazed round base, legs slightly apart, arms stretched out to sides, hands folded to hold jump rope, rough textured black hair w/pigtails out to sides & held in place w/ cobalt blue glossy ties, light blue long sleeved shirt, cobalt blue overblouse w/straps, rough textured cobalt blue short skirt & socks, inkstamp on unglazed bottom, "Hedi Schoop Hollywood, Cal.," 8 1/2" h. **$240**

Figural group, cowboy & woman dancing, bisque faces & hands, cowboy wears hat & kerchief, woman wears black top & ruffled yellow full-length skirt, cowboy has one hand around woman's waist, woman holds skirt out w/one hand, incised unglazed mark "Hedi Schoop, California," 11" h. **$400**

Jardiniere, cylindrical, incised stylized design of a kneeling Chinese woman w/Ming trees & animals, base & design in gold glaze on a light green body, 7" h. **$148**

Planter, model of a horse, rough textured mane & tail, white glossy glazed body w/mint green face accents, saddle, bows in assorted areas & scalloped edging at the base, inkstamp mark "Hedi Schoop," 7 1/2" h. **$126**

Vase, 9" h. at highest point, 4 1/2" h., at lowest point, 9" l., seashell-form, footed oval base, fluted edge rising from the low end to the higher end, dark green base w/dark green & gold fading to light green, rim trimmed in gold, transparent textured glossy glaze, marked w/a silver label w/red block letters, "Hedi Schoop Hollywood, Calif." on two lines **$110**

Flower holder, figure of kneeling woman, short light textured hair, white dirndl-type dress w/blue trim & h.p. flowers on skirt, one hand holds apron out for holding flowers, on light blue oval base, inkstamp underglaze "Hedi Schoop, Hollywood, Cal.," 8 1/2" h. **$125**

Flower holder, figure of woman w/long light hair & a wide picture-style hat, dressed in ruffled teal off-the-shoulder long-sleeved full-length dress & teal picture hat w/scalloped rim, hands clasped in front holding matching basket, all w/applied pink flowers, inkstamp underglaze "Hedi Schoop, Hollywood, Cal.," 11" h. **$245**

Tray, figural, divided w/irregular leaf-shaped raised edges, the rim mounted w/the figure of a cherub on her knees, arms outstretched beside her, head tilted, beige & gold tray interior, beige w/pink-tinged cherub, gold wings, rose on left wrist, belt of roses around her waist w/rose-glazed bowl exterior & rose hair, bottom of tray also in a glossy rose, incised "Hedi Schoop," 11 1/2" l., overall 6" h. **$268**

Spatterware

This ceramic ware takes its name from the "spattered" decoration, in various colors, generally used to trim pieces handpainted with rustic center designs of flowers, birds, houses, etc. Popular in the early 19th century, most was imported from England.

Related wares, called "stick spatter," had freehand designs applied with pieces of cut sponge attached to sticks, hence the name. Examples date from the 19th and early 20th century and were produced in England, Europe and America.

Some early spatter-decorated wares were marked by the manufacturers, but not many. Twentieth century reproductions are also sometimes marked, including those produced by Boleslaw Cybis.

Teapot, cov., Thistle patt., a flared base tapering to a wide bulbous ovoid body tapering to a cylindrical neck w/flat rim, serpentine spout & C-form handle, low domed cover w/button finial, bright yellow spatter ground centered by a large red & green thistle design, end of spout damaged, English-made, ca. 1830, 7" h. **$4,140**

Tea set: child's size, two cov. teapots, two cov. sugar bowls, two creamers, four handleless cups & one saucer; Peafowl patt., teapots & sugars w/footed squatly bulbous bodies w/flaring necks & inset domed covers w/pointed knob finials, each piece decorated w/a green spatter center band decorated w/a yellow, red & blue peafowl, similar designs w/slightly varying colors, England, ca. 1830, some damage & repair, teapots 4 1/4" h., the set (ILLUS. of part) **$1,610**

Tea set: child's, cov. teapot, cov. sugar bowl, two handleless cups & saucers; Fort patt., the teapot & sugar w/footed squatty bulbous bodies w/wide tapering paneled shoulders supporting domed covers w/button finials, teapot w/serpentine spout & C- scroll handle, sugar w/rolled tab handles, each piece w/a blue spatter ground centered by a painted fort building in black & brown w/green trees, England, ca. 1830, spout & rim flake on teapot, hairline on base of sugar, one cup w/repaired rim, teapot 4 3/8" h., the set **$825**

CERAMICS

■ Spongeware

Spongeware's designs were spattered, sponged or daubed on in colors, sometimes with a piece of cloth. Blue on white was the most common type, but mottled tans, browns and greens on yellowware were also popular. Spongeware generally has an overall pattern with a coarser look than Spatterware, to which it is loosely related. These wares were extensively produced in England and America well into the 20th century.

Bowl, 8 3/4" d., 3 1/2" h., three bands of blue on white sponging alternating w/two narrow white bands, minor surface wear, late 19th - early 20th c. **$88**

Butter crock, wide flat-bottomed cylindrical form, overall dark blue sponging on white w/the printed word "Butter," excellent condition, 6 1/2" d., 4 1/4" h. **$143**

◀Canister, cov., cylindrical w/molded rim & inset flat cover, light blue fine overall sponging on cream, very tight hairline through bottom, stack mark on cover, late 19th - early 20th c., 7" h. **$303**

Chamber pot, miniature, cream w/overall light blue sponging, ca. 1900, 1 1/2" h............................**$88**

Chamber set: washbowl & pitcher, round soap dish, shaving mug & master waste jar w/cover; cream background w/overall coarse blue sponging, minor losses to pitcher, late 19th - early 20th c., pitcher 10" h., the set....................**$546**

Charger, round dished form w/overall dark blue sponging on white, minor wear, late 19th c., 10 1/8" d. **$173**

Creamer, bulbous wide body tapering to a wide cylindrical neck w/wide spout & loop handle w/pointed thumb rest, the lower body molded in relief w/a scene of a heron holding a snake in its beak in a garden setting, dark blue overall sponging on white, late 19th - early 20th c., 5 1/2" h. **$495**

Pitcher, 6 1/2" h., cylindrical body w/molded rim & pointed rim spout, pointed scroll loop handle, overall dark blue sponging on white, minor interior stains, late 19th - early 20th c. **$201**

Harvest jug, beehive-shaped w/high arched handle across the top above the short angled shoulder spout & round raised back shoulder opening, overall heavy blue sponging on white w/the incised & blue-tinted name "A. Noland," long U-shaped glued crack on the back, rare, ca. 1860, 13" h. **$688**

▶Pitcher, 9 1/2" h., bulbous ovoid body tapering to a cylindrical neck, pinched spout & long C-form handle, overall medium blue sponging on white, marked on the base by the Uhl Pottery Co., Huntingburg, Indiana, early 20th c., excellent condition **$303**

CERAMICS

Pitcher, 9" h., tall slightly tapering cylindrical body w/a molded rim w/pointed spout, C-form long handle, overall bold blue sponging on white, minor crazing in glaze, late 19th - early 20th c. **$303**

Pitcher, 9" h., cylindrical body w/a flat rim & large pointed spout, small C-form handle, overall coarse banded blue sponging on white, early 20th c............. **$403**

Pitcher, 9" h., cylindrical body w/ flat rim & pointed spout, squared loop handle, overall fine medium blue sponging on white, flake on base, early 20th c.............. **$288**

Pitcher, 9" h., slightly tapering cylindrical body w/pointed rim spout & small C-form handle, dark overall navy blue on white wavy design, hairline from rim near handle, late 19th - early 20th c. **$176**

Pitcher, 9" h., slightly tapering cylindrical body w/pointed rim spout & small C-form handle, overall blue on white "chicken wire" design, tight T-shaped hairline in bottom rim up into the sides, late 19th - early 20th c. **$165**

Pitcher, 9" h., swelled bottom below the cylindrical body w/a pointed rim spout & angled loop handle, overall blue sponging on white, minor glaze flake at spout, late 19th - early 20th c. **$303**

Pitcher, 9" h., paneled cylindrical form w/rim spout & C-form handle, all over scattered large blue dot sponging on white, professional restoration to a large chip at spout & a couple of interior glaze flakes at rim, overall glaze crazing, late 19th - early 20th c. (ILLUS. second from left with three larger sponged pitchers)... **$143**

◀Pitcher, 9" h., cylindrical w/rim spout & C-form handle, medium blue repeating wavy vertical bands of sponging on white, interior rim flake near spout... **$275**

Salt & pepper shaker, one-piece, ovoid body divided into two halves w/two short spouts w/metal caps, overall blue & brown sponging on white, some small cap dents, excellent condition, early 20th c., 3" h. . **$154**

Whimsey, model of a standing pig, white Bristol glaze w/scattered blue spots, some surface chipping, ca. 1990, 5" l... **$303**

Toothbrush vase, footed baluster-form, wide dark blue on white sponged bands alternating w/two narrow white bands, excellent condition, late 19th - early 20th c., 5" h.. **$440**

Syrup jug, advertising-type, bulbous beehive-shaped w/short rim spout & wire bail handle w/black turned wood grip, overall blue sponging w/lower oval reserve stenciled "Grandmother's Maple Syrup of 50 Years Ago," relief-molded vine design around top half, bottom molded in relief "Mfg'd by N. Weeks - Style XXX Pat. Pending - Akron, O.," surface chips on spout, late 19th - early 20th c., 5 1/4" h. **$495**

Washbowl & pitcher, bulbous ovoid pitcher tapering to a wide flaring neck, C-scroll handle, matching bowl w/rolled rim, the pitcher w/overall coarse blue sponging on white w/a wide band in blue & white around the bottom, sponged rim & base bands on the bowl flank the wide blue & white bands, attributed to Red Wing, Minnesota, early 20th c., minor hairline & glaze flake on pitcher, pitcher 12" h. **$633**

CERAMICS

■ Stoneware

Stoneware is essentially a vitreous pottery, impervious to water even in its unglazed state, that has been produced by potteries all over the world for centuries. Utilitarian wares such as crocks, jugs, churns and the like were the most common productions in the numerous potteries that sprang into existence in the United States during the 19th century. These items were often enhanced by the application of a cobalt blue oxide decoration. In addition to the coarse, primarily salt-glazed stonewares, there are other categories of stoneware known by such special names as basalt, jasper and others.

Crock, bulbous ovoid body w/a wide slightly flared mouth flanked by eared handles, large brushed cobalt blue tulip design below the impressed mark of C. Hart & Co., Ogdensburg, New York, & impressed number, some glaze spider cracks & crazing on back, ca. 1855, 2 gal., 10" h. **$220**

Jug, cylindrical body tapering to a small molded mouth & strap handle, cobalt blue slip-quilled long parrot perched on a vertical leafy sprig below the impressed mark "F.B. Norton and Co. - Worcester, Mass. - 2," excellent condition, ca. 1870, 2 gal., 13 1/2" h. **$1,485**

Jug, cylindrical body w/rounded shoulder tapering to a molded mouth, applied strap handle, unusual bold slip-quilled cobalt blue four-petal starburst w/arrows & dots design, impressed mark of Cortland, New York, minor glaze wear, surface chip on back base, ca. 1860, 1 gal., 11" h. **$578**

Jug, flat-bottomed beehive shape w/small mouth & strap handle, advertising-type w/brushed cobalt blue inscription reading "R.H. Gilgallon - Scranton - Pa" & "2," made by Co-operative Pottery Co., Lyons, New York, cinnamon clay color in the making & some staining from use, ca. 1890, 2 gal., 12 1/2" h. **$275**

Model of a dog, seated begging spaniel in cream w/dark bluish green applied accents under the Bristol glaze, probably from Ohio, possibly early 20th c., minor surface wear, 5 1/2" h. **$495**

Water cooler, disk foot supporting tapering urn-form body w/loop shoulder handles, incised birds trimmed in cobalt blue, mark of the Somerset Potters Works, Massachusetts, kiln burn on front, glued crack on front, in-the-making chip out of bung hole frame, ca. 1870, 3 gal., 15" h. **$3,960**

Wedgwood

Reference here is to the famous pottery established by Josiah Wedgwood in 1759 in England. Numerous types of wares have been produced through the years to the present.

WEDGWOOD

BASALT

Ewer, Classical urn-form body on a square foot & ringed & reeded pedestal, the body w/a fluted lower body & narrow molded band below large molded grapevine swags, the angled shoulder w/a cylindrical neck & high arched spout w/the figure of a crouching satyr reaching around the base of the spout to grasp the horns of a goat mask below the spout, the loop handle issuing from the shoulders of the satyr, 19th c., 15 1/2" h............. **$863**

Figure of a nude male, standing w/legs crossed & playing a flute, leaning against a tall tree trunk w/his cloak pinned at one shoulder & draping down around the stump, 19th c., 17 1/4" h.......... **$920**

MISCELLANEOUS

Boston cup, Fairyland Lustre, a low cylindrical footring supporting the wide rounded bowl, the exterior decorated w/the Leaping Elves patt., yellowish brown upper sides decorated w/fairing w/transparent gold wing frolicking on a green & blue ground w/mushroom, the upper section sprinkled w/printed gold stars, the interior decorated w/the Elves on a Branch patt. w/ two small elves perched on a prickly branch w/black bat & bird around the leafy rim, base w/the Portland Vase mark & "ZXXXX," 5 1/4" d......................... **$1,725**

Bowl, 10 3/4" d., 4 3/4" h., Fairyland Lustre, a narrow footring supports the deep rounded sides, exterior Poplar Tree patt. decorated w/a fanciful landscape of stylized trees against a midnight blue lustre ground, interior decorated w/the Woodland Elves V, Woodland Bridge patt., some minor scratches on the interior... **$5,175**

CERAMICS

Bowl, 8 1/2" d., 4" h., Fairyland Lustre, Woodland Elves VI patt., a narrow footring supports the octagonal bowl, the exterior w/a continuous design of tree trunks in dark bluish green & all the elves in brown on a flame lustre background of orange over crimson, the interior w/the Ship & Mermaid patt. w/a flame lustre center, Pattern No. Z5360 .... **$7,475**

Bowl, 11" d., Fairyland Lustre, wide rounded shape, the interior decorated w/the Garden of Paradise (Variation I) patt. w/daylight lustre, the arch in the design is missing but the black pillars remain against a mother-of-pearl sky, two different idol figures appear in violet & the dancing beetle faces the opposite way, the green "Cake" tree w/a companion tree w/a curvaceious black trunk & copper brown foliage, the exterior w/the Flight of Birds patt. printed in gold outline on a very dark green & blue lustre ground encircling the sides, the under rim & foot decorated w/ gold pebble & grass border, signed on the base, Pattern No. Z4968 (ILLUS. of interior).............. **$4,600**

Bowl, 8" w., Fairyland Lustre, footed octagonal form, the exterior in the Woodland Elves VI patt., the Fiddler in Tree against a midnight blue lustre background, the interior decorated w/the Ship & Mermaid patt. against a white lustre ground, some minor scratches to interior bottom... **$4,600**

Bowl, 8" w., Fairyland Lustre, footed deep octagonal shape decorated in the Willow patt., the exterior in Coral & Bronze decorated w/a printed gold Willow Ware style decoration, the interior w/a Willow patt. in the bottom & a blue leafy band around the rim, Portland Vase mark & "Z5406".................... **$3,450**

Bowl, 9 3/8" w., 4 1/2" h., Fairyland Lustre, footed octagonal shape, Fairy in a Cage patt., the exterior w/ each side w/a lacy gold border enclosing a landscape scene, the interior decorated w/fantastic creatures in an exotic landscape, No. Z5125 .... **$3,450**

◄Bowl, miniature, 2 1/4" w., Lustre Ware, footed octagonal shape, the exterior w/a mottled orange lustre glaze decorated w/various gold mythological beasts between gold rim & base bands, the dark blue mottled interior decorated w/a stylized spider **$260**

Jar, cov., Fairyland Lustre, malfrey pot Shape No. 2312, bulbous ovoid body fitted w/a domed cover, the exterior includes various patterns including Demon Tree, Roc Bird, Bat in the Demon Tree, Black Toad & Dwarf, Red Monkeys & the Scorpion w/a long yellow tail & spines, a narrow dragon bead border around the base & rim of the collar, inside of collar decorated in the Pan-Fei border, the cover decorated w/Owls of Wisdom w/purple bodies & bright copper-colored faces, blue eyes & red pupils, the cover w/a Red Fei border band & the Scorpion, cover also w/a Pan-Fei border around the inside surrounding Elves on a branch in the center, Pattern No. Z-4968, very light wear to gold cover trim, 14" h..............**$57,500**

Plates, 11" d., Lustre decoration, octagonal w/eight alternating panels of gold geometric designs alternating w/panels showing Oriental men, the figures in gold against a dark blue lustre ground, Portland Vase mark & retailer mark for William H. Plummer & Co., New York, set of 12...**$900**

Punch bowl, Fairyland Lustre, wide flaring foot supporting the wide deep rounded bowl, exterior decorated w/the Lahore patt. featuring swags of brilliant colors & hanging lanterns, the interior decorated w/ three elephants, two of which have riders, a camel, a war horse w/lancer & a flying goose in the center, all figures in black mother-of-pearl outlined in gold against a yellow lustre ground, Pattern Z5266, 11" d., 5 5/8" h..**$8,625**

Vase, 17" h., Fairyland Lustre, footed squatty bulbed base band below the tall slightly flaring cylindrical body, decorated w/daylight lustre background w/crimson & violet Imps crossing a red bridge w/a light yellow top against green bushes, the sky in reddish pink & the river in deep blue w/a yellow canoe, the bubbles boy & bat are black & the Roc bird is vermilion, the base band w/a blue lustre background w/green flaming wheel border, the treehouse above the bridge w/a green roof w/yellow, red & black walls, signed on the base & numbered "Z4968" **$43,125**

Vase, 11" h., Fairyland Lustre, Serpent Tree patt., a flaring base tapering to a tall cylindrical body w/a flaring rim, the abstract tree & landscape design in bright colors against a flame lustre sky, base signed, Pattern No. Z4968..**$7,475**

CERAMICS

Weller Pottery

Weller Pottery was made from 1872 to 1945 at a pottery established originally by Samuel A. Weller at Fultonham, Ohio and moved in 1882 to Zanesville, Ohio.

Mr. Weller's famous pottery slugged it out with several other important Zanesville potteries for decades. Cross-town rivals such as Roseville, Owens, La Moro, and McCoy were all serious fish in a fairly small and well-stocked lake. While Mr. Weller occasionally landed some solid body punches with many of his better art lines, the prevailing thought was that his later production ware just wasn't up to snuff.

Samuel Weller was a notorious copier and, it is said, a bit of a scallywag. He paid designers such as William Long to bring their famous discoveries to Zanesville. He then attempted to steal their secrets, and, when successful, renaming them and making them his own.

After World War I, when the cost of materials became less expensive than the cost of labor, many companies, including the famous Rookwood Pottery, increased their output of less expensive production ware. Weller Pottery followed along in the trend of production ware by introducing scores of interesting and unique lines, the likes of which have never been created anywhere else, before or since.

In addition to a number of noteworthy production lines, Weller continued in the creation of hand-painted ware long after Roseville abandoned them. Some of the more interesting Hudson pieces, for example, are post-World War I pieces. Even later lines, such as Bonito, were hand painted and often signed by important artists such as Hester Pillsbury. The closer you look at Weller's output after 1920, the more obvious the fact that it was the only Zanesville company still producing both quality art ware and quality production ware.

For more information on Weller pottery, see *Warman's Weller Pottery Identification and Price Guide* by Denise Rago and David Rago.

◀Ewer, Aurelian, ruffled rim, painted by T.J. Wheatley with nasturtium, 10". ....**$500-$700**

MARKS

An important factor collectors should familiarize themselves with is the markings found on Weller pottery. There are many different markings found on pieces and here are some examples.

Incised script mark.

Impressed WELLER mark.

Ink stamp mark.

Incised script mark on a Patra vase.

Incised script mark on a star vase.

Rhead Faience incised mark.

One of several black stamp marks used by Weller.

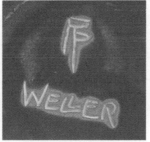

Another variation of the incised Rhead Faience mark.

This is an example of the etched marking found on Clewell's metal-covered pieces; this particular piece was produced using a Weller blank.

Impressed numerals found on several of their forms.

A very rare raised mark, found on a Stellar vase.

Occasionally a piece will be found with a sequence of numbers in crayon or pencil.

EARLY ART WARE

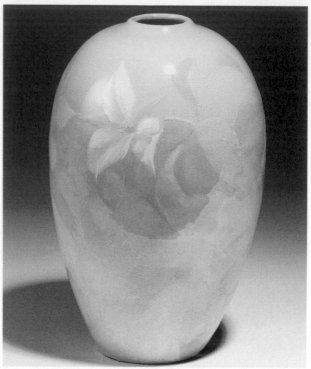

Vase, Auroro-type, very finely decorated in unusual colors, 9-1/4". ....**$3,000-$4,000**

Vase, Aurelian, tall ovoid, finely painted by R. G. Turner with a full-figure portrait of a monk, incised mark and artist's signature, 19" x 6-3/4". .... **$1,500-$2,000**

Ewer, Dickensware II, decorated with loons along the bank of a river, incised mark with numbers, 9" x 6". ....**$400-$600**

Vase, Dickensware I, bulbous, beautifully decorated by Frank Ferrell with chrysanthemums in polychrome, impressed mark and signed Ferrell, 7" x 6-1/2" ....**$1,500-$2,500**

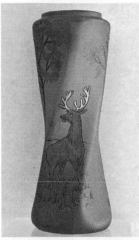

Vase, Dickensware II, decorated with a deer near trees, impressed Dickensware mark, 11-1/4" x 4-1/4"................. **$1,250-$1,750**

Vase, Dresden, tall cylindrical, painted by Levi Burgess with a panoramic Delft scene, signed LJB, stamped Weller Matt, 16" x 4-1/2"....................... **$500-$750**

Vase, Eocean, tall, cylindrical, beautifully painted by Eugene Roberts with pink and ivory thistle, incised mark, 20-1/2" x 5-3/4". .... **$2,500-$3,000**

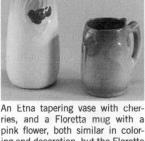

An Etna tapering vase with cherries, and a Floretta mug with a pink flower, both similar in coloring and decoration, but the Floretta has a hint of brown in the shaded background; both bear impressed marks; the vase is 9-1/2" and the mug is 5-1/4". ...... **$50-$100 each**

Jardinière, Etched Floral or Modeled Etched Matt, by Frank Ferrell with sunflowers in burnt orange on ivory over celadon ground, artist's signature, 10" x 13-1/2". .... **$450-$650**

Vase, Fru Russet, bulbous, exceptionally decorated by Pickens with pink lilies on a heavily curdled pale green ground, 13"..**$3,000-$4,000**

Vase, Fudzi, ovoid, leaves and berries around the rim, impressed numbers, 10-1/2". **$1,500-$2,000**

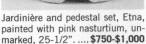

Jardinière and pedestal set, Etna, painted with pink nasturtium, unmarked, 25-1/2". .... **$750-$1,000**

CERAMICS

Floor vase or umbrella stand, Greenaways, incised S. A. Weller, 22"..................... **$1,500-$2,500**

Vase, Rhead Faience, ovoid, blue with birds, signed Weller Faience with numbers, 11"...**$3,000-$5,000**

Vase, Hunter, rare, slightly flared, incised with seagulls flying over waves, marked with impressed numbers, 7-1/4" x 3". **$600-$900**

Hair receiver, Jap Birdimal, closed-in rim, painted by Hattie Ross with Viking ships, artist's initials, 2" x 4"..............**$450-$650**

Vase, L'Art Nouveau, shell-shaped, painted with maidens and flowers, impressed mark, 10" x 8-3/4". ....**$500-$700**

Fine cabinet jug, Louwelsa, painted with small yellow blossoms, overlaid with silver, impressed mark, 3-3/4" x 2-3/4"......**$1,000-$1,500**

Vase, Louwelsa, red, painted with pink teasel in pink, ivory, and purple on a red ground, unmarked, 10-1/2" x 4"........ **$1,500-$2,000**

Ewer, Matt Floretta, incised with pears on a branch, incised mark, 10-1/2" x 4-1/2"........**$250-$350**

Vase, Matt Green, corseted with reticulated rim and embossed poppy decoration, unmarked, 12-1/4" x 6-1/2".. **$1,500-$2,500**

Vase, Perfecto, ovoid, very finely painted by Albert Haubrech with chrysanthemums, on a matt green ground, unmarked, 14-1/2" x 4-1/2"................. **$2,000-$3,000**

Jardinière, Turada, massive with banded floral decoration in orange and ivory on an olive ground, impressed Turada 217 mark, 17" x 18"..................... **$1,000-$1,500**

Floor vase, Sicard, fine and large, extensively decorated with flowers and leaves, signed on body and dated 1902, 25" x 13". .... **$5,000-$7,500**

◄Vase, Weller Matt Ware, two-handled with swirled design, incised Matt Ware mark, 8-3/4" x 7". ....**$400-$600**

CERAMICS

MIDDLE PERIOD TO LATE ART WARE AND COMMERCIAL WARE

Batter jug, Ansonia, covered in a mottled green and yellow glaze, signed Weller in script, 10" x 8". ....**$100-$200**

Large Ardsley flaring bowl and Kingfisher flower frog, stamped mark, 9-1/2" x 16" diameter. Both are fine examples of these forms. ....**$650-$950**

Vase, Athens, with mythological medallions, 9-3/4" x 6", unmarked. ....**$750-$1,000**

Planter or bowl, Baldin, blue, unmarked, 4-1/4" x 8"...........**$200-$300**

Vase, Atlas, flaring, in blue and ivory, script mark, 6" x 9-1/4". ....**$150-$250**

►Umbrella stand, Baldin, brown, unmarked. ....**$1,000-$1,750**

Vase, Barcelona, large baluster, stamped Barcelona Weller, Barcelonaware paper label, 11". ....**$300-$400**

Umbrella stand, Bedford Matt, covered in the standard matt green glaze, unmarked, 20" h. ....**$600-$900**

Vase, Blo' Red, ovoid, covered in a bright orange mottled glaze, 9" x 4"................................**$200-$300**

Jardinière and pedestal set, Blue Drapery, unmarked, 29" overall. ....**$600-$900**

Pair of tall candlesticks, Besline, decorated with berries and leaves, unmarked, 11" h each. ....**$250-$350/pair**

Vase, White and Decorated Hudson, classically shaped, with branches of pink and ivory roses, impressed mark, 13" x 6 1/2" ....**$600-$800**

▶Vase, Blue and Decorated, faceted, painted with a bluebird and cherry blossoms, impressed mark, 11-1/2" x 5"........ **$1,000-$1,500**

◀Vase, Blue Ware, large, has maidens dancing and playing instruments, stamped mark, 12" x 6-1/2".......................**$300-$400**

CERAMICS

Wall pocket, Bonito, unmarked, 10-1/2" x 6" .... **$450-$650**

Pair of colorful parakeets on a branch, Brighton, 9". **$950-$1,450**

Vase, Bronze Ware, tall, curdled reddish bronze glaze, unmarked, 13" .... **$600-$800**

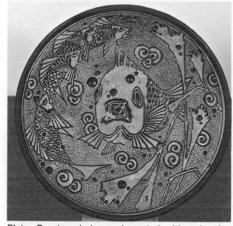

Plate, Burntwood, large, decorated with swimming fish, unmarked, 12" diameter. .... **$450-$650**

Jardinière, Clinton Ivory, rare, with squirrels, birds, and owls in trees, unmarked, 7" x 8". ..... **$400-$600**

Vase, Camelot, corseted, gray-green and white, un-marked, 11-1/2". .... **$1,750-$2,750**

Two Cameo pieces: one blue and one orange, both marked in script, 7-1/2" and 5-1/4". .... **$75-$150 and $50-$75**

Umbrella stand, Cameo Jewell, impressed mark, 22-1/2". .... **$1,000-$2,000**

Vase, Chase, bulbous, marked in script, 8" x 5". ....**$300-$400**

Vase, Chengtu, faceted, stamped mark, 9-1/4" x 4". ......**$200-$300**

Vase, Cloudburst, ovoid, in brown, orange, and ivory, unmarked, 10-1/2" x 4". ....**$300-$400**

Figure, dancing frogs, Coppertone, extremely rare, 16-1/2". .... **$7,000-$9,000**

Basket, Copra, painted with daisies, impressed mark, 10" x 7-1/2". ....**$250-$350**

Vase, Cornish, blue, corseted, marked in script, 7-1/4" x 4-1/4". ....**$100-$200**

Tobacco jar, Creamware, lidded, embossed with pipes and flowers, unmarked, 7-1/2" x 5-1/2". ....**$250-$350**

Vase, Cretone, black, bulbous, with flowers and animals in ivory, signed Hester Pillsbury and incised mark, 7". ....**$700-$900**

Bowl, Dupont, decorated with birds on a wire between puffy green trees, unmarked, 3-3/4" x 8"...**$75-$150**

Jardinière, Flemish, decorated with colorful birds, leaves, and flowers, unmarked, 10-1/2" x 15".
....**$500-$700**

Wall pocket, Fairfield, impressed mark, 9" x 5".............**$100-$200**

Vase, Elberta, large bulbous, marked in script, 10" x 10".
...................................**$400-$600**

Wall pocket, Florala, conical, unmarked, 9-1/2" x 5"...**$250-$350**

Fish bowl holder, Flemish, shows fishing boy, 12".
....**$750-$1,000**

Vase, Frosted Matt, baluster, with heavily curdled pale lime green over sheer brown glaze, 13-1/2".
....**$1,500-$2,500**

Two Forest high-glaze pieces: a teapot and a pitcher, both covered in glossy glaze, both marked, 6" and 5"................................ **$250-$350 and $200-$300**

Vase, Fruitone, large squat, unmarked, 5-1/2" x 7-1/4"...**$650-$950**

Vase, Geode, ivory, bulbous, painted shooting star design in blue, incised mark, 3-3/4" x 4-1/2". ....**$500-$700**

Vase, Stellar, bulbous, blue, painted by Hester Pillsbury, incised mark and artist's initials, 6" x 6-1/2". ....**$700-$900**

Vase, Glendale, baluster, embossed with birds, flowers, and butterflies, 12"........**$850-$1,250**

Covered jar, Greora, marked in script, 6-1/4" x 5"......**$450-$650**

Vase, Graystone Garden Ware, large, two handles, embossed with a wreath of laurel leaves, stamp mark, 15-1/2" x 13"...**$400-$600**

◄Figure of a woman holding her dress out to her sides, Hobart, impressed mark, 11" x 8". ....**$750-$1,250**

CERAMICS

Vase, Kenova, two-handled, decorated with hanging branches of roses, unmarked, 10".........**$800-$1,200**

Vase, "Hudson on Silvertone," rare and hand-carved, decorated by Dorothy England with a pelican flying beneath branches of cherry blossoms, signed D.E., 12"..**$12,000-$16,000**

Fine planter, Knifewood, carved with bluebirds in an apple tree, unmarked, 6" x 7". ....**$750-$1,250**

Vase, Hudson Perfecto, tall, painted by Claude Leffler with flowers, marked with artist's signature. ....**$600-$800**

Cabinet vase, Lamar, unmarked, 2-1/2" x 2-1/4". ....**$200-$300**

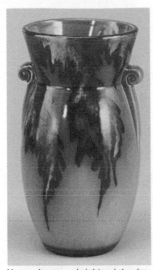

Vase, Juneau, bright pink, impressed mark, 10"......**$150-$250**

Four wall pockets: One Woodrose in pale blue, one basket-shaped Klyro, one tapered Klyro, and one Roma conical, all unmarked, 6-1/2", 5-1/2", 6-3/4", 7"... **$75-$150 each**

Pair of bud vases, LaSa, corseted, unmarked, 7-1/4". **$200-$300 each**

Vase, Marengo, pink, faceted, unmarked, 9-1/2" x 3-1/2". ....**$400-$600**

Vase, Louella, painted with irises, 9-1/2"........................**$150-$250**

Vase, Lustre, unusual gold bulbous, Weller Ware and LP Ball Jeweler and Optometrist labels still intact, 3-3/4" x 4". ..... **$100-$200**

Pillow vase, Malverne, marked in script, 8" x 6"............**$100-$200**

Vase, Manhattan, green with tall leaves, marked in script, 9" x 5". ....**$100-$250**

CERAMICS

Pitcher, Marvo, pink, unmarked, 8" x 8"..**$250-$350**

Fish bowl holder, Muskota, playing cat, impressed mark, 10" x 11"............................. **$1,750-$2,750**

Vase, Neiska, blue bulbous with twisted handles, incised mark. ....**$100-$200**

Wall pocket, Orris, with flowers and trellis pattern, unmarked, 8" x 4-1/2". ....**$100-$200**

Wall pocket, Parian, in pale blues and ivory on a pale gray ground, unmarked, 10-1/2" x 6". ..**$300-$400**

Large and small dachshunds, Novelty, both marked, 5" x 3". .... **$100-$150 and $75-$125**

Form duck planter or bowl, Patricia, covered in an Evergreen glaze, incised mark, 8" x 16".**$150-$250**

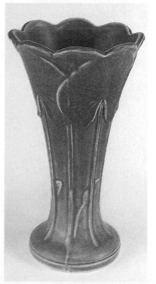

Vessel, Patra, handled, incised mark, 4-3/4" x 6".......**$100-$200**

Pillow vase, Sabrinian, sea horses along the sides, stamped mark, 7" x 7-1/2". ....**$200-$300**

Vase, Pumila, brown, flaring, stamped mark, 10-1/4" x 6". ....**$150-$250**

Planter, Roma, large ovoid with clusters of red roses, unmarked, 5-1/2" x 16". ....**$300-$400**

Vase, Rochelle, bulbous, painted by Hester Pillsbury with blue and yellow flowers, a highly decorated example, incised mark and artist's initials, 6-1/2" x 3-1/4". ....**$700-$900**

Planter, Rosemont, unmarked, 7-1/2" x 9-1/2". ....**$600-$800**

Jardinière, Silvertone, has clusters of hydrangea, stamped mark, 11" x 10-1/2". ....**$600-$900**

Wall pocket, Souevo, conical, unmarked, 12-1/4". ....**$200-$300**

Vase, Turkis, flaring, marked in script and Turkis paper label, 8-3/4" x 6". ....**$100-$200**

Vase, Tutone, rare, green leaf design around the rim, 12-3/4". ....**$500-$800**

Wall pocket, Tivoli, conical, impressed mark, 9-3/4" x 5". ....**$75-$150**

Potpourri jar, Warwick, lidded, 5". ....**$200-$250**

◄Vase or ginger jar, Velva, brown, lidded, marked in script, 11-1/4" x 6". ....**$350-$450**

CERAMICS

Two Wild Rose tall pieces: a bulbous vase and a ewer, in pale orange and green blended glaze, marked in script................................ **$75-$125 each**

Wall hanging, Woodcraft, rare, with branch-shaped pockets, decorated with large pink flowers and applied blue birds nesting in branches, impressed mark, 15" x 13"...................................... **$1,250-$1,750**

Wall pocket, Woodrose, unmarked, 6-3/4" x 3". ....**$75-$120**

Pitcher, Zona, with lightly colored panels of king-fishers and cattails, impressed mark, 8-1/2" x 9". ....**$200-$300**

Lamp base, Xenia, finely decorated with pink flowers on a matt deep green-blue ground, impressed mark, 14-1/4"... **$1,500-$2,000**

Civil War Collectibles

This section covers items of a collectible nature related to the Civil War period of the United States of America. The war began April 12, 1861, at Fort Sumter, the Confederates surrendered at Appomattox Courthouse on April 9, 1865, and all official fighting ceased on May 26, 1865.

All war is tragic and is full of tragedies; however, the American Civil War was especially devastating in the loss of human lives and capital. It nearly destroyed our nation while paving the way for today's society.

Between the beginning and end of the Civil War, the way wars were fought and the tools soldiers used changed irrevocably. When troops first formed battle lines to face each other near Bull Run Creek in Virginia on June 21, 1861, they were dressed in a widely disparate assemblage of uniforms. They carried state-issued, federally supplied, or brought-from-home weapons, some of which dated back to the Revolutionary War, and marched to the orders and rhythms of tactics that had served land forces for at least the previous 100 years. Four short years later, the generals and soldiers had made major leaps in the art of warfare on the North American continent, having developed the repeating rifle, the movement of siege artillery by rail, the extensive employment of trenches and field fortifications, the use ironclad ships for naval combat, the widespread use of portable telegraph units on the battlefield, the draft, the organized use of African-American troops in combat, and even the levying of an income tax to finance the war.

For some Civil War enthusiasts, collecting war relics is the best way to understand the heritage and role of the thousands who served. Collecting mementos and artifacts from the Civil War is not a new hobby. Even before the war ended, people were gathering remembrances. As with any period of warfare, the first collectors were the participants themselves. Soldiers sent home scraps of flags, collected minie-ball shattered logs, purchased privately marketed unit insignias, or obtained a musket or carbine for their own use after the war. Civilians wrote to prominent officers asking for autographs, exchanged photographs ("carte de visites") with soldiers, or kept scrapbooks of items that represented the progress of the conflict.

After the war, the passion for owning a piece of it did not subside. Early collectors gathered representative weapons, collected battlefield-found relics, and created personal or public memorials to the veterans. Simultaneously, surplus sales emerged on a grand scale. Dealers made hundreds of Civil War relics available to the general public.

Following World War II, a new wave of collecting emerged. Reveling in the victories in Japan and in Europe, Americans were charged with a renewed sense of patriotism and heritage. At the same time, newspapers started to track the deaths of the last few veterans of the Civil War. As the nation paid tribute to the few survivors of the Rebellion, it also acknowledged that the 100-year anniversary of the war was fast upon them. In an effort to capture a sense of the heritage, Civil War buffs began collecting in earnest.

Excavated, Leech & Rigdon, Memphis, Tennessee, C.S.-molded officer's cavalry spur. ..... **$1,850-$2,000**
Middle Tennessee Relics

During the Civil War Centennial in the 1960s, thousands of outstanding relics emerged from closets, attics, and chests, while collectors eagerly bought and sold firearms, swords, and uniforms. It was during this time that metal detectors first played a large role in Civil War collecting, as hundreds donned headphones and swept battlefields and campsites, uncovering thousands of spent bullets, buttons, belt plates, and artillery projectiles.

By the 1970s, as this first wave of prominent and easily recognized collectibles disappeared into collections, Civil War buffs discovered carte-de-visites, tintypes, and ambrotypes. Accoutrements reached prices that far outstretched what surplus dealers could have only hoped for just a few years prior. The demand for soldiers' letters and diaries prompted people to open boxes and drawers to rediscover long-forgotten manuscript records of battles and campaigns.

By the end of the twentieth century, collectors who had once provided good homes for the objects began to disperse their collections, and Civil War relics reemerged on the market. It is this era of Civil War relic reemergence in which we currently live. The fabulous collections assembled in the late 1940s and early 1950s are reappearing.

It has become commonplace to have major sales of Civil War artifacts by a few major auction houses, in addition to the private trading, local auctions, and Internet sales of these items. These auction houses handle the majority of significant Civil War items coming to the marketplace.

The majority of these valuable items are in repositories of museums, universities, and colleges, but many items were also traded between private citizens. Items that are being released by museums and from private collections make up the base of items currently being traded and sold to collectors of Civil War material culture. In addition, many family collections amassed over the years have been recently coming to the marketplace as new generations have decided to liquidate some of them.

Civil War items are now acquired by collectors in the same fashion as any material cultural item. Individuals interested in antiques and collectibles find items at farm auction sales, yard sales, estate sales, specialized auctions, private collectors trading or selling items, and the Internet and online auction sales.

Provenance is important in Civil War collectibles—maybe even more important than with most other collectibles. Also, many Civil War items have well-documented provenance as they come from family collections or their authenticity has been previously documented by auction houses, museums, or other experts in the field.

For more information on Civil War memorabilia, see *Warman's Civil War Collectibles Identification and Price Guide*, 3rd edition, by Russell L. Lewis.

Privately purchased McClellan-style saddle attributed to Confederate General A.R. Lawton. The entire seat, pommel, and cantle are covered in black bridal leather. The pommel has a stamped brass shield reading "11 inch seat." .... **$7,500-$9,000**
James D. Julia Auctioneers

Accoutrements

Artillery fuse pouch and belt. Fuse box brightly marked on outside flap "U.S. WATERVLIET ARSE-NAL." This is an unusual box with brown leather surfaces. Box and belt are complete with very good surfaces.. **$862**
James D. Julia Auctioneers

The square-shaped front and lead-finial are two characteristics often associated with Confederate cap boxes.. **$1,250-$1,700**
Middle Tennessee Relics

Extremely rare Bartholomae patent filter canteen, cover and partial strap. Invented and patented by Charles Bartholomae, the tin canteen is about 6" h. x 6" w. and is kidney-shaped in cross section with a wide, funnel-like spout with an applied brass label reading "PATENTED JULY 3rd 1861" and two other lead spouts (one retaining its lead cap and chain). In his patent, Bartholomae described his invention "as a canteen which may be worn with greater facility than those of usual construction, more readily filled and more convenient to drink from, and one supplied with an efficient filtering device, which may be used whenever necessity requires". This example retains its original brown wool cover and part of its narrow brown bridle leather strap. These canteens, mostly private purchase, saw actual use in the field, which accounts for their rarity today. Good condition.
.... **$3,737**
James D. Julia Auctioneers '07

Black leather cartridge box with double tin insert attached to leather shoulder strap with brass eagle breastplate attached by leather thong through metal loops. Cartridge box has double closure flaps with inside flapped implement pocket. A complete cartridge box with sling will sell for................. **$650-$1,100**
Wisconsin Veterans Museum

The square-shaped front and lead-finial are two characteristics often associated with Confederate cap boxes.. **$1,250-$1,700**
Middle Tennessee Relics

Artillery and Accessories

A limber was a two-wheeled carriage used to transport a cannon and its carriage. This U.S. field artillery limber retains 50 percent of its original paint. ....**$6,000-$10,500**
James D. Julia Auctioneers

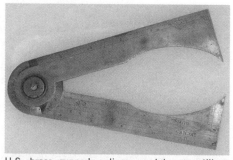

U.S. brass gunner's calipers used by an artilleryman to check the diameter of cannon balls. Marked, "INCHES," "GUNS" and "SHOT.".... **$3,200-$3,500**
James D. Julia Auctioneers

Confederate artillery crate. 16-1/2" x 13-1/2" x 22" wooden crate constructed to contain artillery projectiles, fuses, and primers. Wooden lid is retained by two forged hinges and is secured by chain tie. Stencils on each side of box reads, "JULY xx 1864 / 168 Lbs / 6 24 PDR / HOWT. CASE / FIXED / FUZES & / FRICTION PRIMER". Stencil inside lid reads, "INSPECTED 1864 / LIEUT / H.L. DUNCAN". Box is sound and solid. **$7,475**
James D. Julia Auctioneers

Belt Buckles and Plates

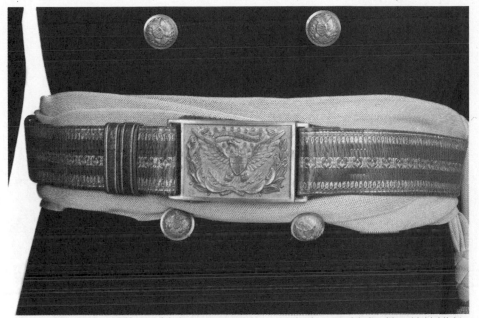

Officer's quality Model 1851 sword belt plate on red Moroccan leather sword belt with gold highlights.
.... **$1,300**

Tommy Haas/Paul Goodwin

C.S. Breckenridge belt plate on brown belt. A scarce, non-excavated plate. Hooks on this buckle appear re-soldered, and one hook appears replaced. Surface of plate exhibits numerous small dents and scratches and old cleaning. Belt is crazed, but sound and solid. **$4,600**

James D. Julia Auctioneers

Oval gilt die-struck rolled brass Maryland buckle with brass stud belt hooks attached with lead .... **$1,500-$2,000**

Cowan's Auctions, Inc.

This officer's-grade sword belt plate was made for troops from Ohio; rare. .... **$2,800-$3,000**

S.E.L.L. Antiques/Paul Goodwin

◾ Projectiles

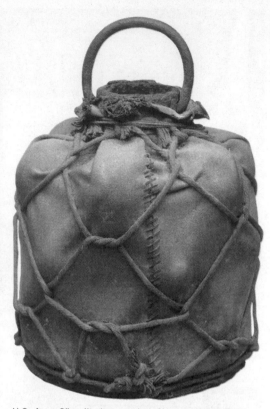

U.S. 6 lb. canister round, unfired and non-excavated, complete with wooden sabot.
....**$2,200-$2,500**

James D. Julia Auctioneers

U.S. Army 9" quilted grape shot. Non-excavated. The canvas covering is in excellent condition. This exact specimen is pictured on page 120 of Jack Bell's book, Civil War Heavy Explosive Ordnance. Near mint museum quality.......**$4,600**

James D. Julia Auctioneers

Confederate 3.8" Schenkl shell with wooden sabot, unfired but excavated. ....
$4,000-$4,600

James D. Julia Auctioneers

U.S. 12 lb. Bormann-fused cannon ball with original wooden sabot, non-excavated. ....**$3,000-$3,350**
James D. Julia Auctioneers

British 6.4" Armstrong bolt, non-excavated. This shell was imported by the Confederates. Written in old lettering on the shell is "CONFEDERATE RIFLE PROJECTILE, NORFOLK NAVY YARD, C.S.A." On the opposite side is "CSA 100," .... **$6,800-$7,350**
James D. Julia Auctioneers

■ Buttons

General Service, Cavalry, cuff-size button........... **$35**
S.E.L.L. Antiques/Paul Goodwin

Solid cast "CSA" coat-sized button with fine patina. This is a difficult button to find in non-dug condition. .... **$800-$1,000**
James D. Julia Auctioneers

Marine Corps cuff-size button made by Horstmann. **$275**
S.E.L.L. Antiques/Paul Goodwin

Excavated, coat-size, Wisconsin state-seal button. .... **$95-$125**
Middle Tennessee Relics

Confederate General Staff coat-size button, marked "S&K Rivet'd & Solder'd." **$1,100**
S.E.L.L. Antiques/Paul Goodwin

Non-dug Louisiana coat-size button marked "Hyde & Goodrich, N.O." **$750**
S.E.L.L. Antiques/Paul Goodwin

Ephemera

Lincoln signature. Authentic signature of "A. LINCOLN MARCH 4, 1864" on a sheet of plain yellow stationery measuring approximately 7" by 9" folded to the approximate size of an envelope. The autograph is accompanied by a copy print of a photograph of Lincoln originally taken by C.G. German of Springfield, Illinois. Near excellent condition..............**$2,012**
James D. Julia Auctioneers

Two autographs by Confederate General J.E.B. Stuart. An envelope addressed to Mrs. J.E.B. Stuart in J.E.B. Stuart's hand. There is an added, clipped autograph from letter placed on envelope to show that the other signature was an in situ autograph. Hinged above the address line is this clip. Envelope has 5¢ Jefferson Davis stamp from 1862 and an imprint, "Headquarters Cavalry Brigade / Army of the Potomac." Attached, clipped autograph has been closely trimmed, removing portion of the "S" in Stuart. Hinge has stained paper. Envelope is soiled with numerous small tears and reductions. Stamp is partially missing. **$2,530**
James D. Julia Auctioneers

Cook & Brother two-dollar bill. On yellow paper, a 6-1/2" x 2-3/4" two-dollar bill issued by Cook & Brother, New Orleans. Note is serial numbered, dated March 15, 1862, and signed "Cook & Brother". Vignettes include two crossed rifles, sailing ship, plow, etc. Note has green overprinted "TWO". **$345**
James D. Julia Auctioneers

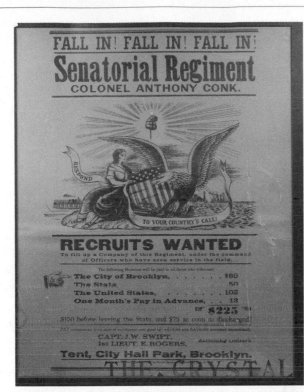

Recruiting broadside for Colonel Anthony Conk's "Senatorial Regiment.".............................$2,200
Tommy Haas/Paul Goodwin

John Hunt Morgan broadside proclamation to the people of Estill County, Kentucky, dated September 22, 1862.. $4,000-$4,200
Cowan's Auctions, Inc.

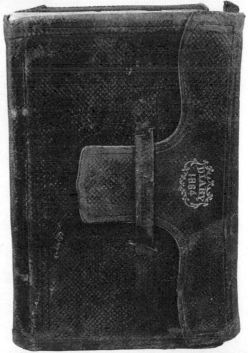

Diary in a small fold-over booklet, 1864, kept by Corporal J.R. Braley, Co. G, 30th Maine Regiment.
.... $1,410
Skinner, Inc.

Flags and Musical Instruments

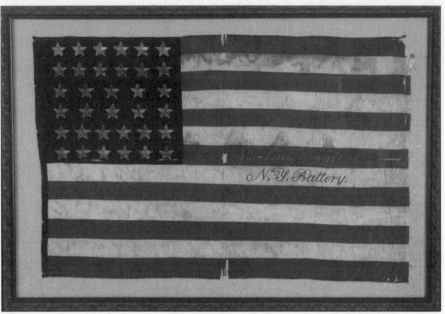

Thirty-four-star (1861-1863), U.S. national color of famous New York Battery that fought at Gettysburg. Tiffany & Co., all silk, U.S. national color of the 4th Independent Battery New York Volunteer Artillery. It is likely that this flag served with the unit during its 1862 and 1863 campaigns. For its age, as a silk flag, this national color is in remarkably good condition, with only minor damage to the fly end due to service wear and a cracking separation starting where the flag was once folded in half. The flag has been professionally framed, and only minor water staining is noticeable in the upper pair and central stripes..**$40,250**
James D. Julia Auctioneers

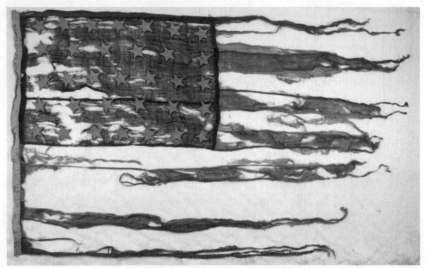

The first American flag captured. "This flag was hauled down by secessionists on January 12, 1861, fully three months before the firing on Fort Sumter, and so far as known was the first United States flag so desecrated in the Great Conflict"—so reads the provenance from the Soldier and Sailors Memorial, where this flag has been since 1912 just being de-accessed in 2007. Much of the stripes are worn and missing; however, the canton is fairly complete with all 33 stars. The hoist is sound. Markings on hoist are very good. Attached pennant is intact with one approx. 2" x 2" hole and several large stains...**$33,350**
James D. Julia Auctioneers

Carrying a regiment's "National colors" was a mark of distinction. The flag served as a rallying point as well as badge of honor for each unit. Each Union infantry regiment carried a National color. In many cases, a regiment's battle honors were recorded on the flag's stripes. **$5,000**
Wisconsin Veterans Museum

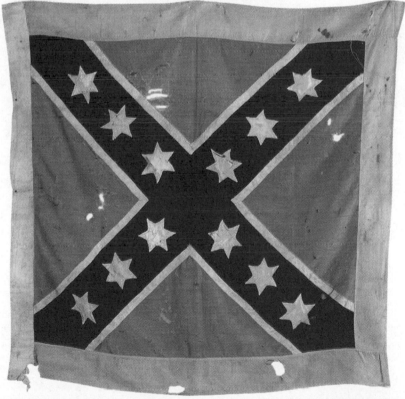

Confederate 1862 contract battle flag of the 4th Tennessee Infantry, made by New Orleans contractor Henry Cassidy and delivered to the Confederate Army of the Mississippi (afterward the Confederate Army of Tennessee).. **$115,000-$125,000**
James D. Julia Auctioneers

Confederate battle flag with alternate coloration of the St. Andrew's cross and stars (orange/red stars on white cross), measuring 28-1/2" high by 37". Although not identified to a specific military unit, oral tradition associates it with South Carolina. ....**$45,000-$57,500**

James D. Julia Auctioneers

Nickel-plated brass E-flat alto horn made by E.G. Wright, a Boston maker of fine instruments. The horn was used by Merrill Sherman, 24th Wisconsin Infantry.............. **$2,950**

Wisconsin Veterans Museum

Above left: Captured Confederate drum. Standard military drum used by both North and South; 16" x 14" with about 2" high red-painted hoops, a natural wood body with a geometric design, a bone vent hole plug, and original tied-on carrying strap. The drum came from a direct descendant of the soldier, who captured this drum and carried it home as a souvenir. There is a 15-line ink inscription on the top head that is no doubt contemporary to the capture of the drum. Because of its bulk, a drum would have been a difficult souvenir for a soldier to obtain, unless he were stationed on a ship such as soldiers fighting at Port Royal, at Hilton Head Island, South Carolina, where other large souvenirs have been known to have been collected. The inscription though worn and weathered, is still mostly discernible as follows: "This drum was found 3 miles from Fort Walker, Hilton Head, S.C. on the 8th of November 1861, by WM. Car.... the Steward of Steamship Manion. The drum was left in that spot by one of the drummers of the Berry Infantry of ... 7th day of ... Georgia on the named month..... after their defeat in the battle for Port Royal. The drummer ... in the hand during his... was on the drum...SECESSION DRUM FROM PORT ROYAL, S.C."..**$20,700**

James D. Julia Auctioneers

Above right: U.S. regulation drum, 15-1/2" tall with 16-1/2" diameter. The painted ribbon reads "__ REG. U.S. INFANTRY." The maker's label inside reads "MANUFACTURED BY HORSTMANN & BROTHERS & CO. MILITARY FURNISHERS. FIFTH & CHERRY STREETS, PHILADELPHIA." ....**$10,000-$13,500**

James D. Julia Auctioneers

Insignia and Medals

Cavalry items seem to be a favorite area among collectors. This pair of sergeant chevrons made of yellow worsted tape sewn to a wool backing sold for **$3,737.50**
James D. Julia Auctioneers

U.S. major's epaulettes, 2nd Cavalry, in japanned tin box. **$2,500**
Tommy Haas/Paul Goodwin

This bullion-embroidered palmetto tree device applied to black velvet measuring 3" x 2" is quite similar to an embroidered Model 1858 hat device. It was found with reunion memorabilia of a South Carolina Confederate veteran. .... **$700-$800**
James D. Julia Auctioneers

An infantry officer was entitled to wear a maroon silk sash under his sword belt. .... **$500-$900**
Tommy Haas/Paul Goodwin

Confederate Southern Cross of Honor was made by Charles Crankshaw of Atlanta in the late 19th century. The United Daughters of the Confederacy gave these medals to any Confederate soldier who was honorably discharged or surrendered with his army or died during the Civil War. These medals were not issued named, and it was up to the soldier to have a jeweler inscribe or scratch his name himself into the name bar. "R. W. Jenkins" inscribed his name quite nicely. R. W. Jenkins appears on the rolls of the 6th and 8th South Carolina Infantry as a sergeant and later lieutenant. Medal is in "as found" condition with pleasant patina on all surfaces. **$805**
James D. Julia Auctioneers

■ Medical Instruments and Equipment

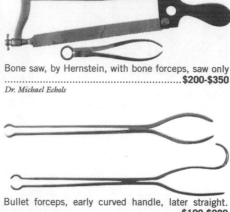

Bone saw, by Hernstein, with bone forceps, saw only
....**$200-$350**
Dr. Michael Echols

Bullet forceps, early curved handle, later straight.
....**$100-$280**
Dr. Michael Echols

Tourniquet, petit brass screw frame, fabric strap,
maker. ....**$200-$270**
Dr. Michael Echols

A Manual of Military Surgery, by Samuel Moore, M.D., Richmond: Ayres & Wade, 1863. With 30 plates and 174 figures, this was the first of only two illustrated military surgical manuals to have been compiled and printed in the Confederacy. During the Civil War, Dr. Moore was the surgeon general of the Confederate States Army Medical Department. **$4,500**
Dr. Michael Echols

Brown leather medical saddle bags owned by Dr. E. Karn M.D., an assistant surgeon in the 93rd Indiana Infantry.. **$750-$1,000**
Cowan's Auctions, Inc.

Prosthetic leg originally worn by soldier injured Feb. 7, 1865 at Hatcher's Run. The soldier had his right leg amputated below the knee at a hospital in Baltimore, Maryland. $1,150
Wisconsin Veterans Museum

Cammann Binaural Stethoscope, unusual for Civil War. ....$300-$600
Dr. Michael Echols

Bone cutting forceps, end cutting, U.S.A. Hosp. Dept....$200-$200
Dr. Michael Echols

Gutta percha irrigation syringe $190
S.E.L.L. Antiques/Paul Goodwin

A Civil War military issue set by Kolbe, Philadelphia, marked "U.S.A., Hosp. Dept." for amputation and major bone surgery. $15,500
Dr. Michael Echols

An outstanding, like-new, three-tier, U.S.A. Hospital Department, major surgical set by Hernstein, New York, 1865. The brass plate is marked for the U.S.A. Hosp. Dept., the large instruments are marked, and there is not one item missing from this extensive Civil War capital surgery set. Most likely it was made at the end of the war, never saw action, and is still in mint condition. **$32,500**
Dr. Michael Echols

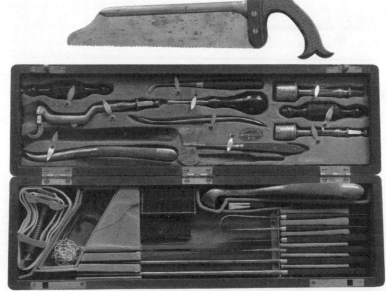

An unusual surgical-dental military set by Wade & Ford, New York, 1861-65. The mahogany case has bilateral military-style sliding latches and contains both dental and surgical instruments. The suspicion is this set was intended for use on naval vessels, as the owner was in the U.S. Navy during the Civil War, but that is not for sure as there is no engraved brass plate on the top of the case. The lid of the case is reinforced with multiple brass screws, which is typical military construction. **$14,000**
Dr. Michael Echols

Personal Items

Soldiers spent far more time in camp passing time than they did marching or fighting. A variety of board games can be a fine representation of one of the ways soldiers passed their hours. This checkerboard belonged to George Stinchfield, a member of Company G, 12th Maine Volunteer Infantry. **$750**
Tommy Haas/Paul Goodwin

Union cards, Standard, American Card Company, 1862, maker's mark on front card, TS inside box, front card also inscribed with "entered according to act of Congress in the year 1862 by Benj. W. Hitchcock in the Clerk's Office for the District Court of the United States for the Southern District of New York", four suits comprised of eagles, shields, stars and flags, court cards comprised of major for jack, goddess of liberty for queen, and colonel for king, original box with elaborate illustration on front and advertisement for first "Genuine American Cards" on back, 52 complete, near mint condition. Hargrave p. 343, Encyclopedia of American Playing Cards W5.
.... **$1,293**
Skinner, Inc.

Blue-painted trunk that belonged to Charles H. Beardsley, 5th New York Artillery. The interior is lined with early hand-colored map of New York and New Jersey. ....**$250-$500**
Cowan's Auctions, Inc.

Patent checkerboard and writing case. H.C. Small of East Lemington, Maine, patented this wooden roll-up checkerboard/writing desk, January 14, 1862, and is so marked. A group of old wooden checkers in a box appears to be similar vintage but did not come with this checkerboard. One small chip on checkerboard, scattered scratches, some loss of red paint. Tarred linen backing is very good. One small 1" x 1/4" area is missing. Copies of original patent drawings are included. **$1,725**
James D. Julia Auctioneers

Gray and black painted trunk decorated with pinstriped borders and starburst on lid panel and "A. Sanders" (Lt. Austin W. Sanders, Co. D, 74th USCT) on front. .... **$1,000-$1,250**
Cowan's Auctions, Inc.

Two-piece carved walnut shaving kit that opens to reveal an old straight razor and a nickel watch fob with pasted-in typed paper label that reads "Shaving box that belonged to General Conrad F. Jackson killed at Fredericksburg December 13, 1862." .....**$300-$350**
Cowan's Auctions, Inc.

Quilt, appliquéd cotton made by Margaret Hazzard, Bainbridge Township, Berrien County, Michigan, 1864.
.... **$82,250**

Skinner, Inc.

Bells in sight musical box by Bremond with American Civil War Tune, No. 24245, playing "Stonewall Jackson, La Fille du Regiment" and six other airs, Gamme No. 518, accompanied by nine optional engine-turned bells with finial strikers, with zither attachment, flat-topped winding lever and tune-sheet, in burl walnut veneered case with tulipwood banding and retailer's transfer of "Alfred Hays, Manufacturer & Importer of Musical Instruments, 4 Royal Exchange Buildings and 82 Cornhill," 23" wide, cylinder 13". The second track is named after the Confederate general of the American Civil War, Thomas Jonathan "Stonewall" Jackson (1824-1863). Its inclusion on a musical box retailed by an English firm, whose program also includes French, German, and Scottish tunes, is unusual, suggesting a special order from an original owner with broad musical tastes. Movement has been recently cleaned and overhauled and plays well. Case has old finish with an attractive mellow patina. Inner glass replaced. **$4,444**

Skinner, Inc.

Photographs and Paintings

Albumen print (probably by Brady) of Major John Buford with his staff officers. .... **$900-$1,100**
Cowan's Auctions, Inc.

Stereoview by Anthony & Co., entitled "Abraham Lincoln, President of United States." Two hand-canceled, two-cent revenue stamps on back....... **$1,500-$1,725**
Cowan's Auctions, Inc.

Quarter-plate ambrotype of an unknown armed artillery soldier, ca. 1860, wearing a red-trimmed frockcoat and M1858 dress hat conforming to Virginia militia regulations of 1858 and carrying a common straight-bladed NCO militia sword worn with a black leather cross-strap. .... **$1,000-$1,500**
Cowan's Auctions, Inc.

Half-plate ambrotype of seven West Point cadets. (General) Ranald Slidell Mackenzie is shown second from the right in the front row. He was born in 1840, graduated at the top of his class at West Point in 1862. He was wounded at Second Manassas, Petersburg, and Cedar Creek. He was made brigadier general after Cedar Creek. Ulysses S. Grant called him the most promising young officer in the Army. During the Indian Wars he was wounded four more times. By the age of 42, his health was so poor he retired. He died in 1889. This is a wonderful ambrotype in excellent condition with good contrast and content........ **$1,265**
James D. Julia Auctioneers

Quarter-plate tintype of an African-American Union soldier uniformed in standard nine-button frock coat and slouch hat. .... **$2,800-$3,300**
Cowan's Auctions, Inc.

A Gettysburg resident, 69 year-old John L. Burns, gained instant fame by picking up "his flint-lock and powder horn" and becoming the only documented civilian to join the battle. After the war, Burns lived off the proceeds of his fame. Though relatively common, signed carte de visites of the citizen soldier are still very desirable. ....**$1,000-$1,200**
Cowan's Auctions, Inc.

Outdoor CDV of three mounted Union cavalry troopers by L.W. McSchooler, Weston, Missouri. Such scenes are extremely rare. ....**$2,000-$2,250**
Cowan's Auctiowns, Inc.

General William Tecumseh Sherman tintype, 3" x 3-3/4". Bust profile of a seated, bearded Sherman in his uniform in a gold foil frame and mounted in a pressed cardboard, hinged case. Generally very good to excellent condition, with an excellent, strong image of Sherman. Case is separated at the hinge and shows wear. **$2,012**
James D. Julia Auctioneers

Outdoor sixth-plate image showing a 6" ordnance rifle with a young cannoneer leaning casually on the barrel. ....**$2,450-$2,700**
Cowan's Auctions, Inc.

The clarity, tinting, and warlike pose of this cavalry trooper with his saber drawn confirm the value of this quarter-plate tintype. **$1,200**
S.E.L.L. Antiques/Paul Goodwin

Large oil portrait of Col. Ezra A Carman, 13th New Jersey Volunteers, in gilt frame........................ **$955**
S.E.L.L. Antiques/Paul Goodwin

Military portrait / Lincoln-signed Congressional resolution to Commander John L. Worden of the *U.S.S. Monitor*. Portrait is oil on board and is a copy of an identical portrait hanging in the U.S. Naval Academy Museum in Annapolis, Maryland, by Philipp Albert Gliemann (1822-1871). This portrait and genre painter was born in Germany in 1822 and died in 1871. The portrait measures 19-3/4" x 24" (slightly smaller than the signed portrait in the Naval Academy Museum), and is unsigned, but obviously from the hand of the same artist. He is depicted in U.S. Navy, regulation uniform of dark blue with brightly highlighted, gold, full dress epaulets on each shoulder, bearing a single star. On his right sleeve is the regulation braid for a rear admiral, being two slightly raised bands on a broad band of gold embroidered lace with a five-pointed gold star above. Cuff of his white shirt is showing. Both of his hands hold the grip and knuckle bow of his elaborate, gold-plated, eagle pommel sword. Frame is of fancy gilded gesso and wood measuring 28" x 32". Portrait is accompanied by Worden's Congressional Resolution, which is a framed, partially printed document on vellum, measuring 15" x 18". Framed oil painting is in very good condition but unrestored. Scratches on Worden's forehead and chipped paint loss on canvas near corners. Light paint flaking at the upper left hand corner and in the lower right hand corner. Painting has darkened with the age of its varnish. No defects affect the subject. Frame is in excellent condition with one broken scroll at the bottom. Partially printed Congressional Resolution is framed and in very good condition with some fading to the ink and signatures. **$40,250**
James D. Julia Auctioneers

■ Pistols and Revolvers ─────────────────────────

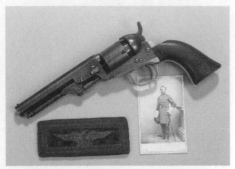

Colt pocket pistol belonging to Civil War Col. Samuel W. Black, c. 1861, the pistol with serial no. 177142, all numbers matching with photo and insignia as well... **$7,050**
Skinner, Inc.

Unmarked .50 caliber percussion pistol with Confederate association. Accompanying the pistol is a note that was found in the barrel that reads, "This pistol was taken from a dead rebel by John Meeker Co. B, 51 Regiment [Pennsylvania Infantry] at the battle of Roanoke Island Presented to B.M. Ganell by J. Meeker.".. **$1,000-$1,725**
James D. Julia Auctioneers

Confederate Augusta Machine Works twelve-stop revolver. Serial number R. Cal. 36. 7-15/16" octagonal barrel. Serial number "R" occurs on most major parts. This is a very rare Confederate revolver with probably no more than 10 examples known of this variety, carried in the Civil War by Turner Fisher who fought in the Civil War under the command of cavalry General, John Hunt Morgan. This gun is accompanied by original Confederate holster and an odd cleaning tool, which descended with gun. Gun is gray/brown overall with scattered dings, gouges, scratches, and pitting... **$37,950**
James D. Julia Auctioneers

Civil War engraved and inscribed Smith & Wesson No. 2 Army revolver. Serial number 14456. Cal. 32 RF. Usual configuration with 6" octagonal barrel with integral rib and German silver front sight and two-piece rosewood grips numbered to this revolver. Frame, cylinder and barrel are engraved in period chiseled foliate arabesque patterns with punch dot background and a wave and dot pattern on each side of barrel. Backstrap is inscribed in period script "Col. John T. Wilder". Both sides of receiver have an engraved lightning bolt representing Col. Wilder's "Lightning Brigade". Col. Wilder joined the Indiana 17th Infantry as a lieutenant colonel on June 4, 1861, and resigned on Oct. 5, 1864, as a brevette brigadier general. He was born Jan. 31, 1830, and died Oct. 20, 1917. Good to very good condition. Metal retains a dark plum/brown patina with blue in some of very sheltered places. Grips are fine. Good mechanics, strong dark bore. **$20,125**
James D. Julia Auctioneers

Left: Colt Model 1849 pocket revolver, .31 caliber, serial number 1798xx, with a hand engraved inscription on the back strap that reads, "F.M. Hewett, 3d S.C. Inf." .... **$3,500-$4,000**
James D. Julia Auctioneers

Right: Colt Navy carried by Captain Thomas Chubb of the Confederate schooner Royal Yacht. Serial number 23167. This Model 1851 Colt Navy was recently found in the state of Vermont, where Chubb died at his summer home in 1886. Chubb's son had a business of manufacturing fishing rods and reels with the Thomas H. Chubb brand, which are highly collectible today. This business was near Chubb's summer home in Post Mills, Vermont. The commemorative inscription on backstrap of gun reads "CAPT T. H. CHUBB, 1861-1865" and "CSN ROYAL YACHT" back of trigger guard. Accompanying this gun is a large folio of history. Mechanically fine, tight with sharp edges in "as found" condition. Gun overall is gray with scattered pitting over 20 or 30%, bright blue on barrel. Cylinder scene is complete but with scattered pitting. Backstrap and trigger guard retain a portion of silver plate. Stocks are very good with original varnish; a small chip is present on inside toe of left stock. **$9,200**
James D. Julia Auctioneers

▨ Uniforms

This dark blue wool forage cap features an embroidered infantry bugle insignia with regiment number "2" in the center. The cap was worn by Col. Lucius Fairchild, 2nd Wisconsin Infantry during the Gettysburg campaign. Because of the association with the famous Iron Brigade, this cap, which would normally sell for around $3,850, is valued at about.... **$22,000**
Wisconsin Veterans Museum

Colonel Lewis Merrill of the 2nd Missouri Cavalry ordered royal blue caps with orange welts from a St. Louis supplier. Being able to identify in what regiment a cap was worn strongly boosts the value. **$14,500**
S.E.L.L. Antiques/Paul Goodwin

U.S. Model 1858 forage cap with original tag that reads "Size #6 U.S. Army TG & Co." Two cards with the cap indicate that it once belonged to a U.S. Commissary Captain John Foley. .... **$4,000-$4,500**
James D. Julia Auctioneers

This is an enlisted cavalry soldier's version of the Model 1858 hat, complete with yellow hat cord and single ostrich plume held in place by a rosette. .... **$8,000-$9,000**
Tommy Haas/Paul Goodwin

Union enlisted man's frock coat worn by Corporal Charles Fisk, 11th Massachusetts Volunteer Infantry
.... **$6,000-8,000**
James D. Julia Auctioneers

South Carolina major's frock coat worn by Robert Jefferson Betsill, 18th South Carolina Volunteer Infantry. It is double breasted with 14 large three-piece U.S. staff officer buttons. The coat suffered major losses, particularly on one side of the breast. Numerous holes in the sleeves, skirts, and back have been professionally conserved and backed with a similar appearing gray wool cloth. Buttons and rank insignia are modern replacements. ....**$20,000-$25,000**
James D. Julia Auctioneers

Confederate artillery officer's butternut shell jacket with eight Louisiana state seal buttons. Jacket has undergone extensive conservation. The body of jacket is totally re-backed and the original lining has been restored. Additionally, the red collar insignia and cuff trim are new. .... **$8,500-$9,200**
James D. Julia Auctioneers

Confederate battle shirt, linen with black silk trim with old tag attached that reads, "Rebel shirt captured at Chattanooga, Sept. 1863." Shirt is handmade from polished cotton with 1/2" Greek key type of silk trim around collar, pocket, and buttons. Shirt fits a bit like a sack, being only retained with three buttons at top. This is a truly rare artifact. This shirt originally sold in a 1985 Ohio auction, where numerous great identified items had been de-accessed from various institutions. Very good condition and sound overall. **$16,100**
James D. Julia Auctioneers

Clocks

The measurement and recording of time has been a vital part of human civilization for thousands of years, and the clock, an instrument that measures and shows time, is one of the oldest human inventions.

Mechanical, weight-driven clocks were first developed and came into use in the Middle Ages. Since the 16th century Western societies have become more concerned with keeping accurate time and developing timekeeping devices that were available to a wider public. By the mid-1600s, spring-driven clocks were keeping much more accurate time using minute and seconds hands. The clock became a common object in most households in the early 19th century.

Anniversary clock, Le Coultre, upright rectangular gilt-bronze footed frame w/glass sides, a large white dial w/Arabic numerals w/ the works visible behind, France, ca. 1955, 9 3/4" h. **$518**

Banjo clock, Grant (William) attribution, Boston, Massachusetts, a round bell mounted at the very top above the round painted dial w/Roman numerals enclosed by a brass bezel & convex glass cover, dial signed by the maker, a tall tapering throat, reverse-painted stylized leaves & scrolls on a white ground & flanked by tall narrow openwork brass brackets above the rectangular pendulum box w/a reverse-painted panel decorated in color w/a rural landscape, eight-day weight-driven alarm movement, imperfections, ca. 1820, 32" h. (ILLUS. second from right with other banjo clocks & the mirror clock).. **$2,468**

Bedside clock, Caldwell (J.E.) & Co., Philadelphia, Art Deco style, an upright square pink quartz block w/beveled edges inset w/a square glass-covered dial w/ Arabic numerals & an eight-day Swiss movement, a rectangular black onyx base w/molded edges, key-wound base, running, 3 x 3" **$748**

Bracket clock, Linden, Germany, mahogany case w/a domed top & metal loop handle, the square glass front w/molding over a dial w/Roman numerals & applied gilded spandrels, stepped bottom molded on flat tab feet, eight-day time & triple chime movement, ca. 1940s, 7 1/2 x 11", 14 1/2" h. **$350**

Bracket clock, Thomas (Seth) Clock Co., Thomaston, Connecticut, walnut case w/a domed top & brass loop handle, brass & enamel dial w/Roman numerals, based on an 18th c. English design, eight-day time & strike movement w/ floating balance, ca. 1950s, 3 3/4 x 7 1/2", 10 1/2" h. . **$180**

Calendar desk clock, DuBois & Fils, Switzerland, tall silver case w/round top dial section w/notched rim & topped by spread-winged eagle finial, a white porcelain time dial w/Arabic numerals framed by a/polychrome scene at top showing a man holding dog & looking toward draped columns, two subsidiary dials for date & days of the week, raised on a flattened waisted support w/a bulbous lower body w/applied flower decoration, all supported by two figural satyrs standing on a rectangular stepped base w/bands of notched decoration & leaf & bead trim, keywind calendar movement, chain fusèe movement w/monometallic balance just visible behind the fancy gilt cock that fits in dial, both dial & movement signed, replaced crystal, ca. 1830, 7" h. .. **$1,960**

Calendar shelf or mantel clock, Ithaca Calendar Clock Co., Ithaca, New York, upright walnut case w/ ebonized trim, the top section w/ an arched & pierced leaf-carved crest above columns flanking the round bezel & paper dial w/Roman numerals, the slightly stepped-out deep lower case enclosing a large glass calendar dial exposing the crystal gridiron pendulum & date roles, molded base, eight-day time & strike movement, second half 19th c., 20 1/4" h. **$3,600**

Crystal regulator, Ansonia Clock Company, New York, New York, ornate upright gilt-bronze case w/the domed top centered by a swag-draped urn above the floral-cast rounded scroll corners, ornate leafy scroll frame enclosing glass sides & front panel below the round dial w/Roman numerals & an open escapement surrounded by a brass bezel, a squared flaring scroll-cast base w/projecting scroll feet, late 19th c., 16 1/2" h. **$1,380**

Crystal regulator, gold-painted cast-spelter upright case w/an arched top w/five flower basket finials, an egg-and-dart cornice over a scroll-cast panel above the long beveled glass door & sides, porcelain dial w/Arabic numerals & decorated w/flower swags, glass tube pendulum, rectangular platform base cast w/a scroll & floret band on flat tab feet, eight-day time & strike movement, early 20th c., 5 3/4 x 8 3/8", 15" h. **$600-650**

◄Cuckoo wall clock, American Cuckoo Clock Co., Philadelphia, Pennsylvania, fumed oak Neo-Gothic Arts & Crafts case, stepped flat top above Gothic arched & flat pilasters flanking the cuckoo door & brass dial w/ Arabic numerals, eight-day weight-driven movement, time & strike, oak pendulum bob in a wheel design, tall obelisk-shaped iron weights, early 20th c., 5 1/4 x 9 1/4", 12 3/4" h. plus chain & weights (ILLUS. disassembled) **$200-250**

Desk clock, clock-inkstand combination, cast-brass, Rococo style, the small clock w/a round dial w/ Roman numerals framed by ornate pierced scrolls in an upright case above a rectangular inkstand w/ ornate scroll trim & fitted w/two inkwells w/domed covers, on small peg feet, 30-hour movement, probably French, late 19th - early 20th c., 6 x 10 1/2", 8 1/8" h. **$180- 200**

Grandfather, Herschede Clock Co. (attributed), Cincinnati, Ohio, the dark mahogany case w/an arched & molded cornice & frieze panel above the tall arched door, the upper arched glass panel over the ornate dial w/silvered metal chapter ring on the gilt face w/ Arabic numerals & a h.p. moon dial w/ship scene, the long lower glass door panel showing the nine tube chimes & cylindrical weights & pendulum, the door flanked by round columns, glass sides, flat molded base, ca. 1910, 88" h. **$2,300**

Above left: Grandfather, Reynolds (John), Hagerstown, Maryland, Federal-style inlaid mahogany case, a broken-scroll pediment w/inlaid rosettes & an inlaid paterae centered by an urn-form finial above a shell-inlaid frieze panel above the arched top door flanked by colonettes & opening to a painted dial w/Roman numerals & a moon phase dial, the body of the case fitted w/a tall narrow door w/small leaf inlays at each corner & a central shell inlay, the stepped-out lower base w/an inlaid square band w/inlaid leaf corners & an oval reserve inlaid w/a spread-winged American eagle, a serpentine apron & short French feet, 1797-1814, restorations to feet & tympanum, 104 1/2" h. **$23,900**

Above right: Grandfather, Phillips & Sons (James), Bristol, England, ornately carved Chippendale Revival mahogany case, the inlaid broken- scroll pediment topped w/ball spiked finials above an arched molded cornice above an arched leaf-carved glazed door flanked by heavy carved corner scrolls, opening to the ornate silvered metal dial w/Arabic numerals & enhanced w/ chased & engraved pierced gilt-bronze surround, a molded flaring molding above the tall waist section w/a tall glazed door w/delicate scrolling & lattice-carved wood overlay & flanked by heavy carved corner scrolls, the door showing the large pendulum & chime tubes, another flaring molding above the bottom section centered by a shell-and-scroll carved raised panel enclosing an inlaid leafy scroll panel surrounding a basket of flowers, carved scrolls at the corners, all resting on a heavy molded base w/stepped flattened block feet, the movement playing bow bells, St. Michael, Westminster & Withington chimes, ca. 1892, 18 1/2 x 29", 111" h. **$37,950**

Novelty shelf or mantel clock, Haddon Clock Co., electric motion clock, "Home Sweet Home," model of a house in plastic & composition, a square large window over the dial on the left, a window on the right w/a scene of an old woman in a rocker, when plugged in woman rocks & fire shimmers, 20th c., 3 1/2 x 12 1/4", 7 3/8" h. **$185**

Shelf or mantel clock, Ansonia Clock Co., Ansonia, Connecticut, black marble temple-style case, thin flat rectangular top above the blocked front w/a central brass bezel around the dial w/Roman numerals, the side panels w/incised scrolls & small inset blocks of tan marble, deep rectangular flat base w/inset tan marble trim, eight-day movement, time & strike, open escapement, ca. 1890, 7 x 17 1/2", 10 1/4" h. **$400-450**

Novelty shelf or mantel clock, Mastercrafter electric motion clock, the brown plastic case designed to resemble an open stage w/railing showing a boy & girl who sit on moving swings, the large round top centering a steel dial w/ Arabic numerals & a sweep seconds hand, ca. 1950s, 5 x 7 1/4", 10 3/4" h........................... **$180**

Shelf or mantel clock, Ansonia Clock Co., Ansonia, Connecticut, simple dark hardwood case w/veneering removed, upright rectangular case w/a two-pane door, the large upper pane over the large faded dial w/Roman numerals & gilt trim above a narrow rectangular glass panel reverse-painted black w/geometric gilt loops, deep molded base, time & strike, second half 19th c., 4 x 8 1/2", 11 3/4" h. **$90**

Shelf or mantel clock, Ansonia Clock Co., New York, New York, "La Charny" model, Royal Bonn china case, the upright arched case molded at the top w/a grotesque mask & scrolls continuing down the sides flanked at each corner by a stylized figure of a seated griffin, the borders in gold & brown shaded to golden yellow & green & decorated w/large red & yellow iris-like flowers, brass door & bezel around the porcelain dial w/Roman numerals, eight-day movement, time & strike, ca. 1900, 5 1/2 x 11 1/4", 11 3/4" h..................... **$700-800**

Shelf or mantel clock, Ansonia Clock Co., Ansonia, Connecticut, "Opera" model cast-metal case, the tapering rectangular base w/sawtooth apron & cast-metal scroll feet supporting a large cast-metal figure of a seated classical woman on an elaborate stool & holding a wreath w/a lyre at the side, the ornate upright cast-metal clock case to one side enclosing a brass bezel around the porcelain face w/Roman numerals, eight-day movement, time & strike, open escapement, minor surface wear, ca. 1885-95, 8 x 21", 16 1/4" h. **$800-1,000**

Shelf or mantel clock, Ansonia Clock Co., Ansonia, Connecticut, ornate Royal Bonn "La Mine" model china case, the tall upright arched case w/waisted sides molded at the top w/a central scroll flanked by long open scrolls w/ further scrolls down the sides & across the base w/incurved scroll feet, painted a deep magenta at the top w/pale yellow in the center shading to dark green at the base, decorated on the front w/large h.p. white & magenta blossoms & green leaves, the large brass bezel around the porcelain dial, Arabic numerals, open escapement, eight-day movement, time & strike, ca. 1900, 6 1/4 x 11", 13 1/2" h. **$1,000-1,200**

Shelf or mantel clock, Ansonia Clock Co., Ansonia, Connecticut, Victorian walnut Renaissance Revival style case w/a high scroll-carved crest centered by a classical head over the arched, molded cornice w/urn-form finials above an arched glass door w/gilt stencil decoration of cupids & ferns, white dial w/Roman numerals, the door flanked by tall narrow angled mirrors backing gilt-metal standing cupid figures, base w/curved, molded sides flanking a front panel w/gilt-metal scroll boss, eight-day movement, time & strike, third-quarter 19th c., 5 1/2 x 16 1/2", 24 1/4" h. **$750-800**

Shelf or mantel clock, Brewster & Ingrahams, Bristol, Connecticut, Kirk's patent movement, beehive form rosewood case w/molded frame & round molding around the round white signed dial w/black Roman numerals, the lower pane reverse-painted w/an image of Ballston Springs, eight-day time & strike rack & snail movement w/ original brass springs, age cracks to dial paint, key escutcheon repaired, pendulum a later Seth Thomas type, hands are old but incorrect for this model, ca. 1845, 19" h. **$560**

Shelf or mantel clock, French Victorian Renaissance Revival-style, gilt-bronze case w/a large swag-draped urn finial on the upright case topped w/ornate scrolls & grape clusters above the round gilt-trimmed enameled dial w/Roman numerals flanked by caryatids, the blocked rectangular base w/leafy scrolls & grapes flanking the case & decorated w/scroll bands & florets, pinwheel movement, third quarter 19th c. **$5,200**

Shelf or mantel clock, figural "Bonapart's Son" model, high stepped ormolu case w/a figure of a seated boy on the top w/his elbow resting on a draped table holding world map & books (one a "Memorial" of Napoleon, the other titled "Code Napoleon"), the table enclosing the round dial w/patterned gilt bezel & black Roman numerals, all on rectangular stepped base w/panels of scroll, floral & shell decoration, notched design & ribbing, waveform feet & corner decorations, engine-turned time & strike movement, dial w/a stress fracture, ca. 1870, 17" h. **$1,232**

Shelf or mantel clock, Forestville Mfg. Co., Bristol, Connecticut, tall upright "column & cornice" case in crotch-grained mahogany veneer, a deep ogee molded blocked cornice over tall half-round columns w/ringed capitals & bases flanking a two- pane door, the upper pane over the polychrome wooden dial w/spandrels, black Roman numerals, open escapement & marked "Forestvill [sic], Manufacturing Co. - Bristol, CT. U.S.A.," the lower pane w/an original Wm. B. Fenn monochromatic silver-colored decoration of a vase w/floral stems, bottom ogee-front block feet flank another glass pane w/an original Wm. B. Fenn monochromatic silver-colored decoration of a bird on limb, good label, hand-colored lithograph of Saturday night scene on backboard, time & strike movement, ca. 1850, 34" h...................... **$1,456**

Shelf or mantel clock, cast spelter, figural case, a large spread-winged eagle atop a rockwork base enclosing a round brass bezel & small dial w/Arabic numerals, Germany, late 19th - early 20th c., 6 x 8 3/4", 13 1/2" h. . **$250-300**

Shelf or mantel clock, Gilbert (Wm. L.) Clock Co., Winsted, Connecticut, walnut "Necho" model, a pointed scroll-carved pediment above scroll-cut & line-incised cornice above the rounded & reeded glazed door w/ornate silver stenciled drapery design over the large dial w/Roman numerals & a brass pendulum w/applied grape leaves, scroll cutouts at the lower sides above the flaring stepped base, eight-day movement, time, strike & alarm, ca. 1890, 5 x 13 1/4", 20 3/4" h. **$300-350**

Shelf or mantel clock, Gilbert (Wm. L.) Clock Co., Winsted, Connecticut, walnut kitchen-style case, Victorian Eastlake design, the sawtooth-cut central cornice flanked by tall corner blocks w/knob finials above reeded sides flanking the tall glazed door w/ornate silver stenciled arches below the dial w/Roman numerals, brass pendulum w/applied grape leaves, molded & blocked base w/line-incised decoration, original varnish, eight-day movement, time & strike, ca. 1885, 4 x 12 1/4", 21 1/4" h. **$450-550**

Shelf or mantel clock, Gilbert (Wm. L.) Clock Co., Winsted, Connecticut, "Acheron" model, walnut case w/fan-carved crest & line-incised scrolls above the arched molded glazed door opening to a dial w/Roman numerals, the lower door w/original silver stenciled leaves, flowers & a checkerboard design, deep flared platform base, paper label inside, late 19th c., 4 1/2 x 13", 19 1/4" h. **$200-250**

Shelf or mantel clock, Gilbert (Wm. L.), Winsted, Connecticut, miniature steeple-type clock, walnut case w/pointed pediment flanked by turned finials above the pointed two-pane glazed door, the upper pane opening to the white metal dial w/Roman numerals & painted spandrels, the lower panel w/a reverse-painted windmill scene, flat base, possibly a salesman's sample, eight-day time & strike movement, mid-19th c., 4 1/2 x 6 1/2", 10 3/4" h. **$250**

Shelf or mantel clock, Jennings Bros. Mfg. Co., Bridgeport, Connecticut, gilt spelter, the tall Art Nouveau design case bulbous at the top & tapering down to a wide serpentine foot, openwork leaves & cherries at the top & down the front w/loop side handles, the round dial w/Arabic numerals, ca. 1900, 4 3/4 x 5 1/4", 12" h. **$200**

Shelf or mantel clock, Kieninger, Germany, skeleton movement in an upright walnut case w/beveled glass front door & back, open ring steel dial w/Roman numerals, brass movement & bell, eight-day movement, 7 3/4 x 10 7/8" d., 16" h, overall **$600**

Shelf or mantel clock, Ingraham Company, Bristol, Connecticut, temple-style, black enamel over wood, the long, high rectangular case w/applied stamped metal columns & cast-metal paw feet, metal lion head mask end handles, top panels on the front inset w/ slag glass framed by metal simulating curtained windows, eight-day movement, time & strike, ca. 1900, 5 1/2 x 20", 10 7/8" h. **$300-400**

Shelf or mantel clock, Lux Clock Mfg. Co., Waterbury, Connecticut, miniature domed celluloid case, dial w/Arabic numerals, flat molded base, early 20th c., 2 1/4 x 6 1/4", 3 1/4" h. **$40**

Shelf or mantel clock, Thomas (Seth) Clock Co., Plymouth, Connecticut, Classical-style ogee rosewood veneer case, the front w/rounded molding around the two-pane long door w/rounded molding, the upper pane over the painted metal dial w/Roman numerals, the lower pane showing the pendulum & works, eight-day movement, time, strike & alarm, face wear, ca. 1880, 4 x 10 3/4", 16 1/2" h. **$200-250**

CLOCKS

Shelf or mantel clock, music box clock, fruit wood case w/domed top w/ring-turned finial & crosshatch & scroll carving w/matching corner finials above the stepped flaring cornice, a large brass bezel around the white dial w/ Arabic numerals & scrolled brass spandrels flanked by ring-turned finials at each corner, flaring stepped base on small bun feet, eight-day movement, Germany, ca. 1930s, 4 1/4 x 7 1/4", 13" h.
.... **$250-300**

Shelf or mantel clock, New Haven Clock Co., New Haven, Connecticut (attributed), Victorian Neo-Gothic style walnut case, a steeply pointed top w/Gothic scroll cutout border & trefoil finial flanked by sunburst side finials on thin blocks over roundels & shaped side panels w/incised scrolls, the tall steeply pointed door w/heavy molding around the glass decorated w/a fancy gilt stencil border band w/Oriental motifs, the dial w/a brass bezel & Roman numerals printed w/patent date "Feb. 11, 1879," brass pendulum w/unique inset compensating needle indicator, deep rectangular platform base w/incised scrolls, original finish, eight- day movement, time & strike, 4 3/4 x 14 5/8", 22 1/4" h.
.... **$350-400**

Shelf or mantel clock, Thomas (Seth) Clock Co., Plymouth, Connecticut, Classical Revival tall case, mahogany veneer, the deep ogee cornice w/blocked corners above a pair of gilt columns flanking the two-pane door, the large upper pane over the worn painted metal dial w/Roman numerals, clear lower pane, the lower section w/ogee corner blocks flanking a panel w/a small round pendulum window, eight-day movement, time & strike, some veneer damage, last quarter 19th c., 4 1/2 x 8 1/2", 16" h.
.... **$225**

Shelf or mantel clock, Thomas (Seth) ogee-case clock, mahogany veneer w/tall two-part door, the upper section over the dial w/Roman numerals, a clear lower pane showing the printed label inside, time-and-strike movement, ca. 1850-70 .... **$175**

Shelf or mantel clock, Thomas (Seth) Clock Co., Plymouth, Connecticut, round-topped rosewood veneer case, the front forms a door w/a molded ring around the dial w/ Roman numerals, eight-day movement, time & strike, ca. 1865, 4 x 8 3/8", 12 1/4" h. **$200**

Shelf or mantel clock, Thomas (Seth) Clock Co., Plymouth, Connecticut, mahogany, the angled domed case top above a conforming glazed door opening to a dial w/Roman numerals above a brass & silvered metal pendulum w/inset brass star, rectangular stepped base, paper label inside, eight-day movement, time & strike, 1850-80, 4 3/4 x 10 3/8", 16" h.
.... **$150**

Shelf or mantel clock, Thomas (Seth) Clock Co., Plymouth, Connecticut, simulated adamantine wood finish on temple-style case, gently arched top w/flat cornice above the blocked case centering a brass-framed glass door over the porcelain dial w/ Arabic numerals, deep platform base on tiny brass knob feet, eight-day movement, time & strike w/Sonora chimes, early 20th c., 7 x 15 1/4", 13 1/2" h. **$700-800**

Shelf or mantel clock, Thomas (Seth) Clock Co., Plymouth, Connecticut, temple-style case, beige marbleized wood w/cast-metal scroll feet & lion heads at each end, flat rectangular top w/a stepped cornice over the blocked center w/an ornate brass bezel & dial flanked by stepped-back side panels w/applied gilt-metal scroll cartouches, a deep molded flat base, eight-day movement, time & strike, ca. 1890, 7 x 16 1/2", 10 3/4" h. **$250-300**

Shelf or mantel clock, Thomas (Seth) Clock Co., Plymouth, Connecticut, Classical-style two-deck decorated mahogany veneer case, the deep ogee blocked top above large gilt-decorated half-round columns flanking the tall two-pane door, the upper pane over the dial w/Roman numerals, the lower pane decorated w/elaborate reverse-painted gilt decor of a scalloped frame enclosing lattice centered by a colored urn of flowers, the deep lower case w/heavy ogee scrolls flanking a small glazed door reverse-painted w/further gilt stencil decoration centering a diamond & bowl of colored flowers, flat base, dated 1863, eight-day movement, time & strike, original finish, 5 1/8 x 18 1/2", 32 1/2". **$1,200-1,500**

Shelf or mantel clock, Waterbury Clock Co., Waterbury, Connecticut, mahogany veneer "steeple" clock, pointed top flanked by turned tapering finials above a pointed two-pane glazed door, the top pane over the dial w/Roman numerals, the replaced pane w/a frosty & etched leafy vine design, half-round columns down the sides, stepped base, one finial replaced, eight-day movement, strike & alarm, ca. 1860-80, 4 3/8 x 11 1/4", 19 1/4" h. **$250-300**

Shelf or mantel clock, Waterbury Clock Co., Waterbury, Connecticut, round-top walnut case, an arched top molding continuing to tapering gilt spear points at the front flanking the tall glazed door w/gilt scroll decoration & opening to the replaced dial face w/Roman numerals, rectangular molded base, eight-day movement, strike & alarm, adjustable mercury pendulum, late 19th c., 4 3/4 x 11 1/4", 17 1/4" h. **$200-300**

Shelf or mantel clock, Welch, Spring & Co., Forestville, Connecticut, Classical Revival rosewood veneer case, the paneled arched top above conforming molding framing a round molding around the dial w/Roman numerals & two roundels over a trapezoidal glass panel showing the pendulum, rectangular base w/ogee border, label inside, ca. 1880, 5 x 11 1/4", 16 1/4" h. **$200-250**

Shelf or mantel, Ansonia Clock Co., New York, New York, gingerbread-style kitchen shelf clock, the stamped oak case w/a high arched & scroll-cut crest molded w/overall ornate scrolling leaf & shell-like design above the arched panel w/tall glazed door opening to a metal dial w/Roman numerals, the lower door decorated w/gilt-stenciled swag design, smaller tapering scroll- stamped wings flanking the lower door, molded flat flaring base, late 19th c., 22" h. **$184**

Shelf or mantel, Atkins Clock Mfg., Bristol, Connecticut, upright stepped rosewood veneer case, a flat top w/blocked front corners above an upper case w/canted corner panels flanking a glazed door over the painted dial w/Roman numerals & gilt- stenciled on black border, a mid-molding w/canted corners stepped out slightly above canted paneled front corners flanking a short, long rectangular mirrored door opening to an iron & brass patent equalizing lever spring thirty-day movement, labeled on the back of the case, ca. 1855-58, 17 3/4" h........ **$3,525**

Shelf or mantel, Art Deco-style, walnut & rosewood veneer, the long gently arched case w/fine veneered designs centering a domed glass round door w/brass bezel opening to a yellow chapter ring w/silvered Arabic numerals, ca. 1920s, 18 1/2" l. **$81**

▶Shelf or mantel, Birge & Fuller, Bristol, Connecticut, Gothic Revival double-steeple style mahogany veneer case, the pointed upper case w/pointed corner steeple finials above the pointed two-part glazed door, the upper panel showing the painted dial w/Roman numerals & an open escapement, the short lower panel reverse-painted w/a green border surrounding a silver, white & red diamond design, the stepped-out lower case w/two pointed corner steeple finials above a case w/a long low rectangular glazed door reverse-painted w/a blue border around a design w/a large oval in white on grey reverse-painted w/stylized red & white blossoms & leaves, flat base, thirty-hour movement marked "J. Ives Patent Accelerating Lever Spring Movement," ca. 1845, 24 1/4" h. **$3,290**

Shelf or mantel, Classical-style, mahogany veneer & stenciled case, the arched crestrail w/a gilt-stenciled basket of flowers on black flanked by mahogany corner blocks, the tall case w/half-round turned columns in black w/gilt stenciled designs flanking the tall two-part glazed door, the upper glass panel showing the floral-painted white dial w/Roman numerals, the taller lower panel w/a reverse-painted gilt-stenciled black border around the reverse-painted bust portrait of General Lafayette, probably produced about the time of his death in 1831, missing weights & pendulum, minor damage to case, unmarked, 33" h. **$1,115**

Shelf or mantel, commemorative-type, the flat upright bronzed-metal case front w/scrolled sides topped by a wreath enclosing a bust portrait of Admiral Dewey, hero of the 1898 Spanish-American War, "Dewey - Manila" cast below the bust & above the round dial w/a brass bezel & Arabic numerals, the lower case cast w/cannon, weapons & an American shield, non-working, ca. 1898, 9 1/2" h. **$348**

Below left: Wall clock, Atkins Clock Co., Bristol, Connecticut, rosewood veneer cottage-style, arched paneled top over a conforming door w/two glass panes, upper pane over the original painted dial w/Roman numerals, lower pane w/original gilt-stenciled rose & wreath decor, interior label coming loose, 30-hour movement, time & alarm, ca. 1865, 10 1/4" h. **$252**

Swinging arm clock, bronzed white metal, a round plinth base supporting a tall cast-metal figure of a Classical maiden painted in natural colors, one arm to her chin, the other raised to support the swinging clock movement composed of a large gilt-metal ball mounted w/ Arabic numerals & enclosing the clock movement & attached to the swinging open bar pendulum w/a heavy ball base drop, late 19th c., 28" h. **$1,064**

Wall clock, Black Forest-type, ornate carved walnut case w/a large carved crest of a spread-winged eagle attacking a mountain goat, the wide sides of the rounded case finely carved w/evergreen trees & roots entwining around the round black glass dial w/white Roman numerals, two further carved goats at the bottom of the case, eight-day movement, Germany, late 19th - early 20th c., dial possibly replaced, overall 47" h. **$3,600**

CLOCKS

Wall clock, Bourgis-Chevalier, Billom, France, brass, the top case front composed of a large rectangular stamped brass plate topped by scrolls w/fruits & flowers around the sides & bottom all enclosing a large white enameled dial w/Roman numerals & signed by the maker, a long openwork wire pendulum w/a large brass lyre-topped pendulum bob, 19th c., 13" w., 54 3/4" h. **$805**

Wall clock, Mauthe Clock Co., Germany, Berliner style, walnut & softwood case, a cast-metal spread-winged eagle finial atop the high stepped pediment w/shell carving flanked by corner blocks w/urn-turned finials over the stepped flat cornice above boldly ring-and-baluster-turned half-columns flanking the dial panel w/leaf carvings in each corner around the wide brass bezel enclosing the celluloid chapter ring w/Arabic numerals centered by an embossed brass Art Nouveau floral center disk, turned drop finials at the front base corners backed by a large, long scroll-cut board behind the free-hanging ornate floral-stamped pendulum bob, eighth-hour time & strike movement w/hour & half hour gong strike, ca. 1895-1910, 15" w., 36" h. **$1,200-1,500**

Wall clock, Junghans, Germany, mahogany-finished hardwood box-style, arched pediment w/applied brass classical wreath & swags above top corner blocks w/similar brass trim flanking the two-pane glass front, the top pane over the celluloid dial w/Arabic numerals, the lower long pane w/slender brass wire overlay showing the pendulum & large brass bob, half-round base apron w/applied brass wreath, eight-day time & strike movement, ca. 1920, 12" w., 33" h. **$900-1,000**

Wall clock, Kroeber (Frederick J.) Clock Co., New York, New York, Model No. 46, Victorian Neo-Gothic style walnut case, the pointed pediment w/blossom finial flanked by matching corner finials above shaped sides w/applied half-round bobbins flanking the rounded tall glass door opening to the dial w/Roman numerals & pendulum w/large brass bob, deep base drop w/Gothic-style curved bracket trim, eight-day movement, time & strike, original finish, ca. 1890, 4 3/4 x 9 1/2", 33 1/2" h. **$800-1,000**

Wall clock, Sessions Clock Co., Bristol, Connecticut, miniature "Aztec" model Mission Oak case, a square molded frame enclosing the square wood dial face w/applied brass Arabic numerals, the free-hanging pendulum w/brass bob backed by a lattice framework, eight-day time & strike movement, ca. 1915-20, 10" w., 19" h. **$500-600**

Wall clock, novelty movement, hand-carved landscape w/a waterwheel & stream, trees & an onion-dome church w/the clock dial set in the tower, framed, eight-day seven-jewel movement, string on reverse runs from waterwheel to clock & is wound by turning the wheel, Germany, ca. 1950s, 15 x 31" **$300**

Wall clock, Waterbury Clock Co., Waterbury, Connecticut, Classical Revival style rosewood veneer case, the flat stepped cornice over an ogee panel flanked by end blocks above half-round maple columns w/gilt capitals & bases flanking the two-pane door, the large upper pane over the painted tin face w/Roman numerals & green-stenciled leaves, the lower door pane reverse- painted w/a bluebird in a gilt ring surrounded by flowers on a tan ground, deep blocked ogee base, open escapement, paper label inside, ca. 1890, 4 3/8 x 14 3/4", 24 3/4" h. **$600-700**

Wall clock, Waterbury Clock Co., Waterbury, Connecticut, short-drop salesman's sample, stained softwood, dial w/Arabic numerals, eight-day movement, time-only, ca. 1920, 4 3/8 x 8", 12 1/2" h. **$200-300**

Above right: Wall clock, Waterbury Clock Co., Waterbury, Connecticut, "Galesburg" model, long oak case, the molded arched crest centered by a block w/turned urn finial flanked by turned corner finials, short reeded columns & turned drops flank the top sides above the tall arched & glazed door, a wood molding encloses the brass bezel & original paper dial w/Roman numerals, the long lower pane shows the pendulum & large brass bob, short reeded columns & finials flank the bottom of the door, a long stepped & tapering base drop w/a turned finial, two drop finials at the bottom case corners, original finish, late 19th - early 20th c., eight-day time & strike movement w/half-hour gong strike, 52" h. **$1,069**

CLOCKS

Wall clock, Thomas (Seth) Clock Co., Plymouth, Connecticut, "World" model, oak case w/a large octagonal top framing the brass bezel enclosing the dial w/Roman numerals & sweep seconds hand, the long pointed drop base enclosing a pointed glass door over the pendulum w/a brass bob, double spring 15-day movement w/Graham dead beat escapement, ca. 1905-15, 17" w., 32" h. **$1,500-1,750**

Wall clock, Welch (E.N.) Mfg. Co., Bristol, Connecticut (attributed), hanging oak kitchen-style, the high arched crest w/a carved shell above scrolls & blocked corners above carved scrolls & notch-cut sides flanking the angled arched door w/ beaded edging & ornate gilt stencil decoration, dial w/Roman numerals, flat built-in shelf above a scroll-stamped apron centered by an inset level above the pointed scallop-cut drop, eight-day movement, strike & alarm, old case refinish, late 19th c., 4 1/2 x 14 3/8", 27 3/4" h. **$350-400**

Wall clock, Welch (E.N.) Mfg. Co., Bristol, Connecticut, octagonal drop wall case, original dark varnish finish, the stepped octagonal top w/a large brass bezel enclosing the dial w/Roman numerals, sweep seconds hands & an outer day-of-the-month band, the short pointed drop case w/a small glass door w/gilt trim, eight-day movement, time, strike & calendar, open escapement, minor wear on face, ca. 1890, 4 1/2 x 17", 22" h. **$350-400**

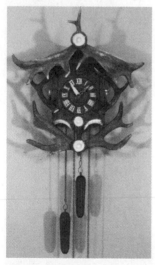

►Wall mirror-clock, Classical style, large rectangular frame in gilt & black w/corner blocks w/metal florettes joined by half-round ring- & rod-turned spindles, the deep pine case hinged to open, the top panel of the front reverse-painted w/a brown ground & gold, black & reddish-brown leaves framing a clear round center showing the clock dial w/Roman numerals above the long rectangular mirror, the case holding the brass works w/weight, pendulum & key, dial signed "B. Morrill, Boscawen," New Hampshire, first half 19th c., some edge damage & touch-up, hinges & reverse-painted panel replaced, 18 1/4 x 38 1/4". **$1,265**

▲Wall cuckoo clock, antler-mounted carved lindenwood, the small central wooden case centered w/a chapter ring mounted w/carved bone Roman numerals & handles, suspending long chains w/long weights, the clock case enclosed by a pair of peaked carved & polished antlers joined by a carved roundel, a smaller pair of antlers below the case forming the pendulum counterweight, Schwarzwald region of Germany, late 19th c., lower antler counterweight broken & spliced, one bone hand replaced w/an aluminum one, 18" w., 21" h. **$201**

Wall regulator clock, oak, a simple arched paneled crestrail above a narrow molded cornice above a case w/a long paneled door, the upper wood panel around a brass bezel & enameled dial w/Roman numerals, the lower door panel composed of geometric beveled glass sections, flat base above a pair of quarter-round brackets & an arched drop backboard, Germany, early 20th c., 33" h. **$316**

Wall regulator clock, Ingraham & Co., Bristol, Connecticut, "Western Union" model, long oak case w/a flat rectangular top w/a wide cornice lightly carved & centered by a fan device above the flat case molding enclosing the tall, wide two-pane glazed door, the upper pane w/black corners centered by the large brass bezel & dial w/Roman numerals, the lower pane w/a gilt Greek key border band & the word "Regulator" over the pendulum & large brass bob, short base brackets flank the scroll-cut & carved drop backboard, late 19th - early 20th c., 37" h. **$338**

Wall regulator clock, Sessions Clock Co., Bristol, Connecticut, oak case w/wide flaring flat cornice above the large two-pane door, the top pane reverse-painted in black w/a gold ring over the paper dial w/Arabic numerals, the lower pane banded in gold & printed "Regulator," showing the pendulum w/ brass bob, molded base above cutout side scallops & a scroll-cut backboard w/stamped designs, eight-day movement, time-only, original finish, foxing on paper dial, ca. 1900, 5 1/8 x 17 3/4", 36" h. **$700-800**

Wall regulator clock, Sessions Clock Co., Bristol, Connecticut, "Regular E" model, pressed oak case, a large wide octagonal top w/ molded bands around the brass bezel enclosing the original paper dial w/Roman numerals & outer calendar date band w/Arabic numerals, the pointed drop case w/stamped molding on the glazed door printed w/"Regulator," pendulum w/large brass bob, eight-day time & strike movement, ca. 1915, 16 1/2" w. top, 38" h. **$850-950**

Wall regulator clock, Ansonia Clock Co., Ansonia, Connecticut, "Regulator A" model, walnut veneer case w/a large octagonal top section w/molded black ring around the brass bezel enclosing the paper dial w/Roman numerals & an outer calendar date ring w/Arabic numerals, the long drop case w/a pointed bottom w/ conforming molding framing the glazed door printed w/"Regulator A," pendulum w/large brass bob, eight-day time & strike movement, ca. 1900-10, 17" w., 32" h. **$900- 1,000**

Wall regulator clock, tall rectangular mahogany case w/a long glazed door w/small carved scrolls flanking the arched top, a wide brass bezel enclosing the porcelain dial w/Roman numerals, a long gridiron brass pendulum w/ harp design over the large brass disk bob, eight-day time-only pinwheel movement, France, late 19th - early 20th c., 61" h. **$2,138**

Wall regulator clock, Thomas (Seth) Clock Co., Plymouth, Connecticut, "No. 2" model, tall oak case w/a large molded round top enclosing the brass bezel & painted dial w/Roman numerals & sweep seconds hand, the long rectangular drop base w/a tall rectangular molding enclosing a glass pane over the cylindrical brass weight & large brass pendulum bob, ca. 1890-1900, 17" w., 36" h. **$1,800-2,000**

Wall Vienna Regulator clock, fancy carved walnut case, a high crest w/a flat top molding above a scroll-carved & pierced panel fitted w/pairs of small turned spindles flanking half-round spindles centered by a carved classical face, the corner blocks w/urnform finials, the tall arched glass front showing the white enamel dial w/Roman numerals & large brass pendulum, the case sides w/ring-turned columns resting on blocks on a flat base above turned round corner droops & a curved & blocked central drop w/knob finial drop, Europe, late 19th c., 31" h. **$259**

Coca-Cola Collectibles

Collectibles provide a nostalgic look at our youth and a time when things were simpler and easier to understand. Through collecting, many adults try to recapture this time loaded with fond memories.

The American soft drink industry has always been part of this collectible nostalgia phenomenon. It fits all the criteria associated with the good times, fond memories, and fun. The world of soda pop collecting has been one of the mainstays of modern collectibles since the start of the genre, and who can deny that Coca-Cola has been at the top of the soda pop world?

Organized Coca-Cola collecting began in the early 1970s. The advertising art of The Coca-Cola Company, which used to be thought of as a simple area of collecting, has reached a whole new level of appreciation. Because of their artistic quality, these images deserve to be considered true Americana. Coca-Cola art is more than bottles and trays, more than calendars and signage, more than trinkets, giveaways, and displays. It incorporates all the best that America has to offer. The Coca-Cola Company, since its conception in 1886, has taken advertising to a whole new level. So much so, that it has been studied and dissected by scholars as to why it has proved to be so successful for more than 120 years.

Can soda pop advertising be considered true art? Without a doubt! The very best artists in America were an integral part of that honorary place in art history. Renowned artists like Rockwell, Sundbloom, Elvgren, and Wyeth helped take a quality product and advance it to the status of an American icon and all that exemplifies the very best about America.

This beautiful advertising directly reflects the history of our country: its styles and fashion, patriotism, family life, the best of times, and the worst of times. Everything this country has gone through since 1886 can be seen in these wonderful images.

For more information on Coca-Cola collectibles, see *Petretti's Coca-Cola Collectibles Price Guide*, 12th edition, by Allan Petretti.

Calendars

1891 calendar, 6-1/2" x 9"
....$25,000

1910 calendar, 15" x 26", "Happy Days" $15,000

1936 calendar $1,000

Trays

1897, 9-1/4", serving tray..**$37,000**

◀1931, 10-1/2" x 13-1/4", serving tray **$900**

1916, 8-1/2" x 19", serving tray **$500**

◀1953-60, 10-1/2" x 13-1/4", serving tray **$45**

▲1903, 5-1/2", bottle tray **$12,000**

Signs

1908, 14" x 22", "Good to the Last Drop," paper, metal strip top and bottom, very rare **$19,000**

1897, 6-1/2" x 10-1/2", "Victorian Girl," hanging sign, cardboard..**$25,000**

1936, 29" x 50", "50th Anniversary," cardboard
.... **$3,000**

1957, 16" x 27", cardboard with gold wood frame
.... **$600**

1940s, 20" x 36", cardboard with gold wood frame ... **$1,500**

▼1960s, 16" x 27", cardboard **$200**

Circa 1912, 30" x 46", cardboard cutout **$12,000**

1950, 10" x 12", Phil Rizzuto, cardboard cutout **$1,000**

1941, 32" x 42", cardboard Santa Claus cutout **$1,600**

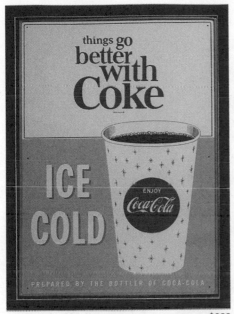

1964, 20" x 28", tin.....................................$300

1950s, metal and Masonite menu board...........$400

Pre-1900, 8" x 24", porcelain, rare $10,000

Circa 1941, 9-1/2", stamped composition, rare
....$2,000

1907, 8" x 10", celluloid, manufactured by Whitehead and Hoag Co., Newark, N.J. **$20,000**

Note: The celluloid "Satisfied" sign is very rare. The price range is for examples in high quality collector condition and complete with ornate corners as shown. Examples in lesser condition will be valued much lower.

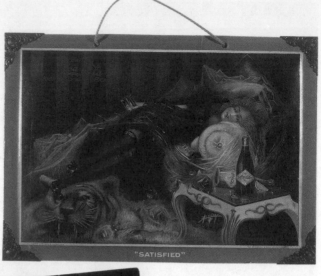

"SATISFIED"

Early 1900s, reverse glass, gold foil backing, beveled edge, very rare **$25,000**

Late 1930s, 12" x 14" reverse glass, The Brunhoff Mfg. Co., Near Mint condition **$5,000**

Note: This Brunhoff sign is highly desirable to collectors. In Mint condition at auction, it has been known to bring above the value listed.

Toys, Games & Entertainment

1948, Buddy-L, wood truck **$5,000**

1930-31, 36", Coca-Cola Flyer, three-wheel scooter **$2,500**

1978, Japanese R2D2 radio, mint in box, toy made by Takara **$1,200**

1933, 24", bottle radio **$7,500**

◀1950s, 12" Buddy Lee, plastic or composition **$1,200**

Note: Must be complete and all original to warrant value shown.

Bottles & Related Items

1960, first domestic can **$400**

Early 1900s, ceramic jug, paper label **$3,000**

Note: Label must be at least 90% intact to warrant this value.

◄1958, Acton No. 10 Jr. picnic cooler, different versions **$325**

1903-08, paper label amber, first paper label, rare............. **$600**

1960s, 10 oz., diamond paper label. **$550**

1940s, six bottle carrier, wood, rare **$600**

1950s, twelve bottle carrier, aluminum...... **$125**

Circa 1929, Glascock cooler, single case, junior size **$1,600**

Paper & Related Items

Circa 1892, 3-1/2" x 5-1/2", trade card **$2,000**

1900, fan, showing both sides **$225**

1914, Verigraph (early 3-D) glasses **$825**

Miscellaneous

1908, pocket mirror, "Bastian Bros. Co., Rochester, NY, Duplicate Mirrors 5¢ Postage, Coca-Cola Company, Atlanta, GA." **$700**

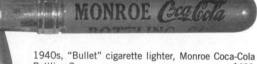

Circa 1929, 12-1/2", axe, "For Sports Men," mint in original box...........**$2,800**

1940s, "Bullet" cigarette lighter, Monroe Coca-Cola Bottling Co..**$400**

1940s, match holder, tin.....**$385**

Circa 1920, 4", hat pin, chrome..**$300**

Circa 1913-1915, brass door knob.................................**$500**

1910, "The Coca-Cola Girl" matchbook, shows both sides **$1,600**

Comics

Brent Frankenhoff, editor of Krause Publications' *Comics Buyer's Guide* (*http://cbgxtra.com*) said, "2010 was marked by three comics cracking the $1 million barrier, and 2011 added another member to that group before the end of the first quarter."

The record-setting 2010 sales were for comics from the 1930s, the beginning of what collectors call the Golden Age: two copies of *Action Comics* #1 (June 1938, featuring the first appearance of Superman, one graded 8.0, Very Fine, one graded 8.5, Very Fine +) and a copy of *Detective Comics* #27 (May 1939, the first appearance of Batman, graded 8.0).

Both of the copies of *Action* #1 were sold through ComicConnect.com, whose co-founder, Vincent Zurzolo, said at the time, "The only comics that are worth more are higher-grade copies of *Action Comics* #1."

Just over a year since he made that statement, Zurzolo helped broker the first $1 million sale of a comic book from the Silver Age of comics, when ComicConnect.com sold a copy of *Amazing Fantasy* #15 (August 1962, the first appearance of Spider-Man) for $1.1 million March 7. Graded 9.6 (Near Mint+) by third-party grading service Certified Guaranty Company, the issue is the only copy graded that high to date. There are no copies graded higher.

So do *you* have a $1 million comic book in your attic, basement, or closet? "Probably not," said Frankenhoff. "These high-end comics are few and far between, which is much of what makes them so valuable. Their outstanding condition is another factor. Time and again, I see sellers who don't take condition into account when pricing their comics at a show or in a shop,

Amazing Fantasy #15 (Aug 62).............$10,000-$100,000

only focusing on the highest value listed in any price guide. A collector with any level of experience is going to know that those prices are wrong for copies that show even slight damage."

Comics Buyer's Guide Senior Editor Maggie Thompson agreed that a major factor in prices realized for rare comics of historic importance is determination of their condition by the CGC third-party grading service. Though usually not a factor in buying and selling most back issues, confirmation of near-perfect condition by CGC can boost the price. "But," she added, "most back-issue comics can't meet CGC's stringent requirements for a Near Mint copy."

Super-hero films usually have only a short-term effect on back-issue prices. When films featuring Spider-Man were released, prices on the early appearances of Spider-Man and those issues containing each film's foes rose. Similar price jumps happened with Batman films and, to a lesser degree, with other movies including the Iron Man franchise. However, it's a bubble

COMICS

Courtesy Heritage Auction Galleries

Batman No. 1, 1940, the character's first solo, sold at auction for $55,269 on Aug. 5, 2010. It was graded 5.5 on a scale of 1 to 10.

that bursts quickly, especially if the movie in question doesn't turn out to be a blockbuster.

Speaking of bubbles, remember the huge comics output of the late 1980s and early 1990s? Two decades later, people continue to try and cash in on those speculations, only to find that the demand is so low and the supply of high-grade copies so high that such items are only being bought by the pound, if then, by most dealers.

So what *should* the collector getting into (or returning to) comics seek out? Buy comics you *enjoy*. If the price goes up, that's a bonus. Visit a comics convention (there are hundreds around the country each year) to see what creators, companies, and even dealers are pushing at their booths. You may discover the next sleeper hit. Early issues of such recent series as *Walking Dead*, *Chew*, and *Mouse Guard* have skyrocketed in price and are holding those values over a longer period. Even with paperback and hardcover reprint collections available, collectors eagerly seek early issues of now-popular series that had low initial print runs. In any case, if you buy what you like, you'll have invested in your own pleasure.

VALUES

◆ Comics have been avidly collected for years. Prices for scarce, early issues of a particular series are often higher than for later issues. However, key events (the first appearance of a character, a creator's first work, or other factors) can also affect value. Prices listed below show a range for copies from "Good" to "Near Mint" condition. "Near Mint" means a nearly perfect copy, whereas "Good" is applied to a copy that's complete but is worn, with visible defects. Note the wide difference between the prices because of condition.

Action Comics #484 (Jun 78)
.... 75¢-$8

Adolescent Radioactive Black Belt Hamsters #7 (Aug 87) ..... 25¢-$2

Adventures into the Unknown #147 (Mar 64)................ $4-$40

All-Star Squadron #7 (Mar 82)
.... **50¢-$3**

Amazing Adventures (3rd series) #21 (Nov 73).................. **75¢-$8**

Amelia Rules #1 (Aug 01) **25¢-$2**

Archie Comics #31 (Apr 48)
.... **$20-$200**

Archie's Girls Betty & Veronica #229 (Jan 75) .... **$1-$10**

Archie's Madhouse #48 (Aug 66)
.... **50¢-$4**

Astro City #1 (Aug 95) ..... **30¢-$3**

Atom #19 (Jul 65)......... **$10-$95**

Badger #1 (Sep 83)......... **50¢-$4**

Batman #134 (Sep 60).**$20-$200**

Batman #260 (Feb 75).... **$6-$56**

Betty #19 (Nov 94) .... **40¢-$4**

Blackest Night #0 (Jun 09)
.... **50¢-$5**

Bone #1 (Jul 91)............. **$8-$80**

Boy Comics #112 (Jun 55)
.... **$2-$22**

Brave and the Bold #1 (Apr 07)
.... **30¢-$3**

Bugs Bunny #34 (Jan 54) **$5-$50**

Captain Marvel Adventures #100
(Sep 49)......................**$10-$125**

Boy Commandos #1 (Win 42) ......**$900-$9,300**

Chew #3 (Aug 09) .... **50¢-$6**

Chip 'n' Dale #31 (Jan 75) .... **50¢-$3**

Civil War #1 (Jul 06)........ **50¢-$5**

Crime and Punishment #48 (Mar 52) .... $3-$30

Crisis on Infinite Earths #7 (Oct 85) .... 75¢-$6

Damage Control #1 (May 89) .... 25¢-$1

Daredevil (2nd series) #1 (Nov 98) .... $2-$15

Dennis the Menace #120 (May 71) .... $1-$12

Dick Tracy Comics #112 (Jun 57) .... $2-$26

Eternal Warrior #1 (Aug 92) .... 35¢-$4

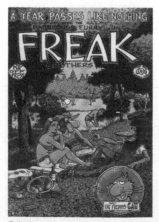

Fabulous Furry Freak Brothers #3 (1973) .... $2-$15

Fantastic Four #51 (Jun 66) .... $12-$118

Fightin' Army #76 (Oct 67)
.... **$3-$25**

Four Color Comics #1030: The Little Rascals (Nov 59) .... **$5-$50**

Four Color Comics #257: Little Iodine (Dec 49) .... **$6-$60**

Four Color Comics #892: Maverick (Apr 58) ....**$20-$200**

F-Troop #4 (Apr 67).........**$4-$35**

G.I. Combat #155 (Sep 72)
.... **$2-$15**

Gene Autry Comics #92 (Oct 54)
.... **$3-$30**

Ha Ha Comics #58 (Oct 48)
.... **$2-$18**

Incredible Hulk #182 (Dec 74)
.............................**$200-$2,000**

Jughead #134 (Jul 66) .... **$3-$25**

Justice League America #28 (Jul 89) .... **35¢-$2**

Justice League of America #7 (Nov 61)......................**$75-$750**

Legion of Super-Heroes #301 (Jul 83) .... **25¢-$2**

Li'l Abner Comics #62 (Feb 48) ....**$12-$125**

Little Lulu #121 (Jul 58) . **$4-$42**

Lone Wolf and Cub #1 (May 87) .... **60¢-$6**

Love Diary #44 (Jun 54) .. **$1-$10**

Marvel Super Heroes Secret Wars #8 (Dec 84)....................**$2-$16**

COMICS

Marvel Team-Up #45 (May 76)
.... 50¢-$5

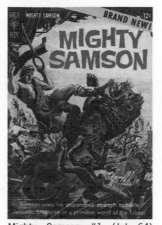

Mighty Samson #1 (Jul 64)
.... $8-$75

Mouse Guard #1 (Feb 06) **$9-$90**

Mr. District Attorney #54 (Dec 56) .... **$5-$50**

Ms. Tree #10 (Aug 84) .... 25¢-$2

New Teen Titans #1 (Nov 80)
.... $1-$9

Pogo Parade #1 (Sep 53)
....$30-$275

Popeye #9 (Nov 49)......$10-$100

Preacher #1 (Apr 95)....... **$2-$15**

Quantum Leap #5 (May 92) .... **30¢-$3**

Real Clue Crime Stories Vol. 2 #11 (Jan 48) .... **$4-$40**

Richie Rich #59 (May 67) **$3-$25**

Roy Rogers Comics #32 (Aug 50) .... **$8-$75**

Savage Dragon (mini-series) #1 (Jul 92) .... **25¢-$2**

Sgt. Fury #75 (Feb 70) .... **$2-$16**

Spider-Man #1 (Aug 90) .. **40¢-$4**

Star Spangled Comics #26 (Nov 43) ....**$85-$850**

Star Spangled War Stories #90 (May 60).......................**$30-$330**

Showcase #17: Adventures on Other Worlds (Dec 58)
.... $275-$2,750

Showcase #37: Metal Men (Apr 62, 1st Metal Men)
.... $125-$1,300

Showcase #22: Green Lantern (Oct 59) .... $550-$5,600

Star Wars #10 (Apr 78).... **$1-$10**

Static #1 (Jun 93)........... **25¢-$2**

Strange Fantasy #7 (Aug 53)
.....................................**$15-$150**

Sugar and Spike #24 (Sep 59)
.....................................$15-$150

Superman (2nd series) #75 (Jan 93) Unbagged first printing **$1-$6**
Bagged collector's set ...... **$2-$14**

Superman's Pal Jimmy Olsen #72 (Oct 63) .... **$7-$70**

Tarzan #53 (Feb 54)........ **$8-$80**

Thor (3rd series) #1 (Sep 07)
.....................................**30¢-$3**

Tower of Shadows #1 (Sep 69)
.....................................**$6-$65**

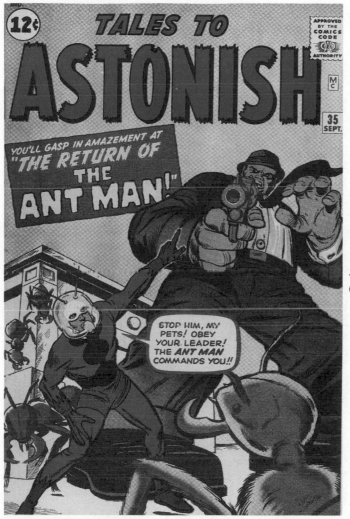

Tales to Astonish #35 (Sep 62) .... **$175-$1,750**

Ultimate Spider-Man #1 (Oct 00)
.... **$6-$60**

Uncanny X-Men #180 (Apr 84)
.... **40¢-$4**

Uncle Scrooge Adventures #5
(Jun 88) .... **35¢-$4**

Walking Dead #1 (Oct 03).. **$5-$50**

Veronica #202 (Nov 10)... **75¢-$7**

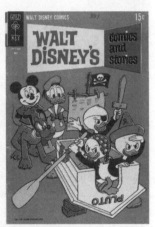

Walt Disney's Comics & Stories #344 (May 69)................ **$2-$20**

Walt Disney's Vacation Parade #4 (Jul 53) .... **$10-$90**

Watchmen #1 (Sep 86).... **$2-$20**

What If? #24 (Dec 80) ..... **35¢-$4**

Wolverine (mini-series) #1 (Sep 82) .... $5-$50

X-Men #123 (Jul 79) .... $4-$40

Yosemite Sam #45 (Jul 77) .... $2-$15

Young Men #28 (Jun 54) ....$75-$750

With first editions, buyers must beware

BRENT FRANKENHOF, MAGGIE THOMPSON, PETER BICKFORD

Action Comics #1 is historically significant because it contains the first appearance of Superman, written by Jerry Siegel and drawn by Joe Shuster.

With Superman jump-starting the super-hero genre and what is known as The Golden Age of comics, the issue has been reprinted several times in the past 72 years, so collectors should be wary of copies presented as the original printing. This is *especially* true of an over-sized reprint from the early 1970s that was one of DC's *Famous First Editions* titles. That reprint was roughly the size of a *Life* magazine, and there have been several cases of buyers being told, "Comics back then were that much bigger than comics of today," and informed that the reprint was the original. (Such sellers would remove the cardboard identifying outer cover, leaving what appeared to be a complete copy of Action #1, including the glossy cover and all the original ads.)

Action Comics was an anthology series, containing several stories featuring other characters, and The Man of Steel's first outing was actually a late addition to the package. Long considered one of the "holy grails" of the collecting hobby, copies of the issue in collectible condition have been selling at gradually higher and higher prices over the years. These 2010 sales surpassed all previous sales by a wide margin. It is estimated that, of its 200,000 copy initial print run, around 100 copies still exist — and approximately half of those have been graded by CGC.

Just shy of a year after Superman's introduction, Batman (written by Bill Finger and drawn by Bob Kane) first appeared in *Detective Comics* #27, another anthology title — and the series whose initials gave DC its identity.

Initially an anthology of mystery stories, Detective quickly embraced super-heroes with The Caped Crusader's adventures. The issue hasn't been reprinted as often as *Action* #1, but there is an oversized early 1970s *Famous First Edition* out there, as well as a 1984 reprint. It's estimated that 175,000 copies of this key issue were printed in 1939, with approximately 100 copies surviving and 50 being CGC-graded.

Cookie Jars

Cookie jars evolved from the elegant British biscuit jars found on Victorian-era tables. These 19th century containers featured bail handles, and were often made of sterling silver and cut crystal.

As the biscuit jar was adapted for use in America, it migrated from the dining table to the kitchen and, by the late 1920s, it was common to find a green-glass jar (or pink or clear), often with an applied label and a screw-top lid, on kitchen counters in the typical American home.

During the Great Depression—when stoneware was still popular, but before the arrival of widespread electric refrigeration—cookie jars in round and barrel shapes arrived. These heavy-bodied jars could be hand-painted after firing. This decoration was easily worn away by eager hands reaching for Mom's bakery. The lids of many stoneware jars typically had small tapering finials or knobs that also contributed to cracks and chips.

The golden age of cookie jars began in the 1940s and lasted for less than three decades, but the examples that survive represent an exuberance and style that have captivated collectors.

It wasn't until the 1970s that many collectors decided—instead of hiding their money in cookie jars—to invest their money in cookie jars. It was also at this time that cookie jars ceased to be simply storage vessels for bakery and evolved into a contemporary art form. And it's because of this evolution from utility to art that—with some exceptions—we have limited the scope of this book to jars made from the 1930s to the early 1970s.

The Brush Pottery Co. of Zanesville, Ohio, produced one of the first ceramic cookie jars in about 1929, and Red Wing's spongeware line from the late 1920s also included a ridged, barrel-shaped jar. Many established potteries began adding a selection of cookie jars in the 1930s.

The 1940s saw the arrival of two of the most famous cookie jars: Shawnee's Smiley and Winnie, two portly, bashful little pigs who stand with eyes closed and heads cocked, he in overalls and bandana, she in flowered hat and long coat. And a host of Disney characters also made their way into American kitchens.

In the 1950s, the first television-influenced jars appeared, including images of Davy Crockett and Popeye. This decade also saw the end of several prominent American potteries (including Roseville) and the continued rise of imported ceramics.

A new collection of cartoon-inspired jars was popular in the 1960s, featuring characters drawn from the Flintstones, Yogi Bear, Woody Woodpecker, and Casper the Friendly Ghost. Jars reflecting the race for space included examples from McCoy and American Bisque. This decade also marked the peak production era for a host of West Coast manufacturers, led by the twin brothers Don and Ross Winton.

For more information on cookie jars, see *Warman's Cookie Jars Identification and Price Guide* by Mark F. Moran.

Baby #561, 11" tall, 1941-42. The Witch is the most valuable of the Abingdon jars, but the Baby is much harder to find. It comes in Frost Blue, Fern Green, Cameo Pink, Antique White, Jonquil Yellow (shown), and Gunmetal Black............................... **$500+**

Fat Boy by Abingdon, cold-paint decoration, 8-1/4" tall, late 1940s, lid with impressed "495," bottom ink-stamped "Abingdon U.S.A."............................. **$950+**

Hippo "Bar Jar" by Abingdon, with atypical under-glaze decoration including hair, 8-1/4" tall, 1942, lid with impressed "549," ink-stamped "Abingdon U.S.A." and impressed "549.".............. **$500+**

TOP LOT!

This glazed ceramic figural cookie jar by American Bisque Co. depicts Harvey Cartoons characters Herman and Katnip hunkered down while Herman the mouse stands atop his back, serving as the lid handle; "Herman And Katnip" names are incised on the base and "USA" is incised on the opposite side; 10" by 11" by 6-3/4" deep, early 1960s... $10,143.67

Courtesy Hake's Americana

Humpty Dumpty by Abingdon, 10-1/2" tall, late 1940s, ink-stamped on bottom, "Abingdon USA," and impressed "663." .... **$500+**

Little Bo Peep by Abingdon, with atypical green trim, 12" tall, late 1940s, ink-stamped, "Abingdon USA," impressed mark on bottom, "694," and original gold label, "Abingdon Made in USA.". **$400+**

Little Old Lady by Abingdon, 9" tall, circa 1950, ink-stamped, "Abingdon USA," and impressed, "471." (Also found with other under-glaze decorations, and in solid colors, similarly priced.) .... **$600+**

Acorn corner jar by American Bisque, 9-1/2" tall, 1940s, raised mark on back, "U.S.A.".... **$400+**

Baby Huey by American Bisque, 13-1/2" tall, early 1960s, impressed on side, "U.S.A." Beware of reproductions. .... **$2,000+**

Boy Pig (with patch on knee) by American Bisque, 11-3/4" tall, late 1950s, impressed mark on back, "U.S.A." .... **$300+**

Casper the Friendly Ghost (candy jar, with lollipops) by American Bisque, 11-3/4" tall, early 1960s, impressed mark on reverse, "U.S.A." Beware of reproductions............................. **$2,500+**

Chick (with tam, which lifts off) by American Bisque, 13" tall, 1950s, impressed mark on tail, "U.S.A." .... **$350+**

Dancing Baby Elephant by American Bisque, 11-1/2" tall, 1950s, unmarked. .... **$200+**

Dino the Caddie by American Bisque, 12-3/8" tall, 1960s, bag marked, "Property of Fred Flintstone," impressed mark on side of Dino's tail, "U.S.A."....... **$1,500+**

Dutch Shoe by American Bisque, 10-1/4" long, 1950s, unmarked, very rare. .... **$3,000+**

Kittens on Yarn Ball by American Bisque, 9-1/2" tall, 1950s, raised mark on side, "U.S.A." ..... **$200+**

Mickey Mouse two versions, by American Bisque, distributed by Leeds China Co. of Chicago, one with rare cold-painted red pants, both 12" tall, 1940s, impressed mark, "Mickey Mouse Copyright (symbol) Walt Disney U.S.A."...**$3,000+ each**

Olive Oyl by American Bisque, 10-1/2" tall, 1950s, impressed mark on side, "U.S.A." Beware of reproductions. .... **$1,800+**

Popeye by American Bisque, with original corncob pipe, 10-1/2" tall, 1950s, impressed mark on back, "U.S.A." Beware of reproductions. .... **$1,200+**

Spaceship by American Bisque, with stencil, "Cookies Out of This World," 10-3/8" tall, late 1950s, raised mark on back, "U.S.A." .... **$700+**

Mammy by Brayton Laguna, in rare red dress, 11-3/4" tall, 1940s, hand inscribed, "Brayton 2"; Adding to the confusion caused by reproductions is the fact that the genuine Brayton Laguna Mammy has been found in sizes up to almost 13" tall.
With red dress .... **$800-$900**
Other colors .... **$600+**

Balloon Boy by Brush, one of the company's last production jars, 11" tall, 1971, unmarked, also found with paper label, "W56." .... **$1,000+**

Chick on Nest. The version of this jar that went into production, the green and white one with the feather, is marked "W38." It was made in 1966 and is worth $350. It is very hard to find one with an undamaged feather. The tan, featherless chick was an experimental piece, and it comes with a letter of authenticity from the man who took it home from the factory. The letter, written by Robert Bush, age 89, is dated Feb. 14, 1999. It reads, in part: "I worked on the kiln when the kiln foreman gave me the chicken jar. I drew it out of the kiln and told the foreman I liked it. A couple of weeks later he called me into his office and said that I could have it. ... It is the only one made like it to my knowledge. We made many other test jars trying things out, like the Squirrel and the Bear jar, but not many of them got out of the shop. Didn't want people copying our ideas." Special Chick: .... **$3,000+**

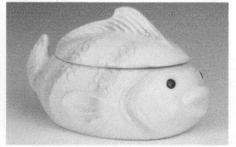

Cow with Cat Finial by Brush, 12-1/2" long, 1950s, raised mark, "Brush USA" in an artist's palette, and "W10." Prices vary widely depending on colors used, from about $200 for typical tan and yellow, to near $2,000 for purple or blue combinations, or with gold trim.................................... **$200-$2,000**

Fish by Brush in hard-to-find yellow glaze (more common with blue or green stripes), 11-1/2" long, introduced 1971, impressed mark, "W-52 Brush USA."
As shown .... **$500+**
In blue or green .... **$350+**

COOKIE JARS

Lady in the Blue Dress, unmarked. According to collector Kathleen Moloney, "This jar is rare, valuable, and shrouded in mystery. It was obviously produced by Brush. The pottery is pure Brush; the colors are identical to those of the Little Girl, Little Angel, and Little Boy Blue jars, to name a few; and the base of the jar is similar to the Clown Bust." There is only one of these jars known to exist, but there are probably more out there...**$3,500+**

Littl* Red "Ridding"-hood by Brush, 10-1/2" tall, late 1950s, with misspelled words "Little" and "Ridding."..**$1,000+**

Card King by California Cleminsons, 10-1/2" tall, 1950s, ink-stamped on bottom, "The California Cleminsons–Hand Painted–Copyright (symbol)." Found in other color combinations. .. **$500+**

Pinocchio by California Originals, 12-1/4" tall, 1950s (?), impressed mark on bottom, "Calif. Orig. G-131 USA." Also found unmarked or with only an impressed "USA." .... **$1,200+**

Sailor Elephant, unmarked but known to be Cardinal. The Cardinal catalog sheet from 1961 included a picture of several jars that had been thought to be American Bisque. This Sailor Elephant, who has "SS Cookie" in black letters on his hat, was one of them. .... **$200+**

Halo Boy by DeForest, 12" tall, 1950s, impressed mark on bottom, "DeForest of California Copyright (symbol) 1956." .... **$600+**

Humpty Dumpty by Doranne of California, 11-1/2" tall, late 1960s, unmarked............. **$500+**

Mammy by Gilner, 11" tall, 1950s, found in other colors, unmarked. Beware of reproductions. .... **$1,500+**

Gleep by Haeger, 11" tall, 1960s, ink-stamped on bottom, "Haeger USA Copyright (symbol)," and a foil label, "Glaze Tested United States Pottery Association.". **$300**

Gim-me by Helen Hutula, 10-1/2" tall, 1940s, marked on bottom, "Helen's Gim-me Original–Helen Hutula Originals." .... **$1,500+**

Little Boy Blue, marked "Hull-Ware Boy Blue U.S.A. 971-122," with cold paint. This jar was not produced, and there are only a few known to exist. **$5,000**

Little Red Riding Hood by Hull, with open basket, with transfer-decorated flowers, 13" tall, 1940s, marked on the bottom, "967 Hull Ware Little Red Riding Hood—Patent Applied For USA." .... **$400+**

Bum on a Barrel by Imperial Porcelain, 12" tall, 1950s, marked on bottom, "Imperial Porcelain Corp. Zanesville O." .... **$700+**

Indian Chief by Lane, 12-1/2" tall, marked "Copyright 1950 Lane & Co. Los Angeles Calif.," and another indistinct raised mark. (May also have hand-written artist initials on base.) ...... **$400+**

Donald Duck by Leeds China, air-brush decoration, 13" tall, 1940s, unmarked. .... **$500+**

Christmas Tree by McCoy, 11" tall, late 1950s to early 1960s, raised mark, "McCoy USA." ..... **$1,000+**

Cookie Boy in turquoise with crisp mold detail, early 1940s, McCoy mark. (Rarely found bare headed.) ....**$300-$350**

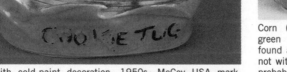

Cookie Tug with cold-paint decoration, 1950s, McCoy USA mark. ....**$8,000-$10,000**

Corn (prototype) by McCoy in green and yellow (sometimes found all yellow or all white, but not with two glazes), 9-1/2" tall, probably late 1950s, unmarked. .... **$500+**

Grapes with bird on lid in air-brushed colors, non-production piece, McCoy mark, 9-1/2" tall. .... **$7,000+**

Hamm's Bear, early 1970s, USA mark, also found with white tie. .... **$225-$250**

Kissing Penguins or Lovebirds in typical factory cold paint decoration, 1940s, McCoy mark. (Rarely found in brown and green.) .... **$90-$110**

Mammy. Left, reproduction Mammy jar; right, real Mammy jar with checked apron (paint touched up). ....**$150-$200**

Mammy in yellow, also found in white and aqua with cold paint decoration (widely available as a slightly smaller reproduction), 1950s, McCoy mark. (Rarely found with two other phrases around base: "Dem Cookies Sure Am Good" and "Dem Cookies Sure Got Dat Vitamin A.") ...**$200-$225**

Mother Goose, late 1940s, McCoy USA mark, cold-painted details. ....**$90-$110**

Oak Leaf and Acorn corner jar (previously thought to have been produced by American Bisque), 1948, McCoy mark. ....**$200-$225**

Picnic Basket by McCoy, early 1960s, USA mark, with cold paint on the lid, 1960s. ....**$90-$110**

Apple (yellow) by Metlox, 9" tall, 1960s, marked on bottom, "Made in USA." ....**$300+**

Bluebird on Pine Cone by Metlox, 11-1/2" tall, marked on bottom, "Made in USA," and gold and brown foil label, "Metlox Manufacturing Co." ....**$350+**

Brownie by Metlox, 9-1/4" tall, made from 1963 to 1967, with gold and brown foil label, "Metlox Manufacturing Co.". ...... **$2,000+**

Cow (lavender/purple) and Butterfly by Metlox, 10" tall, 1960s, impressed mark, "Made in Poppytrail Calif." .... **$800+**

Donald Duck by Metlox, 11-3/4" tall, late 1950s, unmarked, made for distribution to Disney executives, very rare. .... **$5,000+**

Humpty Dumpty by Metlox, 10-7/8" tall, with original silver foil label, "Made in California–Poppytrail Pottery by Metlox." .... **$1,200+**

Little Red Riding Hood by Metlox, 12-3/4" tall, 1960s, with original silver foil label, "Made in California–Poppytrail Pottery by Metlox," also marked on bottom, "Made in Poppytrail Calif. USA."... **$1,800+**

Pretty Ann by Metlox, 11" tall, 1960s, marked on bottom, "Made in Poppytrail California" over an outline of the state. .... **$500+**

Schoolhouse by Metlox, 11-1/2" tall, late 1950s, with gold foil label, "Metlox Manufacturing Co." .... **$1,500+**

Turkey by Metlox, one of only a handful known to exist, 13-1/2" tall, late 1960s (?), with original silver foil label, "Made in California–Poppytrail Pottery by Metlox." . **$2,000+**

Washtub Mammy attributed to Metlox, 11" tall, late 1940s (?), unmarked. .... **$1,800+**

Hen and Chicks by Morton Pottery, cold paint and under-glaze decoration, 8-1/2" tall, 1930s, unmarked. .... **$100+**

Black Chef by Pearl China, marked in gold on front, "Cooky," 10-1/4" tall, 1940s, stamped on bottom, "Pearl (in a seashell) China Co. Hand decorated 22 Kt. Gold U.S.A." and impressed, "639." (A companion to the Chef was a Mammy jar, same marks, $900+.) .... **$600+**

Albert Apple by Pitman-Dreitzer (also called PeeDee), cold painted, 12-1/4" tall, late 1940s (?), impressed mark, "Pitman-Dreitzer & Co." and an indistinct mold number. .... **$150+**

Chef by National Silver, with cold-paint highlights on mouth, 10" tall, 1940s, marked on bottom, "USA NSCO." (Sometimes found with foil labels, and the mark "NASCO.") .... **$500+**

Carousel by Pfaltzgraff, lid 9-1/2" wide, 1950s, unmarked. ... **$500+**

Elsie on a Barrel by Pottery Guild, 11-3/4" tall, 1940s, ink-stamped, "Hand Painted Pottery Guild of America" and indistinct mold number. .... **$400+**

Baking Angel, unmarked. This jar was identified because a photo of it appeared in a Pearl China catalog. **$300**

Derby Dan Muggsy by Pfaltzgraff, 8-1/2" tall, 1950s, marked, "Derby Dan Muggsy–The Pfaltzgraff Pottery Co., York, Pa.–Designed by Jessop." .... **$500+**

Chicken by Purinton, 11-3/8" tall, late 1940s, stamped "Purinton Serve Ware." .... **$175+**

COOKIE JARS

Howdy Doody by Purinton, 9-1/4" tall, 1950s, unmarked. ..... **$700+**

Davy Crockett by Ransburg, stoneware, 10" tall, 1950s, marked on bottom, "Ransburg Genuine Hand Painted Indianapolis USA" inside an artist's palette..........**$80-$100**

Barrel (Spongeware) with stepped profile by Red Wing, stoneware, 8-1/4" tall, 1930s, unmarked. .... **$400+**

Advertising jars by Red Wing; left, 8-1/2" tall, with daisy pattern on lid, late 1930s, ink-stamped, "Red Wing Saffron Ware"; right, glossy, 8-1/2" tall, brown and white trim lines, plain lid, late 1930s, ink-stamped, "Red Wing Saffron Ware." .... **$400+ each**

Cattails by Red Wing, in glossy blue and tan, with "Cookies" in raised lettering, very crisp mold, 8-5/8" tall, late 1930s, ink-stamped, "Red Wing Union Stoneware Co.-Red Wing Minn.". **$600+**

Chef Pierre, unusual jar by Red Wing with post-factory black and white paint, 11-3/4" tall, early 1940s, impressed mark, "Red-Wing U.S.A." with what collectors call a "ski" line, which resembles the profile of a snow ski..... **$200+**

Drummer Boy by Red Wing, all original, 9" tall, early 1960s, faint mark. .... **$800+**

King of Tarts by Red Wing, multicolored, 9-3/4" tall, 1950s, impressed mark on bottom, "Red Wing USA," and ink-stamped, "Red Wing Pottery Hand Painted." .... **$1,000+**

Jack Frost by Red Wing, 8-1/4" tall and 12" tall, early 1960s, both unmarked. Short version.. **$600+**
Tall version,... **$700+**

Diaper Pin Pig by Regal China, 11-1/2" tall, 1950s, marked on bottom, "404." .... **$800+**

Dutch Girl by Regal China, 10-3/4" tall, 1940s, unmarked. (Also found in predominant pale blue, yellow, and orange. $1,000+) .... **$800+**

Little Red Riding Hood by Regal China, with closed basket, large transfer-decorated flowers, and gold trim, also note blue petticoat under dress, 13-3/8" tall, 1940s, marked on bottom, "Little Red Riding Hood Patent Design No. 135889 USA."................ **$700+**

Frightened Alice in Wonderland by Regal China, 13-1/4" tall, late 1950s, marked "Walt Disney Productions Copyright (symbol) Alice in Wonderland." .... **$4,000+**

Far left: Oriental Lady by Regal China, in rare white with gold trim, 11-5/8" tall, late 1940s, unmarked....... **$1,500+**

Left: Uncle Mistletoe by Regal China, 11-1/2" tall, early 1960s, marked on back, "Uncle Mistletoe Cookie Jar Patent D. 1-50028."**$3,000+**

COOKIE JARS

Dutch Girl by Robinson Ransbottom, 12" tall, 1940s, marked on bottom, "RRPCo. Roseville Ohio No. ... (obscured)." .... **$300+**

Hey Diddle Diddle by Robinson Ransbottom, 10" tall, 1940s, impressed marked, "RRPCo. Roseville Ohio #317." (Also found with slight glaze variations and rarely in gold trim. Beware of solid-color reproductions marked "Brush McCoy" available on the Internet for $50.) .... **$400+**

Whale by Robinson Ransbottom, 8" tall, 1950s, impressed mark, "RRPCo. USA Roseville O." **$900+**

Clematis green cookie jar by Roseville (3-8"), raised mark, 9" by 10-1/4". .... **$800-$900**

Freesia blue cookie jar by Roseville (4-8"), half-inch bruise to rim and lid, a few small glaze nicks to high points (some from firing), raised mark. .... **$400-$450**

Magnolia green cookie jar by Roseville (2-8"), raised mark, 8-3/4" by 10-1/2". .... **$575-$625**

Water Lily brown cookie jar by Roseville (1-8"), strong mold, raised mark. .... **$400-$450**

Cooky by Shawnee, 12" tall, transfer-decorated with flowers and "COOKY" in gilt letters on her right shoulder, 1940s, impressed mark, "U.S.A." .... **$600+**

Cottage House by Shawnee, 7" tall, 1940s, impressed mark, "U.S.A. 6." (Other Cottage-theme pieces include teapot, sugar bowl, and S&P shakers.) .... **$1,400+**

Jo Jo the Clown by Shawnee, 9-1/4" tall, 1940s, raised mark, "Shawnee U.S.A." and an impressed "12." .... **$600+** With gold trim .... **$1,200+**

Lucky by Shawnee, with gold trim, transfer-decorated flowers, and original label, "Hand Painted Fired Ceramic Colors 22 Kt. Gold," 11-3/8" tall, 1940s, otherwise unmarked. .... **$1,400+**

Muggsy by Shawnee, with transfer-decorated flowers and gold trim, 10-1/2" tall, impressed marked, "Patented Muggsy U.S.A." .... **$2,000+**

Smiley by Shawnee, with gold trim and transfer-decorated roses, 11-1/4" tall, early 1940s, raised mark, "U.S.A." .... **$800+**

Smiley by Shawnee in butterscotch pants, with bank head, 11-1/4" tall, 1940s, impressed mark, "Patented Smiley 60," raised mark, "Shawnee U.S.A." ... **$900+**

Winnie by Shawnee in brown coat, with gold trim and bank head, 11-1/2" tall, 1940s, impressed mark, "Patented Winnie 61," raised mark, "Shawnee U.S.A." **$1,200+**

Winnie by Shawnee, with bank head and butterscotch coat, 10-3/4" tall, 1940s, impressed mark on the bottom, "Patented Winnie 61," and raised, "Shawnee U.S.A." .... **$700+**

Woven Bowl of Fruit by Shawnee, 8-1/2" tall, 1940s, raised mark, "Shawnee U.S.A." and an impressed "84." ....**$150-$200**

Boy with Crown by Sierra-Vista, 8-1/4" tall, 1950s, marked on the bottom, "USA." .... **$1,000+**

COOKIE JARS

Pinocchio and Whale by Sierra-Vista, 8-3/4" tall, 1950s, unmarked. .... **$600+**

Rocking Horse by Starnes, 10-1/2" tall, late 1950s, unmarked. .... **$350+**

Tuggles by Sierra-Vista, 9" tall, late 1940s, impressed mark, "Sierra-Vista California." .... **$300+**

Corn by Stanford, 9-1/2" tall, 1950s, impressed mark on bottom, "215." .... **$100+**

Practical Pig designed by Don Winton, made by Hagen-Reneker, 12-5/8" tall, early 1960s. . **$500+**

Champ designed by Don Winton, 11-1/4" tall, 1960s, also found with green or yellow sweater, unmarked. ....**$2,500+**

Santa Claus by Twin Winton, 13-3/4" tall, 1960s, impressed mark on back, "Original Sculpture by Don Winton - Copyright (symbol)." ....**$500-$600**

Cross-eyed Chick by Ungemach, 10-3/4" tall, late 1950s, impressed mark, "CJ-6 USA."**$600+**

Pinky Lee by Ungemach, 10-1/2" tall, 1950s, impressed mark on back, "U.S.A.," found in other colors. ....**$700+**

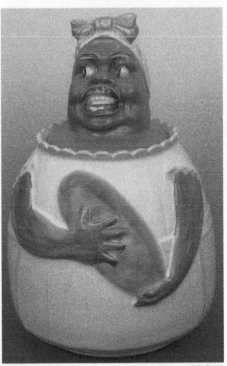

Above: Mammy with Watermelon by Weller, 10-3/4" tall, mid-1930s, impressed mark in script, "Weller Pottery Since 1872." Beware of reproductions. ....**$4,000+**

Left: Raggedy Ann (sitting), attributed to William Hirsch, and also found other colors including wood-tone brown, 9-3/4" tall, 1960s. (The head, face, and general attitude of this jar are similar to a standing Raggedy Ann made by Brush.) ....**$350+**

Above left: Winkie by Vallona-Starr, 8-1/4" tall, marked "Vallona-Starr 302 Copyright (symbol) 51 California." This jar is widely available as a reproduction. ....**$1,000-$1,200**

Currier & Ives Prints

This lithographic firm was founded in 1835 by Nathaniel Currier, with James M. Ives becoming a partner in 1857. Current events of the day were portrayed in the early days, and the prints were hand-colored. Landscapes, vessels, sport and hunting scenes of the West all became popular subjects. The firm was in existence until 1906. All prints listed are hand-colored unless otherwise noted. Numbers at the end of the listings refer to those used in *Currier & Ives Prints - An Illustrated Checklist*, by Frederick A. Conningham (Crown Publishers).

◄A Good Chance, large folio, 1863, framed, 2424, mat stain, subtle toning, minor foxing, repaired tear in corner edge, old tape residue on face edges & back **$4,700**

American Country Life - October Afternoon, large folio, N. Currier, 1855, framed, 122, margins trimmed, stains & small tears framed **$2,070**

American Field Sports: Flush'd, large folio, 1857, framed, 149, hinged at top, mat stain, small loss on lower corner **$3,173**

American Forest Scene - Maple Sugaring, large folio, 1856, N. Currier, framed, 157, mat staining, toning, staining on back **$19,975**

◄American Winter Scenes - Evening, large folio, 1854, framed, 207, hinged at top, several repaired tears, minor toning **$3,408**

American Winter Sports - Deer Shooting "On the Shattagee," large folio, N. Currier, 1855, framed, 209, several repaired tears, some into image, light toning & stains **$3,055**

American Winter Sports - Trout Fishing "On Chateaugay Lake," large folio, 1856, N. Currier, framed, 210, light mat stains, minor tears, loss on margin edge. **$4,994**

Camping Out "Some of the Right Sort," large folio, 1856, framed, 777, small loss in upper right corner. **$3,408**

Cares of a Family (The), large folio, 1856, N. Currier, framed, 814, repaired margin tear, light toning, mat stains, framed **$2,468**

Catching a Trout, large folio, after Arthur Tait, 1854, framed, minor foxing & corner staining. **$3,819**

Celebrated Horse Lexington (The), large folio, 1855, framed, 887, toning, light stains, hinged at top. **$2,233**

Central Park, Winter. The Skating Carnival, small folio, undated, framed, 953, repaired tear in lower margin **$3,173**

City of New York (The), large folio, 1870, bird's-eye view looking north, framed, 1105, bands of pale staining, repaired tears at lower margin, minor margin damage & repairs... **$8,963**

Clipper Ship "Nightingale," large folio, 1854, framed, 1159, scattered light spotty stains & few light vertical streaks **$2,938**

Clipper Ship "Red Jacket," large folio, 1855, framed, 1165, hinged at top, toning, light stains, few fox marks **$4,994**

Clipper Ship Dreadnought Off Tuskar Light, large folio, 1856, N. Currier, framed, 1144, toning, vertical light brown stains, scattered black stains in margins, faded inscriptions **$2,350**

General Tom Thumb...Now Performing with Barnum's Travelling Museum and Menagerie, small folio, 1849, N. Currier, standing on chair w/six small views up each side, evenly toned, framed . **$231**

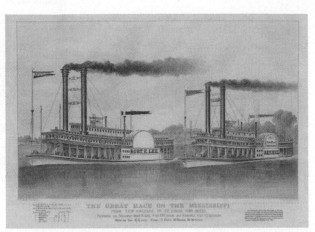

Great Race on the Mississippi from New Orleans to St. Louis (The), large folio, 1870, unframed **$3,738**

Grand Drive (The) - Central Park, N.Y., large folio, 1869, framed, 2481, light stains in lower margin, light toning **$4,700**

Hunter's Shanty (The), large folio, 1861, in a narrow modern frame, overall toning & foxing, No. 2993. .... **$1,035**

Landscape, Fruit and Flowers, large folio, 1862, 3440, framed, top corners reinforced, minor toning. **$2,820**

Life of a Hunter (The) - A Tight Fix, large folio, 1861, 3522, repair to margin, framed **$44,063**

Life on the Prairie - The Buffalo Hunt, large folio, 1862, framed, 3527, several repaired tears, subtle toning, retouch to sky & margins **$5,288**

"Lightning Express Trains" (The) - Leaving the Junction, large folio, 1863, framed, 3535, tear left corner, toning, old ink inscription on back **$25,850**

Midnight Race on the Mississippi (A), large folio, 1860, 4116, margins reinforced, touch-up to scratch, repaired corners, framed **$11,163**

Mink Trapping - Prime, large folio, 1862, framed, 4139, tears in right edge, repaired tear in upper right edge, old tape remaining on back, light mat staining & minor foxing... **$15,275**

Peytona and Fashion. In Their Great Match for $20,000, large folio, undated, N. Currier, ca. 1845, framed, 4763, several repaired tears, subtle toning. **$4,700**

Preparing for Market, large folio, 1856, framed, 4870, repaired margin tears, light toning & stains, framed **$3,055**

Rail Shooting. On The Delaware, large folio, 1852, framed, 5054, light toning & mat stain, five repaired tears in margin edges, small surface abrasions. **$2,703**

Ready For the Trot - "Bring Up Your Horses," large folio, 1877, framed, 5085, hinged at top, repaired tears to upper corner, light stains & toning. **$1,998**

Splendid Naval Triumph on the Mississippi, April 24, 1862 (The), large folio, 1862, framed, 5659, repaired tear in margin, slight abrasions, part of bottom title trimmed **$1,058**

Western Farmer's Home (The), small folio, 1871, framed, 6619, some staining. **$161**

Whale Fishery, (The) - Sperm Whale "In a Flurry," large folio, 1852, 6627, repaired tear in margin, light staining **$8,813**

Winter in the Country - The Old Grist Mill, large folio, 1864, framed, repaired tear in lower title, light mat stain **$8,813**

Decoys

Decoys have been used for years to lure flying water fowl into target range. They have been made of carved and turned wood, papier-mâché, canvas and metal. Some are in the category of outstanding folk art and command high prices.

Bluewing Teal drake, carved & painted wood, Mason factory, Challenge grade, original paint w/ minor to moderate flaking & wear, several tiny dents & shot marks, branded "DWH" **$8,250**

Canada goose, Marcel Dufour, Verdun, Quebec, Canada, swimming position, head turned slightly, original paint, shot marks **$1,100**

Canada goose, Sam Soper, Barnegat, New Jersey, swimming pose, hollow-carved w/good feather detail, original paint w/good patina, minor wear, repair to crack in neck, early **$2,200**

Canada goose, Ben Schmidt, Detroit, Michigan, good feather carving detail, hollowed out from underside, detachable head w/small metal plate at neck seam, original paint, crack in tail, second quarter 20th c. **$5,500**

Canvasback drake, Lee Dudley, Knott's Island, North Carolina, humpback "classic" style w/"V" wing carving, original paint w/some overpaint removed, branded "ELM" for E.L. Mayer, vice president of Morse Point Gunning Club & Pocahontas Fowling Club, very rare, professional repair to bill, ca. 1900 .... **$25,300**

Canvasback drake, Ward Brothers, Crisfield, Maryland, 1932-36 model, original paint **$10,450**

▼Canvasback hen & drake, Ken Anger, Dunnville, Ontario, Canada, original paint, pr. **$4,620**

Gull, standing position, relief wing carving w/crossed wing tips, old black overpaint removed to show original paint, Long Island, New York, ca. 1900 .... **$12,650**

Goldeneye drake, Ward Brothers, Crisfield, Maryland, "Fat Jaw" model, head turned approximately 20 degrees & lifted slightly, dry original paint w/alligatored surface, old replaced glass eyes, ca. 1918 (ILLUS. left)
.... **$28,600**

Merganser drake, carved & painted wood, Mason factory, Challenge grade, taken down to original paint w/ minor wear, numerous dents & shot marks, some old neck filler replaced, first quarter 20th c. **$3,575**

Merganser drake, George Huey, Friendship, Maine, large red-breasted body w/slightly turned inlet head attached to body w/small wooden dowel, carved eyes, "G R HUEY" carved in underside, original paint, second quarter 20th c., professional repair to bill
.... **$11,275**

DECOYS

Old squaw, Gus Wilson, South Portland, Maine, w/ characteristic carved eyes & raised shoulder & wings, dry original paint, swivel heads, rare, second quarter 20th c., pr. **$5,500**

Pintail drake, Mason Factory, Detroit, Michigan, hollow body, original paint w/crazed & crackled surface, original feathering still visible, thin crack in tail secured from bottom w/two small nails, first quarter 20th c. **$9,900**

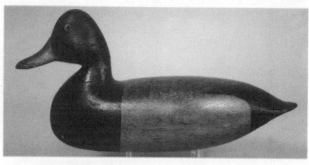

Redhead drake, Harry V. Shourds, Tuckerton, New Jersey, carved & painted wood w/original paint & minor wear, slight roughness on bill edge, some tiny dents, last quarter 19th c. **$1,540**

Trout, metal fins & tail, original paint, Lake Chautauqua, New York, 6 1/4" l. **$2,420**

Wood drake & hen, carved & painted wood, glass eyes & highly detailed bill carving, both were used as stick-ups & floaters, each w/painted initials "GRW" on the bottom, original paint w/fine patina & very minor wear, slight roughness on hen's tail & tiny chip under her bill, very small chip on top of drake's tail, both lightly hit by short, only five of these are known, Ontario, Canada, ca. 1900, pr. **$110,558**

Disney Collectibles

Collectibles that feature Mickey Mouse, Donald Duck and other famous characters of cartoon icon Walt Disney are everywhere. They can be found with little effort at flea markets, garage sales, local antiques and toys shows and online, as well as through auction houses and specialty catalogs.

Of the Disney toys, comics, posters, and other items produced from the 1930s through the 1960s, prewar Disney material is by far the most desirable.

Alice in Wonderland movie cel, the White Rabbit running, shown in profile, gouache on celluloid, 1951, 3 x 4". **$239**

Donald Duck toy, windup tin, Donald Duck walker, by Schuco, original colorful box w/one inside flap missing, ca. 1950s, 6" h. **$480**

Donald Duck toy, windup tin, Donald the Drummer, Donald sways back & forth & nods & drums, Line-Mar, Japan, 6" h. **$210**

Disney characters card set, "Walt Disney Cartooning Cards," each w/a color picture of a different Disney character including Dumbo, Lady & the Tramp, Pinocchio & Mickey Mouse, the back of each w/instructions on how to draw the character, 1959, complete set of 18 cards (ILLUS. of part) **$278**

Donald Duck & Goofy toy, windup tin, Donald & Goofy Duet, large Goofy standing on a large drum w/a small Donald on a drum in front of him, 1946, Marx, Goofy missing one arm, replaced ears, 10 1/4" h. **$201**

Dwarf Dopey movie cel, half-length portrait of Dopey wearing an oversized jacket, applied to a wood veneer background, original descriptive label on the back, 1937, cel 3" w., overall 5 1/2 x 6". **$1,793**

Dwarfs Doc & Dopey movie cel, Dopey & Doc looking at diamonds, applied to a wood veneer background, original sticker on the back, minor chipping & some wrinkling on the cel, 1937, cel 4" sq., overall 7 x 9". **$3,346**

Fantasia pre-production sketch, pastel on paper, a scene of two centaurettes frolicking, in shades of green, yellow & blue, 1940, matted & framed, 7 x 11". **$1,315**

Ferdinand the Bull toy, windup tin, Ferdinand & the matador, each figure on a platform joined by a wheeled base, Louis Marx & Co., 1938, working, 7" l. **$240**

Fantasia movie premier program, large format souvenir-type printed on the cover w/a large black title panel surrounded by colored sketches of various characters from the movie, virtually mint, 1940, 9 1/2 x 12 1/2". **$225**

►Ferdinand the Bull toy, key-wind tin, walking Ferdinand w/fabric flowers in his mouth, marked "Japan - Walt Disney Productions," 1938, all original w/box, 5 1/2" l., 4" h. **$360**

Mickey Mouse game, "Pin The Tail On 'Mickey'," a large cloth banner printed in red, black & white w/a rear few of Mickey, comes w/original cloth tails & original cardboard box, Marks Bros., Boston, apparently never used, early 1930s, box 9 x 10 1/2", banner 17 x 21", the set **$604**

Mickey Mouse bank, cast pot metal, a standing pie-eyed Mickey w/his arms spread beside a spherical bank marked "Delaware Water Gap," on a thin rectangular base, base marked "Germany," original paint & miniature padlock on the bank, 1930s, base 3 1/4" l., Mickey 3 1/2" h. **$1,553**

Mickey Mouse & Pluto toy, windup tin & celluloid, celluloid figure of Mickey standing on two-wheeled platform joined by a wire to a larger wheeled platform w/a figure of Pluto running, Japan, 1930s, original paint, missing string reins, working, overall 8" l. **$2,990**

Mickey Mouse figure, celluloid nodder, flattened standing figure of Mickey w/a nodding head, holding a square banjo, on a blue round base, excellent original paint & rare paper label reading "Mickey Mouse Copt. 1928, 1930 by Walter E. Disney," made in Japan, 7" h. **$805**

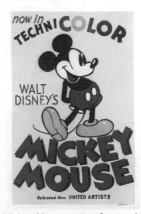

Mickey Mouse pencil sharpener, celluloid, rounded upright figure of Mickey w/sharpener in the base, 1930s, original paint, slight rim damage at back, 3" h. **$98**

Mickey Mouse toy, windup tin, "Jazz Drummer," plunger causes a lithographed two-dimensional Mickey to play the drum, by Nifty, Germany, ca. 1931, 6 3/4" h., good working condition ... **$2,100**

Mickey Mouse poster, for a color cartoon, a bright yellow background printed w/a large image of Mickey & colorful wording reading "now in Technicolor - Walt Disney's Mickey Mouse - Released thru United Artists," one-sheet, 1935, linen-backed, 27 x 41" .. **$14,350**

Mickey Mouse toy, windup tin, Mickey Mouse Ferris Wheel, colorful printing w/the head of Mickey at the side of the base, other Disney characters on the baskets, by Chein, mechanism replaced, other restoration, 17" h. **$230**

Minnie Mouse toy, windup tin, "Minnie Mouse Knitter," Minnie sitting in rocking chair knitting, colorful, Line Mar, Japan, 1950s, mechanism works but skips, 6 1/2" h. **$288**

Pluto toy, windup tin, "Drum Major," seated Pluto holding a horn, cane & bell, Line Mar, Japan, replaced ears, 5 1/2" h. **$201**

Pluto toy, pull-type w/bell, lithographed paper on wood figure of a racing Pluto pulling a four-wheeled platform w/bell, three small lithographed cardboard figures of Mickey Mouse are detached from the platform & one is missing, early 1930s, overall 20 1/2" l. **$1,898**

Sleeping Beauty movie cel, a forest landscape w/a small figure of Briar Rose walking w/her basket, gouache on celluloid applied to an airbrushed background, 1959, 1 1/2 x 3" . **$837**

Snow White & the Seven Dwarfs dolls, Snow White in stockinet w/painted features, black mohair wig & wearing a velvet & silk dress w/the hem silk screened w/images of the Dwarfs, made by Ideal, the seven Dwarfs in jointed composition w/molded shoes & felt outfits & hats w/their names, made by Knickerbocker, 1930s, Dwarfs 9" h., Snow White 15 1/2" h., the set **$1,610**

Snow White & the Seven Dwarfs lawn ornaments, cast cement, small airbrushed & hand-painted figures of each Dwarf & a reclining Snow White, minor chipping & fading, Doc missing right arm, break in right elbow of Snow white, largest 9 1/4" h., the set **$230**

Snow White & the Seven Dwarfs candy containers, hand-painted papier-mâché, many w/original tags marked "© W.D.P. Container made in Germany," four w/fixed heads, 1930s, large 5 1/2" h., the set ... **$180**

Snow White & the Seven Dwarfs movie cel, scene of Snow White gazing down into the wishing well w/eight doves perched around the rim, gouache on celluloid applied to an airbrushed background, vintage matte board w/handwritten pencil notation, also marked on the back & w/copyright stickers, 1937, 4 x 5 1/2". **$4,541**

Walt Disney photograph, black & white image signed by Walt Disney, framed & mounted on an 8 x 10" mat board, photo 7 x 9" **$3,123**

Drugstore & Pharmacy Items

The old-time corner drugstore, once a familiar part of every American town, has now given way to a modern, efficient pharmacy. With the streamlining and modernization of this trade, many of the early tools and store adjuncts have been outdated and now fall in the realm of "collectibles." Listed here are some of the tools, bottles, display pieces and other emphemera once closely associated with the druggist's trade.

Apothecary storage jar, cov., free-blown clear cylindrical jar w/two applied cobalt blue bands around the body, high domed clear cover w/cobalt blue rim band & hollow blown knob finial, pontil scar, ca. 1850, 11" h. **$532**

Apothecary jar w/fitted lid, cobalt blue-glazed pottery, cylindrical w/ waisted neck, wide gold banner printed in black "Pulv. Lapis P.," probably English, ca. 1860-80, 6 5/8" h. **$448**

Apothecary show bottle, blown bulbous ovoid ruby glass body w/ tapering cylindrical neck & flaring rim, raised on an applied clear pedestal & round foot, original clear hollow-blown stopper, probably American, ca. 1870-90, 10" h. **$504**

Apothecary show globe w/original stopper, Art Deco style, a large clear glass teardrop-shaped globe w/a stepped shoulder, short cylindrical neck & tall oblong stopper, fitted in cast- and polished aluminum three-footed stand, American, ca. 1920-35, 18 1/8" h. **$420**

Balance scales, brass, central shaft w/the balance arm suspending a fixed tray on one side & a suspended small tray on the other, on a rectangular wooden base, w/five weights, crossbar marked "W & T Avery Lt. - To Weigh 2 lb.," minor scuffing, 19th c., 10 3/4 x 20", 22" h. **$259**

Countertop display jar, square tall clear glass w/a wide mouth w/fitted mushroom-style stopper, the front w/a large rectangular label-under-glass reading "Dr. D. Jayne's Sanative Pills for Constipation, Biliousness, Sick Headache, Etc. - Sugar-Coated - 25 Cents," ca. 1880-95, 8" h. **$1,456**

Drug bottle, "C.W. Snow & Co., Druggists (design of eagle w/shield & mortar & pestle), Syracuse, N.Y.," square w/tooled lip, ca. 1885-95, deep cobalt blue, 8 1/4" h. **$468**

Drug bottle, "Jacob's Pharmacy (motif of eagle on mortar & pestle) Atlanta GA," tooled mouth, "W.T. Co. U.S.A." on smooth base, 70% original label for "Strychnine Sulphate," ca. 1885-1910, amber, 2 1/2" h. **$77**

Drug bottle, rectangular w/sloping shoulder, embossed "Jozeau" & "Pharmacien" on opposite ends, rolled lip, pontil-scarred base, ca. 1840-1855, deep olive green, 4 1/2" h. **$165**

Pill roller, walnut device on a brass base w/a star stamp & a separate two-handled device which glides along top, 19th c., 12" h. **$220**

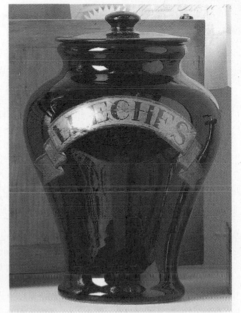

Apothecary storage jar, pottery, wide baluster-form body w/flattened disk cover w/small pierced holes & knob finial, deep cobalt blue glaze w/an arched red-bordered gold banner reading "Leeches," impressed "Royal Doulton England," label probably repainted, late 19th - early 20th c., 9 1/2" h. **$8,625**

Apothecary storage jar, porcelain, cylindrical w/ringed white base & rim, domed cover w/small air holes & button finial, the sides & cover in dark moss green, the base h.p. w/ a gilt crown & scrolls above a red-bordered white banner reading "Leeches," early, 9 1/2" h. **$5,980**

Drug bottle, narrow rectangular w/beveled sides, embossed "Maximo M. Dia - Druggist - Ybor City, Fla.," tooled lip, "W.T. & Co. U.S.A." on smooth base, ca. 1890-1910, cobalt blue, 5 1/8" h. **$190**

Apothecary storage jar, earthenware, wide baluster-form body w/a flaring round foot, fluted band around the lower body & short flaring neck w/flattened inset cover w/small pierced holes & knob finial, leaf-molded loop shoulder handles, sea green at the bottom & top w/the white center area h.p. w/leafy scrolls & a large sea green banner decorated in gold w/the word "Leeches," impressed "Alcock" mark, England, some damage on lid, late 19th - early 20th c., 13 1/2" h. **$8,625**

Figurines

Hummel Figurines & Collectibles _____

The Goebel Company of Oeslau, Germany, first produced M.I. Hummel porcelain figurines in 1934, having obtained the rights to adapt the beautiful pastel sketches of children by Sister Maria Innocentia (Berta) Hummel. Every design by the Goebel artisans was approved by the nun until her death in 1946. Goebel produced these charming collectibles until Sept. 30, 2008. Manufaktur Rodental GmbH resumed production in 2009.

For more information on M.I. Hummel collectibles, see *The Official M.I. Hummel Price Guide* (Krause Publications, a division of F+W Media, Inc.).

HUMMEL TRADEMARKS

Since 1935, there have been several changes in the trademarks on M.I. Hummel items. In later years of production, each new trademark design merely replaced the old one, but in the earlier years, frequently the new design trademark would be placed on a figurine that already bore the older style trademark.

The Crown Mark (TMK-1): 1934-1950

The Crown Mark (TMK-1 or CM), sometimes referred to as the "Crown-WG," was used by Goebel on all of its products in 1935, when M.I. Hummel figurines were first made commercially available. The letters WG below the crown in the mark are the initials of William Goebel, one of the founders of the company. The crown signifies his loyalty to the imperial family of Germany at the time of the mark's design, around 1900. The mark is sometimes found in an incised circle.

Another Crown-type mark is sometimes confusing to collectors; some refer to it as the "Narrow Crown" and others the "Wide Ducal Crown." This mark was introduced by Goebel in 1937 and used on many of its products.

Often, the Crown Mark will appear twice on the same piece, more often one mark incised and the other stamped. This is, as we know, the "Double Crown."

When World War II ended and the United States Occupation Forces allowed Goebel to begin exporting, the pieces were marked as having been made in the occupied zone.

These marks were applied to the bases of the figurines, along with the other markings, from 1946 through 1948. They were sometimes applied under the glaze and often over the glaze. Between 1948 and 1949, the U.S. Zone mark requirement was dropped, and the word "Germany" took its place. With the partitioning of Germany into East and West, "W. Germany," "West Germany," or "Western Germany" began to appear most of the time instead.

Incised   *Stamped*   *Wide Ducal*
Crown Mark   *Crown Mark*   *Crown Mark*

The Full Bee Mark (TMK-2): 1940-1959

In 1950, Goebel made a major change in its trademark. The company incorporated a bee in a V. It is thought that the bumblebee part of the mark was derived from a childhood nickname of Sister Maria Innocentia Hummel, meaning bumblebee. The bee flies within a V, which is the first letter of the German word for distributing company, Verkaufsgesellschaft.

There are actually 12 variations of the Bee marks to be found on Goebel-produced M.I. Hummel items.

The Full Bee mark, also referred to as TMK-2 or abbreviated FB, is the first of the Bee marks to appear. The mark evolved over nearly 20 years until the company began to modernize it. It is sometimes found in an incised circle.

The very large bee flying in the V remained until around 1956, when the bee was reduced in size and lowered into the V. It can be found incised, stamped in black, or stamped in blue, in that order, through its evolution.

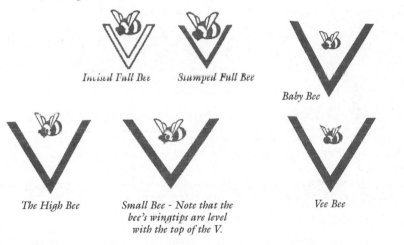

Incised Full Bee   *Stamped Full Bee*

Baby Bee

The High Bee   *Small Bee - Note that the bee's wingtips are level with the top of the V.*

Vee Bee

The Stylized Bee (TMK-3): 1958-1972

A major change in the way the bee is rendered in the trademark made its appearance in 1960. The Stylized Bee (TMK-3), sometimes abbreviated as Sty-Bee, as the major component of the trademark appeared in three basic forms through 1972. The first two are both classified as the Stylized Bee (TMK-3), but the third is considered a fourth step in the evolution, the Three Line Mark (TMK-4).

The Large Stylized Bee: This trademark was used primarily from 1960 through 1963. The color of the mark will be black or blue. It is sometimes found inside an incised circle. When you find the Large Stylized Bee mark, you will normally find a stamped "West" or "Western Germany" in black elsewhere on the base, but not always.

The Small Stylized Bee: This mark is also considered to be TMK-3. It was used concurrently with the Large Stylized Bee from about 1960 and continued in this use until about 1972. The mark is usually rendered in blue, and it too is often accompanied by a stamped black "West" or "Western Germany." Collectors and dealers sometimes refer to the mark as the One Line Mark.

Large Stylized Bee   *Small Stylized Bee*

FIGURINES

The Three Line Mark (TMK-4): 1964-1972

This trademark is sometimes abbreviated 3-line or 3LM in print. The trademark used the same stylized V and bee as the others, but also included three lines of wording beside it. This major change appeared in blue.

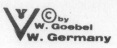

Three Line Mark

The Last Bee Mark (TMK-5): 1972-1979

Developed and occasionally used as early as 1970, this major change was known by some collectors as the Last Bee Mark because the next change in the trademark no longer incorporated any form of the V and the bee. However, with the reinstatement of a bee in TMK-8 with the turn of the century, TMK-5 is not technically the "Last Bee" any longer. The mark was used until about mid-1979. There are three minor variations in the mark shown in the illustration. Generally, the mark was placed under the glaze from 1972 through 1976 and is found placed over the glaze from 1976 through 1979.

Last Bee Mark

The Missing Bee Mark (TMK 6): 1979-1991

The transition to this trademark began in 1979 and was complete by mid-1980. Goebel removed the V and bee from the mark altogether, calling it the Missing Bee. In conjunction with this change, the company instituted the practice of adding to the traditional artist's mark the date the artist finished painting the piece.

Missing Bee Mark

The Hummel Mark (TMK-7): 1991-1999

In 1991, Goebel changed the trademark once again. This time, the change was not only symbolic of the reunification of the two Germanys by removal of the "West" from the mark, but very significant in another way. Until then, Goebel used the same trademark on virtually all of its products. The mark illustrated here was for exclusive use on Goebel products made from the paintings and drawings of M.I. Hummel.

Hummel Mark

The Millennium Bee (TMK-8): 2000-2008

Goebel decided to celebrate the beginning of a new century with a revival in a bee-adorned trademark. Seeking once again to honor the memory of Sister Maria Innocentia Hummel, a bumblebee, this time flying solo without the V, was reinstated into the mark in 2000 and ended in 2008. Goebel stopped production of the M.I. Hummel figurines on Sept. 30, 2008.

Millennium Bee Mark

The Manufaktur Rödental Mark (TKM-9): 2009-Present

Manufaktur Rödental purchased the rights to produce M.I. Hummel figurines from Goebel in 2009. This trademark signifies a new era for Hummel figurines while maintaining the same quality and workmanship from the master sculptors and master painters at the Rödental factory. This trademark has a full bee using yellow and black for the bumblebee, which circles around the words "Original M.I. Hummel Germany" with the copyright sign next to M.I. Hummel. Manufaktur Rödental is underneath the circle with a copyright sign.

EARLY M.I. HUMMEL FIGURINES

For purposes of simplification, the various trademarks have been abbreviated in the list. Generally speaking, earlier trademarks are worth more than later trademarks.

TRADEMARK	ABBREVIATIONS	DATES
Crown	TMK-1	1934-1950
Full Bee	TMK-2	1940-1959
Stylized Bee	TMK-3	1958-1972
Three Line Mark	TMK-4	1964-1972
Last Bee	TMK-5	1972-1979
Missing Bee	TMK-6	1979-1991
Hummel Mark	TMK-7	1991-1999
Millennium Bee/Goebel Bee	TMK-8	2000-2008
Manufaktur Rödental Mark	TMK-9	2009-present

Hum 2: Little Fiddler, trademarks 1-8. . **$110-$2,000**

Hum 1: Puppy Love, trademarks 1-6. ... **$125-$2,400**

Hum 4: Little Fiddler, trademarks 1-8. The left piece features the doll face with pale hands and face, different head position, and lack of neckerchief.
.... **$200-$1,200**

Hum 3: Book Worm, trademarks 1-8..... **$200-$2,500**

FIGURINES

Hum 5: Strolling Along, trademarks 1-6.................**$150-$350**

Hum 6: Sensitive Hunter, trademarks 1-8...............**$125-$1,200**

Hum 7: Merry Wanderer, trademarks 1-8.............**$200-$25,000**

Hum 8: Book Worm, trademarks 1-8. This image shows the comparison between the normal skin coloration (left) and the pale coloration.
....**$200-$300**

Hum 9: Begging His Share, trademarks 1-7..................**$150-$550**

Hum 10: Flower Madonna, trademarks 1-7..................**$200-$800**

Hum 11: Merry Wanderer, trademarks 1-8..................**$100-$575**

Hum 12: Chimney Sweep, trademarks 1-8....................**$99-$450**

Hum 13: Meditation, trademarks 1-8. ....$99-$2,750

Hum 14/A and 14/B: Book Worm bookends, trademarks 1-7. **$350-$800**

Hum 15: Hear Ye, Hear Ye, trademarks 1-8..................$125-$650

Hum 16: Little Hiker, trademarks 1-8. ....$140-$500

Hum 17: Congratulations, trademarks 1-7..............$200-$2,000

Hum 18: Christ Child, trademarks 1-7 .....$125-$250

Hum 20: Prayer Before Battle, trademarks 1-8 ....$200-$450

FIGURINES

Hum 21: Heavenly Angel, trademarks 1-8 ....**$100-$800**

Hum 22: Angel With Bird holy water font, trademarks 1-8 **$50-$275**

Hum 23: Adoration, trademarks 1-8 ....**$250-$900**

Hum 24: Lullaby candleholder, trademarks 1-7...........**$150-$900**

Hum 25: Angelic Sleep candleholder, trademarks 1-6 **$150-$450**

Hum 26: Child Jesus holy water font, trademarks 1-7 .....**$40-$450**

Hum 27: Joyous News, trademarks 1-7 ....**$225-$750**

Hum 28: Wayside Devotion, trademarks 1-8 ....**$275-$1,100**

Hum 29: Guardian Angel holy water font (closed edition), trademarks 1-3 ....**$800-$1,400**

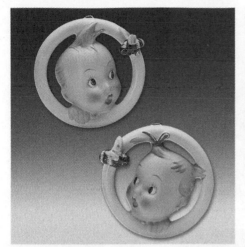

Hum 30/A and Hum 30/B: Ba-Bee Rings wall plaques, trademarks 1-8 .... **$200-$3,700**

Hum 31: Advent Group candleholder, trademark 1 ....**$12,000**

Hum 32: Little Gabriel, trademarks 1-7 .... **$150-$1,300**

Hum 34: Singing Lesson ashtray, trademarks 1-6 ....**$125-$350**

Hum 35: Good Shepherd holy water font, trademarks 1-8 **$50-$350**

Hum 36: Child With Flowers holy water font, trademarks 1-8 ....**$50-$200**

Hum 37: Herald Angels candleholder, trademarks 1-6 **$150-$300**

FIGURINES

Hum 38, Hum 39, and Hum 40: Angel Trio candleholders, trademarks 1-8 ....**$60-$350 each**

Hum 42: Good Shepherd, trademarks 1-7 ....**$195-$5,500**

Hum 43: March Winds, trademarks 1-8.....................**$55-$400**

Hum 44/A and 44/B: Culprits and Out of Danger table lamps, trademarks 1-6 ....**$195-$450 each**

Hum 47: Goose Girl, trademarks 1-8 ....**$120-$780**

Precious Moments

The Precious Moments line of collectibles began more than 30 years ago when artist Sam Butcher and his partner, Bill Biel, started a greeting card company called Jonathan & David Inc. in Grand Rapids, Michigan. They prepared a line of cards and posters with teardrop-eyed children and inspirational messages, called Precious Moments, for the Christian Booksellers Association convention in 1975.

Around that time, Eugene Freedman, then president and CEO of Enesco Corporation, spotted Butcher's artwork and thought the drawings would translate well into figurines. Japanese sculptor Yasuhei Fujioka transformed one of Butcher's drawings into three-dimensional form, and this piece was called Love One Another. Everyone was so pleased with the resulting figurine that 20 more drawings were given to the sculptor, and in 1979, 21 Precious Moments figurines (called the "Original 21") were introduced to the public. Made of porcelain bisque painted pastel colors, the figurines and their inspirational messages were an immediate hit with the public.

So popular was the line of figurines that it spawned several clubs, including the Precious Moments Collectors' Club in 1981, the Precious Moments Birthday Club in 1985, and the Precious Moments Fun Club (which replaced the Birthday Club) in 1998.

Since 1979, more than 1,500 Precious Moments figurines have been produced. Each year approximately 25 to 40 new items are released and 12 to 20 existing pieces are retired or suspended from production.

Besides the Precious Moments line, Butcher produced a collection modeled after his grandchildren, called Sammy's Circus. In 1992 he created Sugar Town, a representation of small-town life.

Today the Precious Moments collection includes figurines, ornaments, plates, bells, musicals, picture frames, and a whole host of giftware and home décor items. Enesco Corporation produced the line until 2005. Precious Moments Inc., based in Carthage, Missouri, currently oversees the distribution of Precious Moments products.

For more information on Precious Moments, see *Warman's Field Guide to Precious Moments Collectibles* by Mary Sieber.

ORIGINAL 21

Come Let Us Adore Him E2011
God Loveth a Cheerful Giver E1378
God Understands E1379B
He Careth For You E1377B
He Leadeth Me E1377A
His Burden is Light E1380G
Jesus is Born E2012
Jesus is the Answer E1381
Jesus is the Light E1373G
Jesus Loves Me (two figurines) E1372B and E1372G

Love is Kind E1379A
Love Lifted Me E1375A
Love One Another E1376
Make a Joyful Noise E1374G
O, How I Love Jesus E1380B
Praise the Lord Anyhow E1374B
Prayer Changes Things E1375B
Smile, God Loves You E1373B
Unto Us a Child is Born E2013
We Have Seen His Star E2010

FIGURINES

PRODUCTION MARKS

A symbol or mark is found on the bottom of each Precious Moments collectible, indicating the year it was produced. Enesco Corporation began putting these marks on Precious Moments pieces starting in 1981. Figurines produced before mid-1981 have no marks and are referred to as "no mark" pieces.

The earliest marks are often the most difficult to locate and, as a result, are continually sought after by collectors. They often have a higher secondary market value as well.

1981 Triangle	1991 Vessel	2001 Sandal
1982 Hourglass	1992 G clef	2002 Cross in heart
1983 Fish	1993 Butterfly	2003 Crown
1984 Cross	1994 Trumpet	2004 Three-petal flower
1985 Dove	1995 Ship	2005 Loaf of bread
1986 Olive branch	1996 Heart	2006 House
1987 Cedar tree	1997 Sword	2007 Hammer
1988 Flower	1998 Eyeglasses	2008 Stylized PM heart
1989 Bow and arrow	1999 Star	2009 Sheaf of wheat
1990 Flame	2000 Cracked egg	2010 Tree

The Lord Bless You and Keep You bell E7179, 1982. ....**$65**

Autumn's Praise 12084, Four Seasons series, 1986............**$50**

Baby Boy Standing E2852A, 1987....................................**$70**

Baby Boy Crawling E2852E, 1987...**$70**

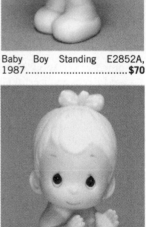

Baby Girl Sitting E2852D, 1987. ....**$70**

Baby's First Picture E2841, Baby's First series, 1984.................. $110

Be Not Weary in Doing Well E3111, 1979...............$65-$185

Blessed Are the Peacemakers E3107, 1980...............$60-$105

Blessings From My House to Yours E0503, 1983.......................$70

Dawn's Early Light PM831, Precious Moments Collectors' Club, 1983...................................$40

Brotherly Love 100544, 1985. ....$70

But Love Goes On Forever E3115, 1979....$40-$100

FIGURINES

Eggs Over Easy E3118, 1980.
....**$60-$120**

The End is in Sight E9253,
1982.............................**$55-$100**

Get Into the Habit of Prayer
12203, 1984.......................**$49**

Fishing for Friends BC861, Precious
Moments Birthday Club, 1986...**$102**

Friends Never Drift Apart 100250, 1985................................. **$68**

God Bless America 102938, America
Forever series, 1985.................. **$39**

God Bless Our Home 12319, 1985...**$77**

God Bless Our Years Together 12440, 1985..... **$265**

God Bless You With Rainbows nightlight 16020, 1986............ **$100**

God Blessed Our Year Together With So Much Love and Happiness E2854, Anniversary series, 1984. .... **$61**

God Loveth a Cheerful Giver E1378, 1979, one of the Original 21 figurines. **$798**

God is Love E5213, 1980. ....**$55-$120**

God is Love, Dear Valentine thimble 100625, 1986. **$15**

God's Speed E3112, 1980...**$50-$105**

FIGURINES

Grandma's Prayer PM861, Precious Moments Collectors' Club, 1986......................................**$58**

He Cleansed My Soul 100277, 1986. ....**$55**

He Watches Over Us All E3105, 1980.............................**$50-$70**

The Heavenly Light E5637, Nativity series, 1981.............**$35-$65**

His Burden is Light E1380G, 1979, one of the Original 21 figurines............................**$85-$160**

▲How Can Two Work Together Except They Agree E9263, 1983. **$175**
◄His Sheep Am I E7161, Nativity series, 1982................**$60-$70**

I Believe in Miracles E7156, 1982............................ **$50-$75**

I Get a Bang Out of You 12262, 1985................................ **$42**

I'm a Possibility 100188, 1986. .... **$40**

I Get a Kick Out of You E2827, 1984........................... **$185**

I'm Following Jesus PM862, Precious Moments Collectors' Club, 1986. .... **$35**

Isn't He Precious E5379, Nativity series, 1984. .... **$36**

It Is Better to Give Than to Receive 12297, 1985. .... **$42**

Jesus is Coming Soon 12343, 1985................................... **$29**

Jesus Loves Me E9278, 1983.
.... **$35**

Jesus Loves Me E1372B, 1979.
.... **$30-$81**

Jesus Loves Me E1372G, 1979, one of the Original 21 figurines.
..................................**$45-$130**

The Joy of the Lord is My Strength 100137, 1986.....................**$48**

Just a Line to Wish You a Happy Day 520721, 1989. .... **$60**

Let Love Reign E9273, 1982.
..................................**$105-$245**

Let Us Call the Club to Order E0303, 1982................. **$45-$50**

The Lord Bless You and Keep You E3114, 1980................ **$50-$75**

Lord Help Us Keep Our Act Together 101850, 1986.**$100-$125**

Love Cannot Break a True Friendship E4722, 1980.
....**$85-$130**

Love is the Glue That Mends 104027, 1987......**$55**

Love is Kind E5377, 1984....**$32**

Love is Sharing E7162, 1982.
................................**$105-$130**

Love Never Fails 12300, 1985.
....**$55**

Love Lifted Me E5201, 1980. .... **$65-$130**

Love Lifted Me E1375A, 1979, one of the Original 21 figurines...**$60-$140**

FIGURINES

Love One Another E1376, 1979, one of the Original 21 figurines. ....$50-$120

Loving is Sharing E3110B, 1980. ....$50-$120

Make a Joyful Noise E1374G, 1979.................................$100

Two variations of Make a Joyful Noise E1374G, 1979, one of the Original 21 figurines..............................$60-$100

May Your Christmas Be Warm E2348, 1982. ....$120-$155

Mommy, I Love You 109975, 1987.................................$31

Mommy, I Love You 112143, 1987.................................$40

Mother Sew Dear E3106, 1980. ....$35-$55

Mow Power To Ya PM892, Precious Moments Collectors' Club, 1989. .... **$32**

My Guardian Angel boy E5205 and My Guardian Angel girl E5206, 1981.
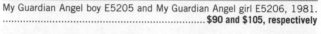 .... **$90 and $105, respectively**

Nobody's Perfect E9268, 1982.........................**$60-$85**

O, How I Love Jesus E1380B, 1979, one of the Original 21 figurines.
....**$85-$140**

Onward Christian Soldiers E0523, 1983............................ **$55-$95**

Far left: Our First Christmas Together E2377, 1982....**$69**

Left: Part of Me Wants to Be Good 12149, 1985... **$84**

FIGURINES

The Perfect Grandpa E7160, 1982. .... **$65-$80**

Praise the Lord Anyhow E1374B, 1979, one of the Original 21 figurines. ....**$65-$110**

The Purr-Fect Grandma E3109, 1980............................ **$35-$75**

Seek and Ye Shall Find E0105, 1985....................................**$38**

Smile, God Loves You E1373B, 1979, one of the Original 21 figurines............................. **$40-$95**

Sew in Love 106844, 1988. ....**$60**

Sharing Our Season Together E0501, 1983. .... **$116**

The Spirit is Willing, But the Flesh is Weak 100196, 1987.........**$53**

Trust in the Lord to the Finish PM842, Precious Moments Collectors' Club, 1984...............**$55**

Waddle I Do Without You 12459, Clown series, 1985...............**$46**

Wishing You a Season Filled With Joy E2805, 1980. ....**$80-$120**

We're In It Together E9259, 1982. ....**$55**

Wishing You a Cozy Season 521949, 1989......................**$38**

You Can't Run Away From God E0525, 1983...............**$85-$155**

You Have Touched So Many Hearts E2821, 1984........................**$47**

FIGURINES

■ Wade Ceramics

In 1967, Brooke Bond Foods, the then-parent company of Red Rose Tea, contracted with George Wade and Son Ltd., a British ceramics manufacturer with roots dating back to 1867, to produce a line of miniatures to be included in specially marked boxes of Red Rose Tea in certain parts of Canada. The original 32 miniatures — known as "Whimsies" — were comprised of an assortment of animals.

The company was pleased with the results, and launched a similar promotion in 1970, this time targeting the British market. In 1983, the company started including the miniatures in tea sold in the United States. In all, there have been a total of 206 different Whimsies issued by Wade for Red Rose Tea promotions.

Collectors of Wade Whimsies congregate on sites like the Wade Whimsies group on Yahoo! (visit WadeWhimsies.com for more information), and there's also the Official International Wade Collectors Club (WadeCollectorsClub.co.uk).

Ian Warner, a longtime collector and co-author of *The World of Wade Figurines and Miniatures II*, which was released in March, says that in the early days of the promotion, quality control was virtually nonexistent. "Many figurines came from the pottery with flaws or even broken but with a glaze over the broken area," he says. "Collectors are only interested in figurines without flaws, cracks, etc., which makes it more interesting for collectors to hunt down the more 'perfect' pieces. Many figurines came from the pottery with slightly differing decorations as the early figurines were hand-painted. These variations are very collectible and highly sought after by collectors."

In recent years, says Warner, the variations in Whimsies have actually increased because of a change in the method of production. "For many years the figurines were produced using hand-crafted steel forms or molds. Each mold could produce up to 30,000 figurines before being discarded or remade," he says. "Starting with the Pet Shop series [in 2006], Wade started to use a new method of production called 'solid casting.' Only about 30 figurines could be produced from a mold, so many molds had to be made. This has caused a large number of size and mold variations."

Wade figurines also have a long history outside of their association with Red Rose Tea. Wade first began manufacturing Whimsies in 1953 and had been producing other figurines since the 1930s. Some of these early figurines fetch prices many times that of the most valuable Red Rose figurines.

Zac Bissonnette, for Antique Trader *magazine*

OFFICIAL INTERNATIONAL WADE COLLECTORS CLUB (OIWCC)

The Official International Wade Collectors Club (OIWCC) was formed in 1994 with the intention of uniting collectors of both new and old Wade figurines from around the world.

Members receive a quarterly magazine, *The Official Wade Collectors Club Magazine*, which has news and views, details of the Wade events throughout the year, sales and wants, and members-only exclusive offers; for 2011 the members-only set will be a set of whimsies: the Survival Set.

Members also receive a membership certificate and card, a membership Whimsie plaque showing the year of membership, and a free exclusive figurine each year; for 2011, the club exclusive will be a Whimsie Elephant, part of the Survival Whimsies series of 2011.

To become a member of the OIWCC, write to The Official International Wade Collectors Club, PO Box 3012, Stoke-on-Trent, ST3 9DD, England, UK. For more information on the OIWCC, contact club@wadecollectorsclub.co.uk or visit www.wadecollectorsclub.co.uk. The OIWCC can be contacted via telephone at 0845 2462525 or from the U.S. +44 845 2462525.

Wade Whimsies, collection of boxed and unboxed ceramic miniatures, including Whimsey-on-Why, "a beautiful miniature English Village in red porcelain," consisting of eight buildings, mint within excellent box; Nurseries Set, five pieces including Little Bo Peep, Old Woman Who Lived In A Shoe, etc., mint in excellent plug packaging; plus No. 4 Kitten; No. 3 Mongrel; No. 1 Fawn; No. 2 Rabbit; No. 15 Trout; No. 5 Spaniel; Nursery Favourites No. 15 Tommy Tucker; No. 8 Polly Kettle; plus large quantity of unboxed, mainly mint to excellent condition. **$1,112**
Courtesy Vectis Auctions LTD, Halls Fine Art, Tom Harris Auctions, DuMouchelles

Set of six Whimsies from 1971, Set No. 1... **$20**
Courtesy Vectis Auctions LTD, Halls Fine Art, Tom Harris Auctions, DuMouchelles

Complete set of Wade first edition Whimsies, set of five; horses, issued 1956-1959, including mare, foal, colt and beagle in addition to a leaping fawn.
.... **$50**
Courtesy Vectis Auctions LTD, Halls Fine Art, Tom Harris Auctions, DuMouchelles

Boxed edition of Wade Whimsies of horses and a dog, set of five...................................... **$90**
Courtesy Vectis Auctions LTD, Halls Fine Art, Tom Harris Auctions, DuMouchelles

Furniture

■ Antique _____

Furniture collecting has been a major part of the world of collecting for over 100 years. It is interesting to note how this marketplace has evolved.

Whereas in past decades, 18th century and early 19th century furniture was the mainstay of the American furniture market, in recent years there has been a growing demand for furniture manufactured since the 1920s. Factory-made furniture from the 1920s and 1930s, often featuring Colonial Revival style, has seen a growing appreciation among collectors. It is well made and features solid wood and fine veneers rather than the cheap compressed wood materials often used since the 1960s. Also much in demand in recent years is furniture in the Modernistic and Mid-Century taste, ranging from Art Deco through quality designer furniture of the 1950s through the 1970s.

These latest trends have offered even the less well-healed buyer the opportunity to purchase fine furniture at often reasonable prices. Buying antique and collectible furniture is no longer the domain of millionaires and museums.

Today more furniture is showing up on Internet sites, and sometimes good buys can be made. However, it is important to deal with honest, well-informed sellers and have a good knowledge of what you want to purchase.

As in the past, it makes sense to purchase the best pieces you can find, whatever the style or era of production. Condition is still very important if you want your example to continue to appreciate in value in the coming years. For 18th century and early 19th century pieces, the original finish and hardware are especially important as it is with good furniture of the early 20th century Arts & Crafts era. These features are not quite as important for most manufactured furniture of the Victorian era and furniture from the 1920s and later. However, it is good to be aware that a good finish and original hardware will mean a stronger market when pieces are resold. Of course, whatever style of furniture you buy, you are better off with examples that have not had major repair or replacements. On really early furniture, repairs and replacements will definitely have an impact on the sale value, but they will also be a factor on newer designs from the 20th century.

As with all types of antiques and collectibles, there is often a regional preference for certain furniture types. Although the American market is much more homogenous than it was in past decades, there still tends to be a preference for 18th century and early 19th century furniture along the Eastern Seaboard, whereas Victorian designs tend to have a larger market in the Midwest and South. In the West, country furniture and "western" designs definitely have the edge except in major cities along the West Coast.

Whatever your favorite style furniture, there are still fine examples to be found. Just study the history of your favorites and the important points of their construction before you invest heavily. A wise shopper will be a happy shopper and have a collection certain to continue to appreciate as time marches along.

For more information on furniture, see *Antique Trader Furniture Price Guide* by Kyle Husfloen.

BEDROOM SUITES

Victorian Eastlake substyle: double half-tester bed, a marble-topped chest of drawers w/mirror, a marble-topped washstand w/mirror; walnut & burl walnut, the half-tester on the bed w/a stepped angular cornice w/panels carved w/stylized flowers between corner blocks, flat serpentine brackets supporting it above the high headboard w/a matching carved cornice, the lower flat-topped footboard w/floral-incised arched & burl panels above rectangular panels, the other pieces w/matching crests, while marble tops & arrangements of drawers w/stamped brass pulls w/angular bails, marble on chest w/old repair & cracks, ca. 1880, bed 63 1/2 x 79 1/2", 8' 3" h., 3 pcs. **$7,188**

Victorian Renaissance Revival substyle: canopied double bed & mirrored armoire; ebonized beech, the bed headboard w/a broken-scroll crestrail centered by a scroll-carved plaque centered by a classical female mask, low spindled galleries on each side between the blocked stiles w/turned finials, all above an arched frieze band over a solid panel, the low footboard w/a flat top rail above two large rectangular raised panels centered by large roundels & flanked on each side by slender columns, the bed w/an appropriate giltwood canopy frame centered w/a scroll & palmette finial, Napoleon II Era, France, ca. 1860, bed 60 x 82", 72" h. **$11,213**

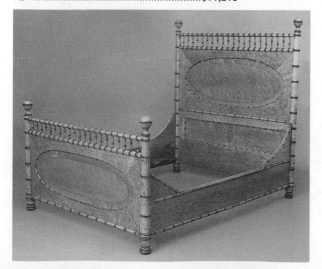

Victorian Faux Bamboo: double bed, chest of drawers, octagonal side table & pair of side chairs; turned wood & bird's-eye maple, the high-backed bed w/a tall rectangular headboard w/a top low gallery of bamboo-turned spindles above the bird's-eye maple headboard w/a large oval recessed panel, the bamboo-turned side stiles topped w/large ball finials, the side rails w/bamboo-turned trim & the low footboard matching the highboard, the chest of drawers w/a large oval mirror swiveling between bamboo-turned uprights above the rectangular case w/ three long graduated drawers, attributed to R. J. Horner & Co., New York, New York, ca. 1875, bed 60 x 81", 68" h., the set **$13,800**

BEDS

Federal tall-poster canopy bed, maple, the slender ring-turned & tapering posts joined by a rectangular canopy frame, the headposts joined by a simple arched headboard w/incurved sides, original rope rails, raised on tall ring- and baluster-turned legs w/ knob feet, possibly Connecticut, 1790-1810, 55 1/4 x 78 3/4", 84 1/2" h. **$3,840**

Classical tall-poster canopy bed, mahogany, a large rectangular canopy w/a deep frame & wide flaring cornice supported on four matching slender spiral-twist turned posts topped by pineapple carving & ending in a ring-turned section w/an acanthus leaf-carved section, all supported on short ring- and, rod-turned legs ending in ball feet, the high headboard w/scroll-cut top ending in rosettes, early 19th c., 62 x 82", 122" h. **$51,750**

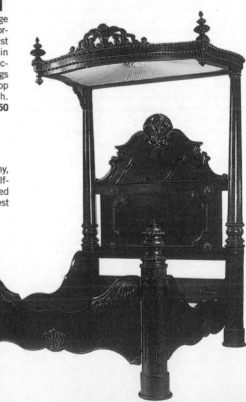

Victorian Rococo half-tester bed, carved mahogany, the tall tapering columnar head posts support a half-tester w/a deep serpentine-sided frame w/gadrooned bands, an ornate arched & pierced scroll-carved crest & double-knob turned corner finials, the high headboard panel w/a tall arched & scroll-carved top centered by a leafy scroll finial above a carved grape cluster, two triangular raised panels above a long molded rectangular recessed panel w/a carved rosette at each corner, a short columnar foot posts carved w/Moorish arch panels below the heavy ring- and knob-turned tops flank the serpentine leafy scroll & shell-carved footboard, matching fancy siderails, ca. 1850s, 65 x 84", 110" h. **$26,450**

BENCHES

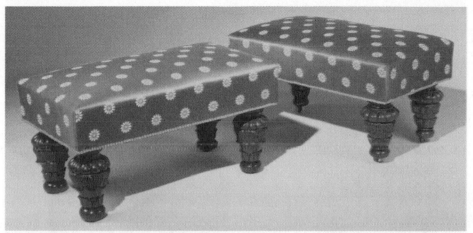

Classical benches, carved mahogany, the long deep upholstered top raised on four heavy tapering ring-turned & gadrooned legs w/knob feet, American or English, ca. 1815-25, 20 x 35", 18" h., pr. **$7,200**

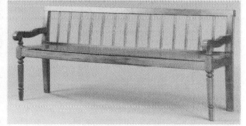

Country-style bench, hardwood, a long flat crestrail above a spindled back flanked by square stiles continuing to the rear legs, shaped open arms on low turned supports flanking the long plank seat, ring- and rod-turned tapering front legs, 19th c., 71" l. **$1,016**

▲Classical window bench, carved mahogany, the long rectangular upholstered seat flanked by open end arms w/baluster- and ring-turned spiral-carved crestrails on scrolled spiral-carved stiles continuing to form the sabre legs, each back w/a lower horizontal splat w/a central shaped tablet flanked by scrolls, old refinish, possibly Pennsylvania, ca. 1820-25, minor imperfections, 16 x 41", 33" h. **$5,875**

Louis XVI-Style window bench, giltwood, the padded rectangular top w/padded & outscrolled upholstered low ends, above a narrow apron centered by a cornucopia-carved pendant, raised on eight tapering fluted legs ending in peg feet, France, mid-19th c., 22 x 48", 18 1/2" h. **$4,830**

FURNITURE

BOOKCASES

Arts & Crafts (Mission-style) bookcase, glazed oak, the rectangular top w/blocked ends above a frieze band w/blocked corners & incised w/the word "Roycroft," above a tall glazed cupboard door opening to three wooden shelves, a single deep drawer at the bottom w/a small metal knob & two incised Roycroft logos, simple bracketed front apron, Roycrofters, East Aurora, New York, ca. 1908, 16 1/4 x 33 1/4", 67 7/8" h. **$16,730**

Classical bookcase, mahogany & mahogany veneer, in the Louis Philippe taste, the rectangular top w/a deep flaring ogee cornice above a pair of tall four-pane glazed doors framed by ogee molding & opening to three wooden shelves above a pair of shorter paneled doors, deep flat apron w/low bracket feet, second quarter 19th c., 19 x 58", 98 1/2" h. **$8,050**

Country-style bookcases, painted & decorated pine, a rectangular top w/narrow molded cornice above a tall case w/a very tall 28-pane glazed door opening to five wooden shelves, a mid-molding above a long deep drawer w/two turned wood knobs, flat molded base, original reddish brown grain painting, central Massachusetts, ca. 1830, minor imperfections, 14 x 33", 82 3/4" h., pr. **$10,575**

BUREAUX PLAT

Louis XV-Style bureau plat, ormolu-mounted kingwood & marquetry, the rectangular top w/serpentine ormolu-mounted edges set w/a leather writing surface, above a conforming frieze, the front w/three drawers fronted w/foliate srigs within scrolling frames, the sides & back similarly decorated, the C-scrolled ormolu long leg mounts trailing foliage down the cabriole legs tapering & ending in scrolled sabots, after the model by Jacques Dubois, France, last quarter 19th c., 31 x 53", 31" h. **$12,000**

CABINETS

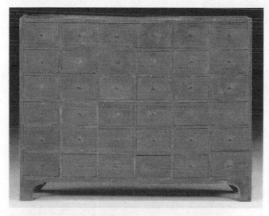

Apothecary cabinet, country style, the narrow long rectangular top above a case fitted w/ six rows of six small drawers each, on simple bracket feet, old powder blue paint, 19th c., 9 3/4 x 58 1/2", 45 3/4" h. **$10,800**

China cabinet, Victorian Golden Oak substyle, side-by-side type, the top w/a wide broken-scroll crest centered by a carved fruit finial above small open shelf w/upturned ends supported on a scroll-carved bracket & slender turned spindle, above the two-section case w/the wider left side topped by a large shaped rectangular beveled mirror above a stepped top w/a shaped side panel carved w/an animal head & a serpentine front above two long serpentine drawers w/fancy pierced-brass pulls & keyhole escutcheons above a pair of wide paneled cupboard doors w/ornately scroll-carved panels & projecting flat cabriole legs, the right side of the case w/a tall glazed door w/a scroll-carved top & base opening to adjustable wooden shelves, original finish, late 19th c., 52" w., 5' 7" h. **$1,645**

FURNITURE

Collector's cabinet on stand, Oriental style, parcel-gilt black lacquer, two-part construction: the upper cabinet w/a rectangular top, sides & pair of doors richly decorated w/scenes of flowers & birds, the doors w/ molded panels decorated w/landscapes in heavy gold enamel & mounted w/brass fitting, opening to an interior composed of 12 drawers of varying sizes each w/ornate flower & insect decoration; the lower stand section made in Europe & features similar decoration, the cabinet made in Japan, ca. 1850, some brass loose, minor wear, 21 x 40 1/4", 62" h. **$12,650**

China cabinet, Chippendale-Style, mahogany & mahogany veneer, breakfront-style, the rectangular top w/a projecting central section, the narrow flaring bead-carved cornice above a conforming blind fret-carved frieze band above a wide tall glazed central door opening to three long wood shelves & flanked by tall narrow geometrically-glazed doors & glazed side panels above the slightly stepped-out base cabinet w/a gadrooned band above a blind fret-carved frieze band above a pair of center doors decorated w/veneered panels framing a large oval reserve carved in relief w/Chinese figures & a small temple, flat side doors decorated w/veneered panels & a diamond-shaped burl center panel, narrow molded base raised on four carved ogee bracket feet, England, early 20th c., 19 1/2 x 60 1/2", 81" h. **$5,750**

Curio cabinet, Rococo style, walnut & burl walnut, an ornate arched & stepped deep front crestrail centered by shell-carved crest flanked by small stepped platforms on each side, all above a pair of tall arched 8-pane glazed doors w/delicate ornate pierced carving over the top two center panes & lower two center panes, the sides composed of four glass panels, the deep ogee apron fitted w/a pair of drawers w/fancy brass pulls in the front, a molded base raised on heavy paw-carved front feet, Holland, ca. 1880, 17 x 63", 99" h. **$4,600**

CHAIRS

Far left: Arts & Crafts style side chair, oak, the tall slightly canted band w/ square stiles joined by two rails centered by a tight grouping of slender square spindles, raised above the leather-upholstered slip seat above square legs joined by high flat front & rear stretchers & low side stretchers joined by a tight grouping of slender square spindles to the bottom of the seatrail, Model No. 384, red decal mark of Gustav Stickley, ca. 1907, 46" h. **$3,585**

Left: Chippendale armchair, carved mahogany, the ox-yoke crestrail w/scrolled ear centered by a carved shell above the pierced vasiform splat, serpentine open arms ending in scroll-carved hand grips above incurved arm supports, wide upholstered slip seat w/a flat seatrail centered at the front by a carved shell, cabriole front legs w/shell-carved knees ending in claw-and ball foot, canted turned rear legs, descended in the Stevenson Family, Philadelphia, ca. 1770, 40 7/8" h. **$36,000**

Classical side chairs, carved mahogany, a narrow curved flat crestrail above a large pierced harp-shaped splat raised on a narrow lower rail, flanked by the scrolled & reeded stiles continuing down to flank the upholstered slip seat, incurved acanthus-carved front legs ending in hairy paw feet, canted square rear legs, attributed to Duncan Phyfe, New York, New York, ca. 1815-25, 32 3/4" h., pr. **$19,120**

Federal side chairs, carved mahogany, the shield-back centered by a pierced oval splat trimmed w/carved drapery swags, over-upholstered seat on square tapering front legs & canted square rear legs, Salem, Massachusetts, 1790-1810, 38 3/8" h., pr. **$13,145**

FURNITURE

Modern style armchair, leather & tubular steel, "Ox" design, the wide curved & rolled black leather crestrail resembling ox horns above the wide upholstered back & wide seat flanked by low rolled leather arms, the curved steel tubular frame w/short outswept rear legs & taller angled front legs, designed by Hans Wegner, manufactured by Johannes Hansen, Model No. EJ 100, Denmark, ca. 1960, 35" h. **$15,534**

Queen Anne corner chair, maple & walnut, the curved low backrail w/a raised center section & forming flat scroll arms raised on three columnar-turned spindles & two vasi-form splats, wovan rush seet, cabriole front legs ending in a pad foot, three column-, block- and knob-turned side & rear legs all joined by a turned, tapering cross-stretcher, New England, 1730-50, 31" h. **$21,510**

William & Mary armchair, painted soft maple & birch, the very tall narrow back w/a high ornate scroll-carved crestrail above a tall narrow caned back panel, the ring- and block-turned stiles w/small knob-turned finials, shaped open arms w/scroll-carved grips raised on columnar-turned arm supports above the wide caned seat, knob- and block-turned front legs ending in knob feet & joined by a ball- and rod-turned front stretcher, matching turned rear stretcher & turned H-stretcher joining the legs, old black paint, Massachusetts or Europe, 1690-1730, 55" h. **$31,200**

Windsor "comb-back" armchair, painted hardwood, the slender serpentine crestrail above seven tall turned spindles continuing through the U-shaped medial rail, the flat narrow shaped arms raised on two more spindles & a canted baluster-turned arm support, the oval shaped seat on widely canted baluster- and ring-turned legs joined by a swelled H-stretcher, old worn red paint over yellow & early paints, overall 41 1/4" h. **$20,700**

CHESTS & CHESTS OF DRAWERS

Blanket chest, country-style, painted & decorated, the hinged rectangular lid w/molded edges opening to a deep well, a molded base raised on shaped bracket feet, decorated overall w/grain painting w/a yellow ground covered w/red burl-style graining, Maine, 1820-40, 21 1/2 x 51 1/2", 27" h **$5,975**

Chippendale "reverse-serpentine" chest of drawers, mahogany, the rectangular top w/molded edges & a reverse-serpentined front edge projecting over a conforming case w/four long graduated drawers w/butterfly brasses & keyhole escutcheons & blocked ends, the conforming base molding over fancy scroll-cut returns & a central drop raised on short claw-and-ball front feet, Salem, Massachusetts, 1760-80, 22 3/4 x 41 3/4", 22 3/4" h. **$27,485**

Country-style sugar chest, cherry, the rectangular hinged top opening to a deep divided well, above a lower section w/a single drawer w/two small turned pulls, raised on ring- and knob-turned legs, Tennessee, mid-19th c., 18 x 24 1/2", 32 1/2" h. **$3,800**

Chippendale "block-front" chest of drawers, mahogany, the rectangular top w/a blocked front above a conforming case of four long graduated drawers w/butterfly brasses & keyhole escutcheons, molded blocked base on tall bracket feet, Massachusetts, 1760-80, original brasses, 18 x 31", 31 1/2" h. **$28,800**

Classical chest of drawers, mahogany grain painting & mahogany veneer, the top w/a very high scroll-carved arched crest w/brass florettes at the scroll tips, above a two-tier section w/a pair of very narrow drawers above a pair of slightly deeper drawers all on the rectangular top slightly overhanging the case w/a projecting long curve-fronted top drawer above three set-back long graduated mahogany-veneered drawers, all drawers w/old pressed lacy glass pulls, the lower drawers flanked by turned black columns, molded base raised on tall heavy ring- and baluster-turned legs w/large ball feet, tiered drawers & case sides decorated w/red & black mahogany graining, State of Maine, first half 19th c., 20 1/2 x 44", overall 64" h. **$4,313**

Dower chest, painted & decorated, the rectangular hinged top w/a molded edge opening to a well, the front elaborately decorated w/brightly painted Pennsylvania Dutch designs, a large central twelve-point star in red & yellow below a facing pair of birds & w/tulips & starflowers below, a rearing unicorn at each side below a large parrot & a cluster of a star, tulip blossoms & starflowers at each end, a German inscription across the top front, all on a dark blue ground, a dark red base molding on dark blue scroll-cut ogee bracket feet, attributed to John Flory (1754-after 1824), Rapho Township, Lancaster County, Pennsylvania, dated 1794, 22 x 51 3/4", 22 1/2" h. .. **$45,410**

Above: Federal "bow-front" chest of drawers, mahogany, rosewood & flame birch veneer, the mahogany rectangular top w/ bowed front edge w/inlay overhangs the conforming case of four long graduated drawers w/flame birch panels & mahogany veneers interspersed w/rosewood-veneered escutcheons, round turned wood pulls, molded base & flaring front French feet w/contrasting crossbanded mahogany veneers, shaped sides, refinished, Portsmouth, New Hampshire, ca. 1800, imperfections, 22 1/2 x 41 1/4", 36 1/2" h. **$14,100**

Left: Federal tall chest of drawers, inlaid walnut, the rectangular top w/a flat-molded cornice above a row of three thumb-molded drawers over a pair of drawers over a stack of four long graduated drawers all w/simple bail handles, string inlay & escutcheons flanked by meandering vines continuing to vases, on cut-out feet & a shaped skirt centered by an inlaid fan, old pulls, old refinish, probably Pennsylvania, ca. 1800, imperfections, 20 1/2 x 40", 71" h. **$5,825**

Above left: Federal sugar chest, inlaid cherry, a hinged rectangular top w/molded edges opening to a deep interior w/a single (missing) divider, dovetailed corners & the front w/fine line inlay w/tiny fans at each corner, a central inlaid oval & a diamond-shaped keyhole escutcheon, fitted in a separate stand w/molded edge above a single long drawer w/matching inlay & inlaid corners raised on four square tapering legs w/ further line inlay, restoration, Mid-Atlantic States, early 19th c., 16 1/2 x 32 1/4", 34 3/4" h. **$12,925**

CUPBOARDS

Corner cupboard, Federal country-style, cherry, the flat top w/a narrow molding above a pair of full-length two-panel cupboard doors w/diamond inlays in the center of the inner rails, scroll-carved apron on high bracket feet, later robin's-egg blue interior paint, made in Louisiana, early 19th c., 23 x 42", 68" h. **$79,500**

Corner cupboard, Federal style, painted pine, barrel-back architectural style, two-part construction: the upper section w/a flat top & deep covered cornice w/wide blocked ends above a corning dentil-carved band over a wider lattice-carved band, projecting lattice-carved side blocks flank the arched & molded top to the wide open display compartment fitted w/ three shelves flanked by fluted pilasters; a conforming mid-molding above the lower case w/a pair of paneled cupboard doors opening to one shelf, deep molded base w/scroll-cut brackets at the front, remnants of old blue & red paint, Mid-Atlantic region, late 18th - early 19th c., 17 3/4 x 52", 84" h. **$8,050**

Jelly cupboard, country-style, painted wood, a narrow rectangular top above an open compartment w/shaped sides over a tall flat single door w/wooden thumb latch opening to three shelves, simple bracket feet, old red paint, 19th c., 13 3/4 x 38", 59 3/4" h. **$5,400**

Corner cupboard, painted pine w/rose head nail construction, one-piece construction, architectural-type; the flat top w/a deep ogee cornice centered by a keystone above a molded arch above the conforming open display section w/ three shaped shelves, the lower cabinet w/a single raised panel door w/original wrought-iron "H" hinges, old blue paint, from a 1748 home in Richmond, Massachusetts, cornice replaced, age splits & edge damage, 18th c., 20 1/4 x 42 1/2", 90 3/8" h. **$2,875**

FURNITURE

Linen press, Chippendale style, mahogany, two-part construction: the upper section w/a rectangular top w/a narrow flaring cornice above a pair of molded panel cupboard doors opening to three linen slides; the lower section w/a hinged slant top w/two simple bail pulls opening to a desk fitted interior w/small drawers above a lower case w/a pair of drawers over two long drawers, all w/simple bail pulls, narrow base molding on scroll-cut bracket feet, one desk drawer signed "J. McCormick" in pencil, Virginia, 1787-1791, 21 x 49", 81" h. **$9,560**

Pewter cupboard, Chippendale country-style, painted pine, two-part construction: the upper section w/a rectangular top w/a deep flaring stepped cornice above a scallop-cut frieze over the tall open compartment w/two long shelves flanked by serpentine-cut sides; the stepped-out lower section w/a pair of drawers w/small old brass knob pulls above a pair of raised-panel cupboard doors, flat molded base on bun feet, old red paint over earlier salmon & black paint, some edge wear & splits, feet old replacements, early 19th c., 23 1/2 x 56", 79 1/4" h. **$6,038**

Step-back wall cupboard, country-style, painted pine, one-piece construction, the rectangular top w/a deep flaring covered cornice above a pair of tall solid raised panel cupboard doors w/cast-iron latches opening to three shelves above an arched pie shelf, the stepped-out lower case w/a pair of drawers w/oval brasses above a pair of raised panel cupboard doors w/simple apron & simple bracket feet, old red paint, interior old light blue paint, one iron latch missing, mid-19th c., 19 1/2 x 48 1/2", 84" h. **$4,000-8,000**

Pie safe, cherry, a rectangular top above a pair of drawers w/pairs of simple turned wood knobs above a pair of wide cupboard doors each mounted w/four pierced tin panels w/pinwheel medallions & floral spandrels, flat apron, raised on baluster- and ring-turned legs w/peg feet, two matching punched tins in each side, opens to three interior shelves, original dark finish, old walnut pulls, Virginia, mid-19th c., restored splits on one door, 18 3/4 x 53", 49" h. **$10,350**

Step-back wall cupboard, country-style, stained poplar, two-part construction: the upper section w/a rectangular top w/a flared ogee cornice above a pair of tall paneled cupboard doors w/thumb latches opening to three shelves; the slightly stepped-out lower section w/a shorter pair of cupboard doors, cut-out base w/angled feet, old red-stained surface, original hardware, Watervliet, New York, ca. 1860, minor imperfections, 19 x 25", 78" h. **$9,988**

DESKS

Chippendale "block-front" slant-front desk, carved mahogany, a narrow rectangular top above a hinged slant-lid w/a pair of large blocked panels flanking a central recessed panel & opening to a fitted interior above a case of four long graduated blocked & recessed drawers all w/large butterfly brasss, molded conforming above w/an arched central drop & scroll-carved bracket feet, Boston or Salem, Massachusetts, 1760-80, 24 1/4 x 40", 44 1/4" h. **$42,000**

Chippendale "oxbow-front" slant-front desk, mahogany, the narrow rectangular top above a wide hinged fall-front opening to an interior fitted w/a central blocked fan-carved prospect door flanked by valanced compartments & small drawers, the case w/ four long serpentine drawers w/simple bail pulls & oval brass keyhole escutcheons, serpentine molded apron w/a central carved fan drop, raised on short cabriole legs ending in claw-and-ball feet, replaced brasses, refinished, imperfections, North Shore, Massachusetts, late 18th c., 23 x 41", 44" h. **$5,875**

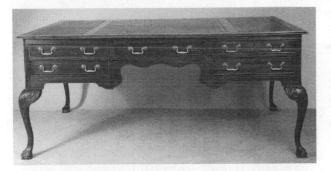

Chippendale-Style partner's desk, mahogany & mahogany veneer, the large rectangular top w/three tooled green leather inserts, the case fitted on each side w/a stack of two narrow drawers w/simple bail pulls flanking the arched serpentine kneehole opening w/a single drawer, scroll-carved cabriole legs w/claw-and-ball feet, late 19th - early 20th c., 48 x 72", 32" h. **$4,715**

Classical Plantation desk, walnut, the long top centered by a wide hinged & slightly slanted writing surface opening to a well & flanked on each side by a pair of small arched compartments, bold scroll-cut ends above an apron fitted w/a small drawer w/two turned wood knobs at each end, raised on ring-, knob- and rod-turned legs ending in ball-and-peg feet, ca. 1830-40, 33 x 60 1/2", 37" h. **$28,750**

Federal "tambour" lady's writing desk, inlaid mahogany, two-part construction: the upper section w/a rectangular top & narrow cornice above a narrow inlaid frieze band above flute-inlaid pilasters flanking a pair of tambour doors opening to fitted interior & centered by a central rectangular door w/banded inlay centered by an oval reserve inlaid w/an American eagle; the stepped-out lower section w/a fold-out writing surface above a case of three long graduated drawers w/inlaid banding & inlaid fans in each corners, oval brasses, inlaid fluted panel heading each side stile continuing into the square tapering legs w/tapering block feet, Northshore, Massachusetts, 1800-10, 19 1/4 x 38 3/4", 46 1/2" h. **$12,000**

George III-Style Carlton House desk, polychromed satinwood, the upper concave stage w/wavy gallery above open compartments, swelled drawers & doors decorated w/festooned garland, portrait medallions & an allegory, the sloped lidded end compartments painted w/musical trophies, the green tooled leather-lined writing surface over three frieze drawers decorated w/floral garlands, the square tapering legs decorated w/classical urns, wreaths & floral pendants, the reverse fully paint-decorated w/matching Adam designs, in the manner of Wright & Mansfield, England, ca. 1875, 23 x 42", 37" h. **$8,050**

Queen Anne "block-front" kneehole desk, walnut, the rectangular top w/a blocked front w/rounded blocks above a conforming case w/a single long top drawer above two stacks of deep graduated drawers all w/ butterfly brasses & flanking the central kneehole w/a scalloped top rail & an inset arched & paneled door w/exposed H-hinges, molded apron on arched, scroll-carved bracket feet, original brasses, Massachusetts, ca. 1740-70, 20 5/8 x 32 1/2", 29 1/4" h. **$72,000**

William & Mary slant-front desk, figured maple, a narrow rectangular top above a wide hinged slant-top opening to a fitted interior, above a case of four long graduated drawers w/simple turned wood pulls, molded base on shaped bracket feet resting on casters, New England, 1740-60, 17 1/2 x 36", 42 1/4" h. **$7,200**

◆ Tambour refers to the narrow strips of wood glued on canvas as found on a rolltop desk.

DINING ROOM SUITES

FURNITURE

Art Deco: dining table & 10 dining chairs; inlaid & inset rosewood, the table w/a long rectangular top composed of large squares of tan travertine, wide corner legs curved at the base w/the central opening fitted at the bottom w/another travertine piece, the chairs w/tall slightly flaring backs w/cream-colored upholstery above half-round upholstered seats, on square tapering legs, chairs stamped "Breveté Sornay France Etranger," Andre Sornay, France, ca. 1935, table 39 x 118", 30" h., chairs 40 7/8" h., the suite **$50,190**

Modern Style: dining table & four "Mira" chairs; walnut, the table w/a square top supported on a simple pedestal on a cross-form foot, each chair w/a wide curved crestrail above seven spindles over a triangular saddle seat, three simple turned & canted legs, by George Nakashima, ca. 1965, table 26 1/4 x 32", 26" h., chairs 27 1/4" h. **$14,340**

◆ The Art Deco movement is considered to have begun with the May 1925 International Exposition of Decorative Arts, although the movement wasn't known by that name until 1968, when a Parisian museum exhibited original items from the 1925 Exposition. The German version of Art Deco was known as Bauhaus.

GARDEN & LAWN

Settees, Laurel patt., the long scallop-topped back composed of openwork panels of large vertical leafy branches curving around to tapering scrolled arms, the long half-round seat composed of leafy scrolls, the front legs in the form a bird head & large wing curving down to a claw foot, old white paint, ca. 1900, 42" l., 29" h., pr. **$5,520**

Settees, the long arched back composed of entwining leafy vines w/various birds all centered by a large relief-molded oval plaque showing a seated classical nymph, the cast-iron slatted seat above curved legs ending in hoof feet, painted black, second half 19th c., 24 x 63", 38" h., pr. **$8,050**

Table & chairs, painted metal, the table w/a round metal meshwork top & curlicue apron raised on a pedestal of tapering & then flaring bar clusters centered by a looped metal ring, each chair w/the tapering back composed of slender bars rolled at the top, armchairs w/matching rolled top arms, round metal mesh seats, simple metal bar chair legs joined by a crossstretcher, painted white, designed by Mathieu Mategot, ca. 1950, table 39 1/2" d., 29" h., chairs 32" h., the set **$14,340**

HIGHBOYS & LOWBOYS

Highboys

Queen Anne "flat-top" highboy, maple w/areas of figure, two-part construction: the upper section w/a rectangular top above a flaring stepped cornice over a pair of beaded overlapping drawers w/batwing brasses over a stack of the long graduated drawers w/matching brasses; the lower section w/a medial rail above a long shallow drawer w/three brasses above a row of three deep drawers w/brasses, shaped apron w/ two drops w/turned knob drop finials, raised on cabriole legs ending in raised pad feet, refinished, old replaced leg returns & brasses, minor splits in top case & minor corner chip on cornice, mid-18th c., 19 x 38 3/4", 67" h. **$5,175**

Chippendale "bonnet-top" highboy, carved mahogany, two-part construction: the upper section w/a very high broken-scroll pediment w/the heavy molded scrolls terminating in large sunflowers flanking a tall cartouche-shaped scroll-pieced finial & mounted w/ corner blocks supporting urn-turned & flame finials, the wide upper frieze ornately carved w/bold leafy scrolls centered by a large pierce-carved shell device, the tall case w/quarter-round reeded corner columns flanking a row of three drawers over a pair of drawers above three long graduated drawers, all w/pierced butterfly brasses; the lower section w/a mid-molding above a case w/a single long drawer over a pair of small square drawers flanking a large central drawer w/finely carved leafy scrolls centered by a large shell all flanked by quarter-round reeded columns, the serpentine apron centered by a small carved shell, raised on tall cabriole legs w/scroll- and leaf-carved knees & ending in claw-and-ball feet, attributed to the shop of Henry Clifton & Thomas Carteret, Philadlephia, 1755-65, descended in the family of Benjamin Marshall, unique, 23 5/8 x 45", 94 1/2" h. . **$1,808,000**

Lowboys

Queen Anne lowboy, walnut & mahogany, the rectangular top w/chamfered corners above a case w/a long drawer over a pair of small square drawers flanking a larger, deeper center drawer, all w/butterfly brasses, fluted & canted side stiles, fancy scroll-cut apron, raised on cabriole legs w/leaf- and shell-carved knees & ending in drake feet, ca. 1780, 19 1/4 x 31 1/2", 28 1/4" h. **$4,830**

FURNITURE

LOVE SEATS, SOFAS & SETTEES

Récamier, grain-painted, stenciled & gilded wood, the low upholstered half-back w/the long crestrail ending in a carved lion head & curving up to a gadroon-carved section joining the outward rolled high end back w/a cornucopia-carved front rail continuing into the low seatrail below the upholstered seat & curving up to the low upholstered foot w/a fan- and scroll-carved rail, raised on heavy leaf-carved & ring-turned tapering legs on casters, New York City, ca. 1826-30 ....$11,950

Settee, Art Deco, upholstered Macassar ebony, the long gently arched wooden crestrail above a tufted back flanked by rolled upholstered arms w/flat heavily grained front supports continuing into simple shaped front legs, the scalloped seatrail connected by four flat front legs, long cushion seat, made by Sue et Mare, France, ca. 1925, 27 x 75", 37 1/2" h. $71,700

Settee, Federal, carved mahogany, the long flat upholstered back flanked by fluted downswept rails above the closed upholstered arms w/baluster-turned reeded arm supports, cushion seat above a long slightly bowed seatrail raised on four ring-turned & reeded tapering front legs ending in turned tapering feet & four square canted rear legs, New England, 1800-20, 24 x 65", 34 1/2" h. $14,400

Settee, Windsor "sack-back" style, the very long slender bowed crestrail above numerous slender turned spindles continuing down through the medial rail that curve to form the flat shaped arms on pairs of spindles & baluster- and ring-turned canted arm supports, the long plank seat raised on eight canted baluster- and ring-turned legs joined by three swelled H-stretchers, old finish, label of John DeWitt, New York City, 1797, 22 x 81", 37" h. ...$31,200

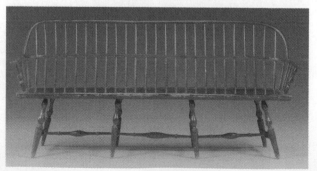

Settle, Spanish Colonial, carved hardwood, a long scrolling foliate-carved crestrail centering religious cartouche flanked by stiles topped w/tall ring-turned finials, the lower back w/a shaped panel raised on pairs of knob-turned spindles, wide flat serpentine arms above floral-inlaid supports & legs flanking the long plank seat, the six-leg trestle-form base w/a flat floral-carved front stretcher, missing much mother-of-pearl inlay, round burn mark on right side of seat, 18th c., 26 x 81 7/8", 43 1/2" h. **$6,325**

Sofa, Chippendale camel-back style, mahogany, the long serpentine upholstered back flanked by outswept scrolled upholstered arms above the long upholstered seat, raised on eight square legs joined by box stretchers, late 18th c., 88" l. **$5,019**

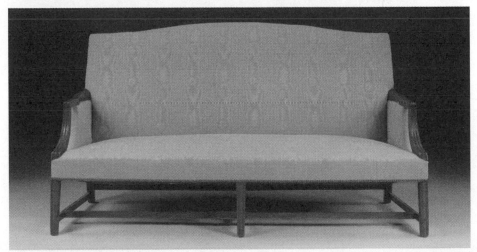

Sofa, Chippendale style, mahogany, the long, high upholstered back w/a gently arched crest above shaped arm rails above upholstered panels & w/incurved fluted arm supports, long upholstered seat raised on three square tapering front legs joined by flat stretchers & three square canted rear legs, Massachusetts, 1770-1780, 77 3/4" l., 42 3/4" h. **$3,840**

Sofa, Classical " Grecian" style, carved mahogany, the long flat crestrail carved w/a repeating design swags & tassels w/a pair of addorsed cornucopia issuing grain above the low upholstered back flanked by outswept upholstered arms w/matching carved on the crestrailrails & continuing down into the long fluted seatrail raised on outswept fluted legs w/brass paw caps & raised on casters, attributed to the shop of Duncan Phyfe, New York City, ca. 1810-20, 88" l., 32 3/4"h. **$13,200**

Sofa, Edwardian style, the long back upholstered in brown leather & flanked by outswept leather-upholstered arms above the two-cushion leather-upholstered seat & seatrail w/brass tack trim, short bulbous turned mahogany legs on brass casters, England, early 20th c., 33 1/2" h. **$3,450**

Sofa, Victorian Rococo sub-style, triple-back design, carved mahogany, the long crestrail w/a long arched center crest pierce-carved w/ fancy scrolls & a floral-carved crest, the rail continuing to high arched balloon-form end sections w/matching ornately scroll & flower-carved crests, the rail continuing down to the low upholstered arms w/ incurved front supports flanking the long upholstered seat w/a double-serpentine scroll-and leaf-carved seatrail raised on three demi-cabriole front legs on casters, New York City, ca. 1855, 87" l. **$3,680**

SECRETARIES

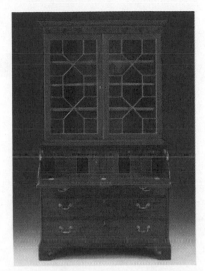

Chippendale secretary-bookcase, mahogany, two-part construction: the upper section w/a rectangular top w/a flaring dentil-carved cornice above a pair of tall geometrically-glazed doors opening to three wooden shelves; the lower stepped-out section w/a hinged fold-down slant front opening to an interior composed of small drawers, pigeonholes & a central door, the lower case w/three long graduated drawers w/simply bail pulls, molded base on scroll-cut bracket feet, underside of interior drawer w/original paper label reading "Elbert Anderson - Makes all kinds of - CABINET WARE - on the most Modern & Approved - Methods & on the most reasonable terms - No. 5 or 53 - Maiden Lane in- NEW YORK," one drawer w/a later inscription, New York City, 1786-96, 24 1/4 x 49 3/4", 88 7/8" h. **$21,600**

Federal secretary-bookcase, carved & inlaid mahogany, two-part construction: the upper section w/a high broken scroll pediment w/scroll-pierced scrolls flanking a central black w/an urn-turned finial above a narrow veneer-paneled frieze band above a pair of tall geometrically-glazed doors opening to three wooden shelves; the stepped-out lower section w/a stack of five long graduated drawers w/line-inlaid panels, oval brasses & diamond-shaped key-hole escutcheons, serpentine apron continuing to tall outswept French feet, Maryland, 1790-1810, 23 1/4 x 42 1/2", 97 1/4" h. **$26,400**

SIDEBOARDS

Arts & Crafts sideboard, oak, the rectangular top w/a low three-quarters gallery above a case fitted w/a row of three short drawers above a pair of flat cupboard doors flanking a stack of three drawers, a single long drawer across the bottom, each fitted w/a rectangular copper & bail pull, the long arched apron flanked by bootjack ends, original dark finish, Model No. 804, red decal mark of Gustav Stickley, ca. 1904, 22 x 54 1/4", 42 3/8" h. **$14,340**

Federal sideboard, inlaid mahogany, the long rectangular top w/a bowed central section flanked by concave sections all above a conforming case, the ends w/concave flat-front doors w/inlaid fans in each corner flanking a long bowed top drawer w/rectangular brasses projecting over a slightly bowed pair of smaller doors w/fan inlay flanked by narrow vertical panels each w/an inlaid Liberty Cap, raised on six square tapering legs, the four in front w/bellflower inlay, New York City, ca. 1790-1810, 27 1/2 x 73 1/2", 38" h. **$65,725**

STANDS

FURNITURE

Candlestand, Queen Anne, cherry & maple, the round top above a turned columnar pedestal w/a knobbed base raised on a tripod base w/cabriole legs ending in snake feet, probably Pennsylvania, late 18th - early 19th c., 17" d., 24 1/2" h. **$9,000**

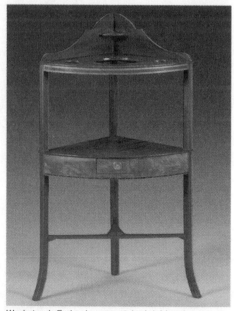

Washstand, Federal corner-style, inlaid mahogany, the quarter-round top w/a delicate arched backsplash w/a tiny shelf above a top w/a large central hole flanked by smaller holes, the edge of the top w/delicate banded inlay, raised on three slender square supports above a medial shelf above an inlaid apron centered by a small drawer, raised on three slender outswept legs joined by a T-form stretcher, probably Portsmouth, New Hampshire, 1800-10, 16 1/2 x 23", 41" h. **$11,400**

Kettle stand, Chippendale, mahogany, square top w/low undulating gallery & candle slide raised on a ring-turned columnar post on a tripod base w/cabriole legs ending in arris pad feet on platforms, old refinish, probably Massachusetts, imperfections, 12 x 12 1/4", 24" h. **$11,163**

◆ Chippendale legs were made in six basic forms: the lion's paw, the ball and claw, the late Chippendale, the Marlborough, the spade, and the club.

◆ The Chippendale style cabriole leg is associated with the ball and claw foot which has its origins in China and represents a dragon clutching a pearl.

◆ Mahogany's dense fine grain is especially prized for its ability to show exquisite detail in carvings. Thus, it was used extensively for handcarved ball-and-claw feet. The golden age of mahogany extended from 1720 to 1860.

TABLES

Art Deco side table, fruitwood, "Soleil" design, round top on a flat round apron w/four low blocks above the square tapering legs capped by turned brass disks & resting on square brass foot caps, designed by Andre Arubs, France, ca. 1940, 27 1/2" d., 25 3/4" h. **$17,925**

Classical pier table, rosewood, ormolu, gilt gesso & marble, the rectangular white marble top on a conforming base w/applied ebonized molding & rosewood veneer frieze w/gilt-brass mounts showing Psyche & Cupid in a chariot being drawn by peacocks, flanked by similarly dressed female figures watering flowers, the bottom edge w/a brass reticulated band, raised on white columnar front legs w/gilt acanthus leaf capitals & ring-turned bases resting on a rectangular concave-front medial shelf w/matching square rear pilasters flanking a large rectangular mirror, the bottom rail w/gilt scrolling designs of flowers & cornucopias & an applied brass beaded edge, raised on short carved hairy paw feet topped by gilt gesso carved leaves, New York City, ca. 1825, restoration, imperfections, 19 1/2 x 50 1/2", 37" h. **$7,050**

Chippendale game table, carved mahogany, the foldover top w/serpentined front & incurved sides above a conforming deep apron w/gadrooned edging, five-legged design w/cabriole legs w/leaf-carved knees & ending in claw-and-ball feet, missing small interior drawer, New York City, 1760-90, 16 3/8 x 34 1/4", 27 1/2" h. **$42,000**

Country-style kitchen table, cypress, the wide rectangular top overhanging an apron fitted w/a long drawer w/a carved wood pull, raised on square legs beveled at the base & joined by an H-stretcher, natural weathered finish, made in Louisiana, mid-19th c., 49 x 64", 31" h. **$14,950**

Queen Anne "tray-top" tea table, mahogany, the rectangular top w/raised molding above a narrow flat apron raised on four simple cabriole legs ending in slipper feet, Newport, Rhode Island, 1740-60, 21 x 32 3/4", 26 1/2" h. **$66,000**

FURNITURE

Hutch (or chair) table, country-style, pine, the wide three-board top hinged above a single-board cut-out ends flanking a lift-seat opening to a compartment, possibly New England, early 19th c., refinished, 41 x 70", 29 3/4" h. **$5,581**

Modern style side table, oak, three-tier 'flower table,' a thick rectangular top overhanging a framework w/a short narrow top shelf raised on four square supports enclosing a medial shelf & joined to four square legs w/outswept feet & joined by a wider bottom shelf, designed by Frank Lloyd Wright in collaboration w/ George Mann Niedecken of Niedecken-Walbridge, for the Second Story Hall of the Avery Coonley House, Riverside, Illinois, ca. 1910, 16 x 29 7/8", 25 1/4" h. **$59,750**

WARDROBES & ARMOIRES

Armoire, Colonial Louisiana, inlaid mahogany, the rectangular top w/a deep flaring corner w/rounded front corners above a deep frieze band centered by a finely inlaid design of a drapery swag above an oval inlaid w/the monogram "EM" all flanked by long line-inlaid panels, the pair of tall cupboard doors centered by tall line-inlaid panels w/a short angled band of inlaid bellflowers at each corner, mounted w/long pierced & scrolled brass escutcheons & centered by a long stile delicately inlaid the full length w/delicate entwined flowering vines & urns, the deep serpentine front apron centered by another double-swag drapery, simple cabriole legs, the interior fitted w/cypress shelves, a center belt of three drawers & a lower belt of two drawers, replaced brasses, late 18th - early 19th c., 23 1/2 x 60", 90 1/2" h. **$140,000**

Kas (a version of the Netherlands kast or wardrobe), gumwood, the rectangular top w/a very deep, stepped & widely flaring cornice above a pair of tall paneled doors opening to a shelved interior, centered & flanked by stiles each w/two tall narrow molded panels, set into a base w/a long single narrow drawer w/the face centered by an applied diamond panel flanked by rectangular molded panels w/turned knob pulls, a raised applied diamond at each outside edge, raised on bulbous turned front feet & cut-out rear feet, Hudson River Valley, New York, early 18th c., old refinish, minor imperfections, 22 x 62", 79" h. **$22,325**

Modernism

By Noah Fleisher

Modern design is everywhere, evergreen and increasingly popular. Modernism has never gone out of style. Its reach into the present day is as deep as its roots in the past. Just as it can be seen and felt ubiquitously in the mass media of today – on film, television, in magazines and department stores – it can be traced to the mid-1800s post-Empire non-conformity of the Biedermeier Movement, the turn of the 20th century anti-Victorianism of the Vienna Secessionists, the radical reductionism of Frank Lloyd Wright and the revolutionary post-Depression thinking of Walter Gropius and the Bauhaus school in Germany.

"The Modernists really changed the way the world looked," said John Sollo, a partner in Sollo Rago Auction of Lambertville, N.J. Sollo's partner in business, and one of the most recognizable names in the field, David Rago, takes Sollo's idea a little further by saying that Modernism is actually more about the names behind the design than the design itself, at least as far as buying goes.

No discussion of Modern can be complete, however, without examining its genesis and enduring influence. Modernism is everywhere in today's pop culture. Austere Scandinavian furniture dominates the television commercials that hawk hotels and mutual funds. Post-war American design ranges across sitcom set dressings to movie sets patterned after Frank Lloyd Wright houses and Hollywood Modernist classics set high in the hills.

You have to look at the dorm rooms of college students and the apartments of young people whose living spaces are packed with the undeniably Modern mass-produced products of IKEA, Target, Design Within Reach and the like.

There can be no denying that the post-World War II manufacturing techniques and subsequent boom led to the widespread acceptance of plastic and bent plywood chairs along with low-sitting coffee tables, couches and recliners.

"The modern aesthetic grew out of a perfect storm of post-war optimism, innovative materials and an incredible crop of designers," said Lisanne Dickson, director of 1950s/Modenr Design at Treadway-Toomey.

"I think that the people who designed the furniture were maybe ahead of society's ability to accept and understand what they were doing," Sollo said. "It's taken people another 30 to 40 years to catch up to it."

There are hundreds of great Modern designers, many of whom worked across categories – furniture, architecture, fine art, etc. – and many contributed to the work of other big names without ever seeking that glory for themselves.

For more information on Modernism, see *Warman's Modernism Furniture & Accessories Identification and Price Guide* by Noah Fleisher.

FURNITURE

BEDROOM FURNITURE

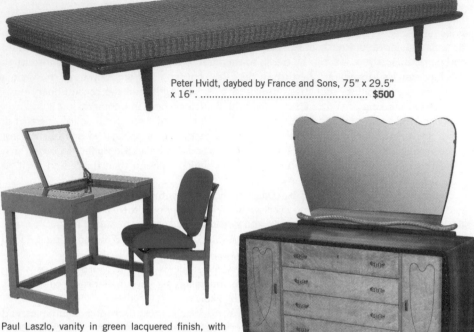

Peter Hvidt, daybed by France and Sons, 75" x 29.5" x 16". **$500**

Paul Laszlo, vanity in green lacquered finish, with pink embossed leather top, fitted with single drawer and lift-up mirror, the matching chair with pink ultrasuede cushions, circa 1952; vanity 29" x 37" x 24", chair 33" x 20" x 22"...........................**$4,000 set**

▲Dresser and mirror, 1940s, Italy; cabinet 62" x 23" x 36", mirror 50" x 31", overall 67"............... **$1,200**

◀Jean Royere, daybed with tan cushion and bolster pillows on oak frame with inset cobalt glass panels, 32.5" x 65" x 32.75"......... **$4,000**

▶Finn Juhl/Baker, full-size bed in teak and maple with slatted headboard, marked with Baker metal tag, 31.5" x 57" x 88". **$1,700**

DESKS/CREDENZAS

Desk, single-drawer, in wood veneer, one end faceted, the other curved, 29.5" x 45.5" x 22.5". **$1,000**

Gordon Bunshaft desk, 66" x 30" x 30". **$1,500**

Hans Wegner/Ry Mobler, Oak credenza with two sliding doors enclosing four sliding trays and four adjustable shelves, with contrasing oak feet, stamped RY, 31" x 78.75" x 19.25". **$2,500**

Portenzac, single-pedestal desk covered in composite with six shaped drawers and steel leg, 30" x 63" x 26.75". **$6,500**

Gio Ponti/Singer & Sons, two-drawer rosewood desk with tooled leather top and integrated magazine rack, circa 1950, 28.75" x 53.25" x 25.5". **$19,000**

Jean Prouve, oak and painted steel student desk and chair unit, with sliding iron inkwell, 25.5" x 23.5" x 32". **$1,900**

Edward Wormley, kneehole desk, curved form, 58.25" x 30" x 29.25". **$3,250**

George Nakashima, walnut credenza, with two grass cloth-backed grilled doors enclosing two drawers, 28.5" x 22" x 20". **$7,500**

FURNITURE

SEATING

George Nelson, Steelframe chair, 29" x 27" x 27". **$375**

Shiro Kuramato/XO, "Sing, Sing, Sing" anodized steel armchairs, marked XO, 33.5" x 20.5" x 23.5". .... **$2,700 pair**

Hans Wegner, CH25 armchairs, 28" x 28" x 28". .... **$2,000 pair**

Le Corbusier, LC/1 Basculant chairs brown leather, 25" x 27.5" x 26"................................... **$550 pair**

Edward Wormley, vanity seat by Dunbar, 28" x 20" x 22.5"... **$850**

Eero Saarinen/Knoll, womb settee upholstered in green fabric on black metal frame, 35" x 60" x 32" **$3,250**

Vladimir Kagan, omnibus sofa upholstered in striped Knoll fabric on Plexiglas base, reupholstered in Knoll fabric, 27.5" x 72" x 32". **$1,000**

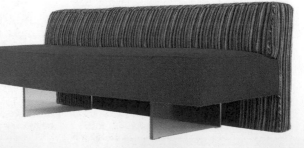

Parzinger, "American Modern" sectional sofa, leopard print fabric, 109" x 30.5" x 28"...**$5,000**

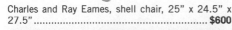

Charles and Ray Eames, shell chair, 25" x 24.5" x 27.5"...**$600**

Lounge chair, possibly Milo Baughman, 1960s, 42" x 38" x 34".......................................**$900**

Arne Jacobsen, Seagull chairs in original white finish, marked in Denmark by Fritz Hansen 1972, 31.5" x 21.5" x 18"..**$3,000 pair**

Phillip Lloyd Powell, New Hope chair in walnut with webbed seat support, 32" x 29.5" x 30.5"... **$7,500**

Charles and Ray Eames, 670/671 lounge chair and
ottoman, chair 33" x 35" x 32", ottoman 26.5" x
21" x 17.5".. **$1,500**

Poul Kjaerholm/E. Kold Chris-
tensen, PK22 lounge chairs
covered in tan leather on steel
bases, impressed marks, set
of four, 28" x 25" x 25".
.................................**$4,250 set**

Isamu Noguchi/Knoll, teak rocking stool with steel wire frame,
circa 1954, 10.5" x 14".
.....................................**$5,500**

SHELVING & STORAGE

Skovmand & Andersen, corner cabinet, 36.5" x 25.5" x 61.25". **$375**

George Nelson, cabinet by Herman Miller, 40" x 18.5" x 39.75".. **$1,100**

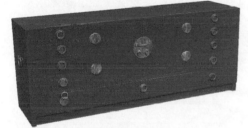

Edward Wormley, sideboard, 59.25" x 18" x 28.25". **$1,600**

Paul Evans, Aluco Bond cabinet with burled walnut doors, 30" x 39.5" x 18". **$3,750**

Osvaldo Borsani, mahogany mirrored sideboard with beige marble top and brass-capped feet, 77.5" x 107.25" x 17.75". **$7,500**

Charlotte Perriand and Jean Prouve, bibliotheque with enameled aluminum and pine shelving unit on pine long bench, 1953, 63.5" x 138" x 21".......**$70,000**

TABLES

Jens Risom Design Inc. coffee table, 40" x 18". ..**$300**

Coffee table, 1960s, 43" x 14.75"...............**$500**

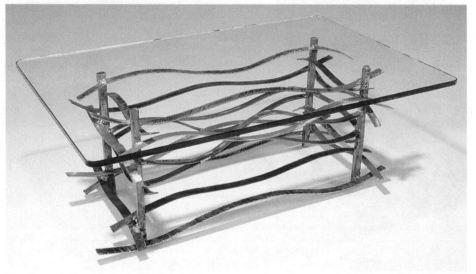

Silas Seandel, ribbon coffee table with glass top on copper, brass, bronze and steel base, 16" x 42" x 27".
....**$7,000**

Donald Deskey/W. & J. Sloane, 10-piece dining suite in Madrone burl veneer and Macassar ebony, extension table with six fabric-upholstered chairs and two 15" leaves, server with interior drawers and shelves, bar cabinet and china cabinet circa 1936; table (closed) 29.5" x 66" x 40", armchairs 34.5" x 23" x 20", server 36" x 66" x 20", bar 32" x 29" x 18", china cabinet 60" x 32.5" x 16".
..............................**$14,000 set**

Jonathon Singleton, dining table with "cerused" (pickled) oak top on curvaceous steel base, metal tag, Jonathan Singleton SIG Furniture, 31" x 89" x 55". **$4,000**

Jay Spectre, occasional table, wedge shaped, 15.5" x 15.5" x 18". **$125**

Vladimir Kagan, tri-symmetric side table with biomorphic plate glass top on sculpted walnut base, 19" x 31" x 24". **$2,100**

George Nakashima, early walnut side table with round top on four tapered, angular legs, 26" x 24". **$2,700**

Saporiti, dining table with concrete and chrome pedestal base under a circular plate glass top, 27.75" x 60". **$4,250**

Philippe Starck, steel console table with glass top, 16" x 47" x 18"................................. **$2,000**

Isamu Noguchi/Herman Miller, chess table with rotating, inlaid biomorphic top over cast-aluminum tray and ebonized base, 20.75" x 25" x 25". **$65,000**

▲Eliot Noyes, telephone stand, 15.5" x 13.5" x 23"........... **$550**

◀Franziska & James Hosken, rolling bar cart, 41" x 23" x 27". **$900**

Glass

■ Art Glass Baskets

Popular novelties in the late Victorian era, these ornate baskets of glass were usually hand-crafted of free-blown or mold-blown glass. They were made in a wide spectrum of colors and shapes. Pieces were highlighted with tall applied handles and often applied feet; however, fancier ones might also carry additional appliquéd trim.

Spatter, rounded body w/flaring crimped rim pulled into points, arched applied clear thorn handle, yellow & pink spatter, white lining, 6" d., 6" h. **$165-185**

Bluerina, round foot below the widely flaring, flattened Hobnail patt. rim w/two sides pulled up, tall applied clear twisted thorn handle, 9 1/2" h. **$633**

Cased, bulbous rounded form tapering to a lobed rim, deep pink interior cased in alternating stripes of pulled-up dark red & white and yellow & white, applied clear double entwined overhead handle, raised on four clear applied peg feet, attributed to Northwood, England, 11 3/4" d., 12" h. **$863**

Cranberry, bulbous cranberry body w/a widely flaring crimped & ruffled applied opalescent rim, applied clear sharply pointed handle, 4 3/4" d., 6 3/4 h. **$66**

Mother-of-pearl satin, shaded pink Herringbone patt., a round foot below the deep rounded bowl w/ deeply folded & crimped flaring rim, applied pointed frosted clear thorny branch handle, interior cased in bright pale green, Mt. Washington Glass Co., museum exhibit label from the New Bedford Whaling Museum, 11" d., 9" h **$570**

Spangled, bulbous body w/two sides folded down & Grimped, white exterior & butterscotch-cased interior w/overall mica flecks, applied clear twist handle, 6 1/2" h. **$66**

Spangled, deep bulbous lobed body w/a flaring ruffled rim, colorful spatter & silver mica fleck exterior cased in white, applied lightly reeded clear looped handle, 6 3/4" h. **$66**

■ Baccarat

Baccarat glass has been made by Cristalleries de Baccarat, France, since 1765. The firm has produced various glassware of excellent quality as well as paperweights. Baccarat's Rose Tiente is often referred to as Baccarat's Amberina.

Model of a bear, colorless crystal, a stylized walking animal, signed on the bottom & side, 11" l.... **$2,300**

Pitcher, 9 1/4" h., 6 3/4" d., Rose Tiente Swirl patt., spherical body tapering to a cylindrical neck w/ pinched spout, applied clear handle **$300-325**

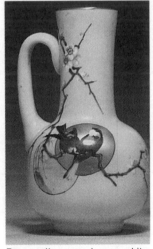

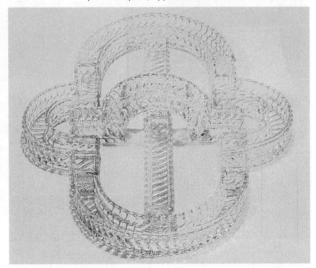

Ewer, yellow cased over white, footed bulbous body tapering to a tall cylindrical neck, large applied yellow handle, decorated in the Japanese taste w/two overlapping round reserves highlighted w/a pair of brick red & brown birds perched on long blossoming branches, ca. 1880, 8 1/8" h. **$956**

Vases, 7 1/4" h., Art Nouveau style, the wide flattened colorless crystal urn-shaped body fitted on an openwork rectangular bronze base issuing stylized leafy vines behind the vase, vases signed, holders marked on the bottom "E. Enot Paris," gh ca. 1900, pr. **$2,280**

Centerpiece, colorless crystal, seven-part, the long open oval design composed of bowed side tray sections, two rectangular center tray sections & a bridged center tray section, marked, one piece w/rim nick, early 20th c., 18 x 24", the set **$633**

▨ Bride's Baskets & Bowls _____

These berry or fruit bowls were popular late Victorian wedding gifts, hence the name. They were produced in a variety of quality art glasswares and sometimes were fitted in ornate silver plate holders.

Amethyst opalescent, the plain bowl w/two sides curled up & inward, enameled on the interior w/white flowers, in an ornate footed brass frame w/ropetwist scrolls & a large, tall arched ropetwist handle, late 19th c., overall 10 1/2" h. **$323**

Butterscotch to yellow, widely flaring ruffled & crimped edges w/ overall swirled ribbing & V-form ribs at the rim flutes, 9 5/8" d., 3 1/4" h. **$92**

Cased bowl, pink shaded to white interior, white exterior, deeply ruffled & crimped rim, in a fancy footed silver plate frame w/overhead bail handle, ca.1900, overall 12" h. **$235**

Cased bowl, green cased w/translucent peach on the interior, white opaque exterior, the deep ribbed bowl w/a wide rolled & finely notched & scalloped rim in green decorated w/tiny enameled blossoms & gilt scrolls, in a very ornate silver plate frame by Barbour, overall 14" l. (ILLUS. top row, center, with other five bride's baskets & bowls)................ **$920**

Cased bowl, apricot shaded to white interior w/a fancy tri-ruffled & fluted rim, white exterior, fitted in a fancy silver plate frame marked by the Rockford Silver Plate Co., small size, bowl 5 1/2" d., overall 5 1/2" h. . **$161**

Satin shaded blue, the wide shallow shaded blue bowl w/a ruffled & crimped rim, molded interior draped pattern, attached atop a silver plate pedestal foot, late 19th c., bowl 10" d. **$147**

Above right: Cased bowl, turquoise blue interior & deep shaded pink exterior, wide cylindrical body w/a squared crimped & ruffled rim, fitted in a fancy silver plate frame w/figural cherries applied to the high arched handle, marked by Meriden, two leaves missing on frame, ca. 1890s, bowl 4" h., overall 10 1/2" h. **$345**

GLASS

Cambridge

The Cambridge Glass Company was founded in Ohio in 1901. Numerous pieces are now sought, especially those designed by Arthur J. Bennett, including Crown Tuscan. Other productions included crystal animals, "Black Amethyst," "blanc opaque," and other types of colored glass. The firm was finally closed in 1954. It should not be confused with the New England Glass Co., Cambridge, Massachusetts.

NEAR CUT

CAPRICE PATTERN

Bowl, 8" d., salad, four-footed, pressed Caprice patt., No. 49, Moonlight Blue **$110**

Candy dish, cov., three-footed, pressed Caprice patt., No. 165, Moonlight Blue, 6" d. **$155**

Cruet w/original stopper, pressed Caprice patt., oil, No. 117, clear, 3 oz. **$42**

Cup & saucer, pressed Caprice patt., Moonlight, pr. **$42**

Rose bowl, pressed Caprice patt., No. 236; Moonlight Blue, 6" d. **$145**

Vase, 8 1/2" h., ball-shaped, pressed Caprice patt., No. 339, pattern on the neck, Amber **$175-195**

Candleholder, three-light, No. 74, 9 1/2" l., 4 1/4" h. **$35**

Salt & pepper shakers, all-glass ball, individual, pressed Caprice patt., Crystal, pr. **$45**

CROWN TUSCAN LINE

Vase, 7" h., footed, crimped square form, No. 3500 Gadroon patt. **$100**

Vase, 12" h., footed, keyhole stem, tall trumpet-form bowl w/gold-encrusted etched Rosepoint patt. **$350**

Ivy ball, keyhole stem, No. 1236, 7 1/2" h. **$175**

►Vase, 7" h., Sea Shell line, No. 46 .... **$185**

ETCHED ROSE POINT PATTERN

Bowl, 12" w., 4-footed, flared squared sides, No. 3400/4, Crystal ... **$90**

Compote, No. 3900/136, Crystal, 5 1/2" d., 5 1/2" h. **$85**

Candlestick, two-light, keyhole stem, No. 3400/647, Crystal, 5 3/4" h., pr. **$125**

Dinner service: six round 8" d. plates, 17 3/4" d. round serving platter, small plates & small serving dishes, salt & pepper shakers, clear, set of 15 pcs. (ILLUS. of part)................................. **$403**

◄Ice bucket, No. 3900/671, Crystal w/chrome handle, scalloped top, 5 3/4" h. **$170**

STATUESQUE LINE

Cocktails, clear bowl, Ebony Nude Lady stem, 6 1/2" h., set of 9 .... **$1,064**

MISCELLANEOUS PATTERNS

Asparagus platter, almond-shaped w/a molded round rim section & molded bars down the center, etched Cleo patt., Emerald (medium green), chip on the base, 14 1/2" l. **$138**

Beverage set: ball-form pitcher & nine tumblers; Optic Swirl design, Moonlight Blue, the set (ILLUS. of part) **$150-200**

Bowl, 9" d., three-footed, Seashell patt., Amber **$68**

Bowl, 9 1/2" d., shallow flared shape, Honeycomb patt., "sponge" acid etching, Rubina **$375**

Center bowl, round w/domed & widely flaring sides, Mold No. 1125 molded on the underside w/a continuous buffalo hunt scene w/figures on horseback, Mystic Blue, 16" d. **$150**

Cocktail, Statuesque line, Nude Lady stem, Carmen bowl, 3 oz. **$220**

GLASS

Console set: 11" d. console bowl w/etched gold border band & a pair of matching square tapering 8" h. candlesticks, Azurite (blue opaque), the set **$196**

Creamer & open sugar bowl, individual size, Gadroon (No. 3500 line), Crystal, pr. **$19**

Decanter w/crystal stopper, Mt. Vernon line, Amber, 40 oz. **$60**

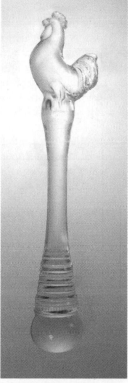

Drink muddler, figural rooster top, clear, 5 1/2" l. **$25**

Pitcher w/ice lip, bulbous ovoid body, Gyro Optic patt., No. 3900/115, Mandarin Gold, 76 oz. **$67**

Salt, open, oval urn-form w/two handles, Mt. Vernon line, Carmen, 2 1/2" l. **$48**

Vase, 8" h., ivy ball-style w/key-hole stem, optic ribbed spherical pale green bowl **$75**

Model of a swan, table centerpiece, Ebony, 13" l. **$795**

GLASS

Carnival Glass

Carnival glass is what is fondly called mass-produced iridescent glassware. The term "carnival glass" has evolved through the years as glass collectors have responded to the idea that much of this beautiful glassware was made as giveaway glass at local carnivals and fairs. However, more of it was made and sold through the same channels as pattern glass and Depression glass. Some patterns were indeed giveaways, and others were used as advertising premiums, souvenirs, etc. Whatever the origin, the term "carnival glass" today encompasses glassware that is usually pattern molded and treated with metallic salts, creating that unique coloration that is so desirable to collectors.

Early names for iridescent glassware, which early 20th century consumers believed to have all come from foreign manufacturers, include Pompeiian Iridescent, Venetian Art, and Mexican Aurora. Another popular early name was "Nancy Glass," as some patterns were believed to have come from the Daum, Nancy, glassmaking area in France. This was at a time when the artistic cameo glass was enjoying great success. While the iridescent glassware being made by such European glassmakers as Loetz influenced the American market place, it was Louis Tiffany's Favrile glass that really caught the eye of glass consumers of the early 1900s. It seems an easy leap to transform Tiffany's shimmering glassware to something that could be mass produced, allowing what we call carnival glass today to become "poor man's Tiffany."

Carnival glass is iridized glassware that is created by pressing hot molten glass into molds, just as pattern glass had evolved. Some forms are hand finished, while others are completely formed by molds. To achieve the marvelous iridescent colors, a process was developed where a liquid solution of metallic salts was put onto the still hot glass form after it was unmolded. As the liquid evaporated, a fine metallic surface was left, which refracts light into wonderful colors. The name given to the iridescent spray by early glassmakers was "dope."

Many of the forms created by carnival glass manufacturers were accessories to the china American housewives so loved. By the early 1900s, consumers could find carnival glassware at such popular stores as F. W. Woolworth and McCrory's. To capitalize on the popular fancy for these colored wares, some other industries bought large quantities of carnival glass and turned them into "packers." This term reflects the practice where baking powder, mustard, or other household products were packed into a special piece of glass that could take on another life after the original product was used. Lee Manufacturing Co. used iridized carnival glass as premiums for its baking powder and other products, causing some early carnival glass to be known by the generic term "Baking Powder Glass."

Classic carnival glass production began in the early 1900s and continued about twenty years, but no one really documented or researched production until the first collecting wave struck in 1960. It is important to remember that carnival glasswares were sold in department stores as well as mass merchants, rather than through the general store often associated with a young America. Glassware by this time was mass-produced and sold in large quantities by such enterprising companies as Butler Brothers. When the economics of the country soured in the 1920s, those interested in purchasing iridized glassware were not spared. Many of the leftover inventories of glasshouses found their way to wholesalers who, in turn, sold the wares to those who offered the glittering glass as prizes at carnivals, fairs, circuses, etc. Possibly because this was the last venue people associated the iridized glassware with, it became known as "carnival glass."

COMPANY HISTORIES

Much of vintage American carnival glassware was created in the Ohio valley, in the glasshouse-rich areas of Pennsylvania, Ohio, and West Virginia. The abundance of natural materials, good transportation, and skilled craftsmen that created the early American pattern glass manufacturing companies allowed many of them to add carnival glass to their production lines. Brief company histories of the major carnival glass manufacturers follow:

Cambridge Glass Company (Cambridge)

Cambridge Glass was a rather minor player in the carnival glass marketplace. Founded in 1901 as a new factory in Cambridge, Ohio, it focused on producing fine crystal tablewares. What carnival glass it did produce was imitation cut-glass patterns.

Colors used by Cambridge include marigold, as well as few others. Forms found in carnival glass by Cambridge include tablewares and vases, some with its trademark "Near-Cut."

Fenton Art Glass Company (Fenton)

Frank Leslie Fenton and his brothers, John W. Fenton and Charles H. Fenton, founded this glassmaker in 1905 in Martins Ferry, Ohio. Early production was of blanks, which the brothers soon learned to decorate themselves. They moved to a larger factory in Williamstown, WV.

By 1907, Fenton was experimenting with iridescent glass, developing patterns and the metallic salt formulas that it became so famous for. Production of carnival glass continued at Fenton until the early 1930s. In 1970, Fenton began to re-issue carnival glass, creating new colors and forms as well as using traditional patterns.

Colors developed by Fenton are numerous. The company developed red and Celeste blue in the 1920s; a translucent pale blue, known as Persian blue, is also one of its more distinctive colors, as is a light yellow-green color known as vaseline. Fenton also produced delicate opalescent colors including amethyst opalescent and red opalescent. Because the Fenton brothers learned how to decorate their own blanks, they also promoted the addition of enamel decoration to some of their carnival glass patterns.

Forms made by Fenton are also numerous. What distinguishes Fenton from other glassmakers is its attention to detail and hand finishing processes. Edges are found scalloped, fluted, tightly crimped, frilled, or pinched into a candy ribbon edge, also referred to as 3-in-1 edge.

Northwood Glass Company (Northwood)

Englishman Harry Northwood founded the Northwood Glass Company. He developed his glass formulas for carnival glass, naming it "Golden Iris" in 1908. Northwood was one of the pioneers of the glass manufacturers who marked his wares. Marks range from a full script signature to a simple underscored capital N in a circle. However, not all Northwood glassware is marked.

Colors that Northwood created were many. Collectors prefer its pastels, such as ice blue, ice green, and white. It is also known for several stunning blue shades.

Forms of Northwood patterns range from typical table sets, bowls, and water sets to whimsical novelties, such as a pattern known as Corn, which realistically depicts an ear of corn.Millersburg Glass Company (Millersburg)

John W. Fenton started the Millersburg Glass Company in September 1908. Perhaps it was the factory's more obscure location or the lack of business experience by John Fenton, but the company failed by 1911. The factory was bought by Samuel Fair and John Fenton, and renamed the Radium Glass Company, but it lasted only a year.

Colors produced by Millersburg are amethyst, green, and marigold. Shades such as blue and vaseline were added on rare occasions. The company is well known for its bright radium finishes.

Forms produced at Millersburg are mostly bowls and vases. Pattern designers at Millersburg often took one theme and developed several patterns from it. Millersburg often used one pattern for the interior and a different pattern for the exterior.

GLASS

Dugan Glass Company (Dugan)

The history of the Dugan Glass Company is closely related to Harry Northwood, whose cousin, Thomas Dugan, became plant manager at the Northwood Glass Co, in 1895. By 1904, Dugan and his partner W. G. Minnemayer bought the former Northwood factory and opened as the Dugan Glass Company. Dugan's brother, Alfred, joined the company and stayed until it became the Diamond Glass Company in 1913. At this time, Thomas Dugan moved to the Cambridge Glass Company, later Duncan and Miller and finally Hocking, Lancaster. Alfred left Diamond Glass, too, but later returned.

Understanding how the Northwood and Dugan families were connected helps collectors understand the linkage of these three companies. Their productions were similar; molds were swapped, re-tooled, etc.

Colors attributed to Dugan and Diamond include amethyst, marigold, peach opalescent, and white. The company developed deep amethyst shades, some almost black.

Forms made by both Dugan and Diamond mirrored what other glass companies were producing. The significant contribution by Dugan and later Diamond were feet – either ball or spatula shapes. They are also known for deeply crimped edges.

Diamond Glass Company (Diamond)

This company was started as the Dugan brothers departed the carnival glass-making scene in 1913. However, Alfred Dugan returned and became general manager until his death in 1928. After a disastrous fire in June of 1931, the factory closed.

Imperial Glass Company (Imperial)

Edward Muhleman and a syndicate founded the Imperial Glass Company at Bellaire, Ohio, in 1901, with production beginning in 1904. It started with pressed glass tableware patterns, as well as lighting fixtures. Imperial also became a major exporter of glassware, including

Acorn vase, maybe U.S. Glass or possibly Millersburg, green, one of two known. **$9,000**

its brilliant carnival patterns. During the Depression, it filed for bankruptcy in 1931, but was able to continue on. By 1962, it was again producing carnival glass patterns. By April 1985, the factory was closed and the molds sold.

Colors made by Imperial include typical carnival colors such as marigold. It added interesting shades of green, known as helios, a pale ginger ale shade known as clambroth, and a brownish smoke shade.

Forms created by Imperial tend to be functional, such as berry sets and table sets. Patterns vary from wonderful imitation cut glass patterns to detailed florals and naturalistic designs.

United States Glass Company (U.S. Glass)

In 1891, a consortium of 15 American glass manufacturers joined together as the United States Glass Company. This company was successful in continuing pattern glass production, as well as developing new glass lines. By 1911, it had begun limited production of carnival glass lines, often using existing pattern glass tableware molds. By the

GLASS

time a tornado destroyed the last of its glass factories in Glassport in 1963, it was no longer producing glassware.

Colors associated with U.S. Glass are marigold, white, and a rich honey amber.

Forms tend to be table sets and functional forms.

Westmoreland Glass Company (Westmoreland)

Started as the Westmoreland Speciality Company, Grapeville, Pennsylvania, in 1889, this company originally made novelties and glass packing containers, such as candy containers. Researchers have identified its patterns being advertised by Butler Brothers as early as 1908. Carnival glass production continued into the 1920s. In the 1970s, Westmoreland, too, begin to re-issue carnival glass patterns and novelties. However, this ceased in February of 1996 when the factory burned.

Colors originally used by Westmoreland were typical carnival colors, such as blue and marigold.

Forms include tablewares and functional forms, containers, etc.

U.S. Glass Big Butterfly tumbler, one of four known, green. **$10,000**

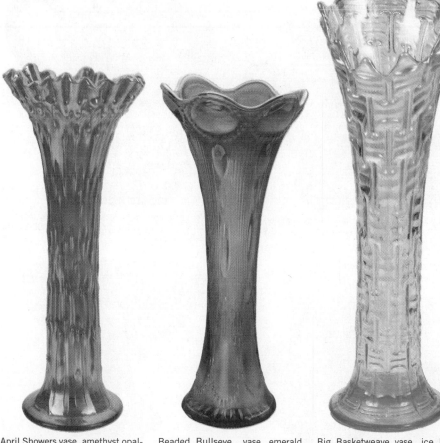

April Showers vase, amethyst opalescent, 11-1/4" h, made by Fenton. **$1,450**

Beaded Bullseye vase, emerald green, 11", made by Imperial. .... **$700-$1,100**
Outstanding example **$2,300**

Big Basketweave vase, ice blue, 11-1/4" h, made by Dugan-Diamond................................. **$600**

GLASS

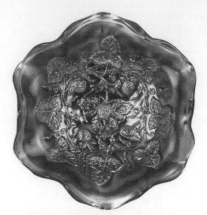

Blackberry Wreath large bowl, ruffled, purple, made by Millersburg. **$40**

Blackberry Block water pitcher and one tumbler, green, made by Fenton. **$4,000**

Blueberry water pitcher and three tumblers (one shown), white, made by Fenton. **$1,450**

Blueberry ruffled-top tankard, blue, 10" h, made by Fenton. .... **$1,000-$1,400**
Outstanding example **$4,500**

Bouquet water pitcher and six tumblers (one shown), marigold, made by Fenton. **$265**

Broken Arches punch bowl and base, purple, 13" d, made by Imperial. .... **$1,000-$1,300**
Outstanding example **$2,000**

Butterfly and Berry water pitcher, amethyst, made by Fenton.. **$3,000**

Butterfly and Tulip bowl, purple, made by Dugan. .... **$2,000-$3,500**

Butterfly and Fern water pitcher and six tumblers, amethyst.. **$1,050**

Captive Rose plate, green, scarce, made by Fenton, 9".. **$725**

Captive Rose plate, emerald green, rare, made by Fenton, 9".. **$600-$1,800**
Outstanding example **$8,000**

GLASS

Captive Rose bowl with 3-in-1 edge, electric blue, made by Fenton.............................. **$500**

Captive Rose plate with great detail, amethyst, made by Fenton, 9".................................... **$575**

Farmyard ruffled bowl, purple, made by Dugan. .... **$5,500-$8,000**
Outstanding example **$12,500**

Fentonia water pitcher and one tumbler, blue, made by Fenton. **$875**

Fluffy Peacock water pitcher and six tumblers, amethyst, made by Fenton.......**$1,050**

Good Luck eight-ruffled bowl with ribbed back, sapphire, by Northwood, 8-1/2". .... **$1,600-$2,300**

Good Luck bowl, enameled, only one known, made by Northwood, blue. **$800**

Good Luck stippled plate with ribbed back, pastel marigold, 9", made by Northwood. .... **$650-$950**
Outstanding example **$2,400**

Good Luck stippled plate with ribbed back, purple, 9", made by Northwood. .... **$1,000-$1,500**
Outstanding example **$2,200**

Good Luck ruffled bowl, electric blue, 8-1/2", made by Northwood ....**$300-$500**
Outstanding example **$900**

Good Luck plate, electric blue, 9", made by Northwood .... **$3,500-$5,000**
Outstanding example **$8,000**
These plates come in a variety of colors and some have a ribbed back, while some have a basketweave back.

GLASS

Imperial Grape carafe, purple, 9", made by Imperial........**$200-$400**

Imperial Grape carafe, emerald green, 9" h, made by Imperial .... **$2,000-$3,000** Outstanding example **$4,300 (rare)**

Imperial Grape water pitcher, purple, 10-1/2" h, made by Imperial ....**$250-$400** Outstanding example **$800**

Imperial Morning Glory funeral vase, purple, 14-1/4" h, 8-1/2" mouth. ....**$700-$1,000** Outstanding example **$2,400**

Imperial Morning Glory vase, purple, 12-1/2" h............**$500-$800**

Imperial Morning Glory miniature vase, vaseline, 5" h. ...**$600-$800** **(very rare)**

Imperial Morning Glory miniature vase, smoke, 4-3/4" h.**$100-$180**

Imperial Morning Glory, miniature vase, marigold, 3-1/2" h, shortest to be known. ....**$150-$250**

Imperial Morning Glory funeral vase, blue, one of only three perfect examples known in this color. ....**$8,000-12,500 (rare)**

Peacocks on the Fence bowl, marigold, pumpkin, ruffled with ribbed back, 8-1/2" d, made by Northwood. **$400**

Peacocks on the Fence stippled plate, electric blue, 9", made by Northwood. .... **$800-$1,200**
Outstanding example **$2,500**

Peacocks on the Fence ruffled bowl, ribbed back, aqua opalescent, 8-1/2" d, made by Northwood. .... **$950-$1,500**
Outstanding example **$3,200**

Peacocks on the Fence plate, electric blue, 9", made by Northwood. .... **$650-$1,000**
Outstanding example **$2,500**

Peacocks on the Fence ruffled bowl, electric green, 8-1/2" d, made by Northwood...................... **$1,350**

Persian Medallion plate, white, covered with pastel yellow iridescence, 9", made by Fenton. **$2,000**

GLASS

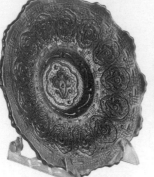

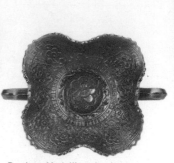

Persian Medallion flat plate, black amethyst, 6-1/4" d, made by Fenton. ....**$250-$400**

Persian Medallion plate, blue, 9" ....**$400-$650** Outstanding example, made by Fenton............................. **$1,200**

Persian Medallion bonbon, two handles, red, made by Fenton. **$700**

Persian Medallion sauce with a six-ruffled edge, blue, 6" d, made by Fenton. .... **$50-$80**

Persian Medallion bonbon with two handles, celeste blue, 7". .... **650-$950** Outstanding example, made by Fenton. **$1,800**

Northwood Poppy Show plate, electric blue, 9". .... **$5,000-$8,000**

Northwood Poppy Show flared plate, ice blue. **$1,700**

Northwood Poppy Show ruffled bowl, electric blue. **$1,500**

Northwood Poppy Show bowl, ruffled, white. **$400**

Northwood Poppy Show plate, marigold, 9" d......... **$900-$1,600**

Ripple squat vase, marigold, 4" h, 2-1/2" base, may be the shortest one there is. .... **$300-$400**

Ripple funeral vase, marigold, 11-1/2" h, made by Imperial. .... **$200-$400**

Ripple squat vase, purple, 6-1/2" h, with a 3" base, made by Imperial. .... **$150-$250**

Ripple vase, purple, 8" h, 2-1/2" base, made by Imperial. .... **$125-$175**

Ripple squat vase, marigold, 5-1/2" h x 3-3/8" base, made by Imperial............ **$200-$300 (rare)**

Rose Show bowl, purple, 8-1/2" d, made by Northwood. **$500**

Ripple vase, blue, 10" h x 3" base, made by Imperial..... **$800-$1,200 (rare)**

Rose Show bowl, aqua opalescent (butterscotch), 8-1/2", made by Northwood. .... **$700-$1,800**

Rose Show bowl, eight ruffles, aqua opalescent, 8-1/2" d, made by Northwood............. **$900-$1,600** Outstanding example **$3,000**

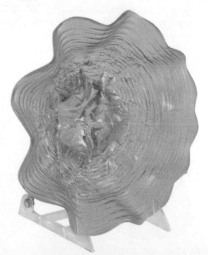

Rose Show bowl, eight ruffles, ice green opalescent, made by Northwood. .... **$2,800-$3,700 (rare)**

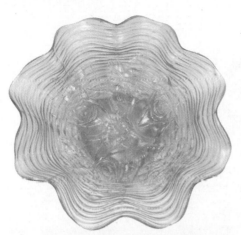

Rose Show ruffled bowl, ice blue, made by Northwood. **$1,300**

Rose Show plate, blue, 9" d, made by Northwood. .... **$1,100-$1,600**

Rose Show plate, marigold over custard, extremely rare, made by Northwood............................**$11,000**

Rose Show plate, ice green opalescent, made by Northwood. **$10,000**

Strawberry Scroll water pitcher and six tumblers, marigold, made by Fenton............. **$2,500**

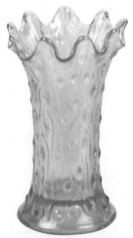

Tree Trunk funeral vase, mid-size, aqua opalescent. **$19,000**

Tree Trunk elephant's foot funeral vase, purple, 13" h. **$1,800-$3,400** Outstanding example **$11,000**

Tree Trunk vases, ice blue, squatty 7"....................................... $400

Tree Trunk mid-size vase, green, 12" h. ....**$350-$650**

Tree Trunk jester's cap vase, marigold, 7-1/2". **$3,000-$4,500 (rare)**

Tree Trunk mid-size vase, blue, 13" h. ....**$550-$950**

Central Glass Works

From the 1890s until its closing in 1939, the Central Glass Works of Wheeling, West Virginia, produced colorless and colored handmade glass in all the styles then popular. Decorations from etchings with acid to hand-painted enamels were used.

The popular "Depression" era colors of black, pink, green, light blue, ruby red and others were all produced. Two of its 1920s etchings are still familiar today, one named for the then President of the United States and the other for the Governor of West Virginia - these are the Harding and Morgan patterns.

From high end Art glass to mass-produced plain barware tumblers, Central was a major glass producer throughout the period.

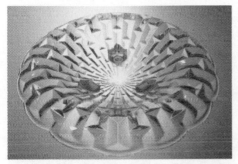

Bowl, 10 1/2" d., 3-footed, rolled edge, Frances patt., pink **$48**

Candleholders, one-light, Brocade etching, No. 2000, green, pr. (ILLUS. of one)................................ **$95**

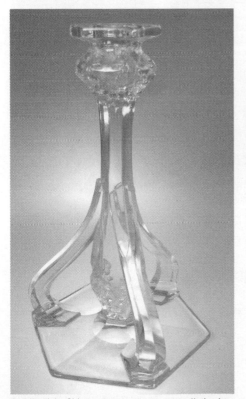

Candlestick, Chippendale patt., three-handled, clear w/cutting, 8 1/2" h. **$77**

Sherbet, low footed, No. 1450 stem, black base w/ clear bowl **$10**

Cigarette jar, round ashtray foot, clear optic bowl on amber foot, gold-encrusted Dunn's Parrot etching **$65**
Cracker plate, octagonal w/a center indentation, Morgan etching, pink, 9 1/2" w. **$75**
Creamer, Roses brocade etching, Pattern #1450, amber **$48**
Vase, 8" h., flip-style w/wide tapering cylindrical body, Roses brocade etching, green **$120**

GLASS

Consolidated

The Consolidated Lamp and Glass Company of Coraopolis, Pennsylvania, was founded in 1894. For a number of years it was noted for its lighting wares but also produced popular lines of pressed and blown tablewares. Highly collectible glass patterns of this early era include the Cone, Cosmos, Florette and Guttate lines.

Lamps and shades continued to be good sellers, but in 1926 a new "art" line of molded decorative wares was introduced. This "Martelè" line was developed as a direct imitation of the fine glasswares being produced by Renè Lalique of France, and many Consolidated patterns resembled their French counterparts. Other popular lines produced during the 1920s and 1930s were "Dancing Nymph," the delightfully Art Deco "Ruba Rombic," introduced in 1928, and the "Catalonian" line, which debuted in 1927 and imitated 17th-century Spanish glass.

Although the factory closed in 1933, it was reopened under new management in 1936 and prospered through the 1940s. It finally closed in 1967. Collectors should note that many later Consolidated patterns closely resemble wares of other competing firms, especially the Phoenix Glass Company. Careful study is needed to determine the maker of pieces from the 1920-40 era.

A book that will be of help to collectors is *Phoenix & Consolidated Art Glass, 1926-1980*, by Jack D. Wilson (Antique Publications, 1989).

CONE

Sugar shaker, w/original top, cylindrical, cased blue, glossy finish **$143**

Sugar shaker, w/original top, cylindrical, cased pale pink, glossy finish **$143**

FLORETTE

Cracker jar, cov., barrel-shaped, cased pink satin, silver plate rim, cover & bail handle not secured, 5 1/2" h. **$121**

GUTTATE

Far left: Pitcher, 7 1/4" h., bulbous w/applied frosted clear handle, cased pink satin **$132**

Left: Pitcher, water, 9 1/4" h., opaque white w/overall gold flecks, applied white handle **$198**

Pitcher, 9 1/2" h., cased pink, glossy finish **$325**

LATER LINES

Bowl, 10" w., deep rounded shape w/a flat rim, blue Vine patt. (Line 700), Martelè Line, mounted w/a ormolu rim band & high arched open floral scroll handles continuing down the sides, raised on a pierced ormolu base w/winged paw feet **$323**

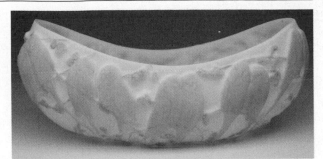

Bowl, boat shaped, 7 1/2 x 13 1/4", 6 1/4" h., Love Birds patt., Martelè line, pale blue birds on custard ground **$154**

Candleholder, one-light, footed bulbous ovoid shape, custard ground w/molded flowers & leaves painted in pink & blue, undocumented pattern, 3 1/2" h. **$130**

Cup & saucer, Dancing Nymph line, frosted pink, pr. **$150**

Lamp, table model, Pine Cone patt., Martelè line, bulbous ovoid body w/brass fittings, custard ground w/blue pine cones design, made from a vase, 6 1/2" h. **$160**

Plate, 8" d., Dancing Nymph line, clear w/brown wash **$145**

Tumbler, iced tea, footed, Catalonian line, honey color **$28**

Vase, 11 1/2" h., Dancing Girls patt., tall ovoid body, girls & Pan relief-molded & colored in deep rose & tan on a creamy custard ground **$518**

Tumbler, Catalonian line, wide tapering cylindrical sides w/a flat bottom, emerald green, 9 oz. **$18**

GLASS

Cranberry

Gold was added to glass batches to give this glass its color on reheating. It has been made by numerous glasshouses for years and is currently being reproduced. Both blown and molded articles were produced. A less expensive type of cranberry was made with the substitution of copper for gold.

Bell, large cranberry bell w/tall applied clear handle, possibly English, late 19th c., 10 1/2" h. **$275-325**

Decanter w/original stopper, bulbous ovoid body tapering to a cylindrical neck w/flared rim, clear pointed bubble stopper, applied clear angled handle, ornate gold enameling of cherry blossoms on branches, Bohemia, early 20th c., 10" h. (ILLUS. bottom row, second from right) . **$100-200**

Pitcher, 10 1/2" h., tankard-type, footed bulbous Optic Ribbed body tapering to a tall neck w/a flaring hexagonal crimped rim, decorated w/enameled white daisies & scattered blue flowers, applied clear handle, light outside residue **$121**

Pitcher, 11 1/4" h., tankard-type, a small cylindrical base flaring to a wide bulbous ovoid body below a tall ringed neck w/a high wide spout, decorated around the body & neck w/polychrome enamel flowers & leaves w/traces of gold, clear applied handle **$110**

Pitcher, 8 1/4" h., tankard-type, tall cylindrical body w/a small pinched spout, decorated in white enamel w/a garden scene of flowers & grasses, an applied twisted rope handle splitting at the base terminal w/two pressed daisy prunts, an applied ropetwist band around the neck **$553**

GLASS

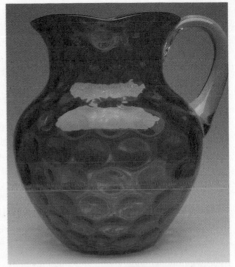

Pitcher, 8 1/2" h., ovoid body tapering to a cylindrical neck w/slightly flared crimped rim, Inverted Thumbprint patt., applied clear handle, engraved presentation "Mrs. M. Goodspeed - Saratoga 1894." ... **$154**

Pitcher, 8" h., ovoid body tapering to a squared neck, Inverted Thumbprint patt., applied clear handle w/ pressed fan design at upper terminal, minor flaws. **$231**

Rose bowl, shaded optic-ribbed bowl w/eight-crimped rim, applied on the side w/clear branch decoration, 4 1/2" d., 3 1/2" h. **$125-150**

Vase, 11 1/4" h., a bulbous ovoid optic ribbed body tapering to a wide neck w/an appliqued clear icicle-style border band pulled into point, raised on three applied clear thorn feet, the side applied w/a large five-petal pink & white flowers on a clear leafy stem. **$288**

◄Vase, 11 3/4" h., footed bottle-form shape w/a squatty bulbous body tapering to a tall stick neck, decorated overall w/ornate white enameled floral clusters, swags, arches & bands, base marked "Lace Art Cameo," late 19th c. **$375**

Vase, 8" h., 3 1/2" d., footed tapering ovoid body w/a short cylindrical neck, decorated w/large enameled blossom-form white reserve w/a worn scene framed w/gold-trim maroon scallops & flanked by leafy branches w/large blue, white & yellow blossoms, late 19th c. **$175-200**

Custard

"Custard glass," as collectors call it today, came on the American scene in the 1890s, more than a decade after similar colors were  made in Europe and England. The Sowerby firm of Gateshead-on-Tyne, England had marketed its patented "Queen's Ivory Ware" quite successfully in the late 1870s and early 1880s.

There were many glass tableware factories operating in Pennsylvania and Ohio in the 1890s and early 1900s, and the competition among them was keen. Each company sought to capture the public's favor with distinctive colors and, often, hand-painted decoration. That is when "Custard glass" appeared on the American scene.

The opaque yellow color of this glass varies from a rich, vivid yellow to a lustrous light yellow. Regardless of intensity, the hue was originally called "ivory" by several glass manufacturers then who also used superlative sounding terms such as "Ivorina Verde" and "Carnelian." Most Custard glass contains uranium, so it will "glow" under a black light.

The most important producer of Custard glass was certainly Harry Northwood, who first made it at his plants in Indiana, Pennsylvania, in the late 1890s and, later, in his Wheeling, West Virginia, factory. Northwood marked some of his most famous patterns, but much early Custard is unmarked. Other key manufacturers include the Heisey Glass Co., Newark, Ohio; the Jefferson Glass Co., Steubenville, Ohio; the Tarentum Glass Co., Tarentum, Pennsylvania; and the Fenton Art Glass Co., Williamstown, West Virginia.

Custard glass fanciers are particular about condition and generally insist on pristine quality decorations free from fading or wear. Souvenir Custard pieces with events, places and dates on them usually bring the best prices in the areas commemorated on them rather than from the specialist collector. Also, collectors who specialize in pieces such as cruets, syrups or salt and pepper shakers will often pay higher prices for these pieces than would a Custard collector

Key reference sources include William Heacock's Custard Glass from A to Z, published in 1976 but not out of print, and the book Harry Northwood: The Early Years, available from Glass Press. Heisey's Custard is discussed in Shirley Dunbar's Heisey Glass: The Early Years (Krause Publications, 2000), and Coudersport's production is well-documented in Tulla Majot's book *Coudersport's Glass 1900- 1904* (Glass Press, 1999). The recently formed Custard Glass Society holds a yearly convention and maintains a web site: www.homestead.com/custardsociety.

- James Measell

BEADED CIRCLE (NORTHWOOD AT INDIANA, PA., CA. LATE 1890S)

Butter dish, cov. **$500**

Berry set, master bowl & 5 sauce dishes; 6 pcs.................... **$495**

Tumbler, polychrome & gilt decoration............................ **$175**

Water set, pitcher & 3 tumblers, 4 pcs................................ **$845**

Water set, pitcher & 4 tumblers, 5 pcs................................ **$850**

GRAPE & CABLE, NORTHWOOD GRAPE, OR GRAPE & THUMBPRINT (NORTHWOOD AT WHEELING, CA. 1913-15)

Bowl, master berry, blue stain **$450-550**

Pitcher, water **$400-550**

Sauce dish, flat **$45-60**

Tumbler .. **$75-85**

INTAGLIO (NORTHWOOD AT INDIANA, PA., CA. 1899)

Pitcher, water **$450-500**

Berry set, pitcher & 6 tumblers, green & gold trim, 7 pcs. **$600-700**

Berry set, 9" d. footed compote & 6 sauce dishes, w/green decoration, 7 pcs. **$393**

Table set, cov. sugar bowl, creamer & spooner, 3 pcs.............. **$180**

Tumblers, blue & gold trim, set of 4 .... **$225**

Water set, pitcher & 6 tumblers, green & gold trim, 7 pcs.. **$575**

INVERTED FAN & FEATHER (NORTHWOOD AT INDIANA, PA., CA. 1900)

▲ Bowl, master berry ... **$200-225**

▶ Sugar bowl, cov. **$275-300**

Bowl, master berry or fruit, 10" d., 5 1/2" h., four-footed **$225**

Berry set, master bowl & 6 sauce dishes, 7 pcs................... **$650**

Berry set, master bowl & 2 sauce dishes, 3 pcs................... **$340**

PAGODA OR CHRYSANTHEMUM SPRIG (NORTHWOOD AT INDIANA, PA., CA. 1899)

Pitcher **$550-650**

Cruet w/original stopper (ILLUS. center with other pieces). **$350-450**

▶ Tumbler **$80-125**

Condiment set, four-footed tray, cruet w/original stopper & salt & pepper shakers w/original tops; 4 pcs.....................**$950-1,000**

Table set, cov. sugar bowl, creamer, cov. butter dish & spooner, 4 pcs. **$740**

GLASS

PEACOCK AND URN (NORTHWOOD AT WHEELING, WV, CA. 1913-15)

Ice cream bowl, master w/nutmeg stain, 9 3/4" d. **$300-375**

TRAILING VINE OR ENDLESS VINE (BASTOW, CA. 1903-04)

Sauce dish **$90**

WILD BOUQUET (NORTHWOOD AT INDIANA, PA., CA. 1899)

Spooner **$200-300**

MISCELLANEOUS PIECES

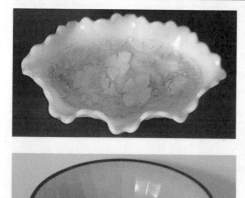

Bowl, Poinsettia Lattice patt., ruffled rim, Northwood. **$90**

Top left: Pickle dish, oval, Poppy patt., Northwood. **$100**

Bottom left: Bowl, shallow w/paneled sides, iridized finish w/black edge trim, Northwood **$250**

Cut

Cut glass most eagerly sought by collectors is American glass produced during the so-called "Brilliant Period" from 1880 to about 1915. Pieces listed below are by type of article in alphabetical order.

BASKETS

Pairpoint, "Cactus," 12" h **$1,595**

BOXES

Dresser, rectangular w/hinged cover w/original metal hardware & key, cranberry cut to clear w/ an overall button & rayed button pattern, 4 3/4 x 9 3/4", 5 1/4" h. **$3,450**

CHAMPAGNES, CORDIALS & WINES

Wines, Dorflinger Russian Cut hock wines in cranberry cut to clear, facet-cut knob stems w/a controlled bubble, each 4 3/4" h., set of 9......... **$3,450**

BOWLS

Blackmer, orange bowl, Columbia patt., 8 x 11 1/2", 4 1/2" h. **$775**

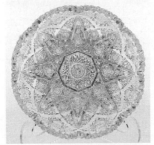

Hawkes low bowl, 9 3/8" d., Kensington patt. **$1,275**

Hoare (J.) & Co., Napoleon's hat fruit bowl, "Carolyn," clear, 9 x 13 1/2", 4" h. **$1,650**

Clark, 14" d., Mercedes patt. **$2,750**

Hawkes, 11 3/4" x 8 1/4" oval, "Kohinoor," clear **$2,700**

Jewel Cut Glass Co., 8" d., 3 1/2" h., Margaret patt. ... **$495**

Pitkin & Brooks, 9" d., 4" h., Cypress patt. **$395**

COMPOTES

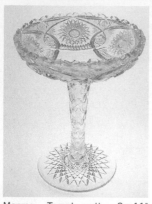

Monroe, Tempt patt., 8 x 11"
.... **$795**

ICE TUBS

Blackmer, Crescent patt., handled tub w/underplate, 6" h. .. **$1,450**

DECANTERS

Clark (T.B.) & Co., whiskey decanter, Lakewood patt., 10" h., signed **$795**

Stevens & Williams, baluster shape with teardrop stopper, amethyst with clear decoration, the body with floral and scrolling designs, a band of cross-cut diamonds on the base & the foot with a single band of beads, rare, 9" h. **$6,500**

Hawkes, ship's decanter, Flutes patt. **$575**

Libbey, Harvard patt., 15 1/2" h. **$975**

MISCELLANEOUS

Ice cream tray, Empire, Seneca patt., 18" l. **$1,775**

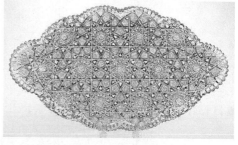

Flower center, Pairpoint, Sillsbee patt., 9 1/2" h. **$1,350**

Finger bowl, Dorflinger, American patt., 4 3/4" d., 2 1/4" h. .. **$145**

Olive dish, Straus, Imperial patt., 7 1/8" l. **$195**

PERFUMES & COLOGNES

Dorflinger, Belmont patt., square shape, 9" h. **$495**

PITCHERS & JUGS

Libbey jug, Harvard patt., 8" h. **$395**

PLATES

8 1/4" d., Alexandrite-type coloring w/strawberry diamond & fan cutting, possibly America, late 19th c. **$2,013**

PUNCH BOWLS

Clark, Mercedes patt., 14" d., 11 1/2" h., signed **$4,950**

Hoare (J.) & Co., Rookwood patt., two-piece **$4,450**

Ohio Cut Glass Co., Fern patt., two-piece, 12" h., 12" d. **$4,250**

ROSE BOWLS

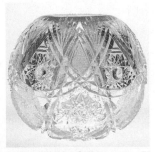

Clark, Baker's Gothic patt., 7" **$650**

TRAYS

Blackmer, Estelle patt., 14" d. **$4,450**

Blackmer, Princess patt., 12" d. **$1,750**

VASES

Cranberry cut to clear, 4" h., footed waisted cylindrical body cut w/vertical flutes, applied clear loop side handles, applied flaring silver rim band **$1,323**

Bergen (J.D.) Co., 12" h., chalice form, Sheldon patt. **$975**

Clark (T.B.) & Co., 14" h., "American Beauty," clear **$795**

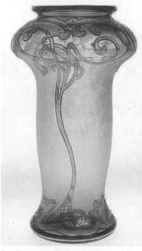

Cranberry cut to clear, 9 1/2" h., chalice-form bowl on a hollow blown lapidary-cut applied stem w/applied cut foot **$1,955**

Dorflinger, 8" h., "Honesdale," sinuous shape w/Art Nouveau-style whiplash design **$1,475**

Dorflinger, 12 5/8" h., green cut to clear, tall form with bulbous base and long, thin neck flaring slightly at rim, decorated overall w/engraved floral & leaf designs. **$4,850**

◄Hawkes, 14" h., "Navarre" variation, clear **$595**

►Hoare (J.) & Co., 12" h., "Marquise," clear **$1,250**

Czechoslovakian

The country of Czechoslovakia, including the glassmaking region of Bohemia, was not founded as an independent republic until after the close of World War I in 1918. The new country soon developed a large export industry, including a wide range of brightly colored and hand-painted glasswares such as vases, tablewares and perfume bottles. Fine quality cut crystal or Bohemian-type etched wares were also produced for the American market. Some Bohemian glass carries faint acid-etched markings on the base.

With the breakup of Czechoslovakia into two republics, the wares produced between World War I and II should gain added collector appeal.

Far left: Bowl, 7" d., deep bulbous tapering body w/closed rim in the Inverted Thumbprint patt., pale blue w/applied yellow rigaree bands & prunts **$81**

Left: Vase, 5 1/4" h., 7 1/2" d., footed squatty bulbous body w/a wide shoulder tapering to a wide flat rim w/a deeply rolled-out flaring rim, overall gold iridescence w/flashes of purple, blue & green, signed. **$300**

Cameo vase, 10 1/4" h., 10" d., footed bulbous ovoid body w/a short rolled neck, pearl overlaid w/ orange & brown & etched w/large orange flowers & brown leaves, signed in cameo "Leopal," ca. 1920s **$1,438**

Dresser set: round hand mirror, oval 11" l. hair brush & 6 1/4" l. clothes brush; Malachite glass inserts, each piece w/a gilt-metal frame, the long handles w/delicate pierced scrolling designs, Malachite w/a pressed putti design, Schlevogt factory, ca. 1935, the set (ILLUS. with vases) **$891**

GLASS

■ Daum Nancy _____

Daum Nancy fine glass, much of it cameo, was made by Auguste and Antonin Daum, who founded a factory in 1875 in Nancy, France. Most of their cameo and enameled glass was made from the 1890s into the early 20th century.

Cameo glass is made by carving into multiple layers of colored glass to create a design in relief. It is at least as old as the Romans.

French art glass vase, Daum Frères, Nancy, France, circa 1900, marked Daum, Nancy, (cross of Lorraine), 12", with varied and vibrant coloration, the shaded orange ground featuring a town scene in one panel... **$9,560**
Photo courtesy Heritage Auction Galleries, Dallas; www.HA.com

French art glass vase, Daum Freres, Nancy, France, circa 1910, marked DAUM, FRANCE, (cross of Lorraine), 11-3/4" x 4-3/4" x 3", with pattern of berried branches in dark mauve shades on dark blue and green modeled ground, surface showing multiple stress lines. **$310**
Photo courtesy Heritage Auction Galleries, Dallas; www.HA.com

Daum Nancy Cameo and Enamel Floral Vase. With delicate blue enameled flowers and green foliage that rest against a mottled background of blue, purple and green. Signed on the underside "Daum Nancy" with the Cross of Lorraine in gold. 5" h. Minor enamel loss to stems........ **$2,400**
Photo courtesy James D. Julia Auctioneers, Fairfield, Maine; www.JuliaAuctions.com

French art glass box and cover, Daum Frères, Nancy, France, circa 1900, marked Daum, Nancy, (cross of Lorraine), 3-3/4" x 5-1/2", squared box with round cover patterned with conforming landscape of birch trees in naturalistic spring palette over frosted, opalescent pink ground. ... **$3,585**
Photo courtesy Heritage Auction Galleries, Dallas; www.HA.com

GLASS

French art glass footed goblet, Daum Frères, Nancy, France, circa 1895, marked Daum, Nancy, (cross of Lorraine), 7" x 7-1/2", patterned with a frieze of field mice in shades of red and orange over shaded and frosted sky. **$5,078**

Photo courtesy Heritage Auction Galleries, Dallas; www.HA.com

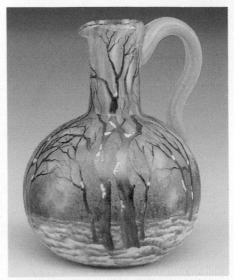

Daum Nancy Cameo Cruet. Winter scene in rare shape. Signed in enamel on the underside "Daum Nancy" with Cross of Lorraine. 3" t. **$3,220**

Daum Nancy Cameo and Enameled Vase. Square vase is decorated on each side with a cameo poppy, stem and leaves against a mottled yellow shading to orange background. Each poppy, in various stages of bloom, is enameled with bright orange flowers and subtle green and brown stems and leaves. The foot of the vase is trimmed with a simple gold gilt line. Signed on the side in cameo "Daum Nancy" with the Cross of Lorraine. 4-3/4" t. **$4,200**

Photo courtesy James D. Julia Auctioneers, Fairfield, Maine; www.JuliaAuctions.com

Daum Nancy Art Deco Vase. With deep acid cut-back Art Deco design against a smoky gray glass. The design has a textured finish in contrast with the polished glass highlights. Signed on the underside with engraved "Daum Nancy France" with Cross of Lorraine. 4" t. **$460**

Photo courtesy James D. Julia Auctioneers, Fairfield, Maine; www.JuliaAuctions.com

▶Monumental Daum Nancy Cameo Vase. With decoration of swans and birch trees. Decoration adorns both from and back of the vase and is finished with enameled scene of islands and trees in the background. A superior example. Signed in enamel on the foot rim "Daum Nancy". 25-1/4" t.**$18,400**

Photo courtesy James D. Julia Auctioneers, Fairfield, Maine; www.JuliaAuctions.com

GLASS

Daum Nancy Cameo Vase. Acid etched and enameled winter scene. Signed in enamel on the underside "Daum Nancy" with the Cross of Lorraine. 4" t.
.... **$6,325**
Photo courtesy James D. Julia Auctioneers, Fairfield, Maine; www.JuliaAuctions.com

Daum Nancy Snail Vase. Design of grapes, leaves and vines in autumn-colored vitreous glass against a mottled yellow, orange and brown background. The unusually large egg-shaped vase is finished with two applied glass snails (second view). Vase is signed on the side in cameo "Daum Nancy" with the Cross of Lorraine. 8-3/4" t. **$10,925**
Photo courtesy James D. Julia Auctioneers, Fairfield, Maine; www.JuliaAuctions.com

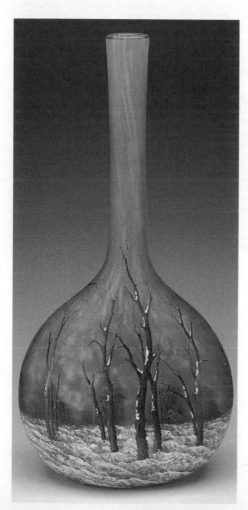

Daum Nancy Cameo Rose Bowl. Winter scenic decoration, strongly colored and detailed. Engraved signature "Daum Nancy" with Cross of Lorraine on underside. 3-3/4" t x 5" diameter. **$8,625**
Photo courtesy James D. Julia Auctioneers, Fairfield, Maine; www.JuliaAuctions.com

◀Daum Nancy Cameo Vase. Winter scenic banjo vase. Unusual shape. Signed in enamel on the underside "Daum Nancy" with Cross of Lorraine. 12" t.
.... **$10,350**
Photo courtesy James D. Julia Auctioneers, Fairfield, Maine; www.JuliaAuctions.com

Daum Nancy Cameo Vase. Canoe shape with acid-etched and enameled winter scene. Enameled signature on the underside "Daum Nancy" with the Cross of Lorraine. 6-3/4" w. **$6,325**
Photo courtesy James D. Julia Auctioneers, Fairfield, Maine; www.JuliaAuctions.com

Daum Nancy Rain Scene Vase. Extremely rare, square form is enameled with earthen-hued trees with green grass and foliage in the background. This design is set against a gray, rose and green ground. The "rain" effect is created by scoring the glass down to its transparency. Signed "Daum Nancy" with the Cross of Lorraine. 4-1/4" h. **$8,625**
Photo courtesy James D. Julia Auctioneers, Fairfield, Maine; www.JuliaAuctions.com

Early Daum Cameo and Enameled Vase. Decorated with a large, central heavily enameled thistle and flower with gold highlights. The flower is set against an acid-etched background of creamy yellow shading to clear. The back and sides of the vase are decorated with all-over cameo thistle design with black enamel highlighting the stems and leaves with gold gilt thistle flowers and red enamel highlights. The vase is finished with an enameled floral band at the lip. Signed on the underside in red enamel "Daum Nancy" with the Cross of Lorraine. 8" h. Some minor wear to gilt trim on lip. **$5,750**
Photo courtesy James D. Julia Auctioneers, Fairfield, Maine; www.JuliaAuctions.com

Daum Nancy Cameo Vase. Acid etched and enameled vase with red berries and green leaves on a yellow to brown mottled background. Vividly colored. Signed on the side in enamel "Daum Nancy France" with the Cross of Lorraine. 15-1/4" h. **$8,050**
Photo courtesy James D. Julia Auctioneers, Fairfield, Maine; www.JuliaAuctions.com

▶ Daum Nancy Cameo Vase. Spring scenic vase with acid-etched and enameled trees. Signed in enamel on the side "Daum Nancy" with the Cross of Lorraine. 10-1/2" h. **$6,325**
Photo courtesy James D. Julia Auctioneers, Fairfield, Maine; www.JuliaAuctions.com

Daum Nancy Cameo Vase. Acid etched and enameled pillow vase with red berries and green leaves on a yellow to brown mottled background. Vividly colored. Signed on the side in enamel "Daum Nancy France" with the Cross of Lorraine. 4-3/4" h. **$5,175**

Photo courtesy James D. Julia Auctioneers, Fairfield, Maine; www.JuliaAuctions.com

Daum Nancy Floral French Cameo Vase. Pillow-shaped vase has a frosted mottled ground which flows into a golden yellow hue. Accenting this is a pattern of violets enameled in purple with green foliage front and back. Signed "Daum Nancy" with Cross of Lorraine. 4-1/2" x 4-1/2"................................. **$4,312**

Photo courtesy James D. Julia Auctioneers, Fairfield, Maine; www.JuliaAuctions.com

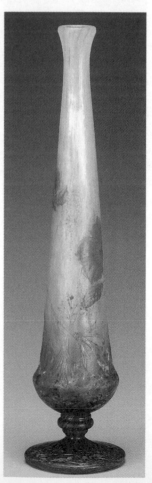

Daum Nancy Cameo Vase. Padded and wheel-carved lavender and brown iris flowers and buds on a frosted to chartreuse background together with acid-etched, deep purple leaves. Acid etched signature on the side "Daum Nancy" with the Cross of Lorraine. 12" h. **$7,200**

Photo courtesy James D. Julia Auctioneers, Fairfield, Maine; www.JuliaAuctions.com

Daum Nancy French Cameo Berry Vase. Deep blue berry decoration with foliage in colors of amber and green atop a muted yellow mottled ground. Unusual tapered bulbous form. Signed "France" and also "Daum Nancy" in cameo with the Cross of Lorraine. 4-1/2" h. **$1,380**

Photo courtesy James D. Julia Auctioneers, Fairfield, Maine; www.JuliaAuctions.com

▶Daum Nancy Padded and Wheel-Carved Vase. Orange poppies on striated blue to green wheel-carved background with simulated hammered texture, brown and yellow mottled foot. Intaglio carved signature on the foot "Daum Nancy" with the Cross of Lorraine. 16-1/4" h. **$9,200**

Photo courtesy James D. Julia Auctioneers, Fairfield, Maine; www.JuliaAuctions.com

Daum Nancy Cameo and Enameled Floral Vase. Cornflowers in blue are accented by russet stamens with green foliage. This pattern wraps itself around the entire vase. The background glass is a softly mottled frost rose and green with an electric cobalt blue base. Signed "Daum Nancy" with the Cross of Lorraine. 3-3/4" h x 4" w. **$4,255**
Photo courtesy James D. Julia Auctioneers, Fairfield, Maine, www.JuliaAuctions.com

Daum Nancy Cameo Vase. Single wheel-carved parrot tulip in shades of purple with wheel-carved leaves on a shaded clear to purple background with simulated hammered texture. Signed on the underside with engraved "Daum Nancy" with the Cross of Lorraine. 6" h. **$6,000**
Photo courtesy James D. Julia Auctioneers, Fairfield, Maine; www.JuliaAuctions.com

Daum Nancy Cameo and Applied Covered Jar. Rare example with one green-gold applied cabochon, one green applied insect and one red applied leaf on body with acid-etched maple leaves. The lid with applied and wheel-carved handle with red applied insect on top (second view). Signed on the underside with engraved and gilded "Daum Nancy" with the Cross of Lorraine. 4-1/2" h. **$9,200**
Photo courtesy James D. Julia Auctioneers, Fairfield, Maine; www.JuliaAuctions.com

Daum Nancy Cameo Vase. Acid-etched green daffodils on wheel-carved green to frosted to green background with simulated hammered texture and foot with opalescent interior. Signed on the underside with engraved "Daum Nancy" with the Cross of Lorraine. 7-3/4" h. **$6,000**
Photo courtesy James D. Julia Auctioneers, Fairfield, Maine; www.JuliaAuctions.com

GLASS

■ Depression Glass _____

Depression glass is the name of colorful glassware collectors generally associated with mass-produced glassware found in pink, yellow, crystal, or green in the years surrounding the Great Depression in America.

The housewives of the Depression-era were able to enjoy the wonderful colors offered in this new inexpensive glass dinnerware because they received pieces of their favorite patterns packed in boxes of soap, or as premiums given at "dish night" at the local movie theater. Merchandisers, such as Sears & Roebuck and F. W. Woolworth, enticed young brides with the colorful wares that they could afford even when economic times were harsh.

Because of advancements in glassware technology, Depression-era patterns were mass-produced and could be purchased for a fraction of what cut glass or lead crystal cost. As one manufacturer found a pattern that was pleasing to the buying public, other companies soon followed with their adaptation of a similar design. Patterns included several design motifs, such as florals, geometrics, and even patterns that looked back to Early American patterns like Sandwich glass

As America emerged from the Great Depression and life became more leisure-oriented again, new glassware patterns were created to reflect the new tastes of this generation. More elegant shapes and forms were designed, leading to what is sometimes called "Elegant Glass." Today's collectors often include these more elegant patterns when they talk about Depression-era glassware.

A time line that highlights the beginnings, major events, and endings of American glassware manufacturers is included in this edition to show the scope of the companies that helped produce glassware in this era. Also included in this edition is a color time line that is designed to help identify colors and when they were manufactured. Combining all these clues, along with the pattern identification sketches, will help determine when a pattern was made, by whom, when, and in what colors.

Depression-era glassware is one of the best-researched collecting areas available to the American marketplace. This is due in large part to the careful research of several people, including Hazel Marie Weatherman, Gene Florence, Barbara Mauzy, Carl F. Luckey, and Kent Washburn. Their books are held in high regard by researchers and collectors today

Regarding values for Depression glass, rarity does not always equate to a high dollar amount. Some more readily found items command lofty prices because of high demand or other factors, not because they are necessarily rare. As collectors' tastes range from the simple patterns to the more elaborate patterns, so does the ability of their budget to invest in inexpensive patterns to multi-hundreds of dollars per form patterns.

To maintain the fine tradition of extensive descriptions typically found in Warman's price guides, as much information as possible has been included as far as sizes, shapes, colors, etc. Whenever possible, the original manufacturer's language was maintained. A glossary is included to help you identify some of those puzzling names. As the patterns evolved, sometimes other usage names were assigned to pieces. Color names are also given as the manufacturers originally named them.

The Depression-era glassware researchers have many accurate sources, including company records, catalogs, magazine advertisements, oral and written histories from sales staff, factory workers, etc. The dates included in the introductions are approximate as are some of the factory locations. When companies had more than one factory, usually only the main office or factory is listed.

For more information on Depression glass, see *Warman's Depression Glass Identification and Price Guide*, 5th Edition, or *Warman's Depression Glass Field Guide*, 4th Edition, both by Ellen T. Schroy

Adam, pink covered casserole **$80**

American Sweetheart, pink soup bowl **$80**

American, crystal candlesticks, 3"
h, round foot **$12**
6" h, octagon foot **$35**

Avocado, green sugar **$40**
creamer **$40**

Aunt Polly, blue vase, 6-1/2" h
.... **$40**

Beaded Block, opalescent 4-1/2" d lily bowl **$30**
opalescent vase with two handles **$110**

Block Optic, pink candlesticks, pr **$100**
green ice bucket **$40**

Bowknot, green tumbler **$20**
footed berry bowl **$25**

GLASS

Bubble, royal ruby 8-3/4" d berry bowl **$18**
Royal Ruby bowl on metal pedestal, marble base **$20**
iridescent 4" d berry bowl **$5**

By Cracky, green cup.. **$5**
cone-shaped pitcher **$20**

Cameo, green 56 oz pitcher ... **$90**

Capri, azure blue bowl, 8-3/4" d swirled bowl............................. **$12**
4-3/4" d swirled berry bowl **$7.50**

Christmas Candy, crystal sugar **$15**
creamer **$15**

Cherry Blossom, pink sugar **$35**

Coin, amber 4-1/2" h candlesticks, pr **$60**
9" d center bowl.. **$40**

Circle, green sugar, ftd **$12**

▶Cloverleaf, green sherbet **$15**

Colonial, pink divided grill plate
.... **$27.50**

Colonial Block, green covered butter dish........... **$50**

Colony, crystal sugar **$6.50**
crystal creamer... **$6.50**

Coronation, royal ruby handled berry bowl **$20**

Cracked Ice, pink creamer **$35**
pink covered sugar.. **$35**

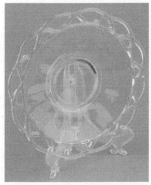

Crocheted Crystal, luncheon plate
.... **$12.50**

Crow's Foot, amber square plate,
8-1/2" d **$7**

Cube, pink covered candy jar . **$30**

Cupid, pink low pedestal-foot comport, 6-1/4" **$290**

Daisy, amber luncheon plate .. **$10**

GLASS

Diamond Quilted, green 4-3/4" d cream soup ...... **$12** green 10" d bowl .... **$20** green 5-1/2" d bowl with one handle **$15**

Dogwood, pink sugar **$22.50**
pink creamer **$25**
pink luncheon plate **$10**

English Hobnail, green 6" mayonnaise............... **$22**
green 6-1/2" plate **$10**

Fairfax, topaz ice bucket with metal handle........ **$35**
whipped cream pail with floral etching, metal handle
.... **$40**

Doric and Pansy, ultramarine child's sugar **$60**
ultramarine child's creamer **$50**

Early American Prescut, crystal 10" h vase **$15**
crystal 8-1/2" h vase.. **$8**

Floral, green 8" d covered vegetable bowl **$50**
pink butter dish.. **$80**

◆ Run your fingertips around the around the edges of pressed glass or Depression glass for chips. One can never overemphasize the importance of condition in collecting.

Floral and Diamond Band, green luncheon plate . **$40**

Florentine No. 1, pink sherbet **$15**
cup **$12**

Flower Garden with Butterflies, blue comport, 5-7/8"
h, 11" w.. **$95**

Florentine No. 2, yellow cup
.... **$14.50**

Fortune, pink berry bowl, 7-3/4"
.... **$28**

Fruits, green luncheon plate .. **$15**

Georgian, green 4-1/4" berry bowl................................. **$10**
green 6" plate **$6.50**

Heritage, crystal cup................ **$4**
crystal saucer **$2**

Hex Optic, green 5" h milk pitcher..................... **$25**
green 9" h footed pitcher **$48**

Hobnail, pink sherbet... **$5**

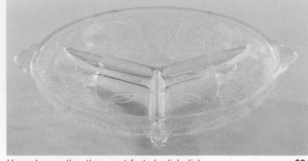

Horseshoe, yellow three-part footed relish dish $24

Jamestown, blue footed creamer $25

Iris, crystal candlesticks $50
iridescent plate $48

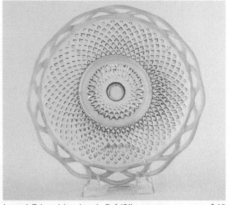

Laced Edge, blue bowl, 5-1/2" $42

Jubilee, yellow goblet. $75

Lorain, green cup and saucer $32

Madrid, amber bowl .. $17.50

Lincoln Inn, cobalt blue goblet $30

Mayfair Federal, amber dinner plate $20

Mayfair, Open Rose ice blue sweet pea vase $160

Melba, amethyst luncheon plate $9

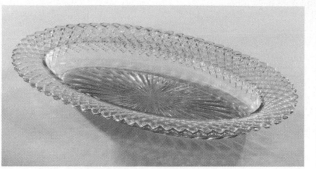

Miss America, pink 10-1/2" oval celery dish $45

Moondrops, red sugar.. $18
red creamer.. $16

Moderntone, cobalt blue salt shaker $25

Monticello, clear compote, stemmed $15

Moonstone, crystal heart-shaped bonbon with opalescent hobnails $16

Moroccan, amethyst cocktail shaker $50

Mt. Pleasant, black scalloped fruit bowl $40

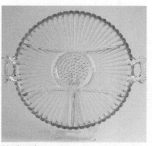

National, crystal tray with two handles $17.50

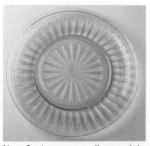

New Century, green dinner plate $24

Newport, cobalt blue 5-1/4" d cereal bowl **$45**

Old Colony Lace Edge, pink 7-3/4" d salad bowl. **$60**

Normandie, iridescent cup.....................**$6**

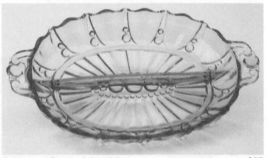

Oyster and Pearl, pink relish **$35**

Old English, green compote **$24**

Patrician, amber covered butter **$95**

Paneled Grape, white milk dinner plate. **$40**

Petalware, pink cream soup bowl **$17**

Pineapple and Floral, crystal cone vase **$42.50**

Pioneer, pink luncheon plate, fruit center...................................... **$8**

Pretzel, crystal leaf-shaped olive dish.. **$7**

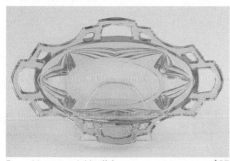

Pyramid, green pickle dish **$35**

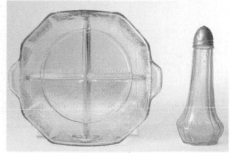

Princess green four-part relish........................... **$35**
green salt shaker **$30**

Queen Mary pink footed sherbet........................ **$12**
pink small tumbler...................................... **$19.50**

Radiance ice blue 6" comport with ruffled edge.. **$35**

Ribbon green covered candy dish **$45**

Ring, crystal with multicolored rings decanter with stopper
.... **$35**
green pitcher, 80oz... **$36**

Rock Crystal, amber plate, 8-1/2" d...**$12**

Rosemary, amber vegetable bowl **$18**
amber berry bowl **$7**

Roulette, green 9" fruit bowl **$25**

Royal Ruby 3-1/2" h flat tumbler with original label
....**$15**
4-1/2" h tumbler with original label **$12**
5" h tumbler **$10**
86 oz pitcher **$35**

S-Pattern, yellow 3-1/2" h flat tumbler **$6.50**
4-3/4" h flat tumbler **$8.50**
5" h flat tumbler **$15**

Sandwich, Hocking, smooth desert gold bowl, 6-1/2" d...**$9**

Sandwich, Line No. 41, crystal salad plate.........**$10**

Sharon, pink 10-1/2" fruit bowl **$50**

Sierra Pinwheel, green butter dish......................**$80**
pink cup..**$17.50**
pink saucer..**$10**

Spiral, green sandwich plate with center handle . **$30**

Strawberry, green 7-1/2" d berry bowl...............................**$20**
pink 5-3/4" d footed comport **$60**

Sunburst, crystal candelabra, two-light **$20**

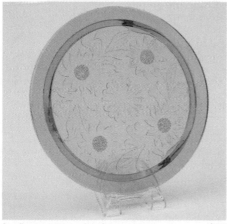

Sunflower, green cake plate **$20**

Swirl, ultramarine cup and saucer **$22.50**

Tea Room, green sugar and creamer on tray with center handle **$95**

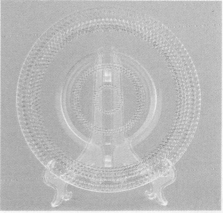

Teardrop, crystal salad plate **$6.50**

GLASS

Thumbprint, green vase......... **$65**

Vernon, yellow tumbler **$45**

Wexford, crystal goblet **$12**

Waterford, crystal 7-1/8" d salad plate **$9**
5-1/4" h goblet **$18**

◀Twisted Optic, green covered flat candy dish ... **$40**

Windsor, pink 11-1/2" oval platter (in back)......**$25**
10-1/2" oval bowl with pointed ends **$32**
8-1/2" l oval bowl..**$30**

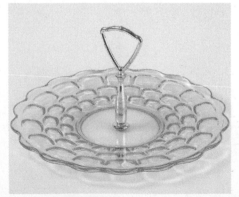

Yorktown, yellow sandwich server with gold metal
center handle **$8**

Duncan & Miller

Duncan & Miller Glass Company, a successor firm to George A. Duncan & Sons Company, produced a wide range of pressed wares and novelty pieces during the late 19th century and into the early 20th century. During the Depression era and after, they continued making a wide variety of more modern patterns, including mold-blown types, and also introduced a number of etched and engraved patterns. Many colors, including opalescent hues, were produced during this era, and especially popular today are the graceful swan dishes they produced in the Pall Mall and Sylvan patterns.

The numbers after the pattern name indicate the original factory pattern number. The Duncan factory was closed in 1955.

Basket, Hobnail patt., applied handle, blue opalescent, 9 x 14"a **$200**

▶Epergne, one-lily, three-piece, fruit & flower-type, a tall English Hobnail patt., lily above the wide Early American Sandwich patt. dish, raised on a pedestal base w/swirled foot, clear, 15" h. **$165**

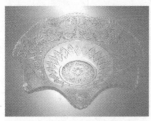

Bowl, 11 1/2" d., Early American Sandwich patt., flared & ruffled rim, clear **$50**

Bowl, 6" d., garden-type w/five deep lobes, blue opalescent.. **$68**

Candy dish, cov., three-part, Canterbury patt., clear w/cutting, 7" d. **$45**

Coaster-ashtray, green, 4 1/4 x 6" **$25**

▶Honey jug, miniature, Mardi Gras patt., clear, 2 1/2" h. ... **$28**

Plate, 8 1/2" d., pressed Ship patt. in center, amber **$16**

GLASS

Relish dish, Sylvan patt., two-part, milk white w/green handle, 8 1/2" l. **$125**

Rose bowl, Canterbury patt., Jasmine, yellow opalescent, 6" **$125**

Salt dip, individual, footed, No. 63 Homestead patt., clear, 2" h. **$18**

Vase, 5 1/2" h., deep flaring sides pulled into six ruffles, clear . **$24**

◄Vase, 10" h., tall trumpet-form body on a short stem & round foot, Early American Sandwich patt., #108, clear **$78**

Vase, 5" h., Early American Sandwich patt., fanned shape, clear **$49**

Vase, 10 1/2" h., footed, Venetian No. 126 patt., ruby **$225**

Vase, 5" h., 6" d., Hobnail patt., pink opalescent **$65**

Vase, 6" h., footed trumpet form, Spiral Flutes patt., green **$20**

Vase, 8" h., Canterbury patt. (No. 115), crimpted, straight sided, clear... **$35**

Fenton Art Glass

The Fenton Art Glass Co. was founded in 1905 by Frank L. Fenton and his brother, John W., in Martins Ferry, Ohio. They initially sold hand-painted glass made by other manufacturers, but it wasn't long before they decided to produce their own glass. The new Fenton factory in Williamstown, W.V., opened on Jan. 2, 1907. From that point on, the company expanded by developing unusual colors and continued to decorate glassware in innovative ways.

Two more brothers, James and Robert, joined the firm. But despite the company's initial success, John W. left to establish the Millersburg Glass Co. of Millersburg, Ohio, in 1909. The first months of the new operation were devoted to the production of crystal glass only. Later iridized glass was called "Radium Glass." After only two years, Millersburg filed for bankruptcy.

Fenton's iridescent glass had a metallic luster over a colored, pressed pattern, and was sold in dime stores. It was only after the sales of this glass decreased and it was sold in bulk as carnival prizes that it came to be known as carnival glass.

Fenton became the top producer of carnival glass, with more than 150 patterns. The quality of the glass, and its popularity with the public, enabled the new company to be profitable through the late 1920s. As interest in carnival subsided, Fenton moved on to stretch glass and opalescent patterns. A line of colorful blown glass (called "off-hand" by Fenton) was also produced in the mid-1920s.

During the Great Depression, Fenton survived by producing functional colored glass tableware and other household items, including water sets, table sets, bowls, mugs, plates, perfume bottles and vases.

Restrictions on European imports during World War II ushered in the arrival of Fenton's opaque colored glass, and the lines of "Crest" pieces soon followed.

In the 1950s, production continued to diversify with a focus on Milk-glass, particularly in Hobnail patterns.

In the third quarter of Fenton's history, the company returned to themes that had proved popular to preceding generations, and began adding special lines, such as the Bicentennial series.

Innovations included the line of Colonial colors that debuted in 1963, including Amber, Blue, Green, Orange and Ruby. Based on a special order for an Ohio museum, Fenton in 1969 revisited its early success with "Original Formula Carnival Glass." Fenton also started marking its glass in the molds for the first time.

The star of the 1970s was the yellow and blushing pink creation known as Burmese, which remains popular today. This was followed closely by a menagerie of animals, birds, and children.

In 1975, Robert Barber was hired by Fenton to begin an artist-in-residence program, producing a limited line of art-glass vases in a return to the off-hand, blown-glass creations of the mid-1920s.

Shopping at home via television was a recent phenomenon in the late 1980s when the "Birthstone Bears" became the first Fenton product to appear on QVC (established in 1986 by Joseph Segel, founder of The Franklin Mint).

In the latter part of the century, Fenton established a Web site—www.fentonartglass.com—as a user-friendly online experience where collectors could learn about catalog and gift shop sales, upcoming events and the history of the company.

In August 2007, Fenton discontinued all but a few of its more popular lines.

For more information on Fenton Art Glass, see *Warman's Fenton Glass Identification and Price Guide*, 2nd edition, by Mark F. Moran.

1905-1930

GLASS

Blue Opalescent swung vase in Fenton Drapery, circa 1910, 14" h...**$45+**

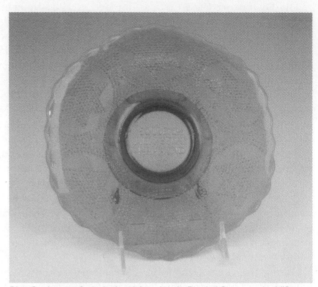

Blue Opalescent footed advertising plate in Beaded Stars, marked "Souvenir Lyon Store Hammond" (Ind.), circa 1910, 8-1/2" diameter. ....**$50+**

Persian Blue handled bonbon, 1915, in Pond Lily with enamel decoration, 7" diameter. **$35**

Crystal bud vase, wheel-cut floral decoration, 1914, 8" h. ......**$20+**

Three candleholders, all 1920s to mid-1930s, from left: Dolphin in Ruby, 3-1/2" h ....**$40+**
Velva Rose and Celeste Blue, 2-3/4" h................................**$35+ each**

Black (Ebony) fan vase, 1926, with thistles in an encrusted pattern done by Lotus Glass Decorating Co., Barnsville, Ohio, 8" h, rare. ....,,, **$250+**

Celeste Blue stretch-glass covered jug and tumbler with cobalt handles, base and coaster, part of a lemonade set that would have included six tumblers, 1920s; jug, 11-1/4" h with base; tumbler, 5" h not including coaster, which is 3-1/4" diameter .... **$700+ for complete set**

Ruby dolphin-handle comport in Diamond Optic, late 1920s, 6" h.. **$110+**

Tangerine stretch-glass tidbit tray in Diamond Optic, late 1920s, 10" diameter............................. **$125+**

Pair of Velva Rose candleholders in style No. 316, 1926 33, 3-1/2" h. ....**$75+ pair**

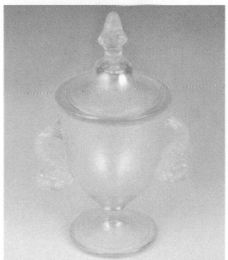

Topaz stretch-glass covered candy jar with dolphin handles, early 1920s, 8" h............................ **$110+**

GLASS

Fenton Carnival Glass

The golden era of carnival glass was from about 1905 to the mid-1920s. It is believed that by 1906 the first cheap, iridized glass to rival the expensive Tiffany creations was in production. Carnival glass was originally made to bridge a gap in the market by providing ornamental wares for those who couldn't afford to buy the fashionable, iridized pieces popular at the height of the art nouveau era. It wasn't until much later that it acquired the name "carnival glass." When it fell from favor, it was sold off cheaply to carnivals and offered as prizes. Fenton made about 150 patterns of carnival glass.

Here are some of the basic colors:

Amethyst: A purple color ranging from quite light to quite dark
Aqua opalescent: Ice blue with a milky (white or colored) edge
Black amethyst: Very dark purple or black in color
Clam broth: Pale ginger ale color, sometimes milky
Cobalt blue (sometimes called royal blue): A dark, rich blue
Green: A true green, not pastel
Marigold: A soft, golden yellow
Pastel colors: A satin treatment in white, ice blue, ice green
Peach opalescent: Marigold with a milky (white or colored) edge
Red: A rich red, rare
Vaseline (Fenton called it topaz): Clear yellow/yellow-green glass

Black amethyst vase in April Showers, 12" h.............**$80- $150**

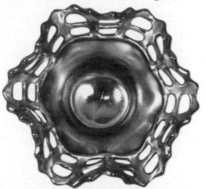

Amberina basket in Open Edge. **$75**

Amethyst banana boat in Thistle. **$185**

Aqua bowl with 3-in-1 edge, Holly, rare, 8-1/2" d.
....**$200-$350**

Blue flat plate in Leaf Chain, 9" d........ **$700-$1,200**

Green water pitcher and tumbler in Blackberry Block.. **$4,000**

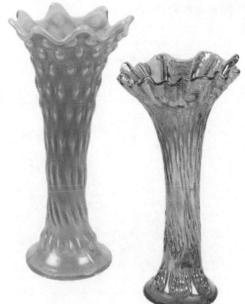

Left: Lime green opalescent vase in Rustic, 9-1/4" h.
.... **$1,250**
Right: Sapphire vase in Knotted Beads. **$450**

Marigold spittoon in Blackberry Wreath, whimsy.
.... **$700**

Peach opalescent bowl in Kittens, ruffled......... **$150**

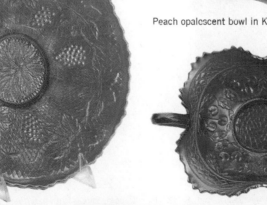

Purple flat plate in Concord, 9" d...... **$2,000-$3,000**

Red large bonbon in Cherry Chain. **$5,000**

1930-1955

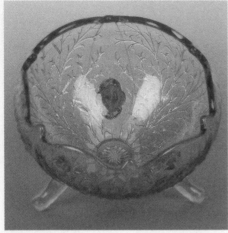

Amber cupped footed bowl in Silvertone, 1937, 5" diameter. .... **$30+**

Amber console bowl, 10" diameter, and footed candleholder, 4-1/2" diameter, both in Silvertone, 1937.
Bowl.. **$35+**
Candleholder.. **$22+**

Green Ming paneled bowl and underplate, mid-1930s: bowl, 10" diameter; plate, 15" diameter.
.... **$125+ set**

Two Crystal wine glasses in Flower Window, late 1930s, each 4" h. ....**$30+ each**

Black (Ebony) Empress vase, 1935, 7-1/2" h. **$110+**

Dancing Ladies Ruby flared vase, mid-1930s, 8-1/2" h.
.... **$450+**

GLASS

Early Milk-glass flared vase in Basket Weave with Open Edge, circa 1933, 4" h............................ **$35+**

Jade Green fan vase with dolphin handles, 1931, 6" h.. **$55+**

Mandarin Red flared bowl with applied gold decoration and Ebony base, mid-1930s, 8" diameter **$200+ pair**

Nymph in footed bowl in Green Transparent, 1930s, 7-1/2" h. .... **$275+ set**

Three cornucopia candleholders from left: Aqua Crest ribbed, Blue Opalescent in Hobnail and Milk-glass in Diamond Lace, 1940s, 5-1/2" to 6-1/2" h. ....**$35+ each**

Blue Opalescent biscuit jar in Hobnail, 1940s, 7-1/2" h. **$900+**

Far left: Cranberry Opalescent covered candy in Hobnail, with clear lid, 1940s, 5-1/2" diameter. .... **$300+**

Left: Gold Crest hat basket with gold handle, mid-1940s, 6-1/2" h.. **$50+**

Rose Overlay pieces on Opal, mid-1940s, from left: crimped jug, 5-1/2" h **$50**
small hat basket, 4" h .... **$50+**

Topaz Opalescent creamer and sugar in Hobnail, early 1940s, each 2" h .... **$50 pair**

Milk-glass spooner in Hobnail, 1950s, 7" l. ... **$100+**

Black Rose basket, 1953-54, 8" h .... **$175+**

New World shakers, two sizes, in Cranberry Opalescent Rib Optic, 1953, 5" h and 4" h. ...**$175 pair**

Crystal Crest 70-ounce jug with original label, 9-1/2" h...... **$450+**

Emerald Green platter in Priscilla, early 1950s, 12" diameter. . **$40+**

French Opalescent petite epergne in Hobnail (the horn sits in a shallow ring rather than a hole), with original label, early 1950s, 4-1/2" h.. **$90**

Peach Crest melon-form vase with Charleton decoration by Abels, Wasserberg of New York, mid-1950s, 5-1/2" h................. **$75+**

Ruby basket in Hobnail, circa 1950, 12" .... **$100+**

Turquoise candleholders in Block and Star, one with finger ring, 1955, 4" diameter not including ring. .... **$30+ each**

1955-1980

Cranberry Polka Dot and Milk-glass covered butter with twig-form handle, 1955-6, 5 1/4" h and 8-1/4" diameter (base)..............................**$400**

Topaz Opalescent crimped bowl in Hobnail, 1959-60, 8" diameter. ....**$75** h...**$125+**

Jamestown Blue Overlay ribbed pillar vase, late 1950s, 5" h...**$45**

Ruby candleholders in Thumbprint, 1950s, each 9" h. ....**$125+**

Colonial Blue and Colonial Amber apothecary jars, 1960s, 11" h.
Blue..**$85**
Amber **$60**

Plum Opalescent and Green Opalescent footed covered candy jars in Hobnail, late 1950s to early 1960s, 8-1/2" h.
Plum **$175**
Green **$100**

Milk-glass shell dish, late 1950s, 5" l. .... **$10+**

Milk-glass covered candy jar in Daisy and Button, 1969, 6" h. **$35**

Honey Amber Overlay crimped vase in Bubble Optic with Gold Crest, early 1960s, 5" h...... **$70+**

Wild Rose cased-glass electric lamp in Blown Out Roses, 1960s, made for L.G. Wright, 18-1/2" h with chimney. .... **$400+**

Vasa Murrhina crimped melon vase in Autumn Orange, mid-1960s, 8" h....................... **$45+**

Crystal covered cruet in Hobnail, 1968, 11-1/2" h. .... **$250+**

Leaves on Burmese fairy lamp, 1970s, 6" h...................... **$200+**

Burmese apothecary jar with hand-painted flowers, mid-1970s, made for L.G. Wright, 10" h. .... **$300+**

Ruby baluster vase with crimped top in Diamond Optic, 1970s, 11" h... **$80+**

Blue Opalescent creamer and covered sugar in Cactus, 1979, 5" h and 6" h. .... **$100+ pair**

Yellow shaker in Rib Optic, made for Foreman, 1970s, 4" h (would have been paired with a taller example)...................... **$45+ each**

Cameo Opalescent basket in Lily of the Valley, 1979, 7-1/2" h. **$45**

Original Formula Carnival Glass swan candleholder, 1971, 6-1/2" h.. **$50+**

Rosalene cracker jar in Cactus, circa 1980, 8" h......................... **$115**

Wisteria bell in Threaded Diamond Optic, 1977, 5-1/2" h. **$50**

GLASS

1980-2007

Black (Ebony) miniature basket novelty with pink crest, 1980s, 4-1/4" h. .... **$90+**

Custard Satin ginger jar with hand-painted log cabin, early 1980s, 7-3/4" h. .... **$100+**

Blue Opalescent 44-ounce pitcher in Spiral Optic, circa 1980, 8" h. .... **$100+**

Original Formula Carnival Glass Red wine decanter and wine goblet in Hobnail, purchased from the "special" room at the Fenton factory, early 1980s, 12" h and 4-1/2" h. .... **$300+ pair**

Lamp with interior and exterior hand-painted autumn-scene shade by Michael Dickinson, 1992, 21" h. **$500**

Cranberry cameo glass platter with sand-carved floral decoration by Martha Reynolds, 1994, one of 500, 14-1/2" diameter... **$275+**

Ruby Iridized paneled pitcher, 2002, 4-1/2" h. **$55+**

Sand-carved iris on Amethyst vase, 1982, 11" h .... **$90+**

Blue Burmese (shiny) ribbed hexagonal vase, 1984, 5" h **$70**

Roselle on Cranberry basket, 1990s, 11-1/2" h .... **$160+**

Ruby Overlay shaker in Leaf, 1990s, 3-1/2" h .... **$50+**

Cobalt and Amber cornucopia candleholders, style No. 950, late 1990s, 6" h. Cobalt .... **$45+**

Amber .... **$25+**

Favrene "Seasons" vase, part of the Connoisseur Collection, limited to 1,350 pieces, 1998, 8-1/2" h. .... **$300+**

Burmese ginger jar, three pieces with base, decorated with butterflies, 2000, designed by J.K. (Robin) Spindler, with facsimiles of Fenton family signatures, 8-1/2" h. **$275**

Rosalene three-piece fairy light in Spiral Optic, with clear candleholder, 1999 for QVC, 7-1/4" h. **$100**

◄Contemporary slippers, 1990s to 2000, each 6" l. From left: Blue Topaz in Daisy Button pattern, Sea Green in Rose pattern, Champagne with hand-painted floral decoration in Rose pattern, and Golden Amber Carnival with hand-painted "ice gold and white daisies" in Daisy Button pattern. These were made for QVC in 1994 **$35+ each.**

GLASS

Pink Iridized trinket box made for Cracker Barrel, 2000, 4-1/2" l. .... **$50+**

Cobalt Snowflake ornaments, various winter scenes, 2000-2005, 3-1/4" diameter. .... **$35 each**

Green iridized vase with hand-painted flowers, 2000 QVC Designer Showcase Series, signed by Bill Fenton, 8-1/2" h. .... **$100+**

Dave Fetty handmade pitcher in Willow Green Opalescent Hanging Hearts, with iridized cobalt trim and handle, Connoisseur Collection, 2003, 8-1/2" h........... **$425**

Lotus Mist Burmese decanter, hand painted, 2004, 11-1/2" h. **$120**

Aubergine Overlay covered candy in Wave Crest, with hand-painted decoration and applied metal trim, 2005, 5" h. **$150**

Topaz Blue Overlay Grasshopper vase made for QVC, 2004, hand painted, 6-3/4" h. **$50**

▶Chocolate Cat, available exclusively to dealers, 2005, signed by George Fenton, 3-1/2" l. ..... **$35+**

Dave Fetty handmade bowl with a sand-carved stars-and-stripes motif (underside cobalt blue), 2006, 9-1/2" w. **$275**

Fostoria

Fostoria Glass company, founded in 1887, produced numerous types of fine glassware over the years. Its factory in Moundsville, West Virginia, closed in 1986.

Fostoria

Almond dish, square foot, flaring bowl, No. 4020, Wisteria, 2 3/4" d. **$32**

▶Ashtray/place card holder, rectangular w/low fluted sides & upright shell-shaped back, Azure Blue, Pattern #2538, 3" h. .. **$22**

Beverage set: 48 oz. 10" h. pitcher & 11 footed & handled tumblers; Priscilla patt., amber, the set (ILLUS. of part) **$250-300**

Bonbon, low ribbed swan-like shape w/arched end handle, ruby, Pattern #2517, 4 1/2" l. **$16**

Bowl, 5 1/2" w., ice cream-type, square, Colony patt., clear ... **$28**

Bowl-vase, footed wide squatty bulbous heavy body w/a thick rolled rim, crystal iridescent, Designer Collection "Impressions" patt., ca. 1970s, 8 1/2" d., 5" h. **$120**

Candleholder, three-light, Pattern #2383, Rose, 4" h. **$38**

Candleholder, three-light, Baroque patt., clear **$29**

Candleholders, one-light, Onyx Lustre, No. 2324, 3" h., pr. (ILLUS. of one) **$425**

Candle lamp, three-part, American patt. footed base, clear blown bell-shaped shade, clear **$100**

GLASS

Candlesticks, one-light, Coin patt., Emerald Green, 4 1/2" h., pr. 4 3/4" h. **$65**

Cigarette holder with ashtray foot, Pattern #2349, green, 3 1/4" h. **$35**

Candlesticks, one-light, Navarre etching, Baroque blank, No. 2496, clear, 4" h., pr. (ILLUS. of one) **$45**

Cocktail, No. 5099, Azure Blue, 3 oz. **$22**

◄Cruet w/original stopper, oil-type, Sunray patt., clear, 3 Oz. **$32**

►Cruet w/original stopper, oil-type, footed, Coronet patt., clear, 3 Oz. **$37**

Champagne, Pattern #5099, clear stem & Wisteria flaring bowl, 6 1/4" h. **$47**

Cup & saucer, Lafayette patt., translucent Jade green, rare color **$150**

►Goblet, American Lady patt., Amethyst bowl, 10 oz. water, 6 1/8" h. **$36**

Mayonnaise bowl w/two ladles, American patt., divided, clear, 3 1/4" d., 6 1/4" h., 3 pcs. .. **$65**

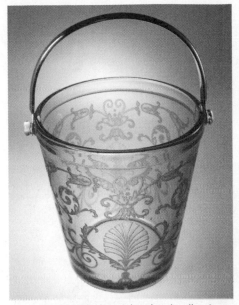

Relish dish, American patt., four-part, rectangular, clear, 6 1/4 x 9" **$42**

Ice bucket w/arched metal swing handle, tapering cylindrical form, Versailles etching, Rose, 6" h. **$135**

Salt & pepper shakers w/original tops on tray, individual size, Colony patt., clear, the set **$15**

Vase, 6" h., footed bulbous ovoid optic-ribbed body tapering to a low cylindrical neck, Pattern #4108, Rose **$49**

Vase, bud, 6" h., clear foot & tall trumpet-form Empire Green body tapering to a wide low neck, Pattern #6102, original company sticker **$32**

Vase, 10 1/2" h., footed w/tall slender waisted bowl, etched Brocade Palm Leaf patt., green **$450**

▶Vase, 9" h., pitcher-style, Heirloom patt., ruby **$90**

GLASS

Gallé

Gallé glass was made in Nancy, France, by Emile Gallé, a founder of the Nancy School and a leader in the Art Nouveau movement in France. Much of his glass, both enameled and cameo, is decorated with naturalistic motifs. The finest pieces were made in the last two decades of the 19th century and the opening years of the 20th.

Pieces marked with a star preceding the name were made between 1904, the year of Gallé's death, and 1914.

Gallé Nancy Déposé

Cameo bowl, 4 1/4" d., 3 1/8" h., low squatty bulbous form tapering to a low four-lobed neck, "Verre Parlant" (speaking glass), internally decorated in pale yellowish green w/thin swirled bands of color granules overlaid in a deep mauve & etched w/an underwater scene of an octopus among seaweed, cameo etched around the neck "L'Etoile du Matin et L'Etoile du Soir - Victor Hugo" (The Morning Star and The Evening Star - Victor Hugo), cameo signature, ca. 1895 (ILLUS. center with two internally decorated & etched cameo vases) **$8,365**

Cameo lamp, the base w/a wide round dark purple foot tapering to a slender ovoid body in pale shaded yellow & overlaid in light blue & olive green & cameo-cut w/a cluster of blue daisy-like flowers above green leafy stems, the peaked mushroom-form shade w/matching decoration, base & shade signed in cameo, shade 8" d., overall 17 1/2" h. ..**$10,350**

Cameo perfume lamp, bulbous body in frosted deep yellow cased in dark maroon shaded to red & cameo- cut w/fuschia blossoms & leaves, signed in cameo, the neck fitted w/a cylindrical brass lamp collar, also w/paper label reading "Gallé Nancy Paris," & the brass collar marked "Made in France," 6" h. **$2,160**

Cameo scent bottle w/original stopper, footed flaring cylindrical body w/a wide rounded shoulder centering a small cylindrical neck w/a pointed stopper, pale green & opalescent white ground overlaid in green & cameo-cut w/stylized Queen Anne's lace blossoms trimmed in white & green leafy stems, cameo-signed, 6 1/2" h. **$1,323**

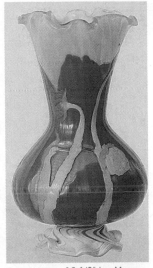

Cameo vase, 15" h., flat-bottomed bulbous spherical lower body tapering sharply to a very tall gently flaring cylindrical neck, mottled salmon pink & frosted white ground overlaid in green & chartreuse & cameo-cut w/long leafy stems & seed pods, signed in cameo on the side **$2,185**

Cameo vase, 17 1/4" h., large ovoid body tapering to a small trumpet neck, clear frosted & peach overlaid w/shades of turquoise & dark blue & etched w/a landscape w/tall trees in the foreground w/a lake & mountains in the distance, cameo signed, ca. 1900 .... **$10,120**

Cameo vase, 10 1/2" h., Marquetry-style, the round ruffled foot supporting a squatty bulbous body tapering to a tall trumpet neck w/a crimped & ruffled rim, mottled creamy white ground overlaid w/brown further overlaid w/white & finely wheelcarved w/ large blossoms on tall leafy stems, engraved signature "Gallé 1900" **$39,675**

Cameo vase, 11" h., wide ovoid body tapering to a short rolled mouth, frosted grey overlaid in amethyst, yellow & blue & cameo- etched w/a continuous landscape of Lake Como w/trees in the foreground, a castle in the mid-ground & the lake & mountains in the distance, cameo signed, ca. 1900 .... **$8,625**

Cameo vase, 7" h., wide swelled & slightly tapering cylindrical body w/a thin rolled rim, yellow shaded to frosted white background overlaid in brown & green & deeply cameo-cut w/a stylized forest landscape w/ large leafy trees in the foreground, cameo signature on the side.. **$2,990**

Cameo vase, 6 3/4" h., banjo-style, bulbous flattened base tapering to a tall slender stick neck w/small cupped rim, frosted pale yellow shaded to dark blue ground overlaid in dark purple & cameo cut around the lower body w/a landscape w/large leafy trees in the foreground & a river & mountains in the distance, cameo signature on the back **$1,725**

Cameo vase, 7 1/2" h., cushion foot tapering to a large ovoid body w/a flat mouth, frosted white shaded to dark blue ground overlaid in orange, pink & dark green & cameo cut w/a design of large pink poppies above green leafy stems, cameo signature w/star on the side **$1,610**

Cameo vase, 7" h., round foot below the ovoid body tapering slightly to the molded flat mouth, mottled citrine yellow & frosted ground w/ an applied blown-out design of deep purple   leaves suspending long pale pods, molded signature **$5,405**

Cameo vase, 8 1/4" h., a round ringed cushion foot supporting a very wide bulbous ovoid body tapering to a short flaring neck, mottled amber & frosted white ground overlaid in dark brown & pale green & cameo-cut w/a landscape of leafy trees around a lake, etched signature on side **$2,300**

Pitcher,   9 3/4" h.,   Marquetry-style, a low squatty round lower body tapering to bell-shaped sides below the high cylindrical neck w/ rim spout, marquetry-carved body decorated w/stylized pink magnolia flowers & green leaves against a lightly martelè clear to white mottled background, long applied peach-stained handle, engraved signature in one of the leaves **$18,400**

Vase, 12" h., "Lion of Lorraine" design, rum-colored blown tapering ovoid body w/a flaring flat rim, raised on three applied rum- colored peg feet & w/two large rigaree bands of rum up the sides & around the rim, finely enameled overall w/scattered flowers in gold, maroon & blue & w/a dark blue griffin near the bottom, signed "E. Gallé Nancy Dèposè" **$2,588**

Cups, clear flat-based cylindrical shape w/an applied twisted rope handle, overall enameled decoration of fleurs-de-lis w/a gilded rim, engraved "E. Gallé Nancy," late 19th c., 2" h., pr........................ **$345**

Heisey

Numerous types of fine glass were made by A.H. Heisey & Co., Newark, Ohio, from 1895. The company's trademark, an H enclosed within a diamond, has become known to most glass collectors. The company's name and molds were acquired by Imperial Glass Co., Bellaire, Ohio, in 1958, and some pieces have been reissued. The glass listed below consists of miscellaneous pieces and types.

Candlesticks, toy-size, one-light, Patrician patt., clear, 4 1/2" h., pr. **$85**

◄Basket, fruit-type, No. 466, round w/high, arched handle, crystal w/cutting, 7 1/4" d., 9 1/2" h. . **$275**

Cruet w/original stopper, oil-type, Yeoman patt., Moongleam, 2 oz. **$80**

Bell, Victorian Belle, hollow figure of girl made into bell, crystal satin, 4" h. **$98**

Candleholder-vase, one-light, two-piece, Ipswich patt., square foot, flaring rim hung w/twelve prisms, clear, 10" h. **$155**

GLASS

GLASS

Cruet w/original stopper, Double Rib & Panel patt., low squatty body & squared handle, No. 417, clear, 3 Oz. **$52**

Crushed fruit jar, cov., Colonial Pattern No. 352, clear, 10" h. **$295**

Water set: 63 oz. pitcher & four tumblers; Renaissance etching, clear, tumblers 3 3/4" h., pitcher 7 1/2" h., the set (ILLUS. of pitcher) **$250-300**

Dresser set: two 4 oz. cologne bottles & stoppers & a 2 3/4 x 4" rectangular covered box; Ridgeleigh patt., each piece in clear w/fancy brass filigree mounts, the set **$225**

Vase, 5" h., cornucopia-shaped, Warwick patt., clear (ILLUS. front with larger Warwick vase)... **$48**

Cornucopia-Vase, Crystolite patt., ornate Calcutta overall cutting, notching & crosshatching, signed, 9" h., pr.......................................**$650**

Plate, 8" d., Minuet etching, luncheon, clear **$28**

Punch bowl, spherical, Ridgeleigh patt., clear, 11" d....................**$225**

Punch set, 9 qt. Dr. Johnson punch bowl, six cups & ladle; Plantation patt., clear, 8 pcs...**$1,100**

Syrup pitcher, cov., Colonial Panel patt., No. 331, clear w/clear applied handle, marked, 5 1/2" h...**$28**

Toothpick holder, Pineapple & Fan patt., green............................**$295**

Higgins Glass

Fused glass, an "old craft for modern tastes" enjoyed a mid-20th century revival through the work of Chicago-based artists Frances and Michael Higgins of the Higgins Glass Studio. Although known for thousands of years, fusing had, by the 1940s, been abandoned in favor of glassblowing. A meticulous craft, fusing can best be described as the creation of a "glass sandwich." A design is either drawn with colored enamels or pieced with glass segments on a piece of enamel-coated glass. Another piece of enameled glass is placed over this. The "sandwich" is then placed on a mold and heated in a kiln, with the glass "slumping" to the shape of the mold. When complete, the interior design is fused between the outer glass layers. Additional layers are often utilized, accentuating the visual depth. Sensing that fused glass was a marketable commodity, the Higginses opened their studio in 1948 and applied the fusing technique to a wide variety of items: tableware such as bowls, plates, and servers; housewares, ranging from clocks and lamps to ashtrays and candleholders; and purely decorative items, such as mobiles and jewelry.

Unlike many of their contemporaries, the Higginses received national exposure thanks to an association with Chicago industrial manufacturer Dearborn Glass Company. This collaboration, lasting from 1957 through 1964, resulted in the mass marketing of "higginsware" worldwide. Since nearly every piece carried the lower-case signature "higgins," name recognition was both immediate and enduring.

The Dearborn demand for new Higgins pieces resulted in more than 75 identifiable production patterns with such buyer-enticing names as "Stardust," "Arabesque," and "Barbaric Jewels."

In 1965, the Higginses briefly moved their base of operations to Haeger Potteries before opening their own studio in Riverside, Illinois, where it has been located since 1966. Although Michael Higgins died in 1999 and Frances Higgins in 2004, the Studio today continues under the leadership of longtime artistic associates Louise and Jonathan Wimmer. New pieces celebrate and expand on the traditions and techniques of the past. Higgins pieces created from 1948 until 1957 are engraved on the reverse with the signature "higgins" or the artist's complete name. A raised "dancing man" logo was added in 1951. Pieces created at Dearborn or Haeger (1957-65) bear a gold "higgins" signature on the surface or a signature in the colorway. The marking since 1966 has been an engraved "higgins" on the reverse of an object, with the occasional addition of the artist's name. Pieces produced since the death of Frances Higgins are signed "higgins studio."

Once heralded as "an exclamation point in your decorating scheme," Higgins glass continues, nearly 60 years since its inception. The company is located at 33 East Quincy Street, Riverside, IL 60546 (708-447-2787), www.higginsglass.com.

Price ranges given are general estimates covering all available patterns produced at Dearborn Glass Company and Haeger Potteries (1957-1965). The low end of the scale applies to the most commonly found patterns (e.g., "Mandarin," "Siamese Purple"), the upper end to those found less frequently (e.g., "Gemspread," "Carousel").

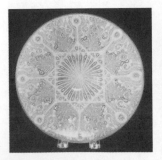

Far left: Bowl, 9" d., round, controlled bubble pattern, green & yellow, by Frances Higgins **$700-750**

Left: Clock, wall or table, gold & black, General Electric, 1954, 8" d. **$900-1,000**

Ashtray, circular, scalloped edge, Stardust patt. only, 11 1/2" d. **$150-200**

Candleholders, Petal patt., 4 1/2" h., pr. **$150-225**

Jewelry set: necklace & earrings; coral glass nuggets & brass spirals, the set **$900-1,000**

Plaque, oblong, "Green-Eyed Snowy," cat face design, by Frances Higgins, 4 1/2 x 7" **$350-400**

Vase, 7 3/4" h., dropout style, signed "Frances Stewart Higgins, 1967" **$78**

Plaque, rectangular, "Ugly Duchess A" patt., by Michael Higgins, framed, 12 x 20" .. **$3,500-3,750**

Vase, 11" h., 14" d., oversized dropout style, multicolored **$1,500-1,750**

▶Platter, 15" l., irregular shape, "Summer Trees" patt., by Frances Higgins **$3,500-3,750**

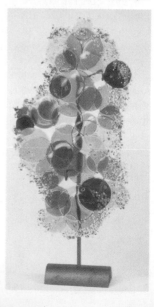

▶Sculpture, "Bubbles" patt., multi-colored glass circles & chipped glass, brass stem, by Frances Higgins, 13" h. **$1,500-1,700**

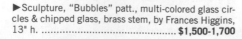

◼ Imperial

From 1902 until 1984 Imperial Glass of Bellaire, Ohio, produced hand made glass. Early pressed glass production often imitated cut glass and may bear the raised "NUCUT" mark in the interior center. In the second decade of the 1900s Imperial was one of the dominant manufacturers of iridescent or Carnival glass. When glass collecting gained popularity in the 1970s, Imperial again produced Carnival and a line of multicolored slag glass. Imperial purchased molds from closing glass houses and continued many lines popularized by others including Central, Heisey and Cambridge. These reissues may cause confusion but they were often marked.

CANDLEWICK

Basket, No. 400/40/0, clear, 6 1/2" l., 4 1/2" h. **$38**

Cake stand & dome cover, No. 400/10D, beaded stem, cover made by West Virginia Glass Specialty & sold w/the stand, cover 10" d., stand 11" d., 2 pcs. **$135**

Compote, 10" h., crimped, three-bead stem, No. 400/103, clear w/h.p. pink roses & blue ribbons **$260**

Cruet w/stopper, No. 400/274, flat, bulbous bottom, clear, 4 oz. **$52**

Relish dish, three-part, three-toed, No. 400/208, clear, 9" l.... **$98**

Candleholder, No. 400/40C, flower-type w/crimped rim, clear, 5" h. **$47**

Jam set: oval tray w/two cov. marmalade jars w/ladles; No. 400/1589, clear, 5 pcs. **$125**

Punch set, punch bowl, underplate, 12 cups & ladle; No. 400/20, bowl & cups w/cut Mallard patt., 15 pcs. **$650**

Vase, two open beaded arms, crimped top, clear............................ **$38**

Cream soup bowl wi/underplate, two-handled, No. 400/50, clear, 5" d. bowl & 6 3/4" d. underplate, 2 pcs. **$75**

CAPE COD

Pitcher, No. 160/239, clear, 60 oz. **$95**

Plate, 16" d., cupped, No. 160/20V, clear........**$50**

Punch set: punch bowl, underplate & twelve cups; clear, 1 gal., 14 pcs. **$220**

Salt & pepper shakers w/original tops, original factory label, No. 160/251, clear, pr. .**$20**

Sherbet, tall, No. 1602, Verde green, 6 oz. **$15**

Sundae, No. 1602, ball stem, clear, 4" h. **$7**

Tumbler, iced tea, No. 1602, amber, 6" h. .**$15**

Tom & Jerry punchbowl, footed, No. 160/200, clear....................**$290**

Wine carafe & stopper, footed, handled, No. 160/185, crystal...**$220**

Candlestick, two-light, No. 160/100, crystal $85

Finger bowl, No. 1604 1/2A, ruby, 4 1/2" d. **$24**

Goblet, dinner, ball stem, Azalea Pink, 11 oz. **$17**

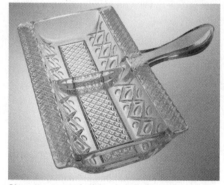

Cigarette server/relish, handled, two-part, No. 160/223, clear, 8 1/2" l. **$40**

Pitcher w/ice lip, No. 160/24, clear, 60 oz., 2 qt... **$92**

◄Pepper mill & salt shaker, chrome base & covers, No. 16/236 & 160/238, clear, pr. **$55**

FREE-HAND WARE

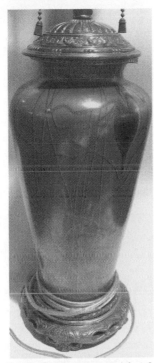 

Lamp, electric, cast metal foot & cap, tapering ovoid glass body in iridescent orange w/cobalt blue Hanging Hearts patt., 10" h. **$1,650**

Vase, 8" h., flat flaring foot & tall slender gently flaring cylindrical body, iridescent cobalt blue exterior & orange interior **$235**

Vase, 10 1/2" h., tall slender waisted shape w/flaring top, iridescent cobalt blue exterior w/ white Hanging Heart decoration **$1,175**

MISCELLANEOUS PATTERNS & LINES

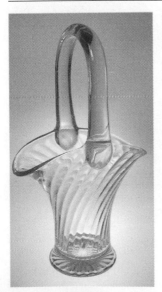 

Cake plate, hexagonal w/two open handles, Brocaded Daffodils etching, green, 7" w. **$49**

◄Basket, Twisted Optic patt., pale blue, 10" h............................. **$85**

GLASS

Candlestick, single-light, Cathay Line, figural Candle Servant (female), No. 5035, clear satin **$195**

Goblet, water, Chroma patt. No. 123, Burgandy, 5 1/2" h. **$24**

Pitcher, Reeded patt., No. 701, green w/clear applied handle **$80**

Decanter w/crystal mushroom stopper, No. 451, spherical body w/ringed foot & cylindrical neck, ruby **$120**

Epergne, one-lily, two-piece, Pattern #1950/196, Doeskin (milk glass), 9" d., 11" h. **$78**

Plate, 8" w., Beaded Block patt., pink **$20**

Tumbler, footed, Parisian Provincial patt., milk glass stem & foot & amethyst bowl, 7 oz. **$22**

Vase, 8" h., pressed, trumpet-shaped, Pattern #G 505, gold on crystal **$28**

◄Punch bowl & base, Broken Arches patt., No. 733, clear, 12 1/2" d., 10 1/2" h. **$65**

Lalique

René Jules Lalique was born on April 6,1860, in the village of Ay, in the Champagne region of France. In 1862, his family moved to the suburbs of Paris.

In 1872, Lalique began attending College Turgot where he began studying drawing with Justin-Marie Lequien. After the death of his father in 1876, Lalique began working as an apprentice to Louis Aucoc, who was a prominent jeweler and goldsmith in Paris.

Lalique moved to London in 1878 to continue his studies. He spent two years attending Sydenham College, developing his graphic design skills. He returned to Paris in 1880 and worked as an illustrator of jewelry, creating designs for Cartier, among others. In 1884, Lalique's drawings were displayed at the National Exhibition of Industrial Arts, organized at the Louvre.

At the end of 1885, Lalique took over Jules Destapes' jewelry workshop. Lalique's design began to incorporate translucent enamels, semiprecious stones, ivory, and hard stones. In 1889, at the Universal Exhibition in Paris, the jewelry firms of Vever and Boucheron included collaborative works by Lalique in their displays.

In the early 1890s, Lalique began to incorporate glass into his jewelry, and in 1893 he took part in a competition organized by the Union Centrale des Arts Decoratifs to design a drinking vessel. He won second prize.

Lalique opened his first Paris retail shop in 1905, near the perfume business of François Coty. Coty commissioned Lalique to design his perfume labels in 1907, and he also created his first perfume bottles for Coty.

In the first decade of the 20th century, Lalique continued to experiment with glass manufacturing techniques, and mounted his first show devoted entirely to glass in 1911.

During World War I, Lalique's first factory was forced to close, but the construction of a new factory was soon begun in Wingen-sur-Moder, in the Alsace region. It was completed in 1921, and still produces Lalique crystal today.

In 1925, Lalique designed the first "car mascot" (hood ornament) for Citroën, the French automobile company. For the next six years, Lalique would design 29 models for companies such as Bentley, Bugatti, Delage, Hispano-Suiza, Rolls Royce, and Voisin.

Lalique's second boutique opened in 1931, and this location continues to serve as the main Lalique showroom today.

René Lalique died on May 5, 1945, at the age of 85. His son, Marc, took over the business at that time, and when Marc died in 1977, his daughter, Marie-Claude Lalique Dedouvre, assumed control of the company. She sold her interest in the firm and retired in 1994.

For more information on Lalique, see *Warman's Lalique Identification and Price Guide* by Mark F. Moran.

(In the descriptions of Lalique pieces that follow, you will find notations like this: "M p. 478, No. 1100." This refers to the page and serial numbers found in *René Lalique, maître-verrier, 1860-1945: Analyse de L'oeuvre et Catalogue Raisonné*, by Félix Marcilhac, published in 1989 and revised in 1994. Printed entirely in French, this book of more than 1,000 pages is the definitive guide to Lalique's work, and listings from auction catalogs typically cite the Marcilhac guide as a reference. A used copy can cost more than $500. Copies in any condition are extremely difficult to find, but collectors consider Marcilhac's guide to be the bible for Lalique.)

GLASS

ASHTRAYS

"Archers" in deep red glass, circa 1922, 5-1/2" diameter. (M p. 269, No. 278) .... **$2,500+**

"Statuette de la Fontaine" in clear and frosted glass, circa 1925, 4-1/2" tall. (M p. 272, No. 288) .... **$900+**

"Irene" in deep green glass, circa 1929, stenciled R. LALIQUE FRANCE, 3-3/4" diameter. (M p. 276, No. 304)..........................**$1,200-$1,500**

"Medicis" in blue glass, circa 1924, molded R. LALIQUE, 5-3/4" long. (M p. 270, No. 280)..**$1,500-$1,600**

BOWLS

▲ "Perruches" circa 1931, in opalescent glass with blue patina, stenciled R. LALIQUE FRANCE, 9-5/8" diameter. (M p. 302, No. 419) .... **$4,000-$4,500**

"Calypso" shallow bowl, opalescent glass, circa 1930, 14-1/2" diameter. (M p. 301, No. 413) ....**$1,200+**

"Nemours" circa 1929, in clear and frosted glass with sepia patina and brown enameled highlights, molded R. LALIQUE FRANCE, 10" diameter. (M p. 299, No. 404) ....**$900-$1,000**

"Marguerites" a center bowl, circa 1941, in clear and frosted glass with green patina, stenciled R. LALIQUE FRANCE, 4-3/4" diameter. (M p. 312, No. 10-404) ....**$900-$1,000**

GLASS

BOXES

"Cleones" circa 1921, in amber glass, molded R. LALIQUE, engraved France, 6-3/4" diameter. (M p. 231, No. 9) .... **$900-$1,100**

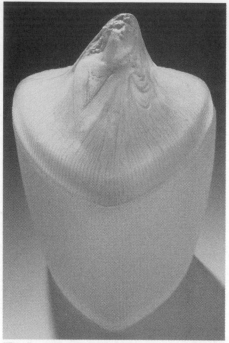

"Tete Femme" powder box for Coty, in satin glass with traces of sepia patina, circa 1912, 3-3/4" tall. (M p. 967, Coty 4) ....**$2,500+**

"Quatre Scarabees" in cobalt blue glass with white patina, circa 1911, engraved R. Lalique France, No.15, 3-3/8" diameter. (M p. 225, No. 15) .... **$2,500-$2,800**

◆ Cobalt blue is one of the most popular glass colors because of its rich, deep hue. It has been a favorite for more than a century and because it coordinates so well with various decorating schemes, will likely remain one of collectors' top choices for the foreseeable future.

"Georgette" circa 1922, in opalescent glass with satin and card base, molded R. LALIQUE, 8-1/4" diameter. (M p. 30, No. 45) .... **$1,700-$2,000**

GLASS

CAR MASCOTS (HOOD ORNAMENTS)

"Chrysis" in clear and frosted glass with sepia patina, stenciled R. LALIQUE, with an ebonized wood display stand. (M p. 505, No. 1183.) .... **$5,000-$6,000**

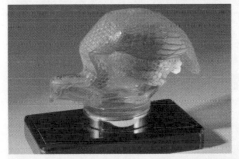

"Libellule" Grande Modele, circa 1928, in clear and frosted glass with pale amethyst tint, molded R. LALIQUE FRANCE and engraved R. Lalique France, 8-1/4" tall, accompanied by a letter authenticating the mascot as the one formerly used by Gary Cooper on his Duesenberg, and presented by Cooper as a gift. (M p. 501, No. 1145).....................**$9,000-$12,000**

◄"Pintade" circa 1929, in clear and frosted glass, with original chrome collar, molded R. LALIQUE, 6" long. (M p. 504, No. 1164).............. **$4,000-$5,000**

▼"Victoire" circa 1928, in clear and frosted glass, molded R. LALIQUE FRANCE, 10-1/4" long, together with an original Lalique wood display mount. (M p. 502, No. 1147) ....**$24,000-$26,000**

GLASS

FIGURES

"Suzanne" a statuette, in amber glass, with original bronze illuminating stand, molded R. LALIQUE, statuette 9-1/8" tall. (M p. 399, No. 833).....**$30,000+**

"Groupe de Six Moineaux" a decoration, in clear and frosted glass with gray patina, circa 1933, 11-5/8" long. (M p. 492, No. 1218) .... **$2,500+**

INKWELLS

"Serpents" in amber glass, circa 1920, 6" diameter. (M p. 317, No. 432)..................................$4,000+

"Quatre Sirenes" in opalescent glass with sepia patina, circa 1920, 6" diameter. (M p. 317, No. 434) ....$4,500+

LIGHTING

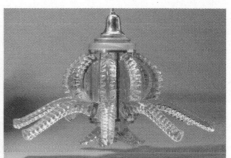

"Monaco" a hanging chandelier, designed by Marc Lalique, circa 1950, in clear, polished glass, formed as eight tentacle-like arms issuing from a metal cage with star-form finial, includes original ceiling cap, lacks hanging rod and one glass finial, engraved Lalique, 32" diameter. .... **$2,800-$3,200**

◄"Six Danseuses" a table lamp, circa 1931, in clear and frosted glass with sepia patina, molded R. LALIQUE, 10" tall. (M p. 625, No. 2179) ....**$15,000-$17,000**

PAPERWEIGHTS

"Toby" circa 1931, in clear and frosted glass, stenciled R. LALIQUE FRANCE, 3-1/3" tall. (M p. 391, No. 1192) .... **$1,700-$2,000**

◄"Deux Tourterelles" circa 1925, in topaz glass, stenciled R. LALIQUE FRANCE, 4-3/4" tall. (M p. 381, No. 1128) .... **$2,200-$2,600**

GLASS

PERFUME BOTTLES

"Bouchon Mures" bottle in clear glass with enamel decoration, stopper in amber glass, circa 1920, 4-1/3" tall. (M p. 329, No. 495) .... **$3,000+**

"Clairefontaine" in clear and frosted glass, circa 1931, 4-3/4" tall. (M p. 338, No. 526) **$1,800+**

"Clamart" in smoky satin glass with black patina, circa 1927, 4-1/2" tall. (M p. 336, No. 517) .... **$1,800+**

"La Violette" a perfume bottle for Gabilla, circa 1925, in clear glass with violet enamel, molded LALIQUE, 3-1/3" tall. (M p. 940, No. 2) .... **$3,000-$3,500**

"Satyre" in clear and frosted glass, circa 1933, 3-1/1/2" tall. (M p. 338, No. 527) ...... **$3,500+**

"Roses" a clear and frosted glass perfume bottle for D'Orsay, circa 1912, molded LALIQUE, 4" tall. (M p. 933, No. 3). **$2,700-$3,200**

"Helene" (Lotus), a perfume bottle, circa 1928, in clear and frosted glass, stenciled R. LALIQUE FRANCE, 2-5/8" tall. (M p. 337, No. 522) .... **$1,800-$2,100**

"Quatre Soleils" in satin glass with sepia patina, circa 1912, 3" tall. (M p. 333, No. 505) .... **$3,000+**

GLASS

TABLEWARE

"Satyr" a carafe, circa 1923, in clear and frosted glass with sepia patina, engraved R. Lalique pour Cusenier, 10-1/4" tall. The mark indicates this is one of a group sold through the wine merchant Cusenier in the 1920s. (M p. 741, No. 3167). **$2,400-$2,800**

◀ "Coqs et Raisins" a cocktail shaker, in clear and frosted glass with sepia patina, circa 1928, 8-7/8" tall. (M p. 813, No. 3879) ....**$5,000+**

"Calypso" a plate, in opalescent glass, circa 1930, 14-1/8" diameter. (M p. 301, No. 413) .... **$5,800+**

VASES

"Acanthes" circa 1921, in red glass, 11-1/1/2" tall. (M p. 417, No. 902) ....**$15,000+**

"Aras" circa 1924, in iridescent teal green glass with white patina, molded R. LALIQUE, 9-3/8" tall. (M p. 421, No. 919)...... **$8,000+**

"Archers" circa 1921, in cherry red glass with strong white patina, 10-3/8" tall. (M p. 415, No. 893) ....**$24,000+**

"Bacchantes" in topaz glass, with original (?) display stand, circa 1927, vase 9-7/8" tall. (M p. 438, No. 997) ....**$15,000+**

"Ceylan" circa 1924, in opalescent glass, wheel-cut R. LALIQUE FRANCE, 9-1/2" tall. (M p. 418, No. 905) .... **$5,500-$6,000**

"Davos" circa 1932, in amber glass, engraved R. Lalique, 11-1/2" tall. (M p. 455, No. 1079) .... **$3,500-$4,000**

"Escargot" in dark red glass, circa 1920, 8-5/8" tall. (M p. 424, No. 931).................................**$15,000+**

"Fontainebleau" circa 1930, in deep blue glass with grayish patina, engraved R. Lalique France No. 1011, 6-7/8" tall. (M p. 446, No. 10-36) ... **$5,500-$6,000**

"Gros Scarabees" circa 1923, in cased jade green glass with white patina, stenciled R. LALIQUE FRANCE, 11-5/8" tall. (M p. 415, No. 892) .... **$30,000+**

"Languedoc" circa 1932, in cased green glass with white patina, engraved R. Lalique France, 8-3/4" tall. (M p. 443, No. 1041) ....**$30,000+**

"Milan" in blue glass with white patina, circa 1929, 11-1/4" tall. (M p. 444, No. 1025) ....**$20,000+**

"Oranges" circa 1926, in clear and frosted glass with brown enamel decoration, molded R. LALIQUE, 11-1/1/2" tall. (M p. 431, No. 964) ....**$30,000+**

"Penthivere" circa 1926, in cobalt blue glass with white patina, engraved R. LALIQUE, 10-1/4" tall. (M p. 441, No. 1011) ....**$15,000+**

"Serpent" in purple glass, circa 1924, 10-1/4" tall. (M p. 416, No. 896) **$40,000**

GLASS

Libbey

In 1878, William L. Libbey obtained a lease on the New England Glass Company of Cambridge, Massachusetts, changing the name to the New England Glass Works, W.L. Libbey and Son, Proprietors. After his death in 1883, his son, Edward D. Libbey, continued to operate the company at Cambridge until 1888, when the factory was closed. Edward Libbey moved to Toledo, Ohio, and set up the company subsequently known as Libbey Glass Co. During the 1880s, the firm's master technician, Joseph Locke, developed the now much desired colored art glass lines of Agata, Amberina, Peach Blow and Pomona. Renowned for its cut glass of the Brilliant Period (see CUT GLASS), the company continues in operation today as Libbey Glassware, a division of Owens-Illinois, Inc.

Bowl, 12" d., 4 1/4" h., a wide shallow bowl w/a flattened rim, white ground decorated in the center w/a lime green pulled feather design, raised on an applied clear pedestal foot, signed **$210**

Champagnes, a wide flaring bowl on a slender tapering stem & round foot, wheel-cut & polished crystal in the "Patrician" patt., each w/Libbey mark, early 20th c., 6" h., set of eight (ILLUS. of part) **$300-500**

Maize cruet w/original stopper, tall ovoid body w/tricorner rim, applied clear handle, pale iridescent ground w/pale blue husks, pointed corn-molded stopper w/shallow chip at tip, 7" h. **$605**

Cocktails, Silhouette patt., clear bowl on a moonstone figural kangaroo stem, ca. 1930s, one w/very slight rim chip, 6" h., set of four
.... **$288**

Maize bowl, 7 3/4" d., 3 5/8" h., iridized clear w/light blue-stained leaves, minor inner rim flakes **$165**

Maize spooner, creamy opaque w/
yellow husks, 4 1/4" h. **$132**

Punch cup, pressed clear petal-
form marked "World's Fair
1893," impressed "Libbey
Glass Co., Toledo, Ohio - World's
Fair" inside **$75**

Stemware set, two champagnes,
nine red wines, a water goblet,
eight white wines, seven high-
balls & one liqueur; Art Deco design, clear w/a drawn ovoid bowl,
fluted rectangular stem & circular foot, etched Libbey mark, the
group **$2,645**

Table service, six wine goblets w/
polar bear stems, four candlesticks w/camel stems, one
compote w/giraffe stem; Silhouette patt., opalescent stems on
colorless glassware, each piece
stamped "Libbey," designed by
Nash, compote 7" h., the group
.... **$2,300**

Vase, 10" h., trumpet-form, clear
ribbed body w/green "zipper"
design, stamped "Libbey". **$165**

Maize salt shaker, original top,
creamy opaque w/yellow husks,
slight damage to metal top, 4" h.
.... **$143**
▶Vase, 8 1/2" h., footed gently
flaring cylindrical crystal body w/
internal optic thumbprints alternating w/fronds of laurel leaves,
the exterior decorated w/thin lilac
threading down the sides, Nash
design, acid-stamped mark on
base **$374**

Maize toothpick holder, creamy opaque w/yellow
leaves trimmed in gold, 2 1/4" h. **$345**

Toothpick holder, Little Lobe patt., opaque white w/
pink shaded rim & enameled floral decoration, satin
finish, 2 1/4" h. **$110**

■ Mary Gregory

Glass enameled in white with silhouette-type figures, primarily of children, is now termed "Mary Gregory" and was attributed to the Boston and Sandwich Glass Company. However, recent research has proven conclusively that this was not decorated by Mary Gregory, nor was it made at the Sandwich plant. Miss Gregory was employed by Boston and Sandwich Glass Company as a decorator; however, records show her assignment was the painting of naturalistic landscape scenes on larger items such as lamps and shades, but never the charming children for which her name has become synonymous. Further, in the inspection of fragments from the factory site, no paintings of children were found.

It is now known that all wares collectors call "Mary Gregory" originated in Bohemia beginning in the late 19th century and were extensively exported to England and the United States well into this century.

For further information, see The Glass Industry in Sandwich, Volume #4 by Raymond E. Barlow and Joan E. Kaiser, and the book Mary Gregory Glassware, 1880-1900 by R. & D. Truitt.

Right: Pitcher, 11" h., tankard-type, gently tapering cylindrical green body w/an arched rim & pinched spout, applied long clear handle, decorated across the front in white enamel w/the standing figure of a Victorian girl in a garden, late 19th c. **$125-150**

Far right: Vases, 8" h., cylindrical ring-type, mottled white & clear cased in light blue, white enameled figure of a Victorian girl in a garden, Muhlhaus factory, Bohemia, late 19th c., facing pr. **$431**

Below: Dress box w/hinged cover, squatty bulbous Prussian blue optic-ribbed base decorated w/a band of white enamel dots, the rim & cover w/brass fittings, the low domed cover decorated w/a white enamel scene of a young Victorian boy in a garden holding a butterfly net, colored enamel face & hands, late 19th c., 4 1/4" d., 2 3/8" h. **$138**

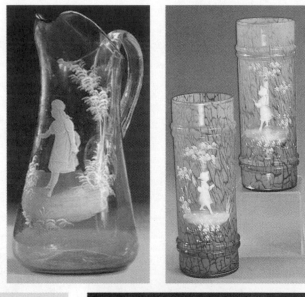

▶Vases, 17 1/2" h., cranberry body w/a flaring scalloped rim, each decorated w/the white enamel portrait of a Victorian lady standing in a garden, band of white beads around the neck, attributed to Mulhaus, Bohemia, ca. 1885, facing pr. **$2,070**

■ McKee

The McKee name has been associated with glass production since 1834, first producing window glass and later bottles. In the 1850s a new factory was established in Pittsburgh, Pennsylvania, for production of flint and pressed glass. The plant was relocated in Jeanette, Pennsylvania, in 1888 and operated there as an

independent company almost continuously until 1951, when it sold out to Thatcher Glass Manufacturing Company. Many types of collectible glass were produced by McKee through the years including Depression, Pattern, Milk Glass and a variety of utility kitchenwares. See these categories for additional listings.

KITCHENWARES

Flour shaker, original metal cover, Seville Yellow **$37**

Flour shaker w/original metal lid, Skokie Green **$75**

Measuring cup, Custard, four-cup **$55**

Reamer, butterscotch, embossed "SUNKIST," marked "Pat. No. 18764 Made in USA," 6" d. **$850**

ROCK CRYSTAL PATTERN

Bowl, 8 1/2" d., center handle, cupped, plain edge, ruby .. **$195**
Bowl, 10 1/2" d., salad, scalloped edge, pink **$55**
Candleholders, two-light, cobalt blue, pr. **$345**
Candlesticks, clear, 8 1/2" h., pr. **$45**
Candy dish, cov., green, 7" d. **$85**

Candleholders, orange slag, 5" d., pr. **$375**

Candlestick, one-light tall, amber, 8 1/4" h. **$62**

Cup & saucer, scalloped edge on saucer, ruby, pr. (ILLUS. w/plate) **$90**

MISCELLANEOUS PATTERNS & PIECES

Creamer & sugar, child's, French Ivory, Laurel patt. **$45-55**

Clock, Tambour Art-style, blue, 14" l. **$550**

Mayonnaise set: footed bowl, ladle & underplate; Brocade etching, pink, 3 pcs. **$75**

Sherbet, Clico patt., green bowl on square black base **$38**

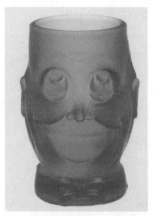

Tumbler, "Jolly Golfer," missing cap, green, 4" h. **$48**

Vase, 8" h., Art Deco-style triangular "Art Nude" design, Skokie Green **$375**

Whiskey set: "Jolly Golfer," figural decanter in the form of a stocky male golfer wearing knickers & cap & grasping a golf club, cap form the stopper, together w/four matching head-shaped glasses w/cap-shaped lids, frosted pink, marked "Pat. Applied For" on smooth base of decanter, some tiny checks & bruise, late 1930s, decanter 11 5/8" h., the set **$616**

Whiskey tumbler & base, Bottoms-Up patt., Skokie Green, satin finish, 2 pcs. **$275**

Milk Glass

Though invented in Venice in the 1500s, the opaque glass commonly known as milk glass was most popular at the end of the 19th century. American manufacturers such as Westmoreland, Fenton, Imperial, Indiana, and Anchor Hocking produced it as an economical substitute for pricey European glass and china.

After World War I, the popularity of milk glass waned, but production continued. Milk glass made during the 1930s and 1940s is often considered of lower quality than other periods because of the economic Depression and wartime manufacturing difficulties.

Milk glass has proven to be an "evergreen" collectible. When asked about milk glass, *Warman's Depression Glass* author and expert Ellen Schroy said, "Milk glass is great. I'm seeing a new interest in it."

"Milk glass" is a general term for opaque colored glass. Though the name would lead you to believe it, white wasn't the only color produced.

"Colored milk glasses, such as opaque black, green, or pink usually command higher prices," Schroy advises. "Beware of reproductions in green and pink. Always question a milk glass pattern found in cobalt blue. (Swirled colors are a whole other topic and very desirable.)"

The number of patterns, forms, and objects made is only limited by the imagination. Commonly found milk glass items include dishes – especially the ever-popular animals on "nests" – vases, dresser sets, figurines, lanterns, boxes, and perfume bottles.

"The milk glass made by Westmoreland, Kemple, Fenton, etc., was designed to be used as dinnerware," Schroy explains. "Much of the milk glass we see at flea markets, antique shows, and shops now is coming out of homes and estates where these 1940-1950s era brides are disposing of their settings." Schroy follows up with some practical advice: "Care should be taken when purchasing, transporting, and using this era of milk glass as it is very intolerant of temperature changes. Don't buy a piece outside at the flea market unless you can protect it well for its trip to your home. And when you get it home, leave it sit for several hours so its temperature evens out to what your normal home temperature is. It's almost a given if you take a piece of cold glass and submerge it into a nice warm bath, it's going to crack. And never, ever expose it to the high temps of a modern dishwasher."

So how do you tell the old from the new? Schroy says many times, getting your hands on it is the only way to tell: "Milk glass should have a wonderful silky texture. Any piece that is grainy is probably new." She further reveals, "The best test is to look for 'the ring of fire,' which will be easy to see in the sunlight: Hold the piece of milk glass up to a good light source (I prefer natural light) and see if there is a halo of iridescent colors right around the edge, look for reds, blues and golds. This ring was caused by the addition of iridized salts into the milk glass formula. If this ring is present, it's probably an old piece." She does caution, however, that 1950s-era milk glass does not have this tell-tale ring.

Old milk glass should also carry appropriate marks and signs, such as the "ring of fire"; appropriate patterns for specific makers are also something to watch for, such as Fenton's "Hobnail" pattern. Collectors should always check for condition issues such as damage and discoloration. According to Schroy, there is no remedy for discolored glass, and cracked and chipped pieces should be avoided, as they are prone to further damage.

Karen Knapstein, Print Editor for Antique Trader *magazine*

ONLINE RESOURCES:

Milkglass.org is an informational website. It includes historical and identification details, in addition to a collection of categorized links to milk glass items for sale on the Internet (primarily eBay).

The National Westmoreland Glass Collectors Club's mission is to promote the appreciation for the artistry and craftsmanship of Westmoreland glass and to continue the preservation of this important part of American history. (westmorelandglassclub.org)

GLASS

Child's mug, Heisey by Imperial, featuring an elephant-theme. **$5**

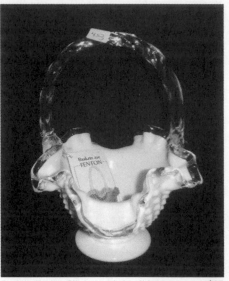

Basket, Fenton Silvercrest hobnail basket. **$35**

Punch bowl, Heisey beaded panel and sunburst opal with crystal base "rare" (Heisey called its milk glass "opal glass"). **$325**

Plate, Heisey No. 46 opal novelty "rare." **$280**

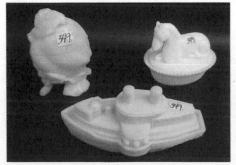

Three covered dishes and boxes depicting the Battleship Maine, 8-3/4" wide x 3-3/4" high; an apple raised on leaves, 5-3/4" high (with chips); together with a reclining horse on oval ribbed base, 5-1/2" long x 4-1/2" high. **$50**

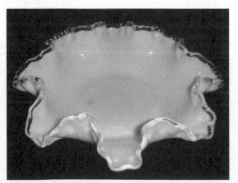

Basket, made by Fenton in the Silvercrest ruffled edge pattern... **$10**

GLASS

Blue milk glass, unsigned, containing hen on nest, six eggcups, small container, and tray, some chips on cups and tray. **$148**

Nesting bird covered dish, opaque white/milk glass showing some opalescence, base raised on three twig-form feet. Late 19th/early 20th century. 4-3/4" high overall, 4-1/2" diameter rim **$180**

Three American milk glass animals on nest; all with glass eyes, including opaque blue Westmoreland lion and eagle, and Atterbury white cat on rectangular dish, 7" high.. **$90**

Collection of eight nesting chickens and roosters in milk glass and slag glass; set includes four rooster tops, four hen tops, four with blue and white decoration, no markings... **$48**

Set of two covered dishes by Westmoreland, the first a two-part covered dish, a rabbit with ruby eyes, 5" high x 4-1/2" x 9-1/4"), and the other a two-part dish, a swan with raised wings setting on a woven nest, 6" x 6" x 10-3/4"; swan is marked with Westmoreland logo of W with superimposed G; rabbit is unmarked but likely Westmoreland but is marked "Pat'd March 9-1888" on bottom; both date to the first half of the 20th century. **$90**

Three souvenir milk glass dishes relating to the Spanish American War, including the Battleship Maine (5" x 4" x 8"), Commodore Dewey (4-3/4" high x 3-1/4" x 7" long) and "The American Hen" (4-1/2" x 3-3/4" x 6") which is the American Eagle with outspread wings protecting three eggs: "Porto Rico," "Cuba" and "Philippines." All date to the first quarter of the 20th century. **$50**

GLASS

◼ Morgantown (Old Morgantown) ——————————————

   Morgantown, West Virginia, was the site where a glass firm named the Morgantown Glass Works began in the late 19th century, but the company reorganized in 1903 to become the Economy Tumbler Company, a name it retained until 1929. By the 1920s the firm was producing a wider range of better quality and colorful glass tablewares; to reflect this fact, it resumed its earlier name, Morgantown Glass Works, in 1929. Today its many quality wares of the Depression era are growing in collector demand.

Candle/vase, Guild, No. 83 Patrician, Pineapple (deep yellow), 8" h. **$36**

Candlestick, No. 7640 Art Moderne, one-light, clear stem & foot, Ritz Blue socket, 4 1/4" h. . . **$200**

Compote, cov., 4 7/8" h., No. 7801 Cumberland, Ebony w/green foot & finial **$475**

Goblet, Tiburon (No. 7634) blank w/Westchester Rose cutting, water, Anna Rose color, 9 oz. ... **$48**

Goblet, water, Queen Anne shape, Sunrise Medallion etching, crystal **$72**

Tumbler, No. 7682 Ramona, footed iced tea, Stiegel Green **$45**

Mt. Washington

A wide diversity of glass was made by the Mt. Washington Glass Company of New Bedford, Massachusetts, between 1869 and 1900. It was succeeded in 1900 by the Pairpoint Corporation. Miscellaneous types are listed below.

Bowl, miniature, 2 3/4" d., 2 1/4" h., squatty melon-lobed shape w/a flat rim, satin opal w/shaded pink rim, decorated w/simple polychrome florals, enamel-beaded rim **$50-75**

Box w/hinged cover, molded colorless round swirled form decorated in the Royal Flemish manner w/ dancing flamingos, gilt-metal hinged rims, 7" d., 4" h. (wear, soiled lining) **$3,450**

Cameo compote, 4 7/8" d., 3 3/4" h., round gold-banded alabaster white foot & baluster-form stem supporting the wide shallow bowl in alabaster white cased on the interior in pink & carved w/a leafy scroll rim band & cluster of central stylized blossoms, gilt rim band, slight gold wear **$259**

Cracker jar w/silver plate rim, cover & bail handle, "Colonial Ware," the squatty bulbous white opaque body decorated at the front w/an oblong reserve of a Colonial couple dancing, framed by gold scrolls, pale cream background, metal fittings marked "MW 4419," base numbered "520," 6" h. **$316**

Cracker jar, cov., barrel-shaped, shaded pink & creamy white ground decorated w/delicate flowering branches, silver plate rim w/crimped edge, domed cover & arched bail swing handle, silver w/Pairpoint logo, slight wear to silver plate, 7" h. **$345**

Cracker jar w/silver plate rim, cover & bail handle, mold-blown squatty tapering round base w/ small scrolls around the bottom, pale yellow background h.p. w/ large pink & white blossoms & green leaves, gold-washed metal fittings marked "MW 4436," base marked "3930/230," 5 3/4" h. **$345**

Cracker jar, cov., barrel-shaped, cased rose satin exterior decorated overall w/pale blue blossoms outlined in yellow enamel, white interior, silver plate rim, floral-embossed domed cover & twisted rope bail handle, 7 1/2" h. **$523**

Cracker jar w/silver plate rim, cover & bail handle, barrel-shaped, satin fired-on pale pink to white ground decorated w/color enameled pansies, silver plate mounts marked "MW - 4404," base marked "3926," 6" h. **$468**

GLASS

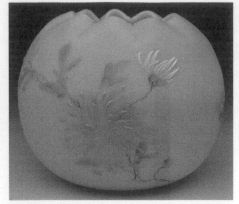

Rose bowl, eight-crimp rim, spherical, fired-on Burmese-like ground w/satin finish enameled w/yellow, pink & white chrysanthemums, pontil marked w/No. 617, 6 1/4" d., 5" h. **$231**

Rose bowl, eight-crimp rim, spherical, peach to white ground w/a satin finish, enameled w/scattered small blue violets, polished pontil w/No. 616, 7" d., 6" h. **$154**

Sugar shaker w/original silver plate cap, egg-shaped, unfired Burmese h.p. w/white & yellow daisies on green leaves & stems, 4" h. **$575**

Sugar shaker w/original silver plate cap, fig-shaped, unfired Burmese w/an overall h.p. decoration of tiny blue, pink & yellow blossoms, 4" h. **$2,185**

Sugar shaker w/original silver plate cap, tomato-shaped, opaque white w/a pink band around the top & delicate h.p. floral sprigs, 4" d., 2 1/4" h. **$480**

Scent bottle w/original stopper, milk white ground w/an overall decoration of color enameled florals, acid-etched on the base "Trademark of Mt. Washington Glass Co.," late 19th c., 9" h. **$116**

Tazza, cornflower blue bowl w/engraved floral decoration, silver plate pedestal base w/three dolphin-shaped feet, signed **$450**

Toothpick holder, transfer-printed scene of three Brownies in a group on front & a Brownie dressed as an Indian w/hatchet on the reverse, light blue shaded to white (very minor flake on rim) **$250**

Tumbler, cylindrical, Colonial Ware line w/a white glossy ground decorated around the body w/ two raised gold bows suspending garlands of assorted flowers, crown & wreath mark on bottom, 3 3/4" h. **$550**

Vase, 8" h., eight-ribbed body w/a flared rim, colored base w/green thistle decoration outlined in gold in the Verona manner **$201**

Vase, miniature, 2 3/4" h., 3 3/4" d., squatty bulbous body tapering to a short fluted neck, satin opal ground w/a pale blue rim band, enameled w/scattered violets **$176**

Nailsea

Nailsea was another glassmaking center in England where a variety of wares similar to those from Bristol, England were produced between 1788 and 1873. Today most collectors think of Nailsea primarily as a glass featuring swirls and loopings, usually white, on a clear or colored ground. This style of glass decoration, however, was not restricted to Nailsea and was produced in many other glasshouses, including some in America.

Bellows on pedestal cranberry red body w/white loop pattern throughout & applied clear glass rigaree, pedestal & foot, pontil scarred foot, applied mouth & neck rings, America or England, ca. 1860-90, 8 3/4" h. **$420**

Sugar bowl base, clear heavy disk foot & short ringed pedestal supporting a bulbous bowl w/a tooled rim in milk white decorated overall w/dark blue looping, pontil scar, Pittsburgh district, ca. 1840-60, some white casing lost in manufacture, 5 3/4" h. **$504**

Vase & witch ball, 12" h., free-blown vase w/a flaring funnel pedestal base supporting a squatty bulbous body below the tall widely flaring trumpet neck, milk glass decorated overall w/cranberry looping, supporting a round matching ball, American, possibly New England, ca. 1850-70, 2 pcs. **$2,240**

Wine glass, free-blown w/an aqua cup-shaped bowl w/white looping, applied to a simple aqua pedestal base, probably South Jersey, ca.1840-60,   3 1/8" h. **$448**

Witchball on stand, round ball w/ white loopings on clear, matching trumpet-form base w/cushion foot, New Jersey, 1850-70, overall 12 1/4" h., 2 pcs. **$952**

Vase, 11 1/2" h., bulbous lower body w/a tall cylindrical neck w/a widely rolled rim, clear w/heavy white looping down the sides, on an applied clear short pedestal foot w/pontil, probably Pittsburgh (some Interior residue & cloudiness) **$605**

Vase & witch ball, 13 1/2" h., free-blown vase of trumpet form w/ cushion foot, clear w/white loopings, supporting a round clear ball w/white loopings, probably New Jersey, ca. 1850-70, 2 pcs. **$840**

Vase w/witch ball, clear w/white & fiery opalescent looping, the tall slender trumpet-form vase w/a swelled base on an applied clear foot, the large witch ball sitting atop the flared rim, probably South Jersey, vase 11" h., overall 16 1/2" h., 2 pcs. **$4,290**

New Martinsville

The New Martinsville Glass Mfg. Co. opened in New Martinsville, West Virginia, in 1901 and during its first period of production came out with a number of colored opaque pressed glass patterns. Also developed was an art glass line named "Muranese," which collectors refer to as "New Martinsville Peach Blow." The factory burned in 1907 but reopened later that year and began focusing on production of various clear pressed glass patterns, many of which were then decorated with gold or ruby staining or enameled decoration. After going through receivership in 1937, the factory again changed the focus of its production to more contemporary glass lines and figural animals. The firm was purchased in 1944 by The Viking Glass Company (later Dalzell-Viking).

Ashtray, figural, model of a wheelbarrow, clear, 4 x 5 1/2" **$24**

▶Basket, oval w/flaring sides & high applied handle, Janice patt., light blue, 9" h. **$120**

Bowl, 9" l., swan-shaped, Janice patt., clear **$58**

Cordial, Moondrops patt., ruby, 3/4 oz. **$32**

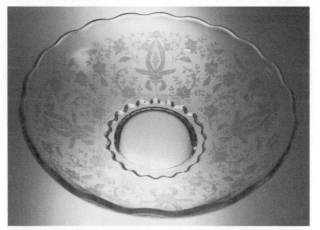

Bowl, 9 1/2" d., shallow w/lightly scalloped rim, Princess patt., Prelude etching, clear **$42**

▶Butter dish w/chrome lid, round, Moondrops patt., cobalt blue, 6" d. **$120**

■ Opalescent

Presently, this is one of the most popular areas of glass collecting. The opalescent effect was attained by adding bone ash chemicals to areas of an item while still hot and refiring the object at tremendous heat. Both pressed and mold-blown patterns are available to collectors and we distinguish the types in our listing below. Opalescent Glass from A to Z by the late William Heacock is the definitive reference book for collectors.

ARABIAN NIGHTS (POSSIBLY BEAUMONT)

Pitcher, 9" h., bulbous ovoid body, short cylindrical ringed neck w/ruffled rim & arched spout, applied handle, blue w/applied blue handle **$990**

Pitcher, 9" h., bulbous ovoid body, short cylindrical ringed neck w/ruffled rim & arched spout, applied handle, cranberry w/clear applied handle **$2,000-3,000**

Water set: 9" h., pitcher & four tumblers; blue w/applied blue handle, tumblers w/rim flakes, rim flake on pitcher, the set **$880**

GLASS

BEATTY RIB

Right: Sugar shaker w/original metal lid, blue, 5" h. **$248**

Far right: Sugar shaker w/original metal lid, clear, chip to top of one rib, 5" h............................ **$110**

BUTTONS & BRAIDS (JEFFERSON & FENTON)

Right: Pitcher, 9 1/2" h., footed bulbous body w/a cylindrical neck & round flaring crimped rim, cranberry w/applied clear handle .. **$1,430**

Far right: Pitcher, 9 1/2" h., footed bulbous body w/a cylindrical neck & round flaring crimped rim, blue w/applied blue handle **$250-300**

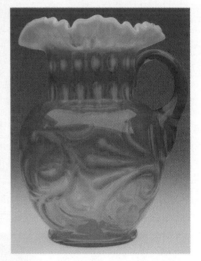

Pitcher, 9 1/2" h., footed bulbous body w/a cylindrical neck & round flaring crimped rim, green w/applied green handle **$200-225**

Pitcher, 9 1/2" h., footed bulbous body w/a cylindrical neck & round flaring crimped rim, clear w/applied clear handle **$132**

Tumbler, blown, blue Jefferson **$80-100**

Tumbler, pressed, green, Fenton **$65-80**

Tumbler, pressed, green, Fenton **$50-60**

Water set, pitcher & eight tumblers; blue, 9 pcs............. **$450**

Water set, pitcher & six tumblers, blue, 7 pcs................**$800-900**

Water set, 9 3/4" h. pitcher & four tumblers; pitcher w/bulbous ovoid body, short cylindrical neck & flaring ruffled rim, tumblers w/cylindrical shape tapering out slightly at rim, blue, 5 pcs. (rim chip to one tumbler) **$550**

CHRISTMAS SNOWFLAKE (NORTHWOOD/NATIONAL & DUGAN)

Pitcher, 9" h., slightly ovoid body w/tapering shoulder, cylindrical neck & ruffled rim, cranberry w/ clear applied handle...... **$2,400**

Pitcher, water, bulbous, cranberry w/applied clear twisted handle **$3,000-3,500**

Pitcher, 9" h., ribbed mold, cranberry w/applied clear handle **$2,400**

Sugar shaker w/original top, cobalt, 4 3/4" h. **$2,400**

Tumbler, cranberry (open bubble on rim) **$170**

Tumbler, blue **$160**

Pitcher, 9" h., ribbed mold, clear w/applied clear handle **$400-600**

COINSPOT

Pitcher, 8 1/2" h., bulbous ovoid body tapering to a cylindrical neck w/round flaring & crimped rim, cranberry w/applied clear handle **$200-300**

Pitcher, 10" h., baluster-form body w/a wide neck & tall upright ruffled rim, Northwood Glass Co., signed in the base, blue w/applied blue handle **$385**

Salt shaker w/old metal lid, cylindrical ring-neck mold, blue, minute flake near base, 4" h....... **$88**

Salt & pepper shakers w/original lids, cranberry, pr. **$375**

Sugar shaker w/original lid, nine-panel mold, cranberry....... **$265**

Sugar shaker w/original lid, nine-panel mold, cranberry....... **$165**

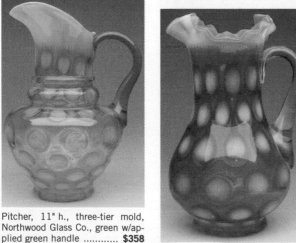

Pitcher, 11" h., three-tier mold, Northwood Glass Co., green w/applied green handle **$358**

◄Pitcher, 11" h., footed bulbous lower body tapering to a tall cylindrical neck a/tri-corner ruffled rim, Jefferson Glass Co., cranberry w/ applied clear handle **$660**

DAISY & FERN (NORTHWOOD, VARIOUS LOCATIONS)

Pitcher, 8 3/4" h., bulbous body tapering to a flaring upright squared & ruffled neck, applied clear handle, cranberry. **$400-550**

Pitcher, 9 1/4" h., footed shoulder-shape mold, triangular ruffled rim, blue, applied blue reeded handle **$250-300**

Pitcher, 9" h., bulbous body tapering to a flaring upright squared neck w/crimped rim, applied clear handle, clear **$150-175**

Sugar shaker w/original lid, ring-neck mold **$150**

Sugar shaker w/original lid, nine-panel, Jefferson variant, cranberry................................ **$295**

Syrup pitcher w/original metal lid, blue................................ **$145**

Sugar shaker w/original lid, Apple Blossom mold, blue **$358**

Sugar shaker w/original lid, Apple Blossom mold, clear **$176**

NORTHWOOD/NATIONAL, INDIANA, PA., CA. 1899-1901

Pitcher, 11 1/2" h., nine-panel mold tankard-style, green w/green applied handle **$1,000-1,500**

Pitcher, 11 1/2" h., nine-panel mold tankard-style, clear w/clear applied handle **$300-500**

Pitcher, 12" h., ribbon tie mold, tankard-style, green w/applied green handle **$200-300**

Pitcher, 9 1/2" h., tall ovoid body, ruffled rim, blue w/blue applied handle **$500**

Pitcher, 9 3/4" h., ovoid body tapering to a cylindrical neck w/a tri-corner crimped rim, clear w/ applied clear handle ... **$100-150**

Pitcher, 9 3/4" h., tall ovoid body tapering to a tri-corner ruffled rim, applied clear handle, cranberry **$1,250-1750**

Pitcher, 8 1/2" h., squat mold, wide cylindrical body tapering to cylindrical neck w/upright flaring & ruffled rim, blue w/applied blue handle **$600**

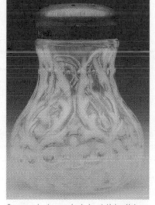

Sugar shaker w/original lid, ribbon tie mold, canary, minor damage, 3 1/4" h. **$231**

Sugar shaker w/original lid, wide waist mold, clear, 4 3/4" h. **$132**

RIBBED OPAL LATTICE

Pitcher, water, 10" h., tankard-type, blue w/translucent blue applied handle **$1,430**

Pitcher, water, 10" h., tankard-type, clear w/clear applied handle **$660**

Pitcher, water, 10" h., tankard-type, cranberry w/clear applied handle **$1,500-1,700**

GLASS

Right: Salt shaker w/early metal lid, cranberry **$88**

Far right: Sugar shaker w/period lid, clear, 4 1/4" h. **$99**

STRIPE

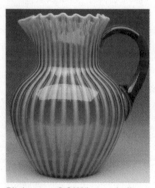

Pitcher, 8 3/4" h., bulbous ovoid body tapering to neck, flared crimped rim, light blue w/ translucent blue applied handle **$300-500**

Pitcher, 9 1/2" h., footed nearly spherical body w/a cylindrical neck & squared flaring crimped rim, clear w/applied clear handle **$75-125**

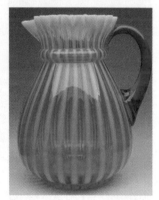

Pitcher, 9 1/4" h., ring-neck mold, blue w/applied blue handle **$400-600**

Pitcher, 9" h., ring-neck mold, clear w/applied clear handle **$150-250**

Pitcher, 9" h., ring-neck mold, tapering ovoid body, ruffled rim, cranberry w/clear applied handle **$1,600**

Pitcher, 9" h., ring-neck mold, tapering ovoid body, ruffled rim, cranberry w/clear applied handle **$600**

Pitcher, 9 1/2" h., spherical body, short cylindrical neck w/tricorner rim, canary w/translucent canary applied ribbed handle w/unique faint opalescent striping within **$800**

Salt shaker w/original lid, cylindrical w/narrow molded rings & a tapering ringed shoulder, pale canary, Belmont Glass, 4 1/4" h. **$99**

Salt shaker w/original lid, six-lobed mold, blue, 3" h, .. **$50-75**

Sugar shaker w/original lid, footed tapering cylindrical body w/ringed neck, blue, possibly Buckeye, 5" h. **$660**

SWIRL

Pitcher, 8 1/2" h., bulbous ovoid body tapering to a cylindrical neck w/squared rim, cranberry w/applied clear handle **$605**

Pitcher, 11" h., footed bulbous lower body tapering to a tall cylindrical neck w/a tri-corner ruffled rim, Jefferson Glass Co., blue w/ applied blue handle **$400-600**

Pitcher, 8 3/4" h., bulbous ovoid body tapering to neck, flared squared rim, blue w/translucent blue applied handle w/pressed fan design at upper terminal **$385**

Salt shaker w/original lid, cylindrical, cranberry, 3 3/4" h. **$99**

GLASS

▪ Pairpoint

Originally organized in New Bedford, Massachusetts, in 1880 as the Pairpoint Manufacturing Company on land adjacent to the famed Mount Washington Glass Company, this company first manufactured silver and plated wares. In 1894, the two famous factories merged as the Pairpoint Corporation and enjoyed great success for more than forty years. The company was sold in 1939 to a group of local businessmen and eventually bought out by one of the group who turned the management over to Robert M. Gundersen. Subsequently, it operated as the Gundersen Glass Works until 1952 when, after Gundersen's death, the name was changed to Gundersen-Pairpoint. The factory closed in 1956. Subsequently, Robert Bryden took charge of this glassworks, at first producing glass for Pairpoint abroad and eventually, in 1970, beginning glass production in Sagamore, Massachusetts. Today the Pairpoint Crystal Glass Company is owned by Robert and June Bancroft. They continue to manufacture fine quality blown and pressed glass.

Candlesticks, a round foot & disk stem supporting a tall hollow baluster-form stem below the applied cylindrical candle socket w/a flattened rim, sulfur yellow, the stem & base engraved w/lush pods on a vine w/florets scattered around the sockets, 10 1/8" h., pr. **$633**

Candlesticks, tall blown baluster-form w/a cylindrical socket & flattened rim, clear optic ribbed design w/dark blue swirls, 12" h., pr. **$1,200-1,800**

Compote, open, 5" h., 8" d., the widely flaring & gently ruffled bowl w/a wide cobalt blue border around spirals in clear & blue, on an applied clear stem & foot **$780**

Vase, 12 1/2" h., Crown Pairpoint Ware, painted overall w/dark earth-tone colors w/a large realistic owl on the front, signed, ca. 1895, rare **$3,500-5,000**

Compote, open, 6" d., cut overlay, Lincoln patt., a shallow wide round bowl in cobalt blue cut to clear, on a tapering facet-cut stem & star-cut round foot ... **$650-750**

Tazza, Fine Arts line, a rib-cut cylindrical flaring amber glass bowl mounted in a swag-cast brass-plated metal holder supported by a figural putto standing on a square onyx platform w/a cast brass-plated border, signed, ca. 1920s, 10" h. **$500-750**

Vase, 12" h., blown chalice-form, the cobalt blue ovoid body w/a flaring rim supported by a clear controlled bubble connector to the cobalt blue foot .. **$450-650**

Pattern

Though it has never been ascertained whether glass was first pressed in the United States or abroad, the development of the glass pressing machine revolutionized the glass industry in the United States, and this country receives the credit for improving the method to make this process feasible. The first wares pressed were probably small flat plates of the type now referred to as "lacy," the intricacy of the design concealing flaws.

In 1827, both the New England Glass Co., Cambridge, Mass., and Bakewell & Co., Pittsburgh, took out patents for pressing glass furniture knobs; soon other pieces followed. This early pressed glass contained red lead, which made it clear and resonant when tapped (flint.) Made primarily in clear, it is rarer in blue, amethyst, olive green and yellow.

By the 1840s, early simple patterns such as Ashburton, Argus and Excelsior appeared. Ribbed Bellflower seems to have been one of the earliest patterns to have had complete sets. By the 1860s, a wide range of patterns was available.

In 1864, William Leighton of Hobbs, Brockunier & Co., Wheeling, West Virginia, developed a formula for "soda lime" glass that did not require the expensive red lead for clarity. Although "soda lime" glass did not have the brilliance of the earlier flint glass, the formula came into widespread use because glass could be produced cheaply.

An asterisk (*) indicates a piece which has been reproduced.

BELLFLOWER

Creamer, double vine, fine rib, applied handle **$110**

Creamer, single vine, fine rib, applied handle, unpatterned band at rim, star in foot **$660**

Lamp, kerosene-type, all-glass, single vine, fine rib, squatty bulbous font applied to a high waisted & paneled pedestal on a round scalloped foot, 7 1/2" h. **$242**

BROKEN COLUMN (IRISH COLUMN, NOTCHED RIB OR BAMBOO)

Carafe, water **$143**

Compote, cov., 7 1/2" d., high stand, minor flaking **$88**

Cracker jar, cov., clear **$143**

Right: Pitcher, water, ruby-stained notches **$550**

Far right: Sugar shaker w/metal top, clear, minor flaws, 4 3/4" h. **$66**

CATHEDRAL

Cake stand, canary, 10" d. . **$143**

COLUMBIAN COIN

Mug, beer, handled, gilded coins **$66**

Lamp, kerosene-type, milk white, 10" h. **$187**

DAISY & BUTTON

Bowl, 10" d., 4" h., round w/eight-scallop rim, canary **$110**

Gas shade, sapphire blue, flaring octagonal shape w/scalloped rim, 9" d. rim **$77**

Gas shade, canary, scallop & point rim, 8 3/4" d. rim **$110**

Bowl, 9 1/2 x 11 1/2", 2 1/2" h., rectangular w/curved & flared sides, canary..................... **$110**

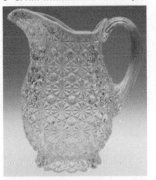

Pitcher, 9 3/4" h., 5" d., water, footed ovoid body w/a high arched spout & applied reeded handle, clear **$55**

*Pickle castor, apple green insert, w/silver plate frame & tongs **$165**

◄Spoon holder in silver plate frame, horizontal blue oblong bowl in a footed oval silver plate frame w/a high arched end handle, over-all 2 1/8 x 6 1/4", 6 1/2" h. **$220**

Novelty, model of a wheelbarrow w/pewter front wheel, normal flakes, amber, 5 3/4 x 10" . **$187**

DAISY & BUTTON - SINGLE PANEL
(ELROSE OR AMBERETTE, WHEN AMBER- STAINED)

Compote, open, 11" d., 7" h., widely flaring bowl, amber panels
.... **$1,760**

Compote, open, 11" d., 7" h., widely flaring bowl, apple green
.... **$55**

Water set: water pitcher & two tumblers; amber panels, the set
.... **$385**

Compote, open, 9 1/2" d., 9 1/2 h., very deep bell-form bowl w/ flared & scalloped rim, foot reduced in size, canary **$176**

Gas shade, flaring ruffled sides, canary, 9 1/2" d. rim **$209**

Table set: cov. sugar, cov. butter dish, creamer & spooner; amber panels, minor nick on sugar, the set **$250-350**

Compote, open, 9 1/2" d., 9 1/2" h., very deep bell-form bowl w/ flared & scalloped rim, clear **$99**

Salt & pepper shakers w/original tops, amber panels, pr. **$176**

DAISY & BUTTON WITH CROSSBARS (MIKADO)

Celery vase, canary yellow **$40-60**

Compote, cov., canary, 8" d., high stand **$154**

Compote, cov., canary, 8" d., low stand.................................. **$154**

Goblets, canary, set of 3 .... **$132**

Sugar bowl, open, individual size, blue.................................**$35**
Syrup pitcher, w/original top ..**$70**
Toothpick holder, ruby stained **$45**
Tumbler, amber **$45**

Pitcher, water, canary yellow **$121**

Cruet w/original stopper, canary yellow, minor interior residue, 8" h. **$176**

Wines, canary yellow, set of 6 .... **$154**

DAISY & BUTTON WITH THUMBPRINT PANELS

Cake stand, four-lobed top & squared pedestal base, minor flaws, canary, 10" w., 7 1/4" h. **$143**

Compote, cov., 5 3/4" w., high stand, blue.......................... **$55**

FROSTED LION (RAMPANT LION)

Cheese dish, cov., rampant lion finial **$300-400**

▶Compote, cov., 9" d., high stand, lion head finial . **$150-250**

*Pitcher, water **$300-400**

GLASS

HOBNAIL

Barber bottle, Frances decoration w/an amber-stained neck & frosted clear body, Hobbs, Brockunier & Co., some loss to knobs, 6 5/8" h. **$143**

Pitcher, 8 1/4" h., bulbous body tapering to a squared rim, Rubina Verde opalescent, applied canary handle, Hobbs, Brockunier & Co. **$495**

Creamer, bulbous body w/a squared neck, applied clear handle, clear opalescent, Hobbs, Brockunier & Co., 4 1/2" h. **$303**

Pitcher, 7 3/4" h., bulbous body w/a squared neck, applied clear handle, clear opalescent, Hobbs, Brockunier & Co. **$110**

Carafe, ovoid body tapering to a tall neck w/flared rim, Rubina Verde, ruby neck above yellowish green body, losses to numerous hobs, Hobbs, Brockunier & Co., 8 1/2" h. **$264**

Pitcher, 8" h., bulbous body tapering to a squared rim, applied clear handle, cranberry opalescent, Hobbs, Brockunier & Co. damage to numerous hobs **$209**

Pitcher, 8" h., bulbous body tapering to a squared rim, applied clear handle, Frances decoration in frosted amber above frosted clear, Hobbs, Brockunier & Co., flake on one hob **$143**

Tumblers, cylindrical, Rubina Opalescent, Hobbs, Brockunier & Co., one w/minor flaws, 4" h., pr... **$187**

HORN OF PLENTY (MCKEE'S COMET)

Plate, 6 1/4" d., canary .. **$1,150**

Butter dish & cover w/Washington's head finial (ILLUS. center with large creamer and celery vase) **$2,600**

HORSESHOE (GOOD LUCK OR PRAYER RUG)

Cake stand, 8" d., 6 1/2" h. **$75-100**

Compote, open, 9" d., 8 3/4" h., wide flaring shallow bowl on a plain stem w/domed foot **$77**

Cheese dish, cov., w/woman churning butter in base, minor flaws **$100-150**

Goblets, knob stem, minute flakes on some, set of 8 .... **$154**

Pitcher, water, 9" h. **$88**

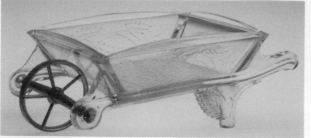

Relish, model of a wheelbarrow, clear, embossed "Pat. Apld. For" on bottom, metal wheel, minor flaws, 4 1/4 x 8" **$77**

Wine **$121**

◄Water tray, double horseshoe handles **$70-90**

MAGNET & GRAPE WITH FROSTED LEAF

Celery vase, scalloped rim, 8 1/2" h. **$240-250**

POLAR BEAR

Goblet, flared rim, frosted .. **$121**

Tray, water, frosted, 16" l. **$300-500**

Waste bowl, clear..................**$90**

Water set, water pitcher, two goblets, flared waste bowl & oval water tray; frosted & clear, some minor flaws, the set....**$300-500**

Water tray, oval, frosted, flakes on interior of table ring, 11 x 15 1/2" **$100-150**

RUBY THUMBPRINT

Castor set, 4-bottle, in clear glass frame, wire loop center handle, minor flakes on frame, one shaker w/minor pattern flake, 9 1/2" h. **$280**

Berry set: master boat-shaped, engraved bowl & 4 sauce dishes, 5 pcs. **$65**

Goblet, engraved vintage band **$70**

Pitcher, milk, tankard, 8 3/8" h., engraved souvenir inscription dated 1900 .... **$90**

SUNK HONEYCOMB (CORONA)

Cake stand, ruby-stained, 8 1/2" d., 5 1/4" h. **$275**

Cruets, ruby-stained & enameled w/leaves & flowers, 6 1/2" h. **$120**

Decanter, ruby-stained & engraved leaf & vine design, 13 5/8" h. **$160**

Wines, ruby-stained & enameled leaf & flower decoration, 4" h., set of 4 .... **$125**

SHELL & TASSEL

Bride's bowl, a clear squared 8" w. bowl w/pegged base raised on a tall ornate silver plate stand w/ twig-like legs trimmed w/a hummingbird & leaves, bowl w/partial loss to one scallop, 10 1/4" h. **$121**

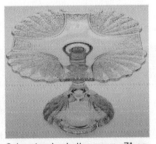

Cake stand, shell corners, 7" sq. **$55**

Dish, 5 3/4 x 8" rectangle, blue, light rim flakes **$50-75**

Salt shaker w/original top **$77**

Tumblers, clear, set of 3 ... **$77**

◀Pitcher, water, round **$99**

U.S. COIN

Lamp, kerosene-type, handled finger style, frosted twenty cent pieces, 5" h......................... **$660**

Goblet, straight top, frosted dimes, 6 1/2" h. **$154**

Water tray, frosted coins, two interior rim flakes, 10" d. **$400-600**

Lamp, kerosene-type, square font, frosted half dollars & dollars, 10 1/4" h. **$935**

WASHINGTON CENTENNIAL

Cake stand, 11" d. **$55**

Celery vase, flint **$165-175**
Lamp, kerosene-type, brass stem & marble base **$45**
Relish, bear paw handles, dated 1876.................................**$45**
Salt dip, master size, flat, round, flint **$35-45**
Salt dip, individual size, flint . **$20**
Spooner, flint **$29**
Syrup pitcher, w/original metal top, applied handle, milk white **$140**
Syrup pitcher, w/dated pewter top w/tiny figural finial, clear .. **$165**
Toothpick holder, w/enameled floral decoration **$30**

▶Pitcher, water **$110**

■ Quezal

In 1901, Martin Bach and Thomas Johnson, who had worked for Louis Tiffany, opened a competing glassworks in Brooklyn, New York. The Quezal Art Glass and Decorating Co. produced wares closely resembling those of Tiffany until the plant's closing in 1925.

Quezal

Bowl, 9 1/2" h., a low gold foot supporting the shallow round bowl w/a widely flaring flattened rim, gold w/overall green shading to blue iridescence, unsigned **$748**

Compote, 9 1/2" d., a low flaring round foot supporting the wide shallow bowl w/a widely flaring flattened rim, gold iridescent foot & bowl decorated w/a wide green iridescent rim band, unsigned **$575**

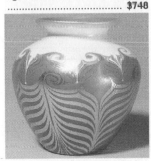

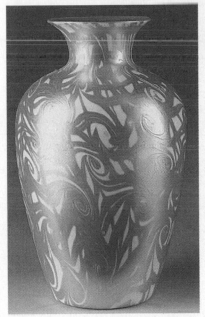

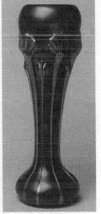

Vase, 7 5/8" h., wide bulbous tapering ovoid body w/a short widely flaring neck, the exterior decorated w/a dark green double-hooked design under a silver iridescent hooked & feathered decoration, gold banding separates the green from the ivory white shoulder & neck, gold iridescent interior, polished pontil engraved "Quezal 121" **$5,290**

Vase, 12 1/2" h., wide flat-bottomed ovoid body tapering to a short trumpet neck, King Tut design, overall scrolling gold iridescence against a cream background, interior in gold iridescence, signed in the pontil **$2,645**

Vase, 14 1/4" h., the bulbous foot tapering to slender flaring cylindrical sides below the bulbous upper body w/a wide flat mouth, dark green iridescent applied up the sides w/ribbed lily pad decoration w/blue & purple iridescence, signed in the pontil **$4,715**

Vase, 5 3/8" h., flower-form, a round cushion foot & slender stem supporting a deep rounded bowl w/a widely flaring six-ruffle rim, the exterior in white w/green & gold pulled-feather decoration up from the foot, iridescent gold interior, signed "Quezal P 413" **$2,160**

◄Punch bowl, a wide funnel foot supporting the deep wide rounded bowl w/a widely flaring angled rim, amber w/ overall gold iridescence, signed, ca. 1920, 14" d. **$1,265**

GLASS

Sandwich

Numerous types of glass were produced at The Boston & Sandwich Glass Works in Sandwich, Massachusetts, on Cape Cod, from 1826 to 1888. Those listed here represent a sampling. Also see BLOWN THREE MOLD, and LACY.

All pieces are pressed glass unless otherwise noted. Numbers after salt dips refer to listings in Pressed Glass Salt Dishes of the Lacy Period, 1825-1850, by Logan W. and Dorothy B. Neal.

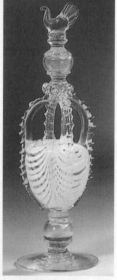

Bank, free-blown, a clear disk base & hollow knob stem supporting the blown ovoid body w/a center opening in clear w/white loopings, applied w/four arching rigaree ribs joined above the body & topped w/a rigaree band supporting a hollow knob applied w/a stylized rooster on a disk in clear, the base & top hollow knob each containing an 1833 American half-dime coin, extremely rare, w/a matching dug fragment, overall 11" h. **$19,975**

Inkstand, pressed flint glass, a squatty round ribbed inkwell w/ metal rim & cap & matching sand shaker, each set on a raised platform on rectangular stand w/peg feet, several edge nicks & small cracks on stand, ca. 1835-55, extremely rare, 6 1/3" l., bottles 2" h., the set **$32,900**

Candlestick, figural dolphin stem w/petal socket, on a stepped square base, light lavender alabaster-clambroth, minute petal & base nicks, 10" h., pr. **$3,300**

Compote, open, 8 1/4" h., 8 1/4" w., a pressed flaring octagonal pedestal base wafer-joined to the pressed openwork bowl w/16 vertical staves below the 32-point rim & above a 34-point star in sloping base, bright deep amethyst, 1840-55, minor flaws, very rare **$17,600**

Candlesticks, pressed flint glass, figural dolphin stem w/a petal socket, on a single-step square base, ca. 1845-70, dark blue, minor base roughness, 10 1/4" h., pr. **$9,988**

Decanter w/bar lip, pressed flint glass, Ashburton patt., pewter stopper, ca. 1840-60, canary yellow, small chip on neck ring, light scratches, 11 5/8" h. **$1,410**

Lamp, whale oil-type, hexagonal base & knop below the three-printed block font w/early burner & collar, ca. 1840-60, minor chips on base edge, amethyst, 9" h. **$881**

Lamps, whale oil type, hexagonal base & knopped stem, slender four-printed block font, original pewter collar & camphene burners, base edge chips, canary yellow, 12 7/8" h., pr. **$2,115**

Vase, 9 1/2" h., 5" d., pressed flint glass, Twisted Loop patt. top w/flaring ruffled rim, on wafers above the waisted & paneled standard & round foot, amethyst, ca. 1850, tiny rim nick, very small rough spot on foot rim, some interior residue **$1,760**

Vase, 10 1/4" h., tulip-style, deep amethyst, octagonal base, wafer construction, ca. 1850 .... **$3,575**

Tiffany

Tiffany & Co. was founded by Charles Lewis Tiffany (1812-1902) and Teddy Young in New York City in 1837 as a "stationery and fancy goods emporium." The store initially sold a wide variety of stationery items, and operated as Tiffany, Young and Ellis in lower Manhattan. The name was shortened to Tiffany & Co. in 1853, and the firm's emphasis on jewelry was established.

The first Tiffany catalog, known as the "Blue Book," was published in 1845. It is still being published today.

In 1862 Tiffany & Co. supplied the Union Army with swords, flags and surgical implements.

Charles' son, Louis Comfort Tiffany (1848-1933) was an American artist and designer who worked in the decorative arts and is best known for his work in stained glass. Louis established Tiffany Glass Co. in 1885, and in 1902 it became known as the Tiffany Studios. America's outstanding glass designer of the Art Nouveau period produced glass from the last quarter of the 19th century until the early 1930s. Tiffany revived early techniques and devised many new ones.

Tiffany Studios picture frame, circa 1906, in the Grapevine pattern with green and white opalescent glass, easel back, 7-3/8" x 8-3/4"............... **$1,673**
Photo courtesy Heritage Auction Galleries, Dallas; www.HA.com

Tiffany Studios, nine Favrile glass tiles, circa 1900, four with molded "PAT. APPL'D. FOR", largest 4" square, four tiles with chips to the prongs on the reverse. .... **$1,195 all**
Photo courtesy Heritage Auction Galleries, Dallas; www.HA.com

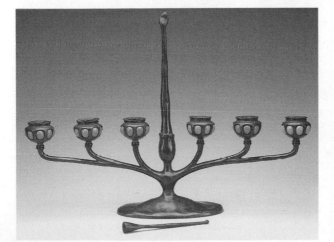

Tiffany Studios Blown-Glass Candelabra. Six-arm candelabra is made of bronze and has patina finish of brown with hints of green and red. From the oval-shaped platform base arises a single center stem with three candle cups on either side. Each of these candle cups has green blown-glass ornamentation and a bobeche. In the center stem of the candlestick rests a Tiffany snuffer that is concealed when in place. Signed on the underside "Tiffany Studios New York 1648". 15" x 21". One tight hairline to blown glass and one blown glass insert is slightly different color.................. **$6,900**
Photo courtesy James D. Julia Auctioneers, Fairfield, Maine; www.JuliaAuctions.com

GLASS

Tiffany Studios rose-water sprinkler, circa 1900, goose-neck form in iridescent Favrile glass with pink undertones, marked "L.C. Tiffany - Favrile W2714", 10" x 4". **$5,078**
Photo courtesy Heritage Auction Galleries, Dallas; www.HA.com

Tiffany Blue Favrile Cabinet Vase. Blue iridescence at the foot shading to platinum iridescence at the shoulder and neck. Signed on the bottom "L.C.T. D3473". 2-1/2" h. minor scratches to iridescence.
.... **$805**
Photo courtesy James D. Julia Auctioneers, Fairfield, Maine; www.JuliaAuctions.com

▶Tiffany Studios Mini Flower-Form Vase. Blue iridescent with vertical ribbing and applied foot. Irregular iridescence to top quarter of the vase shading down to deep purple mirror iridescence on the foot. Engraved signature "7311N 1522 L.C. Tiffany-Inc Favrile" on the underside. 6-1/4" t. **$2,400**
Photo courtesy James D. Julia Auctioneers, Fairfield, Maine; www.JuliaAuctions.com

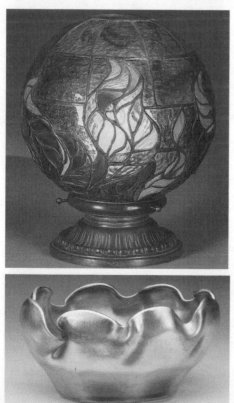

Tiffany Studios Footed Candy Dish. With applied gold iridescent border on opaque blue body and foot. Scratched in "59" on the underside. 6" diameter. Multiple chips to foot rim, some scratches on interior. **$60**
Photo courtesy James D. Julia Auctioneers, Fairfield, Maine; www. JuliaAuctions.com

◀Tiffany Studios Fireball Lamp. One of two known examples. Exceptional early Tiffany Studios leaded orb shade has flame design in mottled red and orange glass against a textured green and brown swirled background. The flames are made up of numerous types of glass, including heavily rippled to lightly textured, giving the effect of dancing flames when lit. The shade rests atop a bronze saucer base with single socket. Base is finished with rich brown patina with green highlights. Shade and base are unsigned. Shade is 12" diameter. Overall 15" h. Few tight hairlines. **$48,875**
Photo courtesy James D. Julia Auctioneers, Fairfield, Maine; www.JuliaAuctions.com

◀Tiffany Studios Ruffled Bowl. Deep gold iridescent finish with magenta, blue and pink highlights. Signed on the underside "L.C.T.". 4-1/2" diameter. **$287**
Photo courtesy James D. Julia Auctioneers, Fairfield, Maine; www. JuliaAuctions.com

Tiffany Studios Lemon Leaf Table Lamp. Heavily mottled apple-green background glass with heavily mottled maize-colored lemon-leaf band. Shade is signed "Tiffany Studios New York 1470". Base is signed "Tiffany Studios New York 531". Original patina on base and shade. Shade is 18" diameter. Overall 25-1/2" h. Some tight hairlines primarily in lower border with no missing glass. Slight lead separation in one small area where lemon-leaf band meets lower geometric bands. Slight dent in heat cap. **$17,250**
Photo courtesy James D. Julia Auctioneers, Fairfield, Maine; www.JuliaAuctions.com

Tiffany Studios Geometric Table Lamp. Colors of butterscotch and caramel striated with white. Shade is supported by a Colonial-style, four-socket base with inverted saucer foot. Shade is signed "Tiffany Studios NY 1469". Base is marked "Tiffany Studios New York 532". Shade is 18" diameter. Overall 25" h. Base has replaced pull chains and has been cleaned down to copper finish. **$8,050**
Photo courtesy James D. Julia Auctioneers, Fairfield, Maine; www.JuliaAuctions.com

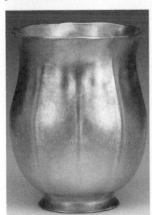

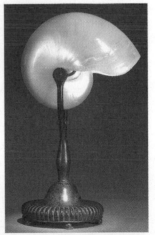

Tiffany Studios Art Glass Shade. Vertical ribbing and deep gold with purple and blue iridescence. Shade is finished with a gently scalloped border. Signed "L.C.T. Favrile" in rim. 2-1/4" fitter x 4-3/4" h. **$862**
Photo courtesy James D. Julia Auctioneers, Fairfield, Maine; www.JuliaAuctions.com

Tiffany Reactive Glass Shade. Green and orange flame design extending from the foot to near the rim. The smokey gray body of the shade has a slightly swirling rib running vertically. When shade is lit in a darkened room, it appears like a dancing flame. Shade is unsigned. 5" t x 2-1/4" fitter. **$4,025**
Photo courtesy James D. Julia Auctioneers, Fairfield, Maine; www.JuliaAuctions.com

Tiffany Studios Nautilus Lamp. Natural shell shade on a patina harp base with additional hook on the underside for possible wall hanging as well as five ball feet. Impressed on underside "403 Tiffany Studios New York". 12-1/2" h. Minor wear to patina. ... **$6,900**
Photo courtesy James D. Julia Auctioneers, Fairfield, Maine; www.JuliaAuctions.com

Tiffany Pastel Tulip Candlestick. With raspberry opalescent cup applied to blue-to-green opalescent stem with white pulled striping and applied raspberry foot with opalescent ribbing. Signed on the underside "1845 L.C. Tiffany-Favrile". 16" t. **$6,612**
Photo courtesy James D. Julia Auctioneers, Fairfield, Maine; www.JuliaAuctions.com

Tiffany Studios Mosaic Pentray. Inlaid blue decorated Favrile glass. Impressed on the underside "TIFFANY STUDIOS NEW YORK 24336" together with the monogram of the Tiffany Glass & Decorating Co. 7-3/4" l. Patina may be enhanced. **$8,000**
Photo courtesy James D. Julia Auctioneers, Fairfield, Maine; www.JuliaAuctions.com

Tiffany Studios Lily & Prism Chandelier. With six gold lily shades and 19 prisms in colors of oyster, gold, amber and green with a deep iridescence over the lilies and complimentary prisms. All of this Tiffany glass surrounds a decorated stalactite Tiffany shade with deep vertical ribbing and a hooked-feather pattern. The shade is supported by a bronze collar, three chains and hooks. The shades are supported by a Moorish-style bronze hanging fixture with openwork at the top, medallions of roping above six lily shade holders, nineteen prism hooks and a single stem for the stalactite shade. Further accenting this lamp, alternating between the prisms, are 19 beaded chains that end in bronze balls. This entire lamp is supported by a bronze decorated ceiling cap, chain and S hook. Stalactite shade is signed "S323" and one lily shade is signed "L.C.T. Favrile" and another is signed "L.C.T." and the remainder are unsigned. Overall 42" l. Some parts are authentic while other parts are exact replications of Tiffany Studios hardware. Three lily shades have broken fitter rims, one has roughness to fitter rim. Stalactite shade has chips to fitter rim that are concealed when in place. All prisms either have chips or are cracked. **$32,775**
Photo courtesy James D. Julia Auctioneers, Fairfield, Maine; www.JuliaAuctions.com

Tiffany Studios early experimental Favrile glass vase lamp base, circa 1900, engraved "X103 Louis C. Tiffany-Favrile", 14-3/4", significant surface scratches along interior, flaw on the body about-1/3 down from rim with some losses. . **$3,585**
Photo courtesy Heritage Auction Galleries, Dallas; www.HA.com

◄Tiffany Studios Flower-Form Vase. Pulled-feather vase on opalescent ground with everted rim and decorated foot. Engraved signature "L.C. Tiffany Favrile 539A". 11-1/4" h. Some staining to the interior. **$3,680**
Photo courtesy James D. Julia Auctioneers, Fairfield, Maine; www.JuliaAuctions.com

Tiffany Studios Favrile Desk Lamp. Gold Favrile shade with rainbow iridescent finish with stretched edge. The cased white-lined shade is supported by a three-arm, leaf-decorated base with a statuary finish. The lamp is completed with a top cap in a patina finish. Shade is signed on the fitter "L.C.T. Favrile" and base is signed on the underside "Tiffany Studios New York 426". Shade is 7" diameter. Overall 14" t. **$4,200**
Photo courtesy James D. Julia Auctioneers, Fairfield, Maine; www.JuliaAuctions.com

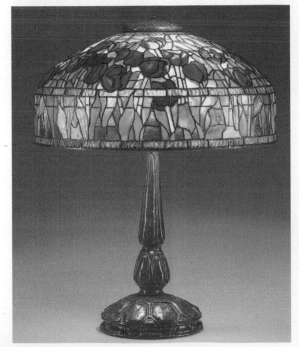

Tiffany Studios Red Tulip Table Lamp. The shade depicts the tulip flower in every stage of bloom (second view). The colors used encompass the entire range of the red family from pink to purple. Some blossoms are entirely constructed of the softer colors, while others use striations of light, medium and dark to give a three-dimensional effect. There are other blossoms that used only the deepest colors and represent the flower in its later stage of bloom. This tulip pattern also shows the foliage in most every color of green. Glass used in this shade is also of a wide variety from striated to cat's paw to rippled and finally granular. The shade is completed with three geometric bands of rippled glass in earthen hues of fiery orange with hints of green. The shade is supported by a mock-turtleback base. This three-socket base is complete with riser, wheel and top cap all in a rich patina finish. Shade is signed "Tiffany Studios New York 1596". Base is signed "Tiffany Studios New York 587". Shade is 18" diameter. Overall 22-1/2" h. A few tight hairlines in shade. Patina has been enhanced on shade and base. ... **$109,250**
Photo courtesy James D. Julia Auctioneers, Fairfield, Maine; www.JuliaAuctions.com

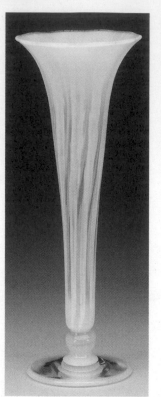

Tiffany Studios Blue Favrile Vase. Classic Egyptian form with elongated neck and squared shoulder. Vase begins with a platinum iridescence over the neck area that recedes into a medium blue and a cobalt blue at the foot. Signed "L.C. Tiffany Inc. Favrile X1421024". 5-3/4" h. Tiny spot of missing iridescence on shoulder. **$920**
Photo courtesy James D. Julia Auctioneers, Fairfield, Maine; www.JuliaAuctions.com

Tiffany Studios Pastel Vase. Clear foot with white opalescent rim. Foot gives way to a white opalescent stem with white opalescent ribs vertically extending to the slightly flaring lip. Interior of the mouth is finished with a rich pastel yellow. Signed on the underside "L.C. Tiffany Favrile 1886". 9-3/4" t **$1,380**
Photo courtesy James D. Julia Auctioneers, Fairfield, Maine; www.JuliaAuctions.com

▶ Tiffany Stalactite Hanger. Shade has gold iridescent hooked-feather design extending from the bottom of the shade. There is an additional hooked-feather design descending from the fitter. Design is set against a lighter gold iridescent background of the vertically ribbed body of the shade. Interior of the shade has a light chartreuse color. Shade is unsigned and numbered "L2400". It is suspended from three chains attached to hooks on a center light post which terminates to a ceiling cap having beaded rim. The bronze replacement hardware is finished in a rich brown patina with strong red and green highlights. Shade is 8" l x 6" diameter x 4-3/4" fitter. Overall 24" h. **$7,187**
Photo courtesy James D. Julia Auctioneers, Fairfield, Maine; www.JuliaAuctions.com

Tiffany Studios Damascene Table Lamp. Green Favrile shade with a damascene-wave pattern decoration in gold shading to platinum having eight vertical ribs, which give it highlights of blue. The cased lined shade is supported by a patinated single-socket, three-arm bronze base with elongated rib decoration over an ornate root-style foot resting on four ball feet. Lamp is completed with a bronze heat cap. Shade is signed on the fitter rim "L.C.T.". Base is signed "Tiffany Studios New York 431". Shade is 9-1/2" diameter x 3-3/4" fitter. Overall 19-1/2" t. ... **$6,612**
Photo courtesy James D. Julia Auctioneers, Fairfield, Maine; www.JuliaAuctions.com

Tiffany Studios Favrile Cabinet Vase. Round squat body with pulled handles on each side and a slightly flaring mouth. The gold Favrile finish shows purple and blue highlights at foot and lip. Signed on the underside "L.C. Tiffany-Favrile 4014L". 2" t. **$540**
Photo courtesy James D. Julia Auctioneers, Fairfield, Maine; www.JuliaAuctions.com

Tiffany Studios Pine Needle Card Case. Constructed of green slag panels with darker striations. These panels are set in a bronze frame with decorative pine needle decoration overall. Exceptional patina finish. Signed on underside "Tiffany Studios New York 875". 4" x 3" x 1" **$1,495**

Photo courtesy James D. Julia Auctioneers, Fairfield, Maine; www.JuliaAuctions.com

Tiffany Studios Tel El Amarna Vase. With applied and decorated collar. Engraved "Exhibition Piece" and "6340N L.C. Tiffany – Favrile" on the underside. 5-3/4" h. Hairline crack to applied rim........... **$5,750**

Photo courtesy James D. Julia Auctioneers, Fairfield, Maine; www.JuliaAuctions.com

Tiffany Studios Pomegranate Table Lamp. Shade has an allover geometric background of green striated glass with hints of blue, yellow and white. The shade is decorated with a single band of pomegranates in fiery mottled yellow and orange glass. Shade is supported by a three-socket, three-armed Grecian urn that is supported by four flaring feet on a pedestal stand. Shade is signed on "Tiffany Studios New York" with a small early tag. Shade is 16" diameter. Overall 20" h. Several spider cracks. **$16,100**

Photo courtesy James D. Julia Auctioneers, Fairfield, Maine; www.JuliaAuctions.com

Tiffany Studios Geometric Table Lamp. With leaded "dichroic" glass shade glass (containing multiple micro-layers of metal oxides) that shows colors of green, tan and mauve when unlit. When lit, the glass turns a rich orange. Shade is signed "Tiffany Studios New York 1436" and rests atop an early Tiffany Studios base with an incised and slightly raised wave design. Base is finished with three attached arms to support the shade. Marked on the underside "25778". Shade is 16" diameter. Overall 20" h. A few tight hairlines in the shade. Bottom of font has been drilled.................... **$15,525**

Photo courtesy James D. Julia Auctioneers, Fairfield, Maine; www.JuliaAuctions.com

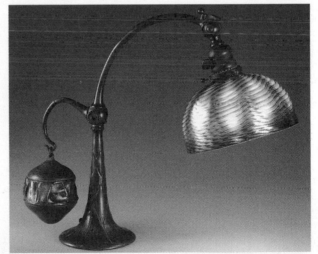

Tiffany Studios Counterbalance Desk Lamp. With pendulous turtleback tile counterweight. Artichoke design stand and blue decorated damascene shade. Shade is signed "L.C.T. Favrile". Base is marked "Tiffany Studios New York". Shade is 8" diameter. Overall 14-1/2" h. Minor chips to three turtleback tiles in the counterweight, one tile with tight hairline, some minor wear to patina... **$32,775**

Photo courtesy James D. Julia Auctioneers, Fairfield, Maine; www.JuliaAuctions.com

◄Tiffany Studios Bell Shade. Decorated with a translucent green pulled-feather motif with gold trim on an oyster ground. Signed "L.C.T.". 2-1/4" fitter rim x 4-1/2" h. Minor grinding to fitter rim. **$2,530**

Photo courtesy James D. Julia Auctions.com

GLASS

■ Tiffin

A wide variety of fine glasswares were produced by the Tiffin Glass Company of Tiffin, Ohio. Beginning as a part of the large U.S. Glass Company early in the 20th century, the Tiffin factory continued making a wide range of wares until its final closing in 1984. One popular line is now called "Black Satin" and included various vases with raised floral designs. Many other acid-etched and hand-cut patterns were also produced over the years and are very collectible today. The three "Tiffin Glassmasters" books by Fred Bickenheuser are the standard references for Tiffin collectors.

Ashtray, shallow oval form, molded stag & wolf design, Black Satin, 6" l. **$55**

Atomizer, footed tall slender waisted body, blue satin, new atomizer fitting, 7" h. **$120**

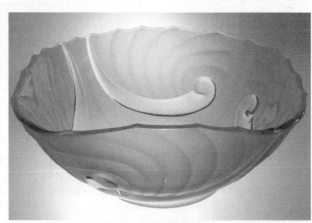

Bowl, 9 1/2" w., square w/flaring sides, Velva patt., frosted blue **$87**

◄Atomizer, round foot & slender stem w/a tall slender ovoid body, amber satin, new atomizer fitting, 7" h. **$115**

Candleholder, three-light, Art Deco style Pattern 308, Sky Blue, 7 1/4" w., 6 3/8" h. **$65**

Candleholders, one-light, figural stylized frogs, black satin, 5 1/2" h., pr. **$250**

Candlestick, one-light, floral cut decoration, Royal Blue, pr. (ILLUS. of one) **$160**

Candlestick, one-light, No. 82 w/ Jack Frost decoration, canary, 8 1/2" h., pr. (ILLUS. of one) **$130**

Candlesticks, one-light, figural Dolphin stem, round base, light green, 4 1/4" h., pr. **$68**

Candlesticks, round foot & large knob below the flaring stem below a ringed collar & tulip-form socket, Pattern No. 17350, clear w/cut decoration, 10" h., pr. **$145**

Stemware set: 23 - 4 3/4" h. wines, 13 - 6" sherbets, 10 - 10 1/2" goblets, 2 - 5 1/2" tumblers & one cordial; etched Athens-Diana patt., platinum rim bands, the set **$949**

Candlesticks, one-light, Pattern No. 151, Black Satin w/gold band trim, 8" h., pr. **$85**

Candlesticks, one-light, Velva patt., blue satin, 5 3/4" h., pr. **$115**

Candlesticks, Twist Stem patt., Pattern 315, Amberina, 8 3/4" h., pr. (ILLUS. left & right with Twist Stem compote).. **$95**

Compote, open, 6 1/4" d., 3" h., wide shallow Killarney Green bowl raised on four applied clear pointed feet, Pattern No. 17430 (ILLUS. right with Killarney Green vase).. **$48**

Candy jar, cov., Pattern No. 179, footed widely flaring base & wide pagoda-style cover w/Gold Ship decoration, Black Satin, 6 1/2" d., 7 1/2" h. **$95**

▶Candy jar, cov., mold-blown, No. 6106, diamond optic ovoid body tapering to a very slender stem & foot, domed cover w/pointed finial, Plum **$125**

Console set: footed round bowl & pair of tall candlesticks; bowl No. 8098 & No. 300 candlesticks, Royal Blue w/ satin finish, bowl 9 1/2" d., candlesticks 8 1/2" h., the set............ **$230**

Serving tray, flaring open center handle, Pattern No. 15320, Black Satin w/gold border bands, 10 1/2" d. **$58**

Ivy ball, mold-blown, No. 6120 patt., bulbous diamond optic bowl on a tall faceted stem w/faceted rings on a round foot, original label, Golden Banada **$72**

Decanter w/original stopper, Pattern No. 17437, a clear applied foot & heavy clear swirled ribs supporting the tall slender ovoid Killarney Green body, tall rounded clear stopper, 12" h. **$140**

Vase, 20" h., swung-type, Green Fantasy Line, green & crystal **$235**
▶Sherbet, tall stem & deep rounded bowl, Topaz stretch glass, 4 1/2" h. **$24**

Vase, 16" h., swung-type, Empress Line, ruby & crystal .. **$175**

Rose bowl, spherical w/wide flat mouth, Killarney Green bowl w/gold Melrose etching, on four applied clear pointed feet, 6 1/4" h. **$250**

Westmoreland

In 1890 Westmoreland opened in Grapeville, Pennsylvania, and as early as the 1920s was producing colorwares in great variety. Cutting and decorations were many and are generally under appreciated and undervalued. Westmoreland was a leading producer of milk glass in "the antique style." The company closed in 1984 but some of their molds continued in use by others.

Basket, English Hobnail patt., high arched handle, clear, 5" w. **$24**

Bowl, 9 1/2" d., scalloped rim, American Hobnail patt., blue opalescent **$50**

Bowl, 11" d., flat bottom w/flaring crimped sides, Wakefield patt., clear w/ruby stain **$120**

Cheese compote, Marguerite patt., No. 700, pink, 4 1/2" d., 2 3/4" h. **$18**

◀Basket, English Hobnail patt., fan-shaped body w/high arched handle, milk glass, 5" w., 10" h. **$30**

Compote, 7" d., 7 3/4" h., hexagonal foot & tall figural dolphin stem supporting a wide shallow round bowl, milk glass w/h.p. Charlton Leaf decoration **$85**

Compote, 8" h., sweetmeat-type w/ball stem, Della Robbia patt., clear w/ruby stain **$125**

Compote, 5 1/4" w., 6" h., two-handled, tall stem, Colonial patt., Blue Mist **$22**

Compote, oval, 6 1/2" l., 4 1/4" h., pressed cut glass-style design, Pattern No. 240, clear **$25**

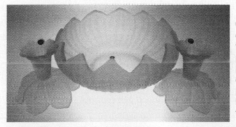

Console set: 9" d. cupped petal-form bowl & pair one-light 4" petal-form candleholders; Lotus patt., original labels, pink satin, the set **$95**

Lamp, table model, hexagonal foot & figural dolphin stem supporting a large flaring cylindrical paneled font, made to resemble an antique lamp, pink, 9 1/4" h. **$200**

Plate, 8" d., openwork Forget-Me-Not patt., black decorated in white enamel w/a scene of a running deer, modern version of an early design **$40**

Tumbler, iced tea, English Hobnail patt., square foot, clear, 11 oz. **$14**

Compote, 5 1/2" d., 3 1/2" h., open stem, Lotus patt., Flame red **$30**

Compote, 7 1/2" h., 8" d., ball stem, spray-cased black, amber stain, cut to clear.............**$150**

Compote, 8" h., Mother of Pearl Dolphin & Shell line, shell-shaped bowl w/dolphin base, milk white w/mother of pearl finish.................................... **$85**

Mayonnaise dish & underplate, Paneled Grape patt., milk white, 3 1/2" d., 2 pcs. **$23**

Vase, 8 1/4" h., Jack-in-the-pulpit style, Corinth patt., Amethyst Carnival **$49**

Nappy, round, handled, Paneled Grape patt., milk white, 5" d. **$17**

Planter, Paneled Grape patt., square, milk white, 4 1/2" w. **$40**

Puff box, cov., Paneled Grape patt., milk white, 4 1/2" d. **$32**

Sweetmeat, cov., Old Quilt patt., high-footed, milk white, 6 1/2" h. **$35**

Tumbler, Beaded Edge patt., No. 64-2 fruit decoration, milk white **$19**

Hallmark Keepsake Ornaments

For nearly 40 years, Hallmark Keepsake Ornaments—produced by Hallmark Cards Inc. of Kansas City, Missouri—have transformed Christmas trees everywhere into 3-D scrapbooks of memories that capture and preserve times, events, and special occasions. When the first 18 ornaments were introduced in 1973, Christmas tree decorations went from simple colored glass balls to creative and fun designs. Soon, Americans started a new tradition that changed the way they viewed ornaments. No longer were ornaments just pretty decorations for the tree. Suddenly they became unique, year-dated and available only for a limited time, making them an instant hit with collectors

In 1973 Hallmark issued a handful of ornaments, six in ball shape and 12 made of yarn. Today the Keepsake line releases more than 200 new ornaments each year. Collectors eagerly anticipate Hallmark's Keepsake Ornament Premiere every July, where they have their first opportunity to purchase that year's new ornaments. In October Hallmark holds its Keepsake Ornament Debut, offering even more new releases. Each year Hallmark also publishes a full-color catalog, called the Dream Book, showcasing the new ornaments

A total of more than 6,000 Hallmark ornaments have been produced since the company began issuing them in 1973, and more than 11 million U.S. households collect them

For more information, see *Hallmark Keepsake Ornaments: Warman's Companion* by Mary Sieber.

1970s

Angel, 1976, from the Twirl-Abouts series......................**$100**

Angel, 1978.........................**$70**

Ornament Title	Series	Year	Price	Value
25th Christmas Together 350QX269-3	Commemoratives	1978	$4	$15
Angel 125XHD78-5	Yarn Ornaments	1973	$1	$29
Angel 150QX103-1	Yarn Ornaments	1974	$2	$29
Angel 175QX220-2	Cloth Doll Ornaments	1977	$2	$45
Angel 250QX110-1	General Line	1974	$2	$80
Angel 300QX176-1	Tree Treats	1976	$3	$85
Angel 350QX354-3	Colors Of Christmas	1978	$4	$50
Angel 400QX139-6	Handcrafted Ornaments	1978	$4	$70
Angel 450QX171-1	Twirl-Abouts	1976	$4	$100
Angel 500QX182-2	Nostalgia	1977	$5	$62
Angel 600QX172-2	Yesteryears	1977	$6	$70
Angel Delight 300QX130-7	Little Trimmers	1979	$3	$72
Angel Music 200QX343-9	Sewn Trimmers	1979	$2	$19
Angel Tree Topper 900HD230-2	Tree Topper	1977	$9	$425
Angels 800QX150-3	Handcrafted Ornaments	1978	$8	$200
Animal Home 600QX149-6	Handcrafted Ornaments	1978	$6	$160
Antique Car 500QX180-2	Nostalgia	1977	$5	$40
Antique Toys Carousel 1st Ed. 600QX146-3	Carousel Series	1978	$6	$175
Baby's First Christmas 250QX211-1	General Line	1976	$2	$129
Baby's First Christmas 350QX131-5	General Line	1977	$4	$85
Baby's First Christmas 350QX200-3	Commemoratives	1978	$4	$31
Baby's First Christmas 350QX208-7	Commemoratives	1979	$4	$28
Baby's First Christmas 800QX154-7	Commemoratives	1979	$8	$100
Behold The Star 350QX255-9	Decorative Ball Ornaments	1979	$4	$30
Bell 350QX154-2	Christmas Expressions Collection	1977	$4	$40
Bell 350QX200-2	Colors Of Christmas	1977	$4	$40
Bellringer 600QX192-2	Twirl-Abouts	1977	$6	$62
Bellswinger 1st Ed. QX147-9	Bellringer Series	1979	$10	$170
Betsey Clark (2) 350QX167-1	General Line	1975	$4	$38
Betsey Clark (3) 450QX218-1	General Line	1976	$4	$60

Angel, 1978, from the Colors of Christmas series **$50**

Angel Delight, 1979, from the Little Trimmers series............ **$72**

Antique Car, 1977, from the Nostalgia series.......................... **$40**

Ornament Title	Series	Year	Price	Value
Betsey Clark (4) 450QX168-1	General Line	1975	$4	$35
Betsey Clark 1st Ed. 250XHD110-2	Betsey Clark	1973	$3	$100
Betsey Clark 250QX157-1	Adorable Adornments	1975	$2	$230
Betsey Clark 250QX163-1	General Line	1975	$2	$20
Betsey Clark 250QX210-1	General Line	1976	$2	$45
Betsey Clark 250XHD100-2	General Line	1973	$2	$45
Betsey Clark 2nd Ed. 250QX108-1	Betsey Clark	1974	$3	$45
Betsey Clark 3rd Ed. 300QX133-1	Betsey Clark	1975	$3	$40
Betsey Clark 4th Ed. 300QX195-1	Betsey Clark	1976	$3	$60
Betsey Clark 5th Ed. 350QX264-2	Betsey Clark	1977	$4	$350
Betsey Clark 6th Ed. 350QX201-6	Betsey Clark	1978	$4	$40
Betsey Clark 7th Ed. 350QX201-9	Betsey Clark	1979	$4	$19
Bicentennial '76 Commemorative QX203-1	Bicentennial Commemoratives	1976	$2	$20
Bicentennial Charmers 300QX198-1	Bicentennial Commemoratives	1976	$3	$50
Black Angel 350QX207-9	Decorative Ball Ornaments	1979	$4	$25
Blue Girl 125XHD85-2	Yarn Ornaments	1973	$1	$25
Boy Caroler 125XHD83-2	Yarn Ornaments	1973	$1	$19
Buttons & Bo (2) 350QX113-1	General Line	1974	$4	$50
Buttons & Bo (4) 500QX139-1	General Line	1975	$5	$38
Calico Mouse 450QX137-6	Handcrafted Ornaments	1978	$4	$50
Candle 350QX203-5	Colors Of Christmas	1977	$4	$60
Candle 350QX357-6	Colors Of Christmas	1978	$4	$85
Cardinals 225QX205-1	Decorative Ball Ornaments	1976	$2	$30
Caroler 175QX126-1	Yarn Ornaments	1976	$2	$22
Charmers (2) 350QX215-1	General Line	1976	$4	$25
Charmers 250QX109-1	General Line	1974	$2	$20
Charmers 300QX135-1	General Line	1975	$3	$50
Charmers 350QX153-5	General Line	1977	$4	$60
Chickadees 225QX204-1	Decorative Ball Ornaments	1976	$2	$40
Choir Boy 125XHD80-5	Yarn Ornaments	1973	$1	$27
Christmas Angel 350QX300-7	Holiday Highlights	1979	$4	$100
Christmas Carousel 2nd Ed. 650QX146-7	Carousel Series	1979	$6	$115
Christmas Cheer 350QX303-9	Holiday Highlights	1979	$4	$40
Christmas Chickadees 350QX204-7	Decorative Ball Ornaments	1979	$4	$32
Christmas Collage 350QX257-9	Decorative Ball Ornaments	1979	$4	$40
Christmas Eve Surprise 650QX157-9	Handcrafted Ornaments	1979	$6	$70
Christmas Heart 650QX140-7	Handcrafted Ornaments	1979	$6	$45
Christmas Is For Children 500QX135-9	Handcrafted Ornaments	1979	$5	$45
Christmas Is Love 250XHD106-2	General Line	1973	$2	$75
Christmas Mouse 350QX134-3	Decorative Ball Ornaments	1977	$4	$60
Christmas Star Tree Topper QX702-3	Tree Topper	1978	$8	$40
Christmas Traditions 350QX253-9	Decorative Ball Ornaments	1979	$4	$40
Christmas Treat 500QX134-7	Handcrafted Ornaments	1979	$5	$42
Christmas Tree 350QX302-7	Holiday Highlights	1979	$4	$50

The original Baby's First Christmas ornament, 1976 .... **$129**

Baby's 1st Christmas, 1979 .. **$28**

Bell, 1977, from the Colors of Christmas series **$40**

Bellringer, 1977, from the Twirl-Abouts series...........................**$62**

Betsey Clark, 1973...............**$45**
Christmas 1973, 1st in the Betsey Clark series **$100**

Betsey Clark, 1978, 6th in the Betsey Clark series................**$40**

Betsey Clark, 1979, 7th in the Betsey Clark series................**$19**

Calico Mouse, 1978 ....**$50**

Candle, 1978, from the Colors of Christmas series **$85**

Ornament Title	Series	Year	Price	Value
Colonial Children (2) 400QX208-1	Bicentennial Commemoratives	1976	$4	$10
Currier & Ives (2) 250QX164-1	Currier & Ives	1975	$2	$40
Currier & Ives (2) 350QX112-1	Currier & Ives	1974	$4	$38
Currier & Ives (2) 400QX137-1	Currier & Ives	1975	$4	$40
Currier & Ives 250QX209-1	Currier & Ives	1976	$2	$40
Currier & Ives 300QX197-1	Currier & Ives	1976	$3	$50
Currier & Ives 350QX130-2	Currier & Ives	1977	$4	$50
Della Robia Wreath 450QX193-5	Twirl-Abouts	1977	$4	$42
Desert 250QX159-5	Beauty Of America Collection	1977	$2	$42
Disney (2) 400QX137-5	General Line	1977	$4	$55
Disney 350QX133-5	General Line	1977	$4	$70
Disney 350QX207-6	General Line	1978	$4	$42
Dove 350QX310-3	Holiday Highlights	1978	$4	$50
Dove 450QX190-3	Handcrafted Ornaments	1978	$4	$45
Downhill Run, The 650QX145-9	Handcrafted Ornaments	1979	$6	$120
Drummer Boy 175QX123-1	Yarn Ornaments	1975	$2	$13
Drummer Boy 175QX123-1	Yarn Ornaments	1976	$2	$26
Drummer Boy 250QX136-3	Little Trimmers	1978	$2	$78
Drummer Boy 250QX161-1	Adorable Adornments	1975	$2	$175
Drummer Boy 350QX130-1	Nostalgia	1975	$4	$168
Drummer Boy 350QX252-3	Decorative Ball Ornaments	1978	$4	$42
Drummer Boy 350QX312-2	Holiday Highlights	1977	$4	$62
Drummer Boy 400QX130-1	Nostalgia	1976	$4	$83
Drummer Boy 500QX184-1	Yesteryears	1976	$5	$85
Drummer Boy, The 800QX143-9	Handcrafted Ornaments	1979	$8	$75
Elf 125XHD79-2	Yarn Ornaments	1973	$1	$26
Elf 150QX101-1	Yarn Ornaments	1974	$2	$26
Elves 250XHD103-5	General Line	1973	$2	$40
First Christmas Together 350QX132-2	Commemoratives	1977	$4	$48
First Christmas Together 350QX218-3	Commemoratives	1978	$4	$48
For Your New Home 350QX217-6	Commemoratives	1978	$4	$25
For Your New Home 350QX263-5	Commemoratives	1977	$4	$35
Friendship 350QX203-9	Commemoratives	1979	$4	$25
Granddaughter 350QX208-2	Commemoratives	1977	$4	$19
Granddaughter 350QX211-9	Commemoratives	1979	$4	$38
Granddaughter 350QX216-3	Commemoratives	1978	$4	$38
Grandma Moses 350QX150-2	General Line	1977	$4	$34
Grandmother 350QX252-7	Commemoratives	1979	$4	$18
Grandmother 350QX260-2	Commemoratives	1977	$4	$50
Grandmother 350QX267-6	Commemoratives	1978	$4	$18
Grandson 350QX209-5	Commemoratives	1977	$4	$35

Hallmark's Antique Card Collection Design, 1978 .... **$44**

Joan Walsh Anglund, 1979....**$35**

Joy, 1977, from the Holiday Highlights series.........................**$50**

Ornament Title	Series	Year	Price	Value
Grandson 350QX210-7	Commemoratives	1979	$4	$40
Grandson 350QX215-6	Commemoratives	1978	$4	$40
Green Boy 200QX123-1	Yarn Ornaments	1978	$2	$28
Green Girl 125XHD84-5	Yarn Ornaments	1973	$1	$25
Green Girl 200QX126-1	Yarn Ornaments	1978	$2	$28
Hallmark's Antique Card Coll. 350QX220-3	Decorative Ball Ornaments	1978	$4	$44
Happy Holidays Kissing Balls QX225-1	General Line	1976	$5	$225
Happy The Snowman (2) QX216-1	General Line	1976	$4	$50
Heavenly Minstrel Tabletop QHD 921-9	Table Decor	1978	$35	$145
Holiday Memories Kissing Ball QHD 900-3	General Line	1978	$5	$120
Holiday Scrimshaw 400QX152-7	Handcrafted Ornaments	1979	$4	$135
Holiday Wreath 350QX353-9	Colors Of Christmas	1979	$4	$42
Holly & Poinsettia Ball 600QX147-6	Handcrafted Ornaments	1978	$6	$60
Holly & Poinsettia Table Decor QHD320-2	Table Decor	1977	$8	$132
House 600QX170-2	Yesteryears	1977	$6	$70
Ice Hockey Holiday 1st Ed. 800QX141-9	Snoopy & Friends	1979	$8	$160
Jack-In-The-Box 600QX171-5	Yesteryears	1977	$6	$67
Joan Walsh Anglund 350QX205-9	General Line	1979	$4	$35
Joan Walsh Anglund 350QX221-6	General Line	1978	$4	$40
Joy 350QX132-1	Nostalgia	1975	$4	$143
Joy 350QX201-5	Colors Of Christmas	1977	$4	$50
Joy 350QX254-3	Decorative Ball Ornaments	1978	$4	$44
Joy 350QX310-2	Holiday Highlights	1977	$4	$50
Joy 450QX138-3	Handcrafted Ornaments	1978	$4	$44
Light Of Christmas, The 350QX256-7	Decorative Ball Ornaments	1979	$4	$30
Little Girl 125XHD82-5	Yarn Ornaments	1973	$1	$25
Little Girl 175QX126-1	Yarn Ornaments	1975	$2	$22
Little Miracles (4) 450QX115-1	General Line	1974	$4	$60
Little Miracles (4) 500QX140-1	General Line	1975	$5	$40
Little Trimmer Collection QX132-3	General Line	1978	$9	$320
Little Trimmer Set QX159-9	General Line	1979	$9	$340
Locomotive (Dated) 350QX127-1	Nostalgia	1975	$4	$113
Locomotive 350QX356-3	Colors Of Christmas	1978	$4	$60
Locomotive 400QX222-1	Nostalgia	1976	$4	$110
Love 350QX258-7	Commemoratives	1979	$4	$38
Love 350QX262-2	Commemoratives	1977	$4	$27
Love 350QX268-3	Commemoratives	1978	$4	$60
Love 350QX304-7	Holiday Highlights	1979	$4	$55
Mandolin 350QX157-5	Christmas Expressions Collection	1977	$4	$40
Manger Scene 250XHD102-2	General Line	1973	$2	$90
Marty Links (2) 400QX207-1	General Line	1976	$4	$55
Marty Links 300QX136-1	General Line	1975	$3	$50

Locomotive, 1976, from the Nostalgia series.........................**$110**

Merry Christmas, 1978, from the Colors of Christmas series......**$55**

Mother, 1979.......................**$18**

Nativity, 1977, from the Nostalgia series $97

Nativity, 1978.....................$125

Norman Rockwell, 1974 ....$62

Partridge, 1976, from the Twirl-Abouts series.......................$100

Partridge, 1976, from the Yester-years series $62

Partridge in a Pear Tree, 1979, from the Colors of Christmas se-ries $40

Ornament Title	Series	Year	Price	Value
Mary Hamilton 350QX254-7	General Line	1979	$4	$28
Matchless Christmas 400QX132-7	Little Trimmers	1979	$4	$39
Merry Christmas (Santa) 350QX202-3	Decorative Ball Ornaments	1978	$4	$20
Merry Christmas 350QX355-6	Colors Of Christmas	1978	$4	$55
Merry Santa 200QX342-7	Sewn Trimmers	1979	$2	$8
Mother 350QX251-9	Commemoratives	1979	$4	$18
Mother 350QX261-5	Commemoratives	1977	$4	$35
Mother 350QX266-3	Commemoratives	1978	$4	$40
Mountains 250QX158-2	Beauty Of America Collection	1977	$2	$35
Mr. & Mrs. Snowman Kissing Ball QX225-2	General Line	1977	$5	$100
Mr. Claus 200QX340-3	Yarn Ornaments	1978	$2	$23
Mr. Santa 125XHD74-5	Yarn Ornaments	1973	$1	$25
Mr. Snowman 125XHD76-5	Yarn Ornaments	1973	$1	$24
Mrs. Claus 200QX125-1	Yarn Ornaments	1978	$2	$22
Mrs. Santa 125XHD75-2	Yarn Ornaments	1973	$1	$22
Mrs. Santa 150QX100-1	Yarn Ornaments	1974	$2	$22
Mrs. Santa 175QX125-1	Yarn Ornaments	1975	$2	$19
Mrs. Santa 175QX125-1	Yarn Ornaments	1976	$2	$19
Mrs. Santa 250QX156-1	Adorable Adornments	1975	$2	$125
Mrs. Snowman 125XHD77-2	Yarn Ornaments	1973	$1	$24
Nativity 350QX253-6	Decorative Ball Ornaments	1978	$4	$125
Nativity 350QX309-6	Holiday Highlights	1978	$4	$95
Nativity 500QX181-5	Nostalgia	1977	$5	$97
New Home 350QX212-7	Commemoratives	1979	$4	$24
Night Before Christmas 350QX214-7	Decorative Ball Ornaments	1979	$4	$40
Norman Rockwell 250QX106-1	General Line	1974	$2	$45
Norman Rockwell 250QX111-1	General Line	1974	$2	$84
Norman Rockwell 250QX166-1	General Line	1975	$2	$62
Norman Rockwell 300QX134-1	General Line	1975	$3	$20
Norman Rockwell 300QX196-1	General Line	1976	$3	$78
Norman Rockwell 350QX151-5	General Line	1977	$4	$65
Old Fashion Customs Kissing Ball QX225-5	General Line	1977	$5	$147
Ornaments 350QX155-5	Christmas Expressions Collection	1977	$4	$45
Our First Christmas Together 350QX209-9	Commemoratives	1979	$4	$68
Our Twenty-Fifth Anniversary 350QX250-7	Commemoratives	1979	$4	$14
Outdoor Fun 800QX150-7	Handcrafted Ornaments	1979	$8	$120
Panorama Ball 600QX145-6	Handcrafted Ornaments	1978	$6	$140
Partridge 450QX174-1	Twirl-Abouts	1976	$4	$100
Partridge 500QX183-1	Yesteryears	1976	$5	$62
Partridge In A Pear Tree 350QX351-9	Colors Of Christmas	1979	$4	$40
Peace On Earth (Dated) 350QX131-1	Nostalgia	1975	$4	$93

Ornament Title	Series	Year	Price	Value
Peace On Earth 350QX311-5	Holiday Highlights	1977	$4	$60
Peace On Earth 400QX223-1	Nostalgia	1976	$4	$90
Peanuts (2) 400QX163-5	Peanuts Collection	1977	$4	$90
Peanuts 250QX162-2	Peanuts Collection	1977	$2	$80
Peanuts 250QX203-6	Peanuts Collection	1978	$2	$60
Peanuts 250QX204-3	Peanuts Collection	1978	$2	$70
Peanuts 350QX135-5	Peanuts Collection	1977	$4	$80
Peanuts 350QX205-6	Peanuts Collection	1978	$4	$70
Peanuts 350QX206-3	Peanuts Collection	1978	$4	$60
Peanuts: Time To Trim 350QX202-7	General Line	1979	$4	$45
Praying Angel 250QX134-3	Little Trimmers	1978	$2	$40
Quail, The- 350QX251-6	Decorative Ball Ornaments	1978	$4	$40
Rabbit 250QX139-5	Decorative Ball Ornaments	1977	$2	$90
Raggedy Andy 175QX122-1	Yarn Ornaments	1975	$2	$40
Raggedy Andy 175QX122-1	Yarn Ornaments	1976	$2	$40
Raggedy Andy 250QX160-1	Adorable Adornments	1975	$2	$275
Raggedy Ann & Raggedy Andy 400QX138-1	General Line	1975	$4	$65
Raggedy Ann & Raggedy Andy 450QX114-1	General Line	1974	$4	$90
Raggedy Ann 175QX121-1	Yarn Ornaments	1976	$2	$40
Raggedy Ann 175QX121-1	Yarn Ornaments	1975	$2	$40
Raggedy Ann 250QX159-1	Adorable Adornments	1975	$2	$160
Raggedy Ann 250QX165-1	General Line	1975	$2	$50
Raggedy Ann 250QX212-1	General Line	1976	$2	$40
Ready For Christmas 650QX133-9	Handcrafted Ornaments	1979	$6	$50
Red Cardinal 450QX144-3	Handcrafted Ornaments	1978	$4	$150
Reindeer 300QX178-1	Tree Treats	1976	$3	$55
Reindeer 600QX173-5	Yesteryears	1977	$6	$71
Reindeer Chimes 450QX320-3	Holiday Chimes	1978	$4	$35
Reindeer Chimes 450QX320-3	Holiday Chimes	1979	$4	$35
Rocking Horse 350QX128-1	General Line	1975	$4	$65
Rocking Horse 400QX128-1	General Line	1976	$4	$170
Rocking Horse 600QX148-3	General Line	1978	$6	$90
Rocking Horse, The 200QX340-7	General Line	1979	$2	$20
Rudolph & Santa 250QX213-1	General Line	1976	$2	$90
Santa & Sleigh 350QX129-1	Nostalgia	1975	$4	$150
Santa 150QX105-1	Yarn Ornaments	1974	$2	$18
Santa 175QX124-1	Yarn Ornaments	1975	$2	$25
Santa 175QX124-1	Yarn Ornaments	1976	$2	$24
Santa 175QX221-5	Cloth Doll Ornaments	1977	$2	$35
Santa 250QX135-6	Little Trimmers	1978	$2	$28
Santa 250QX155-1	Adorable Adornments	1975	$2	$100
Santa 300QX135-6	Little Trimmers	1979	$3	$28
Santa 300QX177-1	Tree Treats	1976	$3	$100
Santa 350QX307-6	Holiday Highlights	1978	$4	$80
Santa 450QX172-1	Twirl-Abouts	1976	$4	$43
Santa 500QX182-1	Yesteryears	1976	$5	$105
Santa With Elves 250XHD101-5	General Line	1973	$2	$80
Santa's Here 500QX138-7	Handcrafted Ornaments	1979	$5	$30
Santa's Motorcar 1st Ed. 900QX155-9	Here Comes Santa	1979	$9	$294
Schneeberg Bell 800QX152-3	Handcrafted Ornaments	1978	$8	$135
Seashore 250QX160-2	Beauty Of America Collection	1977	$2	$50
Shepherd 300QX175-1	Tree Treats	1976	$3	$70
Skating Raccoon 600QX142-3	Handcrafted Ornaments	1978	$6	$35
Skating Raccoon 650QX142-3	Handcrafted Ornaments	1979	$6	$35
Skating Snowman, The 500QX139-9	Handcrafted Ornaments	1979	$5	$30
Snowflake 350QX301-9	Holiday Highlights	1979	$4	$40
Snowflake 350QX308-3	Holiday Highlights	1978	$4	$65
Snowflake Collection (4) 500QX210-2	Metal Ornaments	1977	$5	$90
Snowgoose 250QX107-1	General Line	1974	$2	$70
Snowman 150QX104-1	Yarn Ornaments	1974	$2	$25

Peanuts, 1977 .... **$80**

Peanuts, 1978 .... **$70**

Peanuts: Time to Trim, 1979 . **$45**

Ready for Christmas, 1979.... **$50**

Santa With Elves, 1973 ....**$80**

Ornament Title	Series	Year	Price	Value
Snowman 450QX190-2	Twirl-Abouts	1977	$4	$78
Soldier 100XHD81-2	Yarn Ornaments	1973	$1	$16
Soldier 150QX102-1	Yarn Ornaments	1974	$2	$24
Soldier 450QX173-1	Twirl-Abouts	1976	$4	$45
Spencer Sparrow 350QX200-7	General Line	1979	$4	$25
Spencer Sparrow 350QX219-6	General Line	1978	$4	$50
Squirrel 250QX138-2	Decorative Ball Ornaments	1977	$2	$95
Stained Glass 350QX152-2	Decorative Ball Ornaments	1977	$4	$36
Star 350QX313-5	Holiday Highlights	1977	$4	$50
Star Chimes 450QX137-9	Holiday Chimes	1979	$4	$29
Star Over Bethlehem 350QX352-7	Colors Of Christmas	1979	$4	$44
Stuffed Full Stocking 200QX341-9	Sewn Trimmers	1979	$2	$24
Teacher 350QX213-9	Commemoratives	1979	$4	$21
Thimble Christmas Salute, A 2nd Ed. 400QX131-9	Thimble Series	1979	$4	$80
Thimble Series-Mouse 300QX133-6	Little Trimmers	1979	$3	$100
Thimble W/Mouse 1st Ed. 300QX133-6	Thimble Series	1978	$3	$120
Tiffany Angel Tree Topper 1000QX703-7	Tree Topper	1979	$10	$25
Toys 500QX183-5	Nostalgia	1977	$5	$67
Train 500QX181-1	Yesteryears	1976	$5	$78
Weather House 600QX191-5	Twirl-Abouts	1977	$6	$35
Wharf 250QX161-5	Beauty Of America Collection	1977	$2	$36
Winnie-The-Pooh 350QX206-7	General Line	1979	$4	$34
Words Of Christmas 350QX350-7	Colors Of Christmas	1979	$4	$78
Wreath 350QX156-2	Christmas Expressions Collection	1977	$4	$38
Wreath 350QX202-2	Colors Of Christmas	1977	$4	$60
Yesterday's Toys 350QX250-3	Decorative Ball Ornaments	1978	$4	$25

Skating Snowman, 1979 ....**$30**

Snowman, 1977, from the Twirl-Abouts series.........................**$78**

Santa's Motorcar, 1979, 1st in the Here Comes Santa series **$294**

◄Weather House, 1977, from the Twirl-Abouts series.................... **$35**

1980s

Ornament Title	Series	Year	Price	Value
Frosty Friends 10th Ed. 925QX457-2	Frosty Friends	1989	$9	$40
Frosty Friends 2nd Ed. QX433-5	Frosty Friends	1981	$8	$325
Frosty Friends 3rd Ed. 800QX452-3	Frosty Friends	1982	$8	$275
Frosty Friends 4th Ed. 800QX400-7	Frosty Friends	1983	$8	$200
Frosty Friends 5th Ed. 800QX437-1	Frosty Friends	1984	$8	$150
Frosty Friends 6th Ed. 850QX482-2	Frosty Friends	1985	$8	$125
Frosty Friends 7th Ed. 850QX405-3	Frosty Friends	1986	$8	$95
Frosty Friends 8th Ed. 850QX440-9	Frosty Friends	1987	$8	$85
Frosty Friends 9th Ed. 875QX403-1	Frosty Friends	1988	$9	$90
Rocking Horse 1st Ed. 900QX422-2	Rocking Horse	1981	$9	$425
Rocking Horse 2nd Ed. 1000QX502-3	Rocking Horse	1982	$10	$315
Rocking Horse 3rd Ed. 1000QX417-7	Rocking Horse	1983	$10	$223
Rocking Horse 4th Ed. 1000QX435-4	Rocking Horse	1984	$10	$85
Rocking Horse 5th Ed. 1075QX493-2	Rocking Horse	1985	$11	$68
Rocking Horse 6th Ed. 1075QX401-6	Rocking Horse	1986	$11	$58
Rocking Horse 7th Ed. 1075QX482-9	Rocking Horse	1987	$11	$67
Rocking Horse 8th Ed. 1075QX402-4	Rocking Horse	1988	$11	$52
Rocking Horse 9th Ed. 1075QX462-2	Rocking Horse	1989	$11	$45

Frosty Friends, 1981, 2nd in the Frosty Friends series **$325**

Rocking Horse, 1984, 4th in the Rocking Horse series............. **$85**

A Cool Yule, 1980, 1st in the Frosty Friends series **$350**

■ 1990s

Barbie: Solo in the Spotlight, 1995, 1st in the Barbie series **$15**

Ornament Title	Series	Year	Price	Value
Holiday Barbie 1st In Ed. 1495QX572-5	Holiday Barbie Collection	1993	$15	$50
Holiday Barbie 2nd In Ed. 1495QX521-6	Holiday Barbie Collection	1994	$15	$25
Holiday Barbie 3rd In Ed. QXI505-7	Holiday Barbie Collection	1995	$15	$18
Holiday Barbie 4th In Ed. QXI537-1	Holiday Barbie Collection	1996	$15	$14
Holiday Barbie 5th In Ed. QXI6212	Holiday Barbie Collection	1997	$15	$13
Holiday Barbie 6th & Final Ed. QXI402-3	Holiday Barbie Collection	1998	$16	$25

The complete set of ornaments from A Charlie Brown Christmas series
.... **$107**
The series includes Charlie Brown, Snoopy, Lucy, and Linus ornaments, plus the Snow Scene display.

Starship Enterprise, 1991, from the Star Trek series **$250**

Illustration Art

Collectors, whether looking for a distinctive decoration for a living room or seeking a rewarding long-term investment, will find something to fit their fancy — and their budget — when they turn to illustration art. Pieces of representational art — often, art that tells some sort of story — are produced in a variety of forms, each appealing in a different way. They are created as the source material for political cartoons, magazine covers, posters, story illustrations, comic books and strips, animated cartoons, calendars, and book jackets. They may be in color or in black and white. Collectible forms include:

• **Mass-market printed reproductions.** These can range from art prints and movie posters to engravings, clipped advertising art, and bookplates. While this may be the least-expensive art to hang on your wall, a few rare items can bring record prices. Heritage Auction Galleries, for example, commanded a price of $334,600 for a Universal 1935 *Bride of Frankenstein* poster (artist unidentified).

• **Limited-run reproductions.** These range from signed, numbered lithographs to numbered prints.

• Tangential items. These are hard-to-define, oddball pieces. One example is printing plates (some in actual lead; some in plastic fused to lightweight metal) used by newspapers and comic-book printers to reproduce the art.

• **Unique original art.** These pieces have the widest range of all, from amateur sketches to finished paintings. The term "original art" includes color roughs produced by a painter as a preliminary test for a work to be produced, finished oil paintings, animation cels for commercials as well as feature films, and black-and-white inked pages of comic books and strips. They may be signed and identifiable or unsigned and generic. "Illustration art" is often differentiated from "fine art," but its very pop-culture nature may increase the pool of would-be purchasers. Alberto Vargas (1896-1982) and Gil Elvgren (1914-1980) bring high prices for pin-up art; Norman Rockwell (1894-1978), James Montgomery Flagg (1877-1960), and J.C. Leyendecker (1874-1951) were masters of mainstream illustration; and Margaret Brundage (1900-1976) and Virgil Finlay (1914-1971) are highly regarded pulp artists.

Taking a look at a specific genre, consider comic-book-related illustration art. Two of the top painters in the field were heroic-fantasy artist Frank Frazetta (1928-2010) and "Disney ducks" artist Carl Barks (1901-2000). Top dollar at Heritage for a Frazetta painting was $150,000 — but, he, too, drew roughs that bring less, when they can be found. In his "retirement," Barks licensed permission to produce and sell illustrations of "his" Disney characters, and full paintings bring six-figure prices. Barks also produced many sketches for fans over the years — some simply quick pencils, that obviously go for much less — when they're available.

The original art for printed comic-book pages and covers also can command high prices, especially if they're from particularly rare or historic comics. This even applies to fairly recent works, if they're connected to important events in stories. On the other hand, it is possible to get started with original-art pages as low as $10 each.

Other comics art forms include magazine cartoons and newspaper strips. Charles Addams (1912-1988) in the former category and Charles Schulz (1922-2000) in the latter have active collecting communities. Spending time with dealers at shows, browsing online auctions, and even following favorite creators on Twitter can turn up low-priced opportunities to get a collection started. Often, art that's returned to the original writers and artists is later sold by those same creators when they need space in their studios, providing excellent opportunities to get that one-of-a-kind collectible and even get it signed by the creator. Remember: Charles Schulz gave away originals of his *Peanuts* strips — originals that bring thousands of dollars to their owners today.

— *Brent Frankenhoff and Maggie Thompson*
CBGXtra.com

All prices and scans courtesy Heritage Auction Galleries

The *Bride of Frankenstein* movie poster (Universal, 1935). **$334,600**

Sketch, black ink sketch of Harvey rabbit signed in blue ink "Harvey James Stewart" by actor James Stewart, who made the invisible rabbit character famous in the classic 1952 film "Harvey,"12-1/2" by x14-5/8". **$632.50**

Sketch, Snoopy accompanied by signature by artist Charles Schulz, on the title page of the third printed edition of the book "The Gospel According to Peanuts," sketch is in ballpoint pen and inscribed "Best Wishes, Charles M. Schulz," January 1965, 5 3/8" by 8". . **$695.75**

▶*Gasoline Alley* daily comic strip dated June 18, 1964 by Dick Moores (Chicago Tribune, 1964). **$155.35**

Carl Barks "Business as Usual" oil painting (1976), featuring Uncle Scrooge and his nephews working deep in his Money Bin, sold for $179,250 at Heritage's Feb. 24-26, 2011, Signature Sale, topping that event.

"Warrior with Ball and Chain," used as cover for *Flashing Swords* Vol. 1 paperback cover (1973). Oil on board by Frank Frazetta.. **$150,000**

Moon Mullins daily comic strip dated March 2, 1974 by Ferd Johnson (New York News Inc., 1974)......... **$10**

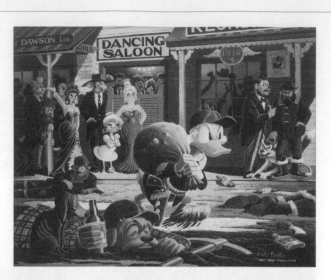

►Carl Barks "Nobody's Spending Fool" oil painting (1974) sold for $101,575 at Heritage's Feb. 24-26, 2011, Signature Sale.

▼Carl Barks "Voodoo Hoodooed" oil painting (1974) sold for $101,575 at Heritage's Feb. 24-26, 2011, Signature Sale.

▲Carl Barks "Only a Poor Old Duck" oil painting (1974) featuring Donald rowing Scrooge across a lake of money, sold for $107,550 at Heritage's Feb. 24-26, 2011, Signature Sale.

◄Wednesday Addams illustration, *Interior Design* magazine, Decorators Walk ad illustration, February 1983, ink and watercolor on paper, 11-1/4" diameter, by Charles Addams. **$3,585**

X-Men #116 cover by John Byrne and Terry Austin (Marvel, 1978)..**$65,725**

Journey into Mystery #83, Page 8, by Jack Kirby and Joe Sinnott (1st Appearance of Thor and his Enchanted Hammer Mjolnir, Marvel, 1962). **$65,725**

"The Ones," *Marvel Science* cover, May 1951. Oil on board. 18" x 11-1/2" by Norman Saunders.
....**$50,787.50**

ILLUSTRATION ART

Zap Comics #1 two-page story "Kitchen Kut-Outs" by Robert Crumb (Apex Novelties, 1968). **$47,800**

Peanuts All-Snoopy Sunday comic strip dated May 19, 1963 (United Feature Syndicate, 1963) by Charles Schulz. **$35,850**

Galaxy Science Fiction Magazine October 1962 painted cover original art, 11" x12" by Virgil Finlay. **$17,925**
▶ Speed Comics #32 Captain Freedom story, Page 2 (Harvey, 1944).............................**$101.58**

"Apocalyptic New York." *Wonder Stories* cover, February 1933. Gouache on board. 22" x 17-1/2" by Frank R. Paul.............**$20,315**

"The Altar of Melek," *Weird Tales* cover, September 1932. Pastel on paper. 20" x 17-1/2" by Margaret Brundage.................**$50,787.50**

Batman: The Dark Knight #3, Page 24, by Frank Miller and Klaus Janson (DC, 1986)........**$38,837.50**

Atomic Bunny #19 cover by Pat Masulli and George Wildman (Charlton, 1959)........................ **$250.95**

Watchmen #1, Page 1, by Dave Gibbons (DC, 1986).
....**$33,460**

Vault of Horror #22 "Fountains of Youth," Page 6, by Johnny Craig (E.C., 1952)........................**$836.50**

ILLUSTRATION ART

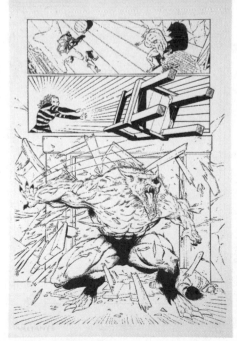

The Hawk and the Dove #3, Page 2, by Gil Kane (DC, 1968). **$507.88**

The Second Life of Doctor Mirage #2, Page 16, by Bernard Chang and Ken Branch (Acclaim, 1993). **$15**

They'll Do It Every Time Sunday comic strip dated July 10, 1949 (King Features Syndicate, 1949) by Jimmy Hatlo.. **$50**

Archie as Captain Pureheart #5, Page 7, by Bill Vigoda and Mario Acquaviva (Archie, 1967).......... **$50**

The Hugh Joseph Ward painting titled "The Evil Flame," produced for the August 1936 cover of "Spicy Mystery Stories," set a record in 2011 at public auction for a pulp magazine cover. **$143,400**

The Shadow cover, March 1932. Oil on canvas.
21-1/2" x 20-1/2" by George Rozen............**$33,460**

▶*Suicide Squad* #53, Page 16, by Geof Isherwood
and Robert Campanella (DC, 1991)....................**$10**

Top: Comic strip from January 1984 depicting Snoopy on top of his dog house by Charles Schulz. **$9,040**
Middle: Comic strip from 1969 with a football theme and Peppermint Patty as the coach by Charles Schulz.
....**$14,125**
Bottom: Comic strip dated Dec. 15, 1956, in which Lucy loses her tooth by Charles Schulz. **$18,080**

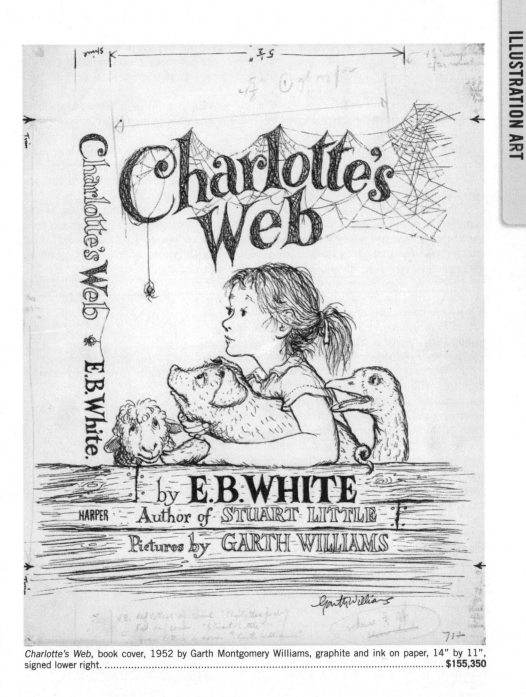

Charlotte's Web, book cover, 1952 by Garth Montgomery Williams, graphite and ink on paper, 14" by 11", signed lower right. **$155,350**

Indian Artifacts (North American)

This section covers collectible items commonly referred to as American Indian artifacts. Our interest in Native American material cultural artifacts has been long-lived, as was the Indian's interest in many of our material cultural items from an early period.

During recent years, it has become commonplace to have major sales of these artifacts by at least four major auction houses, in addition to the private trading, local auctions, and Internet sales of these items.

Anthropologists have written millions of words on American Indian cultures and societies and have standardized various regions of the country when discussing these cultures. Those standard regional definitions are continued here.

We have been fascinated with the material culture of Native Americans from the beginning of our contact with their societies. The majority of these valuable items are in repositories of museums, universities, and colleges, but many items that were traded to private citizens are now being sold to collectors of Native American material culture.

Native American artifacts are now acquired by collectors in the same fashion as any material cultural item. Individuals interested in antiques and collectibles find items at farm auction sales (an especially good place for farm family collections to be dispersed), yard sales, estate sales, specialized auctions, and from private collectors trading or selling items. The most wonderful of all sources is the Internet, especially online auction sales. There is no shortage of possibilities in finding items; it is merely deciding where to place one's energy and investment in adding to one's collection.

Native American artifacts are much more difficult to locate for a variety of reasons including the following: scarcity of items; legal protection of items being traded; more vigorous collecting of artifacts by numerous international, national, state, regional, and local museums and historical societies; frailties of the items themselves, as most were made of organic materials; and a more limited distribution network through legitimate secondary sales.

However, it is still possible to find some types of Native American items through the traditional sources of online auctions, auction houses in local communities, antique stores and malls, flea markets, trading meetings, estate sales, and similar venues. The most likely items to find in the above ways would be items made of stone, chert, flint, obsidian, and copper. Most organic materials will not have survived the rigors of a marketplace unless they were recently released from some estate or collection and their value was unknown to the previous owner.

For more information on Native American collectibles, see *Warman's North American Indian Artifacts Identification and Price Guide* by Russell E. Lewis.

Apache White Mountain Moccasins, early 1900s. Full high top moccasins with toe tab in yellow ocher, 10" long x 30" high. Allard 8-13-05. ....**$475**

Southwest

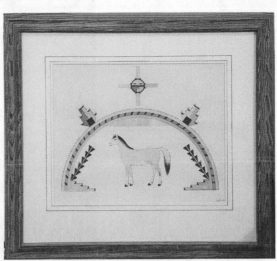

Alfonso Roybal (Awa-Tsireh) (1895-1955) Original Art. Signed pen and watercolor on paper showing a single horse and interesting symbols, image 10-1/4" x 13", framed 18" x 20". Allard 8-13-05. ....**$1,100**

Traditional Hopi Kachina. Made of traditional cottonwood in classic colors, handcarved 10-1/2" doll is placed here as an example of "Art" even though most are under Ceremonial Items below. It is without doubt that these important cultural icons served artistic purposes in addition to the ceremonial purposes in which they were involved. Allard 3-11-05......... **$450**

Acoma Polychrome Olla, circa 1900. Concave base, rounded shoulder and tapered neck with black, red/brown and orange geometric, foliate motifs and a stylized parrots on a cream-colored ground, 11" high x 13-1/2" diameter. Skinner 9-10-05. .**$29,275**

Pima Basketry Bowl, early/mid 1900s. Flat-bottomed with flared sides and zigzag patterns, 8" high x 14" diameter. Allard 3-11-05. .... **$850**

Zuni Olla, circa 1880. Shows use, no cracks, no damage or restoration, museum quality piece, 11" x 15". Allard 8-13-05.. **$16,000**

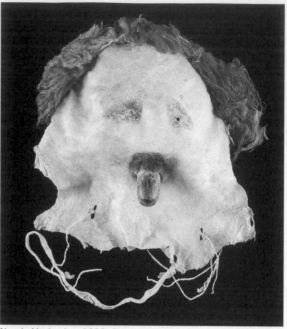

Navajo Mask, circa 1900. Possibly related to Yei-be-chai ceremony. Native tanned leather with angora across the top, painted with clay or kaolin, 17" high x 15" wide. Julia 10-05. .... **$1,610**

Santo Domingo Necklace, circa 1920s. Classic early necklace with chip inlay of turquoise in the Thunderbird design pendant and bone heshi, 24" long. Allard 8-13-05. .... **$250**

Pueblo Woman's Moccasins, circa 1900. Native tanned elk uppers with rawhide soles. Painted with yellow ocher and green, 29" high x 18" wide. Julia 10-05. .... **$575**

►Navajo Weaving, late 1800s. Fine tapestry grade weaving of classic red, gold, brown, green, etc., 45" x 30". Allard 8-13-05. ....**$2,250**

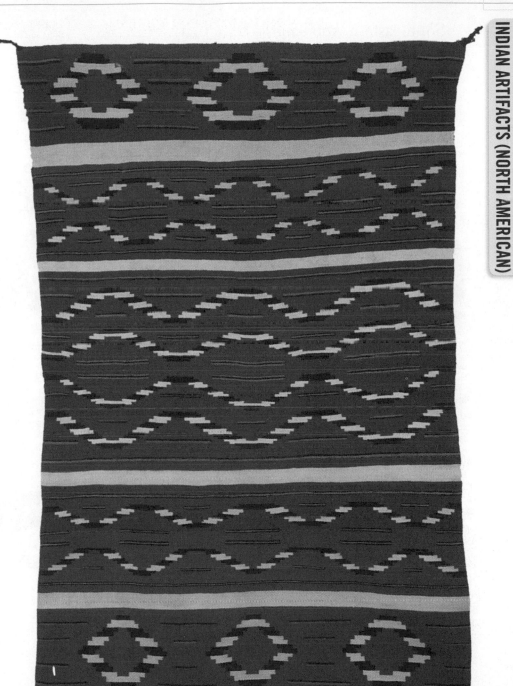

Navajo Late Classic Period Wearing Blanket, circa last quarter 19th C. Tightly woven banded pattern with background in raveled cochineal-dyed red and aniline-dyed light red, separated by ivory stripes, overlaid with deep indigo blue and ivory zigzag and stepped motifs with indigo blue and blue-green stripes, minor wool loss, 70-1/2" x 46". Provenance: Edward Everett Ayer, one of the founders and the first president, and then trustee, of the Field Museum of Natural History in Chicago. This item descended through the family and was personally collected by him prior to his death (1841-1927). Skinner 9-10-05. .... **$35,250**

INDIAN ARTIFACTS (NORTH AMERICAN)

Southeastern Woodlands

Louisiana Polychrome Twilled Lidded Basket, circa 1900. Chitimacha culture lidded form with damage to three corners, squares and rectangular designs, 5" high. Skinner 1-29-05. .... **$2,350**

▶Rare Southeastern Beaded Cloth Sash, Creek, second quarter of 19th C. Sash panel is 26-1/2" long. Black trade cloth backed with an early velvet and beaded on one side. The drops are natural dyed wool with white pony beaded edging and tassels at the ends that appear to have once been braided. Some bead loss and minor damage. Provenance: Given in the 19th C. by Native Americans in Oklahoma to Rev. B. F. Tharpe for services rendered and then descended through his family. Skinner 9-10-05.............**$10,575**

Southeastern Woman's Dress and Handbag, Seminole, circa 1920. Traditional Seminole patterns and colors made of brightly colored traditional cloth skirt and cape, applique and Seminole patchwork on cotton and rayon and a multicolored patchwork handbag, skirt length 30". Literature: "Patchwork Clothing of the Florida Indians," D. Downs, American Indian Art Magazine, Vol. 4, No. 3. Skinner 9-10-05. **$1,292.50**

◀Two prehistoric carved stone discoids from Georgia, the larger one is 5-1/4" and has an old tag reading Etowah River, Bartow Co. Georgia. Provenance: Wistariahurst Museum, Sherman Collection. Skinner 9-10-05.**$11,162.50**

◀Prehistoric carved shell gorget from Georgia, concave 4-1/8" diameter with two holes for suspension with incised and open work representing a rattlesnake. Provenance: Wistariahurst Museum, Sherman Collection. Skinner 9-10-05.
.... **$8,225**

Northeastern Woodlands

Iroquois Birch Baskets, early 1900s. Pair of oval lidded baskets of birch bark, quilled with color floral motifs on each top, 2" x 4" x 6" each. Allard 8-13-05......**$300**

Passamaquaddy Basket, circa 1900. Woven split ash basket with bentwood handles in excellent condition, a style seen throughout both the Northeast and Great Lakes regions, 9-1/2" x 9-1/2". Allard 8-13-05....................**$150**

◀Woodlands Burl Wood Bowl, early 1900s. Hardwood bowl used for mixing and mashing, 11" x 10-1/2". Allard 3-13-05. .....**$160**

▶Woodlands Sash, early 1900s. Hand woven dance sash in purple, green and red designs with woven in and hanging pony bead accents, 31-1/4" long x 4-1/4" wide plus fringe. Allard 3-13-05. ....**$250**

▼Iroquois Bag, early 1900s. Finely detailed two-sided flap pouch with floral design in small beads on brown velvet, some beads missing, 6-1/4" x 6". Allard 8-13-05...**$250**

▪ Great Lakes

Mound Builder Pipe. Prehistoric effigy pipe associated with the Hopewellian cultures of the Ohio River Valley and the Great Lakes, 7" long. Provenance: James Fowler collection. Allard 3-13-05..........................**$500**

▲Two Ojibwa Spoons, circa 1870s. Two small carved spoons found in medicine bundles, 6" x 4-1/2". Allard 3-13-05. ......**$225**

▶Very Rare and Early Huron Baby Moccasins, circa 1780-1810. Excellent and original condition, 5" long. Allard 8-14-05........**$2,500**

Ball Headed War Club, Eastern Great Lakes, 19th C. Carved of hardwood, this is actually an example of a club that would have been carried denoting the bearer was on "men's business" and not a war club. However, the design of the war clubs was similar with ball end clubs being favored in the Great Lakes and the Northeastern Woodlands. Julia 10-05. ....**$1,725**

Winnebago Beaded Cloth Man's Shirt, late 19th C. Calico pullover with wool tape ribbons, loom beaded panels on shoulders and bib, leaf pattern, tabs decorated with trade beads and wood tassels, some minor damage, 29" long. Skinner 1-29-05. .... **$2,233**

Two Great Lakes Bandolier Bags.
Left: Ojibwa, circa late 19th C. similar to ones above, 35" long. Skinner 9-10-05. .... **$2,817.50**
Right: Menominee, circa last quarter 19th C., commercial cloth, 40" long. Skinner 9-10-05. .... **$2,467.50**

Menominee Beadwork, circa 1890. French velvet panel with floral beadwork, 3-1/2" x 11". Provenance: Old tag reads "from Neopit, Wisconsin". Allard 3-13-05. ..... **$60**

■ Prairies ────────────────────────

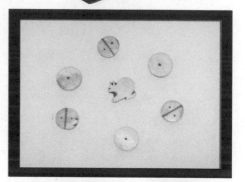

Sauk-Fox Breech Cloth, late 1800s. Early Civil War era wool cloth heavily beaded with Prairie forms, 18" x 54". Allard 3-12-05. ....**$1,100**

▶Osage Dice Game, 19th C. Six dice and one rabbit figure with incised markings and dyed blue and red, as shown in the "Art of the Osage, Saint Louis Art Museum," objects are approximately 1" diameter. Allard 8-13-05. .... **$375**

Mesquakie Sash, circa 1890s. Finger woven yarn and pony bead sash with yarn and bead fringe, excellent condition, 6' 10" x 6" wide. Provenance: Pohrt collection. Allard 3-12-05. .... **$425**

Sauk Fox/Otoe Beaded Moccasins, early 1900s. Rare and in very fine condition, 10-1/2" long. Provenance: Richard Pohrt, Sr. Collection. Allard 3-12-05. .... **$3,000**

Plains

Painted Buffalo Robe, Northern Cheyenne, circa 1880. Provenance to survivors of the Little Big Horn and owned until sale by descendants of the original 1876 Cheyenne artist. The consignor stated it was passed on to him through his family lineage and traces back to a Cheyenne named Wolf and his wife Magpie, descendants of the consignor. The cavalry figures were overpainted by the consignor's grandfather in an attempt to preserve the images. This beautiful piece measures 8' tall x 8' 4" wide and is a wealth of information about Cheyenne culture and very likely the Battle of the Little Big Horn. Apparently, provenance was strong enough to bring healthy bidding at auction. Julia 10-05.................... **$14,950**

Plains Shield and Shield Cover, late 19th C. These items were also shown from the Moon collection in Driebe's book on page 329 and are made with rawhide, tanned hides and turkey vulture buzzard feathers. Diameter of the cover is 17-1/2" and of the shield itself 16-1/4". Julia10-05. ....**$2,875**

Central Plains, Ute, Beaded Hide and Wood Cradle and Cloth Doll, circa last quarter 19th C. Some cloth and bead loss, 21" high. Skinner 9-10-05. ....**$8,812.50**

▼Blanket Strip, Sioux, circa 1870s. 49" long x 5-1/2" wide. Julia 10-05..**$5,980**

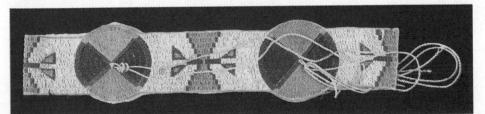

Plains Painted Wood-and-Hide Drum, 19th C. This walking bear image drum has on the opposite side a circle and dot, hide stretched over wood frame, hide strap, 19" diameter. Skinner 1-29-05................**$58,750**

Assiniboine Pipe Bag, circa 1890s. Beaded and quilled sections, native hide pipebag with many tin cone and feather drops and danglers, old tag reads "Ft. Union North Dakota", 34" x 5" wide. Allard 8-14-05. ...... **$2,750**

Lakota Sioux Beaded Hide and Cloth Saddle Blanket, late 19th C. Central panel is canvas, and beadwork is on recycled buffalo hide with cowhide fringe trim. Beads include metallic and glass seed beads and also used are brass hawk bells. Skinner 9-10-05.
.... **$2,585**

Plains Tomahawk, circa third quarter 19th C. Handle has typical Plains adornment of tacks, original beaded drop has been repaired and a newer piece added to the buffalo hide original, head is forged; it is 23-1/2" long. Skinner 9-10-05. ....**$10,575**

Apache Bear Claw Necklace, late 19th C. Provenance: Moon collection. Consists of nine grizzly claws and eight black bear claws attached to buffalo hide and edged with red felt similar to that used for the backing on buffalo lap robes. The metallic and blue beads used as spacers are of an unknown origin. Driebe shows this at page 322 in his book on Moon. Julia 10-05.................... **$3,450**

Kiowa Awl Case, circa 1900. Sinew sewn, yellow ocher stained awl case with lazy stitch beaded designs and a buttoning top flap, 11" x 2-3/4". Allard 8-13-05. .....**$700**

Ute Tail Bag, circa 1870. Beaded tail bag with sinew sewn beadwork on buffalo hide, an early example, 3-1/2" x 13" long. Allard 8-14-05.................... **$1,500**

Sioux Pipe, circa 1860. Black stone pipe bowl with wood stem, 16-1/2" x 2-1/2". Provenance: Collected from Chief Wacoutas Band, Prairie Island, Minnesota Sioux. Allard 8-14-05. .... **$650**

Arapaho Pipe Bag, circa 1890. Sinew sewn buckskin pipebag with lizards beaded on top, terminated with quilled slats and fringe, all original, 8" x 32" long. Allard 3-11-05. .... **$4,000**

Southern Plains Beaded Hide Coat, last quarter 19th C. This yellow stained with red details coat with fringe also has black faceted and mescal beads, 20" long. Provenance: Collected during the 1889 Oklahoma Land Rush by Fred H. Reed and descended in his family. Skinner 1-29-05. .... **$19,975**

Southern Plains, Kiowa, Hard Sole Buffalo Hide Moccasins, circa 1870s. Partially beaded and trimmed with red trade cloth. Skinner 9-10-05. ....**$15,275**

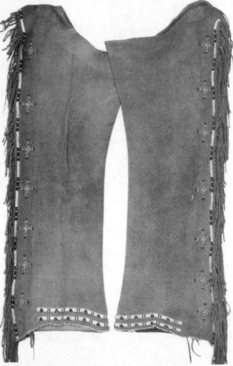

Plains Hide Scraper, circa 1870. 5" x 12". Provenance: Pawnee Bill Museum. Allard 8-14-05. .... **$475**

Plains Trade Axe, mid-19th C. Old fur trade axe with a long haft and leather grip at the end and nice patina, hallmarked P.C. Allard 3-11-05. .... **$275**

Southern Cheyenne Leggings, 1870s. Sinew sewn beadwork on green and yellow ocher stained elk hide, trimmed with brass shoe buttons, 12" x 30". Provenance: Richard Pohrt, Sr. collection. Allard 8-14-05 .... **$3,250**

Plateau Region (Intermountain)

Blackfoot Leggings, circa 1880. Calico-backed leggings with beaded panels, 13" x 13". Allard 8-14-05........................ **$1,300**

Above: Flathead Skirt, early 1900s. Older thread sewn black/navy trade cloth skirt with large floral designs and trim done with glass tube beads, 36" waist and 32" long. Allard 8-13-05. .... **$1,000**

Left: Nez Perce Beaded Flat Bag, circa 1900. Classic Plateau designs with an elk and floral patterns, 11" x 13". Allard 8-14-05. .... **$650**

Above left: Crow Moccasins, circa 1890. Buffalo hide soles, false vamps, partially beaded moccasins, museum quality, 10-1/2". Provenance: Honnen collection. Allard 8-14-05. .... **$1,900**

INDIAN ARTIFACTS (NORTH AMERICAN)

▶Quilled Cloth Bag, Cree, first half 19th C. Made of blue trade cloth with silk applique details, decorated with tightly loomed geometric quillwork with quill wrapped hide loops and white seed bead spacers below the panels. It has a braided cloth strap and is lined with cloth ticking. An old paper label says "This Indian bag was made by squaws and used by Titian Peale during Longs Rocky Mountain Expedition in 1819-1820." The reverse of the paper says "Holmesberg Feb. 4, 1876." The bag has some minor loss and is 10-3/4" long. Provenance: Supposedly purchased from the direct descendants of the Peale family by Wesley Crozier of Red Bank, New Jersey. Exhibitions: Monmouth (NJ) County Library. Skinner 9-10-05....**$94,000**

▼Piegan Pipe Bag, circa 1870. Buffalo hide bag beaded on both sides with beaded bottom fringe, 5-1/2" x 21". Allard 8-14-05. .... **$1,600**

Blackfoot Dress, late 19th C. Made of red trade cloth and decorated heavily with seed beads and pink basket beads; 51" tall and 45" wide. Julia 10-05...**$2,587.50**

California

Pictorial Coiled Basketry Bowl, Yokuts, circa late 19th C. Flared form pictorial bowl with four rows of two color rattlesnake design and a top row of humans holding hands in alternating colors, some restoration done to this piece, 7-1/2" high x 17-1/4" diameter. Skinner 9-10-05...**$14,100**

Hupa Lidded Basket, early 1900s. Rare fine-weave lidded basket with excellent black and red designs and top knot handle on lid, 10" high x 9-1/2" diameter. Allard 8-13-05........**$2,000**

INDIAN ARTIFACTS (NORTH AMERICAN)

◼ Northwest Pacific Coastal ────────────

Skokomish Basket, circa 1900. Large storage basket with dog figures encircling the rim, excellent shape, 13" x 13". Allard 8-14-05. ....**$3,000**

Puget Sound Clam Basket, circa 1880. Cedar root basket in excellent condition and a rare example, 16" x 22". Allard 8-14-05. ....**$650**

NW Coastal Painted and Carved Wood Mask, Tsimshian, second half 19th C. This item was the high of the 9-10-05 Skinner Auction at $259,000, as apparently the provenance was solid and the age of the mask important, as well as the articulating mouth. The mask is a cedar form with both an articulated lower jaw and articulated eyes, part of the articulation device remains on the mask. It is in a form with both human and bird features, it has red lips and nostrils over a graphite-like black pigment. The outer edge of the mask is decorated with cedar bark bundles nailed to the edge, patina on mask from use, 14" high. Provenance: Collected by Garnet West in 1952 from Rev. Shearman, Kitkatla Reserve, Prince Rupert, British Columbia. Note: "Over 200 years old, worn by Chief Gum-I-gum, meaning 'Brave Man'." Skinner 9-10-05. ....**$259,000**

►Haida Totem Pole, 1890. Very detailed old hand-carved totem pole with six figures, concave back and covered in a reddish paint or stain, 16-1/2" high. Allard 3-11-05. **$1,000**

Rare Wasco Bag, 19th C. Loomed octopus bandolier bag with sinew and thread sewn pony beads. Skeletal figures on both sides with shell wampum and abalone drops, 7-1/2" x 39", very rare piece. Allard 8-13-05. .... **$10,000**

Subarctic

▲Blackfoot Telescope, 19th C. Brass telescope covered with beadwork. An old tag reads "Blackfeet Indian Spy Glass, Arrowwood, Alberta, Canada," 2" x 9". Allard 8-13-05. .... **$500**

◄Aleutian Basket, circa 1900. Extremely finely woven lidded treasure basket with checks done in blue and red yarns, 5-1/4" x 6-1/2". Allard 8-13-05.**$550**

Arctic

Inuit Wooden Utility Box and Contents, circa late 19th C. A rare find of numerous early Inuit items from the late 19th C. Box includes five early trade beads inlaid on the lid, contents include ulus, saw, pipe, wood bow drill, animal teeth, kayak cleats, miniature pair of mukluks, and other items; box is 7" high x 17" long. Skinner 1-29-05. .. **$10,575**

Above left: Eskimo Carved Soapstone Figure, late 1800s. Hand-carved mottled soapstone human figure with parka, hood, and boots, arms are missing, 3-3/4" tall. Allard 8-13-05. .... **$225**

Above right: Inuit Moccasins, early 1900s. Rare pair of hard-soled seal skin child's boots, 4" x 5" x 2-1/2". Allard 3-12-05. .... **$70**

Inuit Basketry, circa 1900. Very rare lidded baleen basket tipped with a carved walrus head, 3-1/2" x 4-1/2". Allard 8-14-05. .... **$1,000**

Ivory

Ivory is a term for dentine, which comes from the teeth and tusks of animals such as elephants. Since ancient times, ivory has been used to make a multitude of items, the most notable being carvings. The biggest source of ivory is from elephants, but ivory has also come from hippopotamus, walrus, mammoth, and narwhal. Owing to the rapid decline in the populations of the animals that produce it, today the importation and sale of ivory in many countries is banned or severely restricted.

Box w/hinged cover, rectangular, the sides & top composed of thick pieces of ivory incised & drilled w/bands of roundels of various sizes, the interior of the top lined w/a tartan plaid material centered by a rectangular mirror, 19th c., some old age cracks, 4 x 4 1/2", 2 1/4" h. **$978**

Plaque a pointed pediment carved in high-relief w/a spread-winged American eagle above a shield & long leaves, above a long rectangular panel carved in high-relief w/a scene of Washington Crossing the Delaware, in original embossed leather & velvet fitted case, American, late 19th c., 9 3/4" l., 7 1/2" h. **$5,019**

Sculpture, a parade of elephants, each connected & carved in graduated sizes from a single tusk, mounted on a carved wood stand, probably China, 20th c., 21" l. **$575**

Right: Figure group, a tall slender Chinese mother standing beside her child, flanking a short tree trunk w/a colorful parrot, each figure w/dark polychrome decoration, probably China, late 19th - early 20th c., 5" w., 16" h. **$900**

Far right: Figure of a Buddhist Immortal, a tall gently curved tusk carved as the figure of a bearded man w/a high bald head & a bare chest & belly, holding a fan in one hand & prayer beads in the other, on a round black wood base, Oriental, mid-20th c., minor loss, 13 1/2" h. **$489**

Jewelry

Jewelry has held a special place for humankind since prehistoric times, both as an emblem of personal status and as a decorative adornment worn for its sheer beauty. This tradition continues today. We should keep in mind, however, that it was only with the growth of the Industrial Revolution that jewelry first became cheap enough so that even the person of modest means could win a piece or two.

Only since around the mid-19th century did certain forms of jewelry, especially pins and brooches, begin to appear on the general market as a mass-produced commodity and the Victorians took to it immediately. Major production centers for the finest pieces of jewelry remained in Europe, especially Italy and England, but less expensive pieces were also exported to the booming American market and soon some American manufacturers also joined in the trade. Especially during the Civil War era, when silver and gold supplies grew tremendously in the U.S., did jewelry in silver or with silver, brass or gold-filled (i.e. gold-plated or goldplate) mounts begin to flood the market here. By the turn of the 20th century all the major mail-order companies and small town jewelry shops could offer a huge variety of inexpensive jewelry pieces aimed at not only the female buyer but also her male counterpart.

Inexpensive jewelry of the late 19th and early 20th century is still widely available and often at modest prices. Even more in demand today is costume jewelry, well-designed jewelry produced of inexpensive materials and meant to carefully accent a woman's ensemble. Today costume jewelry of the 20th century has become one of the most active areas in the field of collecting and some of the finest pieces, signed by noted designers and manufacturers, can reach price levels nearly equal to much earlier and scarcer examples.

Jewelry prices, as in most collecting fields, are influenced by a number of factors including local demand, quality, condition and rarity. As market prices have risen in recent years it has become even more important for the collector to shop and buy with care. Learn as much as you can about your favorite area of jewelry and keep abreast of market trends and stay alert to warnings about alterations, repairs or reproductions that can be found on the market.

For more information on jewelry, see *Warman's Jewelry Identification and Price Guide*, 4th edition, by Kathy Flood.

Pearls

Pearls have been with us for ages. The earliest pearl jewelry is almost 45 centuries old.

Pearls became available to the general public in 1921. Ironically, it was the oyster shell's mother-of-pearl lining that was sought after for centuries. In the 1700s, Polynesian divers discarded the pearls. All anyone cared about was the creature's seafood (to eat) and its abalone (to inlay as decoration).

When everything goes as planned and a perfect pearl is formed, its quality is graded by origin, size, shape, nacre thickness, color, luster, surface clarity and matching (one to another in a strand).

Edwardian diamond, pearl, white gold "jabot" (meaning an ornamental cascade of ruffles or frills), Cartier, French, features mine-, single- and rose-cut diamonds, highlighted by a pearl measuring 4.00-3.50mm, set in 18k white gold. Marked Cartier Paris, reference number 2463. French hallmarks, gross weight 7.00 grams, 3-3/8" x 1"......................**$8,365**
Courtesy Heritage Auction Galleries

Ring, natural pearl, diamond and platinum, centering a gray natural pearl measuring 12.80mm, the shoulders with channel-set baguette diamonds and bead-set, full-cut diamond mélée, signed, France.............................**$18,800**

The Cultured Pearl Association of America (CPAA) notes the finest pearls once came from the Persian Gulf. The burgeoning oil industry lured away pearl divers in the 1930s, and subsequent pollution destroyed the pristine environment of the waters. Mexico looked to be big in the cultured-pearl industry, but its oyster banks were over-fished as early as the 1940s.

Most pearls come from Japan, Australia, Indonesia, Burma (officially the Union of Myanmar), China, India, the Philippines and Tahiti. South Seas waters around Australia, Indonesia and Burma are famed for large white pearls, while Japan's are treasured for luster. China has been most known for freshwater pearls, and India is one of the last strongholds of naturally occurring pearls.

No discussion of pearls is complete without mention of Mikimoto Kokichi (1858-1954), who set out to create the cultured-pearl industry. Mikimoto began raising oysters in 1888. Tireless research, experimentation and application of the Mise-Nichikawa method finally led to the day in July 1893 when he successfully created a spherical pearl. He's considered the father of the modern commercial cultured-pearl industry, combining business savvy and marketing acumen to successfully promote them around the world.

◄Onyx, cultured pearl, gold brooch, features an oval-shaped onyx cameo, depicting a lady's profile, framed by cultured pearls, set in 14k yellow gold, completed by a pin stem and catch mechanism on the reverse, 1-3/4" x 1-1/2"... **$717**
Courtesy Heritage Auction Galleries

Golden South Seas cultured pearl, diamond, gold necklace, designed with a dogwood blossom motif, features golden South Seas cultured pearls ranging in size from 13.50 x 12.00mm to 12.00 x 11.00mm, enhanced by rose- and full-cut diamonds weighing a total of 10.49 carats, set in 18k yellow gold with rhodium finished accents, 18" x 5/8". **$13,145**
Courtesy Heritage Auction Galleries

Black South Seas cultured pearl, diamond, white gold suite, includes a graduated necklace, featuring black South Seas cultured pearls ranging in size from 22.50 - 22.00mm to 10.00 - 9.50mm, enhanced by full-cut diamonds, pavé set in 18k white gold; a matching bracelet; a matching ring; together with a matching pair of earrings, each completed by a post with clip back on the reverse. Total diamond weight for the suite is approximately 39.00 carats. Necklace 18" x 13/16"; bracelet 8" x 5/8"; earrings 1-1/16" x 3/4"; ring size 5. .... **$23,900 suite**
Courtesy Heritage Auction Galleries

Natural pearl, diamond, white gold necklace, composed of pearls, ranging in size from 6.00 to 4.00mm, forming a single knotted strand, completed by a barrel clasp, featuring rose-cut diamonds, pavé set in 18k white gold, accented by mine-cut diamonds, 65". **$10,755**
Courtesy Heritage Auction Galleries

"Umbel and Corymb" necklace of "Kasumi" pearls, grown in lake Kazumiga-Ura in northern Japan from a Lake Biwa/Chinese Mussel hybrid. Photo shows unusual bronze and gold colors, and unique characteristic crinkled nacre patterns. Clasp is 14k rose gold with "Padparascha" sapphires; 16" necklace, 12-13mm pearls...**$13,600**
Jewelry © Eve Alfillé; photo by Matthew Arden

"French Lace" bracelet from the Antiquities Series, 18k white gold, cultured Akoya pearls, yellow and white diamonds, 7" long-1/2" wide. **$8,240**
Jewelry © Eve Alfillé; photo by Matthew Arden

"Luscious fruit" earrings from "Umbel & Corymb" series, asymmetrical, 14k gold, diamonds framing large cultured Chinese freshwater pearls; 1"...**$1,960**
Jewelry © Eve Alfillé; photo by Matthew Arden

◄Edwardian pearl and diamond brooch, 15k bar and clasp are topped with a platinum-finished oval, encircled with twelve natural oriental pearls. Rhomboid and fleur de lis diamond accents frame the oval; 12 single-cut and rose-cut diamonds, circa 1905. .... **$900**
Photo courtesy www.Topazery.com

JEWELRY

Jadeite

The term "jade" covers two different rock minerals: nephrite and jadeite. Different chemical compounds compose them. In jewelry, the focus is on gem-quality jadeite, a silicate of sodium and aluminum. The best and most coveted jadeite is from Burma (now generally called Myanmar, but still often referred to as Burma in jade circles). Its color may be one of a rich variety of green shades, Imperial to apple, then lavender, white, and from there the basic color chart varies, with some calling remaining shades red, yellow or black, versus gray, brown, orange and colorless.

Cufflinks, jadeite and diamonds, double link jadeite pi's, 14k gold millegrain accents, gold and platinum mounts, bezel-set old European-cut diamonds, 5/8". **$7,650**

Image courtesy Skinner Inc.

Pagoda brooch, jadeite, polychrome enamel, 14k gold mount, carved, pierced jadeite plaque depicting bird among flowers, Sloan & Co., signed, 1-1/4". . **$4,150**
Image courtesy Skinner Inc.

Peacock brooch, jadeite cabochons, rubies, diamonds, considered excellent design for its balance, detailed execution, use of varied-color gems. Betty Ma notes, "Chinese artists are partial to peacocks, from paintings, embroideries and carvings. The jadeite stones are vibrant, translucent, colors well matched. Use of rubies and sapphires is well integrated. This peacock represents what I would like Chinese-Americans, Americans and all jewelry lovers to think of jadeite: a piece of art in its natural, untreated form, and modern when done tastefully. This piece has it all. The person who created it was well trained and knew when to stop with the materials on hand," 1968-72, 2-1/4". .... **$5,000-$7,000**
Jewelry courtesy Lee Shau Kwan, Esther Woo Jan; image by John F. Pipia

Carved peapod ear pendants, vivid emerald-green translucent jadeite pods linked by diamonds and jadeite beads, brilliant-cut diamond surmount, 18k white gold, peapods approximately 1-5/8". **$591,000**
© *Christie's Images Limited 2009*

Animal bracelet, two dragon heads, white mutton-fat nephrite jade bangle, nine carved balls as tails, mouths hold pearl; very rare; 2 12" diameter, 19th century. **$2,000**

Double-headed tiger bracelet, plastic turquoise cabochons, antique-gold plated metal, crystal baguettes and brilliants, high-domed glass igloo cabochons in heads, 7/8" thick, 1968, signed K.J.L. .... **$1,200-$1,800**

Walter Lampl jadeite dress clip, carved translucent green jadeite frog atop carved white jade leaf; natural seed pearl eyes; clip marked WI STERLING and PAT. 1852188, 1932, 1-1/2".....**$150**
Rocky Day photo

Double dragons simulated carved jadeite spring-hinged cuff bracelet, faux coral cabochons, emeralds and diamonds, fancy cast 22k gold-plated metal, 3-1/2" wide, signed © KJL, 1960s. **$240**
Jewelry courtesy Kenneth Jay Lane

KJL bangle, all-resin bracelet, molded simulated jadeite, wavy shape, 1-1/2" high, 2009, signed © Kenneth Lane.. **$50**
Jewelry courtesy Kenneth Jay Lane

Simulated jadeite comet set, fur clip pin and matching earrings, creamy faux jadeite cabochons and slim blue gold-specked art-glass navettes, 3-1/2" clip, 1-1/4" earrings, signed Hattie Carnegie, 1950s. .... **$179 set**

Walter Lampl jadeite brooch and ring set, 14k gold, highly polished carved green jadeite imported from China, surrounded by tiny natural seed pearls, finished in 14k gold frame. Brooch marked WL 14k; ring marked 14k WL. Fine examples of Lampl jewelry. Pin 2", ring 7/8", 1920s. ....**$1,125 set**
Courtesy Milky Way Jewels; Rocky Day photo

JEWELRY

■ Cameos

An ancient jewelry form dating from 4th century B.C. Alexandria, where the art of engraving precious stones began, the cameo is a carving in relief on materials such as gem, hardstone or shell, showing contrast between foreground and background.

For investment and resale considerations right now, antiques cameos remain where the money is. Qualities that affect value most are crisp, lifelike carving detail; subject or theme; age; materials; setting; size; condition; artist signature.

As far as subjects go, the more unusual, the more valuable.

Not a bore: Rare antique Commesso cameo of mythological goddess; superb example using shell, coral, malachite, mother of pearl and mottled agate, incorporating multiple attributes of mythological goddesses, as well as Maenad (bacchante maiden). Base cameo is shell, different colored stones applied to create total artwork; great example of liberties some Victorian artists took with mythology, this cameo exhibiting attributes of four different mythological figures, all rolled into one: fruits or flowers in hair associated with Flora; crown associated with Hera; animal pelt associated with Omphale or maenads; bow associated with Diana; 14k gold mount; Italian, circa 1870, 2-1/4". **$2,500**
Jewelry courtesy Camelot Cameos and Antiques; photo by Kerry Davidson

Large hardstone cameo of Cupid (Eros) walking with a lion. This cameo is taken from a set of four bas-reliefs by Bertel Thorvaldsen depicting love's power over the elements. It shows love's power over the earth (represented by the lion). Rare subject, Italian, circa 1860, 18k gold and pearl pendant/brooch frame, superbly carved in high relief, 2-1/2". **$6,500**
Jewelry courtesy Camelot Cameos and Antiques; photo by Kerry Davidson

Cameo, "The Cupids Seller," lava carving with pierce work, 14k gold setting, 4-1/2", circa 1850 (with contemporary gold setting)................................. **$2,800**
Cameo courtesy Aesthetic Engineering Fine Jewels and Antiques; photo by Jacquelyn Babush

High relief lava cameo of Medusa, Italian, circa 1850, frontal facing, finely carved, set in 15k gold brooch frame, 1-1/2". **$2,500**

Hardstone Medusa cameo carved using three layers, exquisite high relief carving, drooping wings and snakes in hair, snake fillet under neck, Italian, 18k gold brooch mount, circa 1870, 1-3/4". **$4,500**

Museum-quality cameo, Aphrodite with love doves and eternal flame of love; 15-18k gold, not marked, tested. Only best goldsmiths work this type of setting; circa 1850-60; 2-1/2", rare theme. **$1,895**
Courtesy Jan Campbell Collection; photo by Jan Campbell

Weekdays cameo bracelet, gold-plated silver .925, lava stone from Vesuvius, each stone 7/8", 2009, unsigned, by carver Claudio Terminio.
.... **$850**
Jewelry images courtesy CASCO, www.cascosrl.it

Large hardstone cameo of Athena with Pegasus on her helmet and a large Medusa's head on her breastplate (aegis). Italian, mid 19th century, exquisitely carved and set in superb gold Etruscan-revival bead and wire-work brooch frame, 2-5/8", scratch-signed on back, signature carved into side of left shoulder by Luigi Isler. .. **$7,500-$10,000**
Jewelry courtesy Camelot Cameos and Antiques, photo by Kerry Davidson

Fancy 18-carat gold bracelet containing a high-relief carved malachite cameo of frontal-facing Eros (Cupid) with bow and arrows. In original box with stamp of the jeweler's shop where sold, "Poile & Smith from Pickett's Court Jewelers, 620 Oxford St. W."; mid-19th century. **$7,500**
Jewelry courtesy Camelot Cameos and Antiques; photo by Kerry Davidson

◄Cameo brooch, pretty Twenties Flapper with her equine companion, carnelian helmet shell, 4-point diamond necklace set en habille, silver filigree, 1920, 1-1/2". **$1,595**
Jewelry courtesy CameoHeaven.com; photo by Jan Campbell

JEWELRY

Georgian/Victorian/Edwardian

Georgian jewels were made before the Industrial Revolution of the 1840s, and the crafting of the pieces was labor-intensive. It's not unusual to see tool marks on the backs of Georgian jewels. All the stones, whether precious or imitation, were set by hand.

From 1837-1901—the longest reign of any monarch in the history of England—Queen Victoria set the tempo for England in its totality: fashion, culture, politics, and societal matters. Victoria set the tone for everything, including jewelry.

Three divisions are identified with the Victorian era. The early Romantic period runs from 1837-1860. The Mid (Grand) Victorian period runs from 1860-1885 (but some sources end the mid-Victorian Period as early as 1880). The third division is the Late (Aesthetic) period, which runs from 1880-1901.

Edward was the first son of Victoria and Albert. As King Edward VII, he ruled from 1901 to 1910. These nine years (and several before and beyond) comprise the Edwardian era, which featured jewelry that was lighter, more open and delicate. It was almost colorless in terms of the glass and stones used, although pastel-colored stones were popular. Enameling was used to create color.

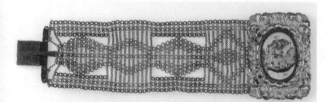

Silesian Ironworks bracelet, early piece of jewelry dating to Georgian era, German, from Silesia, where iron mines were located. Silesian Ironworks and Berlin Ironworks produced iron mesh jewelry, although Berlin examples were less intricately meshed and flexible than Silesian's. The buckle portion is wider, features landscape scene on background of what is possibly mica; 7-1/4", 2" wide, late 1700s. .... **$500+**
Private Collection

Brooch, gold and hand-painted, mourning-type, a thin gold mount and frame enclosing a long oval hand-painted scene of a memorial obelisk centered by a covered urn above initials against a landscape of hairwork poplar trees and inked details, the back inscribed and dated 1782, England, 1-1/4" l.
.... **$2,500**

French portrait miniature brooch, paining on ivory, 18k gallery, 1830s, 2-1/2". **$2,600**
Jewelry courtesy the Steve Fishbach Collection; photo by Linda Lombardo

◄European miniature portrait painting on enamel pin, circa 1880s, 18k gallery with diamonds, 1-5/8". **$2,500**
Jewelry courtesy the Steve Fishbach Collection; photo by Linda Lombardo

English silver locket with inlaid multicolor gold, circa 1880s, 18". **$2,800**
Jewelry courtesy the Steve Fishbach Collection; photo by Linda Lombardo

European carved moonstone pin with rose diamonds and rubies, silver front, gold back, circa 1860, 1".......................... **$9,500**
Jewelry courtesy the Steve Fishbach Collection; photo by Linda Lombardo

Enameled portrait pin, 18k gold, circa 1880s, 1"................... **$950**
Jewelry courtesy the Steve Fishbach Collection; photo by Linda Lombardo

Gutta percha link chain with later Bakelite and Lucite cameo attached, 1870s, 18"............ **$195**
Jewelry and image courtesy Linda Lombardo, Worn to Perfection on Ruby Lane

Gold locket with mine-cut diamonds, rubies and emeralds, 15k gold on 14k gold slide chain, circa 1880s, 2-1/8" on 26" chain.
.... **$12,000**
Jewelry courtesy the Steve Fishbach Collection; photo by Linda Lombardo

English Banded Agate locket with hair aperture, set in 15K gold, Inscribed "from CT Wright to WMS Ainsley", 3".................... **$3,500**
22k gold Indian chain, circa 1900, 21"......................... **$500**
Jewelry courtesy the Steve Fishbach Collection; photo by Linda Lombardo

Black hairwork set, necklace and bracelet, horse hair, metal charms (bracelet charm missing), unmarked, 15" and 7", 1880s-1900.........................**$400-$550**

Bracelets, Bohemian rose-cut garnets, circa 1880s, 3/4" wide.
.... **$1,500 each**
Jewelry courtesy the Steve Fishbach Collection; photo by Linda Lombardo

Victorian earrings, jet, polished, faceted balls dangle from decorative pearl and enamel panel, later converted to screwbacks, 1-1/4", 1900................................. **$100**

JEWELRY

Low-karat gold mourning pin with hair aperture and lock of hair, 1870s, 1-1/4". **$150**
Jewelry and image courtesy Linda Lombardo, Worn to Perfection on Ruby Lane

Essex crystal brooch with enameled edge, European hallmarks, circa 1880s, 2". **$4,500**
Jewelry courtesy the Steve Fishbach Collection; photo by Linda Lombardo

Sash pin with large amber-colored glass, circa 1900, unmarked, 2-1/2". **$125**
Jewelry and image courtesy Linda Lombardo, Worn to Perfection on Ruby Lane

Sash pin with enormous red faceted glass, circa 1900, unmarked, 3". **$120**
Jewelry and image courtesy Linda Lombardo, Worn to Perfection on Ruby Lane

Amethyst cabochon and rose diamond bracelet set in 14k gold, circa 1900s, 7-1/4". **$3,500**
Jewelry courtesy the Steve Fishbach Collection; photo by Linda Lombardo

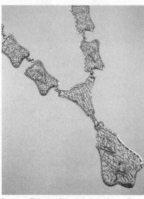

Late Edwardian/early Art Deco pierced segmented rhodium plated necklace, 17-1/2". ... **$195**
Jewelry and image courtesy Linda Lombardo, Worn to Perfection on Ruby Lane

Sash pin with large amethyst colored glass, circa 1900, 2-1/2". **$95**
Jewelry and image courtesy Linda Lombardo, Worn to Perfection on Ruby Lane

Georgian stomacher, chain added to convert to necklace in Victorian period; rose-cut diamonds, emeralds set in silver, with gold pinchbeck; 3-3/4", circa 1820; chain 30". **$8,500**
Jewelry courtesy the Steve Fishbach Collection; photo by Linda Lombardo

Lover's locket, natural pearls and carnelian, two hair compartments, 1800s, 18k gold, 2-1/4". **$550**
Jewelry courtesy the Steve Fishbach Collection; photo by Linda Lombardo

◄German-made 900 silver, ivory and lapis brooch, 1900, 3". **$2,500**
Jewelry courtesy the Steve Fishbach Collection; photo by Linda Lombardo

Art Nouveau

Cited dates for Art Nouveau vary, from as early as 1880 as to as late as 1919. The most widely accepted peak years are usually defined as 1895-1910.

The familiar characteristics of Art Nouveau include sinuous asymmetry; undulating whiplash lines; dreamy, organic ornamental flourishes; stylized interpretations of nature; fantastic symbols with undercurrents of darkness; idealized view of woman; and attempted universal beauty aesthetic.

Art nouveau sterling set, necklace and cuff bracelet, necklace with 6" bird in flight (fits 18" neck), cuff with unique fit, measures 2-1/2" wide; unsigned, hallmarked sterling. .... **$500+**
Private Collection

Liberty & Co. moonstone necklace, circa 1900, 2-1/3" drop, British. **$3,650**
Jewelry courtesy Didier Antiques London; image by Adam Wide

Art Nouveau bat ring, 14k gold, circa 1900, J.F. Chatellier, New York.................................. **$9,200**
Jewelry courtesy Didier Antiques, London; image by Adam Wide

Pendant La Bretonne, Art Nouveau enamel and multi-gem piece, sculpted gold female bust in profile, calibré-cut opal costume, bonnet extending to form scrolling frame, enhanced with single old European rose-cut diamond trim, carved amethyst sleeve against openwork green and yellow enamel floral background suspending drop-shaped amethyst cabochon from detachable rose-cut diamond foliate hoop, mounted in gold, circa 1900, showing a traditional motif (young French Breton woman) in the new style; signed Vever for Henri Vever, Paris. October 2009 auction estimate **$400,000-$600,000, unsold**
© Christie's Images Ltd. 2009

Far left: Bernard Instone pendant/brooch, chrysophase, chalcedony, carnelian, 1920s, 2-3/4", British **$1,245**
Jewelry courtesy Didier Antiques London; Image by Adam Wide

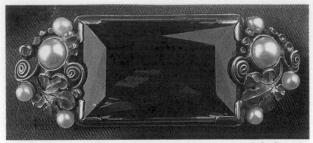

Brooch, green tourmaline, seed pearl and 14k gold, Arts & Crafts style, centered by a long rectangular fancy-cut green tourmaline flanked by scroll and floret gold ends accented with seed pearls, unsigned piece by Edward Oakes, early 20th century, 5/8 x 1-1/2"...................**$5,600**

Choker, gem-set 14k yellow gold, Art Nouveau style, composed of openwork looped & serpentine links highlighted with seed pearls, diamonds, rubies, sapphires or turquoise, joined by trace link chains, American hallmark, late 19th - early 20th century, 13" l................................**$3,800**

Newlyn School large garnet pendant, silver, circa 1900, 3-1/2" drop, British.................... **$2,740**
Jewelry courtesy Didier Antiques London; image by Adam Wide

Art Nouveau gold, plique-a-jour enamel and freshwater pearl brooch, centering three flared leaves applied with green plique-a-jour enamel, accented with gold veins, outlined in gold, the stem continuing to an open modified oval, supporting drooping flowers fashioned as freshwaterpearls, enhanced by gold caps and curved stems, circa 1900, missing one small enamel section at tip of one leaf, center pearl possibly replaced, 3-1/8" x 2". **$3,000**
Photo courtesy Doyle New York

Pendant, emerald, diamond and enamel, Art Nouveau style, a large central cabochon emerald and a teardrop emerald drop, the cabochon within a gold scroll mount framed by 47 old European-cut diamonds, platinum-topped 18k gold mount, chased and engraved on the reverse, by Marcus & Co., later pin stem, some enamel loss. **$17,625**

Above right: Pendant-necklace, black opal, diamond and 14k gold, Arts & Crafts style, the delicate fancy link gold chain fitted with an oblong gold slide decorated with tiny pine cones and leaves, and enclosing an oblong black opal, suspending an ornate long gold-frame pendant with open leafy scrolls with tiny pine cones flanking a large almond-shaped black opal above an openwork spear-point frame set with five old European-cut diamonds suspending a black opal teardrop, mark of William Bramley, Montreal and "14B," 15"..**$17,625**

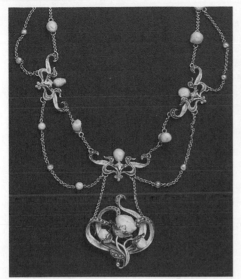

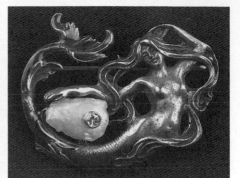

Brooch, enameled 14k gold and freshwater pearl, Art Nouveau style, an openwork design of a swimming mermaid with swirling hair and red basse-taille enameled tail, a freshwater pearl mounted below her extended arm, diamond accents. **$400**

Pendant necklace, enamel, pearl and 14k yellow gold, Art Nouveau style, the bottom pendant in the form of stylized freshwater pearl blossoms on scrolling leafy stems enameled in shaded orange and pale green and trimmed with tiny seed pearls, suspended on delicate trace-link chains below a necklace composed of three leafy scroll enamel and pearl blossoms along double delicate trace-link chains accented with seed pearls, Bippart Griscom & Osborn, late 19th - early 20th century, 15-1/2" l. **$4,400**

Dorrie Nossiter garnet and pearl earrings, 1920s, 1", British. **$1,575**
Jewelry courtesy Didier Antiques London; image by Adam Wide

Slide locket, silver, Art Nouveau style, a flattened waisted rectangular shape, the top embossed with sinuous vine and abstract leaf designs highlighted by green cabochons, gilt interior, European assay marks, early 20th century, 1-3/8 x 2". **$550**

▲Scenic landscape plaque from Art Nouveau dog collar (pin stem added later), gold, opals, diamond, enamels, circa 1900, by Koch. Estimate **$150,000-$200,000, unsold**
Christie's Images Ltd. 2009

◄Newlyn School pansy brooch, enamel and gold, 1900, 1-1/8", British. **$2,740**
Jewelry courtesy Didier Antiques London; image by Adam Wide

■ Art Deco

The Art Deco period fell between World War I and World War II. The jewelry from that era has spoken easily to us through the decades. Each generation seems able to recognize in it a wild joy for the present. Fresh ideas and experimentation emboldened jewelry makers. The icy geometry of Art Deco had the edge, audacity and abstraction women wanted and craved after war. The severe new jewelry suited fashion's leaner silhouettes, shorter hair, simpler lines and showing off in public.

Large Chinaman mask or face brooch, earrings set, silver-plated metal with turquoise enamels and faux onyx cast plastic, hat rimmed with pavé-set rhinestones, five strands light turquoise glass beads mimicking beard or decorative fringe; glass beads as earrings. Copy of an original Georges Fouquet corsage ornament of enamels, onyx, jade beads and brilliant-cut diamonds; 1920-25. Brooch copy signed © Art Deco 89, B 175, 4-3/4"; earrings B 256, 2-1/2". .... **$750 set**

Art Deco New York skyline pin, stamp-molded silver metal with imitation marcasites look; skyscrapers and circle design adorned with prong-set clear rhinestone chaton; 1920s-30s, unsigned, old c-clasp, 3-1/4". .... **$75-$150**

Jewelry courtesy GreatVintageJewelry.com; photo by Veronica McCullough

Art Deco gem-set devant de corsage, Boucheron, Paris, centering diamond-set scrolls among cabochon coral, lapis and jadeite leaves, diamond 11.05 carats, platinum, palladium; 18k gold mount; Maison Boucheron was a major contributor toward success of the 1925 Exposition Universelle, defining event of the Art Deco period. This piece by Hirtz for the Exposition represents some of the period's best innovations. **$189,600**

Image courtesy Skinner Inc.

Art Deco bracelet, crystal rhinestone wide-link bracelet, rhodium plating, 1930s, indecipherable mark, possibly "&", 6-7/8". **$300**

Art Deco buckle, copper and silver-toned heavy base metal with figures of dancers; 1920s, unsigned, 4". **$300**

Art Deco fountain brooch, brilliant and baguette rhinestones in silver plating, reproduction presented in this chapter because fountains were popular motif, especially Mauboussin; this is a rendition of a Mauboussin tiara, also similar to their fountain brooch from the 1925 Paris Exposition; 1991, signed Art Deco, B140, 89; 3"... **$300**

Art Deco style cuff bracelet, monogram initials WM inset into frame, gold-plated brass, probably 1950s 'Deco look,' unsigned, 1-1/2" high. **$25**

Art Deco style figural brooch, sapphire, diamond and ruby squatting lion with sapphire cabochon head, collet-set diamond eyes and mouth, sculpted platinum whiskers extending a sculpted gold mane to circular single-cut diamond and calibré-cut sapphire body; mounted in platinum and gold, circa 1957, signed Yard (for Raymond Yard). **$43,750**

© *Christie's Images Ltd. 2009*

Modern face brooch, sculptural gold-plated and silver chrome-finish metals, copy of original brooch by architect Gustave Miklos, executed by Raymond Templier in 1927, original in yellow gold and white gold; worth seeing because it's known as one of the few pieces of jewelry Miklos designed, 2-5/8", signed 89, © Art Deco, B096. .... **$250**

Art Deco brooch, triple-curtain chain fringe, varied-size crystal rose-cut rhinestones, antiqued-gold-finish base metal, filigree work, 3-1/4", 1940, signed Lidz Bros. N.Y. **$150**

Art Deco bracelet, ball-links rectangle, gold-plated sterling silver vermeil, marked Symetallic Sterling 925, 1940s, 8". **$100**
Jewelry courtesy Past Perfection Vintage Costume Jewelry, PastPerfection.com

Art Deco bar pin, modernist steel-gray aluminum, incised metal, convex domed effect, 4", 1930s, signed Ben Meltzer Inc. N.Y... **$50**

JEWELRY

▪ Plastics

The four chemical formulas that had a huge impact on the jewelry world are celluloid, Bakelite, Lucite, and later modern plastics being used in the trendiest jewelry.

John Wesley Hyatt's the go-to guy as celluloid's inventor, because he came up with the crucial solvent ingredient, camphor, after Alexander Parkes' parkesine couldn't be used widely or well (it cracked, easily). Hyatt dubbed his version of cellulose nitrate "celluloid," and introduced it in 1863.

Leo Hendrik Baekeland brewed his phenol-formaldehyde concoction as early as 1907; perfected it around 1912; and got jewelry designers hooked in the 1920s. A thermoset plastic, Bakelite was durable and cheap. It is some of the most highly artistic jewelry ever carved and so valuable and desirable, Asian factories would be knocking it off with their own "Fakelite" into the 21st century.

Otto Roehm is the scientist who actually patented and registered methyl methacrylate as Plexiglas, also known as Lucite, in 1933. It became available in 1936, and Elliot Handler (early of Elliot Handler Plastics, later of Elzac, later still of Mattel) was one of the earliest design engineers interested in it for furniture and house wares. He made the leap to jewelry when only Lucite scraps were left available on the market after acrylic glass was rerouted to the war effort. Appeal was in Lucite's hardness and transparency, as well as the fact it could be tinted or opaqued. Its most famous and desirable use in jewelry was as shaped globs called "jelly bellies," inserted into mostly figural shapes.

Lucite bangle, large and chunky with crystals, signed Alexis Bittar, 2" high, 2000s. **$500**
Jewelry courtesy Barbara Wood, BwoodAntique.com; image by Mary Cochran

Military-patriotic pins, plastic, soldiers in Jeep, WWII era, 2-1/2".. **$150**
Blue plastic bell brooch, says "In the Marines," 1940s, 2". **$125**

Josephine Baker pin, painted plastic, silver-ball top, purchased in London, 1997, signed Butler Wilson, 3"... **$325**

Lady and guitar pins: Lady's head pin signed Lea Stein Paris, 2", made in France, 1970s...**$165**
Heavily carved Lucite guitar pin, 1940s, 4"...............................**$165**

Fish pendant, painted Lucite, reverse carved with fish, celluloid chain, signed Judy Clarke, pendant 1", 2000s....................**$225**

Jelly starfish brooch, Lucite and sterling silver, rare, signed Mosell, 3", mid-1940s...........**$400-$500**

Tuxedo Tree pins, layered cellulose acetate, black and white herringbone pattern, French, signed Lea Stein Paris, 3", designed 1970s, produced 2000. ....**$75-$150**

Arrow brooch, Lucite and base metal, rare, signed with Phrygian cap for Boucher, 4", 1948-49.
....**$300-$450**

Jelly larval-like winged insect brooch, Lucite and sterling silver, uncommon, signed Jollé, 2-1/2", 1940s.
....**$125-$175**

Jelly sunflower brooch, Lucite and sterling silver, uncommon, Trifari, 3-1/4", 1944. ....**$750-$850**

Jelly bird head brooch, Lucite, sterling silver, emerald rhinestones, rare, signed "Sterling Pat Pend, Trifari," 1-7/8", 1938-42.................................**$800-$1,000**

Jelly basket brooch, Lucite and base metal, rare, signed with Phrygian cap for Boucher, 2-1/4", 1948-49..**$350-$450**

Jelly butterfly brooch, Lucite and sterling silver, rare, signed "Trifari," 2-1/4", 1949...............**$500-$600**

Jelly rabbit brooch, Lucite and base metal, unsigned, designer and manufacturer unknown, 2-3/4", 1938-42..**$250-$300**

Bangle bracelet, four-color laminate in Bakelite bangle measuring 7/8" high, unsigned, 1930s. **$450**

Jelly flower brooch, Lucite and sterling silver, uncommon, maker unknown, 2-3/8", 1944-46. ....**$250-$350**

Jelly rose brooch, Lucite and base metal, signed "Trifari," 2-1/2", mid-1940s.................**$400-$600**

▲"Gone Fishin'" brooch, rare, carved figural butterscotch Bakelite fish, gold-leaf accents, strung onto celluloid fishing pole, 4", unsigned, 1940s...................**$500**

Machine-Age jelly brooch, Lucite and metal, very rare, signed "Trifari," 3-1/2", late 1940s.**$2,000+**

◄Jelly heart brooch, Lucite and base metal, signed "Trifari," 2-1/4", late 1940s. ....**$250-$350**

Silver

Because silver had unique aesthetic attributes and was more affordable to work with, artists could give their talents and imaginations free rein while still enjoying the privilege of creating objects with one of the planet's most precious resources. Jewelry makers also love the lustrous white metal's malleability as well as ductility.

Animals pin, abstract, stylized prehistoric group, tested silver, weighty; glossy silver figural overlay on oxidized silver for high contrast; molded ball overlay accents, 2-1/2", unmarked, 1960s. **$100+**

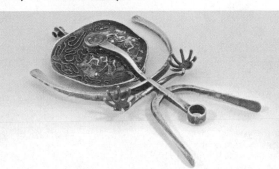

Articulated pendant, transparent pink crystal stone in sterling silver, by Bob Winston, early work of the artist, related to 1955 Walker exhibit; unmarked, 7", 1950s. **$5,000**
Jewelry courtesy Marbeth Schon, mschon.com; photo by Shirley Byrne

Southwestern Indian butterfly pin, silver, handmade, set with turquoise, coral, onyx and carnelian; no marks, purchased 1940, Colorado, Zuni, 2". **$150**

Rare sterling silver cuff (notice outstanding patina), pictured in Jewelry by Ed Wiener, Retrospective Exhibition, Fifty/50 Gallery, 1989, 1-3/8" at widest point, marked ED. WIENER, STERLING, circa 1947....**$1,800**
Jewelry courtesy Victor Alper; photo by Shirley Byrne

Spring Series necklace, fine and sterling silver, copper, resin, and turquoise; 2007, 20" x 3-1/2", signed EllenK..................... **$250**

Story bracelet, sterling silver clamper bangle, amusing narrative involving bull and man or matador unfolds across surface, open cutwork figures overlaying oxidized solid base; 5/8" wide, marked TC-04 Mexico 925, Taxco, 1980s. .... **$150-$200**

JEWELRY

Evald Nielsen canoeist silver brooch circa 1940s, 2-1/2", Danish. **$1,120**
Jewelry courtesy Didier Antiques London; image by Adam Wide

Omar Ramsden garnet and silver pendant, numerous small garnets in circular pattern, circa 1910, English, Arts & Crafts, 1-3/4".
.... **$1,120**
Jewelry courtesy Didier Antiques London; image by Adam Wide

Salvador Teran Bracelet, sterling silver, 7", hallmarked, 2" links, 83.6 grams. **$650**
Jewelry courtesy Alderfer Auction and Appraisal

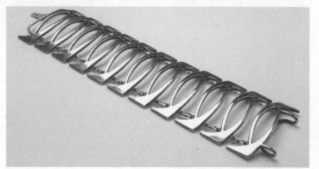

Tostrup bracelet, design by Gene Sommerfelt, silver, 2" wide, 1960s, Norway. **$1,400**
Jewelry courtesy Didier Antiques London; image by Adam Wide

Turquoise hearts cuff bracelet, bezel-set inlaid turquoise and onyx in silver, signed A.P. (presumably for Arthur Platero) .925, 7/8" high, 1970s. **$250**

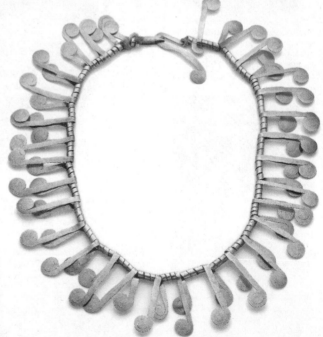

Modernist fish brooch, sterling silver, 1940s, 4-1/3", American, Paul Lobel, 1940s, signed. **$2,500**
Jewelry courtesy Didier Antiques London; image by Adam Wide

Silver fringe necklace by Alexander Calder (1898-1976), untitled, hammered silver on hemp cord, twisted silver bands supporting a continuous fringe of stylized silver musical notes; wedding gift to Mrs. William B.F. Drew in 1940 from her husband, who was best man and lifelong friend of Calder; 1940, 20-1/2". **$170,500**
Jewelry courtesy Doyle New York

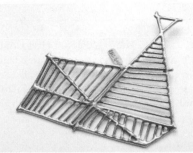

Frances Holmes Boothby silver grid brooch, 1950s, 4-3/4", American. **$2,500**
Jewelry courtesy Didier Antiques London; image by Adam Wide

Sigurd Persson necklace, silver and silver gilt, 14-1/3", 1960s, Sweden. **$5,500**
Jewelry courtesy Didier Antiques London; image by Adam Wide

Rebajes silver face earrings, each 1-1/2", circa 1950s, American.. **$1,325**
Jewelry courtesy Didier Antiques London; image by Adam Wide

Link bracelet, sterling silver, commissioned custom piece, 1950s, handmade to order from silversmith in Taxco taller, four oval and four oblong links, 7", $20 in 1953....................................... **$150+**

Cameo bracelet, sterling "wire wrap" cuff, large central carved MOP oval of anonymous lady in profile, 1-3/4", 1950s, signed "Sterling Original Hand-Wrought Design Rebajes," by Frank Rebajes.............. **$500-$900**

Southwest Indian silver and turquoise cuff bracelet, 45 cabochons in three-row bracelet, purchased 1940, $9, West Yellowstone; five turquoise cabochonss in bias-set ring, purchased Taos, N.M., 1967, $4; no marks or hallmarks, tested as silver; ring 3/8", bracelet 7/8"... **$250 both**

▶Modernist earrings, silver, by Paul Lobel, signed, 1-5/8", 1940s, American. **$1,575**
Jewelry courtesy Didier Antiques London; image by Adam Wide

JEWELRY

▪ Rhinestones

Rhinestones get their name from stones found in the Rhine. Though colored glass stones have been around since the 13th or 14th centuries, today's glass stone gets its name from the colorful quartz pebbles that were found in the river that begins at the Rheinwaldhorn Glacier in the Swiss Alps and flows north and east for 820 miles, through Germany. These glass pebbles were used in jewelry making until their scarcity prompted a search for something similar but more readily available. The name "rhinestone" came to mean any cut glass used in jewelry.

Claudette pin with matching earrings and large red glass stones. Pin is 2-1/8" diameter and earrings are 3/4", only earrings are signed. ....**$200-$250**

Unsigned brooch has a rose gold and gold washed appearance with amethyst and ruby glass stones, 2-3/4" x 2-1/8"..........**$100-$150**

Rare "Original by Robert" ring with enormous opal like stone, ring has a uniquely adjustable shank and is marked with the artist's pallet "Original by Robert" mark, ring measures 1" across. .... **$125-$150**

▶DeLizza & Elster show-stopping bracelet with heliotrope stones, from the early 1960s, a truly remarkable bracelet. ......**$400-$500**

DeLizza & Elster blue set with oval engraved flower stones from the mid-1960s. ....**$1,000-$1,300 set**

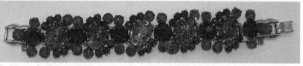

DeLizza & Elster oval red cat's eye cabochon bracelet from the late 1950s. **$275-325**

DeLizza & Elster chalk white and brown striped oval stone bracelet from the mid-1960s. ....**$250-$300**

Rhinestone set, clamper bracelet with buckle-effect design echoed in clip earrings. Pavé-set crystals with aurora-borealis treatment making stones reflect pastel pink-blue-lavender. Soldered rhinestone chain; clamper opens from side. Looks like a DeLizza & Elster product, but unconfirmed. Buckle motif 2-1/4"; earrings 1-1/2", 1960s.................................. **$250 set**

Set with large, oval green and brown stones called "green heliotrope," necklace, bracelet, pin and earrings with other autumnal colors, mid-1960s. .... **$1,200-$1,400 set**

DeLizza & Elster bracelet with blue and black beads that look like seed pods but are called "nugget beads," from the early 1960s, the set was called "Elegance."... **$250-$300**

DeLizza & Elster set with stunning collar necklace and flat bracelet design with rivoli and margarita stones from the late 1960s. .... **$2,100-2,300+ set**

Ciro fur clip with dark green ovals and clear chatons and baguettes, signed CIRO, 1-1/4" diameter. ....**$250-$275**

Calvaire sterling bracelet with large blue oval glass stones, gold wash over sterling. 7-1/2" x 3/4", marked Calvaire in block letters and Sterling. .... **$550-$650**

DeLizza & Elster heliotrope rhinestone pin with dangling beads. ....**$150-$200**

JEWELRY

Trifari bracelet with aquamarine glass stones and chaton, tapered baguette and baguette clear stones, 7-1/2" x 1/2", marked with the crown Trifari mark. ....**$295-$350**

DeLizza & Elster jade matrix navette stones pin leaf from the early 1960s. ....**$95-$150**

Butler & Wilson rhinestone fruit clamper bracelet with tiny gold bee by the orange strawberry, signed inside the back of the apple. Bracelet is 1-1/2" tall. ....**$250-$300**

Rare Zoe Coste bracelet with black and clear Lucite stones, signed "Zoe Coste Made in France." 7-1/4" x 2". ....**$175-$195**

DeLizza & Elster smoky topaz brooch with beads and stones called arrow stones, from 1959. ....**$175-$225**

DeLizza & Elster brooch with hematite and topaz stones from 1963..........................**$175-$200**

Les Bernard leaf pin with pearl center and colored glass cabochons and marcasites, with matching earrings, pin and one earring are marked Les Bernard, pin is 2-1/8" x 1-3/4", earrings are 7/8". Les Bernard was one of the first companies to mix rhinestones with marcasites in the same design............**$95-$125 set**

DeLizza & Elster five-link bracelet with large green emerald-shaped glass stones accented with dark and light green chatons and navettes. ....**$250-$300**

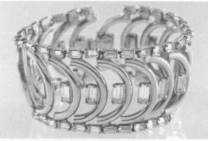

DeLizza & Elster earrings with coral gold floral cabochons called "Rose Limoges," from the early 1960s. ....**$75-$150**

Semi-circles and baguettes bracelet, heavily gold-plated metal, articulated half moons or semicircle links, 20 central crystal baguettes, 58 smaller stones along perimeters, 7-3/4", 1950s, signed Trifari... **$150-$250**

Figurals

Costume-jewelry figurals were (and still may be) so affordable, collectors can indulge a whim for whimsy, whether that means pinning on laughs or choosing a brooch so big it overwhelms a lapel. Aficionados of figural jewelry collect small works of art they may or may not wear, appreciated for craftsmanship, history, and the wit or beauty of the object itself.

Two different types of figurals are avidly collected in modern times. The first group includes such forms as birds, flowers, dogs and people. The opposite category includes crowns, shoes, Christmas trees, angels and umbrellas.

Wood — Wise owl brooch, college grad or professor, massive size, 3-D, painted wood, google-eyes, early Elzac, unsigned, 1940, 5". **$50**

People — Eerie gentleman-hobo pin, sometimes referred to as W.C. Fields but unlikely, gold-plated base metal, probably unsigned Har (exact figural turns up as large charm on signed-Har charm bracelets, as do other related pins);1950s-60s, 2-1/2"... **$100+**

Patriotic — Navy duck brooch, resembles early incarnation of Donald Duck, dressed in navy uniform, gilded pot metal and enamel, rhinestone accents, unsigned, 1942, 2-3/4"..................... **$50+**

Dogs — Pooch brooch, gilded pot metal with 20 emerald-cut amethyst rhinestones, tiny crystal accents; unsigned, 1940s, 3". **$150**

Seasonal — Bushel-basket fruit pin, enameled, gold-plated metal, Venetian glass fruits wired into elaborate 3-D construction, part of a series, signed HAR, 1950s, 1-3/4". .... **$150+**

JEWELRY

Tropical parrot brooch, polychrome enamel on pot metal, rhinestones, twin of Staret bird although enamel work resembles Coro, unsigned, 3-1/2", 1938-42................................... **$150+**

Aquavita — Seahorse pin, gold-plated stamped metal in layers, plastic beads (turquoise and coral) and fluted coral body, enameled in Coro-like polychrome colors; unsigned, 1960s, 2-3/8"... **$50-$75**

Boucher — Brooch, resembles comet, jellyfish or bowl of greenery depending on which way turned; finely plated metal, pavé-set emerald rhinestones in bowl, layered tentacles or streamers, signed © Boucher 9030, 1960s, 2-1/4".
.... **$150**

Left to right, top to bottom:
Crown brooch, clear rhinestones in silver-plated metal, golden sword flourish, 2", 1950s, signed Ora.
.... **$100**
Crown brooch and earrings, clear marquise-cut stones on gold-plated metal, 1-3/4", signed KJL for Avon , 1980s-90s........ **$75 set**
Crown brooch and earrings, large cabochons and color-matched baguettes, gilt sterling silver vermeil, 1-7/8", design patent #139100, 1944, signed Corocraft. (Variations on this mark include Coro Craft, Corocraft, Coro CRAFT, Coro-Craft.) .... **$275 set**
Crown brooches, multicolor rhinestones, gold-plated metal, red and purple velvet, 2", 1950s, signed Art. ....**$100 each**
Cheater's crown clip (shown upside down: "It doesn't look like a crown otherwise!"), large crystal stones of varied cuts, pronged fur clip, design patent 1942, 2-1/8", signed Eisenberg Original. **$300**
Crown brooch, clear and amber rhinestones with small amber-colored cabochons on gilded sterling silver vermeil, 1950s, 2", signed Jollé................................. **$125**
Jewelry courtesy of and photos by Dennis Scheer

Jeweled peacock pin, gilded metal with flamboyant use of rhinestones, amethyst ovals in tail, emerald and ruby oval rhinestones on wing and head comb, signed Coro, 1940s, 3-1/4".......................... **$150+**

Pair of geese in flight pin, highly dimensional, scattered rhinestone accents, sterling silver, 3", unsigned, 1942-46. .... **$50-$100**

Zany tropical bird pin, yellow, white, green enamels, gilt pot metal, 3-1/4", unsigned, resembles Staret work, 1938-42. . **$150**

Roosters — Brooch, painted, molded plastic inset with multicolor rhinestones, riveted to brass die-cut base, probably French, 1950s, unsigned, 2-7/8". ...**$50+**

Elaborate "fruit salad" basket of flowers brooch, gunmetal finish makes multicolor, multi-cut rhinestones pop, clear rhinestone chaton accents, large brilliant red radiant-cut stone in basket, blue and green fruit-salad leaves, 2-3/4", unsigned, 2000s but made to appear vintage. **$150**

Cross pendant-brooch, diamond and 18k gold, the gold mount set with 10 old European- and mine cut diamonds weighing about 3.75 carats, each arm with a pointed and forked tip accented with black enamel, 2-1/8".**$3,525**

Clockwise from left: Floral ribbon-wrapped pump, epoxied gold-plated metal, 2000s, 1-1/2", signed KJL, **$25**. Gold-plated high-heel pendant, 1980s, 1-7/8", signed Cachet, **$25**. Old-fashioned boot, fur clip, enameled gold-plated metal with rhinestone accent, unsigned, 1-1/2", 1940-42, **$100**. Professor Henry Higgins' slippers, fetched by Eliza, part of My Fair Lady jewelry series, signed BSK and My Fair Lady, 1-3/4", 1960s, **$50**. Sandal charm, sterling silver, hallmarked 925, 1970s, 1-1/4". **$25**

JEWELRY

Scene Pins — Home on the range cowboy scene pin, 3-D, gold-plated frame with sun setting on painted backdrop, cowboy on fences with lasso, saddle, cactus; unsigned, 1950s-60s, 2"...........................**$50+**

Aquamarine arrangement of flowers in enameled-white gold basket, gilded pot metal, pink centerpiece stones in decorative raised prong settings, unsigned, 1940s, 3-1/2"..**$150+**

Posy basket, four polychrome enameled blooms, green leaves, in filigree basket, signed Trifari, 1960s, 2-1/4"......................**$50**

Drooping red-hot pokers pin, elongated pink-red rounded skinny navettes in gilded sterling (vermeil) vase, wire stems, crystal rhinestone accents add feminine touch, unsigned, 1940s, 2-3/4".. **$150+**

Sinuous vine floral dress clip, gold-plated metal, multicolor rhinestones in four blooms, emerald navette rhinestone leaves, unsigned, 1950s, 2-1/2". **$25**

Crystal balls dress clip, multicolor faceted glass orbs in pink, sapphire, topaz, aqua, silver-plated metal, pavé-set rhinestone leaves, 2", 1950s, unsigned. **$50**

Glass dress clip, gold-washed metal flowers centered with blue rhinestones set against highly detailed cast leaves, large, faceted crystal glass vase set into prongs; unsigned but has been found signed Mazer and Reinad; 1940s, 2-3/4".................................**$250**

Brooch, diamond and gold, bow-form, the top four-loop fancy openwork gold bow collet-set with table- and rose-cut diamonds, suspending a small bow pendant topped with scrolls also set with diamonds and suspending another cross-form pendant with scrolling details further set with diamonds, gold mount, diamonds possibly foiled, later pin stem, evidence of solder, 3-7/8"..................**$3,819**

Basket pendant-brooch, carved ivory, coral flowers, jade cabochon leaves, 1-3/4", unsigned, 1950s. **$150**

Branched arrangement, enameled leaves and flowers in gilded pitcher jardiniere, rhinestone and moonstone accents, from the "Gardenesque Series," rhodium reverse, signed Reja. 2-1/4", 1940s. .... **$150-$250**

Pot of flowers pin, basket-weave bowl pavé-set with rhinestones, nine flowers set on thin wire stems that move, emerald baguettes invisibly set in one stalk, openwork leaves with emerald rhinestone accents; dimensional, 1950s, unsigned, 2-1/8" **$50**

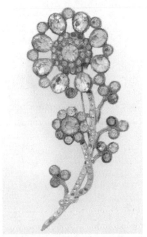

Crystal flower brooch, multi-cut rhinestones all in clear crystal, silvered pot metal, 4-1/4", 1940s, unsigned........................ **$25-$50**

Floral dress clip, faceted oval orchid rhinestones in enameled pot metal setting, 1930s, signed Stempa, 2". **$50**

Tisket-tasket flower basket, 3-D, arranged enamel flowers, unsigned, 1960s-70, 2-1/2". **$25**

Flower basket pin, silvery pot metal, 1930s thick, heavy urn with rhodium plating. Flower spray adorned with clear and amethyst rhinestones. Safety clasp, measures 3", unsigned, attributed to Reinad........................ **$110-155**

Jewelry courtesy GreatVintageJewelry.com; photo by Veronica McCullough

Single-bloom brooch, layered "swedged" (meaning to shape metal using a hammer or crimp), circular arrangement of orchid navettes, clear crystals and pink center rhinestones riveted to gold-plated petals edged with clear rhinestone chaton, unsigned, similar to some Eisenberg-Mazer-Reinad pieces, 2-3/4", late 1940s. .... **$150+**

Three-flower in pot enameled fur clip, 1930s, unsigned, 1-3/4". **$25**

Rose bowl fur clip, gilded bowl of enameled roses, pale metallic green enameling on some leaves (others left gold), rhinestone accents at base, highly dimensional and well made, signed R. DeRosa, 1940s, 2-3/4".. **$250**

Framed flowers pin, rhinestones and enamel rectangle frames vase of enameled flowers, signed Coro, 1930s-40s, 2"... **$50**

Bow-tied sheaf of leaves with simulated blue moonstones, enameled leaves and tie, blue rhinestone accents, 3-1/4", looks like a Chanel Novelty piece but pin mechanism French; 1930s-40s, unsigned............................ **$50+**

Floral hat brooch set (earrings not shown), gilded sterling silver (vermeil), 3-D, wire trim prongset with multicolor rhinestones, unsigned other than hallmark but looks like CoroCraft; 2-3/4", 1940s. .... **$195 set**

Soaring bird brooch, heavy gilt sterling avian figural with topaz teardrop rhinestones in wings, oval in tail feathers, large oval body, 3", 1942-46, unsigned Eisenberg with numeral 3 for stone-setter Scarino in circle. **$500**

Clown charm or pendant, pull tie and eyes roll, tongue sticks out, 1-1/2", 1960s, unsigned but has appeared signed DeNicola................................. **$25+**

Glamorous butterfly brooch, enormous winged thing of heavy sterling silver, crystal accents, and large, horizontally faceted barrel glass stones in wings; hook and latch construction; signed Eisenberg Original Sterling (twice), 3", 1940s........................... **$1,500**

Top: Flower tree, enamel pine with rhinestone florals, 1960s, unsigned Gem-Craft, 2"................. **$50-$75**
Left: Stars tree, layered, enamel, original Gem-Craft design, unsigned, 1960s, 2-1/2"............... **$25-$50**
Center: Fireworks tree, gold-plated metal, multicolor rhinestones, metallic dangling ornament, original Gem-Craft design, unsigned, 1970s, 2-1/2"..... **$50+**
Right: Bow tree, swoosh motif, green enameling, red bow, older pin originally by Gem-Craft, 1960s, 2-3/4"......................... **$50**
Bottom: Beaded cone tree, un plated, raw casting, ultra-rare, probably originally for Hattie Carnegie, pot metal with emerald beads, 1950s-60s, unsigned, 2-1/4".................................**$150-$250**

Left to right, top to bottom:
Polka dots tree, multicolor rhinestones on skinny trunk, original 1950-60s Gem-Craft, signed Craft, 2-5/8".. **$100+**
Metallic ornaments tree, original Gem-Craft design, balls dangle and swing from partitions, unsigned, 2-3/4".. **$100+**
Bottom row, left and right: Teepee trees (bottom left and right), original Gem-Craft designs, similar, one with scalloped edges, the other with more stones, both unsigned, 1960s, 2-3/4".................**$50 each**
Colorful tree, brightly hued rhinestones, original vintage design by Alfeo Verrecchia at Gem-Craft, Austrian coloration, japanned setting, six candles, 1950s-60s, possibly for Kramer, unsigned, 2-1/4"................**$250**

Top: Stars tree, openwork stars, some with rhinestones centers, other stars dangling as ornaments, rounded boughs, gold-plated metal, rare early Lianna, signed Lia, 1980s, 2-1/2"............ **$150**
Left: Shapes tree, lemony glitter epoxy in gem-shape cups, silver plating, 1990s, signed Lia, 2-1/4"................................. **$50**
Center: Circles tree, 10 crystal brilliants in gold-plated circles, early Lianna, 1980s, sold at Accessory Lady, signed Lia, 2".. **$75**
Right: Tall tree, greenery and holly berry colors, epoxy, plated stars, unsigned Lianna, has been copied, 1990s-2000s, 4-3/8". ...**$50**
Bottom left: Bezels tree, gold-plated with emerald rhinestones in raised bezels, unsigned Lia, hard to find, 1980s, 2"............. **$50+**
Bottom center: Hugs & kisses tree, cast, gold-plated metal, early Lianna, sold at Accessory Lady, 1980s, 1-3/4". ....**$75-$100**

JEWELRY

■ Beads

Beads weren't just for ornamentation. Throughout history, they've been used as money, protection, or to broadcast the wearer's place in society. Beads also worked as symbols, so the "blue eye of the heart" served as a third eye to protect the bearer from the so-called "evil eye." Black beads symbolized loss; white, purity; red, strength; green, harmony. Every culture has used beads in one form or another for some purpose. Many religions use beads in prayer; the abacus employs beads to calculate sums.

Nearly life-size grapes bunch pin with beaded flowers and leaves, 5-1/2" x 3-1/2", by Ian Gielar for Stanley Hagler, with both applied tags...........................**$650 -$750**

Annie Navetta Designs fruity necklace with vintage fruit beads, including lemons, apples, pears and oranges, 19" long with centerpiece of 3-1/2". Signed with a metal hangtag. ....**$175-$225**

Ian Gielar for Stanley Hagler Christmas tree pin called Tutti Frutti, 4-1/2" x 3", with both applied tags...................**$350-$450**

Museum quality Bird in Nest pin by Ian Gielar for Stanley Hagler, size overall is 5" x 5", signed with both the Hagler and the Gielar metal tags..........**$2,500+**

◆ Aurora borealis, in jewelry terms, refers to a rainbow-like iridescent finish that is reminiscent of the weather phenomenon also called the Northern Lights. To produce this finish, glass or acrylic beads are coated with thin layers of metal to enhance color and give an extra sparkle and a rainbow look to the base color. Beads with this finish are labeled AB.

Two necklaces by Flying Colors, a ceramic company in business in California in the late 1970s through the early 1980s, sometimes the jewelry comes with dated tags. Chili peppers necklace is 21" long and the chili peppers are 2-1/4" long. ....**$175-$225** Watermelon necklace is 18" long and the center slice is 2-1/2" long, both signed. ....**$175-$200**

Ellen Klamon Summer Series Necklace Set, fabricated from fine and sterling silver, copper, resin and turquoise. Necklace is 1-1/2" x 2" x 20", earrings are 1" x 3/4". **$350**

Annie Navetta Designs necklace in lavender and green with vintage pieces, including German glass flowers and Czech faceted lavender opal glass beads. Signed with a metal hangtag, 18" long with a centerpiece 3" x 3-1/4". ....**$195-$255**

▶Annie Navetta Designs fruity bracelet with beaded strands and a fruitful centerpiece that is 2" x 2", bracelet is 7" long, signed with a metal hangtag. ....**$125-$150**

◼ Diamonds

Penny Preville ring in 18k white gold with 0.50 carat diamonds.
.... **$2,805**

Diamond ring, platinum and vertically set European-cut diamonds, approximately 4.25 carats, elongated pierced openwork mount set throughout with numerous single-cut diamonds, circa 1915, approximately 4 dwt, 1-3/16" long.
....**$12,000**
Courtesy Doyle New York

Cushion-cut fancy natural yellow diamond ring set in platinum, rose gold and 18k yellow gold, ccented by fancy yellow diamonds, fancy pink diamonds and colorless diamonds, 3.49 carats.........**$59,000**
Maidi Corp courtesy of Natural Color Diamond Association

Schlumberger band ring, 18k gold, platinum, diamonds, signed Schlumberger, Tiffany, approximately 4 dwt., 3/16". **$1,200**
Courtesy Doyle New York

"Bird on a Rock" brooch, platinum, 18k gold, pavé-set with 70 round diamonds of 2.75 carats, polished gold beak, feathers and legs, ruby eye, perched atop cushion-cut citrine, 29.0mm, signed Schlumberger, Tiffany, approximately 18.3 dwt.; 2-1/2". Doyle catalog note: In the late 1950s, Jean Schlumberger was invited to design for Tiffany & Co., creating whimsical and surrealist pieces incorporating natural and organic forms in his work. This iconic design was originally created in the 1960s for the Tiffany yellow cushion-cut diamond of 128.50 carats.............................**$25,000**
Courtesy Doyle New York

Fancy natural pink marquise diamond earrings set in 18k rose gold and platinum, 4.97 carat weight.
....**$86,000**
Maidi Corp courtesy of Natural Color Diamond Association

Puffed hearts earrings, 14k white gold, 3.39 carat-weight black diamonds, 3/4"................... **$1,195**
Jewelry courtesy HeavenlyTreasures.com

Left: Diamond, pearl, rock crystal bracelet, eight strands creamy graduated cultured pearls, 3.9 to 5.6mm, platinum, ruby and garnet clasp centering oblong rock crystal panel, 17 rectangular-cut garnets, four horizontal diamond-set bands, two openwork diamond-set sections of heart- and teardrop-shaped segments accented by two round rubies, 12 baguette diamonds, 66 old European-cut diamonds, all approximately 5.75 carats, circa 1935, 2 14" clasp. **$4,250**
Courtesy Doyle New York
Right: A.LINK diamond bracelet in 18k white gold, three-row double-layered bracelet with shared prongs and contains 315 diamonds for a total weight of 16.89 carats. **$37,400**

Kitchenwares

The Vintage Kitchen - 1850-1920

Coffee mills, commonly called grinders, are perfectly collectible for many people. They are appealing to the eye and are frequently coveted by interior decorators and today's coffee-consuming homeowners. Compact, intricate, unique, ornate, and rooted in early Americana, coffee mills are intriguing to everyone and are rich and colorful.

Coffee milling devices have been available for hundreds of years. The Greeks and Romans used rotating millstones for grinding coffee and grain. Turkish coffee mills with their familiar cylindrical brass shells appeared in the 15th century, and perhaps a century or two later came the earliest spice and coffee mills in Europe. Primitive mills were handmade in this country by blacksmiths and carpenters in the late 1700s and the first half of the 19th century. These were followed by a host of commercially produced mills, which included wood-backed side mills and numerous kinds of box mills, many with machined dovetails or finger joints. Characterized by the birth of upright cast-iron coffee mills, so beautiful with their magnificent colors and fly wheels, the period of coffee mill proliferation began around 1870. The next 50 years saw a staggering number of large and small manufacturers struggling to corner the popular home market for box and canister type coffee mills. After that, the advent of electricity and other major advances in coffee grinding and packaging technology hastened the decline in popularity of small coffee mills.

Value-added features to look for when purchasing old coffee grinders include:
- good working order and no missing, broken, or obviously replaced parts
- original paint
- attractive identifying markings, label or brass emblem
- uncommon mill, rarely seen, or appealing unique characteristics
- high quality restoration, if not original.

—Mike White

COFFEE MILLS
Box Mills

Box mill, iron cover w/gear opening & crank & sunken hopper, on wooden box w/pull-out drawer in front, Parker National **$100**

Box mill, iron crank & side handle on wooden box w/ pull-out drawer in front, 1 lb. capacity, Logan & Strobridge Brighton No. 1180 .... **$150**

Box mill, raised brass hopper & crank, Moravian base & inlaid drawer, signed by maker **$200**

Box mill, raised iron hopper w/patented partial cover design & crank on wooden box w/pull-out front drawer, Arcade Favorite No. 357 .... **$100**

Box mill, raised iron hopper & crank on tin canister w/picture of woman painted on front, drawer in back, patented Norton **$650**

Side Mills

Side mill, iron, sliding cover, Kenrick patented, England **$110**

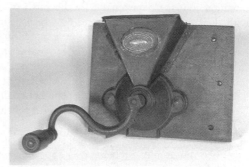

Side mill, tin hopper on wood backing, brass emblem reads "Peck Smith Mfg." **$100**

Upright Mills

Upright mill, cast iron, L.F. & C. New Britain, Conn. Universal, overall green paint w/gold highlights, hand crank w/wooden grip, slide-out base drawer, mounted on wooden board, all-original & like new, late 19th c., 11 1/2" h. **$320**

Upright two-wheel mill, cast iron, single wheel, cup, patented Clawson & Clark No. 1 model .. **$1,000**

Upright two-wheel mill, cast iron, w/nickel-plated brass hopper, 10 3/4" wheels, Enterprise No. 4 .... **$2,000**

Upright two-wheel mill, cast iron, miniature model for children, two 2"-h. wheels, Arcade No. 7, rare, overall about 2 1/2" h. **$350**

Upright two-wheel mill, cast iron, w/17" wheels, pivoting cover on hopper, original red paint, decals & pin striping, 1898 patent date marked on grinding burrs, Enterprise #7 .... **$1,500**

Upright two-wheel mill, cast iron, pivoting lid on hopper, two 12"-h. wheels, Coles No. 4 .... **$950**

Wall Canister Mills

Wall-mounted canister mill, cast iron, decorative design based on Ami Clark's 1833 patent, w/adjusting thumbscrew in back & two-sided grinding burr, only known example **$2,500**

Wall-mounted canister mill, ceramic w/glass measure, marked on front "Douwe-Egberts Koffie," Europe **$140**

Wall-mounted canister mill, iron & glass, w/2-qt. jar, L.F. & C. Universal No. 24 .... **$190**

Wall-mounted canister mill, iron, clamp-on type, w/pivoting lid, red, rare National Specialty No. 0 **$310**

Wall-mounted canister mill, bronzed cast-iron canister w/glass window & cup, embossed canister reads "Golden Rule Blend Coffee The Finest Blend In The World, The Citizens Wholesale Supply Co., Columbus Ohio," 18" h. **$450**

Wall-mounted canister mill, ceramic, children's model, glass measure, "Cafe" on front, Europe, about 6" h. **$420**

Wall-mounted canister mill, tin lithographed canister, pictures a young girl wearing white dress, yellow apron & bonnet, Bronson-Walton Holland Beauty, 13" h. including cup..**$350**

EGG BEATERS

Eggbeaters are pure Americana! No other invention (although apple parers come close) represent America at its best from the mid-19th century to the 1930s or '40s. Eggbeaters tell the unbeatable story of America—the story of demand for a product, competition, success, retreat, failure, faith, and revival.

The mechanical (rotary) eggbeater is an American invention, and ranks up there with motherhood and apple pie, or at least up there where it counts—in the kitchen. American ingenuity produced more than 1,000 patents related to beating eggs, most before the 20th century.

To put it in perspective, try to imagine 1,000 plus ways to beat an egg. Here's a clue, and it's all due to Yankee tinkering: There are rotary cranks, archimedes (up and down) models, hand-helds, squeeze power, and rope and water power—and others. If you ever wanted a different way to beat an egg it was (and is) available.

Today, eggbeaters are a very popular Americana kitchen collectible—a piece of America still available to the collector, although he/she may have to scramble to find the rare ones.

But, beaters are out there, from the mainstay A & J to the cast-iron Dover to the rarer Express and Monroe. There is always an intriguing mix, ranging in price from less than under $10.00 to the hundreds of dollars.

—Don Thornton

S & S Hutchinson, heavy tin rotary marked "S & S Hutchinson No. 2 New York Pat. Sept. 2, 1913," w/ heavy tin apron on ribbed glass jar embossed "National Indicator Co. No. 2 S & S Trade Mark Long Island City," 9 1/2" h. **$450**

A & J, Ecko, wood handle, rotary w/apron marked "A&J USA Ecko," on a two-cup measuring cup marked "A&J" **$35**

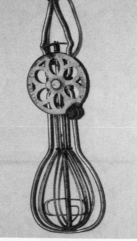

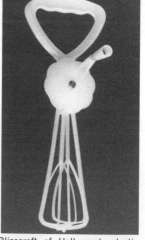

Taplin, cast-iron rotary, marked "The Taplin Mfg. Co. New Britian Conn, U.S.A. Light Running Pat. Nov. 24 '08," 12 1/2" h. **$45**

Master, cast iron w/nickel plate, "Master Pat. Aug. 24-09," 10 3/4" **$1,500**

Blisscraft of Hollywood, plastic, rotary, marked "Blisscraft of Hollywood Pat. USA Pend.," scarce, 12" h. **$75**

MISCELLANEOUS

Apple peeler, cast iron, "Wiggin Pat. Aug. 4, 1868"
.... **$1,000**

▶Basket, wire w/twisted wire center handle, 7" at
widest diameter **$85**

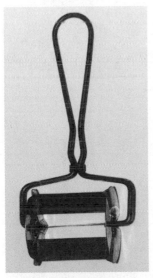

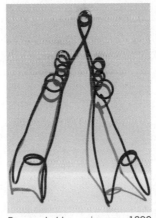

Broom holder, wire, ca. 1890
.... **$65**
◀Biscuit cutter, tin, rolls three
biscuits at a time, Pat. Sept. 12,
1893 .... **$65**

Butter churn, table model, tin &
cast-iron top w/unmarked glass
jar, "The Home Butter Maker,
Kohler Die & Specialty Co. Dekalb,
III USA" **$125**

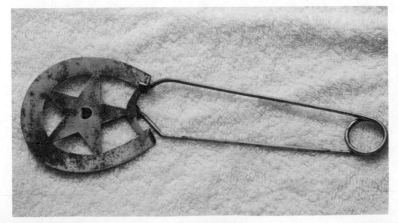

Cake turner, tin,
horseshoe-shaped
w/star marked
"M.C.W. Cake
Turner, Pat. Apr.
2. 07," wire
handle flips it
.... **$115**

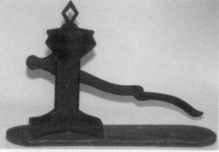

Can opener, cast iron, mounted on board, Williams's Patent of Jan 8, 1878, rare **$275**

Candy kettle, copper, a large half-round form w/a heavy rolled rim & heavy riveted iron loop rim handles, early 20th c., 20" d. **$259**

Cherry pitter, cast iron w/three legs, marked "Pat'd Nov. 17, 1863" **$145**

Cherry pitter, wood, porcelain & cast iron, crack-type, unmarked, 10 1/2" **$125**

Chopper, cast iron handle w/two metal blades, handle marked "Pat'd. May 2, 93 No. 20 Croton, NY" **$45**

Dipper, tole, cylindrical bowl w/ tapering strap handle, the bowl decorated w/red & mustard decorative band on black ground, the handle w/mustard & red leaf decoration, bowl 3 1/2" d., 2 1/4" h., 8" w/handle **$480**

Dish drainer, tin & wire, wire dish rack fits into rectangular tilted pan **$50**

Egg scale, metal, platform-style, "Reliable Mfg Co./Los Angeles Calif," 8 3/4" **$75-85**

Flour sifter, tin, mesh screen in bottom, shake handle from side to side for action, marked "The New Shaker Sifter, Center Drive, Prevents Tipping, Pat. Applied For," two-cup size **$35**

▶Jar lifter, steel w/turned wood handle, marked "Pat Pend," 8 1/2" h. **$30**

Jar opener, cast iron, very unusual screw clamp mechanism, marked "Pat June 18, 1888," 8 3/4" l. **$150**

Kettle stand, brass, the rectangular top w/a slightly bowed front above a conforming scroll-cut front apron w/ front cabriole legs, iron rod back legs, a cast brass handle flanking the top, 19th c., 11 3/4 x 18 3/4", 12" h. **$201**

Food chopper, hand-wrought iron, single blade, wood handle, ca. 1850 .... **$30**

Grater, tin, hand-punched, common **$45**

Kettle, a deep cylindrical form w/a slightly rounded bottom, the slightly domed hinged cover pierced w/ overall decorative holes, iron side rim handle for holding wooden extension, early 19th c., 19" l. **$104**

Kraut cutter, a long flat rectangular board inset w/ an angled metal cutting blade, the heart-shaped top w/a small hanging hole, well scrubbed & used surface, 7" w., 21 1/2" l. ... **$345**

Nut cracker, cast iron, clamp-style for attaching to table edge, clamp-form cracker, marked "Perfection Nut Cracker - Made in Waco, Texas - Patented 1914," 6 x 6 1/2" **$55-65**

Nut grater, tin, half-round w/hanging hole at top, stamped "Acme Nut Grater Rd 114671," English **$40**

Lemon squeezer/slicer, cast iron, combination cutter & squeezer on wood base w/crank action of handle forcing juice from lemon, inserts often missing, approx. 13" h. **$200-225**

Nutmeg grater, cast iron, tin & wood, "The Gem" **$75-85**

Nutmeg grater, tin, marked "H. Carsley, Patented Nov. 20, 1855, Lynn, Mass.," rare **$975**

Nutmeg grinder, sterling silver oval cylindrical case w/engine-turned design & hinged cover holding the grater, touch marks for Thomas Hall, Exeter, England, 1855-56, 1 1/4" w., 3" l. .. **$275**

Peach stoner, cast iron, "Rollman Mfg. Co. Pat Pend Mount Joy PA U.S.A.," 8 3/4" **$250**

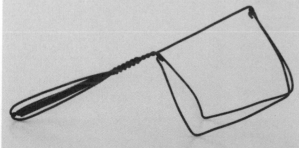

Pie lifter, wire handle w/wood insert, two hinged wings on opposite end which act to grab pan **$95**

Pie pan, tin, pierced star design holes in bottom, used to make crisper crusts **$55**

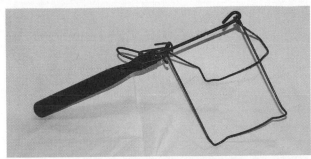

Pie lifter, wire w/long turned black wood handle, an unusual wire lever top opening the wire grips, 12 1/2" l. **$75**

Rolling pin, wooden, turned wood handles, the cylinder carved w/20 springerle designs in rows of blocks, early, overall 17" l. **$250-350**

Spatula, tin & cast iron, mechanical, squeezing handle flips end ... **$75**

Potato masher, double-spring-action type w/two heavy wire wavy sections, one over the other, turned wooden handle **$45**

Rolling pin, peacock blue blown glass, hollow w/closed handles, rare, 19th c., 14" l. **$400**

Spoon holder, tin, oval shape w/seven holes & ridge around edge, w/hook, to be placed on side of kettle for drippings from spoon, unmarked **$35**

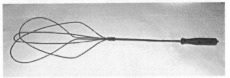

Rug beater, wire w/complex woven design forming three loops of different widths & angles, turned maple handle, late 19th - early 20th c., 9" w., 29" l. **$30-40**

Sugar bucket, cov., stave construction w/three finger lappets w/copper tacks, swing bentwood hickory bail handle, old mustard yellow paint, 19th c., minor wear & edge chips, 13 3/4" h. **$460**

Teakettle, cov., copper, oval cylindrical body w/deep sides below the wide angled shoulder, ringed domed cover w/mushroom finial, angular snake spout, fixed tall brass curved supports joined by a bar handle, tin-lined, 19th c., 11" h. **$201**

KITCHENWARES

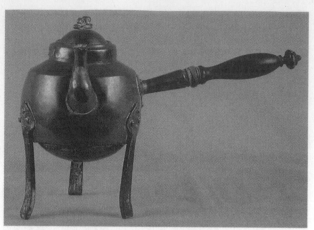

Teakettle, cov., copper, flat-bottomed dovetailed body w/a wide base & tapering sides to a short cylindrical neck w/a fitted low domed cover w/baluster-form finial, angular snake spout, overhead brass strap swing bail handle, stamped number "6," American-made, 19th c., overall 13" l. **$1,208**

Teapot, cov., copper, bulbous nearly spherical body w/an angled shoulder to a short cylindrical neck w/a fitted domed cover w/scroll finial, tapering cylindrical side handle fitted w/a baluster-turned black wood handle w/pointed terminal, body raised on three straight riveted wrought-iron legs, probably Europe, 19th c., wear, spout pressed in, 8" h. **$125**

Trivet, cast-iron, advertises "C D Kenny Teas, Coffees, Sugars, 60 Stores," 5" l. **$145**

Teakettle, cov., copper, Revere Ware, domed beehive body w/applied black Bakelite handle and bird whistle spout, marked on bottom "Revere Solid Copper - Rome, N.Y.," 7 1/4 x 7 1/2"............ **$100**

Toaster, wire w/wood handle, bread was placed between decorative wire, rare............................ **$65**

Toaster, wire w/wood handle, mechanical, lever was pulled to open wire circles to insert bread **$45**

Trivet, wire, rounded starburst design of stamped wire w/double-loop ends & triangles, used as a coffeepot or teapot stand **$45**

Trivet, hand-wrought, model of a coiled snake, on three short scroll legs, incised underside, found in Pennsylvania, 19th c., minor surface corrosion, 4 3/4 x 10 1/2", 3 1/4" h................................. **$978**

Wafer iron, cast iron, traditional scissor-form w/a pair of hinged round disks on long handles ending in a loop catch, one disk intaglio-cast w/a spread-winged American eagle & shield w/a banner in its beak reading "E Pluribus Unum," Pennsylvania, ca. 1800, overall 29 1/4" l.. **$1,610**

Wafer iron, hand-wrought iron, hinged scissor-form w/long slender handles ending in a pair of rectangular plates each incised w/a rectangular zigzag border enclosing a monogram "E.R.D." & heart on one & initials "I.D." & a heart on the other, dated 1763, Pennsylvania, overall 32 1/2" l. **$978**

The Modern Kitchen

The diverse area of kitchenware/household objects offers a world of collecting opportunities. Your interests may lead you to antique rarities more than 100 years old or to items of more recent manufacture. Any and all territory should be considered fair game. As with other collectibles, your primary motivation should be your individual likes and preferences.

There is a great deal of interest in kitchenware and related items from 35 to 60 years old; these objects rekindle old memories and represent a different, less-complicated era for many.

The items here represent a broad spectrum of kitchen items and cooking activities. These include just about every task you would want to try to master in your kitchen of yesteryear. There are gadgets of all types and all sorts of accessories, sets, holders, and miscellaneous gizmos. Most of the items are non-electrical and small in scale.

For more information on kitchen collectibles, see *Spiffy Kitchen Collectibles* or *Warman's Kitschy Kitchen Collectibles Field Guide*, both by Brian S. Alexander.

◀Longhorn Meat Markers, 12 metal cooking level markers, boxed, 1950s, Bar & Barbecue Products, Los Angeles.. **$15-$18**

Arthur Godfrey Barbecue, with charcoal inside, "The charcoal pit for broiling your food," with cardboard insert, 1950s, Marc Mfg. Co., Chicago........ **$28-$35**

Skotch O' matic Hot or Cold Jug, metal and plastic, 1/2 gal, "Press the bulb, it serves a drink, a delight to use!," boxed, 1950s, Hamilton- Skotch Corp., Hamilton, Ohio. .... **$30-$35**

Gadget Master Hot Vegetable Tongs, metal, "No more burned fingers, A star in any kitchen," boxed, 1950s, Popiel Bros, Chicago. .... **$18-$22**

"Handi Hostess" Potato Basket and Noodle Nest, "Makes a delicious potato basket for parties, luncheons," boxed, 1951, Bonley Products Co., Chicago. .... **$18-$22**

KITCHENWARES

Ohio Baster, for roast meat and fowl, in cardboard tube, 1950s, Ohio Thermometer Co., Springfield, Ohio..................... **$18-$22**

Eggbeater, natural and red wooden handle, "Another Androck Product," 1940s-1950s. ...... **$22-$25**

Eggbeater, with green Bakelite side handle, 1940s, Worlbeater, Los Angeles................... **$30-$35**

Tater Baker, metal with plastic handle, "Bakes potatoes, warms buns and leftovers on top of stove," boxed, 1950, The Everedy Co., Frederick, Maryland. .... **$25-$28**

Artbeck Whip Beater, with plastic knob, "Whips, beats, mixes, one hand operation," with tube carton, 1954, Arthur Beck Co., Chicago................. **$15-$18**

Roasting Pan, metal, "Easy to clean, Completely seamless, Sure-hold handles," with label, 1950s, Bake King, Chicago Metallic Mfg. Co., Lake Zurich, Illinois. **$18-$20**

Spud Spikes, set of six, aluminum, "Exclusive knife edge, Bake potatoes fast," with card sleeve, 1950s, Monarch Die Casting, Santa Monica, California. **$18-$20**

Duplex Whipper, metal with green wood handle, "Double action for cream, eggs, and dressings," boxed, 1930s-1940s. .... **$40-$45**

Mirro Spring-Form Pan, aluminum, "Clampless, for Tortes, Cakes, Desserts," boxed, 1950s, Mirro Aluminum, Manitowoc, Wisconsin. .... **$20-$25**

Dazey Mix-er-ator, with graduations and mixing directions, 1950s, Dazey Corp., St. Louis. .... **$20-$25**

Rudolph the Red Nosed Reindeer Cake and Mold Pan Set, 8 pieces, copyright 1939, Robert L. May, boxed, 1950s, Bake King, Chicago Metallic Mfg. Co., Chicago. .... **$45-$55**

Swans Down Cake Pan, "Swans Down cake flour makes better cakes," 1920s. .... **$25-$30**

Alumode Gingerbread House Mold, mentions Woman's Day article on box, with cardboard sleeve, 1950s, Aluminum Specialty Co. .... **$22-$25**

Cake Cover, metal, yellow lid with apple design. Same pattern was used on canister sets, flour sifters, etc., 1940s-1950s. .... **$22-$25**

KITCHENWARES

Cake Cover, locking copper-tone aluminum, square with wooden handle, boxed, has tag, 1950s Mirro Aluminum. .... **$30-$35**

Can-O-Matic Electric Can Opener, pink metal with chrome, 1950s-1960s. ...**$35-$50**

Salt & Pepper with Sugar Container, three-piece styrene plastic set with hand-painted flower decoration, 1950s, Plastic Novelties Inc., Los Angeles.. **$22-$25**

Canister Set, three-piece styrene plastic, "The smart set for smart kitchens. The first and only canister set with a window, a feature to gladden any woman's heart," boxed, 1950s, Janetware Plastic Products, Aurora, Illinois. .... **$40-$45**

Cake Server, Kut-n-Serve, metal with plastic handles, "No fumbling, no crumbling," boxed, 1950s, Krag Steel Products, Chicago. .... **$15-$18**

Aluminum Cake Decorator, Happy Birthday, "for delightful, interesting cakes," with six tips, boxed 1940s, Made in USA. ....**$18-$20**

Cake and Sandwich Cutters, metal bridge set "for luncheons and card parties," boxed 1930s-1940s. .... **$15-$20**

Plastic Cookie Cutters, eight-piece set with figural animal shapes, boxed, 1940s, Hutzler Mfg. Co., Long Island City, New York. .... **$35-$40**

Androck Flour Sifter, three screens, "Hand-I-Sift," red and white "Pantry Pattern" design with bakery items, 1950s. .... **$25-$30**

Telechron Clock, styrene plastic, "floating" bubble clock design with an outer numeral band, 1950s, in red with white numerals................................. **$65-$75**

Sessions Kitchen Clock, plastic teapot-shaped design, 1950s, Sessions Clock Co., Forrestville, Connecticut. .... **$55-$60**

"Sift-Chine" Flour Sifter, three screens with wooden handle and knob, cream with orange bands, 1930s-1940s, Meets-A-Need Co., Seattle, Washington. ...... **$18-$20**

Rooster Measuring Spoon and Hot Pad Holder, styrene plastic, with spoons, 1950s. .... **$22-$25**

Geese Measuring Cups, four-piece set, plastic with colored beaks and eyes, 1950s-1960s. ...... **$18-$22**

Kit Cat Klock, styrene plastic, battery operated with moving eyes and tail, 1950s, California Clock Co., San Juan Capistrano, California. .... **$35-$50**

KITCHENWARES

Nayco Ripple Rolling Pin, "For cookies, pies, cakes, and breads," boxed, 1950s............... **$25-$30**

Krispy Krust Rolling Pin, chrome, with catalin plastic handles and ball bearings, 1940s, Buffalo Toy and Tool Works, Buffalo, New York............................... **$40-$45**

Wear-Ever "Lazy Suzy" Cookie Cutter Wheel, aluminum with styrene plastic center, "Newest easiest way to make fancy cookies every day," boxed, 1950s, Aluminum Cooking Utensil Co. .... **$22-$25**

Federal Onion Choppers, regular, painted metal with wooden knob, graduated, with label, 1940s. .... **$25-$28**

Nutbrown Chipper and French Fry Cutter, metal with wooden handles, simple to operate, "The finest of all chippers!" boxed, 1940s, Thos. M. Nutbrown Ltd., Blackpool, England........ **$25-$28**

Scoop Master Ice-Cream Scoop, "For modern serving, for every kitchen," boxed, 1950s, Bonny Products Co., New York. . **$35-$45**

Bi-Cor Ice-Cream Scoop, stainless with plastic handle, "For ice cream, potatoes, sandwiches," boxed, 1950s, Bloomfield Industries, Chicago. .... **$20-$25**

Cat and Dog Salt and Pepper Shakers, styrene plastic with painted details, promotional set from Ken-L Ration dog food, 1950s, marked F&F Tool and Die, Dayton, Ohio. .... **$25-$28**

Humpty Dumpty on Wall Salt and Pepper Shakers, styrene plastic with contrasting color top, 1950s. .... **$25-$28**

Quick Mayonnaise Maker, steel with glass housing, "Made expressly for the Wesson Oil people," boxed, 1940s-1950s, Wesson Oil, New Orleans.................. **$25-$28**

Tele-Servers, styrene plastic, set of four, server and tumbler sets, "For TV serving, handy, convenient," boxed, 1950s, APCO, Associated Plastic Corp., Chicago..**$25-$28**

Deluxe Serving Tray, styrene plastic, large size in two-tone yellow and green with brown center, 1950s, Another Superlon Product, Superior Plastics, Chicago. .... **$25-$28**

Deluxe Lazy Susan, large size in two-tone green and yellow with clear section covers, 1950s, Federal Tool Corp., Chicago... **$28-$35**

Acme Rotary Mincer, stainless steel blade with wood handle, "For mincing, cutting noodles, etc.," in red or green with instructions, boxed, 1935.......... **$22-$25**

Salad Set, styrene plastic, nine-piece set with flower design, 1950s, Hoffman Industries Inc., Sinking Springs, Pennsylvania. .... **$22-$25**

Tupperware Tumblers, 2 oz. "Midgets" with seals, set of six in pastel shades, 1950s-1960s......... **$12-$15**
Plastic Spice Rack, styrene plastic, non Tupperware, 1950s. .... **$12-$15**

Ekco Tableware, Baguette stainless steel, six place settings, boxed, 1961...**$30-$35**

Wonderlier Bowl Set, five sizes in pastel shades with lids, 1950s-1960s. .... **$45-$50**

Ekco Pastry Kneader, 1940s. .... **$8-$12**

Ekco non-spatter Egg Beater and Bowl Set, (quart), A&J with 1923 patent date. .... **$40-$45**

Jumbo Hamburger Press, wood with painted rooster design, boxed, 1950s, Western Woods Inc., Portland, Oregon. ... **$22-$25**

▶Em-Ree Jar Lifter, metal, "To lift any hot, cold, open, or closed jar with safety," boxed 1940s, Emery & Sons Co., Detroit. .... **$18-$22**

Lighting Devices

Lighting devices have been around for thousands of years, and antique examples range from old lanterns used on the farm to high-end Tiffany lamps. The earliest known type of lamp was the oil lamp, which was mass-produced starting in the 19th century. Bright-burning Aladdin lamps and early electric lamps followed in the early 1900s. Decorative table and floor lamps with ornate glass lampshades reached their height of popularity from 1900-1920, due to the success of Tiffany and other Arts and Crafts lamp makers, such as Handel.

■ Early Non-Electric Lamps & Lighting ——————————

LAMPS, MISCELLANEOUS

Banquet lamp, composite-style, a white metal domed footed base supporting a tall brass stem & embossed brass font w/burner supporting a replaced bulbous frosted & etched clear shade w/ruffled open top, marked "New Juno" burner, electrified, late 19th c., 26" h. **$288**

Left: Banquet lamp, three-section, milk glass baluster-form standard molded w/ acanthus leaves & painted w/pink roses joined to a bulbous matching font w/inset burner supporting the matching tulip-form shade, on a gilt-iron openwork squared foot, Consolidated Lamp & Glass Co., ca. 1890s, overall 35" h. **$1,035**

Center left: Cut-overlay table lamp, kerosene-type, the inverted pear-shaped cranberry cut to clear font in a design of clustered circles, joined by a brass connector to a white opaque Baroque variant pattern base, brass collar w/reducer & late HB&H lip burner, Boudoir-style shade ring soldered to burner, a 3 1/4" h. clear engraved & frosted Oregon shade & early lip chimney, ca. 1870, open bubble on side of font, 10 3/4" h. **$440**

Far left: Gone-with-the-Wind table lamp, decorated milk glass, the domed pierced cast-metal foot supporting a bulbous squatty font w/blown-out lion heads alternating w/small Egyptian landscapes all on a deep rusty brown ground, brass collar & font insert supporting the matching ball shade, some damage, 22" h................... **$403**

Left: Gone-with-the-Wind table lamp, milk glass bulbous base & ball shade h.p. w/a dark shaded green ground & clusters of large white mums & small red daisies & green leafy stems, cast-metal scroll-decorated base & brass collar connector, ca. 1890s, electrified, 22" h. **$316**

Hall lamp, blown spherical deep cranberry swirled ribbed shade w/a brass base cap & drop finial, the top w/a brass crown band w/ hanging chains, electrified, 12" h. **$316**

Hall lamp, gas-type, leaded glass & brass, a tall square form w/each side composed of clear leaded segments centered by an amber & red cross design, metal corner finials & four arched top bars & drop center burner joined to hanging cap, ca. 1890s, electrified, 9" w., 24" h. **$633**

Hanging parlor lamp, kerosene-type, frosted & shaded open-topped domed cranberry shade w/a Diamond Quilted patt. fitted on an ornate shade ring suspending facet-cut prisms above a very elaborate brass framework centered on each side by a red jewel, an ornate brass cap & drop framing the matching Diamond Quilted font, ca. 1880s, shade 14" d. **$3,450**

Hanging parlor lamp, kerosene-type, the open-topped domed milk glass shade h.p. w/large deep red & white flowers & green leaves on a tan ground, pierced brass shade ring suspending facet-cut prisms, looping brass frame supporting the bulbous milk glass font w/decoration matching the shade, complete w/hanging chains, crown & brass smoke bell, solder repair within brass font cup, late 19th c., overall 36" h. **$440**

Parlor table lamps, kerosene-type, mold-blown cranberry glass, each w/a round cushion foot below the large baluster-form ringed body supporting the burner ring & large Diamond Quilted matching tulip-form shades, overall ornate gilt leafy scroll decoration, burner marked "Duplex," some wear & minor flakes, overall 29" h., pr. **$1,610**

▶Sinumbra table lamp, gilt-lacquered bronze, the cut-and-etched clear tulip-form shade resting on a circular shade ring above a tall reeded vasiform standard w/a pair of foliate-cast handles, on a columnar stand joined to a square plinth base, mid-19th c., America or England, electrified, overall 33" h. **$2,185**

Student lamp, double style, the ornate brass body w/raised design of lion heads surrounded by scrolled designs, central bulbous ringed font flanked by upturned large arms each supporting a ring & ribbed white-cased pink open-topped shade & clear chimney, drilled & electrified, width shade to shade 24", shades 10" d., overall 18" h. **$2,300**

Table lamp, kerosene-type, blue opalescent Coin Spot squatty bulbous font joined by a brass connector to a "Detroit" style pedestal base composed of swirls of reds, yellow & white, a brass collar w/a No. 2 slip burner & clear chimney, screw connector, one foot flake, ca. 1880s, 9 1/4" h. . **$605**

Table lamp, kerosene-type, clear Adams Temple - Applesauce design, round plinth-style base supporting four open columns centered by a glass dome w/apparently original contents, the squatly bulbous patterned font w/brass shoulder & shade ring fitted w/a frosted Oregon shade, No. 2 burner & chimney, rim below columns molded "Patented March 20 1883 July 25 1882," cork on center dome w/paper label reading "Fruit Bowl Patented Nov. 15 1881 July 25 1882," Ripley, Vogeley & Adams Co., overall 13" h. **$880**

Table lamp, "Ripley Marriage lamp," two bulbous translucent blue fonts flanking a central covered match holder & joined on a tapering flange to a threaded brass connector on an opaque milk glass stepped, square pedestal foot, connector dated "1868," lamp marked "D.C. Ripley, Patent Pending," brass font collars w/kerosene burners & shade rings supporting clear tulip-shaped etched chimney shades, one shade cracked, overall 19 3/4" h. **$1,265**

Table lamp, pressed Triple Swag & Diamond clear pear-shaped font w/brass collar & connector to the milk white pedestal on a stepped square base, 12 1/4" h. **$77**

Table lamp, 7 1/2" d. domical open-topped porcelain lithophane shade w/four panels showing different ladies in garden settings, colorful tinted interior, raised on a Meissen porcelain base w/a bulbous basketweave font w/applied gilt-trimmed floral sprigs supported by three standing cupids w/delicate coloring all on a round mottled brown base, blue Crossed Swords mark, late 19th c., overall 13 1/2" h. **$2,585**

Table lamp, pressed glass, a kerosene burner & brass collar on the squatty ringed onion-form blue opaline glass font above a turned brass connector & flaring ringed pedestal on a square white marble foot, ca. 1860, 9" h. **$61**

Table lamp, Burmese glass, 10" d. domical shade & base hand-painted & enameled w/Egyptian decoration of five ibis birds in flight in sunrise sky w/pyramids & palm tree oasis scene, original Burmese glass chimney, gilt metal mounts, not electrified, Mount Washington, late 1890s, 20" h. **$10,350**

Whale oil lamp, tin & glass, a clear cylindrical glass font w/brass collar & two-wick whale burner flanked by upright tin round frames enclosing bull's-eye focusing lenses, all on a slender cylindrical tin shaft & round disk weighted base, old worn black finish, first half 19th c., 8 1/2" h. (old repairs, one lens chipped) **$248**

Whale oil table lamp, pressed sapphire blue flint glass, the tapering ovoid fonts w/the Arch patt. fitted w/original pewter collar & double burner, fonts joined w/a wafer to an ornate flaring tiered octagonal pedestal base, Pittsburgh, ca. 1830-50, 10 3/8" h., pr. **$7,425**

Electric Lamps & Lighting_____

HANDEL LAMPS

The Handel Company of Meriden, Connecticut (1885-1936) began as a glass and lamp shade decorating company. It became a major producer of decorative electric lamps which have become very collectible today.

Hanging lamp, domical eight-paneled open-topped caramel slag shade, Hawaiian metal filigree design w/a tropical sunset scene w/palm trees & a lagoon in each panel, hanging hardware & three-light bulb socket, signed, 24" w. **$7,475**

Student lamp, the round bronzed metal reticulated foot centered by a tall reeded shaft issuing two adjustable arching arms ending in electric sockets each fitted w/a 10" d. domical green "Mosserine" shade signed "Handel 6047X," unmarked base, 24" h. **$3,525**

Boudoir lamp, small domical reverse-painted shade decorated w/a continuous meadow landscape w/ tall trees at sunset in shades of yellow, brown, tan & green, raised on a bronze base case in low-relief w/tree trunks, shade signed "Handel 6661," 13" h. **$2,300**

Table lamp, 18" d. domical reverse-painted shade in the Bird of Paradise patt., large exotic birds in shades of deep red, lavender, yellow & orange among shaded brown & yellow foliage against a black background, chipped ice exterior, signed "Handel 7026 - Broggi," atop a heavily enameled urn-form three-legged base w/red enameled berries separating the stylized leaf design around the book, hung w/original amber glass drops & matching glass ball finial, base signed w/label on the felt bottom, 24" h. **$18,300**

Table lamp, 18" d. domical reverse-painted shade in the Mt. Fuji patt., a contiuous Oriental landscape w/tall bamboo in the foreground & a lake & Mt. Fuji in the background, the reverse side shows a bay w/Oriental ships & a dock, signed "Handel 6945 - John Bailley," raised on a Handel cast-bronze bamboo-shaped base w/ Handel cloth tag under the bottom, base w/some minor pitting, rewired, 23" h. **$7,475**

MOSS LAMPS

Clock lamp, No. XT 815, deLee Art male figurine "Siamese Dancer," 2' 11" h. **$275-300**

Floor lamp, No. 2293, "Leaning Lena," butterfly Plexiglas angled standard, 4' 7" h. **$275-300**

Floor lamp, No. 2317, marble pattern plexiglass, Decoramic Kilns figurine "Cocktail Girl," 5' h. **$600-625**

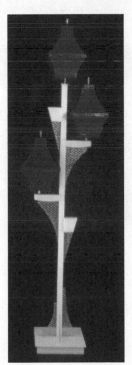

Music box lamp, No. T 534, Lefton "Harlequinade Boy & Girl" figurines, 2' 5" h. **$275-300**

Floor lamp, No. 2328, triple red pagoda-style shade, 6' 5 1/2" h. **$400-425**

▶Partner lamp, No. XT 815, no clock, deLee Art female "Siamese Dancer" figurine, 2' 11" h. **$200-225**

Table lamp, No. T 731, Decoramic Kilns "Prom Girl" figurine, 3' 7 1/2" h. **$300-325**

Table lamp, No. T 544, corner table-style, triple pod shades, Decoramic Kilns "Bell Girl" figurine, 2' 10" h.. **$300-325**

Table lamp, No. XT 835, Johanna "Black Luster Dancer" figurine, 3' h., each (ILLUS. of two) **$125-150**

Table lamp, No. XT 827, torchere shade, Decoramic Kilns "Escort" figurine **$375-400**

Table lamp, No. XT837, "Las Maracas," double pod shades, 3' 8 1/2" h. **$300-325**

Table lamp, No. XT 838, double cone shades, Decoramic Kilns "Mambo" figurine, 4' 4 1/2" h. **$325-350**

Left: Table lamp, No. XT 807, Hedi Schoop "Phantasy Lady" figurine, 2' 5 1/2" h. **$250-275**

Far left: Table lamp, No. T 681, corner table-type, double rectangular shades, Decoramic Kilns "Bali Dancer" figurine, 3'4" h. **$300-325**

PAIRPOINT LAMPS

Well known as a producer of fine Victorian art glass and silver plate wares between 1907 and 1929, the Pairpoint Corporation of New Bedford, Massachusetts, also produced a wide range of decorative lamps.

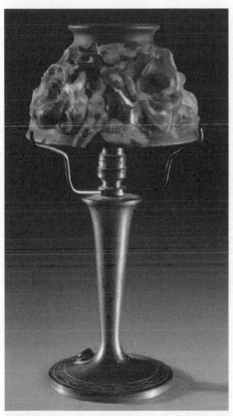

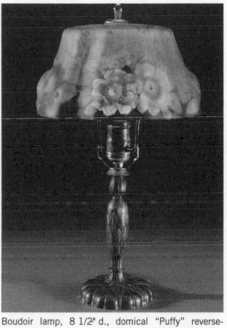

Boudoir lamp, 8 1/2" d., domical "Puffy" reverse-painted "Stratford" shade, flat top & flaring undulating sides decorated around the lower border w/large blue & eyllow dogwood flowers against a pale pink shaded to black ground, signed, raised on a signed slender bronzed metal base w/the swelled shaft cast w/overlapping pointed leaves, the round base w/ribbing, one small flake inside shade rim, 16" h. **$2,350**

▲Boudoir lamp, 5 1/4" d., domical "Puffy" reverse-painted "Pansy" shade, open-topped & decorated w/dark red, yellow & purple pansy flowers on a dark green ground, raised on a spider support above the simple bronzed metal candlestick-style marked base, minor bruise to shade rim, small fitter rim flake, 11 1/2" h. **$1,528**

Far left: Boudoir lamp, 5" d., domical "Puffy" reverse-painted "Rose Bouquet" shade, decorated w/ large red & yellow roses & green leaves on a frosted clear blue-striped ground, raised on a green patinated brown Pairpoint tree trunk base, base signed "Pairpoint B 3079," 10 1/2" h. **$6,000**

Left: Boudoir lamp, 8" w. domical "Puffy" reverse-painted "Bristol" shade, slightly domed top center above four flaring sides, decorated in each panel w/various flowers including roses, daisies, pansies & poppies, rests on a gilt-bronze Pairpoint base w/a swelled four-sided standard impressed on two sides w/flowers & leaves, on a stepped rectangular foot, base signed "Pairpoint Mfg. Co. B 3050," minor discoloration on base, 15" h. **$4,800**

Table lamp, 13 1/2" d., domical "Puffy" reverse-painted "Devonshire" shade, closed-top design w/a wide border band of large yellow, white & red roses below a flying hummingbird, all against a background of light & dark green stripes, signed, raised on an antiqued bronze Art Nouveau-style base w/the tapering four-sided shaft decorated w/ slender leafy vines above the wide swelled four-lobed foot w/further vining, base marked & stamped "B3031," 22" h. **$9,400**

Table lamp, 12" d., domical "Puffy" reverse-painted "Azalea" shade, closed-top design w/the flowers painted in shades of red, pink, white & yellow w/ green leaves against a black ground, signed, raised on an antiqued brass base signed "Pairpoint 3035," w/a shade ring supported by four curved & pierced flat arms tapering to the conical base raised on fancy ornate leaf-scroll feet, overall 22" **$12,925**

Table lamp, 14" d., domical "Puffy" reverse-painted "Papillion" shade, closed-top design decorated w/sections of large red, yellow & orange flowers & green leaves below large yellow & orange butterflies, all against a mottled white ground, signed, on an antiqued brass base w/a slender columnar shaft w/tall narrow oval panels centered by tiny floral sprigs above the paneled & squared foot cast w/shell-like devices, base marked "Pairpoint Mfg. Co. B33202," 21" h. **$10,500**

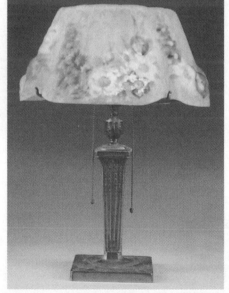

Table lamp, 15 1/2" d., domical "Puffy" reverse-painted "Devonshire" shade, closed-top design decorated on each side w/garlands of colorful flowers against a pale bluish green ground, riased on a green patinated bronze base w/a tall square slightly tapering fluted column above a rectangular foot, interior of shade w/some darkening from light bulb heat, a couple of tiny rim fleabites, 21 3/4" h. **$9,300**

Table lamp, 12" d. domical reverse-painted "Venice" shade, decorated w/large pink rose blossoms w/yellow & green leaves against a frosted white scrolling ground, on a slender bronze base w/a square foot marked "Pairpoint B 3003," 21" h. **$4,485**

TIFFANY LAMPS

Desk lamp, 7" d. domical open-topped shade w/molded ribbing & decorated w/a continuous wavy golden orange banded design, cased in gold iridescence, supported on a Tiffany bronze three-prong base w/a central shaft resting on a round leaf-cast foot w/a brown patina, shade signed "LCT," base signed "Tiffany Studios - New York 426," chips to fitted rim, minor damage to top cap & socket of base, overall 14" h............. **$8,625**

Desk lamp, Arabian-style, a conical shade decorated w/a gold & platinum iridescent snakeskin design on a butterscotch ground, on a slender baluster-form optic ribbed amber iridescent glass standard on a domed foot, shade & base signed, 13" h. **$4,680**

Desk lamp, the shade formed by a large white nautilus shell trimmed in hammered silver & raised on a forked bronze standard above a round domed base w/a ribbed edge & raised on five small ball feet, fine reddish brown patina w/ green highlights, base signed "Tiffany Studios - New York 403," 13" h. **$7,763**

Desk lamp, counter-balance style, a 7" w. domed shade w/platinum damascene iridescent decoration on an orange & purple ground w/cased interior, supported atop a high arched counter-balance arm above the domed base trimmed w/a row of teardrop nodules, fine dark patina, shade signed "LCT Favrile," base signed "Tiffany Studios - New York 415," 16" h. **$16,200**

Table lamp, "Acorn Border," a 16" d. domical leaded glass shade composed of concentric rows of graduated rectangular tiles in heavily mottled yellow opalescent glass above a medial band of mottled green opalescent glass heart-shaped leaves, w/finial, raised on a gilt-bronze slender three-arm standard w/applied thin reeded bands w/small curled ends above the leaf-cast cushion base on scroll feet, shade signed "Tiffany Studios - New York," base signed "Tiffany Studios - New York - 357 - S171," 22" h. .. **$17,825**

LIGHTING DEVICES

Table lamp, "Daffodil," 16" d. domical open-topped leaded glass shade composed of tall clusters of yellow daffodils on leafy stems against a mottled white shaded to mottled green ground, shade marked "Tiffany Studios - New York," raised on a tall slender shaft above a cushion base cast w/rounded teardrops raised on scroll feet, base impressed "Tiffany Studios - New York - 6842," 22 1/2" h. **$37,375**

Table lamp, "Geranium," 16 1/8" d. conical leaded glass shade decorated w/mottled red geranium blossoms above, against a mottled pale blue & green ground, among a profusion of varied colored green leaves below, interspersed w/rippled glass leaves, against a mottled & striated pale pink & green ground, bordered by three bands in mottled pale pink, blue & green, the standard cast w/scrolling tendrils & pods, in rich greenish red patina, tag stamped "TIFFANY STUDIOS - NEW YORK," 23" h. **$32,200**

Table lamp, "Linenfold," the 14 1/2" w. twelve-sided slightly tapering shade w/an arrangement of large square amber linenfold panels between smaller amber linenfold borders between amber smooth borders, intaglio finish, shade impressed "TIFFANY STUDIOS - NEW YORK - 1950 - PAT. APPLIED FOR," the base impressed "TIFFANY STUDIOS - 442," 24 1/2" h... **$5,000**

Table lamp, "Lily," ten-light, the long clambroth & butterscotch optic-ribbed iridescent Favrile glass trumpet-form lily shades on a clustered stem bronze doré lily pad base, shades signed "L.C. T.," base impressed "Tiffany Studios - N.Y." & numbered, 20" h **$40,538**

◆ Louis Comfort Tiffany's lampshades were inspired by the stained glass windows in European cathedrals. But instead of painting powdered glass on the surface of the glass as was done on the cathedral glass, he chose to use solid color glass for his creations.

Little Golden Books

Western Publishing Company, Inc., one of the largest printers of children's books in the world, began in Racine, Wisconsin when Edward Henry Wadewitz purchased the West Side Printing Company in 1907. In 1910, the name was changed to Western Printing and Lithographing Company.

By its seventh year, sales had topped $127,000. Wadewitz was approached by the Hamming-Whitman Publishing Company of Chicago to print its line of children's books. Unable to pay its bills, Hamming-Whitman left Western with thousands of books in its warehouse and in production. Trying to cut its losses, Wadewitz entered Western into the retail book market for the first time. It proved so successful that the remaining Hamming-Whitman books were liquidated.

After acquiring Hamming-Whitman on Feb. 9, 1916, Western formed a subsidiary corporation called Whitman Publishing Company. Whitman grossed more than $43,500 in children's book sales in its first year. Sam Lowe joined the Western team in 1916. Lowe sold Western and Whitman on the idea of bringing out a 10-cent children's book in 1918.

By 1928, sales were more than $2.4 million. Western was able to keep its plant operational during the Depression years (1929-1933) by introducing a jigsaw puzzle and a new series of books called Big Little Books.

Western formed the Artists and Writers Guild Inc. in the 1930s to handle the development of new children's books. This company, located on Fifth Avenue in New York City, had an immense hand in the conception of Little Golden Books.

In 1940, Sam Lowe left the company and George Duplaix replaced him as head of the Artists and Writers Guild. Duplaix came up with the concept of a colorful children's book that would be durable and affordable to more American families than those being printed at that time. The group decided on 12 titles to be released at the same time. These books were to be called Little Golden Books. The books sold for 25 cents each. In September 1942, the first 12 titles were printed and released to stores in October.

The First 12 Little Golden Books
1 Three Little Kittens
2 Bedtime Stories
3 The Alphabet A-Z
4 Mother Goose
5 Prayers for Children
6 The Little Red Hen
7 Nursery Songs
8 The Poky Little Puppy
9 The Golden Book of Fairy Tales
10 Baby's Book
11 The Animals of Farmer Jones
12 This Little Piggy

Within five months, 1.5 million copies of the books had been printed and they were in their third printing. They became so popular with children that by the end of 1945, most of the first 12 books had been printed seven times. When the books were first released, they were sold mainly in book and department stores. From there, they moved into variety, toy, and drug stores, and finally in the late 1940s, to something new called the supermarket.

Sales of Little Golden Books were doing so well that in 1944, Simon & Schuster decided to create a new division headed by George Duplaix, called Sandpiper Press. Duplaix hired Dorothy Bennett as the general editor. She was responsible for many of the subjects used in Little Golden Books through the mid-1950s.

In 1952, on the tenth anniversary of Little Golden Books, approximately 182,615,000 Little Golden Books had been sold. In their eleventh year, almost 300 million Little Golden Books had been sold. More than half of the titles printed by 1954 had sold more than a million copies each.

Little Golden Books have been printed in more than 42 countries. In 1982, Little Golden Books were 40 years old and more than 800 million books had been sold. On Nov. 20, 1986, the one billionth Little Golden Book was printed in the United States, The Poky Little Puppy.

Little Golden Books are still published today.

For more information on Little Golden Books, see *Warman's Little Golden Books Identification and Price Guide* by Steve Santi.

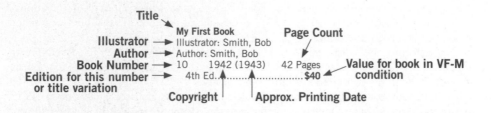

My First Book
Illustrator: Smith, Bob
Author: Smith, Bob
10   1942 (1943)   42 Pages
4th Ed. $40

Title
Illustrator
Author
Book Number
Edition for this number or title variation
Copyright
Approx. Printing Date
Page Count
Value for book in VF-M condition

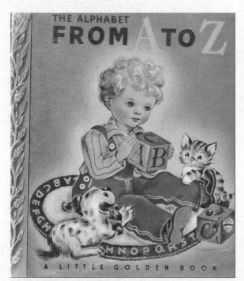

Alphabet From A-Z, The
Illustrator: Blake, Vivienne
3   1942   42 Pages   1st Ed. $50
Four-Color and Black & White
Blue Spine with Dust Jacket .... $50-$200
3   1942 (1950) 42 Pages   18th Ed. $16
Four-Color and Black & White Golden Paper Spine.
  Song added to last page.

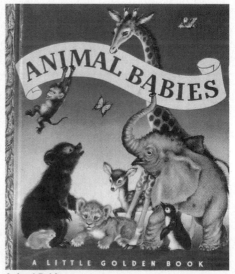

Animal Babies
Illustrator: Werber, Adele
Author: Jackson, Kathryn & Byron
39   1947   42 Pages   1st Ed. $16
Four-Color and Black & White Golden Paper Spine
39   1947 (1949) 28 Pages   3rd Ed. $12
Four-Color

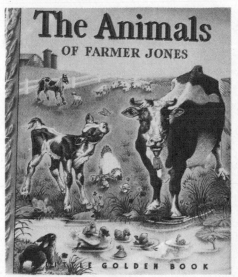

Animals of Farmer Jones, The
Illustrator: Freund, Rudolf
Author: Gale, Leah
11   1942   42 Pages   1st Ed........**$50**
Four-Color and Black & White
Blue Spine with Dust Jacket ....**$50-$200**
11   1942 (1943) 24 Pages   1st Ed........**$22**
Four-Color and Black & White Blue Spine Blue Spine
  with Dust Jacket..................................**$40-$100**
11   1942 (1947) 42 Pages   10th Ed. **$15**
Four-Color and Black & White
Golden Paper Spine

Baby's Book
Illustrator: Smith, Bob
Author: Smith, Bob
10   1942   42 Pages   1st Ed........**$50**
Four-Color and Black & White
Blue Spine with Dust Jacket ....**$75-$300**

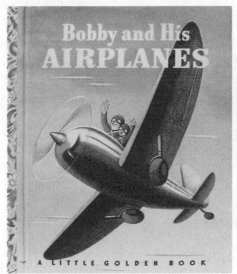

Bobby and His Airplanes
Illustrator: Gergely, Tibor
Author: Palmer, Helen
69   1949   42 Pages   1st Ed........**$18**
Four-Color and Three-Color
Golden Paper Spine

Bedtime Stories
Illustrator: Tenggren, Gustaf
Author: Misc. Authors
2   1942   42 Pages   1st Ed........**$50**
Four-Color and Black & White
Blue Spine with Dust Jacket ....**$50-$150**
Five Stories: Chicken Little, The Three Bears, The Three
  Little Pigs, Little Red Riding Hood, The Gingerbread
  Man
2   1942 (1955) 28 Pages   21st Ed......**$12**
Four-Color. Foil Spine
Three Stories: The Gingerbread Man, Chicken Little,
  Little Red Riding Hood

Busy Timmy
Illustrator: Wilkin, Eloise
Author: Jackson, Kathryn & Byron
50   1948   28 Pages
   1st Ed. **$35**
Four-Color, Golden Paper Spine

Color Kittens, The
Illustrator: Provenson, Alice & Martin
Author: Brown, Margaret Wise
86   1949   28 Pages
   1st Ed. **$25**
Four-Color, Golden Paper Spine

Come Play House
Illustrator: Wilkin, Eloise
Author: Oswald, Edith
44   1948   42 Pages
   1st Ed. **$35**
Four-Color and Black & White
Golden Paper Spine

Chip Chip
Illustrator: Carbe, Nino
Author: Wright, Norman
28   1947   42 Pages
   1st Ed. **$25**
Four-Color and Black & White

Blue Spine with Dust Jacket
.............................**$50-$150**

Circus Time
Illustrator: Gergely, Tibor
Author: Conger, Marion
31   1948   42 Pages
   1st Ed. **$20**
Four-Color and Black & White
31   1948 (1950)   42 Pages
   7th Ed. **$16**
Four-Color and Three-Color
Golden Paper Spine
31   1948 (1952)   28 Pages
   9th Ed. **$12**
Four-Color, Foil Spine

Counting Rhymes
Illustrator: Malvern Corrine
12   1946   42 Pages
   1st Ed. **$25**
Four-Color and Black & White
   Blue Spine with Dust Jacket
.............................**$50-$100**
12   1942 (1948)   28 Pages
   4th Ed. **$16**
Four-Color
Golden Paper Spine

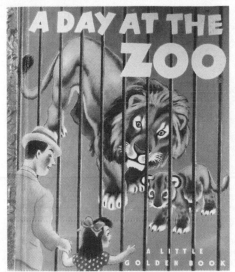

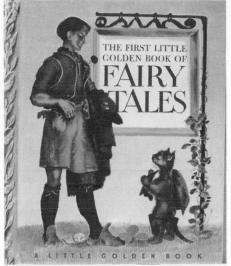

Day at the Zoo, A
Illustrator: Gergely, Tibor
Author: Conger, Marion
88   1949   42 Pages   1st Ed........**$14**
Four-Color, Foil Spine
88   1949 (1952) 28 Pages   2nd Ed.......**$12**
Four-Color, Foil Spine
324   1950 (1958) 24 Pages   4th Ed. **$8**

First Little Golden Book of Fairy Tales, The
Illustrator: Elliott, Gertrude
9   1946   24 Pages   1st Ed........**$20**
Four-Color and Black & White
Blue Spine with Dust Jacket ....**$50-$100**
Three stories: Jack and the Beanstalk, Puss in Boots,
Sleeping Beauty
9   1946 (1947) 42 Pages   2nd Ed...... **$16**
Four-Color and Black & White
Golden Paper Spine

Five Little Firemen
Illustrator: Gergely, Tibor
Author: Brown, Margaret Wise
64   1948   42 Pages   1st Ed........**$30**
Four-Color and Black & White
Golden Paper Spine
64   1948 (1951) 28 Pages   8th Ed. **$15**
Four-Color, Foil Spine
Picture with poem changed.

Fix It, Please
Illustrator: Wilkin, Eloise
Author: Mitchell, Lucy Sprague
32   1947   42 Pages   1st Ed........**$35**
Four-Color and Black & White
Gold Paper Spine

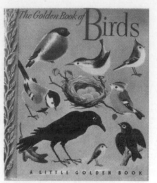

Fuzzy Duckling, The
Illustrator: Provenson, Alice & Martin
Author: Werner, Jane
78   1949   28 Pages
    1st Ed..............................$15
Four-Color
Golden Paper Spine

Gaston and Josephine
Illustrator: Rojankovsky, Feodor
Author: Duplaix, Georges
65   1949   42 Pages
    1st Ed..............................$30
Four-Color and Black & White
Golden Paper Spine
65   1949 (1950)   42 Pages
    4th Ed.............................$25
Four-Color and Three-Color
Golden Paper Spine

Golden Book of Birds, The
Illustrator: Rojankovsky, Feodor
Author: Lockwood, Hazel
13   1943   42 Pages
    1st Ed. $25
Four-Color and Black & White
    Blue Spine with Dust Jacket
    ....$50-$150
13   1943 (1948)   42 Pages
    4th Ed..............................$20
Four-Color and Black & White
Golden Paper Spine

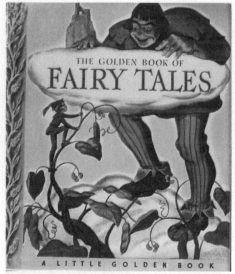

Golden Book of Fairy Tales, The
Illustrator: Hoskins, Winfield
9   1942   42 Pages   1st Ed........$50
Four-Color and Black & White
Blue Spine with Dust Jacket ....$50-$200
Four stories: Jack and the Beanstalk, Cinderella, Puss
    in Boots, Sleeping Beauty
9   1942 (1943) 24 Pages   1st Ed........$22
Four-Color and Black & White
Blue Spine
Three stories: Jack and the Beanstalk, Puss in Boots,
    Cinderella
Blue Spine with Dust Jacket ....$40-$100
Four-Color and Black & White

Golden Book of Flowers, The
Illustrator: Hershberger
Author: Witman, Mabel
16   1943   42 Pages   1st Ed........$30
Four-Color and Black & White
Blue Spine with Dust Jacket ....$50-$150

Golden Sleepy Book, The
Illustrator: Williams, Garth
Author: Brown, Margaret Wise
46   1948   42 Pages
  1st Ed. $25
Four-Color and Black & White
Golden Paper Spine

Good Morning, Good Night
Illustrator: Wilkin, Eloise
Author: Werner, Jane
61   1948   42 Pages
  1st Ed. $35
Four-Color and Black & White
Golden Paper Spine

Guess Who Lives Here
Illustrator: Wilkin, Eloise
Author: Woodcock, Louise
60   1949   42 Pages
  1st Ed. $30
Four-Color and Black & White
Golden Paper Spine
60   1949 (1949)   42 Pages
  3rd Ed.............................$16
Four-Color and Three-Color
Golden Paper Spine

Hansel and Gretel
Illustrator: Weihs, Erika
Author: Bros. Grimm
17   1945   42 Pages
  1st Ed. $30
Four-Color and Black & White
  Blue Spine with Dust Jacket
  ....$50-$150

17   1945 (1952)   28 Pages
  8th Ed.............................$14
Four-Color and Three-Color
Cover art by Eloise Wilkin

►Happy Man and His Dump Truck, The
Illustrator: Gergely, Tibor
Author: Miryam

77   1950   28 Pages
  1st Ed. $20
Four-Color
Golden Paper Spine

Happy Family, The
Illustrator: Elliott, Gertrude
Author: Nicole
35   1947   42 Pages
  1st Ed. $40
Four-Color and Black & White
  Blue Spine with Dust Jacket
  ....$50-$175
Last title with a dust jacket.

How Big
Illustrator: Malvern, Corinne
Author: Malvern, Corinne
83   1949   28 Pages
  1st Ed..............................$20
Four-Color
Golden Paper Spine

How Big
Illustrator: Malvern, Corinne
Author: Malvern, Corinne
83   1949 (1970)   24 Pages
  2nd Ed..............................$6
Four-Color
Foil Spine

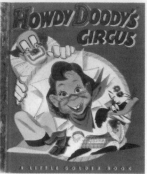

Howdy Doody's Circus
Illustrator: Dauber, Liz
Author: Gormley, Don
99   1950   28 Pages
  1st Ed..............................$25

Jerry at School
Illustrator: Malvern, Corinne
Author: Jackson, Kathryn & Byron
94   1950 (1951)   28 Pages
  2nd Ed..............................$15

Johnny's Machines
Illustrator: DeWitt, Cornelius
Author: Palmer, Helen
71   1949   42 Pages
  1st Ed..............................$16
Four-Color and Three-Color
Golden Paper Spine

Jolly Barnyard, The
Illustrator: Gergely, Tibor
Author: Bedford, Annie North
67   1950   28 Pages
  1st Ed..............................$16
Four-Color

Jolly Barnyard, The
Illustrator: Gergely, Tibor
Author: Bedford, Annie North
67   1950 (1965)   24 Pages
  4th Ed..............................$6
Four-Color, Foil Spine

Katie the Kitten
Illustrator: Provenson,
  Alice & Martin
Author: Jackson, Kath-
  ryn & Byron
75   1949
  28 Pages
  1st Ed............$15
Four-Color
Golden Paper Spine

Let's Go Shopping
Illustrator: Combes, Lenora
Author: Combes, Lenora
33   1948   42 Pages   1st Ed. **$17**
Four-Color and Black & White
Golden Paper Spine
33   1948 (1949) 42 Pages   5th Ed. **$15**
Four-Color and Three-Color
Golden Paper Spine
33   1948 (1950) 42 Pages   6th Ed. **$15**
Four-Color and Three-Color
Golden Paper Spine
Song added to last page.

Little Black Sambo
Illustrator: Tenggren, Gustaf
Author: Bannerman, Helen
57   1948   42 Pages   1st Ed. **$175**
Four-Color and Black & White
Golden Paper Spine
57   1948 (1949) 42 Pages   5th Ed. ... **$125**
Four-Color and Three-Color
Golden Paper Spine
57   1948 (1952) 28 Pages   7th Ed. ... **$100**
Four-Color, Foil Spine
57   1948 (1960) 24 Pages   15th Ed. ... **$75**
Four-Color, Foil Spine

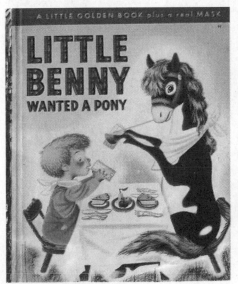

Little Benny Wanted a Pony
Illustrator: Scarry, Richard
Author: Barnett, Olive O'Connor
97   1950   42 Pages   1st Ed. **$60**

Little Boy With a Big Horn
Illustrator: Battaglia, Aurelius
Author: Bezchdolt, Jack
100   1950   42 Pages   1st Ed. **$16**

LITTLE GOLDEN BOOKS

Little Golden Holiday Book, The
Illustrator: Wilkin, Eloise
Author: Conger, Marion
109   1951   28 Pages
   1st Ed. **$25**

Little Golden Book of Poetry, The
Illustrator: Malvern, Corinne
38   1947   42 Pages
   1st Ed. **$16**
Four-Color and Black & White
Golden Paper Spine
38   1947 (1948)   28 Pages
   2nd Ed. **$12**
Four-Color, Golden Paper Spine

Little Galoshes
Illustrator: Miller, J.P.
Author: Jackson, Kathryn & Byron
68   1949   68 Pages
   1st Ed. **$25**
Four-Color and Three-Color
Golden Paper Spine

Little Golden Book of Hymns, The
Illustrator: Malvern, Corinne
Author: Werner, Elsa Jane
34   1947   42 Pages
   1st Ed. **$16**
Four-Color and Black & White
Golden Paper Spine
34   1947 (1949)   28 Pages
   4th Ed. **$8**
Four-Color

Golden Paper Spine
34   1947 (1950)   42 Pages
   8th Ed. **$12**
Four-Color
Golden Paper Spine   42 Pages is
correct.

Little Golden Book of Singing Games, The
Illustrator: Malvern, Corinne
Author: Wessles, Katheryne Tyler
40   1947   42 Pages
   1st Ed. **$15**
Four-Color and Black & White
Golden Paper Spine

Little Golden Book of Words, The
Illustrator: Elliott, Gertrude
Author: Chambers, Selma Lola
45   1948   42 Pages
   1st Ed. **$18**
Four-Color and Black & White
Golden Paper Spine

Little Golden Book of Words, The
Illustrator: Elliott, Gertrude
Author: Chambers, Selma Lola
45   1948 (1949)   42 Pages   5th Ed. $15
Four-Color and Three-Color
Golden Paper Spine
45   1948 (1952)   28 Pages   8th Ed. $8
Four-Color
Foil Spine
45   1948 (1955)   24 Pages   12th Ed. $5
Four-Color
Foil Spine
Title changed to Words.

Little Golden Funny Book, The
Illustrator: Miller, J.P.
Author: Crampton, Gertrude
74   1950   42 Pages   1st Ed........$14
Four-Color, Golden Paper Spine

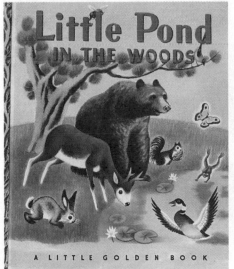

Little Pond in the Woods
Illustrator: Gergely, Tibor
Author: Ward, Muriel
43   1948   42 Pages   1st Ed........$30
Four-Color and Black & White
Golden Paper Spine

Little Red Hen, The
Illustrator: Freund, Rudolf
Author: Potter, Marion
6   1942   42 Pages   1st Ed........$50
Four-Color and Black & White
Blue Spine with Dust Jacket ....$50-$200
6   1942 (1949)   42 Pages   12th Ed. $15
Four-Color and Three-Color

Little Red Hen, The
Illustrator: Freund, Rudolf
Author: Potter, Marion
6 1942 (1952)   28 Pages
  13th Ed............................**$25**
Four-Color and Three-Color
Foil Spine

Little PeeWee Or, Now Open the Box
Illustrator: Miller, J.P.
Author: Kunhardt, Dorothy M.
52   1948   42 Pages
  1st Ed. **$17**
Four-Color and Black & White
Golden Paper Spine

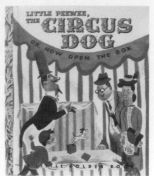

Little PeeWee, The Circus Dog Or, Now Open the Box
Illustrator: Miller, J.P.
Author: Kunhardt, Dorothy M.
52   1948 (1949)   42 Pages
  7th Ed..............................**$25**
Four-Color and Three-Color
Golden Paper Spine

Little Trapper, The
Illustrator: Tenggren, Gustaf
Author: Jackson, Kathryn & Byron
79   1950   42 Pages
  1st Ed. **$18**
Four-Color
Golden Paper Spine

79   1950 (1950)   28 Pages
  2nd Ed.............................**$16**
Four-Color
Foil Spine

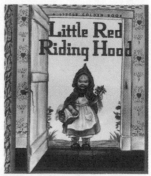

Little Red Riding Hood
Illustrator: Jones, Elizabeth Orton
Author: Jones, Elizabeth Orton
42   1948   42 Pages
  1st Ed. **$40**
Four-Color and Black & White
Golden Paper Spine

Little Yip Yip and His Bark
Illustrator: Gergely, Tibor
Author: Jackson, Kathryn & Byron
73   1950   42 Pages
  1st Ed. **$16**
Four-Color, Foil Spine

Lively Little Rabbit, The
Illustrator: Tenggren, Gustaf
Author: Ariane
15   1943   42 Pages   1st Ed........ **$35**
Four-Color and Black & White
Blue Spine with Dust Jacket ....**$50-$150**
15   1943 (1943) 24 Pages   1st Ed........ **$22**
Four-Color and Black & White
Blue Spine, War Edition
Blue Spine with Dust Jacket ....**$50-$100**
15   1943 (1948) 42 Pages   10th Ed. **$15**
Four-Color and Black & White
Golden Paper Spine
Sleeping owl picture dropped from book.
15   1943 (1951) 42 Pages   14th Ed. **$14**
Four-Color, Foil Spine. Song added to last page.

Lively Little Rabbit, The
Illustrator: Tenggren, Gustaf
Author: Ariane
15   1943 (1954) 28 Pages   15th Ed. **$15**

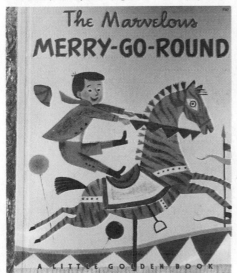

Marvelous Merry-Go-Round, The
Illustrator: Miller, J.P.
Author: Werner, Jane
87   1949   42 Pages   1st Ed........ **$15**
Four-Color, Foil Spine

Mother Goose
Illustrator: Elliott, Gertrude
Author: Fraser, Phyllis
4   1942   42 Pages   1st Ed........ **$50**
Four-Color and Black & White
Blue Spine with Dust Jacket ....**$50-$200**
4   1942 (1943) 24 Pages   4th Ed. **$20**
Four-Color and Black & White
Blue Spine
Abridged for the war.
Blue Spine with Dust Jacket ....**$40-$100**
4 1942 (1953)   28 Pages 22nd Ed.......... **$12**
Four-Color and Three-Color
Foil Spine

Mr. Noah and His Family
Illustrator: Provensen, Alice & Martin
Author: Werner, Jane
49   1948   28 Pages
  1st Ed. $18
Four-Color, Golden Paper Spine

My First Book
Illustrator: Smith, Bob
Author: Smith, Bob
10   1942 (1943)   42 Pages
  4th Ed.............................$40
Four-Color and Black & White
Blue Spine with Dust Jacket

My First Book
Illustrator: Smith, Bob
Author: Smith, Bob
10   1942 (1947)   42 Pages
  8th Ed.............................$20
Four-Color and Black & White
Gold Paper Spine
Laddie the dog's name changed to
  Bow-wow.

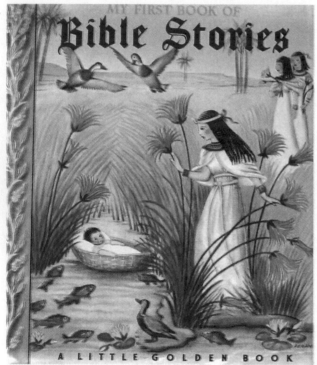

My First Book of Bible Stories
Illustrator: Ferand, Emmy
Author: Walton, Mary Ann
19   1943   42 Pages
  1st Ed. $40

Four-Color and Black & White
  Blue Spine with Dust Jacket
  ....$60-$175

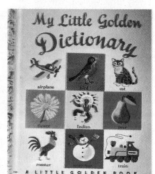

My Little Golden Dictionary
Illustrator: Scarry, Richard
Author: Reed, Mary; Oswald, Edith
90   1949   56 Pages
  1st Ed. $15
Four-Color, Golden Paper Spine

Name for Kitty, A
Illustrator: Rojankovsky, Feodor
Author: Mcginley, Phyllis
55   1948   28 Pages
  1st Ed. $14
Four-Color, Golden Paper Spine

New Baby, The
Illustrator: Wilkin, Eloise
Author: Shane, Ruth & Harold
41   1948 (1948) 42 Pages   2nd Ed.......**$35**
Four-Color and Black & White
Golden Paper Spine
41   1948 (1950) 42 Pages   6th Ed. **$25**
Four-Color and Three-Color
Golden Paper Spine

New Baby, The
Illustrator: Wilkin, Eloise
Author: Shane, Ruth & Harold
41   1948 (1954) 28 Pages   7th Ed. **$15**
Four-Color, Foil Spine

New House in the Forest, The
Illustrator: Wilkin, Eloise
Author: Mitchell, Lucy Sprague
24   1946   42 Pages   1st Ed........**$40**
Four-Color and Black & White
Blue Spine with Dust Jacket ....**$50-$175**

Night Before Christmas, The
Illustrator: DeWitt, Cornelius
Author: Moore, Clement C.
20   1946   42 Pages   1st Ed........**$25**
Blue spine; never printed with dust jacket.
20   1946 (1948) 42 Pages   3rd Ed. **$22**
Four-Color and Black & White
Golden Paper Spine, Two songs added.

Night Before Christmas, The
Illustrator: Malvern, Corinne
Author: Moore, Clement C.
20   1949   28 Pages
  1st Ed. $15
Four-Color. Gilded cover and pages.

Night Before Christmas, The
Illustrator: Malvern, Corinne
Author: Moore, Clement C.
20   1949 (1951)   28 Pages
  5th Ed..............................$18
Four-Color, Foil Spine
Gilded cover and pages.

Noises and Mr. Flibberty-Jib
Illustrator: Wilkin, Eloise
Author: Wilkin, Eloise
29   1947   42 Pages
  1st Ed. $40
Four-Color and Black & White
Gold Paper Spine

Nursery Rhymes
Illustrator: Elliott, Gertrude
59   1948   28 Pages
  1st Ed. $14
Four-Color, Golden Paper Spine

Nursery Songs
Illustrator: Malvern, Corinne
Author: Gale, Leah
7 1942   42 Pages
  1st Ed. $40
Four-Color and Black & White
  Blue Spine with Dust Jacket
  ....$50-$200

Nursery Songs
Illustrator: Malvern, Corinne
Author: Gale, Leah
7 1942 (1949)   42 Pages
  15th Ed............................$15
Gold Paper Spine

Nursery Tales
Illustrator: Masha
14   1943   42 Pages
  1st Ed. $25
Four-Color and Black & White
  Blue Spine with Dust Jacket
  ....$50-$150
14   1943 (1951)   42 Pages
  9th Ed..............................$20
Four-Color and Black & White
Golden Paper Spine
Song added to last page.

Our Puppy
Illustrator: Rojankovsky, Feodor
Author: Nast, Elsa Ruth
56   1948   28 Pages
  1st Ed. $14
Four-Color, Golden Paper Spine
292   1948 (1957)   24 Pages
  5th Ed................................$7

Pat-A-Cake
Illustrator: Battaglia, Aurelius
Author: Mother Goose
54   1948   28 Pages
  1st Ed. $14
Four-Color
Golden Paper Spine

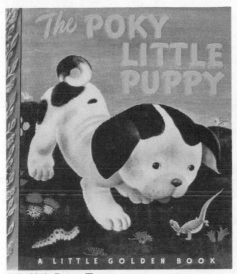

Poky Little Puppy, The
Illustrator: Tenggren, Gustaf
Author: Lowrey, Janet Sebring
8   1942   42 Pages   1st Ed........**$50**
Four-Color and Black & White
Blue Spine with Dust Jacket ....**$50-$200**
8   1942 (1950)   42 Pages   21st Ed......**$15**
Four-Color, Golden Paper Spine
8   1942 (1950)   28 Pages   22nd Ed.....**$10**
Four-Color, Foil Spine

Saggy Baggy Elephant, The
Illustrator: Tenggren, Gustaf
Author: Jackson, Kathryn & Byron
36   1947   42 Pages   1st Ed........**$25**
Four-Color and Black & White, Golden Paper Spine
36   1947 (1949)   28 Pages   4th Ed. **$18**
Four-Color, Golden Paper Spine
36   1947 (1955)   28 Pages   11th Ed. **$8**
Four-Color, Foil Spine
36   1947 (1955)   24 Pages   11th Ed. **$5**
Four-Color, Foil Spine
11th Ed. done with 28 & 24 pages.

Prayers for Children
Illustrator: Dixon, Rachel Taft
5   1942   42 Pages 1st Ed.............**$40**
Four-Color and Black & White
Blue Spine with Dust Jacket**$50-$200**
5   1942 (1948)   42 Pages 12th Ed. **$15**
Four-Color and Black & White, Golden Paper Spine
Prayer "Till the victory is ours" changed to "Good Night."
5   1942 (1950)   42 Pages 18th Ed. **$12**
Four-Color and Three-Color, Golden Paper Spine
Song added to last page.
5   1942 (1950)   42 Pages 19th Ed. **$10**
Four-Color and Three-Color, Golden Paper Spine
Song on last page given solid background.

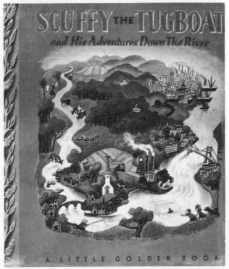

Scuffy the Tugboat
Illustrator: Gergely, Tibor
Author: Crampton, Gertrude
30   1946   42 Pages   1st Ed........**$25**
Four-Color and Black & White
Blue Spine with Dust Jacket ....**$50-$150**
30   1946 (1951)   42 Pages   9th Ed. **$18**
Four-Color, Foil Spine

LITTLE GOLDEN BOOKS

Seven Sneezes, The
Illustrator: Gergely, Tibor
Author: Cabral, Olga
51　　1948　　　　42 Pages
　1st Ed. **$25**
Four-Color and Black & White
Golden Paper Spine
51　　1948 (1948)　　28 Pages
　4th Ed. **$15**
Four-Color, Golden Paper Spine

Shy Little Kitten, The
Illustrator: Tenggren, Gustaf
Author: Schurr, Kathleen
23　　1946　　　　42 Pages
　1st Ed. **$25**
Four-Color and Black & White
Blue Spine with Dust Jacket
　........................... **$50-$150**
23　　1946 (1949)　　28 Pages
　5th Ed. **$12**
Four-Color, Golden Paper Spine

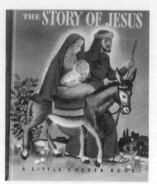

Story of Jesus, The
Illustrator: Lerch, Steffie
Author: Alexander, Beatrice
27　　1946　　　　42 Pages
　1st Ed. **$25**
Four-Color and Black & White
Blue Spine with Dust Jacket
　........................... **$50-$150**
27　　1946 (1949)　　42 Pages
　6th Ed. **$18**
Four-Color and Three-Color
Golden Paper Spine

Surprise for Sally
Illustrator: Malvern, Corinne
Author: Crowninshield, Ethel
84　　1950　　　　42 Pages
　1st Ed. **$22**
Four-Color. Comes in gold paper
　and foil editions.

Susie's New Stove
Illustrator: Malvern, Corinne
Author: Bedford, Annie North
85　　1950　　　　42 Pages
　1st Ed. **$35**
Four-Color, Golden Paper Spine

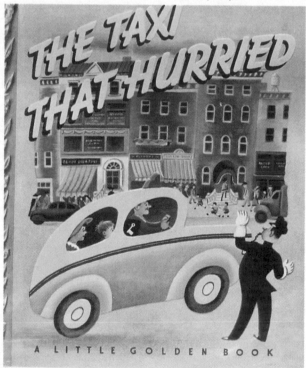

Taxi That Hurried, The
Illustrator: Gergely, Tibor
Author: Mitchell, Lucy Sprague;
　Simonton
25　　1946　　　　42 Pages
　1st Ed. **$25**
Four-Color and Black & White
Blue Spine with Dust Jacket
　........................... **$50-$150**

25　　1946 (1951)　　42 Pages
　6th Ed. **$8**
Four-Color and Black & White
Golden Paper Spine
25　　1946 (1951)　　28 Pages
　10th Ed. **$8**
Four-Color, Foil Spine

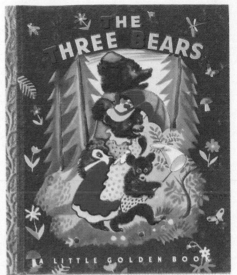

This Little Piggy and Other Counting Rhymes
Illustrator: Paflin, Roberta
12   1942   42 Pages   1st Ed........ **$60**
Four-Color and Black & White
Blue Spine with Dust Jacket ....**$60-$250**

Three Bears, The
Illustrator: Rojankovsky, Feodor
47   1948   42 Pages   1st Ed........ **$95**
Four Color and Black & White
Golden Paper Spine

Three Bears, The
Illustrator: Rojankovsky, Feodor
47   1948 (1948)   42 Pages   2nd Ed....... **$25**
Four-Color and Black & White
Golden Paper Spine
47   1948 (1949)   42 Pages   5th Ed. **$16**
Four-Color and Three-Color
Golden Paper Spine
47   1948 (1955)   28 Pages   10th Ed. **$8**
Four-Color, Foil Spine
47   1948 (1955)   24 Pages   13th Ed. **$4**
Four-Color, Foil Spin

Three Little Kittens
Illustrator: Masha
1   1942   42 Pages   1st Ed........ **$50**
Four-Color and Black & White
Blue Spine with Dust Jacket ....**$50-$200**
1 1942 (1946)   24 Pages   9th Ed. **$30**
Four-Color and Black & White, Blue Spine
"To Albert" no longer written above clothsline.
Blue Spine with Dust Jacket ....**$40-$100**
1   1942 (1951)   42 Pages   17th Ed. **$20**
Four-Color and Three-Color, Golden Paper Spine
Song added to last page.
1   1942 (1952)   28 Pages   19th Ed. **$12**
Four-Color and Three-Color, Foil Spine
Song on page 4.

Tootle
Illustrator: Gergely, Tibor
Author: Crampton, Gertrude
21   1945   42 Pages
1st Ed. $30
Four-Color and Black & White
Blue Spine with Dust Jacket .... $50-$175

Tootle
Illustrator: Gergely, Tibor
Author: Crampton, Gertrude
21   1945 (1945) 42 Pages   2nd Ed. $20
Four-Color and Black & White
Blue Spine with Dust Jacket .... $50-$150
21   1945 (1951) 42 Pages   14th Ed. $15
Four-Color and Three-Color, Foil Spine
21   1945 (1952) 28 Pages   15th Ed. $7
Four-Color and Three-Color, Foil Spine
21   1945 (1957) 24 Pages   17th Ed. $5
Four-Color and Three-Color, Foil Spine

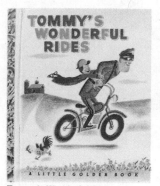

Tommy's Wonderful Rides
Illustrator: Miller, J.P.
Author: Palmer, Helen
63   1948   42 Pages
    1st Ed. $17
Four-Color and Black & White
Golden Paper Spine
63   1948 (1950)   42 Pages
    6th Ed. $15
Four-Color and Three-Color
Golden Paper Spine

Toys
Illustrator: Masha
Author: Oswald, Edith
22   1945   42 Pages
    1st Ed. $25
Four-Color and Black & White
    Blue Spine with Dust Jacket
    .... $50-$150
22   1945 (1949) 42 Pages
    9th Ed. $16
Four-Color and Three-Color
Golden Paper Spine

Two Little Miners
Illustrator: Scarry, Richard
Author: Brown, Margaret Wise
66   1949   42 Pages
    1st Ed. $30
Four-Color and Black & White
Golden Paper Spine
66   1949 (1949)   42 Pages
    2nd Ed. $25
Four-Color and Three-Color
Golden Paper Spine

Up in the Attic
Illustrator: Malvern, Corinne
53   1948   42 Pages
  1st Ed. $18
Four-Color and Black & White
Golden Paper Spine

We Like to Do Things
Illustrator: Lerch, Seffie
Author: Mason, Walter M.
62   1949   42 Pages
  1st Ed. $14
Four-Color and Three-Color
Golden Paper Spine

What Am I?
Illustrator: DeWitt, Cornelius
Author: Leon, Ruth
58   1949   28 Pages
  1st Ed. $14
Four-Color
Golden Paper Spine

When I Grow Up
Puzzle Edition
Illustrator: Malvern, Corinne
Author: Mace, Kay & Harry
96   1950   28 Pages
  1st Ed $150
Missing puzzle......................$12

When You Were a Baby
Illustrator: Malvern, Corinne
Author: Eng, Rita
70   1949   42 Pages
  1st Ed. $17
Four-Color and Black & White
Golden Paper Spine

Wonderful House, The
Illustrator: Miller, J.P.
Author: Brown, Margaret Wise
76   1950   42 Pages
  1st Ed. $17
Four-Color
Foil Spine

Year in the City, A
Illustrator: Gergely, Tibor
Author: Mitchell, Lucy Sprague
48   1948   42 Pages
  1st Ed. $25
Four-Color and Black & White
Golden Paper Spine

Year on the Farm, A
Illustrator: Floethe, Richard
Author: Mitchell, Lucy Sprague
37   1948   42 Pages
  1st Ed. $20
Four-Color and Black & White
Golden Paper Spine

Lunch Boxes

First introduced in the 1950s, a lunch box is the colorful companion of generations of school kids that did more than hold a peanut butter and jelly sandwich. The most popular boxes displayed favorite film and television characters. Steel lunch boxes are most popular among collectors. A "bottle" is the container for holding liquids that came in most lunch boxes. A common term for bottle is Thermos, but that is a trademarked name and not accurate in collecting circles.

As with other collectibles, condition is always king, says veteran collector and dealer Joe Soucy. "Finding a rare box in poor condition will reduce its value considerably. Some collectors are willing to accept a rare box in lesser condition, but you can go overboard and pay too much for a lesser condition box just to have one, so collectors must exercise good judgment."

The Adco 1954 Superman lunch box, in mint condition, is the Holy Grail of lunch box collecting. Pristine examples, which can sell for $16,500, are difficult to find and once acquired rarely resurface.

Annie Oakley, Aladdin, 1955. .... $725

Batman, Aladdin, 1966. .... $700

Beatles, The, Aladdin, 1966.................$2,800

Beverly Hillbillies, The, Aladdin, 1963 .... **$375**

Bonanza, Aladdin, 1968. .... **$120**

Bullwinkle and Rocky, Okay Industries, 1962 .... **$3,500**

Charlie's Angels, Aladdin, 1978. .... **$225**

Davy Crockett at the Alamo, Adco, 1955 .... **$1,800**

Green Hornet, The, King Seeley Thermos, 1967.
.... **$875**

Gomer Pyle, Alladin, 1966. .... **$450**

Dudley Do-Right, Okay Industries. **$3,450**

Gunsmoke, error box (Marshal is misspelled), Aladdin, 1959. .... **$1,350**
Non-error box from same year. **$375**

Hogan's Heroes, Aladdin, 1966. .... **$725**

Hopalong Cassidy, the first full litho lunch box, Aladdin, 1954 .... **$850**

Howdy Doody, Adco, 1954. .... **$1,100**

James Bond, Aladdin, 1966. .... **$775**

Lone Ranger, The, Adco Liberty, 1954........ **$1,150**

Jetsons, The, front of box, Aladdin, 1963.........**$2,650**

Mickey Mouse, Adco, 1954...............**$1,000**

Munsters, The, King Seeley Thermos, 1966. .... **$900**

Muppet Show, The, King Seeley, 1978. .... **$150**

Peanuts, King Seeley Thermos, 1966. .... **$325**

Popeye, Universal, 1962. .... **$900**

Porky's Lunch Wagon, American Thermos, 1959.
.... **$625**

Roy Rogers, this is the first Roy Rogers box, American Thermos, 1953. .... **$360**

Roy Rogers Chow Wagon Dome, King Seeley Thermos, 1958. .... **$525**

Sesame Street, Aladdin, 1983. .... **$125**

Six Million Dollar Man, The, King Seeley, 1978. .... **$225**

Star Trek, front of box shows the U.S.S. Enterprise, Aladdin, 1968. .... **$2,350**

Star Trek: The Motion Picture, King Seeley Thermos, 1980..**$300**

Star Wars, King Seeley Thermos, 1978..........**$300**

Tarzan, Aladdin, 1966. ....**$475**

Underdog, Okay Industries, 1974...............**$3,500**

Superman, front of box, Adco, 1954. ....**$16,500**

Yellow Submarine, The, King Seeley Thermos, 1968....................**$1,300**

Perfume Bottles

Although the human sense of smell isn't nearly as acute as that of many other mammals, we have long been affected by the odors in the world around us. Science has shown that scents or smells can directly affect our mood or behavior.

No one knows for certain when humans first rubbed themselves with some plant or herb to improve their appeal to other humans, usually of the opposite sex. However, it is clear that the use of unguents and scented materials was widely practiced as far back as Ancient Egypt.

Some of the first objects made of glass, in fact, were small cast vials used for storing such mixtures. By the age of the Roman Empire, scented waters and other mixtures were even more important and were widely available in small glass flasks or bottles. Since that time glass has been the material of choice for storing scented concoctions, and during the past 200 years some of the most exquisite glass objects produced were designed for that purpose.

It wasn't until around the middle of the 19th century that specialized bottles and vials were produced to hold commercially manufactured scents. Some aromatic mixtures were worn on special occasions, while many others were splashed on to help mask body odor. For centuries it had been common practice for "sophisticated" people to carry on their person a scented pouch or similar accoutrement, since daily bathing was unheard of and laundering methods were primitive.

Commercially produced and brand name perfumes and colognes have really only been common since the late 19th and early 20th centuries. The French started the ball rolling during the first half of the 19th century when D'Orsay and Guerlain began producing special scents. The first American entrepreneur to step into this field was Richard Hudnut, whose firm was established in 1880. During the second half of the 19th century most scents carried simple labels and were sold in simple, fairly generic glass bottles. Only in the early 20th century did parfumeurs introduce specially designed labels and bottles to hold their most popular perfumes. Coty, founded in 1904, was one of the first to do this, and they turned to Rene Lalique for a special bottle design around 1908. Other French firms, such as Bourjois (1903), Caron (1903), and D'Orsay (1904) were soon following this trend.

People collect two kinds of perfume bottles—decorative and commercial. Decorative bottles include any bottles sold empty and meant to be filled with your choice of scent. Commercial bottles are any that were sold filled with scent and usually have the label of the perfume company.

The rules of value for perfume bottles are the same as for any other kind of glass—rarity, condition, age, and quality of glass.

The record price for perfume bottle at auction is something over $200,000, and those little sample bottles of scent that we used to get for free at perfume counters in the 1960s can now bring as much as $300 or $400.

For more information on perfume bottles, see *Antique Trader Perfume Bottles Price Guide* by Kyle Husfloen.

Perfume bottle & stopper, shoe-shaped black glass w/"jade" knot stopper & enameled & jeweled applied metalwork, Hoffman, stenciled "Made in Czechoslovkia," ca. 1920s, 4 1/2" l. **$18,000**

TOP LOT!

Courtesy International Perfume Bottle Association

Meissen, German porcelain bottle, modeled by Kaendler as a Harlequin, circa 1800s...... **$3,900**

Czech Ingrid bottle, ruby jeweled glass with ivory stopper. **$9,600**

Tappan Cycle Perfume, wirework tricycle, circa 1892...................................... **$2,760**

Roadster enameled silver purse with compartments, 1920s. **$24,000**

R. Lalique for Gabilla "Narcisse," 1926............................ **$11,400**

Perfume Bottles From Around The World ─────

AUSTRIA

Perfume bottle & stopper, amber crystal in an oblong upright shape w/a low angled shoulder to the short neck fitted w/an amber facet-cut stopper, mounted in a gilt-metal base w/a decorative plaque on the side, paper label reads "T&B Austria," ca. 1920s, 8 1/2" h. **$3,000-4,000**

BOHEMIA

Cologne bottle & stopper, cylindrical clear glass w/a rounded shoulder & short neck, flashed in amber & ornately cut overall w/ tall almond-shaped panels alternating w/block & fan panels, amber facet-cut stopper, ca. 1860, 6 3/4" h. **$400-500**

Cologne bottle & stopper, mold-blown square amber bottle w/optic ribbing & a stepped shoulder to the short flaring neck, heavily & ornately enameled overall w/ colorful flowers & leaves, one side applied w/a large salamander, the tall ribbed & lily-form stopper w/an applied rigaree rim band & applied lady bugs on the sides, Harrach factory, ca. 1890, 9" h. . **$750-1,000**

Cologne bottle & stopper, silver-overlay glass, squatty bulbous lower body below slender tapering cylindrical upper body w/a short flaring neck, bulbous pointed stopper, dark green overlaid w/ornate sterling scrolls & flowers w/ lattice panels up the neck, solid silver neck, silver overlaid stopper, Bohemia, 8" h. **$4,320**

Perfume bottle & stopper, domed cylindrical cranberry glass bottle h.p. w/heavy gold shoulder panels above lily-of-the-valley decoration, gilded knopped stopper, Moser, ca. 1900-20, 3 1/2" h. **$650**

Perfume bottle & stopper, annagrun uranium glass in a cylindrical shape deeply cut around the sides w/diamond panels, silver collar & fancy hinged cap w/glass inner stopper, Joseph Riedel, mid-19th c., 4 1/4" h. **$450-500**

Perfume bottle & stopper, cylindrical cranberry glass cased in clear w/a short neck w/a flaring rim, the sides decorated w/a wide center band ornately enameled in color w/leafy scrolls & flowers, flanked by bands decorated w/gold lappets, cranberry ball stopper w/ gold lappet design, probably the Myers-Neffe factory, ca. 1885, 6 3/4" h. **$1,250-1,500**

CZECHOSLOVAKIA

Perfume bottle & stopper, amber crystal molded as a pair of seated nude young maidens on an oblong base & flanking a gilt-metal filigree-framed oval black cameo jewel w/the head of an elegant lady, mounted on a thin filigree base raised on small scroll feet, a flower-molded mushroom-shaped stopper, unmarked, 1920s, 5 3/4" h. **$3,200-4,000**

Perfume bottle & stopper, black glass paneled bell-form shape w/a cylindrical neck w/a flattened faceted oval stopper etched w/a scene of seated lovers complete w/dauber, the neck & shoulders decorated w/ gilt-metal filigree jewel-mounted bands w/a long front panel enclosing a long oval pale green flower-molded jewel, stenciled oval "Made in Czechoslovakia" & metal tag w/"Czechoslovakia - Morlee," 7 1/4" h. **$1,300-1,600**

Perfume bottle & stopper, clear faceted crystal w/a flattened & sharply tapering form & wide shoulders, mounted w/gilt-metal enameled filigree trimmed w/red jewels & centered by a carved white rose, the tall flat spade-shaped crystal stopper etched w/branches of roses & ending in a dauber stub, metal tag marked "Czechoslovakia," 1920s, 5 1/2" h. **$950-1,400**

Perfume bottle & stopper, crystal flat-sided oblong ribbed shape on short feet, overlaid w/ornate gilt-metal enameled filigree bands set w/blue jewels, tall flat cryal shaped oblong stopper etched w/a flying bird-of-paradise & ending in a dauber stub, stenciled oval "Made in Czechoslovakia" & metal tag w/"Czechoslovakia," 1920s, 7 1/4" h. **$1,600-2,100**

Perfume bottle & stopper, clear crystal squatty domed shape resembling a petaled daisy, the tall clear oblong stopper etched w/a tall nude flying female fairy, stenciled oval "Made in Czechoslovakia," 1920s, 8 1/2" h **$1,560**

Perfume bottle & stopper, long low clear crystal shape w/flattened sides & angled shoulders, decorated around the lower half w/ornate gilt-metal triple-arched filigree trimmed w/green jewels, the rounded clear faceted stopper etched w/a scene of seated lovers & ending in a dauber, unmarked, 1920s, 5 3/4" h. **$2,160**

Perfume bottle & stopper, pale blue crystal bulbous shape molded as a flower blossom, fitted w/a figural butterfly stopper w/dauber, unsigned Irice, Czechoslovakia, 1920s, 5 3/4" h. **$2,200-3,400**

Perfume bottle & stopper, dark blue faceted pyramidal shape raised on a filigree-trimmed metal base w/ball feet & wrapped around the neck & shoulders w/enameled & jeweled leaf & blossom mounts, tall crystal stopper molded in the shape of a stylized lady wearing a pleated gown & holding a bouquet of flowers, complete w/dauber, stenciled oval "Made in Czechoslovakia," 1920s, 6" h. .. **$3,900**

Perfume bottle & stopper, pale green crystal, flattened rectangular form w/beveled corners & short neck fitted w/a tall flattened spearpoint stopper, resting on a fancy jeweled openwork gilt-metal stand decorated w/dragons & classic masks, marked "Czechoslovakia," ca. 1920s, 5 1/2" h. **$1,500-2,000**

Perfume bottle & stopper, pale purple crystal w/flattened angled sides, metal band on neck, wide flat diamond-form stopper etched w/a kneeling maiden, complete w/ dauber, a large enameled & jeweled metal plaque on the side centered by a large green jewel, stenciled "Made in Czechoslovakia" & metal tag reading "Czechoslovakia," 1920s, 3 7/8" h. **$1,100-1,800**

▼Perfume bottle & stopper, a Prochaska bottle by J. Viard in clear crystal w/enamel & brown patina, a long low arched container w/molded & colored borders, squatty stopper w/a molded half-figure of a child, ca. 1926, 3 1/4" h. **$3,000**

Perfume bottle & stopper, pale yellow crystal molded as graduated overlapping flattened discs w/the outer two ribbed, matching stopper w/overlapping ribbed discs & ending in a dauber, unsigned, 1930s, 6" h. **$1,800-2,500**

ENGLAND

Perfume bottle & stopper, Dubarry bottle by J. Viard & made by Depinoix, clear wide squatty round shape molded overall w/a repeating wave design & multicolored patina, the upright figural frosted stopper w/a kneeling nude, flea bites to stopper plug, ca. 1920s, 3 1/2" h. **$3,000-4,500**

Perfume bottle & stopper, Chelsea porcelain, upright bulbous molded basket-form lower body w/a molded gold chain around the middle w/a shield-shaped tag inscribed "eau de senteur," tall tapering neck h.p. w/a colorful bouquet of flowers, metal collar & stopper w/tall porcelain finial molded as a model of a butterfly atop a blossom, ca. 1765, 4" h. **$3,000**

EUROPE - GENERAL

Perfume bottle & stopper, boule-shaped cameo glass bottle, citron cased in white & cameo-carved w/large flowers & buds w/on leafy stems, hinged sterling silver cap w/hallmarks for Birmingham, 1891-92, 3 1/2" h. **$1,800-2,200**

Scent holder, Bessamin box or spice tower, silver, a tall tapering stem supporting a bulbous tower-form container set w/colored stones & w/a pierced band around the middle, conical cover w/flag finial, Poland, 19th c., 7 1/4" h. **$1,500-2,000**

FRANCE

Perfume bottle & stopper, white opaline disc-shaped bottle w/fancy gold shoulder mounts & cap w/basse taille enameling, mid-19th c., 3" l. ... **$2,000-2,500**

Perfume bottle & stopper, "Bermuda Angel Fish" by Peniston-Brown, figural opalescent glass fish stopper on short glass bottle base, base marked "A. Jollivet - Made in France," ca. 1937, 4 1/2" h. **$3,500**

Perfume bottle & stopper, clear columnar glass bottle mounted on a flaring silver base cast w/swags & floral designs, a silver collar & silver stopper cast as a sculpted bust of Bacchus, inner glass stopper, ca. 1840, 6" h. **$3,000-3,500**

Perfume bottle & stopper, flattened violin-shaped glass body in red, pink & white twisted filigrana decoration, cylindrical silver cap, Clichy factory, second half 19th c., 4 1/4" h. **$750-1,000**

Perfume bottle & stopper, panel-cut clear crystal bottle on an ornate vermeille over silver base mount & similar scrolling shoulder & neck mounts, crown-style matching cap over inner glass stopper, 19th c., 4" h. ... **$4,500**

Perfume bottle & stopper, "Gai Monmartre" by Deroc, figural red-painted glass windmill w/a pointed metal cap & enameled windmill blades, partial label, ca. 1926, 4 3/4" h. **$2,200-3,200**

Perfume bottle & stopper, novelty-type, "Ouvrez-Moi" by Lubin, figural black glass purse w/metal rim & black glass button stopper, original black silk cord strap, original label on strap, ca. 1937, 3 1/2" h. **$1,100-2,000**

Perfume bottle & stopper, "Isadora" by Isadora, factice bottle from a Pierre Dinand design, squatty cylindrical clear glass bottle printed in gold, a tall frosted clear figural stopper showing a seated female nude w/her hands behind her head, extremely limited Czechoslovakian production, ca. 1990, 12" h. ... **$3,750**

Perfume bottle & stopper, "Madelon" by Depinoix, a Boissard J. Viard bottle in clear & frosted glass, footed squatty disk-form bottle w/a colorful enameled patina band around the sides, the tall figural stopper w/further color trim, ca. 1919, 4" h. **$2,400**

Perfume bottle & stopper, novelty-type, a carved tortoiseshell teardrop-shaped container w/tiny overall inlaid gold stars & an ornate filigree collar, tall bulbous engraved cap over the interior glass bottle, ca. 1849, 4 3/4" l. **$2,000**

RUSSIA

Perfume bottle & stopper, flattened ovoid fancy silver-gilt body w/a stippled background highlighted w/delicate designs in enamels colored red, blue & white, matching ball-form cap, hallmarked, ca. 1880, 3" h. **$1,750-2,000**

◄Perfume bottle & stopper, "Le Roy Le Veult" by Marcel Buerlain, squatty clear glass figural crown bottle trimmed w/gold, figural fleur-de-lis stopper frozen in place, labeled, in original box, ca. 1927, 3 1/8" h. ... **$2,800-3,500**

UNITED STATES

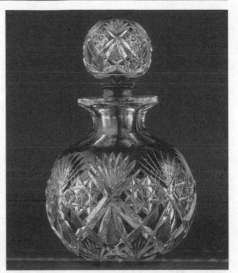

Cologne bottle & stopper, Royal Flemish art glass, squatty bulbous body h.p. w/flowers & butterflies, the neck & base of stopper in dark brown trimmed w/heavy gold scrolls, Mt. Washington Glass Co., marked, ca. 1894, 5 3/4" h. **$6,500-8,000**

Cologne bottle & stopper, squatty bulbous cut glass, clear flashed in green & cut overall in the Marlborough patt., cut ball stopper, unsigned Dorflinger, ca. 1890-1910, 6 1/2" h **$6,500-7,500**

Cologne bottle & stopper, Amberina art glass, tall pedestal base & slender ovoid body tapering to a flared & lobed rim, tall acorn-form stopper, signed by Libbey, ca. 1917, 8 1/4" h. **$2,500**

Perfume bottle & stopper, flat-bottomed squatty base covered in gold tapering to the slender black body trimmed w/slender gilt stripes & scrolls, gilt-metal cap fitted w/an upright flat octagonal finial w/black enameled trimmed w/ blue & lavender enameled scrolls, long slender gilt-metal rods hanging from bottom sides of finial & ending in small black glass balls, w/dauber, marked "DeVilbiss," 1920s, 4 3/4" h. **$4,200**

Perfume bottle & stopper, clear bulbous cut glass in the Venetian patt. by Hawkes, set on a high scroll-decorated sterling silver base & w/silver mounts by Gorham, ca. 1885-90, 7" h. **$1,200-1,500**

PERFUME BOTTLES

▪ Perfume Bottle Designers ─────

CZECHOSLOVAKIA

Perfume bottle & stopper, green tapering bottle w/a short neck trimmed w/metal filigree, flat octagonal stopper etched w/a Cupid & Psyche scene & dauber, mounted in a high fancy metal filigree base trimmed w/enamel & a large oval green jewel, marked in intaglio "Hoffman," one jewel chip, 1920s, 3 1/4" h. **$1,300-1,600**

Perfume bottle & stopper, pale blue crystal w/faceted tapering sides, metal-wrapped neck & tall oval stopper etched w/a dancing nude, on a gilt-metal four-footed jeweled & reeded base, marked in intaglio "Hoffman," 1930s, 6 1/2" h. **$3,000**

Pefume bottle & stopper, dark royal blue flattened domed bottle molded w/a female nude, the arched tiara-style stopper also molded w/nudes, signed by Hoffman, ca. 1920s-30s, 6 1/3" h. **$2,500-3,000**

Perfume bottles & stoppers, green glass, two upright squared bottles w/angled shoulders w/gilt-metal neck band & flattened stoppers etched w/a Cupid & Psyche scene, in a fitted filigree gilt-metal stand, one w/dauber, marked in intaglio "Hoffman," 1920s, 6 1/2" h. **$1,500-3,000**

Perfume bottle & stopper, "Tula" by Dralle of Germany, designed by Hoffman of Czechoslovakia, a low clear crystal bottle w/a heavily notched rockwork-like design, fitted w/a large upright blue disc stopper etched w/the figure of a kneeling nude male archer, w/paper label, ca. 1930, 5 1/2" h. **$1,440**

FRANCE

Julien Viard

Perfume bottle & stopper, "Sous la Charmille" by Brecher, a J. Viard bottle made by Depinoix, squatty bulbous clear glass tapering to a small neck & flattened blossom-form stopper, the sides enameled in shades of green & brown w/leaves, ca. 1924, 2 3/4" h. **$2,520**

Perfume bottle & stopper, "Blue Lagoon" by Dubarry, a J. Viard bottle in clear & frosted glass w/a multicolored patina, squatty four-lobed shape w/Egyptian designs between each lobe, small molded hobs on the shoulder, short neck w/a figural stopper of a kneeling Egyptian woman, ca. 1919, 4" h. **$4,440**

Perfume bottle & stopper, "Enigma" by Lubin, a J. Viard bottle in clear glass, flattened triangle shape molded on the side w/an Egyptian sphinx & stylized vertical label in gold, triangular stopper, in original extremely rare decorative box w/a Nile tableau of flowering lotus blossoms inside & the name & an Egyptian scarab on the exterior, ca. 1921, 3 1/2" h. **$27,600**

■ Perfume Bottle Makers

ENGLAND

Thomas Webb

Perfume bottle & stopper, cameo glass flattened teardrop form, avocado green ground cased in white & cameo-cut w/trumpet-form blossoms on leafy vines, hinged sterling silver cap marked for Birmingham, 1887, Thomas Webb & Sons, 5" l. **$2,400-2,750**

Perfume bottle & stopper, cameo glass, flattened teardrop lay down-type, deep red cased in white & cameo-carved w/large blossoms on leafy stems, screw-off répoussé sterling silver cap, unsigned Thomas Webb, ca. 1890-1900, 4 1/2" l. **$2,000**

Perfume bottle & stopper, cameo glass, boule-form four-color cameo bottle, opal cased in citron under red & white, cameo-carved around the body w/leafy blossoming branches, Thomas Webb butterfly emblem on the reverse, hinged sterling silver répoussé cap, ca. 1885, 4 1/2" h. ... **$4,000-4,500**

Scent bottle w/cap, cameo glass, lay-down type w/a pointed teardrop shape, deep red overlaid in white & cameo-carved w/water lilies & a dragonfly, original gold-washed metal screw-on cap w/répoussé designs, 3 1/4" l. **$3,335**

Stevens & Williams

Perfume bottle & stopper, emerald green cut to clear upright bottle w/ pinched-in sides (also called the "Kettroff" or "glug-glug"), sterling silver collar & emerald cut to clear ball stopper, cut leafy vine design, by Stevens & Williams, silver hallmarked 1897-98, 7 1/4" h. **$2,500-3,000**

PERFUME BOTTLES

FRANCE

Baccarat

Perfume bottle & stopper, "Ta Wao" by Madhva, a Baccarat container designed by J. Viard, wide thin disk-form base tapering sharply w/fluted sides enameled in gold below the black disk stopper w/original bead on stopper, base marked "Baccarat," ca. 1923, 2 1/2" h. **$6,000**

Perfume bottle & stopper, "Cascade" by Gravier, Baccarat bottle in clear & frosted crystal w/pale green patina, the round upright three-tiered shape topped by a frosted figural dolphin stopper, bottom stenciled "Baccarat," 4 1/2" h. **$3,360**

▶ Perfume bottle & stopper, "XII" by Delettrez, a Baccarat container in molded pink opaque glass, a narrow upright rectangular form w/a molded oblong stopper, w/label, in original hand-painted box, first appearance of this bottle, base marked "Baccarat," ca. 1927, 4 1/2" h. **$24,000**

Perfume bottle & stopper, "Kismet" by Lubin, a Baccarat bottle in clear glass, figural design of an elephant w/black draping down the sides, the frosted stopper in the shape of its rider, base stenciled "Baccarat," ca. 1921, 4 1/8" h. **$6,500-9,000**

Perfume bottle & stopper, "Muguet" by Maudy, a Baccarat square crystal bottle w/the beveled corners decorated w/silvery grey stylized florals, the domed decorated cap w/four open arches ending at each rim corner, base stenciled "Baccarat," ca. 1928, 3 1/4" h. **$2,200-3,500**

Almeric Walter

Perfume atomizer w/fittings, pate de verre, upright cylindrical form travel-type in shades of blue & a touch of orange molded w/stylized flowers, gilt-metal fittings, signed by Almeric Walter, ca. 1900-1910, 4 1/2" h. **$4,000-4,200**

Gallé

Perfume bottle & stopper, footed ovoid clear glass bottle w/a short neck & button stopper, enameled around the sides w/dark blue & purple blossoms w/slender green leaves & a butterfly to the side, signed by Gallé, ca. 1870-80, 3 3/4" h. **$1,750-2,000**

Daum - Nancy

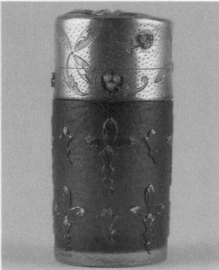

Scent bottle & stopper, cameo glass, cylindrical body in rare raisin color cased in clear & cameo-carved w/a design of fleur de lis trimmed in gold, cylindrical chased silver cap set w/small turquoise stones, Daum - Nancy, ca. 1892, 3" h. **$3,000-4,000**

Scent bottle & stopper, Daum - Nancy cameo glass, spherical white body tapering to a short neck w/a clear stopper w/faceted edges trimmed in gold, the body cameo-cut & enameled w/a leafy vine of shaded red flowers & buds framing a black & white enameled scene of a road leading to a village, base signed w/etched signature, very small old chip inside lip, small flake on corner of stopper, 3 1/4" h. **$2,185**

PERFUME BOTTLES

Lalique

Perfume bottle & stopper, "Amphitrite," green glass in an upright snail shell design w/a small figural stopper, engraved "R. Lalique - France," a. 1920, 3 1/2" h. **$5,100**

Perfume bottle & stopper, "Le Baiser du Faune" by Molinard, clear & frosted Lalique bottle, an upright circle design enclosing an engraved plaque of a woman kissing a faun, small round stopper, molded "R. Lalique" & engraved "Molinard - Paris, France," ca. 1928, 5 3/4" h........................ **$4,800**

Perfume bottle & stopper, "Roses" by D'Orsay, clear & frosted Lalique bottle w/sepia patina, footed spherical bottle w/a short neck & tall figural stopper, molded "Lalique" w/extended "L," some interior residue, stopper frozen, ca. 1912, 4" h. **$3,360**

Perfume bottle & stopper, "Panier de Roses," a Lalique clear & frosted glass container w/a grey patina, designed as a slender upright ribbed cylinder molded around the shoulder w/a band of roses, stopper formed by a cluster of roses, engraved "Lalique," ca. 1912, 3 3/4" h. **$2,040**

Perfume bottle & stopper, "Fleurs de Pommier" by Bouchon, Lalique frosted clear w/blue patina, the ovoid body molded w/bands of graduated arches, the high arched & pierced long stopper molded w/a flowering tree, stopper engraved "R. Lalique - 939," matching number on the base, introduced in 1919, 5 1/2" h. **$10,755**

Perfume bottle & stopper, "La Phalène" by D'Heraud, a Lalique clear & frosted Amberina glass container, molded as a tiny nymph w/butterfly wings, flattened round stopper, molded "R. Lalique," ca. 1925, 3 1/2" h. **$7,200**

Perfume bottle & stopper, "Misti" by Piver, a Lalique clear & frosted glass container w/a blue patina, squatty low round form molded overall w/butterflies, blossom-form button stopper, molded "R. Lalique," ca. 1913, 2" h. **$3,000**

Perfume bottle & stopper, "Flausa" by Roger & Gallet, clear & frosted Lalique bottle w/sepia patina, flattened ovoid body molded w/the seated figure of a half-nude classical maiden, molded "Lalique" on the button-form stopper, matching engraved control numbers, ca. 1914, 4 3/4" h. **$4,200**

▶Perfume bottle & stopper, "Elegance" by D'Orsay, a Lalique bottle in frosted glass w/a brown patina, upright flattened square shape w/an overall molded design of frolicking female figures, partial label, molded "R. Lalique," ca. 1914, 3 3/4" h. **$4,200**

Perfume bottle & stopper, "Le Jade" by Roger & Gallet, jade green Lalique bottle w/grey patina, flattened ovoid body molded overall w/entwined vining, molded "R. L. - France," few flecks on inner rim, 3 3/4" h. **$2,400**

Perfume bottle & stopper, Lalique "Bouchon Fleurs do Pommior" patt., gently swelled clear cylindrical bottle w/panels outlined in thin red stripes, very rare large arched & flower-molded stopper, signed "R. Lalique," ca. 1910-20, 5 2/3" h. ..... **Too rare to price**

Perfume bottle & stopper, "Muguet," a Lalique perfume bottle in clear & frosted glass, a clear squatty bulbous bottle w/a high arched frosted floral stopper, stenciled "R. Lalique," ca. 1931, 4" h. **$4,000-5,000**

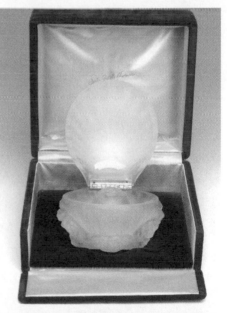

Perfume bottle & stopper, "Trésor de la Mer" for Saks Fifth Avenue, a unique Lalique opalescent glass container, composed of a shell-shape box w/hinged cover opening to expose the pearl-shaped bottle, complete w/original red velvet presentation box lined in gold silk & blue velvet & corded label in the form of a booklet identifying this as No. 72 from a limited editon of 100, box also retains original Saks price tag affixed to the bottom indicating a price of fifty dollars, glass box retains partial label on inside of cover, box stenciled "R. Lalique - France," bottle engraved "R. Lalique - France," ca. 1936, box 5 x 7 1/2 x 8 1/4", glass box 5 3/4" w. **$216,000**

Perfume bottle & stopper, "Quatre Soleils," a Lalique clear & frosted glass container w/a sepia patina, wide flaring lower body below a sharply tapering upper body molded w/four panels enclosing stylized sunburst florettes backed w/reflecting foil, button-form stopper, engraved "R. Lalique," ca. 1912, 2 7/8" h. **$10,200**

Perfume bottle & stopper, "Sirene" pattern by Lalique, the perfume bottle in clear & frosted glass w/a blue patina, clear flattened upright disk shape molded w/ the swirled figure of a siren trimmed in blue, matching mushroom stopper, first documented example w/ conforming stopper, molded "R. Lalique," ca. 1927, 5" h. **$57,000**

UNITED STATES

Steuben

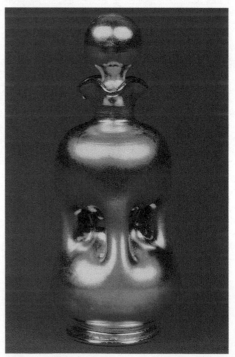

Perfume bottle & stopper, deep purple Steuben glass w/a tapering ovoid shape w/molded columns down each corner forming side panels finely engraved w/ draping flower & leaf swags, pointed disc stopper, variant of No. 6604, factory signature & original paper label, ca. 1920s, 8 1/4" h. .... **Too rare to price**

Perfume bottle & stopper, upright "Atomic Cloud" shaped Steuben blue Aurene bottle w/ball stopper, four indents around the sides, unsigned, 1920s, 3 2/3" h. **$2,800-3,300**

Perfume bottle & stopper, tall slender ovoid body w/a very tall slender neck & pointed button stopper, colorless glass layers enclosing mica flecks, the sides applied w/swirled Topaz drops, ruby stopper & dauber, Steuben Shape No. 6309, ca. 1920s, 6" h. **$2,500-3,000**

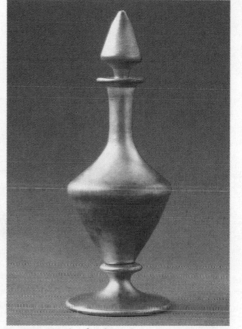

Perfume bottle & stopper, footed wide-waisted shape tapering to a tall slender neck w/flared rim & tall pointed stopper, Steuben blue Aurene glass, Shape No. 3175, signed "Aurene," ca. 1920s, 7" h. **$2,500-3,000**

Tiffany

Perfume bottle & stopper, tapering double-gourd shape w/ eight vertical ribs in Tiffany blue Favrile glass, signed, ca. 1909, 5 3/4" h. **$3,500-4,500**

Scent bottles & stoppers, cut glass, spherical clear bodies cut w/a band of strawberry diamond & hobstars above a panel-cut bottom & shoulder w/a flaring neck, fitted w/an ornate pointed sterling-capped stopper, silver marked by Tiffany & Co., ca. 1900, 5 1/4" h., pr. **$1,150**

Perfume bottle & stopper, boule-shaped body w/short flared neck & ball-shaped stopper, gold iridescent Tiffany Favrile glass w/ an overall green hearts & vines decoration, signed, ca. 1920s, 4 1/4" h. **$750-900**

PERFUME BOTTLES

Perfume Manufacturers

FRANCE

Coty

Perfume bottle & stopper, "L'Effleur," upright rectangular clear & frosted Lalique glass bottle molded in the center panel w/an Art Nouveau female above waves, brown patina, probably first collaboration w/Lalique, ca. 1908, 4 1/3" h. **$4,500-4,750**

D'Orsay

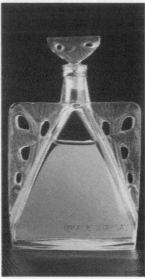

Perfume bottle & stopper, "Grace d'Orsay," an upright square clear & frosted Lalique glass bottle w/reticulated upper corners & flaring reticulated stopper, brown patina, sealed, extremely rare, 1915-20, 5 1/8" h. **$20,000-30,000**

Dior (Christian)

Perfume bottle & stopper, "Dior-ling," clear Baccarat glass footed & ribbed ovoid bottle w/a tall upright gilt-metal stopper composed of flowers on stems, signed & numbered by Baccarat, ca. 1956, 9" h. **$1,000**

LeLong (Lucien)

Perfume bottle & stopper, "Opening Night" by Lelong, a clear glass tiered pyramidal bottle enclosed in a rare amber & black Lucite box, cord sealed, w/labels, ca. 1939, 3" h. **$1,920**

Schiaparelli

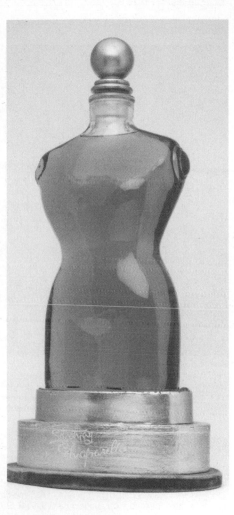

Perfume bottle & stopper, "Le Roi Soliel," clear Baccarat glass round sharply tapering wave-molded bottle w/a large flattened upright stopper representing the sun w/the face composed of doves, designed to celebrate the liberation of France at the end of World War II, designed by Salvador Dali, missing gold metal shell-shaped case, bottle only, ca. 1945, 7" h.
.... **$9,000-10,000**

▶Perfume bottle & stopper, "Shocking" by Schiaparelli, a factice clear glass bottle in the shape of a female mannequin, fitted w/a gold ball stopper, on original velvet display stand, ca. 1936, 18" h.
.... **$3,500-4,000**

Perfume bottle & stopper, "Le Roi Soliel," clear Baccarat glass round sharply tapering wave-molded bottle w/a large flattened upright stopper representing the sun w/the face composed of doves, designed to celebrate the liberation of France at the end of World War II, designed by Salvador Dali, w/gold metal shell-shaped case, ca. 1945, empty in original case, 7" h. **$12,500**

PERFUME BOTTLES

UNITED STATES

Arden (Elizabeth)

Perfume bottle & stopper, "On Dit" by Elizabeth Arden, clear frosted container molded in the shape of two ladies' heads, one whispering to the other, curled topnot stopper, very rare box w/graphics by Rene Bouche, ca. 1948, 3 3/4" h. **$6,600**

Hudnut (Richard)

Perfume bottle & stopper, "Fadette," a J. Viard design in clear & frosted glass, cylindrical w/an overall molded floral swag design trimmed in sepia patina, figural stopper of nude lady, bottom molded "J. Viard," ca. 1924, 4" h. **$1,600-2,300**

Colgate & Company

▶Perfume bottle & stopper, "Orchis," a Lalique bottle in clear & frosted glass w/a light rose patina, upright flattened rectangular shape w/an overall etched design of stylized flowers on the sides, w/label, molded "R. Lalique," ca. 1927, 3 5/8" h. **$2,520**

▼Perfume bottle & stopper, "The Unknown Flower," J. Viard frosted clear upright round bottle w/a sepia patina, the sides molded as a large four-petaled blossom, small blossom stopper, w/original disk-form box w/tassel, ca. 1921, stain to interior of box, 3 1/8" h. **$2,200-3,000**

Petroliana

Items in the section have primarily been selected at the high end of the market. The focus is on the top price items, not to skew the values, but to emphasze the brands and types that are the most desirable. Some less valuable items have been included to help keep values in perspecitive. For example, in many cases, even a large group of common low-end items can be worth just a fraction of a single rare piece. As with all advertising items, factors such as brand name, intricacy of design, color, age, condtion and rarity drastically affect value.

Warning: Beware of reproduction and fantasy pieces. Virtually all categories of antiques are plagued by fakes and reproductions, and petroliana is no exception. For collectors of vintage gas and oil items, the only way to avoid reproductions is experience: making mistakes and learning from them; talking with other collectors and dealers; finding reputable resources (including books and Web sites), and learning to invest wisely, buying the best examples one can afford.

Beginning collectors will soon learn that marks can be deceiving, paper labels and tags are often missing, and those that remain may be spurious. Adding to the confusion are "fantasy" pieces, globes that have no vintage counterpart, and that are often made more for visual impact than deception.

How does one know whether a given piece is authentic? Does it look old, and to what degree can age be simulated? What is the difference between high-quality vintage advertising and modern mass-produced examples? Even experts are fooled when trying to assess qualities that have subtle distinctions.

There is another important factor to consider. A contemporary maker may create a "reproduction" sign or gas globe in tribute of the original, and sell it for what it is: a legitimate copy. Many of these are dated and signed by the artist or manufacturer, and these legitimate copies are highly collectible today. Such items are not intended to be frauds.

But a contemporary piece may pass through many hands between the time it leaves the maker and winds up in a collection. When profit is the only motive of a reseller, details about origin, ownership and age can become a slippery slope of guesses, attribution and—unfortunately—fabrication.

As the collector's eye sharpens, and the approach to inspecting and assessing petroliana improves, it will become easier to buy with confidence. And a knowledgeable collecting public should be the goal of all sellers, if for no other reason than the willingness to invest in quality.

Fortunately, there are entire Web pages devoted to petroliana reproductions. A check of these resources is advised for beginning collectors.

For more information about petroliana, consult *Warman's Gas Station Collectibles* by Mark Moran.

Photo acknowledgments to Aumann Auctions, Rich Gannon, George Simpson, and John Hudson.

Power-lube Motor Oil, five-gallon rocker can, display side excellent condition, reverse side fair ....**$2,100+**

Containers

Petroliana containers are prized by many collectors. Unlike signs and globes, these were meant to be discarded after use, so they fall into the category of ephemera.

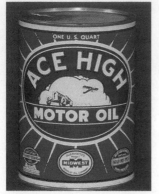

Ace High Motor Oil, quart tin can, near mint.......................... **$875+**

Atlantic Motor Oil, Medium one-gallon tin can, light overall wear .... **$90+**

Babolene Motor, one-gallon flat tin can, display side excellent, reverse good, worn.............. **$500+**

C.A.M. (Indian Motorcycle), quart tin can, good condition...... **$200+**

Cruiser Motor Oil, quart tin can, near mint.......................... **$200+**

Gilmore Lion Head, "Purest Pennsylvania" tin quart, very good condition, dents and minor wear, full .... **$475+**

Harley-Davidson Genuine Oil, one-gallon flat tin can, very good to excellent condition, light wear .... **$2,600+**

Hudson Motor Oil, quart tin can, near mint.......................... **$400+**

Husky Heavy Duty Motor Oil, quart tin can, orange background, excellent condition, small dents .... **$825+**

Indian Motorcycle Oil, quart tin can, excellent condition, dent on reverse.............................. **$300+**

Penntroleum Motor Oil, quart tin can, excellent condition .... **$200+**

PEP Boys Pure as Gold Motor Oil, quart tin can, excellent condition, small dents .... **$150+**

Polly Penn Motor Oil, quart tin can, green stripe at top, excellent condition, light wear and dent on top .... **$875+**

Republic Motor Oil, tin quart, very good condition, small dents and some wear......................... **$150+**

Shamrock Motor Oil, tin quart, very good condition, some wear, small dents, full .... **$150+**

Strata Motor Oil, quart tin can, near mint.......................... **$400+**

Vanderbilt Motor Oil, quart tin can, near mint, small dent in bottom ring............................. **$400+**

Wil-Flo Motor Oil, quart tin can, near mint, extra fine.......... **$475+**

Displays, Holders, Racks

Although this category may be of limited interest to many collectors, those trying to assemble a well-rounded collection that approximates a working garage find them to be the perfect accessories for display. This section also includes rack tops, which many collectors use as wall-mounted decorations.

Chevron Supreme Gasoline, map rack, excellent condition, 20" x 13".. **$300+**

Shell X-100 Motor Oil, display rack .... **$550+**

Gulf, restroom tin key holder, dated 1961, excellent condition, 9" x 11"... **$210+**

Mobil Tires, display rack with ad insert, 8 1/2" x 14" .... **$325+**

Socony Petroleum Products, single-sided tin die-cut display rack, good condition, chip in field, 14" x 16" .... **$300+**

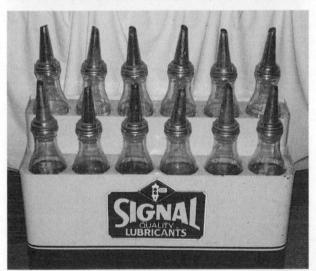

Signal, metal 12-bottle oil rack with 12 generic bottle and spouts, fair to good condition ....**$575+ all**

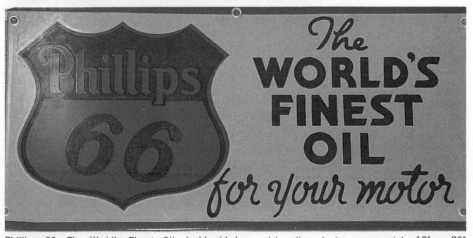

Phillips 66, The World's Finest Oil double-sided porcelain oil rack top, near mint, 12" x 20" ....**$1,300+**

PETROLIANA

■ Globes

The globes that once decorated the tops of gasoline pumps are the holy grail for many petroliana collectors.

Early globes were a single piece of glass, often with etched or painted lettering. "Globe" is a misnomer, since none here is truly spherical, and a complete globe often has three main parts: two lenses and a body, though some came with a single lens.

The body can be made of metal, plastic or fiberglass. A high-profile body has a standing seam around the circumference. A low-profile body has a flattened seam. A gill body has a rubber or metal gasket holding the lenses in place. Later Capco bodies are molded plastic with screw fasteners at the base. A hull body accepts notched lenses, and is open where the lenses are mounted, as opposed to a glass body where the lenses rest on a low dome. Gill and hull bodies take their names from the manufacturers that created them, but as the petroliana field has grown, these names are often found with lower-case spellings.

Some collectors secure the lenses on the bodies using silicone caulk, a practice that many object to because this can contribute to paint loss and it makes the lenses difficult to examine off the bodies.

Ripple and jewel bodies are among the most desirable, and hardest to find. Ripple glass bodies have an irregular textured surface, and come clear, white, and in a range of colors. Jewel bodies have round faceted glass "jewels" set into the surface.

Globes can range in value from $50 for a common or damaged example to almost $20,000 for rarities in near-mint condition.

American Hi-Compression globe, 13 1/2" lenses in a gill-glass body, small chip on one lens ... **$1,800+**

Atlantic Gasoline, one-piece chimney-top globe, etched lettering, slight fading, chimney repainted, small chips on base .... **$5,250+**

Bay globe, 13 1/2" lenses in Capco body, good condition **$175+**

Buffalo Premium, single 13 1/2" lens, excellent condition.... **$275+**

Coastal Gasoline, (with birds) globe, 13 1/2" lenses in a clear ripple body.................... **$2,750+**

Conoco Gasoline, (with Minuteman) globe, 15" lenses in a high-profile metal body (repainted) .... **$5,750+**

Drake's Hi Octane Regular globe, 13 1/2" lenses in a Capco body, excellent condition .... **$3,200+**

Eagle Gasoline globe, 13 1/2" lenses on a yellow ripple gill body, excellent condition .... **$3,750+**

Fyre-Drop globe, 13 1/2" lenses, in a high-profile metal body, near mint .... **$2,200+**

General Gasoline globe, 15" single lens in repainted low-profile body, excellent condition .... **$600+**

Gilmore Ethyl globe, 15" single lens in low-profile body, good condition .... **$3,500+**

Hudson Ethyl, with logo, 13" lenses in an orange ripple gill body, body cracked with paint loss around base .... **$3,250+**

Husky Hi-Power, (with dog) globe, 13 1/2" lenses on a Capco body .... **$3,750+**

Johnson Gasolene Time Tells, (with ethyl logo) globe, 13 1/2" lenses in orange ripple gill body, metal base .... **$5,750+**

Kan-O-Tex Bondified globe, 13 1/2" lenses, in an orange ripple glass body, base chips.... **$3,000+**

Lonas Premium globe, 13 1/2" single lens in original red Capco body with some crazing, lens good condition, scratches in field **$100+**

Magnolia globe, with rose, 16 1/2" lenses in low-profile body, very good condition............... **$4,600+**

Mobilfuel Diesel globe, 13 1/2" lenses in Capco body, excellent condition .... **$250+**

Red Crown Gasoline globe, with crown, 15" lenses in high-profile metal body, display side excellent, reverse very good..... **$3,750+**

Mohawk Gasoline, (orange background) globe, 15" lenses in low-profile metal body (repainted)..**$8,500+**
▶Shamrock oval globe, body damaged, lenses very good condition.. **$200+**

Shell globe, (West Coast), 15" single lens in high-profile body, lenses very good condition, body good original paint..**$2,500+**

Signal globe, 15" lenses in high-profile body, lenses excellent condition, body repainted ....**$10,000+**

Sinclair Aircraft, one-piece globe, baked-on paint faded with some pinholes, chips around base .... **$6,000+**

Texaco, leaded stained-glass metal body globe, slight fading, smaller size................... **$4,500+**

White Rose globe, 13 1/2" lenses on narrow glass body, lenses caulked in place .... **$1,900+**

Pumps

Pumps are not for everybody. They are big machines that—though relatively simple—can require significant maintenance if a collector desires to keep them in working order. That's why most serve as nonfunctioning accessories. Correct components and spare parts can be expensive, and proper restoration in manufacturer's colors can take months. Pumps in untouched original condition are quite rare, and command some of the highest prices.

Some sellers, easily found on the Internet, stock reproduction parts for many gas pumps. Some also offer new-old-stock parts, used parts, and original-condition and restored pumps. Others carry globes, decals, signs, books, oil cans, road maps, and offer restoration, consultation and appraisals.

►National 365 computing pump, with G4 top, Flying A ad glass, good original condition...**$850+**

Far left: Bennett Model 748 pump, restored in Gulf colors, with reproduction globe. ....**$950+**

Left: M&S 80 Script Top pump, Mobilgas Special, with reproduction pump plates. **$1,800**

Tokheim 36-B pump, painted in Texaco colors, with reproduction globe, two original Fire Chief porcelain pump plates dated 1957 and 1962 .... **$1,700+**

Wayne 40 computing pump, fancy face bezel, original paint fair condition, Mobil shield, globe holder .... **$1,400+**

Wayne 60 pump, with sunburst, restored in Gilmore colors, several parts chromed, with reproduction Gilmore globe, also fitted with remote button that makes dial register................................. **$3,500+**

Wayne 519 10-gallon visible pump, restored in Shell colors and decal............................ **$1,200+**

Signs

Signs are some of the most important and desired petroliana collectibles. Their color and design are eye appealing and create wonderful wall displays. Porcelain and metal signs were intended to last for years, so they were made to endure. However, they are susceptible to scratches, chipping, rust, etc. which can dramatically lower their value. Signs in mint or near mint condition command premium prices.

Aristo Motor Oil, porcelain flange, very good condition, small chips in field, reverse has two quarter-size chips, 20" x 20" .... **$2,500+**

Calso RPM Lubrication, porcelain flange, display side excellent condition with few edge chips, reverse near mint, 19" x 22" .... **$2,500+**

Flying A Super Extra, porcelain pump plate, near mint, new old stock, 10" diameter .... **$800+**

Grizzly Gasoline, (Dubbs Cracked) Watch Your Miles double-sided tin sign, display side good condition, light wear and fading at bottom, extremely rare, 36" x 24" .... **$3,500+**

Husky Service, double-sided porcelain die-cut sign, good condition, large chips and re-drilled holes at top and small chips in field, light scratches, larger chips on reverse, 48" x 42" ..... **$4,250+**

Kendall The 2000 Mile Oil, curved single-sided porcelain sign, very good condition and gloss, two quarter-size chips in field, chip at left mounting hole, 30" x 20" .... **$3,700+**

Hancock Gasoline, (early rooster) porcelain pump plate, very good condition with repaired quarter-size hole below "A" in Hancock, 12" diameter .... **$3,100+**

Magnolia Gasoline, for sale here double-sided porcelain sign, excellent condition-plus, light scratches on reverse, 30" diameter .... **$2,700+**

Red Crown Gasoline, GM Ethyl double-sided porcelain sign, professionally restored, 30" diameter .... **$1,500+**

Red Crown Gasoline Zerolene, double-sided porcelain, fair to good condition, chipping in fields and on edges, 42" diameter .... **$4,000+**

Signal Gasoline, porcelain pump plate with stoplight, excellent condition, 12" diameter....... **$2,000+**

Skylark Aviation Grade Gasoline, neon sign, with plane skywriting, replaced neon and housing (or as collectors call it, the "can"), 42" x 66" .... **$8,000+**

Stanocola, Standard Oil Company of Louisiana double-sided porcelain sign, good condition, several areas professionally touched up, 30" diameter .... **$3,000+**

Texaco, (black T) Gasoline-Motor Oil double-sided porcelain sign, very good to excellent condition, two chips in field and chipping around mounting holes, 42" diameter .... **$1,250+**

Union 76 Gasoline, porcelain pump plate, very good condition, chip on one mounting hole, 11 1/2" diameter .... **$125+**

Zerolene, The Standard Oil for Motor Cars single-sided porcelain sign, good condition, three touched-up chips around edge, 24" diameter .... **$1,900+**

Wil-Flo Motor Oil, double-sided tin oval sign, 17" x 23", display side restored, reverse total loss .... **$3,100+**

◄Union Oil Minute Man Service, double-sided porcelain sign, excellent condition, chips around top mounting holes .... **$7,000+**

Related Items

"Related" collectibles—often automotive in nature—that appeal to petroliana collectors, but are not directly tied to the production of oil and gasoline, include things like tires, spark plugs, heaters, etc., and transportation in general.

Atlas Tires, clock, good condition, needs work on motor, 19" diameter .... **$325+**

Eveready Daylo, glass counter top show case, with mirrored back, good condition, 12" x 20" x 12" .... **$200+**

Firestone Tires Badge, rubber and celluloid .... **$75+**

Bus line guides, one Gray Line, one Pickwick Greyhound Lines .... **$35+ pair**

Buss Auto Fuses, metal counter-top display rack, excellent condition, 7 1/2" x 8 1/2" x 3".. **$450+**

PETROLIANA

◀Champion Spark Plug, cardboard display, excellent condition, light wear, framed and matted, 32" x 22" .... **$2,100+**

Seiberling Steel Radial Tire, clock (clock by Sessions), working condition .... **$50+**

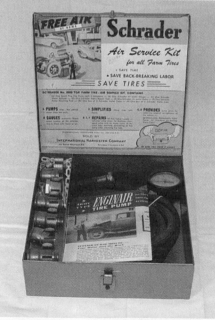

Schrader Air Service, Kit for the Farm, excellent condition, 3" x 8" x 8" .... **$375+**

Rival Auto Lamps, Made in England cardboard display with 12 lamps, 7 1/2" x 7"................. **$225+ all**

Posters

A poster is a large, usually printed placard, bill, or announcement, often illustrated, that is posted to advertise or publicize something. It can also be an artistic work, often a reproduction of an original painting or photograph, printed on a large sheet of paper.

Vintage posters are usually between 20 and 50 years old and must be original and not copies or newer reproductions.

The value of a vintage poster is determined by condition, popularity of the subject matter, rarity, artistic rendering, and the message it conveys.

Concert, "Beach Boys Show," cardboard printed in red, yellow & black on a white ground, three photos of the group, 1968 concert in Lincoln, Nebraska, near mint, 14 x 22" **$2,070**

Concert, colorful images of two French ladies in costume dancing, printed in red & brown "Trianon Concert - Tous Les Soirs - Tableau de la Troupe... Spectacle Variè," marked by H. Gray, style of the 1890s, ca. 1920, laid on canvas, 36 3/4 x 51 1/8" **$316**

◄Concert, "Pink Floyd - Atom Heart Mother Earth Tour," long narrow rectangular form printed in pink & red on white, photos of the band at the top & bottom, 1970 performance in Salt Lake City, 7 x 29" **$1,150**

Liqueur, long colorful design of a horse race w/a central figure of a flying lady wearing a long flowing orange robe & holding aloft a bottle of the product, printed in French across the bottom "Premier Fils - La Vieille Marque Francaise," image by Roby, printed by L. Maboeuf, ca. 1936, framed, 51 1/4 x 79 1/2" **$1,175**

POSTERS

Firearms, "Ithaca Guns," large color picture by artist Louis Agassiz Fuertes of passenger pigeons w/red wording above "Extinct Passenger Pigeon," advertising below the picture reads "Ithaca Guns - Out Shoot Them All - Authorized Agent," ca. 1910, bands at top & bottom, excellent condition, 16 1/2 x 27 3/4" **$1,540**

Magazine, "Le Locataire," French protest-type w/a color image of a group of poor children & their parents, title & information on a protest in black across the top, name of editor in lower left, designed by Steinler, Paris, France, ca. 1913, laid on canvas, 47 x 63" **$489**

Music festival, "Woodstock Music & Art Fair - An Aquarian Exposition in White Lake, N.Y. - 3 Days of Peace & Music," cardboard w/a red background printed in white, blue, green & black, August 1969, excellent condition, 24 x 36" **$993**

Seeds, "Ferry's Seeds," color lithograph w/artwork by Maxfield Parrish of a young girl seated beside a watering can, advertising below reads "Mary Mary quite contrary - How does your garden grow? - Plant Ferry's Seeds," framed, two horizontal creases w/ two softer vertical folds, ca. 1920, 19 1/2 x 27" **$5,520**

Stage play, "Bunco in Arizona," colorfully lithographed design of a cowboy on a bucking bronco, advertising across the top reads "J.L. Veronee Amusement Company's Original Co. in the Queen Bee of All Comedy Drama - Bunco in Arizona," wording at bottom of the scene reads "Billy Craver and His Bucking Pony 'Chub,'" American Show Print Co., Milwaukee, Wisconsin, 1902, minor edge tears, 28 x 42" **$1,485**

Stage play, "Bunco in Arizona," colorfully lithographed design w/a large oval central portrait of a pretty young woman framed by portraits of four Indian chiefs, reads "The Original Company - in The Queen Bee of All Comedy Dramas - Bunco in Arizona - Nae St. Clair Among The Red Skins," American Show Print Co., Milwaukee, 1902, 28 x 42" **$1,925**

Steamship, "Cunard Line," printed in orange & blue on a white ground w/a large image of the steamship Saxonia, reads "Cunard Line - Spend Xmas in Europe...," ca. 1885, minor wear at folds, one small internal tear, 19 x 29" **$255**

Steamship, "Red Star Line," printed in German w/black wording framing an engraving of a passenger steamship, covers trans-Atlantic passages, ca. 1875, some minor loss at folds, small ares of discoloration, 25 x 38" **$230**

Theatre, "Born Yesterday," starring Judy Holliday, Henry Miller's Threatre, colorful yellow, blue & red comic design of the star being carried by a stork, 1940s, window card-type, some minor soiling, 14 x 22" **$1,170**

Theatre, "La Yetta," long narrow color lithograph showing a full-length portrait of an exotic belly dancer in Mideastern attire, by F. Garric, Paris, France, ca. 1900, excellent condition, 22 x 61" **$690**

▶Theatre, "The Electric Spark - Atkinson's Follies," Alcazar Theatre, New York City, November 27, 1882, colorful images of the theatre interior & the crowd, the production featured Illumination by Thomas Edison's new incandescent electric bulbs, mounted on board, loss to top & bottom borders, light uniform toning, w/ an original four-page program for the play, 28 x 42" **$1,072**

Theatre, "The Charity Ball," printed in color on a white ground, printed across the bottom "Daniel Frohman's Lyceum Theatre Success...," ca. 1890, minor edge loss & a small tear, gold colors, 20 x 28" **$414**

Theatre, "The Squaw Man - Liebler & Co's. Production," large color image of a standing cowboy & small child w/a kneeling young woman, title across the top & image titled, Wallack's Theatre, New York City, ca. 1906, mint condition, 20 x 27" **$411**

POSTERS

Left: World War I, "Remember Your First Thrill of American Liberty - Your Duty - Buy United States Government Bonds - 2nd Liberty Loan of 1917," the upper half w/a large color scene of immigrants arriving by ship w/the State of Liberty in the distance, slight border staining, 22 1/2 x 33" **$173**

Far left: World War I, "Boys and Girls! You can help your Uncle Sam Win the War - Save your Quarters - Buy War Savings Stamps," colorful James Montgomery Flagg image of Uncle Sam w/a young girl & boy, minor creasing, tiny corner chips, 20 x 30" **$288**

World War I, "Buy More Liberty Bonds," a grim color image of a young mother grasping her children, printed in the corner "Must Children Die and Mothers Plead in Vain," border tears repaired, 30 x 40" **$76**

World War II, "The Four Freedoms," famous color images by Norman Rockwell, in original mailing envelope w/Office of War Information marking, set of 4 .... **$790**

Travel, "Red Star Line - Antwerpen - New York," lovely color scene of a mother & her young daughter looking out at an arriving ocean liner, artwork by H. Lassiers, printed in Belgium, ca. 1900, near mint, matted & framed, poster 24 x 34" **$1,150**

Records - 45 and LP

Music fans have been collecting records, beginning with 78 RPMs, since they were first mass produced in early 20th century. The fragile shellac 78s were eventually replaced by vinyl 33 RPM albums beginning in 1948, the 45 RPM single beginning in 1949, and the 7-inch extended play (EP) record in 1952. Later, the 8-track tape and cassette tape were introduced. They were popular because they were portable, but didn't enjoy the breadth or longevity of collecting that vinyl experienced. In the late 1980s and 1990s, digital music in the form of compact discs began to replace vinyl, and by 1991, the golden age of vinyl was over. With the rapid technological development in the music industry, CDs in turn, are being supplanted by digital downloads. Ironically, however, in recent years, music afficianados are returning to vinyl as a preferred medium because of its richer sound and its dramatic cover art. Sales of new releases in high quality 180 gram vinyl has been growing rapidly since around 2005, although vinyl sales still comprise only a fraction of all music sales.

The following records are only a broad sampling of music produced between 1950s and the 1970s, the peak of vinyl production. To make the most of the space available, records listed here are relatively scarce and have higher than average value. Common records are often worth only a few dollars in Near Mint condition, and a fraction of that in lower condition. But some rare records in Near Mint condition sell for thousands and even tens of thousands.

Prices listed are for Near Mint (NM) condition.

Very Good+ (VG+) condition = 50 percent of Near Mint value.

Very Good (VG) condition = 25 percent of Near Mint value.

▪ 45

Bobby Darin, "Dream Lover," Atco 6140, 1959...........................$50

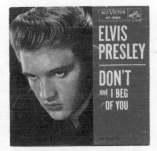

Elvis Presley, "Don't," RCA Victor 47-7150, 1958 ....$90

Elvis Presley, "He Touched Me," RCA Victor 74-0651, 1972.$120

Elvis Presley, "Jailhouse Rock," RCA Victor 47-7035, 1957, picture sleeve $50-100

Jerry Lee Lewis, "Great Balls of Fire," Sun 281, 1957...........$80

John Lennon, "Mother," Apple 1827, 1970.......................$120

Johnny Cash, "Guess Things Happen That Way," Sun 295, 1958 ....$40

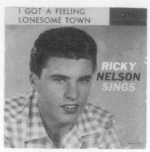

Ricky Nelson, "I Got a Feeling"/ "Lonesome Town," Imperial 5545, 1958.........................$70

Stevie Wonder, "Fingertips Pt. 1 and 2," Tamla 54080, 1963.$50

The Beatles, "And I Love Her," Capitol 5235, 1964, picture sleeve $60-120

The Beach Boys, "Barbara Ann," Capitol 5561, 1965 .....$150-200

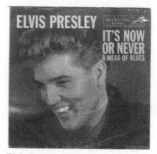

Elvis Presley, "It's Now or Never," RCA Victor 47-7777 1960 ....$60

The Beach Boys, "Ten Little Indians," Capitol 4880, 1962...$200

The Byrds, "The Times They Are a-Changin'," picture sleeve for unreleased single $500

The Ronettes, "Walking in the Rain," Philles 123, 1964....$150

LP

Alan Freed, Rock 'n Roll Dance Party, Coral CRL 57063, 1956 .... **$150**

Annette, Annette's Beach Party, Vista 3316, 1963 .... **$100**

Ann-Margret, The Vivacious One, RCA Victor LPM-2551, 1962 .... **$30**

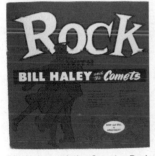

Bill Haley and the Comets, Rock with, Somerset P-4600, 1958 .... **$150**

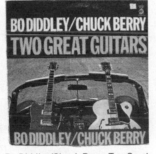

Bo Diddley/Chuck Berry, Two Great Guitars, Checker LP 2991, 1964 .... **$60**

Buddy Holly, Buddy Holly, Coral CRL 57210, 1964 .... **$100**

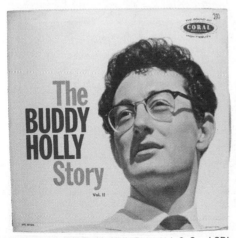

Buddy Holly, The Buddy Holly Story, Vol. 2, Coral CRL 57326, 1959 .... **$200**

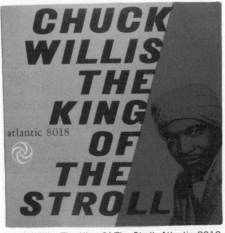

Chuck Willis, The King Of The Stroll, Atlantic 8018, 1958 .... **$300**

Duane Eddy, The Biggest Twang of Them All, Reprise, 6218, 1966 ....$30

Elvis Presley, Blue Hawaii, RCA Victor LPM-2426, 1961, mono, with sticker on cover hyping "Can't Help Falling in Love" and "Rock-a-Hula Baby" $50-100

Elvis Presley, G.I. Blues, RCA Victor LSP-2256, 1960, stereo, "Living Stereo" on label, no sticker on cover $50-100

Elvis Presley, Elvis, RCA Victor LPM-1382, 1956, mono...$300-800

Elvis Presley, Elvis' Christmas Album, RCA Victor LOC-1035, 1957, mono, with gatefold and booklet intact $500

Frank Sinatra, Swing Easy/Songs for Young Lovers, Capitol W 587, 1955, mono, gray label $40

Hank Williams, Honky-tonkin', MGM E-3412, 1957 .... $100

Harry Belafonte, "Mark Twain" and Other Folk Favorites, RCA Victor LPM-1022, 1954, mono ..**$50**

James Brown, Mighty Instrumentals, King 961, 1966..........**$100**

Jefferson Airplane, Surrealistic Pillow, RCA Victor LPM-3766, 1967, mono.........................**$60**

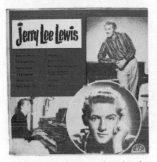

Jerry Lee Lewis, Jerry Lee Lewis, Sun SLP-1230, 1958.........**$200**

Johnny and the Hurricanes, The Big Sound of, Big Top 12-1302, 1960.................................**$250**

Joni James, Joni James, MGM E-3346, mono, yellow label, 1956 ....**$80**

Les Paul and Mary Ford, Time to Dream, Capitol T 802, 1956 .**$50**

Little Richard, His Biggest Hits, Specialty SP-2111, 1963 .....**$50**

Little Richard, Little Richard, RCA Camden CAL-420, 1956.....**$200**

Nat King Cole, Love Is the Thing, Capitol W 824, 1957, mono, gray label....................................**$40**

Neil Sedaka, "Little Devil" and his Other Hits, RCA Victor LSP-2421, 1961.................................**$60**

Ronnie Hawkins and the Hawks, Mr. Dynamo, Roulette, R 25102, 1960.................................**$150**

RECORDS – 45 AND LP

Scatman Crothers, Rock and Roll with Scatman, Tops 1511, 1956 ....$80

The Beach Boys, Surfin' U.S.A., Capitol ST 1890, 1963, stereo $50

The Beatles, Abbey Road, Apple SO 383, 1969 .... **$20-75**

The Champs, Everybody's Rockin' with the Champs, Challenge CHL-605, 1959..........................**$200**

The Dovells, You Can't Sit Down, Parkway P 7025, 1963.........**$50**

The Go-Go's, Swim with the Go-Go's, RCA Victor LPM-2930, 1964....................................**$25**

The Police, Synchronicity, A&M SP-3735, 1983, with gold, silver and bronze stripes on cover ...**$40**

The Shadows, Surfing With The Shadows, Atlantic SD 8089, 1963 ....**$300**

The Surfaris, Hit City '65, Decca DL 74614, 1965..................**$40**

The Trashmen, Surfin' Bird, Garrett GA-200, 1964................**$220**

Scientific Instruments

Collectible scientific instruments were created to make daily life better and simpler, and have been used through the ages to solve scientific problems. Objects include instruments to gauge and forecast the weather, such as barometers and thermometers; medical instruments; astronomy telescopes, lenses, charts and rulers; compasses; globes; abacuses; and much more.

Barometer, banjo-style, inlaid mahogany, the broken-arch pediment above an inlaid rosette, the tall slender neck w/a glazed thermometer above two inlaid sea-shells, the lower circular silvered metal dial above another inlaid rosette, unmarked, old refinishing, minor veneer damage, probably England, 19th c., 38 1/2" h. **$316**

Barometer, banjo-style, inlaid mahogany, the broken-arch pediment above an inlaid rosette, the tall slender neck w/a glazed thermometer flanked by two inlaid paterae, the lower circular silvered metal dial labeled "F. Saltern & Co. London," above another inlaid rosette, thermometer damaged, some edge damage w/ missing or replaced pieces of molding, England, 19th c., 38 1/2" h. **$546**

Barometer, banjo-style, inlaid satinwood, the rounded top & shaped throat mounted w/the thermometer panel above the large above the round silvered metal dial & rounded base drop, narrow mahogany banding around the whole case, dial marked by F. Molton, St. Law, Norwich, England, first half 19th c., minor loss to inlay, minor age crack, in base, 37" h. .. **$3,450**

Barometer, stick-type, gimbeled marine-type, tall slender columnar mahogany case w/turned detail, ivory scale enclosed at the top, cylindrical brass cistern at the base & brass wall bracket, marked by James Bassnett, Liverpool, England, 19th c., mercury tube missing, 38" h. **$3,450**

Compass, cased model, round iron frame w/brass dial enclosed in a square mahogany case w/a hinged front window & top brass handle, a brass cylindrical oil lamp mounted on the side, ca. 1900, case 6 1/2" h. **$172**

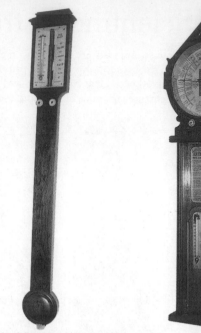

American, Simmons & Company, long narrow rectangular case w/ ripple or piecrust border, Fenton, New York, 19th c. **$950**

English, Adie, rosewood case w/ stepped cornice, double vernier **$3,500**

English, Admiral Fitzroy-type, marked on upper dial "Royal Polytechnic Barometer," top-of-the-line model, one of 12 types **$3,800**

English, bow-front case w/beveled glass, double vernier, Mason of Dublin **$3,800-4,000**

English, Cremonini-Wolverhampton, dark oak case w/angled pediment centered by an urn finial above freestanding columns flanking the central thermometer over the lower case w/a large round dial **$1,800**

English, Fortin or Kew or laboratory-type, long wooden board w/ milk glass inset at top **$1,000**

Silver

Silver is a precious metal used to make ornaments, jewelry, tableware, utensils, silverware, and currency coins. It is a favorite medium for visual arts because of its bright white color.

Sterling silver (standard silver) is an alloy made of silver and copper and is harder than pure silver. It is used in the creation of sterling silver flatware (silverware) and various other tableware, such as tea services, trays and salvers, goblets, water and wine pitchers, candlesticks, and centerpieces.

Hollowware refers to table service items plated in a thin coating of silver. Hollowware is different from regular silverplate in that it has thicker walls and more layers of silverplate. Items include sugar bowls, creamers, coffee pots, teapots, soup tureens, hot food covers, water pitchers, and platters.

American (Sterling & Coin)

Basket, shallow oblong form w/a serpentine scroll-trimmed rim, the sides pierced overall w/delicate scrolls around the oval bottom panel engraved w/a script monogram, Towle Silversmiths, Newburyport, Massachusetts, early 20th c., 9 x 12", 2 3/4" h. . **$431**

Berry server, large oblong gilded bowl w/thin enameled scrolls at the top of the bowl & around the oblong handle, Gorham Mfg. Co., Providence, Rhode Island, ca. 1900, 9" l. **$50-100**

Bowl, the lobed circular bowl w/a wide undulating rim decorated in high relief w/scrolls & foliage, bowl center w/an engraved script monogram, Frank W. Smith Silver Co., Gardner, Massachusetts, early 20th c., 11 7/8" d., 2" h. .. **$316**

Bowl, round w/deep rounded sides w/a flat rim & a thin footring, embossed w/spiral gadrooning separated by a matte band from the milled & applied shell-and-scroll border band, Tiffany & Company, New York, ca. 1884, 8 1/2" d., 3 1/2" h. **$2,185**

Bread tray, oval w/wide rolled & scalloped rim, Francis I patt., Reed & Barton, dated 1949, 7 1/2 x 12" **$690**

◄Bread tray, Art Nouveau style, shallow rounded navette form, the wide everted rim decorated w/ deep repoussé irises on a matte ground, the center monogrammed, Unger Brothers, New York, ca. 1895, 7 1/2 x 12 1/2" **$403**

SILVER

Brandy warmer, squatty bulbous bowl tapering to a flaring double-spout rim, baluster-turned wooded side handle, F.B. Rogers Silver Co., Taunton, Massachusetts, ca. 1900, 4 3/4 x 9 3/4", 3 1/4" h. **$100-150**

Creamer, bulbous shape w/scroll handle & three trifid feet, the front w/crest & "Rand R M 1758," inscription on one side reading "E.S. & S. Rand to Caroline M. Fitch July 4th, 1828" & on other side "Caroline M. Fitch to Mary F. Jenks April 1st, 1882," square hallmark "T.S.," Thomas Barton Simpkins, 3 3/4" h. **$6,900**

Porringer, round shape, 2 1/2" l. pierced handle, engraved "MR to MF," w/"Simpkins" touch mark, William Simpkins, Boston, 18th c., 5 1/4" d. **$2,875**

Tea set: cov. teapot, cov. sugar bowl & creamer; coin, Classical boat-shaped style, round stepped pedestal base supporting bulbous oblong lower body below a wide curved shoulder band w/leafy vine motif below the curved & rounded shoulder & domed hinged cover w/pineapple finial, high arched fancy C-scroll handles, tall serpentine spout on teapot, each piece w/engraved monogram on the side, mark of Peter Chitry, New York, New York, ca. 1830, teapot 9 3/4" h., the set (ILLUS. of teapot & sugar bowl) **$1,195**

Caster, coin, slender baluster-form w/molded banding, raised on an ogee-domed foot, the cap w/pierced & engraved panels, molded banding & baluster-form finial, marked on the base w/initials of Zachariah Bridgon of Boston, & a set of wedding initials of a couple, ca. 1760, 1 3/4" d., 5 1/2" h. **$3,738**

Pitcher, Art Nouveau style, footed bulbous baluster-form body w/a wide flared rim w/high arched spout, ornate floral-cast C-scroll handle, the body chased around the top & base w/sprays of intertwining flowers & leaves, engraved foliate monogram on the side, Gorham Mfg. Co., Providence, Rhode Island, 1903, 9 1/2" h. .. **$5,378**

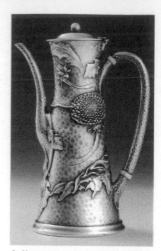

Coffeepot, cov., Aesthetic Movement style, tall slender waisted shape w/a hand-hammered ground, tall slender spout & C-form long handle w/ivory insulators, the sides wrapped w/chased & applied dandelion flowers, buds & leaves, the low domed hinged cover w/chased curly dandelion stem & ball finial, mark of Tiffany & Co., New York, New York, 1881-91, 7 1/4" h. **$19,120**

Pitcher, Neoclassical style, large urn-form body decorated w/milled swag banding & engraved acanthus scrolls, raised on an ogee-domed foot, a waisted neck w/integral spout, angled loop handle w/scroll finial, monogrammed body, Frank M. Whiting, ca. 1920, 10 1/2" h. (ILLUS. left with platter).................................... **$863**

Tea set: cov. teapot, cov. sugar urn & creamer; coin, Classical style, the oval teapot w/flat sides & a concave shoulder band w/a hinged tapering domed cover w/urn finial, tall helmet-shaped creamer & sugar urn w/tall waisted cover w/urn finial, both on a square foot, each w/bright-cut floral swags centering a cartouche w/drapery mantling, monogram in the cartouche, beaded borders, straight spout on teapot & C-scroll black wood handle, mark of William G. Forbes, New York, New York, ca. 1790, teapot 12 1/2" l., the set **$13,145**

Tea set: cov. teapot, cov. sugar urn & creamer; coin, each of Classical form, the teapot oval w/beaded border at foot & rim & the hinged cover w/urn finial, straight spout, wooden loop handle, the creamer & sugar of vase form on a square base, each engraved w/a monogram within a mantle, teapot 12 3/4" l., John Vernon, New York, New York, ca. 1792, the set **$8,365**

Tea set: cov. teapot, cov. sugar bowl & creamer; Neoclassical style, each piece w/a tall ovoid body raised on three long scroll legs ending in paw feet, domed cover & arched C-scroll handles, narrow shoulder & cover bands of classical designs, each leg headed by a Bacchanalian mask, mark of Tiffany & Co., New York, New York, ca. 1860-64, teapot 9 1/2" h., the set **$2,760**

SILVER

Teapot, cov., coin, oval upright body w/a flat shoulder centered by a hinged domed cover w/ pineapple finial, straight angled spout, C-scroll wooden handle w/ silver joins, the sides engraved w/a drapery cartouche enclosing a monogram, mark on base of Daniel Van Voorhis, New York, New York, ca. 1790, 7 1/8" h. **$4,780**

Tray, coin, round w/a foliate-decorated rim band, the center engraved w/a coat-of-arms, raised on four small cartouche-form feet, marked by John Mood, Charleston, South Carolina, ca. 1825, small dent on side of rim, minor body warping, 9" d., 1 1/4" h. . **$3,450**

▲ Teakettle on stand, cov., coin, the bulbous fluted body w/a ring-banded short neck & hinged domed cover w/ flower finial, scroll- trimmed serpentine spout, arched scroll swing handle, raised on a burner base w/four ornate scroll legs ending in shell feet & joined by serpentine straps centered by the burner ring, engraved inscription w/later date, mark of Ball, Tompkins & Black, New York City, ca. 1839-51, no burner, overall 15" h., the set **$1,150**

Teapot, cov., coin, wide bulbous inverted pear-shaped body on a domed foot, domed hinged cover w/a pinecone finial, serpentine spout w/cast shell & scroll decoration, black wooden C-scroll handle w/ scroll-decorated joins, the body engraved w/a rococo cartouche enclosing monogram "HPG," the shoulder engraved w/a strapwork bird & mask border, base w/ mark of Samuel Casey, South Kingstown, Rhode Island, ca. 1760, overall 10" l. **$47,800**

Teapot, cov., coin, inverted pear-shaped body on a disk foot, domed hinged cover w/pointed finial, serpentine spout w/cast leafy scrolls, C-scroll wooden handle w/scrolled silver terminal & leaf-clad joins, the shoulder engraved w/diaperwork, rocaille scrolls & flowering vines, the edge of the cover engraved w/a scallop band, base engraved w/block initials "H" over "IM," also w/mark of maker John Bayly, Philadelphia, ca. 1765, overall 9 1/4" l. **$71,700**

Teapot, cov., coin, footed spherical body w/a hinged double-domed cover w/baluster-form finial, octagonally faceted straight spout, C-scroll wooden handle w/octagonally faceted handle joins, base engraved "E*H," base also w/mark of maker Simeon Soumaine, New York, New York, ca. 1730, overall 10 1/4" l. **$207,500**

English & Other

Basket, oval footring w/pierced diamond & star designs below the deep flaring basket pierced overall w/delicate cross, dot & chevron design, serpentine narrow gadrooned rim band, twisted arched swing handle, mark of William Vincent, London, England, 1773-74, 8 3/4" l. **$863**

Cigarette box, cov., rectangular w/ hinged cover, the sides decorated w/rèpoussè flying birds above turbulent seas, the cover decorated w/bold rèpoussè chrysanthemums & leaves, opening to a cedar-lined interior, raised on narrow bracket feet, Japanese Export, ca. 1900, 3 1/2 x 6 1/2", 3" h. **$1,955**

Frame, for carte-de-visite picture, Art Nouveau style, hallmarked "84," Imperial-era Russia, 3 1/4 x 5 5/8"................................ **$295**
▶Serving spoon, figural relief handle w/a standing figure of Frederick the Great of Prussia, royal emblems at base of handle, chased scrolls in the wide shovel-form bowl, Europe, early 20th c., 11" l................................. **$595**

Beaker, parcel-gilt, a narrow flared gadrooned foot below the tall flaring cylindrical body w/the upper rim engraved w/a band of rocaille & flowers against a matted ground, a gilt molded rim, marked under foot by Johan Andersson Starin, Stockholm, Sweden, 1753, 7 5/8" h. **$2,390**

Cup, flared base & cylindrical sides w/high arched loop handle, the body engraved w/Art Nouveau flowers, gold-washed interior, Russian touch marks, 19th c., 3 1/2" h. **$345**

Bowl, round, w/elaborate raised design of scrolls, flowers & leaves along flaring sides, marked "WC" & hallmarks for London, England, 4 3/4" d. **$155**

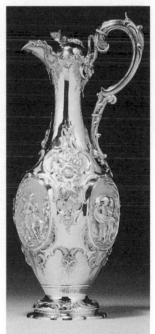

Ewer, cov., tall slender baluster form, a small round flaring foot, the body inset w/four oval plaques decorated w/cast figures representing the Four Seasons, surrounded by large chased flowers & scrolls, the slender neck w/cast scrolls continuing around the high arched spout, hinged domed cover w/flower finial, the ornate C-scroll leaf-clad handle w/ivory insulators, marked by Thomas, James & Nathaniel Creswick, London, England, 1852, 14 1/4" h. .. **$2,629**

SILVER

Serving spoon, figural relief handle w/a standing lady in Victorian dress, above a section of pierced entwined branches, chased musical instruments & sheet music in the wide oblong handle, marked "800," Europe, early 20th c., 11 1/4" l. **$595**

Serving spoon, figural relief handle w/a standing figure of Mary, Queen of Scots, engraved initials in the wreath & swag-trimmed wide shovel-form bowl, back marked "800," Europe, early 20th c., 10 1/2" l. **$645**

Serving spoon, figural relief handle w/a standing figure of Napoleon I above his imperial emblem & his initial & swags in the large shovel-form bowl, Europe, early 20th c., 10 1/2" l. **$550**

Serving spoon, the long oval bowl chased & pierced, a central figure of Moses & cherubs, a classical head below, the long flat handle w/ pierced scrolls & masks & pierced griffins at the base, Europe, late 19th - early 20th c., 12" l. **$750**

Tankard, cov., baluster form w/ round foot & medial body band, hinged stepped domed cover, a heavy scroll handle w/baluster drop & openwork thumbpiece, initial mark probably of John King, London, England, 1770, 8 3/4" h. **$2,629**

Sugar bowl, cov., silver-gilt, inverted pear-shaped body raised on a round domed foot, chased w/ rococo floral garlands & centering a vacant cartouche, the domed cover w/matching decoration & a figural spread-winged bird finial, mark of Samuel Taylor, London, England, 1746, 5 3/8" h. **$1,673**

Soup tureen, cov., Rococo style, the deep undulating oval base raised on four large pierced rocaille feet, the body rèpoussè & chased w/floral garlands & centering two vacant rocaille cartouches, large leafy scroll end handles, the high domed & stepped cover w/conforming decoration & a cast bird on branch figural finial, mark of Gottfried Bartermann, Augsburg, Germany, 1751-53, also later French control marks, overall 15 1/2" l. **$28,680**

Stirrups, foot-shaped flat sole w/ the pointed toe guard elaborately chased & rèpoussè w/leafy scrolls & flowers, Spanish Colonial, probably Peru, stamped "925," 9" l., pr. **$633**

Tea set: cov. teapot, cov. sugar bowl & creamer; each footed piece w/a squatty melon-lobed body, lobed domed covers w/figural flower finials, ornate C-scroll handles, one piece marked "F. Guzman - Mexico," .900 quality, 20th c., the set.. **$1,150**

Tea set: cov. teapot, cov. sugar bowl, cov. creamer, waste bowl, tongs & oval tray; each piece w/a squatty bulbous boldly lobed shape w/ivory handles & ivory lobed finials, designed by Josef Hoffmann & produced by The Wiener Werkstatte, Austria, ca. 1920s, tray 20 1/2" l., teapot 7 3/4" h., the set **$71,700**

Tea set: cov. teapot, cov. sugar bowl, creamer, teakettle on stand & oval tray; the serving pieces w/ upright flat oval bodies w/hinged tapering covers w/brass ball finials, cylindrical rosewood side handles, the kettle on a conforming burner stand w/pierced side holes, designed by Josef Hoffmann, manufactured by The Wiener Werkstatte, tray w/original Wiener Werkstatte lace doily, Austria, ca. 1923, tray 14 1/4" l., teakettle & stand 9 1/2" h., the set . **$53,775**

SILVER

Teapot, cov., George I era, footed spherical body w/small hinged cover w/knop finial, angled faceted straight spout, C-scroll wooden handle, body engraved w/a crest, base engraved w/initials "E.R.," mark of Seth Lofthouse, London, England, 1720, overall 8 1/4" l. **$4,183**

▲Teakettle on stand, cov., George II era, spherical body w/a flat hinged cover w/wooden knop finial, serpentine spout, overhead swing bail handle w/shaped uprights joined by a baluster-turned black wood grip, the body finely engraved w/a border of brickwork, scrolls, putti & foliate as well as a coat-of-arms, on a round stand raised on three leafy scroll legs w/ wooden knob feet joined by shaped braces centered by a deep burner, marks of Peze Pilleau, London, England, 1731, burner dating from 1956, overall 22 1/2" h. **$3,824**

▲Tea urn, cov., George III era, tall Classical urn-form body w/a tall slender tapering cover w/acorn finial, beaded shoulder band, long arched reeded side handles, a projecting spigot near the base w/a dark ivory handle, raised on a slender flaring pedestal on a square foot, interior fitted w/a heating column, cover engraved w/a crest, the body engraved w/a coat-of-arms, mark of John Wakelin & William Tayler, London, England, 1784, overall 20 1/2" h. **$4,780**

Teapot, cov., George II era, footed spherical body w/a small flat detachable cover w/reeded border & wooden disk finial, curved spout w/stylized petal join, C-scroll wooden handle, marked "RP," English provincial maker, ca. 1740, overall 8 5/8" l. **$3,760**

Teapot, cov., George III era, footed wide inverted pear-shaped body w/domed hinged cover w/pointed knob finial, ribbed serpentine spout, C-scroll handle, the body swirl-fluted & decorated w/rèpoussè & chased rococo floral & scroll designs w/a vacant cartouche, mark of Paul Storr, London, England, 1814, 6 7/8" h. **$1,610**

Teapot, cov., George III era, oval upright body w/flat shoulder & hinged flat cover w/wooden disk finial, angled straight spout, wooden C-scroll handle, the body engraved around the base & shoulder w/a floral & foliate band, the body engraved w/a coat- of-arms, mark on base of Richard Gardner, London, England, 1774, overall 9" l. **$3,585**

Tray, footed shell-shaped tray w/elaborate scrollwork & engraved but indistinct initials, England, 9 1/2 x 16" **$995**

Sterling Silver (Flatware)

Bittersweet patt., dinner service: eight each dinner forks, salad forks, cake forks, tablespoons, soup spoons, teaspoons, dinner knives & butter spreaders; Georg Jensen Silversmithy, Copenhagen, Denmark, 64 pcs. (ILLUS. of three) **$5,750**

Old English patt., dinner service: thirty-six each dinner knives & dinner forks, twenty-four each luncheon knives, luncheon forks & dessert spoons, twelve each fish knives, fish forks, dessert knives, dessert forks, tablespoons & teaspoons, four sauce ladles, pair of salad servers, pair of fish servers, one gravy spoon & four-piece carving set; in fitted oak cabinet w/five drawers & double doors, Francis Higgins, London, England, 1936, 229 pcs. (ILLUS. of three).................. **$20,700**

Francis I patt., dinner service: forty two teaspoons, twenty-four each luncheon forks, salad forks, luncheon knives & butter spreaders (twelve w/silver blades), twenty bouillon spoons, twelve each dinner knives, soup spoons, demitasse spoons, coffee spoons, dinner forks, cocktail forks, ice cream forks, eight grapefruit spoons plus fourteen serving pieces, w/ two wood cases; Reed & Barton, Taunton, Massachusetts, 20th c., 276 pcs. (ILLUS. of three) **$9,000-10,000**

Louis XIII Richelieu patt., dinner service: twelve each dinner knives, dinner forks, luncheon knives, luncheon forks, tablespoons, dessert spoons, lobster forks, teaspoons, fish knives, fish forks, demitasse spoons, three butter knives, two serving forks & one each soup ladle, sauce ladle, slice, cake knife & cheese knife; monogrammed, w/rattail bowls, trifid ends & cannon- handled knives w/stainless steel blades, Puiforcat, Paris, France, 20th c., in three fitted trays stamped w/ maker's name, 144 pcs. (ILLUS. of three) **$28,750**

Arcadia patt., dinner service: twelve each dinner knives, dinner forks, dessert spoons, luncheon forks & salad forks, eleven teaspoons & eight luncheon knives; Georg Jensen Silversmithy, Copenhagen, Denmark, post-1945, 79 pcs. **$3,500-4,500**

Imperial Chrysanthemum patt., dinner service: twenty-four each table forks & dessert forks, twenty-one tablespoons, twelve each dessert spoons, teaspoons, fruit spoons, demitasse spoons, fish forks, cocktail forks, fish knives & butter knives, four condiment spoons & one each fish server, fish slice, serving fork, punch ladle & lobster server plus twenty-four table knives & twelve dessert knives & fruit knives w/stainless steel blades; the terminals chased w/flower heads & leaves, also engraved w/a monogram, in fitted wooden case, 222 pcs. **$6,500-8,000**

Lap-Over-Edge Etched patt., dinner service: twenty-four each teaspoons & luncheon forks, twelve each dinner knives, luncheon knives, butter spreaders, dinner forks, dessert spoons & dessert knives, ten tablespoons, one sauce ladle & butter knife; etched w/plants, animals & fish, some identified on the back, engraved w/name "Scoville" in script on back, Tiffany & Co., New York, New York, ca. 1885, 132 pcs. **$20,700**

Versailles patt., dinner service: twelve each salad forks, dinner forks, teaspoons, soup spoons, dinner knives & butter spreaders, ten small teaspoons & eight seafood forks; monogrammed, Gorham Mfg. Co., Providence, Rhode Island, 1888, 90 pcs. **$2,300**

■ Silver Plate (Hollowware)

SILVER

Ash receiver, figural, a small figure of a chick & wishbone beside a round dished base centered by a stem centered by a fan- shaped cigar trimmer below the tall cup-shaped top match holder w/a hammered dot design, mark of the Derby Silver Co., ca. 1880s, 4 1/2" h. **$127**

Biscuit box, upright hinged shell shape w/engraved scrolls, an arched scrolling top border w/ center ring handle, raised on a trestle-style base w/outswept scrolled legs, England, early 20th c., 6 x 81 2/", 10" h. **$225**

Breakfast server set, a footed diamond-shaped base w/engraved edge supporting a ring-engraved footed salt cup & matching shaker flanking the central tall arched handle enclosing a napkin ring w/ an ornate pierced finial & resting atop a tiny seated boy & applied leaf, mark of the Meriden Britannia Co., ca. 1880s, overall 7" h.. **$403**

◄Breakfast server set, a shell-shaped tray on ball feet centered by a tall loop handle w/a napkin holder & a side bracket to support a ruffle-rimmed butter pat above a pair of attached small tapering waste cups flanking the bulbous salt & pepper shakers, all decorated w/floral engraving, impressed mark of the Aurora Silver Plate Mfg. Co., tray 6 3/4" d., overall 7 1/2" h., the set **$633**

▲Card tray, four-lobed squared-shape tray decorated w/engraved flowers & insects, attached to round base by three legs & two applied leaf & flower supports, maker's name indistinct, 5 7/8 x 6 1/4" **$175**

▼Clock, figural, figure of an Art Nouveau bonneted girl holding folds of cloak open, w/clock set in folds on one side, 2 1/2 x 7 x 7" **$795**

Candleholders, a slightly domed round base w/a leaf-tip band centering an upright short leaf & bud issuing two upturned long slender arms ending in tulip-form sockets, marked "Her Majesty 1847 Rogers Bros. 009056 I.S.," 20th c., 10 7/8" w., 6 3/4" h., pr. (ILLUS. of one) **$200**

Condiment holder, in the form of a woven basket containing three egg-shaped holders for salt & pepper shakers & mustard cup, w/ spread-winged baby bird perched on rim, English, indistinct maker's mark on bottom, 5 1/2" h. **$1,295**

Hairbrush, Art Nouveau style, decorated at one end w/the head & shoulders of a woman in profile w/long flowing hair, heavily embossed w/floral & whiplash design, 1 3/4 x 2 1/4 x 7 1/4" **$21**

Cup, cylinder shape on flared base, repeating panels w/stylized floral design around rim & base, made by Rockford Silver Co., style number 288, 3 x 4 x 4 1/4" . **$45**

Jewelry box, cov., Art Nouveau style, footed, decorated w/ roses, marked on bottom "92 DL," possibly a hair receiver, 2 3/4 x 2 3/4 x 3 1/2" **$165**

Jewelry casket, oblong form, the arched top w/two hinged covers flanked by arched sides w/a pierced design of flowers & leaves & raised on four leaf-sprig feet, a slender arched handle from side to side, mark of the Pairpoint Mfg. Co., portions of base reinforced & some leaves missing, 1890s, 6 1/2" l., 9" h. **$633**

Epergne, model of a palm tree w/ sinuous trunk and six palm fronds, w/a fox running at the circular, ringed base, topped w/a cranberry glass trumpet-shaped flower, 6 1/2" h. **$1,495**

►Match holder, model of old oaken bucket w/two branch handles on sides, sitting on raised base ribbed for striking matches, 4" l. **$325**

Hot water urn, Neoclassical style, the large ovoid body w/reeded band & concave top w/a domed cover & vasiform finial, the sides w/ringed lion-mask handles, raised on four flat reeded columnar legs ending in paw feet connected by a concave square base centered by a bowl-shaped burner, the whole w/ four flattened bun feet, plain downturned spout w/pineapple spigot, England, ca. 1890, 10 1/2" d., overall 20 1/2" h. **$863**

SILVER

Napkin ring, domed stepped circular base holding cockatoo perched on stylized branch, ring resting atop tail, marked "738," 4" h. **$595**

Napkin ring, stepped base holding reclining lion figure, ring resting on lion's back and engraved with "HEP" and floral motifs, 1 1/4 x 2 1/4 x 2 1/2" **$475**

Napkin ring, triangular shape on claw-and-ball feet, w/pierced floral rims and crossed wishbones forming a border around engraved leaf frond decoration & "Best Wishes," made by Meriden, style number 630, 1 7/8 x 2 3/8 x 3" **$175**

Salt cellar, in the form of a dolphin carrying a shell on its back, rimmed base w/design depicting ocean waves, handle in the form of a ribbed leaf, 2 x 2 3/4 x 4 1/2" **$275**

Tea set: cov. teapot, cov. sugar, creamer & rectangular tray; Art Deco style, each piece w/a squatty slightly flaring rectangular body & wide tapering shoulder, low domed cover w/reddish amber rectangular Bakelite finials, teapot w/angled Bakelite, tray w/cut corners & matching Bakelite squared end handles, England, ca. 1925, tray 15" l., the set **$196**

Teakettle on stand, cov., Victorian, Orientalist taste, the decagonally paneled body tapering to a short neck w/ thin pierced gallery & hinged domed & stepped cover w/ spherical finial, a pointed Arabesque arch fixed overhead handle, serpentine spout, the panels engraved as arches enclosing ornate quatrefoils above a chain band, raised on a platform base w/a wide top & thin gallery around a narrower pierced & paneled pedestal enclosing the burner, the wide dished & paneled base w/short columns forming the feet, by Elkington & Company, Birmingham, England, 1854, overall 10 1/2" w., overall 8 1/2" h. **$1,150**

Smoking accessory, consisting of model of owl on branch attached to three hollow tree stumps w/removable inserts for holding cigarettes, matches & ashes, 5 x 7 x 7 1/2" **$750**

Teakettle on stand, cov., footed paneled bulbous body w/a wide conforming shoulder centering a short rolled neck, hinged pointed & domed cover w/pointed finial, a fixed reeded loop overhead handle, scroll-trimmed serpentine spout, raised on open serpentine side supports on a paneled round base centered by a burner, mark of Reed & Barton, late 19th - early 20th c., overall 13" h. **$230**

Teapot, cov., round flat base below the wide rounded lower body w/a gadrooned medial band below the tall tapering sides w/a flaring rim, hinged domed cover w/knob finial, tall slender serpentine spout, C-scroll handle, trademark w/a lion on either side of a shield above "Silverplated - Est. 1905," early 20th c., 9 1/4" w., 9 3/4" h. **$65**

Toothpick holder, figural, round stepped base holding figure of monkey holding staff & carrying on its back a basket w/basketweave decoration & rope twist rim, Meriden, 3 1/3" h. **$550**

Teapot, cov., round foot below the wide squatty bulbous body tapering to a short flared neck w/a domed hinged cover, leafy scroll-trimmed spout & C-scroll handle, marked on bottom "Silver on Copper [crown] S [shield]," probably England, late 19th - early 20th c., 8" h. **$100**

Toothpick holder, model of a billy goat next to a large sack w/flared rim, Meriden, 2 1/4 x 2 3/4 x 3" **$375**

Teapot, cov., squatty bulbous boat-shaped body w/ widely flaring flanged rim & hinged stepped, domed cover w/wooden disk finial, ribbed serpentine spout, pointed angular handle, the sides w/an ornate engraved floral cartouche enclosing a gift inscription dated 1911, marks for an English silver plate firm, 11 1/2" l., 5 3/8" h. **$85**

Warming platter, oval frame raised on scroll feet, the scroll-cast side fitted w/a small filling hole, ornate scrolled end handles, fitted w/a well-and-tree insert, base marked "D & S," England, early 20th c., 17 1/2 x 24", 3 1/2" h. **$575**

TOYS

Toys

The collector's appetite for antique and vintage toys, by recent auction standards, shows no signs of going gray. Colorful graphics, fine detail and timeless childhood charm elevated the toy market to dizzying highs in 2011. The toy market's strong sales show remarkable consistency, whether you're at a country auction or the top of the market.

Liquidating the fine automotive collection of KB Toys founder Donald Kaufman required five auctions and generated more than $12.1 million in total sales. The 10,000-piece collection has a new home all over the globe.

After celebrating 50 years in business and it's 200th auction, Hakes Americana & Collectibles of York, Pennsylvania, celebrated the highest-grossing auction in the firm's history in early 2011. Many of the results you'll find in this year's edition feature top lots from these and more auction houses who are finding a bright future in selling playthings from the past.

For more on Donald Kaufman's collection and auctions, visit AntiqueTrader.com and listen as the man, who devoted his life to celebrating the joy of play, discusses amassing a 60-year collection with his wife, Sally, and why he decided to sell every single item in his collection—including his very first toy.

Windup toy, celluloid Mickey figure depicted in cowboy attire including neckerchief and pair of guns tucked in his belt, with string lasso in one hand and reins in the other while seated atop a painted wood horse; missing a paper hat; built-in key makes clockwork move figure forward in a galloping motion; 3" x 7" x 7" tall, Japan, circa 1930s. **$575**

▪ Cowboy Toys

Toy cap pistol, metal gun is 10-1/2" long with "Davy Crockett" name in low relief on frame and star design incised on plastic grips, attached to thin cardboard box is marked "Outlaw Apache," with Davy Crockett label pasted on lid over original text; made in England by BCM, 1-1/4" x 11" wide, circa 1950s.....**$575.58**

Alarm clock, painted metal case with brass luster frame around the glass cover over the clock face, image of Davy in seated position holding a guitar as one squirrel lays against his leg and another rests on his raised arm. This squirrel has a separate head that moves as seconds tick. Unique figural clock hands are a rifle and tomahawk. Circa 1955, 2" x 7-1/2" x 5" tall. **$488.93**

Dexterity Puzzles

Collection of three Maine-inspired dexterity puzzles, first is a 1-5/8" dexterity puzzle with glass cover over full-color cardboard image of ship that has four tiny indents for placing the four tiny white balls; second is a 1-5/16" long white metal replica of the ship with word "Maine" on the lower edge; last is a thin embossed silver luster sheet of metal measuring 1 3/4" x 2-1/4" with eagle surmounting a shield bearing an image of a ship, American and Cuban flags flanking the sides.. **$51.75**

Set of children's toys with dexterity puzzles and clickers, first is 1-3/4" diameter dexterity puzzle depicting an owl on a branch, cardboard edges with glass cover and interior marked "Made In Japan"; next are a pair of litho tin tops for "Red Goose Shoes For Boys And Girls"; next is "Red Goose Shoes" clicker and "Smile" orange drink working clicker followed by a pair of identical "Weather Bird All Leather Shoes" litho tin spinning tops. **$74.75**

Early dexterity puzzle depicting automobile and driver, 2-1/2" with glass cover over embossed cardboard showing driver in hat, goggles, and heavy coat at the wheel of his auto headed down a road with great dust cloud behind; inside puzzle are five white balls to get into small recesses on the radiator front; mirror on underside. **$111.32**

World War II-era dexterity puzzle has metal frame with glass cover over cardboard insert showing "Atomic Bomb" dropping from the sky headed toward the country of Japan with the designation for the cities Tokyo, Hiroshima, and Nagasaki; the latter two have small cut-outs in the cardboard next to the name, and this is where a pair of celluloid pellets with interior bb are to be positioned. A rather gruesome game given the consequences, but emblematic of the era; 3-1/4" x 4-3/8" x 7/8" deep. **$118.28**

Dexterity puzzle, box is cardboard with clear thin plastic lid, Popeye characters around sides include Popeye, Olive Oyl, Wimpy, Swee' Pea, and the Jeep; inside has small die-cut thin paper figures of Popeye, Olive Oyl, and clown with small piece of foil on one side of feet along with star design playing surface with numbers for scoring. Underside has text instructions including "Slap And Rub Firmly Across Top Of Box With Fingertips Or Coat Sleeve Repeatedly. Then Comics Will Dance, Hop And Skip. You Will Be Amazed To See Them Come To Life! Fingers Must Be Absolutely Dry"; copyright King Features Syndicate Inc., circa 1930s, 4-7/8" diameter x 1-1/2" deep. **$382.66**

◄Group of three dexterity puzzles with textured paper-covered cardboard frame and glass cover over the playing surface, circa 1934 by Marks Bros. Co., titles are "Mickey Mouse The Entertainer," "Mickey Mouse In His Garden," and "Mickey Mouse The Farmer" with each measuring 4" x 6" x 3/4" deep.. **$224.11**

TOYS

◼ Pinbacks

Pinback button, 1" celluloid pinback button with intense cream glow-in-the-dark background to show at its center the black silhouetted Shadow in hat and cape with his gun leveled, 1939. ....**$455.40**

Pinback button display, thin cardboard holds full complement of cello buttons, each 1-1/2" diameter with image in center of smiling boy wearing coonskin cap. Only five of the 48 buttons have correct spelling of "Davy" name; 11" x 17". **$354.20**

◀Pinback badge, premium, depicting classic enamel image of Superman shown waist up breaking chest chains with his name in text at bottom coming out of circular border with enamel stars surrounded by brass luster burst design; 1949 Fo-Lee Gum Corp., Philadelphia. 3" x 4-1/4" high; quality leather wallet made by Pioneer has embossed design on front. **$8,475.50**

Set of pinback buttons ranging from 3/4" to 1-5/8", largest of which is a litho from the 1960s with reverse text "Watch Cap'n Bill And The Little Rascals 11:30 A.M. Channel 10"; six other pieces are all from the 1920s-1930s and include images of Joe Cobb, Farina, and three showing Spanky; one early text button apparently issued by a Y.M.C.A. reads "Our Gang Club/Wabash/Y." **$115**

Popeye

Figural string holder depicting Popeye's pet, painted plaster with recessed back to hold string ball and hole in mouth for string. Has hanging loop at top for display, dated 1955 with incised text at top "American Cartoon" and his name incised on underside, 7" x 7-3/4".........................**$2,656.50**

Toy cap gun set, 1961 King Features Syndicate Inc., made by Halco, Pittsburgh, Pennsylvania, die-cut thin cardboard has choice graphics of Popeye dressed as cowboy holding two pistols with horse looking at him, 8" x 12", inside is a pair of 4-3/4" tall thin leather holsters with Popeye image on each and shiny cast metal "Pal" guns made by Kilgore in each pocket. Set also has leather belt wrapped in place at bottom. Reverse side has text: "After The Holster Set Has Been Removed From The Card, The Picture Makes A Fine Wall Plaque For A Child's Bedroom Or Playroom." Die-cut hole at top of display card is unpunched. **$253**

Brass folk art figure produced by fan of Jeep, Popeye's orchid-eating, truth-telling pet who can see the future Jeep. Figure was probably created shortly after Aug. 9, 1936, after Jeep left his 4th dimensional world to join Popeye and us in our three-dimensional world; figure stands 4"tall and is solid brass nearly 3/8" thick.**$230**

Pinback button promoting "Channel 13" complete with tiny text "©King Features Syndicate, Inc.," circa 1960 with a union bug on the yellow metal back, 1-1/4".
....**$44.28**

Toy celluloid figure of Popeye with pipe in mouth; when wound, head goes up and down and figure waddles about; 5-3/4" tall, circa 1930s, made in Japan for Australian market. Thin cardboard box is 1-1/2" x 2-1/4" x 6", box's front and back panels show Popeye throwing a punch with his hat in mid air, side panels show him looking at loop, and end panels show him hatless, throwing a punch with stars in the air; complete with key. **$612.26**

◄Pinback button promoting "Channel 13" complete with tiny text "©King Features Syndicate, Inc.," circa 1960 with a union bug on the yellow metal back, 1-1/4".
....**$44.28**

TOYS

Wristwatch, chrome accent case with dial images of Popeye, Olive Oyl, Swee'Pea, and Wimpy. One of two varieties. This one has Popeye's name in two words and standard hands whereas other version has no name and different hands. Leather band is a replacement; circa 1948, 1-3/4" diameter. **$172.50**

Wristwatch, chrome accent case with dial images of Popeye, Olive Oyl, Swee'Pea, and Wimpy. One of two varieties. This one has Popeye's name in two words and standard hands whereas other version has no name and different hands. Leather band is a replacement; circa 1948, 1-3/4" diameter. **$172.50**

Candy boxes, pair, each 2-1/2" by 3-3/4" by 1" deep, from a 1950s numbered set by Super Novelty Candy Co. Inc. Fronts feature single character image as a perforated card panel, backs have comic panel cartoon with story that continues from box to box. Boxes are No. 12 Oscar and No. 15 Popeye. Additional character images on side panels. **$140.42**

Tin toy car, circa late 1950s, thin cardboard box is 3-1/2" x 8 1/4" wide x 3 3/4" deep with art images on all five sides of lid showing Olive Oyl driving convertible; Number J-4050 with lid text including "Sculptured Figure With Hair"; tin car is 8-1/2" long with smiling Olive Oyl, sporting long ponytail, behind the wheel... **$1,043.62**

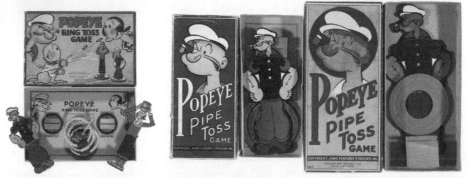

Left: Large and small varieties of mid-1930s Rosebud Art Company pipe toss games. One is 4-1/4" x 9-1/8" boxed variety, the other is 5" x 10-7/8" variety. Each contains die-cut thin cardboard target figure of Popeye with wood block to stand on and three die-cut thin cardboard rings. One figure is 8-1/4" tall, the other is 10" tall. Smaller box has directions printed on inside of lid with wood block glued in place, the other has no instructions and wood block is loose. Right: Ring toss game comes in 10-1/2" x 16" x 1-1/2" deep cardboard box by Rosebud Art Company New York, ©1919-1929-1933 King Features Syndicate Inc., has two attached wooden blocks to hold 10-1/4" tall Olive Oyl figure and 10-1/8" tall Popeye figure, complete with roped rings with wood attachment. **$208.72**

■ Premium Rings

Rare prototype Sky King premium ring, circa 1950, never produced but created by Armstrong for the Robbins Co. to present to the executives of the radio show's sponsor, Peter Pan peanut butter; ring has perfectly formed adjustable bands, base design is same as the 1949 Sky King Electronic Television Picture Ring with image of Sky King's horse "Yellow Fury" and airplane "Flying Arrow"; base joins to a black metal frame that holds a large diameter (15/16" x 2") heavy aluminum tube with slightly recessed center area and features a knurled pattern around the circumference at the eyepiece end, both intended to facilitate rotating the tube with one hand while the other holds the ring towards light to view the interior; interior displays a kaleidoscopic effect with die-cut portrait illustration of Sky King; only one known to exist. **$16,100**

Premium ring depicting Clarabell the Clown character from "Howdy Doody" network television show; on Clarabell's head is mounted a small brass hat fully 1/4" tall; ring base, as on the Howdy version, shows two images of Clarabell with his elaborate collar, and the brass loop to hold a battery has the same maker's name "Brownie Mfg. Co." along with "Pat. No. 2,516,180."; circa 1950, rare. **$4,174.50**

Premium ring, 1934 pulp magazine ring depicting metallic skull image with numeral 5 on forehead with metallic base, the insignia of Jimmy Christopher, fictional undercover ace whose adventures fighting spies and foreign agents took place from 1934 until the beginning of World War II; ring was used for distribution in the United States. **$10,925**

▇ Vehicles & Trains

Bing 1 gauge train set with "Express" electric locomotive and tender, Speisewagon dining car, Wagons-Lits sleeping car. **$12,650**

This early 20th century Marklin steam-powered, horse-drawn fire pumper features a hand-painted body with copper-finished upright boiler and two finely painted figures. Thirteen inches from hitch to platform..**$17,250**

Copyright 1922 Toonerville Trolley train with track, boxed, embossed Fisher (Germany) logos. **$4,025**

Circa-1927 American Flyer President "Special" boxed train set. **$11,500**

Circa-1909 Marklin "Priscilla" steamboat, 19 inches long, formerly in the Bill Bertoia collection. **$63,250**

Windups

Windup toy depicting comic strip character Henry tin litho with celluloid figures and wind-up key in left side. Made in Japan and distributed by George Borgfeldt Corp., New York; original thin cardboard box has lid graphics of Henry smiling and waving while seated in back of three-wheel vehicle being driven by young black boy. Lid top shows him with pyramids and palm trees in the background; front and back panel shows him going past mountain range and waving hanky; circa 1930s; toy is 5" long. **$3,162.50**

Wind up toy clown made in Germany, circa 1900s; 6" tall tin litho figure with built-in key on side and wheels next to feet pushing 4" diameter double hoop. Maker unknown. **$747.50**

Windup Mickey Mouse toy with wire metal tail and built-in key. Underside of one foot has copyright label. Figure's legs move back and forth rapidly as Mickey "rambles about." Made in Japan, distributed by Borgfeldt, 4" x 5" x 7", 1930s. **$659.06**

Windup Boob McNutt toy made by Ferdinand Strauss Corp., New York. No. 41, tin litho wind-up toy depicts Boob standing full figure with note on his back, "I'm Boob McNutt R. L. Goldberg." When wound, Boob's separate upper torso moves back and forth, arms swing, and toy moves about, 8-3/4", accompanied by thin cardboard box that has nice graphics on front and back showing Boob dancing, signed at lower right by cartoonist R. L. Goldberg. Side panels each feature a different daily comic strip with Boob; 2-3/4" x 4" x 9" tall, toy has repairs, 1924...................... **$670.45**

TOYS

Stock German tin three-wheel car, working clockwork, pre-war, circa 1912. Complete with original female driver, 5" long. **$860**

Windup toy marked "Donald Duck Walt Disney Japan" on back and inspection sticker on Donald's stomach. Mickey, Minnie, Donald, and Pluto characters on umbrella above Donald's head; includes original box, distributed by George Borgfeldt, Japanese, pre-war, 11" tall. **$950**

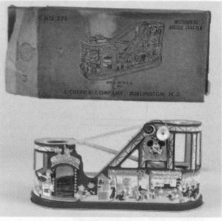

Windup tin litho Chein Disney Roller Coaster, includes original box and two original tin litho roller coaster cars; depictions of Disney characters around base include The Three Little Pigs, Mickey Mouse, Mad Hatter, Pinocchio, Donald Duck, and others; 19-1/2" long. **$475**

▼Windup pair of tin litho "Cruiser" ships, each 1-3/8" x 8-3/4" long with great lithography including waves on side with separate flag and seaplanes on top of decks; both have separate antenna to attach to top of masts; circa 1950s, made in Japan, accompanied by original thin cardboard box, 2-1/5" x 8-3/4" x 1-3/4" deep with paper label on top with graphics of battleship in action on high seas with planes flying overhead. **$521.81**

Toy robot, battery operated with robot face remote control, original wrench and hands, includes very colorful original box, 8-3/4". **$850**

Miscellaneous

Model kits, the first, "Francis The Foul The Way Out Dribbler" box is 1-7/8" x 5-7/8" x 14" tall, Hawk model no. 535-100, showing skinny purple monster basketball player "Francis" dribbling ball, having just knocked over referee; box is complete with unassembled parts, instruction sheet, and decal sheet. "Mother's Worry" box is 6-1/8" x 9-3/8" x 2" deep, Revell #H-1302: 1.00, with photo of Ed "Big Daddy" Roth wearing "Mother's Worry" shirt with his foot on paint spray compressor; lid also has art image of Rat Fink type character driving souped-up hot rod with smoking wheels and dice gear shift; front and back side panels each have a different black and white photo of Roth with one titled "King Of The Monster Painters"; both are copyright 1963................................. **$130.28**

J. & E. Stevens "Fowler" cast-iron mechanical bank, circa 1892. ....**$17,250**

Mechanical "Peek-a-Boo" Cat in pot, pictured in 1893 Ives catalog. **$8,050**

Fischer Father Christmas in auto, circa 1912, one of very few known...............**$25,875**

Rare 26-inch chalkware Father Christmas figure..........................**$10,925**

Vintage Clothing

The history of fashion is a mirror to the future. Nearly every style has already been done in some form and is reproduced with variations today. The popularity and demand for vintage pieces is growing because clothing and accessories are great collectibles that are also a good investment.

Many factors come into play when assessing value. When shopping vintage, keep the following in mind:

Popularity: How well known the designer is affects the price.

Condition: Collectors tend to want the original design condition with no modifications or repairs.

Relevance: The piece should be a meaningful representation of a designer's work.

When you're hot you're hot: As a trend develops, it is shown in fashion magazines, and the original vintage pieces go up in value (and plummet when it goes out of favor).

Location: Prices fluctuate from one geographic region to another.

Value: The appeal of vintage items has greatly increased over the last few years. Our rule of thumb is to buy quality.

◼ 1950-1960

Late 1950s Candy-Striped Bathing Suit Ensemble, all pieces of nylon, the bra-top w/a shaped bustline pieced in chevron stripes w/contrasting red & white striped trim, halter neck tie, center back closure; the short bolero jacket w/a spread collar & lapels, short cuffed sleeves w/a slight puff at shoulders, patch pockets at waist, worn open; the short flared skirt-style bottoms of 14 gored panels pieced in chevron stripes, 2" w. waistband, center back zipper & single button closure, trunks underneath of white nylon tricot, bottoms labeled "I. Magnin & Co.," excellent condition, trunks stained, late 1950s, the set **$350**

Fine 1950s Balenciaga Dress & Wrap, designer-made, both pieces of warp-printed silk in greens varying from emerald to chartreuse w/red & pink flowers, top of dress wraps around waist to form a V-neck & attaches to side-zippered skirt w/snaps, elbow-length sleeved blouse gusseted under the arms, lined in black silk chiffon, skirt of two overlapping panels gently gathered at waist, wraps w/self-fabric belt lined in nylon horsehair, shoulder wrap w/two self-buttons, labeled "Balenciaga - 10, Avenue George V - Paris," perfect condition **$5,000**

◀Lovely 1950s Christian Dior Satin Cocktail Dress, salmon-colored duchess satin, the bodice w/horizontal accordion pleating & a halter neck w/a self-fabric strap around the neck, a 5 1/2" w. waistband above the 33" l. sunburst pleated skirt, self-fabric-covered buttons down the center back stopping 18" from the hem-line & revealing an inverted pleat running the length of the skirt, labeled "Christian Dior Original - Made in U.S.A. - Christian Dior - New York Inc.," excellent condition, four buttons missing, later strapless bra sewn into the bodice **$3,500**

▶Labeled 1950s Schiaparelli Robe, pale pink nylon w/gathered neckline & loosely gathered sleeves, pink velvet ribbon & lace-trimmed yoke, ribbon belt, snap closure on bodice, hook & eye closure at waist, labeled "Schiaparelli - New York," perfect condition **$150**

Late 1950s Dior Wool Skirt Suit, both pieces of grey wool, the short slim-fitting jacked w/a small collar & lapel, oversized buttons & bound buttonholes down the center front, decorative flaps high on the waist suggesting pockets, long sleeves, back buttoned waistbelt & side vents, lined w/grey silk; the straight skirt w/tiny tucks under 1" w. waistband, center back zipper & hook closure, lined w/grey silk, jacket labeled "Christian Dior-New York - Marsal Park Avenue," good condition, some wear to lining, two tiny wear holes on front, late 1950s - early 1960s, the set**$475**

Above left: Labeled 1950s Embroidered Sun Dress, composed of eight panels of white bark cloth ground w/light blue flower embroidery w/green stems & leaves, flower appliquéd straps over ivory muslin, tight bodice & full skirt, center back zipper, labeled "Tina Leser Original," excellent condition **$500**

Above right: 1950s Blue Gabardine Two-Piece Suit, light blue gabardine w/subtle slubs of red & darker blue, the jacket w/a narrow collar & lapels, single patch breast pocket, two oversized patch pockets at hips, single-breasted w/two-button closure at center front, decorative buttons on cuffs, unlined; the trousers feature narrow belt loops, no waistband w/ pleats running the length of the leg, on-seam slit pockets at hips, back welt pockets, tapered legs w/cuffs at hem, zippered fly, jacket labeled "M-H Clothes of Distinction," very good condition, some age darkening to seams & around pockets & jacket cuffs **$500**

A 1950s and 1970s Varsity Jacket, green boiled wool w/ cream-colored leather sleeves & pocket edging, acrylic knit collar, cuffs & waist, lined w/green lustrous fabric, center front snap closure, labeled "Timberline by Bill Bros. - Milwaukee - Size 44," good condition, some discoloration to sleeves, tearing to lining (ILLUS. left with 1970s varsity jacket) **$150**

Lovely 1950s Duchess Satin Formal with Shrug, duchess satin w/sweetheart strapless neckline & sequins & beading overall, self-fabric beaded belt, bodice boned at every seam, gros-grain inner waist belt, side zipper closure, hem faced w/stiff tulle, fair condition, some discoloration, tearing in parts & some beads & sequins missing, the outfit **$1,800**

1960 - 1970

Two Views of a Designer Bathing Suit - Skirt Ensemble by Emilio Pucci, both pieces of cotton printed w/ abstract rendering of fish scales in three shades of green w/black outlining & including the facsimile signature of Emilio Pucci in places, swimsuit bodice fitted w/boning & a generous amount of elasticized ruching on each side, side zipper & neckline w/thin self-strap tie around neck, center bow, ending in a box-pleated mini-skirt w/attached elasticized modified trunks underneath, long, full skirt w/ seams running circularly around the underside for larger skirt protrusion, double wrap w/center bow & box pleats, size 12, labeled "Emilio Pucci - Florence Italy - Made in Italy - 100% pure cotton," excellent condition, never worn, ca. 1960, the ensemble **$2,000**

Fine Pauline Trigere Coat & Dress Ensemble, both pieces of brocaded fabric w/a black ground decorated overall w/gold spheres; the dress features a wide scoop neck, long sleeves tapering to snap cuffs, tucks high on bustline achieving a smock-style effect continuing to the full bodice & skirt w/an 18" l. straight-cut bottom tier, center back zipper, lined w/sheet black organdy, accompanying belt of same fabric w/ fabric-covered buckle & hidden hook closure faced w/ black cotton faille; the swing-style coat w/a 2 3/4" w. stand-up collar structured underneath w/wire for support & overlap hidden hooks & eyes & single oversized wrapped button closure, raglan bracelet-length sleeves, a 2" w. padded band at upper thigh level continuing to 18" l. straight-cut bottom tier, lined w/ black knit jersey, labeled "Pauline Trigere," excellent condition, the set....................................... **$1,200**

Blue Chiffon Cocktail Dress, dusty blue sleeveless design w/minutely tucked chiffon bodice, self-fabric piping at rounded neckline & armscyes, 4" w. mauve satin insertion at high waistline w/side bow finish & trailing ends, purple acetate full skirt w/tucked chiffon overlay, bodice lined w/fine blue net, center back zipper, labeled "R & K Originals," excellent condition, some fading to satin insertion & bow, ca. 1960 .... **$275**

1960s Hattie Carnegie Silk Dress, shantung silk w/a beige ground w/red, pink & yellow flowers & green leaves, wide scoop neck w/a tucked bustline, elbow-length sleeves, rounded waistline & straight skirt, center back zipper, labeled "Hattie Carnegie Blue Room," excellent condition, some alteration work **$500**

Designer Peasant Dress by Geoffrey Beene, gypsy- or peasant-style, silk w/an orange ground w/stylized flowers in shades of yellow, green, pink & black, low scoop neckline & unlined bodice, five pairs of orange grommets & self-fabric cording to lace-up, empire waistline, gently gathered long skirt lined in ivory-colored organza & ending in a doubled flounced tier, fitted armhole & sleeve also ending in a double flounced cuff, low scoop back, center back zipper w/hook & eye closure, labeled by Geoffrey Beene, late 1960s, perfect condition **$1,500-1,800**

1960s Apricot 'Baby Doll' Dress, apricot acetate sleeveless dress w/apricot-colored chiffon overlay, the bodice featuring strips of embroidered chiffon around the square neckline & empire waistline, bishop sleeves made from sturdier organdy w/insertions of the same embroidered chiffon running vertically, band of the same lace over acetate just above the elbows, lower length of sleeves faced w/stiff tulle for fullness & tapering to elastic cuffs, skirt of dress tucked under the waistband for fullness, center back zipper w/a white gros-grain ribbon bow, mid- to late 1960s, good condition, minor tears to chiffon **$175**

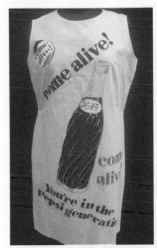

1960s Pepsi-Cola Shift Dress, yellow cotton sleeveless design w/ Pepsi-Cola slogans & a large bottle printed design, round neckline, darts at bustline, center back zipper, labeled "Regatta by Mill Fabrics Corporation - Penney's - 18," mint condition w/original tags **$350**

Late 1960s Wild Floral Print Dress, very thin jersey material in a wild & colorful floral print, bateau neckline, three-quarters length slim-fitting sleeves, skirt falls to lower knee, self-fabric cord tie belt, labeled "42," late 1960s, excellent condition **$350**

1960s Betsey Johnson Minidress, pink cotton w/small bow & ribbon print, shirred & elastic long sleeves, princess seaming front & back, white buttons down center front, labeled "DESIGNED by Betsey Johnson for Paraphernalia," excellent condition, mid-1960s ....**$400-$500**

Two 1960s Men's Plaid Jackets. **Right:** Jacket, blue, yellow, white & brown plaid patchwork madras-style in a cotton blend, deep back vent, white satin lining, two flap pockets, two inside slit pockets & two-button front closure, excellent condition **$125**
Left: Jacket, red, yellow & ivory plaid in an open weave, possibly silk-cotton blend, beige satin monogrammed lining, two flap pockets, single chest slit pocket, two inside slit pockets w/plaid fabric edging, back vent, single button closure center front, labeled "Mark Chrisman - Pompano Beach - Boca Raton - Naples, Florida - Dry Clean Only," excellent condition **$125**

▲1960s Suede & Tweed Jacket & Skirt Ensemble, the loose-bodied jacket of light brown suede w/a stand-up collar & open placket faced w/light brown & white flat tweed fabric, kimono-style short sleeves w/turn-back cuffs also faced w/same tweed, two patch hand-warmer pockets at center front trimmed w/tweed, lined w/beige crepe; the pencil skirt of same tweed falls to mid-calf w/1 1/2" w. suede waistband, tweed-wrapped button & tab closure, center back seam edges w/same suede, kick slit near hem w/suede detail, jacket labeled "Created by Royal Suedes of New York," late 1960s, excellent condition, some age wear to suede, the set **$200**

■ 1970 - 1980

1970s Hungarian Embroidered Blouse, finely textured unbleached gauze featuring floral yarn embroidery at the center front & smocking & overstitching around the neckline, short puff sleeves & waist, light blue cord drawstring at V-neckline, labeled "Hand Embroidery Made in Hungary - Karavan N.Y.," excellent condition, tiny pinhole at front, slight age yellowing over left shoulder ....**$175-$200**

Yellow Wool Dress by Ronald Amey, bright yellow wool knit, mock-turtle neckline, raglan-type long full sleeves w/openings at the shoulders & tapering athe cuffs w/carved Lucite & gold-rimmed buttons & loop closures, bodice gathered from shoulder yoke & at elastic-covered waistline, attached 3" w. self-fabric covered belt w/button & loop closure, skirt lined w/ yellow china silk, rolled hemline, center back zipper closure, labeled "Ronald Amey New York," & a fabric care label, excellent condition, minor pilling mainly at neckline.. **$400**

◀1970s Midnight Blue Silk Velvet Long Dress, w/ wide scoop neck, slightly padded shoulders, long sleeves gathered at shoulders & tapering to wrists w/functioning prong-set rhinestone buttons up the cuff, same buttons down center front of bodice, empire waist w/gathered mid-calf skirt, lingerie straps at shoulder, neckline lined w/blue acetate, excellent condition, lining around neck shows some wear **$200**

1970s Plaid Halter Dress & Shawl, halter-style, plaid twilled polyester, halter bodice w/hook & eye closure at upper neck gathered for fullness, darts at bustline, bias-cut wide skirt, zipper down center back, w/matching shawl, labeled "Lillie Rubin," late 1970s, excellent condition, the set **$125**

Two Views of a 1970s Brocade Gown by Mary Norton, brocade w/bands of light green, orange & pale yellow w/silver lame thread running throughout, bodice features a wide V-neckline w/attached light green organdy swatch that drapes around neck & falls down the back, trimmed w/gold-flecked lace, bodice tucked at center for fullness around the bustline w/ self-fabric bows at center seam, kimono-style three-quarter-length sleeves w/underarm gussets, high waistline & tucks underneath creating a full skirt, center back zipper, lined w/orange satin, labeled "Mary Norton - Coral Way - Miami, Florida - Bay Harbor Islands-Miami Beach - Main St.-Blowing Rock, N.C.," good condition, some tears along seams, discoloration to lining under armscyes, early 1970s **$250**

Saint' Angelo Patchwork Maxi Skirt, all-cotton, the gored skirt of twelve panels separated by crimson soutache braid, each panel w/a different whimsical print including polka dots, bunnies, toadstools & psychedelic flowers & steeply graduated, a 1 3/4" w. woven & embroidered waistband w/long surplus that wraps around waist finishing w/sash tie, labeled "Saint' Angelo - 10," Giogio di Saint' Angelo, ca. 1976 ....**$700**

Tee Shirt & Pants Outfit, circa 1970, peach-colored cotton & polyester blend w/iron-on patch reading "Free Moustache Rides," good condition, some fabric wear & fading, ca. 1970, $55; cotton pants (possible blend) in a madras patchwork design in shades of beige, pink, brown & red, two-inch waistband angle set welt pockets in front & straight welt pockets in back, labeled "A JAYMAR SLACK" & fabric care label, ca. 1970, excellent condition, pants **$175**

1970s Jacket, Pants & Shirt Ensemble, formal yellow shirt of polyester-cotton blend w/tucks & lace on center pront, narrow lace edging at cuffs, labeled "After Six," excellent condition, $55; patterned textured polyester clip-on bow tie, 1960s, excellent condition, $13; plaid trousers of 100% wool w/slight flare at bottom, tab buttoned pocket at right hip, two-inch wide waistband & two-inch wide self-fabric belt loops, top-lined, center front zipper closure & top hooks, excellent condition, $100-125; brown jacket of polyester twill w/satin collar, padding at shoulder, handstitched lining, two deep vents at back, center front button closure, excellent condition, jacket... **$150**

Two Pairs of 1970s Decorated Denim Jeans, w/home-made patchwork embellishments on lower flares, five-pocket styling, perhaps a 'marriage' of two different pairs, excellent condition, intentional fraying of threads & patches, front button missing (ILLUS. left with other denim jeans) **$250**

1970s Orange Velvet Hot Pants, crushed rayon velvet w/patch pockets & self-belt loops, snap button & fly closure, measures 8 1/2" from waistband to cuffs, labeled "Velpanne - Ameritex," mint condition .... **$50-$55**

Two Knitted Wool Ponchos from the 1970s, knitted in green & yellow wool yarn, w/a yellow drawstring & pom-pons, yellow yarn fringe, excellent condition.. **$85**
Knitted, white, brown & orange acrylic yarn in a banded design, excellent condition **$35**

Watches

Watches evolved from portable spring-driven clocks that first appeared in the 15th century. The first timepieces to be worn, made in 16th century Europe, were fastened to clothing or worn on a chain around the neck. Styles changed in the 17th century, and men began to wear watches in pockets instead of as pendants. Patek Philippe created the first known wristwatch in 1868 for the Countess Koscowicz of Hungary.

Lady's hunting case watch, Elgin, delicately engraved gold-filled Duebor case, keywind mechanism, late 19th c., 1 3/4" d. **$173**

Lady's hunting case watch, pendant style, 18k gold case polished & set w/a diamond, sapphire & ruby accent, the white enameled dial w/Arabic numerals, jeweled & adjusted damascened lever escapement movement, late 19th - early 20th c. **$264**

Lady's hunting case watch, the round case decorated in green guilloche enamel centered by a rose-cut diamond starburst & bordered by tiny diamonds, suspended from a double old European- and rose-cut diamond-mounted chain & bail joined to an enameled baton & seed pearl necklace, the silvertone dial w/ Arabic numerals, platinum & 18k gold mount, some enamel loss, Edwardian, England, early 20th c. **$3,878**

Lady's open face watch, pendant-type, enamel, platinum & diamond, the back of the platinum-topped 18k gold case in marine blue guillochè enamel centered by square set w/rose-cut diamonds & decorated in light blue guilloché bordered by a narrow white enamel Greek key band, the goldtone dial w/Arabic numerals, suspended from a platinum, enamel baton & rose-cut diamond fancy link chain, Edwardian, England, early 20th c., overall 22" l. **$2,468**

Lady's hunting case watch, Vacheron & Constantin, 18k gold case w/three bands of rose-cut diamonds ending in cabochon garnets, the white enamel dial w/ Arabic numerals, a jeweled nickel movement, suspended from a scrolling openwork gold pink trimmed w/cabochon garnets & tiny diamonds, triple signed, fitted box, early 20th c. **$2,585**

Lady's pendant watch, Art Deco style, the round silvertone engine-turned dial w/Arabic numerals, a jeweled damascene nickel movement, platinum matte polished hunting case bow-set w/rose-cut diamonds & sapphires w/a cabochon sapphire in the center, w/a 14k white gold & sapphire bar pin, case interior inscribed "Paris," ca. 1920s **$2,115**

Lady's verge watch, L'Epine, Paris, France, designed in the shape of a mandolin w/multicolored enamel decoration on the 18k gold ground, opens to reveal a signed gilt movement, suspended from a trace link chain, late 19th - early 20th c. **$4,700**

Man's hunting case watch, E. Howard Watch Co., 17-jewel movement, 14k yellow gold case w/central shield on engine-turned ground, case marked "Keystone," ca. 1903 .... **$805**

Man's hunting case watch, Elgin, lever-set movement, in a finely engraved 14k gold case applied w/an elk head, w/original Elgin mahogany case, late 19th c., w/ short watch chain **$460**

Man's hunting case watch, Illinois, lever-set movement, finely engraved 14k yellow gold case, slight case wear, minor hairlines in dial, ca. 1880 .... **$1,035**

Right: Man's hunting case watch, Waltham, 14k tri-color gold case engraved w/foral & leaf designs among interlocking circles, the white enamel dial w/Roman numerals & subsidiary seconds dial, jeweled adjusted nickel movement, late 19th - early 20th c.........**$646**

Far right: Man's open-face watch, Art Deco-style, 14k gold, goldtone metal dial w/Arabic numerals & subsidiary seconds dial, stepped bezel, enclosing a 17-jewel nickel lever escapement movement, w/ rectangular trace link fob chain, w/Dreicer & Co. box, ca. 1930s (ILLUS. of watch) **$323**

Man's open-face watch, E. Howard Watch Co., open-faced w/marked dial w/Arabic numerals, small seconds dial, 17-jewel movement, 14k yellow gold case marked "KW.C.C.O.," minor hairline in dial, tiny fleck at numeral 4, ca. 1900 .... **$403**

Man's open-face watch, Patek Philippe, 18k yellow gold, the silvertone dial w/Arabic numerals enclosing an 18-jewel eight adjustment damascened nickel movement, the reverse w/worn monogram, 20th c., triple-signed, boxed **$1,880**

Man's open-face watch, Tiffany & Co., 18k yellow gold & platinum, Art Nouveau design, gold case w/applied platinum wire in a looped clover-style design against a chased & repoussè ground w/a small bird, the gilt dial w/applied free-form Arabic numerals, curved & scrolling bi-color hands, subsidiary seconds dial, jeweled & damscened nickel lver escapment movemont, ca 1890s, triple-signed (ILLUS. of back) **$35,250**

Man's open-face watch, Vacheron, 18k gold, the white enamel dial w/ Roman numerals & a subsidiary seconds dial, enclosing a jeweled lever escapement movement, early 20th c. **$646**

Cartier, lady's Art Deco style, the diamond-shaped silvered dial w/Roman numerals framed by rose-cut diamonds & onyx tablets framed by more diamonds, rose-cut diamond winding stem, completed by a later strap, the platinum-topped 18k gold case enclosing a 19-jewel movement, eight-adjustment, signed by Cartier, Paris, ca. 1920 ....**$15,275**

Patek Philippe, man's Retro style 14k gold, the square silvertone dial w/Roman & abstract numerals under a domed crystal, on a shaped end lugs attached to a pyramidal arched bracelet, an 18-jewel damascened movement, Tiffany & Co., mid-20th c., 6 1/2" l. **$1,880**

World War II

During the years since the end of World War II, veterans, collectors and nostalgia seekers have eagerly bought, sold, and traded the "spoils of war." Soldiers eagerly looked for trinkets and remembrances that would guarantee their place in the historic events that unfolded before them.

As soon as hostilities ended in 1945, the population of defeated Germany and Japan realized they could make money selling souvenirs to the occupational forces. The flow of war material increased. Values became well established.

Over the years, these values have remained proportionally consistent. Though values have increased dramatically, demand has not dropped off a bit. In fact, World War II collecting is the largest segment of the militaria hobby.

The value of military items is greatly affected by variation. The nuances of an item will determine its true value. Also, the amount of World War II material is vast.

Following is a sampling of various items from Germany and the United States. For more information, see *Warman's Civil War Collectibles Identification and Price Guide* by Russell E. Lewis.

Photos courtesy of www.advanceguardmilitaria.com, Rock Island Auction Company, Hermann Historica OHG, Charles D. Pautler, Minnesota Military Museum, Colin R. Bruce II, and John F. Graf.

Germany

Army medical officer's visor cap
..................................**$650-900**

Artillery soldier's Waffenrock
..................................**$475-600**

German Luftwaffe Model 40 single decal helmet...........**$400-650**

German paratrooper's camouflage jump smock **$5,500-6,000**

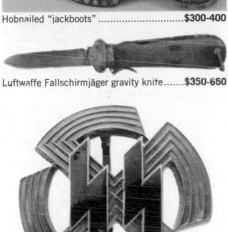

Hobnailed "jackboots" $300-400

Luftwaffe Fallschirmjäger gravity knife.......$350-650

Officer's map case $95-150

German proficiency badge of the SS in bronze.
....$6,500-7,500

Stamped steel Heere belt plate on black leather belt
....$100-175

Krieghoff 1936 Luger pistol................ $1,500-5,000

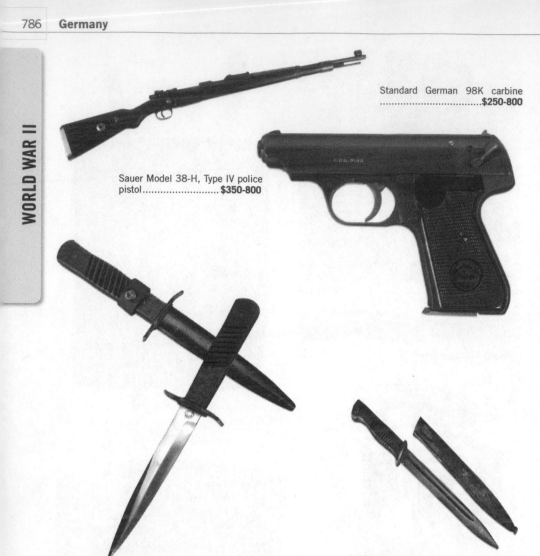

Standard German 98K carbine
....................................**$250-800**

Sauer Model 38-H, Type IV police
pistol..........................**$350-800**

German soldier's fighting knife..................**$150-250**

84/98 Mauser rifle bayonet by "Hörster"
with scabbard............................**$65-85**

German Walther "ac 43" code P.38
pistol............................**$700-900**

United States

Navy Amphibious Petty Officer's jumper............................ **$25-50**

40th Division sergeant's Ike jacket, with bullion patch and combat or tilleryman badge **$75-100**

▶Army Nurse Corps captain's uniform, complete with matching skirt, shirt and necktie ..**$300-350**

A-2 jacket, with a painted squadron insignia **$1,500-2,500**

Model 1944 shoepacs................................... **$50-75**

U.S. Army enlisted visor cap........................ **$45-65**

WAC brown leather shoes **$25-50**

U.S. Navy officer's khaki cap **$145-295**

Navy white fatigue hat...................................**$5-10**

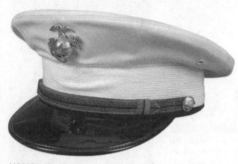

USMC officer's visor cap with white removable cover.
....**$275-325**

M1 fixed bail helmet, with painted 2nd Infantry Division insignia on shell and liner...............**$895-1,200**

Enameled canteen, cup, and cover........... **$100-165**

Radio Receiver and Transmitter BC-611-E ("Handie-Talkie") ...**$250-325**

M1943 folding shovel **$25-45**

U.S. Army Purple Heart with Oak Leaf cluster, signifying an additional receipt of the award **$75-100**

Army Signal Corps compass **$65-95**

U.S. Distinguished Service Cross, numbered **$300-350**

Colt U.S. Army Colt Commando Model revolver..........**$500-900**

Union Switch & Signal Company M1911A1 pistol **$2,000-3,000**

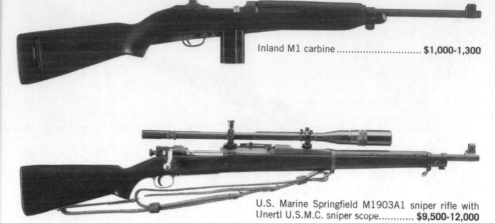

Inland M1 carbine **$1,000-1,300**

U.S. Marine Springfield M1903A1 sniper rifle with Unertl U.S.M.C. sniper scope............ **$9,500-12,000**

M1941 Johnson semi-automatic rifle... **$4,500-6,500**

MK III fighting knife with M8 scabbard (which replaced the earlier leather M6 scabbard)... **$200-300**

Wartime short pattern M1 Garand rifle bayonet also known as the M1905 E1 bayonet........ **$85-165**

M1918 pattern trench knife **$450-600**

Zippo Lighters

History

George Grant Blaisdell was born on June 5, 1895, in Bradford, Pennsylvania. In 1931, at the Bradford Country Club, Mr. Blaisdell met a gentleman who was using a lighter made in Austria. The lighter worked exceptionally well, especially in the wind; however, it required the use of both hands. It intrigued Mr. Blaisdell, who envisioned improving upon the design. The word "Zippo" is a spin-off of the word "zipper." The zipper had recently been patented in a nearby town, and Mr. Blaisdell liked the sound of the word. He established Zippo in October 1932 in Bradford and the first Zippo lighter was produced in January 1933. Mr. Blaisdell's lighter had the lid attached to the body and required the use of only one hand to light it, making it less awkward to use and better looking.

The first Zippo lighters retailed for $1.95 each—a costly investment for most people at that time. But with Mr. Blaisdell's guarantee and marketing strategy, "It works or we fix it for free," folks were more willing to part with that kind of money.

The original patent was applied for on May 17, 1934, and patent number 2032695 was granted on March 3, 1936. The 2517191 patent number was issued on August 1, 1950. The Zippo lighter basically remains the same to this day, with just minor improvements.

In the mid-1930s, Kendall Refining Company placed an order for 500 Zippo lighters. These are believed to be the first company-advertised lighters produced by Zippo and are highly collectible. Decades later, companies continue to use Zippo lighters as an advertising medium.

Zippo Manufacturing Company, Canada, Ltd., was established in Ontario, Canada, in 1949 to negate import duties. The facility closed on July 31, 2002.

In 1954, construction began on new offices at 33 Barbour St. in Bradford, and an open house was held in September 1955. The headquarters remain there today.

Mr. Blaisdell passed away on October 3, 1978. He is remembered not only for inventing the Zippo lighter, a great American icon, but also for his generous and kind spirit. After his passing, his daughters, Mrs. Harriett B. Wick and Mrs. Sarah B. Dorn, inherited the business. Robert Galey was chosen to lead the company. He retired in 1986, and the controller, Michael Schuler, was appointed president and chief executive officer. Today, Mrs. Sarah Dorn and her son, Mr. George B. Duke, own Zippo Manufacturing Company. Gregory W. Booth is president and CEO.

In 1994, Zippo Manufacturing Company began hosting a yearly "National Zippo Day" celebration. Every other year, an international swap meet is held at the same time. Eight thousand people attended the 2004 swap meet.

The Zippo/Case Visitors Center opened in July 1997. It is a 15,000-square-foot facility that includes a store, museum, and the famous Zippo Repair Clinic, where the Zippo lighter repair process can be viewed through expansive windows.

In the fall of 2002, Zippo obtained trademark registration for the "shape" of the Zippo lighter. This was a major milestone for the company. Zippo lighters are often imitated by inferior replicas, but by obtaining this right, Zippo has legally been able to curtail much counterfeiting.

The Zippo Click Collectors Club was formed in 2002 and debuted at that year's international swap meet. At the Zippo/Case International Swap Meet 2004, a members-only get together was held at the Pennhills Country Club, where 54 years earlier Mr. Blaisdell shot a hole-in-one. At this writing, Zippo Click has 9,000+ members from around the world.

 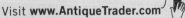

ZIPPO LIGHTERS

By 2004, Zippo lighters had appeared in thousands of movies, on more than 120 television shows, and on stage about 30 times.

Today, though most products are simply disposable or available with limited warranties, the Zippo lighter still comes with its famous lifetime guarantee, "It works or we fix it for free.™" No one has ever spent a cent on the repair of a Zippo lighter regardless of the lighter's age or condition.

For more information on Zippo lighters, see *Warman's Zippo Lighters Field Guide* by Robin and Dana Baumgartner.

Dating Zippo Lighters

Mr. Blaisdell had date codes imprinted on the bottom of the lighter cases. These codes provided him with the date of manufacture, should a defect be found, allowing him to maintain records of repairs. Fortunately, those date codes are a tremendous help today in the ability of collectors to correctly identify the year any given Zippo lighter was made. In this guide, we'll discuss only the bottom stampings of the case. Other factors for dating early Zippo lighters are their height and shape, the number of barrels on the hinge and the case's material. Inserts can also be dated by their material, number of holes in the chimney, flint wheel style, cam style, and markings.

Very quickly, you can determine a broad age of a Zippo lighter based on the three major changes to the style of the word "Zippo" imprinted on the bottom of the lighter. The "Block" Zippo was used from 1933 to 1954; it was changed to the "Script" Zippo in 1955, and the "Flaming i" began in 1980 (see P. 33).

Pat. Pending was stamped from 1933 until the end of 1936, when it was replaced with Pat. 2032695. Pat. 2517191 was stamped from late 1953 until 1967.

Date codes appeared as early as 1955, and the dating system was fully in effect by 1959. Before 1959, dating Zippo lighters can be a bit tricky, as the exact placement of the words must be taken into consideration. We've provided examples of what we believe to be the correct bottom codes for those tricky years. Again, placement of the wording, the material the case is made of and the number of barrels on the hinge play key factors in dating earlier Zippo lighters.

In 1986, the dot and slash date code methods were replaced with Roman numerals representing the year and letters of the alphabet representing the month of production.

In 2001, the last two digits of the year were used along with the same letters for the months, and that system continues today.

Slim Zippo lighters were introduced in 1956 and had no date code on the bottom of the lighter. Slims were first marked in 1957. From 1957 through 1965, slims had different bottom date codes than did regular size Zippo lighters. Beginning in 1966, the same markings were used on both the slim and regular. In 2002, the holes in the chimney of slim lighters were enlarged.

Dating Zippo lighters produced in Canada from 1950 until 1986 is difficult due to the lack of date coding. The bottom stamps shown here generally provide for time spans.

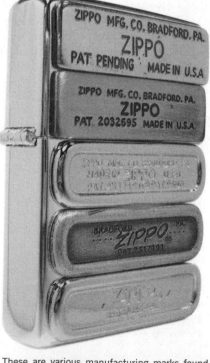

These are various manufacturing marks found on Zippo lighters.

These block letters were used on the bottom of Zippo lighters from 1933 to the mid-1950s.

The 1933-1936 Pat Pending mark.

This is the script logo used circa 1955 to the late 1970s.

The flaming "i" mark used from 1980 to the present.

The Pat 2032695 mark was used from 1936-1940.

Another Pat 2032695 mark used from 1940-1953.

This Pat 2157191, Pat. Pend. mark was used from 1953-1955.

This 1955 mark includes Zippo in script, four dots on the left and right, Pat. 2517191, and Pat. Pend.

This 1956 mark has three dots on the left, four dots on the right, Pat. 2517191, and Pat. Pend.

Four dots on the left and right and Pat. 2517191 make up this 1957 mark. Pat. Pend. has been removed.

This 1958 mark has four dots on the left and right, with Pat. 2517191 centered.

This 1959 mark has three dots on the left, four dots on the right, and Pat. 2517191 centered.

Vertical slashes, with Pat. 2517191 centered, make up this 1966 mark.

The 1974 mark has forward slashes. Pat. 2517191 was removed by 1968.

This 1982 mark has backward slashes.

A 1986 mark has month codes and Roman numerals for years.

Zippo stopped adding Roman numerals to its mark in 2000.

The 2001 mark includes the last two digits of the year.

A Canadian mark from 1949, with Pat. on the left and Pend. on the right.

The Canadian mark used from 1950 to the mid-1960s has Patented on the left and 1950 on the right.

A Canadian mark from the mid-1960s to 1986. Patent information is removed and there is no date coding.

This Canadian mark was used from 1986-2000; shown here is the 1994 version.

This is a Canadian mark from 2001-2002.

■ Early Zippo

The original 1933 lighter was 1/4" taller than the Zippo lighter we know today and the case had square corners. The corners were rounded in the late 1930s. The first method used to decorate Zippo lighters was affixing a piece of metal lace, only 5/1000's of an inch thick, to the front of the case using a cement type glue. The so-called "metallique" was then hand painted with enamel paint and baked to set the paint. This process was used from the mid-1930s to the early 1940s.

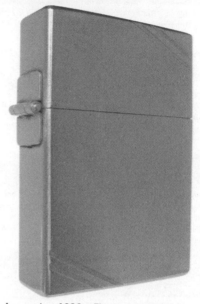

A 1934-35 lighter, Metallique, outside hinge. .... **$2,000-$2,500**

An early 1936 Zippo with outside hinge. .... **$1,500-$1,800**

A 1936-37 lighter, Metallique, Louis the 14th, four-barrel hinge....................................... **$1,500-$1,800**

The back side of the Louis the 14th lighter, with initials.

◼ Advertising

COMPANIES

Cover the Earth,
1951...**$150-$175**

TWA, Lockheed,
1953...**$150-$175**

GE Refrigerators,
1956...**$175-$200**

A 1946 Zippo, Call for Philip Morris, Metallique,
three-barrel. ....**$8,000+**

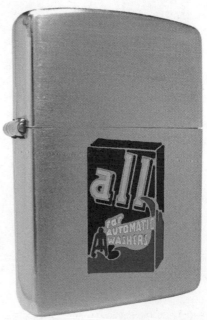

All, For Automatic Washers, 1953...........**$275-$300**

ZIPPO LIGHTERS

Hertz, slim, 1968.......**$500-$550**

Howard Johnson's, slim, 1958.
...................................**$250-$275**

Planters, Mr. Peanut, The Name
for Quality, slim, 1963.**$325-$350**

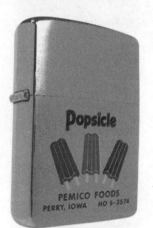

Popsicle, 1961...........**$500-$600**

Holiday Inn, 1970. ......**$225-$250**

Buster Brown Textiles Inc., 1973
...................................**$250-$275**

Drink Coca Cola in Bottles, 1960
...................................**$225-$250**

Campbell's   Soup,   1975.
.... **$275-$300**

Marlboro, 1976..........**$100-$125**

Events

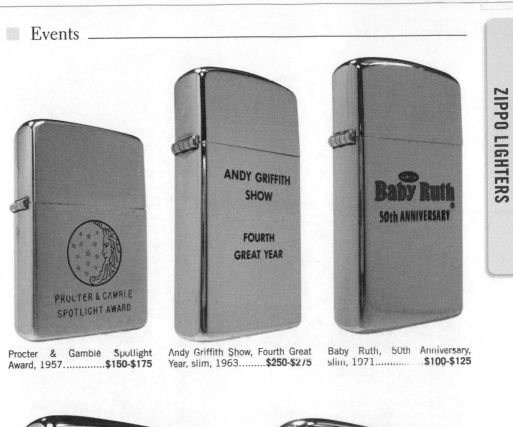

Procter & Gamble Spotlight Award, 1957..............**$150-$175**

Andy Griffith Show, Fourth Great Year, slim, 1963.........**$250-$275**

Baby Ruth, 50th Anniversary, slim, 1971.............**$100-$125**

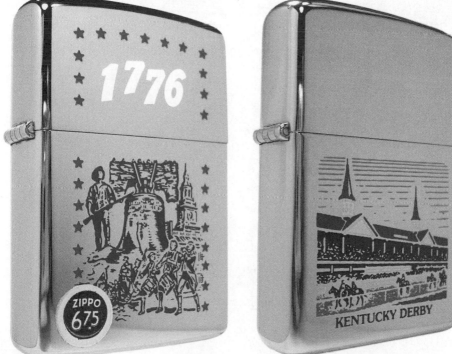

Bicentennial, 1976. ....**$100-$125**

Kentucky Derby, 1980. ....**$125-$150**

People, Places & Things

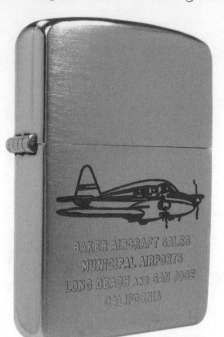

Baker Aircraft Sales, Municipal Airports, Long Beach
and San Jose California, 1955. ....**$175-$200**

Golden Nugget, Las Vegas, Nevada, 1946. **$350-$400**

Ringling Bros. and Barnum &
Bailey, Circus World, slim, 1976.
...................................**$175-$200**

Town & Country

Rooster, slim, 1960. ....$400-$500

Happy Jack, USS Harold J Ellison, DD-864, 1955.
....$800-$900

July 20, 1969, moon landing commemorative,
1969....................................$200-$225

Trout, original series...............................$500-$600

ZIPPO LIGHTERS

Military

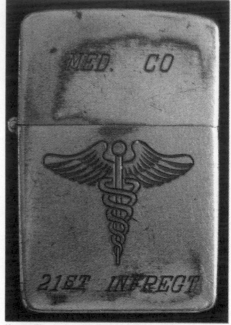

Korea Zippo lighter of Lieutenant Colonel William W. Cox, 2nd Medical Battalion, 1951.................... **$200**

Korea Zippo lighter of Paul Howard, Medical Company, 21st Infantry Regiment, 1951................ **$150**

Zippo lighter of Sergeant Timothy J Kendall, U.S. Army Special Forces, Teams B-24/A-244, 1968.
.... **$350**

Zippo lighter of Combat Medic Guevara, 2nd Battalion, 505th Infantry Regiment (Airborne Infantry), 1968... **$200**

161st Aviation Company, 1967...................... **$300**

620th Tactical Control Squadron, Detachment 2, Pleiku, 1968................................... **$300**

18th Special Operations Squadron, 1971.......................... **$150**

River Division 574, 1969.... **$350**

Coastal Division 17 (Patrol Air Cushion Vehicle), 1969......... **$35**

U.S. Marine Corps Da Nang, 1965................................... **$250**

U.S. Coast Guard Cutter Half Moon WHEC 378 (Coast Guard Squadron Three), 1967....... **$350**

USS Thresher, 1963...**$350-$400**

Sports

Bowler, 1946. ....**$200-$300**

Golfer, 1953. ....**$150-$175**

Fisherman, 1956........**$175-$200**

Hockey player, 1957-59, Canadian. ....**$250-$275**   Hunter, 1953...**$175-$200**

Bowler, 1958, slim. ....$300-$325

Skier, 1965. ....$250-$275

Snowmobiler, 1970. ...$200-$225

Miami Dolphins, slim, 1973. ....$75-$100

NFL, 1974.................$100-$125

Table Lighters

Barcroft personalized "The Wiley's," 2nd model, 1947...**$150-$200**

Barcroft Shakertown Sidewalls Cleveland Ohio, 3rd model..**$250-$300**

Barcroft Mickey Mouse, 4th model. ....**$800-$900**

Barcroft Westinghouse (vending machine), 4th model...**$600-$700**

Lady Bradford, 1950. ....**$175-$200**

Moderne, 1960. ....**$125-$150**

Super Steelers, Super Bowl IX, X, XIII and XIV Champions, 1979..**$150-$175**

Roseart, 1958..**$350-$375**

Special Contributors
and Advisors

The following collectors, dealers, sellers and researchers have supported the *Antique Trader Antiques & Collectibles Price Guide* with their pricing and contacts for more than 25 years. Many continue to serve as a valuable resource to the entire collecting hobby, while others have passed away. We honor all contributors past and present as their hard work and passion lives on through this book.

Andre Ammelounx

Mannie Banner

Ellen Bercovici

Sandra Bondhus

James R. and Carol S. Boshears

Bobbie Zucker Bryson

Emmett Butler

Dana Cain

Linda D. Carannante

David Chartier

Les and Irene Cohen

Amphora Collectors International

Marion Cohen

Neva Colbert

Marie Compton

Susan N. Cox

Caroline Torem-Craig

Leonard Davis

Bev Dieringer

Janice Dodson

Del E. Domke

Debby DuBay

Susan Eberman

Joan M. George

Roselyn Gerson

William A. and Donna J. Gray

Pam Green

Green Valley Auctions

Linda Guffey

Carl Heck

Alma Hillman

K. Robert and Bonne L. Hohl

Ellen R. Hill

Joan Hull

Hull Pottery Association

Louise Irvine

Helen and Bob Jones

Mary Ann Johnston

Donald-Brian Johnson

Dorothy Kamm

Edwin E. Kellogg

Madeleine Kirsh

Vivian Kromer

Curt Leiser

Gene Loveland

Mary McCaslin

Pat Moore

Reg G. Morris

Craig Nissen

Joan C. Oates

Margaret Payne

Gail Peck

John Petzold

Dr. Leslie Piña

Arlene Rabin

John Rader, Sr.

Betty June Wymer

LuAnn Riggs

Tim and Jamie Saloff

Federico Santi

Peggy Sebek

Steve Stone

Phillip Sullivan

Mark and Ellen Supnick

Tim Trapani

Jim Trautman

Elaine Westover

Kathryn Wiese

Laurie Williams

Nancy Wolfe

Contributors by Subject

ABC Plates: Joan M. George

Black Americana: Leonard Davis and Caroline Torem-Craig

Character Collectibles: Dana Cain

Chase Brass & Copper Company: Donald-Brian Johnson

Cloisonné: Arlene Rabin

Compacts & Vanity Cases: Roselyn Gerson

Decals: Jim Trautman

Eyewear: Donald-Brian Johnson

Jewelry (Costume): Marion Cohen

Kitchenwares:

> Cow Creamers: LuAnn Riggs
>
> Egg Cups: Joan M. George
>
> Egg Timers: Ellen Bercovici
>
> Pie Birds: Ellen Bercovici
>
> Reamers: Bobbie Zucker Bryson
>
> String Holders: Ellen Bercovici

Lighting: Carl Heck

Lighting Devices:

> 1930s Lighting: Donald-Brian Johnson
>
> Moss Lamps: Donald-Brian Johnson

Nativity Sets: Donald-Brian Johnson

Plant Waterers: Bobbie Zucker Bryson

Pop Culture Collectibles: Dana Cain and Emmett Butler

Ribbon Dolls: Bobbie Zucker Bryson

Steins: Andre Ammelounx

Vintage Clothing: Nancy Wolfe and Madeleine Kirsh

CERAMICS

Abingdon: Elaine Westover

American Painted Porcelain: Dorothy Kamm

Amphora-Teplitz: Les and Irene Cohen

Bauer Pottery: James Elliott-Bishop

Belleek (American): Peggy Sebek

Belleek (Irish): Del Domke

Blue & White Pottery: Steve Stone

Blue Ridge Dinnerwares: Marie Compton and Susan N. Cox

Brayton Laguna Pottery: Susan N. Cox

Buffalo Pottery: Phillip Sullivan

Caliente Pottery: Susan N. Cox

Catalina Island Pottery: James Elliott-Bishop

Ceramic Arts Studio of Madison: Donald-Brian Johnson

Clarice Cliff Designs: Laurie Williams

Cleminson Clay: Susan N. Cox

deLee Art: Susan N. Cox

Doulton/Royal Doulton: Reg Morris, Louise Irvine and Ed Pascoe

East Liverpool Potteries: William and Donna J. Gray

Flow Blue: K. Robert and Bonne L. Hohl

Franciscan Ware: James Elliott-Bishop

Frankoma Pottery: Susan N. Cox

Gonder Pottery: James R. and Carol S. Boshears

Hall China: Marty Kennedy

Harker: William A. and Donna J. Gray

Hull: Joan Hull

Ironstone: General - Bev Dieringer; Tea Leaf - The Tea Leaf Club International

Limoges: Debby DuBay

Majolica: Michael Strawser

McCoy: Craig Nissen

Mettlach: Andre Ammelounx

Noritake: Tim Trapani

Old Ivory: Alma Hillman

Pacific Clay Products: Susan N. Cox

Phoenix Bird & Flying Turkey: Joan Collett Oates

SPECIAL CONTRIBUTORS

Pierce (Howard) Porcelains: Susan N. Cox

Quimper: Sandra Bondhus

Red Wing: Gail Peck

Royal Bayreuth: Mary McCaslin

Rozart Pottery: Susan N. Cox

R.S. Prussia: Mary McCaslin

Russel Wright Designs: Kathryn Wiese

Schoop (Hedi) Art Creations: Susan N. Cox

Shawnee: Linda Guffey

Shelley China: Mannie Banner; David Chartier; Bryand Goodlad; Edwin E. Kellogg; Gene Loveland and Curt Leiser

Stoneware and Spongeware: Bruce and Vicki Waasdorp

Vernon Kilns: Pam Green

Warwick China: John Rader, Sr.

Zeisel (Eva) Designs: Kathryn Wiese

Zsolnay: Federico Santi/ John Gacher

GLASS

Animals: Helen and Bob Jones

Cambridge: Helen and Bob Jones

Carnival Glass: Jim and Jan Seeck

Central Glass Works: Helen and Bob Jones

Consolidated Glass: Helen and Bob Jones

Depression Glass: Linda D. Carannante

Duncan & Miller: Helen and Bob Jones

Fenton: Helen and Bob Jones

Fostoria: Helen and Bob Jones

Fry: Helen and Bob Jones

Heisey: Helen and Bob Jones

Higgins Glass: Donald-Brian Johnson

Imperial: Helen and Bob Jones

McKee: Helen and Bob Jones

Morgantown: Helen and Bob Jones

New Martinsville: Helen and Bob Jones

Opalescent Glass: James Measell

Paden City: Helen and Bob Jones

Pattern Glass: Green Valley Auctions

Phoenix Glass: Helen and Bob Jones

Wall Pocket Vases: Bobbie Zucker Bryson

Westmoreland: Helen and Bob Jones

PRICING, INDENTIFICATIONS AND IMAGES PROVIDED BY:

LIVE AUCTION PROVIDERS

AuctionZip
113 West Pitt St., Suite C
Bedford, PA 15522
(814) 623-5059
www.auctionzip.com

Artfact, LLC.
38 Everett St.
Suite 101
Allston, MA 02134
(617) 746-9800
www.artfact.com

LiveAuctioneers LLC
2nd floor
220 12th Ave.
New York, NY 10001
www.liveauctioneers.com

AUCTION HOUSES

American Bottle Auctions
2523 J St., Suite 203
Sacramento, CA 95816
(800) 806-7722
americanbottle.com

American Pottery Auction
Vicki and Bruce Waasdorp
P.O. Box 434
Clarence, NY 14031
(716) 759-2361
www.antiques-stoneware.com

Antique Helper Auction House
2764 East 55th Place
Indianapolis, IN 46220
(317) 251-5635
www.antiquehelper.com

Apple Tree Auction Center
1616 West Church St.
Newark, OH 43055-1540
(740) 344-4282
www.appletreeauction.com

Auction Team Breker's
Otto-Hahn-Str. 10
50997 Köln (Godorf), Germany
02236 384340
www.breker.com

Brunk Auctions
P.O. Box 2135
Asheville, NC 28802
(828) 254-6846
www.brunkauctions.com

Charlton Hall Auctioneers
912 Gervais St.
Columbia, SC 29201

Christie's New York
20 Rockefeller Plaza
New York, NY 10020

Cincinnati Art Galleries
225 East Sixth St.
Cincinnati, OH 45202

Dargate Auction Galleries
326 Munson Ave.
McKees Rocks, PA 15136
(412) 771-8700
dargate.com

Fontaines Auction Gallery
1485 W. Housatonic St.
Pittsfield, MA 01210

Garth's Arts & Antiques
P.O. Box 369
Delaware, OH 43015
(740) 362-4771
www.garths.com

Glass Works Auctions
Box 180
East Greenville, PA 18041
(215) 679-5849
www.glswrk-auction.com

Green Valley Auctions
2259 Green Valley Lane
Mt. Crawford, VA 22841
(540) 434-4260
www.greenvalleyauctions.com

Guyette & Schmidt, Inc.
P.O. Box 522
West Farmington, ME 04922

Ken Farmer Auctions and Appraisals
105 Harrison St.
Radford, VA 24141
(540) 639-0939
www.kfauctions.com

Hake's Americana & Collectibles
P.O. Box 12001
York, PA 17402
(717) 434-1600
www.hakes.com

Norman Heckler & Company
79 Bradford Corner Rd.
Woodstock Valley, CT 06282

Heritage Auction Galleries
3500 Maple Ave.
Dallas, TX 75219-3941
(800) 835-3243
 www.HertiageAuctions.com

Jackson's International Auctioneers &
   Appraisers
2229 Lincoln St.
Cedar Falls, IA 50613

James D. Julia, Inc.
P.O. Box 830
Fairfield, ME 04937

Jeffrey S. Evans & Assoc.
2177 Green Valley Lane
Mount Crawford, VA 22841
(540) 434-3939
www.jeffreysevans.com

John Moran Auctioneers
735 West Woodbury Rd.
Altadena, CA 91001
(626) 793-1833
www.johnmoran.com

Legend Numismatics
P.O. Box 9
Lincroft, NJ 07738
(800) 743-2646
www.legendcoin.com

Leslie Hindman Auctioneers
1338 West Lake St.
Chicago, IL 60607
(312) 280-1212
www.lesliehindman.com

Matthews Auctions
111 South Oak St.
Nokomis, IL 62075-1337
(215) 563-8880
www.matthewsauctions.com

McMasters-Harris Auction Company
P.O. Box 755
Cambridge, OH 43725

Metz Superlatives Auction
P.O. Box 18185
Roanoke, VA 24014
(540) 985-3185
Web: www.metzauction.com

Morphy Auctions
2000 N. Reading Rd.
Denver, PA 17517
(717) 335-3435
Web: morphyauctions.com

Neal Auction Company
4038 Magazine St.
New Orleans, LA 70115
(504) 899-5329
Web: www.nealauctions.com

New Orleans Auction Gallery
1330 St. Charles Ave.
New Orleans, LA 70130

O'Gallerie: Fine Arts, Antiques and
   Estate Auctions
228 Northeast 7th Ave.
Portland, OR 97232-2909
(503) 238-0202
www.ogallerie.com

Pacific Galleries Auction House and
   Antique Mall
241 South Lander St.
Seattle, WA 98134
(206) 441-9990
www.pacgal.com

Past Tyme Pleasures
39 California Ave., Suite 105
Pleasanton, CA 94566

Rago Art & Auction Center
333 No. Main St.
Lambertville, NJ 08530

Rock Island Auction Co.
7819 42 St. West
Rock Island, IL 61201
(800) 238-8022
www. rockislandauction.com

Seeck Auction Company
Jim and Jan Seeck
P.O. Box 377
Mason City, IA 50402
www.seeckauction.com

Skinner, Inc.
357 Main St.
Bolton, MA 01740
(978) 779-6241
 www.skinnerinc.com

Slater's Americana, Inc.
5335 No. Tacoma Ave., Suite 24
Indianapolis, IN 46220

Sotheby's New York
1334 York Ave.
New York, NY 10021
(212) 606-7000
www.sothebys.com

Specialists of the South, Inc.
544 E. Sixth St.
Panama City, FL 32401
(850) 785-2577
www.specialistsofthesouth.com

Stanley Gibbons
399 Strand,
London
WC2R 0LX
England
Tel: +44 (0)207 836 8444
www.stanleygibbons.com

Stephenson's Auctioneers & Appraisers
1005 Industrial Blvd.
Southampton, Pa 18966
(215) 322-6182
www.stephensonsauction.com

Stevens Auction Company
301 North Meridian St.
Aberdeen, MS 39730-2613
(662) 369 2200
www.stevensauction.com

Strawser Majolica Auctions
P.O. Box 332
Wolcottville, IN 46795

Swann Auction Galleries
104 E 25th St., # 6
New York, NY 10010-2999
(212) 254-4710
www.swanngalleries.com

John Toomey Gallery
818 North Blvd.
Oak Park, IL 60301

Treadway Gallery, Inc.
2029 Madison Rd.
Cincinnati, OH 45208

Whiterell's Art & Antiques
300 20th St.
Sacramento, CA 95811
(916) 446-6490
witherells.com

ADDITIONAL PHOTOGRAPHS AND RESEARCH PROVIDED BY:

Belleek Collectors International Society, www.belleek.ie/collectors-society;
CAS Collectors, www.cascollectors.com & www.ceramicartstudio.com;
International Perfume Bottle Association, www.perfumebottles.org;
National Assn. of Warwick China & Pottery Collectors; the Red Wing Collectors
Society, www.redwingcollectors.org and Tea Leaf Club International,
www.tealeafclub.com.

Index

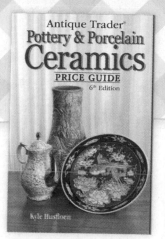

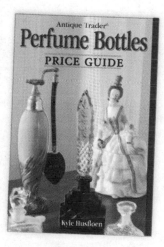

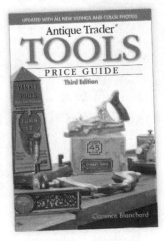